THE

HINDU PANTHEON

श्री
सर्व्व देव सभा

THE
HINDU PANTHEON

EDWARD MOOR, F. R. S.

GYAN

Published by

Gyan Publishing House
5, Ansari Road
Daryaganj, New Delhi-110002
Phone: 011-47034999, 9811692060
E-mail: books@gyanbooks.com

Distribution Network
gyanbooks.com
India, USA, Canada, UK, Australia, France

ISBN : 978-81-212-9158-3 (PB)
First Published, 1810

2nd Impression 2023

Printed at: Gyan Press, Delhi.

THE HINDU PANTHEON
Author: EDWARD MOOR

श्री सर्व्व देव सभा

THE

HINDU PANTHEON.

BY

EDWARD MOOR, F. R. S.

MEMBER OF THE ASIATIC SOCIETY OF CALCUTTA, AND OF THE LITERARY SOCIETY OF BOMBAY.

LONDON:

PRINTED FOR J. JOHNSON, ST. PAUL'S CHURCH-YARD,

BY T. BENSLEY, BOLT-COURT, FLEET-STREET.

1810.

TO THE

Hon. JONATHAN DUNCAN,

GOVERNOR OF *BOMBAY.*

MY DEAR SIR,

It is not, perhaps, usual, but I am little read in the history of such things, for an author to inscribe two works to the same person. Permit me, however, to dedicate a second, though a smaller, work to YOU.

When I compiled the former, we stood in a different relation to each other—YOU A GOVERNOR, I one of your subalterns—now we are merely, what I am not a little proud and happy in saying we at all times have been, FRIENDS. In the first case, a prudent forecast, laudable and honourable will be admitted, of bettering my fortunes, might have been supposed to mingle with other sentiments. Now, continents and oceans are interposed between us, and we may never meet again: this Dedication of my humble Work cannot, therefore, flow from feelings less pure than those of GRATITUDE and ESTEEM. These would, of themselves, necessarily have influenced me; but when I recollect that I dedicate the HINDÚ PANTHEON to the man whose name and character, of all men now in *India*, (and with the exception, perhaps, of WARREN HASTINGS, of all men who have ever been there) are looked up to with the most respect and reverence by the extraordinary race whose prejudices and superstitions on the subject of MYTHOLOGY I here endeavour to illustrate, and who in varied knowledge of that race is exceeded by few — when I recollect these facts, I persuade myself that I am guided by a propriety, independent of personal considerations, not often attainable on such occasions.

The language of adulation would ill become me to adopt, or YOU to approve; nor is it likely that I shall now use it, for the first time. In what I state, those who know me will give me credit for being sincere; those who know us both will see that I am no more than just.

The complimentary style in which dedicators of the last and preceding centuries indulged themselves, is happily now disused; and were it otherwise, I should be backward, not only in following their example, but, knowing who I address, in saying what I feel. But I may, passing over all other instances of public and private virtue, be permitted to state that to YOU, and YOU solely, is humanity indebted for her triumph over unnatural enthusiasm, in the entire and voluntary abolition of that most extraordinary practice, INFANTICIDE; formerly and lately so unhappily prevalent among some misguided classes, both in the East and West of *India*.

Thousands of infants owe a continuation of their existence to YOU :—as many mothers, that they, when with Nature's tenderness nurturing their offspring, have not been forced to "TEAR THE NIPPLE FROM THEIR BONELESS GUMS, AND DASH THEIR BRAINS OUT."— There are few persons who may not envy YOU the feelings legitimately arising from such retrospections. That YOU may long enjoy them, and all that flow from the zealous promotion of the PUBLIC GOOD; and from the extensive exercise of PRIVATE BENEVOLENCE, is my most cordial wish.

EDWARD MOOR.

PREFACE.

It having fallen to my lot to visit, in very early life, the extraordinary people whose Mythology I here endeavour to explain, and to remain among them, in situations frequently favourable to the acquisition of information, until lately, I take the liberty of offering to the Public this Work, the result of my observations and inquiries.

During an intercourse of many years, with natives of almost every description, I often, in conversation on interesting topics, found myself at a loss in comprehending certain terms and allusions, and in seeking what I required; and frequently experienced the utility of pictures and visible objects in directing me in both: hence I began to collect pictures and images, which in the progress of years, without being particularly valuable as a selection, have accumulated to a considerable extent.

Conceiving that the possession of such objects may be of similar use in guiding the inquirer to sources of information that might not otherwise offer, and be agreeable at the same time to those in search of amusement chiefly, I have caused many of those subjects to be accurately copied, and engraved by hands eminent in their respective lines. The greatest attention has been paid by the ingenious artist (*Mr.* Haughton of the Royal Academy) in taking the portraits of the images and the drawings of the pictures for my plates; which may be relied on as faithful representations of the original subjects; and will, I hope, be deemed curious in themselves, as well as possessing, in many instances, a highly creditable portion of elegance in their execution.

Hindu artists being more skilful in metallurgy than in perspective, I farther indulge the hope, that in the latter line my Work may, if haply introduced among them, be ultimately of utility in contributing to their improvement; nor, perhaps, will even the *amateur* or artist of *Europe* easily find more graceful models of outline than some of my plates will afford him.

My Work has, as is generally the case, exceeded in bulk what I originally intended, although, as will appear, I have well filled both page and plate, (for the plates, though but one hundred and five in number, contain nearer two than one thousand mythological figures, attributes, and subjects,) and have resorted to some artifices to increase their contents. Being unable to read the sacred books of the *Brahmans*, as *Mr*. WILKINS, *Mr*. COLEBROKE, *Mr*. WILFORD and others are, and as *Sir* WILLIAM JONES (alas!) was, I have, as acknowledged, very freely availed myself of the labours of these learned Gentlemen, and shall be well pleased if, in return, they can benefit in any way from my publication.

Of such friends as have favoured me with the gift, or loan, of materials, I have made grateful mention; and I will here generally thank many others who made me obliging offers of a sistance that it did not suit me to accept. In this I could do myself honour by names eminent for learning and virtue, both in *England* and in *India*; some of whom, however, and the obligation is the greater, I am not so fortunate as to call friends personally, but they have been such to my work, and I heartily thank them. Other zealous friends in both portions of the globe have most kindly and profitably exerted themselves in favour of my work; such will accept my cordial acknowledgements.

To *Mr*. WILKINS, whose kindness has been so promptly extended to me on every occasion, mythological and miscellaneous, I must, however, thus return thanks in a more pointed manner; and should do it more particularly were it not that the pride, which I cannot conceal, of the countenance and friendship of a man of such rare talents and virtues, might wear the semblance of a display of vanity and egotism. Among other aids he has been so good as to affix the names in *Sanskrit*, to many of the subjects of my plates. But it may be necessary to mention that, however I may have availed myself of his intelligence and communications, he bears no share in their application or arrangement; and that although my advantages so derived are numerous, the errors and follies of my work, whatever they be, are exclusively my own.

Although there can, I think, be but little doubt of the mythological legends of the *Hindus* being the source whence have been derived the fables and deities of *Greece* and *Italy*, and other heathen people of the West, a relationship highly interesting, it is not my purpose, in this publication, to enter into any disquisitions in proof of such origin: I have, indeed, seeing the length it would have carried me, avoided the subject. In the quotations that I have had occasion to make it has been introduced, and I have casually noticed some coincidencies; but I leave to learned writers any general comparison of such deities throughout their manifold agreements in origin, name, character, attributes, and other points of presumable identity.

In orthography I have generally followed *Mr*. WILKINS's System; but strict uniformity has not been observed throughout. I have not always avoided, as I wished, the hard C, initial and medial—KRISHNA is sometimes spelled CRISHNA; KARTIKYA, CARTIKYA, or perhaps, according to *Sir* WILLIAM JONES, CARTICEYA; LAKSHMI, LACSHMI, &c. The *u* for *oo*, medial and final, as introduced by him, and now generally substituted in *Hindu* for *Hindoo*, ARJUN for ARJOON, &c., I have uniformly endeavoured to use; and it was my wish, farther, to have attended to the system of accentuation adopted by the above gentlemen; but, living remotely from the press, I found accuracy on such minute points unattainable, without more frequent corrections than I could give the proofs; and I have, therefore, to avoid the risk of misleading, altogether refrained from the attempt.

It might be becoming were I to offer some apology for the presumption so apparent in my undertaking, and for my conscious comparative incompetence in executing it. Such apology, however in unison with my feelings, might afford an excuse for not publishing at all, but would be insufficient for publishing, if it prove so, a bad book; and I shall urge it no farther than to avail myself of the opportunity of stating, that having been accustomed to an active life, I arranged the materials of this work, during an undesired abundance of leisure, for the sake of the employment it yielded; and in the pleasing hope that my friends and the public will not be altogether disappointed. I assure my READER, that I have done my best; and wish, more earnestly than he can, that it were in my power to offer him a book more worthy of his favourable notice.

The Frontispiece to this work is taken from a brass cast of GANESA, the *Hindu* God of Prudence and Policy, generally invoked at the commencement of all undertakings, whether of a literary or other description, as is more particularly explained in page 169, and in other pages referred to in the Index. The sacred and mystical character seen encircled by a serpent over his head, is the holy monosyllable A U M, or O'M—see page 410, and Index. Above the plate is *Sri* GANESA, in *Sanskrit* characters, from *Mr.* WILKINS's masterly pen; as is also the *Sanskrit* in the title-page—*Sri sarva Déva Sabbá—the Court of all the holy Gods.*

It was my intention to have interspersed the plates among the pages, and facing those wherein the plates are more particularly described, an arrangement adverted to in some passages:—but, on the completion of the work, I found it inconvenient; for plates are referred to from many pages, and placing them at the end was found preferable in several respects, and has been adopted.

INDEX

To the Pages wherein the Plates of this Work are described, or noticed.

For the Forehead (or Sectarial) Mark of any subject, the Reader is referred to Plate 2, and its explanation in *pages* 399 to 409.

THE BINDER

Is requested to be particularly careful not to cut off more of the edges than is absolutely necessary to smooth them—the size of the page and plates will not admit of it. He will place

The Frontispiece opposite the Title-page—the other plates, N° 2 to 105, between page 452 and the Index.

ERRATA.

Page 92. line 2. from bottom, *for* cast—*read* cart.

109. l. 1. for *fig.* 1—read *fig.* 3.

114. l 14 and 21. for *vahara*—read *varaha*.

155. l. 15. from bottom, *for* BHANANI—*read* BHAVANI.

190. l. 7. from bottom, for *Zug*—read *Yug*.

312. l. 10. for *wane*—read *wain*.

352. l. 11. from bottom, *for* clothing—*read* clothing."

356. l. 14. *for* page 515—*read* page 315.

424. l. 9. *for* rather in the house—*read* rather than in the house.

426. l. 2. *for* by a whip—*read* for a whip.

442. l. 6. from bottom, *for* "observe—*read* "I observe.

THE

HINDU PANTHEON.

OF BRAHM.

The religious doctrines of the *Hindus* may be divided, like those of most other people whose scriptures are in a hidden tongue, into *exoteric* and *esoteric*; the first is preached to the vulgar, the second known only to a select number: and while the *Brahmans* are admitted to possess a considerable portion of unadulterated physical, and moral truths, the *exoteric* religion of the *Hindus*, in general, consists in gross idolatry and irrational superstition.

The doctrines thus divided, may be otherwise styled *religion* and *mythology*: the latter is perhaps the invention rather of poets than of priests; but being so well adapted to their purpose, the priests have artfully applied it to rivet the mental chains that, when the scriptures are concealed, they seldom fail to assist in forging for mankind.

Strictly speaking, the *religion* of the *Hindus* is *monotheism*. They worship God in unity, and express their conceptions of the Divine Being and his attributes in the most awful and sublime terms. God, thus adored, is called Brahm: the One Eternal Mind; the self-existing, incomprehensible Spirit.

After this we enter a field of allegory, so wide and so diversified, and at first sight so apparently confused and contradictory, that much ingenious research was found necessary, among its early cultivators, to reduce it to any regular arrangement; and much remains still to be done, before the inquirer can be repaid by the development of those truths that are unquestionably buried in the amazing mass of mythology, that I humbly endeavour to illustrate.

The will of God, that the world should exist and continue, is personified; and his creative and preservative powers appear in BRAHMA and VISHNU, while SIVA is the emblem of his destructive energy; not, however, of absolute annihilation, but rather of reproduction in another form.

In *mythology*, therefore, this triad of persons represent the almighty powers of *creation, preservation*, and *destruction*. In *metaphysics* BRAHMA is *matter*, VISHNU *spirit*, SIVA *time;* or, in natural philosophy, *earth*, *water*, and *fire*.

Once deviating from rational devotion, the ardent mind of man knows no bounds: these three persons are hence fabled to have wives, the executors of the divine will, the energies of their respective lords. The fables arising from sexual allegories can scarcely fail of degenerating into indelicacy, although we may admit that many historical and scientific truths lie concealed in their moral.

The rage for personification is unbounded: the sun, moon, and all the heavenly host; fire, air, and all natural phenomena; all nature indeed is animated—the passions and emotions of human beings, their vices and virtues, are transformed into persons, and act appropriate parts in the turbulent history of man.

The preservative and regenerative powers, being in constant action, are feigned to have descended on earth innumerable times, in divers places, for the instruction and benefit, including the profitable punishment, of mankind. The wives and children of these powers have also, like their lords and parents, descended and assumed an infinite variety of forms on earth for similar purposes. The history of these endless incarnations affords ample scope for the imagination; and they are worked up by the poets with wonderful fertility of genius and pomp of language into a variety of sublime descriptions, interspersed with theological and moral texts, that at length were received as inspired productions, and have become the standard of divine truth.

Of BRAHMA, the deity's *creative* energy, less appears to have been said and sung, than comparatively of the other coequal members of the triad: he has, like them, his consort and offspring, and has had terrestrial incarnations; but the work of creation being past, BRAHMA, its represented power, is no longer especially adored in temples dedicated exclusively to him: associated with the other deities, offerings are gratefully made, and invocations piously addressed to the primary person; but as his portion of divine activity doth not operate on the present hopes and fears of the enthusiastic, or trembling suppliant, the exclusive and especial adoration of BRAHMA has mixed itself with that addressed to VISHNU and SIVA: gratitude is less ardent than hope or fear; in time it becomes overpowered by their superior potency, and its object is in a manner forgotten. But a *Hindu*, spurning at sobriety of narration, cannot plainly state any historical or philosophical fact; it must have a fabulous and mythological origin, progress, and termination: hence the three sects, who separately worshipped the coequal, coeternal powers, have, by a series of poetical persecution and warfare, in which the followers of BRAHMA were discomfited, his temples overthrown, and his worship abolished, been reduced to two; and the sects of *Vaishnava* and *Saiva* now comprise all the individuals of that very numerous race, distinguished by the appellation of *Hindus*.

These two sects, or grand divisions, are variously subdivided, as will be unfolded in the course of our work; but the whole, with the exception of the philosophic few, are influenced by a superstitious and idolatrous polytheism. The ignorant address themselves to idols fashioned by the hand of man; the sage worships God in spirit.

Of that infinite, incomprehensible, self-existent Spirit, no representation is made: to his direct and immediate honour no temples rise; nor dare a *Hindu* address to him the effusions of his soul otherwise than by the mediation of a personified attribute, or through the intervention of a priest; who will teach him, that gifts, prostration, and sacrifice, are good because they are pleasing to the gods; not, as an unsophisticated heart must feel, that piety and benevolence are pleasing to God because they are good.

But, although the *Hindus* are taught to address their vows to idols and saints, these are still but types and personifications of the Deity, who is too awful to be contemplated, and too incomprehensible to be described: still the ardour and enthusiasm of sectaries, when representing the object of their own exclusive adoration, dictate very awful and sublime effusions, exalting him into the throne of the Almighty, and arraying him in all the attributes of the Most High. It is, therefore, under the articles allotted to the description of persons and attributes, and sects and symbols, that our attention will be chiefly arrested and detained. As the *Hindu* erects no altars to BRAHM, so we shall in this place make him but a brief offering of our consideration: in imitation of sectarial devotees, we shall dwell longer on the contemplation of created or imaginary beings, and haply aided by a ray of their philosophic light, look through nature up to nature's God.

"Of Him, whose glory is so great, there is no image," *(Veda.)* I can give no representation in the engraved portion of my work; nor shall I here detain the reader, but proceed to the consideration of the personified attributes of that invisible, incomprehensible Being, "which illumines all, delights all, whence all proceeded; that by which they live when born, and that to which all must return." *(Veda.)*

BRAHMA.

BRAHMA, the personification of the *creative power* of the Deity, although the name of the three most familiar perhaps to *European* readers, is, in fact, not so often heard of in *India* as either of the other two great powers of preservation and destruction; or as of several other deities, or incarnations of deities, of an inferior description. Images are made of BRAHMA, and, placed in the temples of other gods, he is reverently propitiated by offerings and invocations; and he has had, like VISHNU and SIVA, also incarnations, or *avataras*, but he has no temples, as many other deities have, or rites, exclusively dedicated to him. The act of creation is past; the creative power of the Deity has no immediate interference in the continuance or cessation of material existence, or, in other words, with the preservation or destruction of the universe. At a stated time the creative power will again be called into action, as will be noticed when we speak of the period *Calpa:* till when, the powers of preservation and destruction only excite the hopes and fears of the devotee. But as, according to the generally received theory, destruction (as we must occasionally, although in view to such theory, rather unphilosophically, term the effects of the destroying power,) is only reproduction in another form; and as creation is a modification of a pre-existing formation of matter, the creative, as well as the destructive power, is thus admitted to be also, although less evidently, in constant action. Such action is, however, inevitable in its results, and the principle or power exciting it is less ardently, and less conspicuously, invoked and propitiated, than its dreaded destructive and contingent precursor; although their reciprocal action and reaction have caused a sort of unity of character; and BRAHMA and SIVA are sometimes found almost identified with each other: oftener, however, in direct opposition and hostility. BRAHMA creates, SIVA destroys; but to destroy, is to create in another form: SIVA and BRAHMA hence coalesce.

In mythology, therefore, BRAHMA is the first of the three great personified attributes of BRAHM, or the Supreme Being. He is called first of the gods; framer of the universe; guardian of the world: under the latter character, agreeing with VISHNU. In physics, he is the personification of matter generally: from him all things proceeded, and in him pre-existed the universe; comprehending all material forms, which he at once called into creation, or arranged existence, as they are now seen; although perpetually changing their appearances by the operation of the reproductive power. As the oak exists in the acorn, or rather, as the *Hindu* would express it, as the fruit is in the seed, awaiting development and expansion, so all material forms existed in BRAHMA, and their germs were at once produced by him.

> Grain within grain, successive harvests dwell,
> And boundless forests slumber in a shell. DARWIN.

From his mouth, arm, thigh, and foot, proceeded severally the priest, the warrior, the trader, and the labourer; these by successive reproduction people the earth: the sun sprung from his eye, and the moon from his mind.

BRAHMA is usually represented with four faces, said to represent the four quarters of his own work; and said, sometimes, to refer to a supposed number of elements of which he composed it; and to the sacred *Vedas*, one of which issued from each mouth. There are legends of his having formerly had five heads, one having been cut off by SIVA, who is himself sometimes five-headed; these legends will be noticed hereafter.

Red is the colour supposed to be peculiar to the creative power: we often see pictures of BRAHMA of that colour; which also represents fire, and its type the Sun: it is likewise the colour of the earth or matter, which BRAHMA also is; BRAHMA is, therefore, the earth; so we shall, by and by, find is VISHNU— BRAHMA is fire, so is SIVA, and all three are the Sun; and the Sun is a symbol of BRAHM, the Eternal One. Fire is an emblem of the *all-changing*, that is TIME; SIVA generally, and BRAHMA occasionally, correspond with TIME. I thus early notice this agreement, or contradiction, or whatever it be, as I shall have occasion frequently, in the course of my humble work, to bring it to the reader's recollection, that most, if not all, of the gods of the *Hindu* Pantheon, will, on close investigation, resolve themselves into the three *powers*, and those powers into one Deity, BRAHM, typified by the Sun.

Keeping this in view, we may perhaps account for the disagreement discernible in the different accounts relating to the theogony of the *Hindus*. They are, as we shall have occasion often to notice, divided into sects, each sect worshipping some individual deity, or two or more conjoined: such individual deity is gifted by its votary with all the attributes of the Most High, and is made the source whence emanate all other gods. Although there is, I believe, no sect named after BRAHMA, denoting him to be the exclusive object of their adoration, yet by some legends he is described as the Almighty; and even his spouse, or *Sacti*, SARASWATI, as we shall find when we come to notice her, is described as all-productive, all-powerful, and all-wise.

Thus, if a *Vaishnava* speak or write of VISHNU, he is actually described as the Deity: if one of the adored incarnations, or *avataras* of VISHNU, (CRISHNA, or RAMA, for instance,) he is likewise omnipotent and omniscient—he is VISHNU. The same of SIVA, when described by one of his own sect; he is the very God of very God: this may be extended even to inferior gods and goddesses. A poet, meaning to describe their energy, calls them omnipotent; their wisdom, they are omniscient; their activity, they are omnipresent: hence arises a confusion that embarrasses the inquirer at every step; "gods meet with gods, and jostle in the dark;" and being ultimately resolvable into one, as that one is approached, the clashing seems more and more frequent.

Mr. COLEBROKE, in a paper that I shall frequently have occasion to benefit by, has the following paragraph, applicable to this topic.

"The deities invoked appear, on a cursory inspection of the *Veda*, to be as various as the authors of the prayers addressed to them; but, according to the most ancient annotations on the *Indian* scripture, those numerous names of persons and things are all resolvable into different titles of three deities, and ultimately of one God. The *Nighanti*, or glossary of the *Vedas*, concludes with three lists of names of deities: the first comprising such as are deemed synonimous with fire; the second, with air; and the third, with the sun. In the last part of the *Niructa*, which entirely relates to deities, it is twice asserted, that there are but three gods—'*Tisra eva devatah.*' The further inference, that these intend but one deity, is supported by many passages in the *Veda*; * and is very clearly and concisely stated in the beginning of the index to the *Rig Veda*, on the authority of the *Niructa*, and of the *Veda* itself.

"The deities are only three, whose places are the earth, the intermediate region, and heaven; (namely,) fire, air, and the sun. They are pronounced to be (the deities †) of the mysterious names ‡ severally; and (PRAJAPATI) the

* The books of *Indian* scripture, called the *Vedas*, will be hereafter noticed.

† The words between brackets, in this, and in future quotations, are not in the original text of the *Veda*, or other quoted work, but are the gloss of the commentator; concisely interpolated to elucidate the text, otherwise often obscure.

‡ *Bhur*, *Bhuva*, and *Swar*; called the *Vyahritis*. See *Institutes* of MENU, c. 2. v. 76. Mysterious words and symbols will come more particularly under our notice hereafter.

lord of creatures, is (the Deity) of them collectively. The syllable O'M intends every deity: it appertains to (BRAHME) the vast one; to (DEVA) God; to *(Adhyatma)* the superintending soul. Other deities, belonging to these several regions, are portions of the (three) gods; for they are variously named and described, on account of their different operations; but (in fact) there is only One Deity, THE GREAT SOUL, *(Mahanatma)*. He is called the Sun; for he is the soul of all beings; (and) that is declared by the sage: 'The Sun is the soul of *(jagat)* what moves, and of *(tatnush)* that which is fixed.' Other deities are portions of him; and that is expressly declared by the sage: 'The wise call fire INDRA, MITRA, and VARUNA,' &c.

"This passage, taken from different parts of the *Veda*, shows," says *Mr.* COLEBROKE, "(what is also deducible from other texts of the *Indian* scriptures, translated in the present and former essays,) that the ancient *Hindu* religion, as founded on the *Indian* scriptures, recognises but one God; yet not sufficiently discriminating the creature from the Creator."—On the *Vedas*. *Asiatic Researches.* Vol. VIII.* p. 397.

In the above quotation, the places of the three deities are said to be the earth, the intermediate region, and heaven; namely, fire, air, and the Sun. In the usual arrangement of the three deities, viz. BRAHMA, VISHNU, and SIVA, we may, therefore, respectively so apply those terms. VISHNU is commonly said to be air, spirit, space, as well as the all-pervading Sun. Fire is applied typically, as well as the Sun, to both BRAHMA and SIVA, but never, I think, to VISHNU, who is humidity in general. Nor is the earth ever symbolical of SIVA, as it is occasionally both of VISHNU and BRAHMA.

Thus, to recapitulate, I have supposed the three great principles to coalesce, and, in a greater or less degree, participate, or not, in these particulars.—

BRAHMA	and	SIVA	are	*Fire*	in which	VISHNU	does not participate, or participates but remotely.
VISHNU		BRAHMA		*Earth*		SIVA	
SIVA		VISHNU		*Water*		BRAHMA	

All three are the Sun and Time; but it is probable, that these distinctions may not bear strict application in every instance.

* The edition of the *Asiatic Researches*, referred to in this work, is, as far as the eighth volume, the *London* octavo. The ninth volume not being yet republished in *England*, I refer, in that instance, to the *Calcutta* quarto edition.

I shall enter as little as possible into the subject of *Hindu* philosophy; no farther, indeed, than is immediately connected with their mythology. The following passage from *Sir* WILLIAM JONES's Dissertation on the Gods of *Greece*, *Italy*, and *India*, will show how those subjects are connected, and how the three great powers emanate from, and exist in, BRAHM.

"It must always be remembered, that the learned *Hindus*, as they are taught by their own books, in truth, acknowledge only One Supreme Being, whom they call BRAHME, or the Great One. They believe his essence to be infinitely removed from the comprehension of any mind but his own; and they suppose him to manifest his power by the operation of his divine spirit, VISHNU, the *pervader*, and NARAYAN, or *moving on the waters*; both in the masculine gender: whence he is often denominated the *first male*. And by this power it is believed, that the whole order of the universe is preserved and supported; but the *Vedantis*, unable to form a distinct idea of brute matter independent of mind, or to conceive that the work of supreme goodness was left a moment to itself, imagine that the Deity is ever present to his work, and constantly supports a series of perceptions; which, in one sense, they call *illusory*, though they cannot but admit the *reality* of all created forms, as far as the happiness of creatures can be affected by them. When they consider the divine power exerted in *creating*, they call the deity BRAHMA, in the masculine gender also; and when they view him in the light of *destroyer*, or rather *changer* of forms, they give him a thousand names: of which, SIVA, ISA or ISWARA, RUDRA, HARA, SAMBHU, MAHADEVA or MAHESA,* are the most common. The first operations of these three powers are variously described in the different *Puranas*, by a number of allegories; and from them we may deduce the *Ionian* philosophy, of *primeval water*; the doctrine of the mundane egg; and the veneration paid to the *Nymphæ*, or *Lotos*, which was anciently revered in *Egypt*, as it is at present in *Hindustan*, *Tibet*, and *Nepal*."—*Asiatic Researches*. Vol. I. p. 243.

The names of BRAHMA are not so numerous as those of his great coadjutors. VISHNU and SIVA are said to have a thousand each. He is sometimes called KAMALAYONI. *Kamal* is the *lotos*, *Yoni* the *pudendum muliebre*, (a type of BRAHMA, or the creative power,) the mystical matrix, into which is inserted the equally mysterious *Linga* † of SIVA. BRAHMA having, by a generally

* MAHESA is, *maha*, *great*, and ISA, *Lord*; the epithet is prefixed to many names of gods: and when the name has an initial vowel, the final of the epithet is omitted, both in writing and conversation.—MAHISWARA, the same with MAHESA.

† These mysterious subjects will be noticed hereafter.

received system, founded on the doctrines of the *Vaishnavas*, sprang on a lotos from the navel * of VISHNU, to "bid all worlds exist," has hence, and perhaps in other points, relation to the lotos: but it is a more immediate attribute of VISHNU, being the prime of aquatic vegetables; and he, a personification of water. His consort, LACSHMI, in one character, sprang from the sea; and the lotos, being also the emblem of female beauty, is peculiarly sacred to her; and she is called KAMALA, or *lotos-like*.

We shall, in future pages, enter more fully into all the points alluded to in the preceding paragraph; which are here given in outline, by way of introduction to our subjects.

All the principal, and several of the secondary deities, or incarnations of the principal, have wives assigned them, who are called *Sacti*; and, except in sex, exactly represent their respective lords, being their *energy*, or *active power*—the executors of their divine will. The *Sacti* of BRAHMA is SARASWATI, the goddess of harmony and the arts. A separate article will be allotted for a description and account of her, as well as to the *Sactis* in general.

Many deities have, as well as wives, vehicles, or *vahans*, allotted to them: that of BRAHMA, and of his *Sacti*, is the swan, or goose, called *hanasa*; but he is not so frequently seen mounted on it, as other deities are on theirs. In my collection of images and pictures, I have not one of him so mounted; nor do I recollect having met with him on, or with, his goose, except in the celebrated cave on *Elephanta*.

It is said by some authors, that there is no image of BRAHMA.—(CRAUFURD's Sketches. Vol. I. p. 149.) "No image is made of BRAHMA, or God." This is not correct of BRAHMA, but is of BRAHM. The two persons are often confounded by authors who wrote twenty or more years ago.

CRAUFURD appears to have taken his opinion from *M. de la* CROZE; who, however, says, that "no image is ever made of God,"† that is, of BRAHM. At the time CRAUFURD wrote, he might have seen many images and pictures of BRAHMA, both in *India* and in *Europe*.

Of BRAHMA, several pictures are given in this publication; and I will now proceed to describe one or two of them that, in the numerical order in which they are placed, fall into this early portion of our work. In future pages I shall frequently have occasion to point the reader's attention to this deity, represented among others in correspondent plates.

* See PLATES 7. 8.

† *Hist.* du *Christ.* des *Indes.*

In **Plate 3** he is seen in his usual form, with four faces, and four arms, having in his hands, what his descendants, the *Brahmans,* are supposed to have often in theirs, viz. a portion of the *Veda,* or scripture; a spoon, used in the performance of sacred ceremonies, for lustral * water; a rosary for assisting abstraction, in contemplating the attributes of God, a bead being dropped at the mental recitation of each of his names, while the mind is intensely fixed on the idea that the name, which is significant of some attribute, excites; and, fourthly, a vessel to contain water for ablution, a preliminary essential to prayer or sacrifice.

This plate is taken from a cast in metal, made by *Mr.* Wilkins, superintended by *Pandits,* (learned *Brahmans,* theologians,) in *Benares.*

Plate 4 is copied from a beautiful painting, in the collection of *Colonel* Stuart; in which Brahma is officiating as a *Brahman,* at one of the daily sacrifices which individuals of that tribe are compelled to offer. His consort, or *Sacti,* Saraswati, is in attendance, and presenting him with the holy utensils. A sort of magical square is seen near the carpet, the sacrificial fire, and sundry implements used on these occasions: on which points we shall, when describing the plates containing those implements, bestow a further portion of our attention. The grace and elegance of the females, and the general beauty of the plate, will, I trust, bespeak the applausive consideration of the reader.

The subjects in the two compartments of Plate 5 are taken from two sketches that I found among my materials. They came into my hands at *Poona,* and are mere outlines; exactly represented in the plate. The upper compartment contains the three grand attributes of the Deity, personified in Brahma, Vishnu, and Siva: Creation, Preservation, and Destruction. The lower, has the same figure of Siva in a sitting position, with his consort, or energy, Parvati, (*fig.* 5.) We shall hereafter advert descriptively to the other subjects, here only noticing Brahma, (*fig.* 3.) with his four faces and arms, with the rosary, spoon, &c. as before. In the right superior hand, I imagine, is the water vessel for ablution, or sacrifice: it is somewhat equivocal, but the plate is a *fac simile* of the sketch, of the original of which I know nothing, nor by whom the sketch was taken.

Having rather unexpectedly introduced these five important mythological personages at so early a period, (I say *five,* for the lower central little gentleman (*fig.* 6.) I am not acquainted with,) I will make them further known to the

* They are of different forms, as shown in some of our plates.

reader by an appropriate extract of the invocatory part of an inscription, on a plate of copper, found in the district of *Gorakhpur.** The first verse *Mr.* COLEBROKE, in the note, refers, very properly no doubt, to SIVA. I should, I think, unassisted, have fancied it addressed to BRAHM, "the Universal Soul, who pervades all." But as the production of a *Saiva*, MAHADEVA, (or SIVA,) would of course be addressed as THE DEITY. The three next verses are addressed to his three great powers—BRAHMA, VISHNU, and SIVA; the latter propitiated in the person of his *Sacti*, or consort, PARVATI.

"1. SALUTATION to the god, who is manifested in various forms, from the earth, to the performer of a sacrifice†; who is an universal soul, to be apprehended only by contemplation of saints; and who pervades all.

"2. SALUTATION to the unborn ‡ god, who makes the world's production, its continuance, and ultimate destruction; and the recollection of whom, serves as a vessel of transport across the ocean of mundane ills.

"3. SALUTATION be to the husband of LACSHMI; to him who reposed on *Sesha*.‖ as on a couch; to him who is VISHNU, extracting the thorns of the three worlds; to him who appears in many shapes.

"4. SALUTATION be to the blessed foot of PARVATI, which destroyed the demon §MAHISHA, by whom all had been overcome; and which gives felicity to the world."

In this place I will introduce a lengthened extract from *Mr.* WILFORD's Dissertation on *Egypt* and the *Nile*, as an appropriate introduction and illustration of sundry passages of our compilation.

"There is no subject, on which the modern *Brahmans* are more reserved, than when closely interrogated on the title of *Deva*, or God, which their most sacred books give to the Sun: they avoid a direct answer, have recourse to eva-

* From the *Asiatic Researches*. Vol. IX. p. 407. *Calcutta* edition.

† "SIVA manifested himself in eight material forms; viz. earth, water, fire, air, ether, the sun, the moon, and the person who performs a sacrifice." COLEBROKE.

‡ "BRAHMA, the Creator; himself not created, and therefore termed unborn."—*Idem.* The reader will please to note, that BRAHMA, as well as the creative, has the conservative and destructive powers, likewise, attributed to him: in this instance the three coalesce in BRAHMA, as in other instances they do similarly in other deities; of which the reader will have been apprised in the preceding pages.

‖ See PLATES 7. 8.

§ The destruction of the *Asura*, or demon, MAHISHA, a personification of wickedness, is a very popular legend, and is seen as often as any in pictures and casts. It was achieved by PARVATI, in her martial character of DURGA, or active virtue: the subject occurs very often in this work, (PLATES 34. 35. and others,) and will be particularly discussed hereafter.

sions, and often contradict one another and themselves. They confess, however, unanimously, that the Sun is an emblem or image of their great deities, jointly and individually; that is, of BRAHM, or the Supreme One, who alone exists really and absolutely: the three male divinities themselves, being only *Maya*, or delusion. The body of the sun they consider as *Maya*; but since he is the most glorious and active emblem of God, they respect him as an object of high veneration. All this must appear very mysterious; but it flows from the principal tenet of the *Vedantis*: that the only being, which has absolute and real existence, is the Divine Spirit, infinitely wise, infinitely benign, and infinitely powerful, expanded through the universe; not merely as the *soul of the world*, but as the provident ruler of it; sending forth rays or emanations from his own essence; which are the pure vital souls of all animated creatures, whether *moveable* or *immoveable*—that is, (as we should express ourselves,) both *animals* and *vegetables*; and which he calls back to himself, according to certain laws established by his unlimited wisdom. Though BRAHM be neuter in the character of the Most High One, yet, in that of supreme ruler, he is named PARAMESWARA; but, through the infinite veneration to which he is entitled, the *Hindus* meditate on him with silent adoration, and offer prayers and sacrifices only to the higher emanations from him. In a mode, incomprehensible to inferior creatures, they are involved at first in the gloom of *Maya*, and subject to various taints from attachment to worldly affections; but they can never be reunited to their source, until they dispel the illusion by self-denial, renunciation of the world, and intellectual abstraction; and until they remove the impurities which they have contracted, by repentance, mortification, and successive passages through the forms of animals or vegetables, according to their demerits. In such a reunion consists their final beatitude; and to effect it by the best possible means, is the object of their supreme ruler; who, in order to reclaim the vicious; to punish the incorrigible; to protect the oppressed; to destroy the oppressor; to encourage and reward the good; and to show all spirits the path to their ultimate happiness, has been pleased (say the *Brahmans*) to manifest himself in a variety of ways, from age to age, in all parts of the habitable world. When he acts immediately, without assuming a shape, or sending forth a new emanation; or when a divine sound is heard from the sky, that manifestation of himself is called *Acasavani*, or an *ethereal voice*. When the sound proceeds from a meteor, or a flame, it is said to be *Agnipuri*, or *formed of fire*; but an *Avatara*, is a descent of the Deity, in the shape of a mortal; and an *Avantara*, is a similar incarnation of an inferior kind, intended to answer some purpose of less moment.* The Supreme Being, and the celestial emanations from him, are *niracara*, or *bodiless*; in which state they must be invisible to mortals: but when they are *pratyacsha*, or *obvious to the sight*, they become *sacara*, or *embodied*, and expressive of the divine attributes, as CRISHNA revealed himself to ARJUN, or in a human form, which CRISHNA usually bore; and in that mode of appearing, the deities are generally supposed to be born of a woman, but without any carnal intercouse. Those who follow the *Purva Mimansa*, or philosophy of JAIMINI, admit no such incarnations of deities, but insist, that the *Devas* were mere mortals, whom the supreme Being was pleased to endow with qualities approaching to his own attributes: and the *Hindus*, in general, perform acts of worship to some of their ancient monarchs and sages, who were deified in consequence of their eminent virtues."—WILFORD. On *Egypt* and the *Nile*. *As. Res.* Vol. III. p. 374.

* Although the accuracy of this distinction cannot be questioned, I have to remark, that it is seldom observed either in conversation or writing: the term *Avantara*, to distinguish an inferior incarnation from an *Avatara*, or one in shape of a mortal, is rarely heard or met with. In what I am about to notice, I assume the point, that the shape of a mortal means a human shape; and thus the shapes assumed, or to be assumed, by VISHNU, in his ten grand *Avataras*, or *descents*, confirm what *Mr.* WILFORD says above. Four of these are of primary importance, and are in a human form, viz. RAMA, CRISHNA, BUDDHA, and KALKI; the rest were of less moment, for a particular purpose, for the punishment of an impious individual, &c. and were in the forms of other and imaginary beings: still the whole ten are alike called *Avataras*. To this it may be objected, that CRISHNA's usual four-armed form is not exactly that of a human being; he is often, however, seen with but two arms—his sectaries give him four. And further it may be said, that, in the VAMANA, or *dwarf Avatar*, VISHNU *was* in a human shape, and only diminutive: this is admitted; but he retained that form for a very short time only, and then expanded himself miraculously, for effecting the purpose of his *descent*. These *Avataras* will be fully discussed in their place.

VISHNU.

If the term orthodox can, in strictness, be applied to any sect of *Hindus*, it appears most appropriate to that of the *Vaishnavas*, or general worshippers of Vishnu. They admit the independent existence of the other personified attributes, but claim a superiority for that of preservation. Nothing, they say, can be actually destroyed: the operation of the destructive power varies the form of matter; but it is only changed, not annihilated; reproduced, not destroyed: hence they infer the paramount power of preservation. What the essential differences, between the sect of *Vaishnavas* and that of the *Saivas*, or worshippers of Siva, may be, I cannot definitely state; for while the latter deem the object of their own exclusive adoration to be the immediate type of the Supreme Being, the philosophical idea of the eternal duration of matter (that is, its susceptibility of change in form, not of annihilation in principle) seems, under some qualification, common to both. Without attempting a comparison, or contrast, of the theories of these two grand divisions of *Hindus*, I shall, under the head of each, or under that of their several *Sactis* and *Avataras*, offer such suggestions as may incidentally arise; and make such extracts of applicable legends, as may enable the reader to form an opinion himself on these and other points.

Under the head of *Sects* will be explained, how the *Vaishnavas* are subdivided: one adoring Crishna as Vishnu—and this is often considered as the orthodox *Vaishnava*; another adoring his *Sacti*, or Radha; a third, those two persons, Crishna and Radha, conjointly. And similarly, another subdivision, who worship Rama and Sita separately and together. The threefold division of *Bauddhists*, or the followers of the doctrines of Buddha, and of the two sects named after their founders, Jina and Mahiman, may also be considered as branches from the stock of *Vaishnavas*; as they, in fact, worship Vishnu in one incarnation, and the adorers of Crishna and Rama worship him in others. All these sects will be noticed hereafter.

Vishnu is the second person of the *Hindu* triad: he is a personification of the *preserving* power, and has, on the whole, no doubt, a greater number of adorers than any other deity or attribute; if, indeed, we take the sect of *Vaishnava* in its most comprehensive sense, including, as we are warranted in doing, the schism of BUDDHA, he has more than all the others collectively.

Under the several heads of *Avataras*, CRISHNA, RAMA, BUDDHA, &c. such frequent mention will be made of their prototype, VISHNU, who "is every where always," that it is impossible to avoid numerous instances of repetition; and, in our present state of mythological knowledge, some perplexity and contradictions are, I fear, equally inevitable.

He is a personification of the Sun, or, conversely, the Sun is a type of him: this character, as well as that of Time, he shares with BRAHMA and SIVA—in *Hindu* mythology every thing is, indeed, the Sun. VISHNU is sometimes the earth—he is water, or the humid principle generally: hence he is air, which the *Hindus* know to be a form of humidity. He is also space, and his colour is blue, supposed to be its apparent tint.

Mounted on an eagle, or rather an animal composed of the eagle and the man, named GARUDA, VISHNU is seen cleaving his own element, and soaring to the skies, (PLATE 10). This marks the aerial levity of his character, as the sluggish goose is emblematic of gravity, and is given as a *vahan*, or vehicle, to BRAHMA, the personification of matter or substance.

His *Sacti*, or consort, is LACSHMI, of whom, as well as of his vehicle, GARUDA, we shall hereafter take particular notice. In the plate just referred to, she is with him on his *vahan*, or vehicle, GARUDA, of whom several pictures will be given, and duly described in their places.

The following four verses are a literal translation from the *Bhagavat** by *Sir* WILLIAM JONES: they are supposed to have been pronounced by the Supreme Being to BRAHMA. The *Bhagavat*, being the work of a *Vaishnava*, it of course speaks of VISHNU as that Being, or rather of CRISHNA, identified by his sectaries with the preserving power.

"Even I was even at first, not any other thing; that which exists unperceived; supreme: afterwards, *I am that which is*; and he who must remain, am I.

"Except the *First Cause*, whatever may appear, and may not appear in the mind, know that to be the mind's *Maya*, or *Delusion*, as light, as darkness.

* The *Sri Bhagavata* comprises a life of CRISHNA, considering that *Avatara* as VISHNU himself; or, according to the *Vaishnavas*, THE DEITY. The work is esteemed as an inspired production, and ranked with the *Puranas*, of which it is reckoned the eighteenth and last, and is supposed to be more modern than the others. It, with the rest, will be noticed hereafter.

"As the great elements are in various beings, yet not entering, (that is, pervading, not destroying,) thus am I in them, yet not in them.

"Even thus far may inquiry be made by him who seeks to know the principle of mind, in union and separation, which must be *every where always*."—*As. Res.* Vol. I. p. 245.

"As the soul of the world, or the pervading mind, so finely described by VIRGIL, we see JOVE represented by several *Roman* poets; and with great sublimity by LUCAN, in the known speech of CATO, concerning the *Ammonian* oracle: 'JUPITER is wherever we look, wherever we move.' This is precisely the *Indian* idea of VISHNU, according to the four verses above exhibited—not that the *Brahmans* imagine their male divinity to be the *divine essence* of the Great One, which they declare to be wholly incomprehensible; but, since the power of *pervading* created things, by a superintending providence, belongs eminently to the Godhead, they hold that power to exist transcendently in the preserving member of the Triad, whom they suppose to be *every where always*—not in substance, but in spirit and energy. Here, however, I speak of the *Vaishnavas*; for the *Saivas* ascribe a sort of pre-eminence to SIVA."—*Ib.* p. 247.

The following legends, taken from *Mr.* WILFORD's Dissertations on *Egypt* and the *Nile*, in the third volume of the *Asiatic Researches*, will introduce us to the character of VISHNU, and other points connected with him and *Hindu* mythology in general; and will explain several difficulties in a manner superior to what I could furnish from any other source. Such passages as bear more immediately on subjects under discussion, or as may appear to require it, I shall endeavour to illustrate by a concise note or reference.

"It is related, in the *Scanda Purana*, that, when the whole earth was covered with water, and VISHNU lay extended asleep on the bosom of DEVI, a lotos arose from his navel, and its ascending flower soon reached the surface of the flood;* that BRAHMA sprang from that flower, and, looking round without seeing any creature on the boundless expanse, imagined himself to be the first born, and

* PLATES 7. and 8. represent this scene; but VISHNU is there, as I have ever seen him, and the subject is extremely popular, reposing, not on DEVI, but on SESHA, the vast thousand-headed serpent, emblematic of Eternity, or ANANTA, as the serpent, as well as VISHNU, is sometimes named; meaning *Endless*, or *Infinite*. And although, as we shall find in the sequel, the denomination of DEVI is more generally applied to PARVATI, the consort, or *Sacti*, of SIVA, than, as above, to LACSHMI, the *Sacti* and associate of VISHNU, yet the latter goddess is occasionally so called: thus in name, as well as in character, LACSHMI and PARVATI sometimes coalesce with each other, in the manner that, as we shall so often have occasion to notice, do the male divinities, their Lords.

entitled to rank above all future beings; yet, resolved to investigate the deep, and to ascertain whether any being existed in it who could controvert his claim to pre-eminence, he glided, therefore, down the stalk of the lotos, and finding VISHNU asleep, asked loudly who he was? 'I am the first born,' answered VISHNU; and when BRAHMA denied his primogeniture, they had an obstinate battle, till MAHADEVA pressed between them in great wrath, saying, 'It is I who am truly the first born; but I will resign my pretensions to either of you, who shall be able to reach and behold the summit of my head, or the soles of my feet.' BRAHMA instantly ascended; but having fatigued himself to no purpose in the regions of immensity, yet loth to abandon his claim, returned to MAHADEVA, declaring that he had attained and seen the crown of his head, and called as his witness the first born cow. For this union of pride and falsehood, the angry god ordained, that no sacred rites should be performed to BRAHMA, and that the *mouth* of the cow should be defiled, and a cause of defilement, as it is declared to be in the oldest *Indian* laws.* When VISHNU returned, he acknowledged that he had not been able to see the feet of MAHADEVA, who then told him, that he was the first born among the gods, and should be raised above all. It was after this, that MAHADEVA cut off the fifth head of BRAHMA †, whose pride (says the *Scanda Purana,*) occasioned his loss of power and influence in the countries bordering on the river *Cali.*

Whether these wild stories, on the wars of the three principal gods, mean only the religious wars between their several sectaries, or whether they have any more hidden meaning, it is evident, from the *Puranas,* which represent *Egypt* as the theatre of action, that they are the original legends of the wars

* Another legend is given in the *Sivpuran,* accounting for the cow's mouth being impure. SITA, spouse of RAMA, (that is, as we shall by and by see, LACSHMI incarnate as SITA to accompany VISHNU in his *Avatara* of RAMA,) was performing the ceremony of *Puja* on some particular occasion; a hand appeared to her (of which subject I have a picture—the hand holding a pen, and writing on the floor,) in evidence of some fact referring to her tyrannical imprisoner, RAVANA; to counteract the happy effects of which apparition, a river near which she was worshipping, the sacrificial fire, a tree that shaded her, and a cow, a spectator, told her falsehoods, and deceived her. She appropriately cursed each; and the malediction that fell on the cow was, that her mouth should, by a regurgitation from the stomach, (chewing the cud,) be ever in a state of filth and defilement. SURYA (the Sun) revealed the deceit to her, and she added lustre to his beams by the blessing that she gratefully pronounced on him. Under the article LACSHMI, and others, we shall see that this uncleanliness of the cow's mouth is amply made up to her in the purity, and cause of purity, of her other orifices, and their productions.

† This fable will be noticed under the articles DACSHA and NARAYANA. BRAHMA's decapitation, and its cause, is differently related, and the meaning of the allegory is not well understood.

between OSIRIS, HORUS, and TYPHON; for BRAHMA, in his character of all-destroying TIME, corresponds with TYPHON; and MAHADEVA, in that of the *productive principle*,* with HORUS, or HARA, who assumes each of his characters on various occasions, either to restore the powers, or to subdue the opponents of VISHNU, or active Nature, from whom his auxiliary springs."—*As. Res.* Vol. III. p. 375.

The preceding legend, as well as that which will follow, appears to be the composition of a *Vaishnava*; for VISHNU is in fact made pre-eminent, although in one part unable to discover the foot, or termination of MAHADEVA. If the allegory have, as is likely, a meaning throughout, it might be both unprofitable and tiresome to pursue it. We may, however, observe, that the conflict between BRAHMA and VISHNU, mitigated by the interposition of SIVA, refers probably to some historical incident in a religious war, in which the adherents of BRAHMA were discomfited, and his temples consequently overthrown. And although it may be said, that the moral is good, which inculcates the belief that pride and falsehood, even in a God, must meet its deserved punishment, it may be more reasonably maintained, that the example set by a deity of such a reprehensible tendency, is more likely to have a pernicious effect on the imitative frailties of human nature.

Like the gods of *Greece*, those of *India* cannot be at all times commended for the correctness of their conduct or conversation: the reverse, indeed, is too often observable.

Another legend, from the same learned dissertation, makes SIVA the offspring of VISHNU. I shall add it here, as well as the reflections of *Mr.* WILFORD naturally arising from a parentage so apparently inconsistent.

"It is said, in the *Vaishna Vagama*, that CRORASURA was a demon with the face of a boar, who, nevertheless, was continually reading the *Veda*, and performing such acts of devotion, that VISHNU appeared to him on the banks of the *Brahmaputra*, promising to grant any boon that he could ask. CRORASURA requested, that no creature, then existing in the three worlds, might have power to deprive him of life, and VISHNU complied with his request; but the demon became so insolent, that the *Devatas*, whom he oppressed, were obliged to conceal themselves, and he assumed the dominion of the world. VISHNU was then

* Here we see BRAHMA and SIVA changing or joining characters. The former is now all-destroying *Time*; the latter the *productive principle*, in direct opposition to the usual personification of the creative and destructive powers of the Deity. But to destroy is only to change, or reproduce: producing, or creating, is changing, or destroying pre-existing formations.

sitting on a bank of the *Cali*, greatly disquieted by the malignant ingratitude of the demon; and, his wrath being kindled, a shape, which never before had existed, sprang from his eyes. It was MAHADEVA, in his destructive character, who *dispelled* in a moment the *anxiety* of VISHNU: whence he acquired the surname of CHINTAHARA."—*Ib.* p. 376. *Mr.* WILFORD, pursuing the subject, proves, with great learning and ingenuity, the identity of this legend with *Egyptian* and *Grecian* stories.

"No doubt," he continues, "the whole system of *Egyptian* and *Hindu* mythology must at first view seem strangely inconsistent; but since all the gods resolve themselves into one, of whom they were no more than *forms* or *appearances*, it is not wonderful that they should be confounded; especially as every emanation from the Supreme Spirit was believed to send forth collateral emanations, which were blended with one another; sometimes recalled, sometimes continued, or renewed, and variously reflected, or refracted, in all directions. Another source of confusion is, the infinite variety of legends which were invented from time to time in *Greece*, *Egypt*, *Italy*, and *India*; and when all the causes of inconsistency are considered, we shall no longer be surprised to see the same appellation given to very different deities, and the same deity appearing under different appellations."—*Ib.* p. 381.

VISHNU and SIVA are each said to have a thousand names; and as they are in most instances significant compound *Sanscrit* words, there are legends in the *Puranas*, and other books, accounting for the origin and application of such names. In the preceding extract, we have seen on what occasion it was, that MAHADEVA acquired his appellation, *care-dispelling*, or *dispeller of anxiety*, CHINTAHARA. He is also, as well as VISHNU, called HARA *, which has, I think, some reference to distress, or lamentation; as I have, in the interior of the peninsula, heard that name distressfully vociferated, at the close of a *Hindu* funeral, by the relation of the deceased, who was a native of *Canara*.

The thousand names of VISHNU and SIVA are strung together in verse, and are repeated on certain occasions by *Brahmans*, as a sort of litany, accompanied sometimes with the rosary. As each name is mentally recited, with the attention abstractedly fixed on the attribute, or character, that such name excites the idea of, a bead is dropped through the finger and thumb: such operation is supposed to assist and promote abstraction, an attainment that enthusiastic *Hindus* think exceedingly efficacious.

* VISHNU is likewise named HARI and HERI.

Brahmans, and pious men of inferior tribes, are often seen with rosaries in their hands, (PLATE 29.) composed of amber, or of certain rough berries, that are sacred to some of the gods. BRAHMA is frequently seen in pictures or images with the rosary in his hand, (see PLATES 3. 5.) so is SIVA, (PLATES 17. 18. 20.) The hand is sometimes enclosed in a loose bag, as in PLATE 22. where we see a *Brahmani* (female *Brahman*) in the act of worship, called *Linga puja*; that is, adoring the *Linga*, or *Phallus*, of SIVA: which subject, being of a curious nature, will require discussion in a separate article; and the plate last adverted to, will in a future page be more particularly described.

The use of rosaries is adopted in *India*, and perhaps in other countries of the east, *Persia*, for instance, by *Mahommedans*, as well as by *Hindus*. With the *Mahommedans* the rosary seems to answer the same purpose as with the *Hindus*: a bead is dropped through the finger and thumb at the contemplation or repetition of certain names and attributes of God, who, in the "copious rhetoric of *Arabia*" has as many appellations nearly as in *Sanscrit*.

It might be curious to investigate, how the use of rosaries came to be adopted for the same purposes by people so distant and distinct, as *Christians, Hindus*, and *Mahommedans*. I do not recollect, (but my recollection and research are too confined to hang the lightest weight of argument on,) that they were used by *Christians* of the earlier ages, or by the *Jews* anterior to CHRIST; and as there can be very little doubt of the high antiquity of their usage among *Hindus* —it could indeed be demonstrated—it would, if the former supposition be well founded, follow, that it is an implement borrowed into the *Christian* church from the pagan temples of the east. Unless, indeed, we suppose that distant people may, without intercommunication, conceive and adopt a similar practice for the obtainment of a similar end. But it is still difficult to extend such supposition to such congeniality, as that now under consideration.

The Sun, being the glorious and universal measurer of Time, it is easy, with those who have a rage for personation, to imagine one to be the other. All the principal *Hindu* deities are the Sun: they are also Time. The Moon, receiving her glory from the Sun, we may expect to find her his fabled wife; but it is not so universally the case, as their obvious relationship might lead us to suppose: for in *Hindu* mythology the Moon is generally a male deity, CHANDRA; as it is also with some other people, as will be noticed when we arrive at that article. I say generally, for sometimes it is feminine, CHANDRI; and such character is more commonly applied to PARVATI, or DEVI, the consort or *Sacti* of SIVA, than to any other goddess. LACSHMI DEVI, as the consort of VISHNU is often called, sometimes, as is before said, simply DEVI, occasionally coalesces with PARVATI; and both, as well as SARASWATI, spouse of BRAHMA, will, I have no doubt, as *Hindu* mythology becomes more and more investigated, be identified with the Moon, or LUNA. Both Sun and Moon having been originally imagined male deities, farther fables and legends became necessary to render congruous a sexual alliance. But as we shall hereafter find one goddess to be the Moon, and wife to (SIVA, or) the Sun, we are warranted in supposing the three principal female divinities as LUNA, in a similar union with their respective Solar Lords.

Considering VISHNU as TIME, he corresponds with the HORUS of *Egypt*. There are legends of his sleeping, awaking, and turning on his side, evidently alluding to the Sun at the solstices; also to the phenomenon of the overflow and receding of the *Ganges*, so similar to that of the *Nile* in *Egypt*. On the 11th day, (sometimes on the 14th, which is the day of the full moon,) of the bright half of the lunar month *Cartica*, VISHNU is fabled to rise from his slumber of four months. A festival is held in honour of this day, and at an auspicious moment, astrologically determined, the Deity is awakened by this incantation, (or *mantra*).

"The clouds are dispersed, the full moon will appear in perfect brightness, and I come in hope of acquiring purity, to offer the fresh flowers of the season; awake from thy long slumber; awake! Lord of all worlds!"*—*As. Res.* Vol. III. p. 226.

Another festival occurs on the 11th of the bright half of the month *Ashada*, when commences, with the summer solstice, the night of the Gods; and VISHNU reposes four months on the serpent SESHA.—(See PLATES 7. 8.) Nine days afterwards, that is the fifth after the full moon, is a festival in honour of "DEVI, the goddess of nature, surnamed MANASA; who, while VISHNU and all the gods were sleeping, sat in the shape of a serpent on a branch of *Snuhi*, *(Euphorbia,)* to preserve mankind from the venom of snakes."—*Ib.* p. 287. We may here notice, although not immediately in the most appropriate place, that snakes and serpents have a conspicuous niche in the *Hindu* Pantheon. The fifth day of the bright half of the month *Sravana*, which day is called *Nagapanchami*, is "sacred to the demi gods in the form of *serpents*, who are enumerated in the *Padma* and

* See *Asiatic Researches*, Vol. III. *Sir* W. JONES on the Lunar year of the *Hindus*: a very curious article. That about to be referred to, in the eighth volume, is by *Mr*. PATERSON, on the Origin of the *Hindu* Religion. It is to be hoped, that this ingenious writer will continue his lucubrations on the subject that he has so happily chosen.

Garuda Puranas. Doors of houses are smeared with cow dung and *Nimba** leaves, as a preservative from poisonous reptiles."—*Ib.* 288.

"Both in the *Padma* and *Garuda,* we find the serpent CALIYA, whom CRISHNA slew in his childhood, among the deities worshipped on this day: as the *Pythian* snake, according to CLEMENS, was adored with APOLLO at *Delphi.*" †—*Ib.*

VISHNU, during his repose of four months, and when it is just half over, is supposed to turn himself on his side: this is on the 11th of the bright half of *Bhadra.* The coincidence of these astronomical movements, with *Egyptian* allegories of HORUS, is shown by *Mr.* PATERSON, in the eighth volume of the *As. Res.* in his ingenious Essay on the Origin of the *Hindu* Religion.

When we speak of the symbolical marks of the *Hindus,* we shall find the triangle, with the apex downwards, to be the appropriate symbol of VISHNU, considered as the principle of humidity. To descend is the property of water, and it naturally assumes that figure. Nor is the triangle, with the apex pointing upwards, a less appropriate symbol of SIVA, as Fire; it being the unvaried form of the igneous element, whose property is ascension.

The paradise, or celestial abode of VISHNU, is called *Vaikontha,* where he enjoys beatitude in the elysium of LACSHMI's lap. It is remarked in the first number of the *Edinburgh Review,* that *Vaikontha* is placed, by a commentator on the *Khetra Nirmana,* the most ancient of *Hindu* geographical books, in the frozen ocean—a circumstance that would have afforded curious confirmation to an idea of BUFFON and BAILLI, had these eminent philosophers been aware of it. I have called *Vaikontha* the *celestial* abode of VISHNU, perhaps not correctly; but there are inconsistencies in the abodes, as well as in the characters of *Hindu* deities. Sometimes they are in heaven, sometimes on earth, and, indeed, as just noticed, in the waters under the earth: *Vaikontha* is sometimes placed in a subterraneous sea of milk.

Before we close this notice of VISHNU, who will be again frequently brought forward, it may be well to give some particular description of the PLATES that in this portion of the work are introduced, representing the Preserving member of the *Hindu* Triad.

Images and pictures of VISHNU, either representing him in his own person,

* This leaf of the *Nimba,* scattered in bookcases or among clothes, will prevent the destructive approach of moths, weevils, and most reptiles.

† Under the article CRISHNA frequent references will be made to the subject of the serpent, called CALINAGA, or CALIYA. It is represented also in PLATE 13, from a cast in bronze.

or in any of his *Avataras*, or incarnations, may be generally distinguished from those of other deities by a shell, *Chank*, and a sort of wheel, or discus, called *Chakra*. The *Chank* is the large buccinum, sometimes seen beautifully coloured like a pheasant's breast. The *Chakra* is a missile weapon, very like our quoit, having a hole in its centre, on which it is twirled by the fore finger, and thrown at the destined object. Whatever mythological mischief may have ensued from its effects, it does not appear to me as capable of producing much, sent from a mortal finger. It has a sharp edge, and irresistible fire flames from its periphery when whirled by VISHNU. Two other attributes appertain generally to VISHNU: these are the *Gadha* and *Padmu*; the former a mace or club, the latter a lotos. But these last are oftener seen in the hands of his *Avataras*, than in those of VISHNU himself; and of the four attributes, the *Chank* is, I think, that which, on the whole, most distinguishes VISHNU. We do, however, sometimes see it in the hands of other deities.

Fig. 1. in PLATE 5. is VISHNU with his *Chank* and *Chakra*, in his usual four-handed form: he there holds them between two fingers, and is not in the act of hurling the *Chakra*, as he is in some of the plates of the *Avataras*.—(See 48.*) His two foremost hands, right and left, are in a position very common to several deities: it is said to be an invitation to ask, and a promise to grant, or protect. In a former page I have noticed, that PLATE 5. is from sketches of unknown originals. Over *fig.* 1. of VISHNU, is written, in *Mahraty*, NARAYAN MURTI; i. e. a figure or form of NARAYANA.

PLATE 6. *fig.* 1. is the same deity with the same attributes, somewhat differently represented. It is taken from a well executed bronze image, about a foot in height including the pedestal, to which it is joined; the back part, rising to form a sort of glory over the figure, is of brass, and of workmanship comparatively inferior to the rest of the subject. A five-headed snake, *(pancha muki,)* hence called *Naug pancha muki*, convolves behind the cap of the figure; its projected heads, looking downwards, make a kind of canopy over it. The serpent forms a part of the surrounding glory, which is inserted by two pins into corresponding sockets in the pedestal, and, being separate, may be lifted out.

The perpendicular lines, on the forehead of the subject under our notice, are said to be the distinction of the *Vaishnavas* from the *Saivas*, the latter having them horizontal. I intend, hereafter, to allot a page or two to the consideration of these sectarial and symbolical marks; but have not hitherto attended

* See PLATE 13. also.

sufficiently to the subject, to say whether or not such distinction holds universally good.

Fig. 2. of PLATE 6. is from a small cast in brass, representing VISHNU in his *Avatara* of *Varaha*, or the *boar*: his spouse, LACSHMI, is on his knee, with the *Padma*, or lotos, in her hand. In this character she is called VARAHI, the *Sacti*, or *energy* of VARAHA. The *Chank* and *Chakra* are in two of his four hands, another of which supports his *Sacti* (VARAHI), whose right hand rests on her husband's back.

Fig. 3. of PLATE 6. holds the *Chank* and *Chakra*, and I had no hesitation in determining it to be LACSHMI; but my *Pandit*, from the utensil held in the inferior left hand, insisted on its being an image of DEVI, or BHAVANI, the consort of SIVA. This utensil is a sort of cup, called *Pan patra*, often seen in the hand of the avenging DEVI, for the purpose, it is said, of receiving the blood of victims, whose incorrigibility demands a terrible vengeance; but the name means merely a drinking vessel. In placing the images for the engraving, I have been obliged sometimes, to save room, to place different deities in the same plate; but, in this instance, the correction of my *Brahman* had escaped me, and my memoranda on the subject did not meet my eye until the plate was engraved. This image, *fig.* 3. is of bronze, well executed: it is not more than three inches high.

Fig. 4. is about the same size, very well cast in copper, apparently quite new: it is also of DEVI, and is in the original, altogether, a neater and more graceful figure than the plate indicates. In her four hands are a mace, or *Gadda*; a small shield *(Dahl)*; the *Pan patra*; and something resembling a flower bud. The *Pan patra* is in the original decidedly a cup, although it may not appear so in the picture; and what I call a flower bud, may be a fruit sacred to MAHADEVA, spouse to this figure, respecting which, farther notice will be taken. On DEVI's head is a *Linga*, surmounted by a *Naug* hanging straight down her back.

Of this PLATE, *fig.* 5. is from a brass image of the same size as the last described; a good deal worn, as if from age. It is somewhat equivocal, whether it be male or female. I was about setting it down as VISHNU, with the *Chank* only; but, turning to my memoranda, I find it described as LACSHMI, wife to VISHNU, in one of his inferior *Avataras*, called BALLAJI, of which I shall speak farther in a future page.

I am not sorry that an oversight in placing *fig.* 3. of this PLATE, should so early have shown the reader how the deities, male and female, of the *Hindu* Pantheon coalesce in attributes as well as in character: here we see DEVI, the consort of MAHADEVA, bearing the symbols that I had but just stated to be the marks by which VISHNU and his *Sacti* and *Avataras* are chiefly distinguishable.

Two tinted pictures, in *Colonel* STUART's collection, furnish the subjects of our seventh plate. At present I shall describe the upper portion only.

We have said before, that no images or pictures are made of BRAHM, or THE DEITY: this is perhaps generally and strictly correct; but, as if it were impossible for any idea, however abstract, to be conceived and retained *essentially* by a *Hindu* mythologist or metaphysician, they have imagined and personified the *Spirit of God*. It is a difficult subject to discuss, and in this place I shall say little else than that this *person* is named NARAYANA, and with the sect of *Vaishnavas* he is identified with VISHNU, while, in the theogonies of the *Saivas*, NARAYANA and SIVA coalesce. I shall as early as possible again introduce the subject, and endeavour with my poor skill to clear it of some of its difficulties; or, at any rate, I will show some of them.

The portion of PLATE 7. now under our notice, represents, according to the doctrines of the *Vaishnavas*, NARAYANA, or VISHNU, reposing on the vast thousand-headed serpent, SESHA, contemplating and willing the creation of the world: the creative power, BRAHMA, is seen springing from his navel on a lotos to the face of the ocean, in which SESHA forms a couch for the contemplative Deity. BRAHMA is in his usual four-faced form: in three of his hands are the three *Vedas*, and the lustral spoon *(Sruva)* in the fourth—it looks almost as much like a flower as a spoon, and it is equally equivocal in the original; but *Colonel* STUART agreed with me in determining it to be intended for the spoon. The reader will not overlook the divine LACSHMI, *shampoing* (chafing) the foot of her heavenly Lord. As NARAYANA, however, the name of his *Sacti* is not LACSHMI, but NARAYANI. The Deity is here two-handed, and holds none of his usual attributes.

SESHA seems floating in a sea of silver or milk, just above the margin of which are BRAHMA's heads: lotos and fish abound in the sea; and ducks and other aquatic birds, peacocks, &c. sport on its banks, which are of lively green: rocks and trees fill the back and fore grounds. VISHNU is, as usual, of a dark blue colour. The plate is more graceful and elegant than the original, a remark that may be extended also to PLATE 4.

I have a tinted picture of the same subject, in which SESHA is coiled in brownish water, his heads, of which twenty-six are visible, just rising above its green margin, pointing their tongues at BRAHMA, who sits in the cup of the lotos four-faced, four-handed, holding two books and two rosaries of white beads: SESHA is milk white, save where his heads and eyes are skilfully indicated by red lines. VISHNU in colour is dark blue, four-handed; the two right hands holding the *Gadha* and *Padma*, (mace and lotos,) the other two empty, one supporting his head. His eyes, unlike most pictures of this subject, are wide open: his robe is bright yellow, the colour usually worn by VISHNU and CRISHNA; such robe is called *Pitamber*, as is sometimes the God himself. BRAHMA in this picture has also a yellow dress, and is copper-coloured, with his beards and hair white. On VISHNU's breast is usually seen a gem, named *Bhrigulita*, worn also by him in his *Avatara* of CRISHNA, and in others; and his fine head-dress, seen in PLATE 7. and others, is called *Mugut*, (or *Moogoot*). In the picture that I have been describing, LACSHMI is seated as she is in the plate, chafing VISHNU's leg, looking benignly in his face. On the top of the picture are written in *Sanscrit* these words—*Shesheshahi*, NARAYANA, LACSHMI, *sahit*; meaning NARAYANA with LACSHMI, on SESHA. In another part of the picture he is called BHAGVAN, one of VISHNU's names, and is said to be "meditating the creation in *Crirasagara*, or the sea of milk, otherwise called *Chirsamudra*."

With the *Vaishnavas* this is a favourite subject. It is frequently met with in casts, painting, and sculpture. In the notes to WILKINS's *Hitopadesa*, (p. 295.) it is noticed in these terms.—"HARI *sleeping on a serpent*. HARI is one of the titles of VISHNU, the Deity in his preserving quality. Nearly opposite *Sultan Ganj*, a considerable town in the province of *Babar*, there stands a rock of granite, forming a small island in the *Ganges*, known to Europeans by the name of the *rock of Iehangiri*, which is highly worthy of the traveller's notice for a vast number of images carved in relief upon every part of its surface. Among the rest there is HARI, of a gigantic size, recumbent upon a coiled serpent, whose heads, which are numerous, the artist has contrived to spread into a kind of canopy over the sleeping God; and from each of its mouths issues a forked tongue, seeming to threaten instant death to any whom rashness might prompt to disturb him. The whole lies almost clear of the block on which it is hewn. It is finely imagined, and is executed with great skill. The *Hindus* are taught to believe, that at the end of every *Calpa* (creation or formation) all things are absorbed in the Deity, and that, in the interval of another creation, he reposeth himself upon the serpent SESHA (duration), who is also called ANANTA (endless)."

In the outer gateway, entering the *Peshwa's* palace at *Poona*, this subject, among others, is painted in glaring colours, of colossal proportions; but as I never passed it, except on state occasions, I had not time to examine it; and it is sculptured on a large scale among the ruins of *Mabebelipur*, commonly called the Seven Towers, near *Madras*.* *Sir* CHARLES MALET noticed it among the sculptures at *Ellora*. † Among my pictures I have one nearly six feet long, and half as high, in which this is the central and principal figure: it does not differ materially from those already described. GARUDA, the *vahan* or vehicle of VISHNU, stands in a posture of adoration, with green wings, behind LACSHMI; and the whole picture, with the exception of a figure of GANESA, relates to the history of VISHNU, including his ten principal *Avataras*—those of CRISHNA and RAMA are more particularly represented. In all it comprises about fourscore figures; horses, birds, buildings, and trees, in abundance; all in gaudy colouring. SESHA has five heads, and VISHNU four empty hands.

Before we quit PLATE 7. I will extract two or three lines connected (the comprehensive wildness of *Hindu* mythology can connect any thing) with perhaps both upper and lower compartments.

"The *Nymphæa*, or lotos, floating on the water, is an emblem of the world; the whole plant signifies both the earth and its two principles of fecundation. The stalk originates from the navel of VISHNU, sleeping at the bottom of the ocean; and the flower is the cradle of BRAHMA, or mankind. The germ is both *Meru* and the *Linga*; the petals and filaments are the mountains which encircle *Meru*, and are also the type of the *Yoni*." ‡

Probably the lotos, on which the figure in the lower part sits, on the summit of a hill, with water at its base, may refer also to the fabulous or mythological mountain *Meru*, of which we shall speak hereafter. Of that figure I will here notice only, that it is compounded of half man, half woman, called *Ardha Nari*, being MAHADEVA and PARVATI conjoined—the right half, down the face and body, being the person, dress, and attributes of the male, the left of the female power. This subject will require, and obtain, a separate discussion.

The reader will now please to turn to PLATE 8. in which the principal subject, *fig.* 1. is that already discussed, and on which I will not detain him long. This is from a fine cast in bronze, in the collection of *Lord* VALENTIA; obligingly lent to me, with several other subjects of my plates, by my noble friend. In this VISHNU is attended by two wives, LACSHMI and SATYAVAMA: the latter was with him under the same name, in his *Avatara* of CRISHNA; and so was

* *As. Res.* Vol. I. p. 150. Vol. V. p. 71. † *Ib.* Vol. VI. p. 410.

‡ WILFORD.—On the Sacred Isles in the West. *As. Res.* Vol. VIII. p. 308

Lacshmi, under that of Rukmeni. Vishnu is four-handed, in two hands holding the *Chank* and *Chakra*; the *Pedma*, otherwise called *Kamal*, is borne by his ladies, who are, as goddesses of beauty, hence named Kamala—the *Kamal*, or lotos, being with the *Hindus* the emblem of female beauty: with philosophical mythologists, it is a symbol of humidity, and marks an aquatic relation in its bearer. The length of the original is about six inches. I have a cast of this subject in bronze, not so well executed as that given in the plate.

The three females in the upper part of Plate 8. represent the Goddess Lacshmi, and, bearing the lotos, are called Kamala. I selected these three from others in my collection, which, in the whole, contains ten images of this character, as being the most graceful; and perhaps the reader will think the attitude tolerably easy; but I must say that I deem the originals much more so, especially *fig*. 4. which is really an elegant and graceful cast. It is five inches high, and was once, as I was positively assured, among the idols in the domestic chapel of Nana Furnaveese at *Poona*; and was plundered thence, when that great man was so shamefully seized and used by that foolish boy, (as he was then,) the present Dowlut Rhao Sindeah. I was at that time, 1797-8, at *Poona*, but the image did not come into my hands until some years afterwards. It is old, and has apparently been buried; the breasts are very prominent and fine; the features, from age, not so perfect as in the etching.

Fig. 2. is of the size of the original, but not, I think, in so easy an attitude, especially if looked at behind, where the hair is seen very prettily gathered in a thick lock like a horn, similar to *fig*. 2. of Plate 9. but neater. The breasts are fine and full, and the features handsome, but something defaced from age; the image has also been buried. *Fig*. 3. is of the same description, apparently more modern, but less elegant, than the other two; it has likewise been buried.

Before we quit Plates 7. 8. containing the personification of eternity in Ananta, or Sesha, we will notice, that he, as well as his superior, Vishnu, has also had his *Avataras*, or terrestrial incarnations. It is related in the *Puranas*, that in Vishnu's seventh grand *Avatara*, as Rama Chandra, Sesha was born in a human shape, his half brother, son of Dasaratha, *Raja* of *Ayodeba (Oude)*, by his second wife, Sumitra, and named L'acshimana; Rama himself being born at the same time of the *Raja's* first wife, Kahunsilya.

In the *Avatara* of Crishna, Sesha was Bala Rama, Crishna's elder brother by the same parents, Vasudeva and Devaky; the latter sister to Kansa, the Herod of *Hindu* scripture history. All these personages will be again introduced.

PLATE 9. will detain us but a short time. *Fig.* 1. is from a bronze cast, of the size of the etching; it is in all essentials so like *fig.* 1. of PLATE 6. that no farther descriptive particulars are necessary. The *Chank, Chakra, Mugut,* and glory, called *Prabhaval,* (from the *Sanscrit Prabha,* splendour, brightness,) with the five-headed *Naga (Pancha muki),* are the same. The glory lifts out like the former, and the image slides out backwards by a grooved receptacle, or socket, in the pedestal; a plan very common in such subjects.

Figures 2. and 3. are back and front portraits of a woman nursing an infant: bearing a *Kamal,* or lotos, she is very likely meant for LACSHMI as KAMALA; the hair too is dressed in the gathered horn-like shape, adverted to in *fig.* 2. of the last plate; but, in this instance again, is not so neatly gathered up as it is in the original, which is tolerably well cast, but rather ill finished. The infant in *fig.* 3. is more feminine in appearance than the original, to which my *Pandit* gave no name; and I merely find a description of it among my memoranda.

The other four figures (4. 5. 6. 7.) are a form of DEVI, or BHAVANI, in her character of ANNA PURNA. Adverting to the beneficent tenor of this lady's emblem, for it is literally a domestic ladle for serving out grain withal, and her name, *Ana,* grain; *Purna,* abundance; I concluded she was an *Avatara* of LACSHMI DEVI, and, without referring to my mythological memoranda, placed her appropriately; but shall reserve my notice of her until her archetype, BHAVANI, or DEVI, come under our consideration.

PLATE 10. is composed of two pretty pictures, communicated by my liberal friend *Colonel* STUART, of the *Bengal* establishment. The lower part represents VISHNU, with his gloried head, and LACSHMI, sitting on an expanded lotos as on a carpet, and borne by his *vaban* or vehicle, GARUDA. A bow and arrow, the latter of rather a strange formation, and the *Chakra,* occupy three of his hands, while the fourth encircles and holds to his side his delightful LACSHMI. GARUDA has green wings, and a red beak, and bears also a bow and arrows: as he must be particularly introduced by and by, I shall describe him no farther here; and shall quit this pretty etching, with a mere notice, as we shall return to it hereafter, of the upper compartment, representing MAHA KALA, or *Eternity,* at the period of *Maha pralaya,* or grand consummation of all things. In the original he, like his name, is black; he holds the roll of fate, and a scimitar to execute its destructive decrees. He devours man, his own offspring, towns, cities, "the great globe itself, and all that it inherits"—the universe. The great personified powers of the Almighty, BRAHMA, VISHNU, and SIVA, "alike await the inevitable doom:" they also fall into the jaws of inexistence. KALA will then, like SATURN, destroy himself; and nothing will remain but BRAHM—THE ETERNAL ONE.

We proceed now to PLATE 11. in which *fig.* 1. represents NARAYANA and LACSHMI, a subject commonly met with in casts, but not often in pictures. I do not think that I have one picture of it among the hundreds in my possession: of casts I have three, besides the three given in PLATE 11. *Fig.* 1. is tolerably well executed in brass, and rather larger than the etching. As all my images of this subject have the attributes of VISHNU, I have no hesitation, especially as we see LACSHMI on his knee, of referring NARAYANA to that power, rather than to SIVA, with whom he occasionally coalesces, as well as with BRAHMA, as hinted at before, and as will be farther explained when we discuss that difficult subject.

In *fig.* 1. of PLATE 11. NARAYANA holds the *Chank* and *Chakra*; a third hand is on LACSHMI; and the fourth may also have held a lotos, but is now empty. The lotos, or *Pedma*, is in LACSHMI's left hand; her right holds on by her spouse.

Fig. 2. of the same plate, is the same subject in copper, tolerably well cast, somewhat larger than the etching: the *Mugut* (high cap), otherways called *Kirita* and *Toop*, is rather of singular and not inelegant construction.

Fig. 3. of PLATE 11. is also the same subject: it is of gilt brass, with an admixture of some other metal, which, to enhance its price, the vender averred was gold. The eyes of NARAYAN are rubies; rubies form his navel, and his and LACSHMI's breast-ornaments; another ruby is in the *Chank*, and another for the *Padma* in his inferior right hand. In his lower left hand is the *Gadha*; the upper had perhaps the lotos, but it is broken or worn off: a lotos was probably distinguishable in LACSHMI's hand, but it is now shapeless. The sacred thread, *Zennaar*, is conspicuous, flowing from his left shoulder. In the pedestal are three holes, one just behind the larger figure, and two in front, as if for inserting something, flowers, perhaps, at the adoration of the image. I have other images that have ruby eyes and ornaments.

In these three subjects it will be observed, that LACSHMI, as wife to NARAYANA, is out of comparison small, looking more like an infant than his consort; but her name is always put first, the subject being called LACSHMI NARAYANA.

Figures 4. and 5. of PLATE 11. are evidently of VISHNU and LACSHMI; but in this instance said by the *Brahmans* to represent them in their inferior *Avatara* of BALLAJI and his wife, in which LACSHMI retained her name. The attributes and attitudes are the same as have been before described of VISHNU and LACSHMI * as KAMALA. These images are a little larger than the etchings, and of somewhat curious workmanship; the faces, bodies, arms, and feet, being of dark copper, and the robes, head-dresses, pedestals, symbols, and ornaments, either gilt, or of light brass. I was told they were made in the *Carnatic*; and I have no other so manufactured, nor did I ever see any. They are tolerably well executed, but rather clumsily designed. The history of BALLAJI's *Avatara* will be detailed hereafter.

Figures 6. and 7. of PLATE 11. are another subordinate *Avatara* of VISHNU, under the name of WITTOBA, in which he was accompanied by LACSHMI again under her own name. They are in copper, five and six inches high, of modern clumsy workmanship; cast, I apprehend, in or near *Bombay* or *Poona*. As the legend of WITTOBA will be detailed hereafter, I shall here notice merely the apparent inconsistency of his being crowned with a *Linga*, the immediate emblem of SIVA; the singularity of the attitudes, and the marks on his right breast and left foot: all of which will in their places more particularly attract our consideration.

PLATE 12. *Fig.* 1. is another representation of BALLAJI, with his two wives, LACSHMI and SATYAVAMA. It is engraved from a pretty subject in silver, larger than the engraving, that was found in *Gayal Gher*, (otherwise *Gher gawil*,) in *Berar*, when that fort was taken by the army under *General Sir* ARTHUR WELLESLY. The centre figure has been gilt, but the gold is mostly worn off; his bracelets are of gold, put on loose after the image was cast. The figures slide backwards out of their sockets on the pedestal, in which they are farther retained by the insertion of the back, or glory, containing the hooded serpent, *Naga*, here with but one head, commonly called in *India*, from the *Portuguese*, *Cobra de Capella*. This neat subject is said, formerly, to have belonged to RAGOJI BOONSLA, and was, I suppose, plundered by a *Mahrata* on the capture of his fort; and, at length, finding its way to me, I purchased it, with a couple of little silver cups used in *Puja*, for something more than their weight in rupees.†

* As this sheet was going to the press, I noticed in *Lord* VALENTIA's collection a well executed cast of VISHNU and LACSHMI, in their *Avatara* of RAMA and SITA; indicated by HANUMAN, who is holding the foot of his Lord.

† The pedestal of this subject is not, however, engraved from the silver one that I purchased, but is added from another similar subject, the original having been very unjustifiably taken from me at the *India* house by the *King's* custom-house officers; who, in other respects, also, behaving illegally and insolently, I made a formal and specific complaint against, to the commissioners of the customs; but, so far from obtaining redress or restitution, the receipt of my letter of complaint was not even acknowledged.

There are six eyelet-holes projecting behind the back or glory, I suppose to receive sacred flowers in holy ceremonies.

In the fort of RAGOJI BOONSLA, just named, I have heard there were found many curious mythological subjects: one was particularly mentioned of silver, and described as a sort of throne, of great extent, with appropriate niches and places for a great many deities, male and female, of all sorts and sizes. It was brought to *Poona* as public prize, and the agents, not knowing what to do with it, thought of having it coined; but it coming to the knowledge of his *Highness*, SRI MANT, the *Peshwa*, who is very pious, he expressed a wish to preserve it, and he paid its weight in silver, which was found to be equal to about twenty thousand ounces, or 40,000 rupees, worth intrinsically *5000l.* sterling.

Fig. 2. of this plate, from having the *Chank* and *Chakra*, may be called VISHNU: the *Pan patra*, and staff or club, called *Lahu danda*; the bull and *Linga*, indicate MAHADEVA, of whom it is an *Avatara*, under the name of BHAIRAVA. It will, as well as *fig.* 1. be again adverted to.

In PLATE 13. VISHNU is represented from a statue, cast under the directions of *Mr.* WILKINS and learned *Brahmans* at *Benares*. Several others of the elegant set of mythological subjects originating from that classical source, will be given in the course of our work, and duly acknowledged. SIVA, the companion to VISHNU, in PLATE 13. and BRAHMA in PLATE 3. are of corresponding size, ten inches in height, and cast in a style of elegance and accuracy not often met with from the mythological founderies of *India*. VISHNU is here seen with his four hands holding his usual attributes, and whirling the *Chakra* in the mode before described.

His companion in PLATE 13. SIVA, and CRISHNA crushing the serpent CALIYA, (the latter from a small image in my collection,) will be referred to and described in their places.

We cannot better close our general hasty account of the Preserving member of the *Hindu* Triad, than with an animated passage from the conclusion of the *Gita Govinda*, a pastoral mythological dramatic poem in *Sanscrit*, glorifying CRISHNA as VISHNU, by JAYADEVA. It will also afford a pleasing introduction to our next article, the destroying, three-eyed, blue-throated, "disappointed husband of PARVATI." The "all-pervading Deity," is the Sun, or CRISHNA, or HERI, or VISHNU: the "daughter of the ocean," LACSHMI, the "sea-born goddess of beauty"—VENUS *Marina*, who is also called PEDMA, or *Lotos*, the symbol of female beauty; in this instance, RADHA, the spouse of CRISHNA, is identified with LACSHMI, of whom she was an *Avatara*. We shall have frequent occasion hereafter to draw information from the elegant pen of JAYADEVA, the great lyric poet of *India*, as introduced to us by *Sir* W. JONES; and all the mythological allusions in the following passage will unfold themselves in the course of our work.

"Whatever is delightful in the modes of music; whatever is divine in meditations on VISHNU; whatever is exquisite in the sweet art of love; whatever is graceful in the fine strains of poetry, all that let the happy and wise learn from the songs of JAYADEVA, whose soul is united to the foot of NARAYANA.* May that HERI be your support, who expanded himself into an infinity of bright forms, when, eager to gaze with myriads of eyes on the daughter of the ocean, he displayed his great character of the all-pervading Deity, by the multiplied reflections of his divine person in the numberless gems on the many heads of the king of serpents whom he chose for his couch; that HERI, who, removing the lucid veil from the bosom of PEDMA, and fixing his eyes on the delicious buds that grew on it, diverted her attention, by declaring that when she had chosen him as her bridegroom, near the sea of milk, the disappointed husband of PARVATI drank in despair the venom which dyed his neck azure."—*As. Res.* Vol. III. p. 207. JONES's Works, Vol. X.

* CRISHNA, who, by his sectaries, (called, from one of his names, *Goculastha*,) is deemed the same with VISHNU, is here denominated NARAYANA.

SIVA.

In any lengthened description of a *Hindu* deity, it is almost impossible to avoid touching on the character and attributes of another. Of the subject of our present article we have, therefore, been obliged to take some previous notice, as we shall in like manner be forced to do in this article, of the deities discussed in the past; who will also, as well as Siva, be brought forward a hundred times in the course of our descriptive account "of men and gods, and things." Hence, the reader will perceive, the difficulty of so arranging my materials as to prevent numberless repetitions, and, perhaps, contradictions: this I have endeavoured, as far as I have been able, to avoid; but I fear not with success, in a degree satisfactory to my reader—certainly not to myself.

Siva is generally ranked as the third power or attribute of the Deity: he personifies *destruction*, or rather *reproduction*; for the most popular system of *Hindu* philosophy excludes, while time shall exist, the idea of absolute annihilation: to destroy is, therefore, but to *change*, or *recreate*, or *reproduce*. And here we at once see how easy it is to confound the characters and powers of Siva and Brahma, and to imagine the deity of destruction to preside also over generation.

In the obvious arrangement of the three grand powers of the Eternal One, Creation and Preservation precede Destruction; and this is the relative philosophical and mythological rank of the triad, but not always their theological or sectarial station. For as the *Vaishnavas* exalt Vishnu, so the *Saivas* exalt Siva to the place, and describe him with the power, of the Deity, or Brahm: as all things must, at the end of time, suffer destruction, so the personification of that power must be considered as ultimately paramount, although, anterior to that inconceivable period, the preserving member of the Trinity may have apparent predominancy.

Siva being more immediately Fire, and Vishnu Water, the philosophical contests for supremacy on the parts of the adherents of these different doctrines, may remind one of those contests, something similar, although tending to another point, carried on in *Europe* by the parties at length denominated *Vulcanists* and *Neptunists.* The difference is, that in *Europe* the destruction of the world by the deluge, and in *India* its recreation after a *Kalpa,* is the point in contention by their respective *Saivas* and *Vaishnavas*; or, in other words, the *Vulcanists* and *Neptunists.*

But we will avoid the unprofitable discussion of such topics as far as may be, and proceed to notice rapidly the principal points in the character and attributes of SIVA, or MAHADEVA, leaving their illustration to unfold itself in the course of the work.

He is Time, the Sun; he is Fire, the destroyer, the generator. His consort, BHAVANI, is the symbol of created nature, and in that character named PRACRITI. As the deity presiding over generation, his type is the *Linga,* the origin probably of the *Phallic* emblem of *Egypt* and *Greece.* As the God of Justice, which character he shares with YAMA and other deities, he rides a bull, the symbol of divine justice. He holds, as his commonest attribute, a trident, called *Trisula,* in this, and in some other points, resembling our NEPTUNE: his consort also has a relationship to water, although VISHNU be generally the deity presiding over humidity. His colour, as well as that of his bull, is white; I know not why, unless it refer to the unsullied purity of justice *: his hair is of a light or reddish colour. He is sometimes seen with two hands, at others with four, eight, or ten, and with five faces, as will appear on reference to the plates. He has a third eye in his forehead, pointing up and down: this distinction is, I think, peculiar to him, and his children and *Avataras.* As emblems of immortality, serpents are a common ornament with many deities; but MAHADEVA seems most abundantly bedecked with them: bound in his hair, round his neck, wrists, waist, arms, and legs, as well as for rings, snakes are his constant attendants. A crescent on his forehead, or in his hair, is common in pictures and images of MAHESA, or SIVA.

In PLATE 13. the beautiful statue of him represents his *Trisula,* or trident, in one hand; in another, the *Pasha,* a string or rope, often seen also in the hand of his consort, CALI, for binding and strangling incorrigible offenders: his

* An ingenious writer has lately supposed SIVA's white colour to be "in *contrast* to the black night of eternity."—PATERSON. *As. Res.* Vol. VIII. But it scarcely seems allowable, to compare or assimilate, or bring things together by contrast: *Hindu* mythology is, however, very confused and contradictory, and almost any two things may be *mythologically* assimilated.

other hands, in the position before described. The third eye in his forehead seems peculiar to him, and his wife and offspring: if *fig.* 2. in PLATE 6. of the *Varahavatara*, be an exception, and the mark in the forehead of that figure looks like an eye, it is the only one that now occurs to me; but, in the course of our work, other instances may occur, although I do not expect them.

Serpents, emblems of eternity, form his ear-rings, called *Naug kundala*: his pendent collar of human heads *(Mund mala)*, marks his character of destruction, or Time; and his frontal crescent points at its most obvious measurement, by the phases of the moon. These are among the attributes that generally distinguish MAHADEVA.

In a former plate (5.) this deity has been noticed: he is there (*fig.* 2. and 4.) represented with a warlike weapon, *(Gadha*, or *Parasha,)* and an antelope in his superior hands; the former, as with many other deities, denoting vengeance, and almost all of them seem occasionally to act as its ministers; the latter, called *Mrigu*, an attribute of the god CHANDRA, the Moon; called also SASIN,* a name for the antelope, given likewise to CHANDRA. SIVA's loins are wrapped in a tiger's skin, an article that will be frequently seen in the plates of this deity; and the river goddess GANGA (the *Ganges*) beams benignly from his *Mugut*, or headpiece.

This bountiful goddess GANGA is a heroine frequently alluded to in the mythological and historical legends of the *Hindus*; and being intimately connected with the deity now under our consideration, we will in this place proceed to notice her in a variety of relations, and at considerable length; bearing, however, directly on the points that this humble work purposes to discuss.

The *Hindu* poets, in their rage for personification, have not of course forgotten those grand natural objects, Rivers: these prime gifts of beneficent nature are deified. The *Ganga, Yamuna, Saraswati, Brahmaputra, Crishna, Cauveri*, and others, enjoy their apotheosis; and there are extant numerous allegorical poems descriptive of their birth, loves, &c. &c.

Sir WILLIAM JONES, in the true spirit of a *Hindu* bard, has addressed a hymn to the Goddess GANGA, who is fabled to be the offspring of MAHADEVA; and he sings her birth, wanderings, and nuptials, with BRAHMA's son, the BRAHMAPUTRA.

* Some *Sanscrit* scholars refer the word to a hare or rabbit, which, like the antelope, may be considered an appropriate symbol of the Moon, as denoting the apparent celerity of his motion. Of this hereafter, when we discuss the Lunar deity.

"Is that the King of Dread,
With ashy musing face;
From whose moon-silver'd locks fam'd GANGA springs?" *

The pictures offered for sale in *India* are generally coloured; and SIVA, the King of Dread, whose characteristic colour is white, is often painted as if rubbed over with ashes, like anchorites or penitents, with a blue throat. The originals of PLATES 17. 18. 20. are instances of this; and in those pictures we see the river *Ganga*, which in *Europe* we have been taught to call the *Ganges*, falling from his head: and sometimes, as in PLATES 17. 18. she afterwards issues from a cow's mouth. It is said that high up towards its source, the river passes through a narrow rocky passage, that pilgrims, who visit the sacred cleft, imagine resembles a *cow's mouth*. This spot is hence called *Gawmuki*, and is a pilgrimage of great resort.

The following stanza, from *Sir* WILLIAM JONES's spirited hymn to GANGA, (*Works*, *Vol.* XIII.) will introduce and illustrate, in a happier manner than I am otherwise master of, some of the engraved subjects of my work, connected with the personages now more immediately under discussion. See PLATE 17.

"Above the stretch of mortal ken,
On bless'd *Cailasa's* top, where every stem
Glow'd with a vegetable gem,
MAHESA sate, the dread and joy of men;
While PARVATI, to gain a boon,
Fix'd on his locks a beamy moon,
And hid his frontal eye, in jocund play,
With reluctant sweet delay.
All nature straight was lock'd in dim eclipse,
Till *Brahmans* pure, with hallow'd lips
And warbled prayers, restored the day;
When GANGA from his brow, by heavenly fingers prest,
Sprang radiant, and, descending, grac'd the caverns of the West."

In this we see a poetical and popular notion of the cause of a solar eclipse, (for we must bear in mind, that SIVA's frontal eye is the sun, here eclipsed by the interposition of the moon,) and the means of restoring the equilibrium of nature's elements. We see too, that GANGA springs, like PALLAS, from the forehead of SIVA, the JUPITER *Tonans*, and *Genitor* of the *Latins*.

* JONES's Hymn to SARASWATI. Works, Vol. XIII.

PLATE 17. and that of the symbolical marks of the *Hindus*, will show the sol-lunar emblem which SIVA bears on his forehead, when the crescent encircles his frontal eye. It is also borne by some individuals and sects of *Saiva*. MAHADEVA's son, GANESA, is sometimes dignified with it, but not, I believe, in any of the subjects engraved for this work.* The title of CHANDRA-SEKRA, or *moon-crowned*, is given to SIVA when his head is so decorated: a legend, accounting for this epithet, will be given under CHANDRA, or the God LUNUS. *Chandra sekara* is the name of SIVA's terrestrial abode.

GANGA, CHANDRA, and SESHNAGA the prince of serpents, are generally seen on SIVA's head as his commonest ornaments; and poets perpetually advert to him in compound epithets, allusive to those distinguishing attributes.

An ancient grant of land, dated about 1018, A. D. engraven on six sheets of copper, found buried in *Salsette*, near *Bombay*, invokes SIVA in terms illustrative of this. The first stanza is of course, as will be noticed in its place, addressed to GANESA, the God of Prudence and Policy, first-born of SIVA and PARVATI.—(See PLATES 19. 20.)

"O'M—VICTORY AND ELEVATION.

"1. May He, who in all affairs claims precedence in adoration; may that GANAYACA, averting calamity, preserve you from danger.

"2. May that SIVA constantly preserve you, on whose head shines (GANGA) the daughter of JAHNU,† resembling-the-pure-crescent-rising-from-the-summit-of-*Su-meru*."—(A compound word of sixteen syllables.)

* BHAIRAVA, a reputed son of MAHADEVA, is painted with the third eye in the crescent, and DEVI frequently. See PLATE 24. BHAIRAVA will be noticed hereafter.

† GANGA is called the daughter of JAHNU from a supposed second birth, through a pious man of that name; and a fable is given of that incident, enforcing the idea of the extreme potency possessed by that description of persons.

In the *Gita*, when CRISHNA, describing himself to ARJUN, brings the first of all things into the comparison, he says, "Amongst rivers I am GANGA, the daughter of JAHNU." On this text *Mr* WILKINS has a note, informing us, that, when the river was first conducted from its source towards the ocean, by a prince whose name was BHAGIRATHA, it happened that JAHNU was at his devotions at the mouth of the river MAHANADI, at a place now called NAVABGANJ. The goddess, in passing, swept away the utensils for his ablutions, which so enraged him, that he drank up her stream; but, after a while, his anger was appeased, and he let her escape from an incision made in his thigh: and from this circumstance of her second birth, she was afterwards called JAHNAVI, or the offspring of JAHNU.—*Gita*, p. 151.

This story probably relates to the fact of some great man having attempted to turn a stream or creek, in which he was temporarily opposed on the part of the owners or guardians of lands granted to temples, whose devotions or interests would have suffered interruption and injury by the intended channel.

"3. May that God, the cause of success, the cause of felicity, who keeps, placed even by himself, on his forehead, a section of the moon-with-cool-beams-drawn-in-the-form-of-a-line-resembling-that-in-the-infinitely-bright-spike-of-a fresh-blown-*Cetaca*-(who is)-adorned-with-a-grove-of-thick-red-locks-tied-with-the-prince-of-serpents, be always present, and favourable to you."—*As. Res*. Vol. I. Art. 19.

Another royal grant of land (*As. Res*. Vol. III. Art. 3.) invokes MAHADEVA, immediately after the usual *Sri* GANESA *Nama*, "adoration to GANESA," thus:

"Adored be the God SAMBHU, on whom the city of the three worlds rested in the beginning as on its main pillar; and whose lofty head is adorned with a crescent, that kisses it, resembling the point of a waving *Chamara*."*

It is the *Saivas*, of course, who place the source of the GANGA in SIVA's hair, whence she, in graceful flow,

"——— Sprang radiant,
And, descending, grac'd the caverns of the West."

But the *Vaishnavas*, unwilling to attribute so great a boon exclusively to another deity, assert, that the blessed and blessing river flowed originally out of *Vaikontha*, from the foot of VISHNU, and, descending upon *Kailasa*, fell on

By the way, it has occurred to me, that the name *Jahnavi*, as applied to the *Ganges*, might have some connection with the mystical thread that *Brahmans*, and *Hindus* in general of the three highest tribes, wear, flowing loosely from the shoulders across the body down the right thigh; which thread, commonly called *Zennar*, is, about *Poona* and *Bombay*, frequently named *Jahnavi*. I do not recollect ever having inquired of a *Pandit* why it is so called. I shall in another place take some notice of this sacred thread.

* *Sir* WILLIAM JONES, in a note on this stanza, informs us, that the comparison (which I cannot think very happy) is taken from the image of an *Indian* prince, fanned by an officer, who stands behind him, with the tail of a *Chamara*, or wild cow, the hairs of which are exquisitely fine, and of a pale yellow tint.

In PLATES 18. and 20. GANESA himself is seen whisking this implement over his father's head: it is seen also in many others of the plates, used to keep flies off great men or from images, or to cause a cooling motion in the air. It is an article of very common utility to men as well as to gods, usually set in a silver handle: great men have the handles ornamented with gems. At meals, or at visits in the hot weather, the *Chawrie*, as it is called in the western parts of *India*, is constantly used, especially by native gentlemen, *Hindu* or *Mahommedan*. *European* gentlemen, indeed, and ladies frequently, have servants standing behind their chairs or sofas with this elegant implement, to keep off flies, musquitos, or noxious insects, and to cause some agitation in the air, which in *Calcutta* is sometimes stagnant to a degree very oppressive on the lungs of some persons. *Chawrie*, or *Chowry*, is an easy corruption of *Chamara*. Sometimes the implement is made of peacocks', or other feathers, (PLATE 18.) and still generally, but perhaps improperly, retains its name of *Chawrie*; as it does also, when made of fine ivory shavings.

the head of SIVA; who, when he received the divine stream from on high, shook some drops from his hair, which are called *Bindu,* and form a great lake far to the north of *Hindustan,* called *Bindu Sarovara.*

Both the *Vaishnavas* and *Saivas* are naturally anxious to attribute to the deity of their exclusive adoration, as well all power, might, and dominion, the origin of acts of favour and beneficence. Both sects partake of the bountiful blessings of the *Ganges,* and each is desirous of tracing its source to the head or foot of its own deity.

But, although the *Vaishnavas* so far outnumber the adherents of SIVA, it appears to me that the latter god has generally the reputation of having produced this river. I have many pictures—a dozen or more, where it flows from SIVA's hair, but not one in which it proceeds from VISHNU's foot.*

There are fables in which it is made to flow from the fingers of PARVATI, who, on some occasion of "reluctant sweet delay," put her hands over the eyes of her amorous lord, which, they being the primary source of light, involved the universe in immediate darkness. She instantly removed them, but an *instant* with immortals is an age among men; and SIVA, to avert the calamity of such lengthened gloom, placed a third eye in his forehead. PARVATI, perceiving the mischief she was causing, removed her hands, and found them moistened with the perspiration of SIVA's temples; and in shaking it off, the *Ganges* flowed from her fingers. In this fable it is still the offspring of SIVA: others make it arise from water poured by BRAHMA on the foot of VISHNU: others directly from the feet of BRAHMA. There is, indeed, no end to the legends connected with the origin, progress, and sanctity, of this divine stream.

The *Ganga* is also called *Dasahara,* or *ten removing*; meaning to *remove ten* sins. Bathing in her waters, on the day named in the following couplet, effaces ten sins, how heinous soever, committed in ten previous births.

"On the tenth of *Jyaishtha,* in the bright half of the month; on the day of MANGALA, son of the earth, when the moon was in *Hasta,* this daughter of JAHNU burst from the rocks, and flowed over the land inhabited by mortals.

* In the instance of *Shevagunga,* as it is commonly spelled, we find a town and fort of some note named after this deity and his watery offspring. *Sivaganga* is the way in which it ought, perhaps, to be spelled; but, in the southern and western parts of *India,* SIVA is generally pronounced SHIVA, or SHEEWA, or SEEWA. A long list of towns might be given, with names derived from *Hindu* deities. One on the *Malabar* coast, commonly called *Sadashyghur,* is *Sida Sivagher.* The deity is frequently styled SIDA SIVA, especially in the *Siva purana,* or *Seupuran,* as it is in shortness entitled. SIDASIVA is not an uncommon name among *Hindus* in *Bombay*: many of the *Parbhu,* or writer tribe, are so named; spelled and called SEDASEW. Among *Mahratas* and others we hear of SHADASHYBOW, for SIDA-SEU-BAHU.

On this lunar day, therefore, she washes off ten sins, and gives a hundred times more felicity than could be attained by myriads of *Aswamedhas*, or sacrifices of a horse."—*As. Res.* Vol. III. p. 284.

Another legend states, that the anniversary of the first day of the *Satyayug* is sacred, on account of GANGA having thereon flowed from the foot of VISHNU down upon *Himalaya*, where she was received on the head of SIVA, and was afterwards led to the ocean by King BHAGHIRAT'HA. Hence adoration is now paid to GANGA, HIMALAYA,* SANCARA † and his mountain, *Cailasa*; nor must BHAGHIRAT'HA be neglected.—*Ib.* p. 281.

Many writers have described the advantages that the *Hindus* fancy they derive from drinking the water, and dying on the banks of the *Ganga*. A man, supposing himself near death, will desire to be carried thither, that he may enjoy such benefit; but cases have occurred, where it proved more distant than was imagined, and the expectant has been left by his friends to die a lingering death, or to be devoured by alligators: some instances of survival and recovery are related. A story is common in *India* of an *English* gentleman, who, while taking a pleasant sail on the river, saw an old man, whose friends had given him the *Gangetic viaticum* and left him. Humanity induced the gentleman to attempt his restoration, and the readiest means were the application of some ardent spirit to his mouth, after cleansing it of the holy mud left there by his friends as his supposed last morsel. His stomach, altogether unused to such a stimulus, quickly recovered its tone, and the old man was restored to his senses—but not to his relations and friends; for they deemed his reanimation by such a process a thing most abominable and detestable, and refused all intercourse with so contaminated a being. The unhappy old man, now an outcast from his family and tribe, found his life insupportable, and made it his invariable rule to resort daily, while he lived, to the house of this well-meaning, but mistaken, author of his resurrection; whom, in the bitterness of his heart, he cursed as the cause of his misery and disgrace, and poured torrents of abuse on his head for his officious interference—snatching him from the heaven just opening on him, to all the wretchedness of such a life. ‡

Those who are not so happy as to live near the holy river, make pilgrimages

* HIMALAYA, meaning *snowy*, is the name of a mountain, the poetical father of PARVATI—the "*mountain born*," the "*mountain Goddess*," *Monte Domina*.

† SANCARA seems here to be SIVA: of him, something hereafter.

‡ This anecdote is recently related in one of our reviews: I think the *Edinburgh*, but have not, just now, the means of reference. I have heard the story in *India*.

for the purpose of benefiting by its sin-expelling water: if unable to perform the pilgrimage in person, there is considerable efficacy in doing it by proxy, paying the expences of an idler man; who, in return, frequently brings his principal a jar of the precious fluid, to be used in the time of death and need. Many persons are constantly employed in bringing *Ganges'* water to distant parts. Temples of celebrity, however remote—those of *Rameswara* and *Jejury* for instance, are said to use it daily for the ablution of the idol; and in every city it may be purchased from persons who carry it about in two vases, slung at the ends of a bambo carried across the shoulders: these are carefully covered, and of course preserved with superstitious veneration.

One of the holiest spots of the *Ganga* is where it joins the *Yamuna (Jumna)*, near *Illahabad*, below *Dehly*, anciently called *Indraprestha*. The *Saraswati* is supposed to join them under ground, whenee the junction is called *Triveni*, or the *three plaited locks*: pilgrims here begin the ceremonies afterwards completed at *Gaya*. The confluence of rivers is a spot peculiarly dear to *Hindus*; and this, more especially, of the *Ganga* and *Yamuna*, is so highly esteemed, that a person dying there is certain of immediate *moksh*, or *beatitude*, without risk of farther transmigration.

We shall notice in another place, that suicide is not only pardonable, but in some cases meritorious with *Hindus*. Cutting one's throat at the above holy junction is, in reference to its immediate result, an instance of the latter. Widows, who become *Sati*, or *pure*, by burning themselves with the bodies of their deceased husbands, which is generally done at the *Sangam*, or confluence of rivers, perform an act of meritorious suicide. And all acts, in themselves good, are rendered vastly better if done on such a spot. PARASU RAM BHAO, the *Mahrata Brahman General*, to remove an impurity transmitted to him from a cobler's wife, who had been kissed by a *Brahman* who dined with another who dined with the *Bhao*, weighed himself against precious articles at the confluence of the rivers *Toom* and *Badra*; and distributing the amount in charity, to *Brahmans* and poor people, again became pure, and fit society for his sanctified fraternity: many of whom, however, had also derived impure taints, circuitously, from the base-tribed damsel; and the *Bhao's* whole army were at a critical time marched to the confluence of the rivers, that the *Brahmans* might have safe escort thither, and by bathing, charities, and other sin-effacing ceremonies, be restored to their wonted spiritual and corporeal cleanliness.*

* This occurred while I was serving in the *Bhao's* army, in 1792, and is related in a work that I published soon after. The army made several marches to the rivers, uncalled in a military point of view, although some military affairs resulted.

In PLATE 75. is a mythological representation of the *Triveni*, or *three plaited locks*, or mystical union of the three divine rivers personified, GANGA, YAMUNA, and SARASWATI. The idea affords scope for poetical exuberance; and I recollect once seeing at *Poona* a well modelled group, by an ingenious artist, named GANGARAM, representing CRISHNA *plaiting* the *three locks* descending from the head of RADHA.

I shall now proceed to make some extracts of considerable length, in explanation of our present subject, and referring to others of a mythological nature.

"ISWARA in *Sanscrit* signifies *Lord*, and in that sense is applied by the *Brahmans* to each of their three principal deities, or rather to each of the *forms* in which they teach the people to adore BRAHM, or the GREAT ONE; and if it be appropriated in common speech to MAHADEVA, this proceeds from the zeal of his numerous votaries, who place him above their other two divinities. BRAHMA, VISHNU, and MAHADEVA, say the *Puranics*, were brothers: and the *Egyptian* Triad, or OSIRIS, HORUS, and TYPHON, were brought forth by the same parent, though HORUS was believed to have sprung from the mysterious embraces of OSIRIS and ISIS before their birth; as the *Vaishnavas* also imagine, that HARA, or MAHADEVA, sprang mystically from his brother HERI, or VISHNU. In the *Hindu* mythology BRAHMA is represented of a red, VISHNU of a black, or dark azure, and HARA of a white, complexion; but in that of *Egypt*, we find OSIRIS black, HORUS white, and TYPHON red. The indiscriminate application of the title ISWARA has occasioned great confusion in the accounts which the *Greeks* have transmitted to us of *Egyptian* mythology; for the priests of *Egypt* were very reserved on subjects of religion, and the *Grecian* travellers had, in general, too little curiosity to investigate such points with scrupulous exactness. Since OSIRIS, however, was painted *black*, we may presume that he was VISHNU, who on many occasions, according to the *Puranas*, took *Egypt* under his special protection. CRISHNA was VISHNU himself, according to the most orthodox opinions. The title SRI BHAGAVAT, importing *prosperity* and dominion, is given peculiarly to CRISHNA, or the *black* deity; and the *black* OSIRIS had also the titles of SIRIUS, SEIRIUS, and BACCHUS. It is related, indeed, that OSIRIS and BACCHUS imported from *India* the worship of two divine bulls; and in this character he was MAHADEVA, whose followers were pretty numerous in *Egypt*: for HERMAPION, in his explanation of the *Hieroglyphics* on the *Heliopolitan* obelisk, calls HORUS the Supreme *Lord*, and the author of *Time*. Now ISWARA, or *Lord*, and CALA, or *Time*, are among the distinguished titles of MAHADEVA; and obelisks, or pillars, whatever be their shape, are among his emblems. In the *Vrihad-haima*, which appears to contain many curious legends concerning *Egypt*, it is expressly said, that "ISWARA, with his consort PARVATI, descended from heaven, and chose for his abode the land of *Misra*, in *Sancha dwip*." We must observe, that the *Egyptians* feared and abhorred TYPHON, or MAHADEVA, in his character of the *Destroyer*; and the *Hindus* also dread him in that character, giving him the name of BHAIRAVA, or *Tremendous*. The *Egyptian* fable of his attempting to *break the mundane egg* is applied to MAHADEVA, in the little book *Chandi*, which is chiefly extracted from the *Marcandeya Puran*." (The continuation of this extract, from *Mr.* WILFORD's Dissertation on *Egypt* and the *Nile*, from the ancient books of the *Hindus*, *As. Res.* Vol. III. p. 371. will be given in a future page, when speaking of NARAYANA.)

ISWARA is said, in the same learned dissertation, to have descended on earth after a great deluge, from which but few escaped, to restore arts and science to the race of man that had become ignorant and brutal, and even without a regular language: he sent his consort and sister, VAGESWARI, or the goddess of speech, to instruct them in arts and language. In this character he is called VAGISWARA, or VAGISA, which means the lord of speech, commonly pronounced BAGESWAR and BAGIS: he is also called SIRO-DEVA. To DEVI, in the character of BHAGESWARI, offerings are made of a lower mantle, with a red fringe, or border, and an earthen pot, shaped like a coronet. To BHAGISWARA are presented a vase of spirits, and the blood of a hog poured before his image, restoring the carcase to its owner. *Mr.* WILFORD thinks the similar offerings by the *Egyptians* to BACCHUS OSIRIS identifies the characters.—*Ib.* p. 396.

In the preceding extracts we may trace farther instances of the coalition of mythological personages. Red is the colour given by the *Hindus* to BRAHMA; by the *Egyptians*, to TYPHON, or MAHADEVA: and both are named ISWARA. As changers of forms, by re-creation and dissolution, these two powers are perpetually confounded with each other. Again, to restore speech, arts, and science, to the race of man, is evidently the duty of BRAHMA's *Sacti*, SARASWATI, rather than of DEVI, *Sacti*, and it is said sister also, of SIVA. But it is DEVI who, in an *Avatara* named BHAGISWARI, mixes her character with that of SARASWATI, goddess of speech, science, harmony, and arrangement.

Obelisks and pillars, of whatever shape, we have just seen, are symbols of MAHADEVA: as are more especially pyramids, and any thing conical. MAHADEVA is *Fire*; the conical or pyramidal shape is the natural form of fire: hence applied to its representative, and symbolized, as noticed in other places, by a triangle, apex upwards.

Under the article *Linga, Yoni,* &c. an humble attempt will be made to illumine the gloom in which these mysterious subjects are buried. Meanwhile I shall offer an extract, connected with our present subject, from a paper in the second volume of the *Asiatic Researches,* by *Mr.* REUBEN BURROWS.*

"The pyramids of *Egypt*, as well as those lately discovered in *Iceland,* (and probably too the tower of *Babel,*) seem to have been intended for nothing more than images of MAHADEVA." *Mr.* BURROW farther thinks it probable, that the *Sakkara* pyramids, described by NORDEN, and one at *Dashour,* drawn by POCOCKE; CLEOPATRA'S Needle; and the Devil's Belts, at *Boroughbridge*; may have had the same religious origin. He says, that "*Stonehenge* is evidently one of the temples of BUDDHA. The religious ceremonies of the papists seem, in many parts, a mere servile copy of those of the *Gosseins* and *Fakirs*. The different tenets of *popery* and *deism* have a great similarity to the two doctrines of BRAHMA and BUDDHA; and, as the *Brahmans* were the authors of the *Ptolemaic* system, so the *Buddhists* appear to have been the inventors of the *Philolaic*, or *Copernican*, as well as of the doctrine of attraction. That the *Druids* of *Britain* were *Brahmans* is beyond the least shadow of doubt."†—Page 478.

SIVA and JOVE have been compared by *Sir* WILLIAM JONES, and other mythologists; but no where, I believe, is JOVE seen combined with his spouse, or any female, as SIVA is, in pictures and sculptures, with PARVATI, as will be described. JOVE is, however, sometimes called mother as well as father: the following verse might warrant such a combination, in the creative eye of a painter.—

> "JUPITER omnipotens, rerum, regumque, deûmque,
> Progenitor, genitrixque."

* I might have said the *late Mr*. BURROW; for this ingenious and learned gentleman is, unhappily for those who contemplate the development of *Hindu* science, no more.

† It is not my intention to offer any comments on these curious speculations of *Mr.* BURROW.—Other writers have fancied great similarity between the practices of the *Brahmans* and the *Druids* of ancient *Europe*; so great, indeed, as almost to identify them as the same people. However extensive *Druidism* may have been on the continent of *Europe*, it prevailed on a very confined scale in *Britain*; and it would be difficult to prove its existence in any part except on the island of *Anglesey*, which may be called the *Elephanta* of *Britain*. Not, however, that there is any positive proof of there having been any temples of celebrity on that holy island, or, perhaps, any temple at all; for TACITUS notices only the destruction of the *Druidical groves* by SUETONIUS PAULINUS, after his defeat of the *British* army in that neighbourhood. TACITUS is the earliest, if not the only ancient, historian who notices the existence of *Druidism* in *Britain*. See *Edinburgh Review*. July 1804, p. 395.

> "Almighty JOVE; father and mother, both
> Of gods and men, and things."
>
> *Letters on Mythology*, p. 140.

And, in some of their multifarious characters, most of the principal *Hindu* deities might be identified with JOVE or JUPITER, where, in the poetical generation of the world, he is called SATURN'S *youngest child*; that is, the latest production of Time.

"The comparison between SIVA and JOVE runs parallel in many instances. In the capacity of avenger and destroyer JOVE overthrew the Titans and giants whom TYPHON, BRIAREUS, &c. led against the God of *Olympus*, to whom an eagle brought *lightning* and *thunder-bolts* during the warfare. In a similar contest, between SIVA and the *Daityas*, or children of DITI, who frequently rebelled against heaven, BRAHMA is said to have presented the god of destruction with *fiery shafts*. As the *Olympian* JUPITER fixed his court, and held his councils, on a lofty and brilliant mountain, so the appropriated seat of MAHADEVA, whom the *Saivas* consider as the chief of the deities, is mount *Cailasa*, every splinter of whose rocks is an inestimable gem. His terrestrial haunts are on the snowy hills of *Himalaya*, or that branch of them to the east of the *Brahmaputra*, which has the name of *Chandrasichara*, or the *mountains of the moon*. When, after these circumstances, we find SIVA with three eyes, whence he is named TRILOCHAN; and know from PAUSANIAS, not only that *Triopthalmos* was an epithet of ZEUS, but that a statue of him had been found, so early as the taking of *Troy*, with a third eye in his forehead, as we see him represented by the *Hindus*; we must conclude that the identity of the two gods falls little short of being demonstrated.

"In the character of *destroyer* also, we may look upon this *Indian* deity as corresponding with the *Stygian* JOVE or PLUTO, especially since CALI, or *Time* in the feminine gender, is a name of his consort, who will be found to be PROSERPINE.

"There is yet another attribute of MAHADEVA, by which he is too visibly distinguished in the drawings and temples of *Bengal*. To destroy, according to the *Vedantis* of *India*, the *Sufis* of *Persia*, and many philosophers of our *European* schools, is only to *generate* and *reproduce* in another form. Hence the god of *destruction* presides over *generation*: as a symbol of which, he rides on a *white bull*. Can we doubt that the loves and feasts of JUPITER *Genitor*, (not forgetting the *white bull* of EUROPA,) and his extraordinary title of *Lapis*, for which no satisfactory reason is commonly given, have a connection with the *Indian* philosophy and mythology?

"The JUPITER *Marinus*, or NEPTUNE of the *Romans*, resembles MAHADEVA in his *generative* character; especially as the *Hindu* god is the husband of BHAVANI, whose relation to the *waters* is evidently marked by her image being restored to them at the conclusion of the great festival of *Durgotsava*.* She is known also to have attributes exactly similar to those of VENUS *Marina*, whose birth from the sea foam, and splendid rise from the conch in which she had been cradled, have afforded so many charming subjects to ancient and modern artists. And it is very remarkable, that the RHEMBA of INDRA's court, who seems to correspond with the popular VENUS, or goddess of beauty, was produced, according to the *Indian* fabulists, from the froth of the churned ocean. The identity of the *Trisula* and the *Trident*, the weapons of SIVA and of NEPTUNE, seems to establish this analogy. And the veneration paid all over *India* to the large *buccinum*, especially when it can be found with the spiral line and mouth turned from left to right, brings instantly to our minds the music of TRITON."—Dissertation on the Gods of *Greece*, *Italy*, and *India*. *As. Res.* Vol. I. p. 250.

"To SIVA is given three eyes, probably to denote his view of the three divisions of Time: the past, the present, and the future. A crescent on his forehead pourtrays the measure of time by the phases of the † moon: a serpent forms a necklace, to denote the measure of time by years: a second necklace, formed of human skulls, marks the lapse and revolution of ages, and the extinction and succession of the generations of mankind. He holds a trident, to show that the three great attributes are in him assembled and united: in another hand is a kind of rattle, called *damaru*, shaped like an hour-glass, ‡ and I am inclined to think it was really at first intended as such, since it agrees with the character of the deity; and a sand *gheri* is mentioned in the *Sastra*, as one of the modes of measuring time. ||

* When we speak of BHAVANI, the *Sacti* of SIVA, we shall notice her under her different epithets of CALI, DURGA, &c. But I have always supposed LACSHMI to resemble most the VENUS *Marina* of *European* heathens: here, again, we find the principal goddesses, like their lords, blending their characters.

† CALI, the consort of CALA, (PARVATI and SIVA,) has no crescent. She is the Moon; also a personification of eternity; and has no typical measure of Time.

‡ This description answers very well for the subject of PLATES 14. and 17. which will be particularly noticed presently.

|| Whether or not we be disposed to allow that SIVA originally held a sand-glass, the double-headed hand-drum, called *damaru*, it must be admitted, is shaped exactly like one, and may in many pictures be

"In the hieroglyphic of *Maha Pralaya*, or grand consummation of all things, when Time itself shall be no more, he is represented as trodden under foot by MAHA CAL, or Eternity.—(See PLATE 10. and page 30.)

"MAHA CAL, as represented in the caverns of *Elephanta*, had eight arms. In one he holds a human figure; in another a sword, or sacrificial axe; in a third he holds a basin of blood, and with a fourth he rings over it the sacrificial bell. Two other arms are broken off; with the two remaining he is drawing behind him a veil, which extinguishes the Sun, and involves the whole universe in one undistinguished ruin. One of the titles of this tremendous deity is BHAIRAVA,* the terrific; but his principal designation is CAL† AGNI RUDRA."—PATERSON. *As. Res.* Vol. VIII. p. 61.

Having lately been in the *Elephanta* cavern, and when there made some memoranda, I will in this place extract from them what relates to the subject of the preceding passage, MAHA CALA; of which a print was first, I believe, given by NEIBUHR. The compartment containing the group, of which SIVA in this character makes the principal figure, is on the right of the entrance, facing a compartment of like size, containing what, in another part of this work, I have supposed to be a marriage ceremony. Between the two compartments, but advanced into the body of the cave so as not to be interposed, is a room, twenty-two feet square, with a door in each face, and on each side the doors a gigantic male figure, in stature sixteen feet, highly ornamented: this room contains a monstrous *Linga*. Premising this, from which, however, I make no inferences, I proceed to extract from my notes an account of the compartment containing the figure in question.

"It is of SIVA *Vindex*, fourteen feet high, but his lower extremities broken off: his attention is, from his attitude, turned to his left: his aspect is terrific, indicating the immediate execution of some avenging act: he had eight arms; the superior right and left stretched up, and either supporting a cloth or curtain, or pulling it over the terrible event he threatens; the fingers grasp the cloth; the left upstretched arm finely executed; the right broken at the elbow: his next right hand is broken off at the wrist; the corresponding left holds a bell, in good preservation, over a cup in the palm of the next, having a serpent

easily mistaken for it, (see PLATES 7. and 14.) as it probably was by the people in *Europe*, who took from *India* the idea and attributes of personified Time. Giving him a sand-glass, whoever did it, was a very happy thought.

* SIVA's offspring are also called BHAIRAVA.

† These three words are especially descriptive of SIVA: they may be rendered *Time, Fire, Fate.*

twining round near the elbow. A third right hand grasps a long straight sword, uplifted, perfect: the two inferior hands, right and left, are broken off above the elbow; they were in bolder relief, and the left appears to have supported, or to have grasped, the leg of a kneeling figure; the trunk of which only remains, its legs, arms, and head, being broken off: this kneeling figure may have been between five and six feet in height; its back is toward the threatener, and leaning so in his direction as to drop its blood, if spilled, into the cup before noticed. The head of the principal figure has a highly ornamented cap, reminding one of the mitre-shaped caps worn some years ago by our grenadiers: * a skull and serpent are among its frontal ornaments. It has also a pendent necklace, and a long chaplet, if I may so call it, composed of human heads, of which only two or three are plainly discernible, flowing over the left shoulder to the right thigh, where it is broken off; the *Zennaar*, or holy thread, and a broader belt, run in nearly a like direction; on all the wrists are bracelets; and above the elbows of three of the arms are *bazubands*. No figures remain in any preservation to the right of the principal, or under him. On the left, near the supposed victim, are two bearded faces expressive of pity: a compassionate female is just above them, leaning forward over the victim; she holds her scarf in her hands, and is an elegant person: below the bearded men are two or three females with pitying aspects: the same emotion, intermingled with terror, is evident in every face of this compartment, whose features can be traced.

"Over the subjects just described † is a row of males and females of rather diminutive size: in the middle of the row, nearly over the head of SIVA, is a thing like a mitre, with a crosier cut deep in it, and surmounted with a cross; but the limbs of the cross not exactly at right angles: two aged and emaciated males are on the right (the spectator's right) of the mitre holding up their hands, betokening pity and pain; on the other side of the mitre are two similar figures: in front of each pair is a prostrate distressed male child, their heads near the mitre: beyond the last mentioned pair, on the spectator's left, are a male and female in great anxiety and distress, holding scarfs in their hands.

"The subject, supposed to be like a mitre, crosier, and cross, appears also,

* See PLATE 81. where the caps worn by the Triad are in the style of that worn by its brethren of *Elephanta*: the latter are in many instances highly ornamented, and so minute, as to show every pearl or gem of the head-dress.

† And, from recollection, I think not so deeply indented into the rock as the ground-work of the compartment, but (somewhat, however, sunk,) running along the top like the upper part of the frame of a picture.

in a compartment before described,* as containing characters in the background: fancy may, perhaps, have had some share in making this resemblance; but it is really curious, and I think striking, although I believe, hitherto, not remarked."

I shall here close my extract from the memoranda made or corrected in the cave, observing, that I had promised myself the pleasure of accompanying it by a picture of the subject described, drawn, at the time the memoranda were written, by a much respected friend, with whom I visited the temple, but it has not reached me.

Before I proceed farther in my notice of this important and tremendous deity, I will request the reader to turn back to the beginning of this article, and examine the opposite beautiful figure of him, PLATE 14. taken from a bronze statue, equally beautiful, deposited by me in the museum at the *India* house.

My *Pandit* informed me, that this image represents the destruction by MAHADEVA of the *Daitya* TRIPURASURA, so surnamed from his capital city *Tripura*: his name was TARIKA, and a long account of his ambition and overthrow is given in the *Sivpurana*; but it is there stated to have been accomplished, not by SIVA in person, but by his son, CARTICEYA,† (of whom farther notice will be taken hereafter); and, for the production of this predicted champion, it was necessary that MAHADEVA should become incarnated, to espouse PARVATI; incarnate also, in the person of the beauteous daughter of HIMACHALA and MAHINA. As the story embraces many points connected with our work, I will give first its outline briefly from the *Sivpurana*, and will afterwards recur descriptively to PLATE 14. and its original.

This TARIKA was excessively ambitious and oppressive, and forced BRAHMA, by his penances and austerities, to promise him any boon he should demand. Among his austerities he went through the following series, each of the eleven specific mortifications enduring one hundred years.—

1. He stood on one foot, holding the other and both hands up toward heaven, with his eyes fixed on the sun; 2. he stood on one great toe; 3. he took as sustenance nothing but water; 4. he lived similarly on air; 5. he remained in the water; 6. he was buried in the earth, but continued, as under the last infliction, in incessant adoration; 7. the same in fire; 8. he stood on his

* The compartment, here alluded to, is in a distant part of the cave; but most of its numerous figures are sadly defaced: a woman suckling a child is among the most perfect, but was not a principal figure.

† As spelled by *Sir* W. JONES, *Mr.* COLEBROKE, *Mr.* WILFORD, and other *Sanscrit* scholars. In my memoranda I find the name spelled KARTICKYA and KARTEEKYA.

head with his feet upwards; 9. he stood on one hand; 10. he hung by his hands on a tree; 11. he hung on a tree with his head downwards.*

Such merit was irresistible; and INDRA, and the whole host of demi gods, alarmed, lest their sovereignty should be usurped by the potency of the penance, resorted to BRAHMA for consolation; who, however, said, that, although he could not resist such austerities, he would, after rewarding them by granting the boon demanded, devise a method of rendering it ultimately inoffensive to them.

The demand by TARIKA was, that he should be unrivalled in strength, and that no hand should slay him but that of a son of MAHADEVA. He now became so arrogant that INDRA † was forced to yield to him the white eight-headed horse, OOCHISRAVA: † CUVERA † gave up his thousand sea-horses, also white except the left ear, which was black: the *Rishis* † were compelled to resign the all-yielding cow CAMDENU †—rivers and seas the riches of the deep. The Sun in dread gave no heat; and the Moon in terror remained always at full: the winds blew as he dictated; and, in short, he usurped the entire management of the universe.

NAREDA had prophesied the marriage whence should arise the destined deliverer of the world; but MAHADEVA was cold, and could not be influenced with the passion of love. INDRA persuaded CAMA to lie in ambush, and contrived that PARVATI should be seen by SIVA while engaged in the amiable and graceful act of gathering flowers, wherewith to decorate his emblem, the *Linga*. CAMA, accompanied by his wife, RETI, *(affection,)* and his bosom friend, VASANTA, *(Spring,)* took his aim, and launched an arrow at MAHADEVA; who, enraged at the attempt, reduced poor CAMA to ashes (some legends say to a mental essence) by a beam of fire darted from his central eye. At length, however, by ardent devotion and austerities, PARVATI propitiated SIVA, and the warmed deity consented to espouse his persevering devotee.

Passing over the detail of preparations, processions, &c. of the wedding, in which all the gods, demi gods, &c. attended, we will proceed to notice, that, for some time, there was no issue of the marriage; and the distressed and disappointed *Devatas* renewed their lamentations and complaints.

SIVA redoubled his caresses; and the *Devatas* having, at an auspicious moment, deputed AGNI, the god of fire, to represent their case, he arrived in

* PLATE 31. contains some of these devotees, practising similar self-inflicted austerities.

† The mythological beings here named will be duly noticed in their places.

the presence of MAHADEVA just as he had risen from the arms of PARVATI; and, assuming the form of a dove, AGNI received from MAHADEVA, in a manner not easy or necessary to describe minutely, the germ of CARTICEYA, but, unable to retain it, let it fall into the *Ganges*. On the banks of which river arose a boy, beautiful as the moon, and bright as the sun, who was called AGNIBHUVA, (or son of AGNI); otherwise GANGA-PUTRA, (or son of GANGA); also SRIMANA, and SKANDA, and CARTICEYA, and SWA'MICARTICEYA; and by many other names. It happened that six daughters of as many *Rajahs*, coming to bathe, saw the boy, and each called him her son; and, offering the breast, the child assumed to himself six mouths, and received nurture from each: whence he was called *Cshani-matriya*, or *Sesbti-matriya*; i. e. having six mothers.* But, in point of fact, he had no mother; for he proceeded, as just observed, from the father alone, without the intervention of PARVATI: and there seems no apparent reason for the pains taken to bring about a match for the procural of a champion, who proceeded, after all, from the male party only. We may farther observe, that this divine couple seems not to have had their offspring by any ordinary process; for their reputed eldest son, GANESA, was, by some legends that will be noticed when that deity makes his appearance, exclusively PARVATI'S, without the interposition of MAHADEVA, who afterwards adopted him.

But we will quit this tale, observing, that CARTICEYA, being the predicted destroyer of TRIPURASURA, a terrible combat in due time ensued between them, which, after continuing ten days, ended in the death of the oppressive *Daitya*; and the *Devatas* and the world were restored to tranquillity and order.

We now return to the fine statue represented in PLATE 14. It is of bronze, or a similar composition, twenty-four inches high, in a dancing attitude, although, from the action, and the vindictive dignity of its countenance, something avenging is evidently in performance: the right foot rests on TRIPURASURA, who is prostrate on his belly, his face turned upwards, with a snake grasped by both his hands. SIVA'S garment falling nearly to the pedestal, it is continued to it by way of a farther support to the figure. It is four-armed, the two right are joined at the elbow; the fore arms only being distinct, the upper arm is therefore thicker, in correspondence with anatomical accuracy: one right hand holds a double-headed hand-drum *(damaru)*, shaped like an hourglass: the other is empty, the fingers pointing upwards, in the position called

* It will appear in its place, that other legends give the *Pleiades*, the banished wives of the *Rishis*, the seven bright stars in *Ursa major*, to CARTICEYA as wet-nurses.

Abahi-hasta, as promising protection: round the fore arm of the empty hand a *naug*, or snake, five-headed, is twined. The left arms are separate from the insertion at the shoulder: one, slanting across the body, bends inward from the wrist; the empty palm is towards the body, fingers pointing downwards to the right, in the position called *Narada-hasta*, or inviting solicitation. The other left hand is elevated as high as the shoulder, holding in the palm a flame triforked. Under the arm-pit is a round bag, the size of a pistol-ball, retained by a string over the shoulder. My *Brahman* called this *Juli*; and said that *Gusains* commonly carry under the arm a bag of that sort, containing *Bibut*, the fine ashes of cow-dung, for rubbing on the neck and arms, or marking the forehead withal;* the ashes being symbolical of SIVA, or destructive Fire.

The figure has the short breeches called *Chulna*, reaching nearly to the knee, and a *Caciha*, or *Cammer-banda*, round his loins, one end hanging between his thighs, and another falling gracefully down near the pedestal, hiding a prop to the figure. On the four wrists are bracelets of small chain, and above the elbows bracelets, called *bazuband*. He has the *Jahnuwi*, or sacred thread, called, in the secret ceremonies of the *Brahmans*, *Yadnupavita*, a term of occult allusion that my *Brahman* did not seem willing to make me comprehend; also necklaces, and encircling ornamental chains or strings, as the artist's fancy dictated.

The countenance is rather placid, considering the action of the subject as a composition: one may fancy in it too, a mixture of ferocity and dignity, exhibiting, however, neither the sentiment of revenge, nor any of the levity annexed to a dancing attitude, which the position seems to indicate. A third eye is in the forehead, as is common in pictures and images of MAHADEVA: his ears are loaded with pendent rings; in his right ear a snake forms the ornament, hence called *Nag-kundala*: in the lobe of the other a large discus, or wheel, is inserted, after the fashion of some *Malabar* tribes, and as BUDDHA is sometimes seen: his forehead is bound by his hair, but it is not well expressed in the engraving; and it is gathered above his head in the style called *Jetta*, having the goddess GANGA in front, with two snakes twined round her neck, and his hair towering overhead like a feather, or five-leaved fan. Over his right ear is a crescent, representing the god CHANDRA (LUNUS); and over his left ear a female figure with joined palms, as if in the act of prayer, probably CHANDRI,

* *Mr.* WILKINS, when examining this statue, noticed this bag as containing *poison*; and in *Mr.* WILFORD's translation from the *Brahmanda Purana*, the inhabitants of a certain region are said "always to carry, like MAHADEVA, poison about them."—*As. Res.* Vol. VIII. p. 369. I do not find a similar bag in any other of my numerous pictures or images of this deity.

(LUNA, of whom more hereafter,) her leaning posture of adoration, and the pointed bent termination of her robe, giving her also a crescent-like form.

Looking at the figure behind, we see the hair falling down the back in five ringlets of unequal length, surmounted by the five-leaved fan, the crescent, and the crescent-formed female; the *Jahnuvi*, or *Zennaar*, crossing the left shoulder and right hip; the *Damaru* and *Trisula*, or tri-forked flame, in the back hands; the little bag under the arm; and the prostrate *Daitya*.

The pedestal of this statue does not correspond with its bulk and height; it seems indeed unfinished, as well as the *Daitya*, as if it were intended to be inserted in some firmer base. The figure being solid is very heavy.

The image just described was brought from *Malabar*, found, I understand, in the neighbourhood of *Chawghât*, and, together with the subject of PLATE 27. were given to me by the *Hon. Mr.* DUNCAN, Governor of *Bombay*, who kindly thus enriched my collection at the heavy expense of his own. The two statues (that just noticed, represented in PLATE 27. will be described in its place,) are deposited, in *Mr.* DUNCAN's name, in the Company's museum at the *India* House.

I must not forget to notice, that the figure has its left leg broken off at the knee, which the artist, who took its portrait for me, has very ably restored: this is the only addition to, or deviation from, the original, which is altogether as graceful and elegant as the plate (14.) represents it.

As with the *Hindus* a variety of natural objects are personified, so every thing lovely or admirable, or at all striking, is consecrated to, or symbolical of, one or other of their deities; and legends are not wanting to account for such application.

The *Asoca* is a shrub consecrated to MAHADEVA: men and women of all classes ought to bathe, on a particular day, in some holy stream, especially the *Brahmaputra*, and drink water with buds of the *Asoca* floating in it: this shrub is planted near the temples of SIVA, and grows abundantly on *Ceylon*. SITA is said to have been confined in a grove of it while in captivity by RAVANA: other relators say she was confined in a place, or house, called *Asocwan*. The *Asoca* is a plant of the 1st order of the 8th class, of leguminous fructification, and bears flowers of exquisite beauty. VAN RHEEDE (*Hort. Malab.* Vol. V. tab. 59,) calls it *Asjogam*.—See *As. Res.* Vol. III. p. p. 254. 277.

The *Bilva*, otherwise called *Malura*, is also sacred to MAHADEVA: he alone wears a chaplet of its flowers, and they are offered in sacrifice to no other deity; and if a pious *Hindu* should see any of its flowers fallen on the ground, he would remove them reverently to a temple of MAHADEVA. The *Hindu* poets call it *Sriphul*, the flower of SRI, because it sprung, they say, from the milk of SRI, the goddess of abundance; who bestowed it on mankind at the request of ISWARA. The fruit is warm, cathartic, of delicious taste, and exquisite fragrance, and of valuable aperient and detersive qualities: the mucus of its seed is used as a cement.—See *As. Res.* Vol. II. p. 350.

I am not certain, but think the fruit above noticed is that called by the *English* custard-apple, and by the natives on the westward side of *India*, *Ramphul*. It grows to the size of our largest pear, but is not so pointed, and the stalk is inserted at its base; in shape it forms a cone, and is, I imagine, hence sacred to SIVA, as, placed on its base, it resembles a pyramid. Its coat is exceedingly rough, being divided into lozenges by lines deeply indented, drawn spirally right and left, and intersecting each other, from the insertion of the stalk to the tip. This species is called *Ramphul*, or the fruit of RAMA.* Another species is named *Sitaphul*, after SITA, spouse of RAMA (incarnations of VISHNU and LACSHMI): this fruit is delectably smooth and soft outside, and in shape not so conical as the other. It is fancied to resemble the *mamma* of the human female; and legends are popularly related of the origin and application of these appellations, which I shall not explain or detail: it is not always that the popular legends of *Hindu* fabulists will bear expounding to an *European* reader.

SIVA, like VISHNU, is myrionomous, and one of his titles is the god with a thousand names; they are strung together in a sort of litany, as has been noticed iu the preceding article. SIVA's thousand names are given at length in the *Padma Purana*, and the sixty-ninth chapter of the SIVA *Purana* is allotted to their enumeration.

He is, I know not why, called RANGA, and SRI RANGA: hence, as I had occasion to notice in a former work, † the city of SRI RANGA is of course called *Sri-ranga-patana*, altered by *Europeans* to *Seringapatam*, or *Seringapatnam*. This city is the capital of *Mahishasur*, the name of a demoniac giant, slain by the consort of SIVA; sometimes shortened into *Mahesur*, which differs but little from our pronunciation of *Mysore*. The contest between Vice, personified under the name of MAHISHASUR, and Active Virtue, under that of DURGA, will, from the popularity of the subject, claim our particular attention when we discuss the character of DURGA or BHAVANI. PLATES 33. 34. 35. represent the combat.

* This is the fruit I alluded to when (in p. 25.) describing *fig*. 4. of PLATE 6.

† NARRATIVE. 1794. Quarto.—JOHNSON.

SIVA is also called SRI VIRUPACSHA, or the three-eyed god. This name of SRI VIRUPACSHA is, however, differently translated by different *Sanskrit* scholars. The earliest renders it as above: another, "with a disagreeable countenance:" a third, "the auspicious deity with uneven eyes:" and as the title is also given to an inferior deity, who is not fabled to have three eyes, (NIRUT) I am disposed to think the latter interpretations are to be preferred.

A poet, in his extravagant praises of a king, gives the following hyperbolical reason for MAHADEVA's third eye, and for the attributes that distinguish other deities.

"The gods had apprehensions in the beginning of time that the glory of so great a monarch would rapidly diffuse one vast blaze over the universe, and leave them without marks of distinction: thence it was, that PURARI assumed a third eye in his forehead, PEDMACSHA four arms, ATMABHU four faces; that CALI holds in her hands a cimeter, RAMA a lotos, and VANI a lyre."

In this adulation the poet seemed desirous also to show his learning, as among *Hindus* a knowledge of the ridiculous legends of their gods is called; for it is not common to hear MAHADEVA denominated PURARI. I recollect but one instance of it, and I cannot immediately call to mind when or where, in which CAMA, the god of love, is called *foe of* PURARI,* in allusion to his attempt of exciting an amorous passion in the bosom of the angry deity, as will be noticed again in its place. Nor did I ever elsewhere see VISHNU called PEDMACSHA, which alludes to his possession of PEDMA, a name of LAKSHMI, in her character of the goddess of beauty, corresponding with our popular VENUS. ATMABHU, a name derived from soul, or spirit, is as seldom applied to BRAHMA; nor, excepting that the great powers so eternally coalesce, do we at once see the justice of the application. His consort, SARASWATI, is often called VANI, and a lyre, or *Vina*, is one of her usual attributes.—See PLATES 24. 45.

The second of VISHNU's ten grand *Avataras*, or incarnations, was in the form of a *tortoise*, and hence called the *Curmavatara*; the principal incident in which, as represented in PLATE 49. was churning the ocean with the mountain *Mandara*, the huge serpent SESHA serving as a rope to whirl the mountain round withal, and VISHNU, in the shape of a tortoise, sustained the vast load. The result was fourteen precious articles, called *gems*, or *Chaodaratny*, (more classically spelled *Chaturdesaratna*,) and one of the fourteen was poison, which is the only one that

* I have, since the above was written, found him called PURARI. In the 9th stanza, of the inscription quoted in p. 39, mention is made of "IYANTA, son to the foe of VRITTA, (or INDRA);" and of "SHANMUCHA, (or CARTICEYA,) son to PURARI, or MAHADEVA."

we at present have occasion to introduce. Among the *Avataras* this of *Curma* will be duly noticed.

> "To soften human ills dread SIVA drank
> The poisonous flood that stain'd his azure neck."

It might perhaps have been more in character, if the *preserving* power had averted from mankind the calamities incident to the production of this "poisonous flood;" but the legend, which is very popular, gives the action to MAHADEVA: whence the epithet *Nilakantba*, or *blue-throated*, is a name of SIVA. With *Sáivas* it is now not an uncommon name, usually pronounced, as is that of the deity, *Nilkant*, or *Neelkont*. We may hence perceive, that the destroying power is occasionally employed in acts of preservation, as we sometimes see VISHNU in his *Avataras* assuming the form and character of the avenging deity. At the close of the last article (VISHNU) a poetical reason is given for the azure throat of SIVA, in the gallant effusion of CRISHNA, addressed to his delightful RADHA.

VISWASWARA, an epithet derived I apprehend from *Viswa*, all, and ISWARA, Lord, is the name by which SIVA is invoked at a beautiful and famous temple of that name in *Cashi*, or *Benares*; and it is said in the *Puranas*, that "the *Vedas* and *Sastras* all testify that VISWASWARA is the first of *Devas*, *Cashi* the first of cities, *Ganga* the first of rivers, and charity the first of virtues."

Many other names of MAHADEVA will occur in the course of the work, and I shall not trouble the reader with a dry catalogue of them.

MAHADEVA's vehicle, or *Nandi*, is a white bull, on which he is frequently seen riding.—(PLATES 19. 21.) In his temples it is represented, sometimes of vast dimensions, couchant, as in PLATES 83. 84. It is very commonly met with in brass, &c. with and without the other symbols of SIVA.

In *Figures* 1. and 2. of PLATE 24. and in others of this work, the bull will mark their references to MAHADEVA. It is understood to be a personification of divine justice, which moves or conveys the avenging power of the Deity to the deserved punishment of mortals.

Institutes of MENU, c. 8. v. 16.—"The divine form of Justice is represented as *Vrisha*, or a bull; and the gods consider him who violates justice as a *Vrishala*, or one who slays a bull."

Nandi is the epithet always given to the vehicle of SIVA; and it may, I think, but am not quite sure, be applied also to the vehicles of other deities. In my memoranda I sometimes find it used in speaking of GARUDA, the vehicle of

VISHNU, and of the goose or swan, *Hanasa*, the *Nandi* of BRAHMA; but I believe the term *Vahan* would be more correct.

I have noticed in another place, that BRAHMA is not seen mounted on his *Vahan* as other deities are on theirs; nor is it commonly given, in pictures or sculpture, to him, or to SARASWATI, as a distinguishing attribute. Except in the *Elephanta* cave, I do not recollect ever to have seen BRAHMA, or his *Sacti*, attended by the swan; and there it is, in several compartments, seen very well embossed on the calyx of the lotos, on which BRAHMA is sitting: three or four of these animals are there pourtrayed as if swimming after one another. *Fig.* 4. of PLATE 24. is taken from a little picture that I purchased at *Poona*: it is a very indifferently coloured representation of SARASWATI, with her *Vina*, or lyre. She is four-handed: one holds her *Vina*, composed of two gourds; another a roll of paper, perhaps a *Veda*; a third the lotos; and the fourth a cup. Her *Vahan*, or vehicle, is milk white, with long red legs and comb; her *Langi*, or petticoat, is red; the *chehar jammah* (saddle-cloth, if it may be so called,) is green; her coronet, the gourds, and cup, yellow; the lotos red. But why I particularly notice this subject is, that, instead of a swan or goose, which bird is now generally understood to be meant by the *Sanscrit* name *Hanasa*, she is riding a bird which resembles that commonly called in *India Bhagala*, I suppose from flying with its head apparently under its wing; which part in a bird, as well as under the arm in the man, is called *Bhagal*. The *Bhagala*, sometimes called by the *English*, *Batty bird*, from frequenting wet rice fields, is in appearance and habits like our heron, and being of a semi-aquatic nature is not an inapt type of BRAHMA; who, although he represents earth or matter, partakes also, in some little degree, of the aqueous element, in as far as he, by a commonly received legend, sprang out of the sea from the navel of VISHNU, and floated on the aquatic lotos.—(See PLATES 7. and 8.)

The classical mode of spelling the *Vahan* of BRAHMA, in *Sanscrit*, is *Hanasa*: it is commonly pronounced *Hansa*, or *Hans*, or rather with a strong nasal, *Hahns*; sometimes *Hahnsy*; and this latter word is precisely the name that in *Suffolk*, and perhaps in other parts of *England*, is commonly given to the heron, that SARASWATI rides on.

I will in this place mention what other animals are appropriated as vehicles to *Hindu* mythological personages. The swan, eagle, and bull, have been noticed as appertaining respectively to BRAHMA, VISHNU, and SIVA, and severally denominated *Hanasa*, *Garuda*, and *Nandi*. GANESA, eldest son of MAHADEVA and PARVATI, the elephant-headed god of prudence and policy, rides a rat, supposed to be a very sagacious animal.—(PLATE 44. and FRONTISPIECE.) CARTICKA, their second son, the generalissimo of the celestial armies, is seen mounted on a peacock. INDRA, the powerful regent of the firmament, the JUPITER *Pluvius* of the *Hindus*, rides the elephant IRAVATI, symbolical of might.—(PLATE 79) VARUNA, genius of the waters, bestrides a fish; as doth also GANGA, the prime goddess of rivers.—(PLATE 75.) CAMA, the god of love, is carried by a lory, or parrot; AGNI, god of fire, by an ardent ram.—(PLATE 80.)

The *Sacti* or energy of these deities have the *Nandi* of their respective lords: BHAVANI is, however, oftener seen on a lion or tiger than on the bull, the *Nandi* of her spouse. *Avataras* of deities ride a bull, horse, &c. as will be noticed when our several plates, representing them, be described.

We have noticed GANESA and KARTIKA, or CARTICKA, as the first and second sons of MAHADEVA and PARVATI. PLATE 19. represents the father and mother, and two sons, mounted on the family *Nandi*. MAHADEVA has an antelope in one hand, an attribute borne by him in common with CHANDRA, or the Moon: he sometimes is seen, as in PLATE 5. with the antelope *Mrigu* in his hand, and the Moon on his head. In another hand (of PLATE 19.) he holds the conch, or buccinum, the usual attribute of VISHNU, but borne frequently also by MAHADEVA. GANGA is seen in his hair, (which, however, should not have been black—the engraver by mistake made it so,) and the river issuing from her mouth, as she also is in the upper compartment of the plate.

The upper half of the plate represents MAHADEVA in his character of PANCHA-MUKI, or *five-faced*. BRAHMA formerly had five faces, as is elsewhere noticed; and the *Saivas* gift their deity with all the distinctions of the other powers: here we see him faced like ancient BRAHMA, and below armed as VISHNU. Before him is his wife suckling, as she is likewise below, their infant GANESA.* A musician, perhaps NAREDA, is playing on the *Vina* before MAHADEVA, and behind him is an attendant fanning him with the *Chawrie*.

Of the sons of MAHADEVA and PARVATI, GANESA and CARTICEYA are by far the most renowned. Their names, and some particulars relating to them, have already been introduced, and they will hereafter be more particularly

* The critical reader must not notice the little anachronism the painter has fallen into by making GANESA a sucking infant, while his younger brother, CARTICKA, is pretty well grown. I will here remark in passing, that elephants do not suck their mothers by their trunks, but by the mouth like other quadrupeds, and as GANESA is here seen. Until I saw one sucking I had, without consideration perhaps, supposed they sucked with their trunks. The milk of an elephant, which I have tasted, is thick and coarse, but not so much so, in comparison with cow's milk, as one might imagine.

made known to the reader; and some notice will be taken of BHAIRAVA and VIRA BHADRA, two other reputed sons of MAHADEVA; of whom a representation is given in PLATES 24. 25. and 47.

We will now recur to PLATE 19. and conclude what remains to be said thereon, and then describe the rest of the plates allotted more peculiarly to the illustration of this principal subject of our work.

PLATE 19. is taken from two coloured drawings in my possession.* The upper part exhibits MAHADEVA *Panchamuki, (five-faced,)* ten-handed, seated in an expanded red lotos on a tiger's skin. When his hair is done up in the style of this picture he is called DHURJATI, which word signifies, *he who weareth his hair bound about his head in the form of a tiara* †; in which style it is also worn by those penitents called *Yogi*, or *Saniyasi*, and other adherents of SIVA; one of whom is represented in the plate, and has in the original a red mark down his forehead. MAHADEVA is white in both figures, with dusky yellowish hair; and it may be remarked, that in one he has white or grey beards and mustachios, and in the other his chin and lip are smooth. In the lower picture the stream from GANGA's mouth is blue, mixing with the blue water below, *on* which the *Nandi* seems to be walking, I know not if by accident on the part of the painter or design: the fish and aquatic birds farther seem to denote the connexion between this party and water. PARVATI, GANESA, CARTICEYA, the musician, and attendant, are of the same copper colour. SIVA's clothing in both figures is blue: PARVATI's *sari* (the robe that in the most elegant folds forms petticoat, cloak, and veil,) is red; her *chuli* (short light shift with sleeves half way to the elbow) is in one green, the other blue. CARTICEYA's and the musician's clothing is yellow: GANESA is naked.

PLATE 15. is taken from a fine statue, one of the series before mentioned, cast under the directions of *Mr.* WILKINS and *Pandits* at *Benares*. It is ten inches high, five-faced, four-handed; one hand with the antelope, another with the *Trisula*, and two others in the position before described. The skin wrapped round his loins reminds us of that of the *Nemean* lion, worn by HERCULES: the earrings of snakes, frontal crescent and eye, and the sacred string, are all the particulars that, in this plate, I shall direct the reader's attention to.

Figures 1. and 2. of PLATE 16. are back and front views of a neatly cast image in bronze, of the same size, of MAHADEVA *Panchamuki*, called in my de-

* Where it is not otherwise mentioned, the reader will please to understand the subject adverted to as belonging to the author.

† *Hitopadesa.*—Page 293.

scriptive memoranda of this subject PANCHAMUKI PARAMESWARA, which means the *five-faced eternal Lord.* He has ten hands, eight holding nearly the same thing, which may be the *Chank* or *Chakra,* or both: one hand is held up empty, and the other has something in it, but I know not what. Above the five *Muguts* is a conical termination, not well represented in the plate, with a round base, offering the same appearance in whichever direction it be viewed. The sacred thread is not distinguishable in the profusion of frontal ornaments (in *fig.* 2.) but is seen flowing down the bare back of *fig.* 1.

The principal subject of this plate, *fig.* 3. is from an uncommonly well cast image in bronze, representing MAHADEVA with PARVATI on his knee, in the same style that we have before described LAKSHMI NARAYAN. This is called MAHADEVA PARVATI, and she, like LAKSHMI, is not of proportionate size to her divine partner. The pendent heads on his collar, *(Ru mala* or *Mund mala,)* the style in which the hair is neatly braided and bound up, with GANGA peeping out of it, distinguishes this subject from those similar of the other deity and his beneficent spouse. One of SIVA's left hands holds PARVATI to his side, and one of her's embraces his loins, the other is empty. His superior right hand has a sort of battle-axe, called *Parasha,* the other is empty: a left hand held something, which is broken off where he grasped it; what is left may be fancied the stem of a lotos.

This subject was given to me by a much valued friend, a *Poona Brahman*; and it may be worthy of remark, that, of the several similar presents made to me by my friends of the tribe of *Brahman,* not one subject is perfect—in some particular, sometimes trifling, there is a defect, or fracture. The figure lifts off from the pedestal, and just above its insertion there is on each side a loop, or eyelet, as if to receive a string to fasten the image on to something. When it was given to me it had indeed no pedestal; at my request my friend the *Brahman* had the deficiency supplied, getting one cast for it in *Bombay.* The subject is nearly ten inches high, and well proportioned, as may be inferred from the plate, which is not at all neater, or more elegant than the original.

The painting or drawing from which PLATE 17. is engraved is, I think, the most beautiful and highest finished thing I ever saw. I purchased it at *Poona* for forty rupees (five pounds), but for some time the seller demanded a hundred (twelve guineas) for it. Although no larger than the plate the quantity of work must necessarily have occupied a very considerable time, and its excellence indicates the exertion of consummate skill. I was desirous of having the picture exactly copied, in every respect of colouring, &c. like the original, but

I was assured that it could not be done in England; and that even an approximation to its style of finishing, which could be attained only by very superior hands, would require a long period of time, and of course be attended with a heavy expense.

I will attempt to give the reader some idea of its beauties and finishing, but to be fully understood it must be seen.

MAHADEVA is of delicate blue colour, as if rubbed over with fine wood ashes, with faint lines of yellow on his arms, breast, and forehead: his hair is of a brownish yellow, bound very neatly round his head, decorated with braids intertwined of black and gold. SESHNAGA with many mouths convolves several times round the crown of his head, his scaly back tinted azure, and his belly white: his scales and folds are so minute as not to be discerned without magnifying glasses. The crescent in SIVA's forehead is of silver leaf. The snakes in his ears and round his wrists are of gold, tinged with crimson: his rosary, a close and a pendent necklace, PARVATI's wrist and other ornaments, the glories round both their heads, are also of liquid shining gold.* The snake round his neck has a dark brown back, spotted black, and a white belly; its folds and scales surprisingly minute and delicate; those forming *bazubands* above his elbows have gold bellies and crimson backs, finished in a similar style. The ornament just above the snake on the right arm is composed of a large central emerald and two small rubies; and they are exactly represented either by thin *laminæ* of those gems, or by coloured glass, or some highly polished substance. PARVATI's *bazubands* are the same: her pendent crossed chaplet is of large pearls embossed, and square emeralds; and her neck, arms, wrists, ancles, ears, and forehead, are similarly decorated: the ring on his finger is a ruby; her's are rubies and emeralds: through her veil of flowered gold net, thrown back off her forehead, her fine black hair is skilfully shown: her *Langi* is of rich flowered gold brocade: her *Chuli* is yellow, delicately embroidered at the termination of its sleeves on her well turned arms. The divine pair sit on a tiger's skin, spread on a crimson velvet carpet; and the large pillow against which they lean is of the same; and both are embroidered in gold with flowers and birds most delicately: the ends of the pillow are of yellow velvet with a border of green, terminated with gold tassels. The *Prabha*, or glory, encircling their heads are of shining gold, and a golden blaze of light is darting through dark clouds above:

* Artists in *India* have a practice of killing, by certain menstrua, silver and gold, making it permanently liquid, and as easy of application nearly by a hair pencil as our water-colours. If this art be known in *Europe* I never saw any successful instances of its application.

the remainder of the back-ground is black. The falling collar of skulls, and the cow, through whose mouth the *Ganga* flows from SIVA's hair, are white. But I am making my description tiresome, as the reader has not, as I have, the beauties of the original before him; and the plate, elegant as it is, can convey but a very inadequate idea of them. I shall, therefore, farther notice only the golden hand and spouted vessel; the circle near it, which in the picture is blue, of the same tint as SIVA's skin, and what it is meant for I know not. The jet black elephant's skin over his loins and thighs is not often seen with this deity; but I have met with another picture or two where he is girded similarly: the trunk winds round his left leg, bent under him. Red and blue lotoses float on the *Ganga*, and the flowers behind the deities are delicately tinted.

We must not, however, omit to notice the golden goblet in the left hand of PARVATI, with which she supplies her spouse with draughts of *Amrita*, or *Ambrosia*, the beverage of immortals. In the original MAHADEVA looks on PARVATI in a more impassioned manner than in the plate; his eyes are more shut and languishing; and he leans towards her, and looks as if already more than half intoxicated either with *Amrita* or with love: her hands and feet are dyed red, in imitation of the custom of maidens when betrothed; hence poets fancy the hand to blush in modest contemplation of the promised favour in bestowing it, and they call it the *crimson of consent*. PARVATI's heavenly hand reveals this bashful tint; for "the reluctant sweet delay," sung by the eloquent and plaintive JONES,* is on her part but of transient duration. But we must proceed to other and less attractive topics; nor attempt to paint or sing in "what tremendous strains immortals woo."

PLATE 18. is from a large coloured picture representing the same divine pair, attended by others of the immortal host. MAHADEVA is represented in his terrestrial paradise, *Kailasa*, situated on the summit of one of the numerous peaks of the wonderful and mystical mountain *Meru*, which may be called the *Olympia* of the *Hindus*. The picture is well done, in a style not usually met with. I imagine it to have been painted in a very northern country; *Tibet* or *Kashmir* perhaps: the two female attendants behind MAHADEVA are of brown complexion, and not in features like the delineations of southern artists. All the other persons in this picture have the same copper colour except VISHNU, who is straddling on the shoulders of the green-winged GARUDA in a bright blue

* Page 38.

skin, with a yellow *pitamber*, holding the *Chank*, *Chakra*, and *Gadha*; for one of which, however, the *Chank*, which is conspicuous enough, my artists have unaccountably substituted a lotos: they have also transformed the tree *Asoca*, which in the original overspreads, and distils milky streams on, MAHADEVA, into a plantain tree, of whose long broad leaves our engraving exhibits a very good representation.

MAHADEVA has a *blue throat*, hence named NILAKANTHA, and, in the position before described, leans on his *Saniyasi's* crooked staff, with half-closed eyes, musing and listening to the divine minstrelsy of the six *Gandbarvas*, playing and singing before him. They are also called *Apsarasa*, and *Devangana*. The names of three of these celestial choristers I find marked on the margin of the picture; viz. RHEMBA, URVASI, and TILUTAMMA: the first and last of whom, and perhaps the other also, are celebrated for their beauty in the amatory effusions of the *Hindu* poets; the first is, indeed, a name of their popular VENUS. The band is composed of a tambarine *(tamma)*; cymbals, or castanets, *(tal,)* not visible, being behind the person of the *tamma* player; a *vina*, or lute; and a *saranga*, played with a bow like a violin. The other two females hold a fan of feathers, *(pankha,)* and a *chawrie* of peacock's feathers, similar to that borne by one of the female attendants before noticed, behind MAHADEVA.

The *saranga* that the damsel is tuning is an instrument of great compass and sweetness in skilful hands; it has sometimes more than one metallic string: the *vina* is also a sweet soft instrument, sometimes composed of a gourd, sometimes of two, one at each end. I have listened with great pleasure to one at *Poona* belonging to the band of a friend, a celebrated and respectable lady, of very extraordinary dimensions and powers: this gourd was of unrivalled magnitude, save one in the orchestra of his *Highness* ASUF *ud* DOWLA, *Navab Vazir* of *Oude*, and was valued at ten thousand rupees, (1250*l.*).

With a due degree of shame and self-abasement I confess it, but I have been more affected with delicious sensations, resulting from the simple melody of a *Vina*, or a *Saranga*, delicately accompanied, than I can bring myself to feel from the elaborate concord of sweet sounds elicited from an *Italian* orchestra, with its complicated fashionable vocal accompaniments. With *Indian* music the auditor is never in the smallest degree surprised; it has nothing brilliant or wonderful; he knows not why, but he feels enraptured; his heart is filled, and his eyes are suffused. Now, with the astonishing intricacies of *Italian* or fashionable music, one (I speak of an unsophisticated Goth) is apt to be all wonder and amazement, to the exclusion of other and better, and more delectable emotions.

I have had opportunities of listening also to the music of *Malaya* and *China.* Most of their wind instruments, like those of hither *India* and *Persia*, are indeed barbarous; but in favour of those of the *Malays* and *Chinese* there are some exceptions—one or two of their wind instruments are very soft and harmonious. *Malay* music is, indeed, proverbially sweet; so is the language. How happens it, that the promontory of *Malaya* in the *Indian* ocean, like that of *Italy* in the *Mediterranean*, is distinguished by its fine climate, soft language, sweet music, and treacherous inhabitants?

But, begging the reader's pardon for this digression, we will finish our notice of PLATE 18. VISHNU has been noticed bestriding the shoulders of his *Vahan*, GARUDA: BRAHMA, four-handed, holding a book, is near him; both in yellow dresses. Behind SIVA are his sons, GANESA and CARTICEYA, the former dutifully whisking a *Chamara* over his parent; the latter, six-headed, with joined palms, reverently attending him: both sons in a yellow dress, with broad scarfs *(Dupaty)* thrown over their shoulders; one red, the other green. Two bearded *Brahmans* are seen behind GANESA; one bearing, perhaps by way of penance, a jagged staff, on which a heavy chain is sometimes suspended, and seen in the hands of pious pilgrims of the present day; or it may be the finger-board of a lyre in the hands of NAREDA. MAHADEVA's hair, frontal marks, snake-ornaments, *Trisula*, &c. are as before described; and GANGA, falling from his hair, issues through the cow's mouth *(Gaomuki)*, expanding to a river, in which stands *Nandi-keswara* ready caparisoned with housings of crimson and yellow, and golden bells and cords round his neck.

PARVATI, as well as her Lord, have green glories encircling their heads, radiated with gold; and SURYA (the Sun) is seen just rising with his gorgeous face over the eastern summit of *Meru* to add fresh splendour to this congress of divinities. PARVATI seems seated on an elephant's skin, and is presenting to her thoughtful spouse a golden goblet of ambrosia *(Amrita)*. She is very handsome, and elegantly attired; her long black tresses flow luxuriantly down her back, and are seen through the fine texture of her drapery. Some straggling lovely curls play, in the original, over her shoulders, that would not have been overlooked by the keen and ardent eye of a tropical poet, though they have escaped the cold hand of our hyperborean artists.

The upper part of PLATE 20. is the same subject described in 17. and 18.

with some differences and varieties. It is engraved from a pretty coloured picture that came into my hands at *Poona*. MAHADEVA is blue, or ashen coloured, and in the original is leaning his head on his right shoulder, with half-closed eyes, languishing on his lovely partner, who returns his amorous looks in a posture of attentive adoration: this is not so well represented in the plate. MAHADEVA has his usual attributes, *Ganga, Naug*, &c. but his hair is dusky brown, not black, as in the plate: his *Trisula* stands on the palisading near him, with something hanging on it; that in the original is not merely chequered, but has writing or figures, perhaps like that with BRAHMA in PLATE 4. a sort of magic square, or *abracadabra*. The crooked stick lying before him sometimes serves to rest his arm on, as seen with animals carved on it in PLATE 18.

GANESA, their eldest son, fans his father with a white *Chamara* in a gold handle: he holds also a lustral vessel, and an instrument like the end of a boat-hook used by elephant-drivers for guiding and urging the animal; it is called *Ankasa*: a third hand holds a gilt basin full of *batasa*, little cakes of refined sugar, with which he is in pictures often seen feeding himself--elephants are particularly fond of sugar-cane, and all saccharine compounds. GANESA is very fat and clumsy; his ears, head, and trunk, of a blood-red colour; his other parts fair, like his mother: his *Pitamber*, as well as SIVA's, yellow; by the way, unless that part of dress be yellow, it is not, I believe, properly so called. The rat, GANESA's *Vahan* or vehicle, (as seen in the FRONTISPIECE,) is near him, of very small dimensions, with red housings girt and bound on by white bands. SIVA's *Nandi*, the white bull, is behind GANESA, with green, red, and gold, trappings and ornaments; and BHAVANI's (i. e. PARVATI's) *Vahan*, the tiger, called *Veaghra*, stands behind her: and in the next plate (21.) they are severally mounted.

In the picture are three or four well tinted plantain and mango trees, not preserved in the etching; one overspreads MAHADEVA, and purplish streams are distilling from its leaves. The glory round the heads of MAHADEVA and PARVATI are dark green; that of GANESA black, like the back-ground, and terminated, as are the others, with a golden periphery.

The lower part of PLATE 20. will be hereafter described; it has been noticed in a former page.

PLATE 21. is taken from two coloured pictures, the lower representing MAHADEVA and PARVATI on their respective *Vahans* or vehicles. As the *Sacti* or *energy* of SIVA, she would, indeed, be appropriately mounted on his white bull. On the tiger she is, more strictly speaking, in the character of DURGA, under which she will hereafter be more fully described. Being eight-handed she is called DEVI *ashta-buja*: on the tiger, DEVI VYAGHRA-YAHI: except two snakes in her hands, neither deity holds any thing.

The upper part of PLATE 21. represents SIVA starting from his symbol, the *Linga*, to execute an immediate act of vengeance on a *Daitya*, or impious monster, who had presumed to offer it an indignity. The *Linga* and pedestal are of a dark blue or slate colour, and in the original SIVA is issuing from its *top*; but the artist, who made the drawing for the engraver, not understanding the subject, shows SIVA's left leg *behind* the *Linga*: it is, however, of little consequence. His hair in this, and the lower picture, is also improperly made black; in the original it is, as usual, of a brownish red hue: the god is white. All the other persons in both compartments are of the same copper colour.

In PLATE 22. a pious female is represented propitiating MAHADEVA in his generative character, indicated by the *Linga*, inserted in its appropriate receptacle, the *Argha*, or *Yoni*, mysterious types of nature that must, in a future page, come particularly into discussion. The devout female may be imagined as invoking the deities, typified by their symbols, for the blessing of fruitfulness, its reverse being deprecated by both sexes as the most afflicting visitation of divine displeasure. We shall show hereafter that certain ceremonies, called *Sradha*, to be performed by the offspring of defunct parents, are essential to the repose of a departed soul.

The picture from which PLATE 22. is engraved is very delicately executed; the female is younger, handsomer, and more feminine, than in the plate, and is very elegantly dressed and decorated. She is performing the ceremony called *Linga puja*; and I shall describe the implements seen in the plate, and some other points connected with the subject; premising that the terms I use may not, perhaps, be in the classical *Sanskrit*, as I learned them from a *Poona Brahman*, who, although a good scholar, may have answered my inquiries in a more popular language. Some of the terms, indeed, are current in spoken dialects of *India*, but may possibly be of *Sanskrit* origin.

The domestic temple, in which the symbol is placed, is called, as temples generally are, *Dewal*, or *Devel*, from *Deva*, a *deity*, and *havela*, a house; literally a *house of God*. The *English* and other people call it *Pagoda*, a word unknown in

India beyond the reach of *European* colloquial instruction. The dome of the temple is white, its lines gold, and it is surmounted by a gold spire, called *Sekra*: when temples, or other things, have a conical or pine-apple-shaped termination, such ornament is called *Kalasa.* The exterior of the temple is white, its interior *(gab'hara)* ash-coloured, like its patron deity. The *Linga* and *Argha* are of black stone, with gilt edges: the *Linga* (the upright conical stone), which has mystical orange-coloured lines traced on it, is crowned with encircled folds of *Bilva* flowers; and a chaplet of three strings of them, white, with yellow buds at regular distances, hangs pendent from the top of the *Linga,* falling towards the termination or spout of the *Argha.* In a former page (55.) it is noticed, that the *Bilva* is a shrub consecrated to MAHADEVA, who alone wears a chaplet of its flowers, which are offered in sacrifice to no other deity. The other shrub mentioned in the same page, the *Asoca,* is in the picture overshading the *Deval,* and being prettily coloured forms a good back-ground, in which some beautiful flowers behind the suppliant is a delicate finish.

Five lighted lamps *(pancharty)* are used in *puja* to SIVA, as seen in the plate; sometimes one lamp, with five wicks, (PLATE 85. *fig.* 2.): the lamp with a handle to it is called *duparti*; of this description I have several in brass; some also borne by women, elephants, &c. in a style not inelegant. The spouted vessel *(jari)* holds lustral water; a cup beside it *(dipa)* is for *ghee,* (clarified butter,) for feeding the lamps; the other cup for water, with which to sprinkle the flowers and *Linga,* is called *novady.* The bell *(gant'ha),* beyond the four lighted lamps, is essential in holy ceremonies, and is rung at certain times to scare away evil spirits, which was probably the origin of their adoption in the west. Bells are much used in and about *Hindu* temples, but were rejected by *Mahommedans* by order of their prophet, who deemed them relics of superstition. These used by the *Hindus* differ in make according to the deity in whose honour *puja* is performed: I have several with HANUMAN on the handle, denoting it to be peculiarly proper for the sect of *Ramanuj,* who exclusively adore VISHNU, or his *Sacti,* LACSHMI, separately or conjointly, in the *Avatara* of RAMA CHANDRA and SITA. *Fig.* 2. of PLATE 92. represents such a bell; and *fig.* 3. of the same plate is a bell with its handle composed of two images, back to back, of HANUMAN and GARUDA, reminding us a little of JANUS *bifrons.* But those *Indian* deified heroes do not correspond in character with the GANESA of the *Romish* PANTHEON; to whom an article must be duly allotted.

Of PLATE 22. there yet remains the pious damsel to be described. She sits on an embroidered carpet, called *asana*: her right hand is in a bag of gold brocade, *(kamkhab)*; the bag is called *gumuki*; and her hand is supposed to hold a rosary of round beads, *(mala,)* containing in number 108, exclusive of connecting beads, differently shaped: her attention is abstractedly fixed on the deity, assisted by the rosary, in the mode noticed in a former page. Her *langi* is yellow, *(pitamber)*: a very fine sprigged muslin robe, edged with gold, thrown over her person, reveals all its attractive points and *contour*; the robe is called *upervastra*, through which her *chuli*, otherwise called *canchoki*, with its worked flowered border, and *bazuband* and other ornaments, are seen. The ornaments she wears are thus denominated: earrings of gold, and pearls, and emeralds, composed of three parts: the upper *bogri*; the centre *bali*; the lower *karnphula*: the long depending pearl necklace, *har*, or *duleri*; the shorter with rubies intermixed, *garsuli*; the broad round necklace is of flowers: above the elbow *vira*, otherwise *tulbandi*; and the band that terminates the sleeve of the *chuli*, *tayit*: on her wrists *churi*, or *cancana*: on the fingers *angli*, in common language; in higher, *mudnekara*: the ancle-ornament of gold and pearls, *vanki-nipuri*: her forehead has three lines drawn with saffron, which are called *kunka*, with a central mark, *teckly*: on her throat are seven similar lines, called *mangal-sutri*. She is of a delicate copper colour, and her fine black hair is finished in an exceedingly minute and beautiful style. The sole of her foot and her finger-nails are tinged with red.

It is not intended to describe with such painful minuteness the originals of many more of our engravings; some few of early occurrence it was deemed best to explain particularly, that, when occasion may require, reference can be made direct to an already printed page.

Being about to close the account of the three personified *powers* of the Almighty, the reader is referred to PLATE 23. where, in the upper compartment, they are represented together, with their *Sactis* beside them. *Fig.* 1. VISHNU and LACSHMI; 2. MAHADEVA and PARVATI; 3. BRAHMA and SARASWATI. Having already explained, perhaps too minutely, the attributes, &c. severally exhibited by these deities, I shall here tax my reader's patience but triflingly. The plate is engraved from pictures: VISHNU holds the *Chakra*, and a lotos flower, *Pedma*, and is of a dark blue colour. SIVA is, as usual, white, holding VISHNU's emblem, the *Chank*, and his own, the antelope, called, in his hands, *Mrigu*. BRAHMA, a *Veda* in two of his hands: he and the three ladies are copper-coloured. SIVA's necklace is of skulls, the others of flowers,

&c. The trio are seated on a tiger's skin: VISHNU and BRAHMA have the lotos by way of carpet: SIVA has not.

The lower part of PLATE 23. represents an *Avatara* of MAHADEVA and PARVATI, in the characters of KANDARHAHU and MALSARA, under which names they are much respected and worshipped in the southern and western parts of *India*. But we shall hereafter introduce this *Avatara* in a separate article, and postpone till then its farther consideration.

NARAYANA.

WITH the early investigators of *Hindu* mythology the character of NARAYANA must have been the source of considerable embarrassment; nor is it yet entirely cleared from contradiction and obscurity: the latter, perhaps, necessarily attendant on a subject so little within the scope of research, and on which contradictory information will be given according to the religious opinions or sect of the informant.

If inquiry be made of a *Vaishnava*, or one of the exclusive adorers of VISHNU, he will not fail of exalting the object of his own adoration to the throne of the One only Almighty Being; and with that view will call him NARAYANA, although in fact such name is not strictly applicable to that Being, but to his *Spirit*, if such a personification can be conceived. The *Goculast'has*, a branch of the *Vaishnavas*, will similarly exalt CRISHNA, the exclusive object of their adoration; and in other passages we are scarcely able to distinguish the persons of NARAYANA and BRAHMA. It is only, therefore, from their own books that, in this instance particularly, any authentic information can be obtained of the *Hindu* doctrines; and even then, we must keep in mind the probable sectarial bias of both compiler and commentator. Without the valuable matter in the *Asiatic Researches*, and other works of recent date, drawn from books of sacred authority, I should have found myself greatly at a loss in attempting an account of the character under our notice: my own verbal inquiries were always attended with perplexity and contradiction, and their results consequently unsatisfactory.

Sir WILLIAM JONES has addressed a hymn to this deity; * and in the argument prefixed says, " that a complete introduction to it would be no less than a full comment on the *Vedas* and *Puranas* of the *Hindus*, the remains of *Egyptian* and *Persian* theology, and the tenets of the *Ionic* and *Italic* schools: but

* *As. Mis.* Vol. I. and *Works*, Vol. XIII.

this is not the place for so vast a disquisition. It will be sufficient here to notice, that the inextricable difficulties attending the *vulgar notion of material substances,* concerning which

> "We know this only, that we nothing know,"

induced many of the wisest among the ancients, and some of the most intelligent among the moderns, to believe that the whole creation was rather an *energy* than a *work,* by which the infinite Being, who is present at all times in all places, exhibits to the minds of his creatures a set of perceptions like a wonderful picture, or piece of music, always varied, yet always uniform; so that all bodies and their qualities exist, indeed, to every wise and useful purpose, but exist only as they are *perceived*: a theory no less pious than sublime, and as different from any principle of atheism as the brightest sunshine differs from the blackest night. This *illusive operation* of the Deity the *Hindu* philosophers call *Maya,* or *Deception.*

In the first stanza of the hymn are represented the sublimest attributes of the Supreme Being, and the three forms in which they most clearly appear to us—*Power, Wisdom,* and *Goodness*; or, in the language of ORPHEUS and his disciples, *Love.* The second stanza comprises the *Indian* and *Egyptian* doctrines of the Divine Essence, and archetypal ideas. The third and fourth are taken from the *Institutes* of MENU, and the eighteenth *Purana,* entitled *Sri Bhagavat.* From BRAHME, or the *Great Being,* in the *neuter* gender, is formed BRAHMA, in the *masculine*; and the second word is appropriated to the *creative power* of the Divinity.

The Spirit of God, called NARAYANA, or *moving on the water,* has a multiplicity of other epithets in *Sanscrit*; the principal of which are introduced expressly, or by allusion, in the fifth stanza of the hymn. The sixth ascribes the perception of *secondary* qualities by our senses to the immediate influence of *Maya*; and the seventh imputes to her operations the *primary* qualities of extension and solidity.

> "Hail, self-existent, in celestial speech,
> NARAYAN; from thy wat'ry cradle nam'd.—
> Or VENAMALY;
> Or high PEITAMBER."
>
> *Hymn,* v. 5.

Ins. of MENU, c. 1. v. 10.—"The waters are called *Nara,* because they were the first production of NARA, or the Spirit of God; and since they were his first *ayana,* or place of motion, he is thence named NARAYANA, or moving on the waters."

It is commonly understood, in the pictures where BRAHMA is seen seated on a lotos issuing from the navel of a figure recumbent on a vast many-headed serpent, that such figure is VISHNU; but he ought, perhaps, as hath been before stated, to be rather considered as NARAYANA, or VISHNU under that name, given him by the *Vaishnavas.*—See PLATE 7. and the description of it in page 26.

Images of MAHADEVA PARVATI are seen so much in form and posture like those of LAKSHMI NARAYAN, as not to be known one from the other but from their distinguishing attributes. PLATES 16. and 26. contain the former of these subjects. A fine figure of it is also given with *Sir* CHARLES MALET's interesting description of the caves at *Ellora,** in the sixth volume of the *Asiatic Researches.* She is sitting in a graceful attitude in the lap of MAHADEVA; he has one of his four hands on her breast, and another similarly placed on an attendant female; in this instance, were it not for the peculiar style in which MAHADEVA's hair is bound up, the subject might be mistaken for LAKSHMI NARAYAN. PARVATI is, however, of a size proportional to MAHADEVA.

LAKSHMI, as well as BHAVANI, is considered as the queen of beauty; and, indeed, like other deities, their characters will be found to melt into each other. Being commonly seen with a *Kamal,* or lotos, the emblem of female beauty, in her hand, she is called KAMALA: the word is by some—by *Sir* W. JONES, indeed, in his earlier lucubrations on *Hindu* mythology, spelled *Kemel.* In his profound and spirited hymn to NARAYANA, which every inquirer into its subject would do well to consult with attention, that deity, a personification of the Spirit of BRAHME, as "he heavenly pensive on the lotos lay,"† said to BRAHMA, "Go; bid all worlds exist!" and the lotos is thus apostrophized.—

* It is impossible to read the interesting account of the excavations near *Ellora,* and to see the sketches that have been made from them, &c. especially *Mr.* DANIEL's unequalled prints, without lamenting that a much greater number of accurate drawings have not been taken. *Ellora* and *Elephanta,* even in their present state, are inexhaustible sources for mythological research: the materials they offer are, as well as being indubitably the most ancient, of the most authentic kind; and faithful copies should be made while within our reach, and before the hand of time or sacrilege be laid yet heavier on them.

† As represented, perhaps, in PLATE 20.

"Hail, primal blossom! hail, empyreal gem!
Kemel, or *Pedma*, or whate'er high name
Delight thee; say, what four-formed Godhead came,
With graceful stole, and beamy diadem,
Forth from thy verdant stem?—
Full-gifted BRAHMA." V. 4.—(See PLATE 7.)

But BRAHMA himself is sometimes considered as NARAYANA. *Mr.* COLEBROKE, in his most valuable Essay on the *Vedas*, (*As. Res.* Vol. VIII.) adverts to the 30th and 31st chapters of the White *Yajush*, (*Yajur Veda*,) as "relating to the *Purushamed'ha*, a type of the allegorical immolation of NARAYANA, or of BRAHMA in that character."—P. 378; note. And in a note in the next page, alluding to the fabulous origin of the *Vedas*, a commentator is said to have had "recourse to the renovations of the universe. 'In one *Calpa* the *Vedas* proceeded from fire, air, and the sun; in another from BRAHMA, at his allegorical immolation.'" Again in p. p. 430. 437. "the allegorical immolation of NARAYANA" occurs: and the epithet NARAYANA PURUSHA in p. 431.

The *Purushamed'ha* means the sacrifice or immolation of PURUSHA. "PURUSHA means the primeval man, or primeval person."*—COLEBROKE. *As. Res.* Vol. VIII. p. p. 470, 471. The hymn or verses, called *Purusha*, will be referred to from other parts of this work; and being of a very curious nature, I give them here from the seventh volume of the *As. Res.* p. 251. The hymn is recited among the ceremonies of the *Sradha*, or oblations in honour of deceased ancestors, and followed by the music of flagelets, lutes, &c. and will serve as a farther interesting instance of the constant recurrence of mythological allusions in every thing said or done through the mediation of the *Brahmans*.

"1. The embodied spirit which hath a thousand heads, a thousand eyes, a thousand feet, stands in the human breast, while he totally pervades the earth.

"2. That being is this universe, and all that has been, or will be; he is that which grows by nourishment; and he is the distributor of immortality.

"3. Such is his greatness; and therefore is he the most excellent embodied spirit; the elements of the universe are one portion of him; and three portions of him are immortality in heaven.

"4. That three-fold being rose above this world; and the single portion of him that remained in this universe, which consists of what does, and what does not, taste the reward of good and bad actions: again he pervaded the universe.

* CRISHNA by his sectaries is called the Primeval male.

"5. From him sprung VIRAJ, * from whom the first man was produced; and he, being successively reproduced, peopled the earth.

"6. From that single portion, surnamed the universal sacrifice, was the holy oblation of butter and curds produced; and this did frame all cattle, wild or domestic, which are governed by instinct.

"7. From that universal sacrifice were produced the strains of the *Rich* and *Saman*: from him the sacred metres sprung: from him did the *Yajush* proceed.

"8. From him were produced horses, and all beasts that have two rows of teeth: from him sprung cows, goats, and sheep.

"9. Him the gods, the demi gods named *Sad'hya*, and the holy sages, immolated as a victim on sacred grass; and thus performed a solemn act of religion.

"10. Into how many portions did they divide this being whom they immolated? What did his mouth become? What are his arms, his thighs, and his feet, now called?

"11. His mouth became a priest: his arm was made a soldier: his thigh was transformed into a husbandman: from his feet sprung the servile man.

"12. The moon was produced from his mind; the sun sprung from his eye; air and breath proceeded from his ear; and fire rose from his mouth.

"13. The subtle element was produced from his navel; the sky from his head; the earth from his feet; and space from his ear. Thus did he frame worlds.

"14. In that solemn sacrifice which the gods performed with him as a victim, spring was the butter, summer the fuel, and sultry weather the oblation.

"15. Seven were the moats surrounding the altar; thrice seven were the logs of holy fuel at that sacrifice which the gods performed, immolating" (read rather *binding*, or *consecrating*.—See *As. Res.* Vol. VIII. p. 437.) "this being as the victim.

"16. By that sacrifice the gods worshipped this victim: such were primeval duties; and thus did they attain heaven, where former gods and mighty demi gods abide."

Mr. COLEBROKE thought it unnecessary to quote from the commentary the explanation there given of this curious passage in the *Veda*, "because it does not really elucidate the sense; and that the allegory is, for the most part, suffi-

* "See MENU. Ch. I. v. 32." VIRAJ will be considered presently.

ciently obvious." I cannot, of course, regret that the commentary is omitted; but my readers will, I think, lament with me that *Mr.* COLEBROKE did not give some farther illustration of this mysterious allegory. It is, however, adverted to in a future volume.—See *As. Res.* Vol. VIII. p. 436. Under future articles this subject must be again introduced.

The hymn above quoted is translated from the 31st chapter of the White *Yajur Veda*: it occurs also in the beginning of the 19th book of the 4th, or *Atharva Veda*, "some of the verses are indeed transposed, and here and there a word differs: for example; it opens by describing the primeval man *(Purusha)* with a thousand arms, instead of a thousand heads."—COLEBROKE. *As. Res.* Vol. VIII. p. 470.

BRAHMA seems, especially in the 11th verse, to be spoken of in the hymn, which, or the ceremony of *Purushamed'ha* as before quoted, is stated by *Mr.* COLEBROKE to "be a type of the allegorical immolation of NARAYANA, or BRAHMA in that character." BRAHMA and NARAYANA are in this instance identified; and from the circumstance of having LAKSHMI as his wife, and bearing the attributes of VISHNU, as above described, NARAYANA is also unequivocally identified with the preserving power. CRISHNA, indeed, calls himself NARAYANA; at least is made to do so by JAYADEVA, the spirited author of the *Gita Govinda*. In one of CRISHNA's tender songs, addressed to his delightful mistress, the following is the burden.—"Give short raptures, sweet RADHA! to NARAYAN, thy adorer."—*As. Res.* Vol. III. art. 8. on the mystical poetry of the *Persians* and *Hindus*, by *Sir* WILLIAM JONES. The combined learning and elegance of that article, including the *Gita Govinda*, are scarcely to be equalled. I have made several extracts from the latter in different parts of my humble work; but earnestly entreat the reader, if a stranger to it, to peruse the whole of the article referred to: he will, I am sure, thank me for the direction to so much elegance, tenderness, and beauty.

JAYADEVA was doubtless a *Goculastya*, "whose soul is united to the foot of NARAYANA," as he sings at the conclusion of his ardent effusion to the honour and glory of CRISHNA; or that "HERI who, removing the lucid veil from the bosom of PEDMA, and fixing his eyes on the delicious buds that grew on it, diverted her attention by declaring that when she had chosen him for her bridegroom near the sea of milk, the disappointed husband of PARVATI drank in despair the venom which dyed his neck azure."

The *Sivpuran* contains a theogonical narrative, grounded of course on the doctrines of the *Saivas*, that includes various points of mythology, although not, perhaps, materially clearing the subject of its difficulties and contradictions. Here follows a brief abstract of it.

Brahm, willing the creation of the world, produced two beings, male and female, Purusha and Pracriti: the latter with eight arms, most beautiful. They were subsequently called Narayana and Narayani; and from the benignity of Narayana proceeded the five elements—earth, air, water, fire, and ether *(akas)*. From his navel, when reposing, issued a lotos, bearing Brahma; and from her sprung Vishnu: a quarrel ensued; and a third deity, the *Linga*, appeared, and appeased the creative and conservative powers, who respectively, assuming the form of a goose and a boar, sought in vain the source and end of Brahm, who in this *Purana* is of course identified with Siva. It proceeds to state how a *Sacti* sprang from Narayani, named Savitri (the Sun *), whom Brahma espoused; and two others, Lakshmi and Parvati, who were taken to wife by Vishnu and Siva. How another form similar to Siva's sprang from a wrinkle in Brahma's forehead, and was named Rudra, and was in all respects the same as Siva; and also the same as both Brahma and Vishnu. The only distinction between the four was, that three proceeded from Pracriti, but himself, Siva, did not.

Brahma, in view to peopling the world, produced four beings, Sanaca, Sananda, Sanatkumara, and Sanatana; who, being refractory, caused their parent to mourn and weep; and, to comfort him, Siva, in the character of Rudra, issued from a fold in his forehead, with five heads and ten arms; and endowing Brahma with additional strength, he produced Bhrigu and the seven *Rishis*; and after that Narada from his thigh, Kardama, the *Rishi*, from his shadow, and from the fore-finger of his right hand Dacsha. Bhrigu produced Marichi; and Marichi, Kasyapa. Dacsha had sixty daughters; thirteen of whom were married to Kasyapa, twenty-seven to Chandra, and one, who is Bhavani, to Rudra: I do not know how the other nineteen were disposed of. From Dacsha and his daughters have proceeded all things divine and human, animal and vegetable, &c.

A portion of the *Veda* is ascribed to Mahidasa, an incarnation of Narayana, proceeding from Visala, son of Abja. A commentator on the *Veda*

* Saraswati and Savitri seem here to be the same; the spouse of Brahma. This is not an usual identity; but occurs again in an inscription translated by *Mr.* Colebrooke.—*As. Res.* Vol. IX. p. 416. *Calcutta* edition. Under the article Surya, the Sun, his name of Savitri will be noticed.

says, "that, on the sudden appearance of this deity at a solemn celebration, the whole assembly of gods and priests fainted, but at the intercession of BRAHMA they were revived; and after making their obeisance, they were instructed in holy science. This *Avatara* was called MAHIDASA, because those venerable personages *(Mahin)* declared themselves his slaves, *(dasa)*."—See COLEBROKE on the *Vedas*. *As. Res.* Vol. VIII. p. 420.

Of the Black *Yajur Veda* a considerable portion, comprising an *Upanishad*, is called NARAYANA; or, to distinguish it from another *Upanishad* of the *Atharvana*, likewise so called, it is styled *Maha Narayana*, or *Vrihan Narayana*; that is, the *Great Narayana*.—*Ib.* p. 454.

NARAYANA, pronounced and written NARAYAN, or sometimes NARRAIN, is a common name with *Hindus* of several sects, and often occurs in their writings without reference beyond mere mortality. *Dasa*, usually written by the *English*, *Dass*, or *Doss*, is a common termination to *Hindu* names of men, especially among the tribe of *Bania*. BHAGAVAN DASA, for instance, signifies the *slave* of BHAGAVAN, VISHNU, or CRISHNA: similarly to ABD ALLAH, the *slave* of *God*, among the *Mussulmans*. RAMDAS is, in like manner, the slave or servant of RAMA.

In the following extracts we shall, among more relevant matter, meet with some apparent contradictions, which I am not so presumptuous as to attempt to reconcile, seeing the meaning of the legends was professedly undiscovered by the respective learned gentlemen; nor do I extract them for the invidious desire of exhibiting apparent incongruities, attached to names so dear to literature, but to invite an attempt at reconcilement.

"As to the creation of the world, in the opinion of the *Romans*, OVID, who might naturally have been expected to describe it with learning and elegance, leaves us wholly in the dark *which of the gods was the actors in it*. Other mythologists are more explicit; and we may rely on the authority of CORNUTUS, that the old *European* heathens considered JOVE (not the son of SATURN, but of the *ether*, that is of an unknown parent,) as the great *Life-giver*, and *Father* of *gods* and *men*: to which may be added the *Orphean* doctrine, preserved by PROCLUS; that 'the abyss and empyreum, the earth and sea, the gods and goddesses, were produced by ZEUS, or JUPITER.' In this character he corresponds with BRAHMA; and, perhaps, with that god of the *Babylonians*, (if we can rely on the accounts of their ancient religion,) who, like BRAHMA, reduced the universe to order; and, like BRAHMA, *lost his head*, with the blood of which new animals were instantly formed. I allude to the common story, the meaning of which I cannot discover; that BRAHMA had five heads till one of them was cut off by NARAYANA." —*Sir* WILLIAM JONES. *As. Res.* Vol. I. p. 246.

Here we see NARAYANA as the decapitator of BRAHMA, with whom we had just identified him.

In the following, which is the concluding paragraph of an extract given under SIVA, it will be found that it was MAHADEVA who beheaded BRAHMA.

"There is a striking resemblance between the legendary wars of the three principal gods in *Egypt* and *India*. As OSIRIS gave battle to TYPHON, who was defeated at length, and even killed by HORUS, so BRAHMA fought with VISHNU, and gained an advantage over him, but was overpowered by MAHADEVA, who cut off one of his five heads; an allegory, of which I cannot pretend to give the meaning."—WILFORD. *As. Res.* Vol. III. p. 371.

BRAHMA's head seems to have been, on other occasions, an object of successful vengeance. It was fortunate he was so well furnished with that important article.

In another passage NARAYANI, the *Sacti* of NARAYANA, is noticed by *Mr.* COLEBROKE as the same with VAISHNAVI, the *Sacti* of VISHNU. Indeed the *Sacti* of any of VISHNU's *Avataras* will be ultimately resolvable into LAKSHMI, or VAISHNAVI, the immediate *Sacti* or consort of VISHNU himself. RADHA, or ROKMENY, the spouse or *Sacti* of CRISHNA, is an *Avatara* of LAKSHMI, as her husband is of VISHNU; NARAYANI similarly of NARAYANA; NRISINHI of NARSINGA; VARAHI of VARAHA; and so forth: and I suspect that, as we explore farther the fruitful subject of *Hindu* mythology, we shall find that there are a greater number of sects than have hitherto been ascertained. Other *Avataras* of VISHNU, and of other deities, male and female, will perhaps be found, like CRISHNA, RAMA, and BUDDHA, to have also their exclusive worshippers.

A passage in the *Hitopadesa* speaks of NARAYANA as BRAHM, comprehending in himself the three great powers —"The great and mighty Lord, NARAYANA; the author of Creation, Preservation, and Destruction: he will wipe away our sorrows."—Page 152. On which, the learned translator (WILKINS) has this note.—"*Destruction*: Though this attribute more particularly belongs to SIVA, yet it is common to allow the same powers to each of the three persons of the *Hindu* Trinity, BRAHMA, VISHNU, (or NARAYANA,) and SIVA, seeing they mean but one God—BRAHM, or BRAHMA."

It would appear from this passage, that the author of the *Hitopadesa* was a *Vaishnava*, as, indeed, his name, VISHNU SARMA, indicates.

The *Ramayana* being the production of a *Vaishnava*, we may of course expect there to find VISHNU and NARAYANA identified. In Sect. 13. p. 120. 8vo. edit. is this passage.—" BRAHMA, the sovereign of the gods; STHANU," (a name of SIVA,) " and NARAYANA, chief of beings." In p. 127.—" NARAYANA, the all-pervading;" " the imperishable VISHNU." The epithet " chief of beings" is applied to half the deities, or persons, superior or inferior, of the *Hindu* PANTHEON. " Sovereign of the gods," as well as to BRAHMA, is a title applied also to VISHNU in the *Ramayana*, (p. 125.); likewise that of " chief of the celestials; adored by all beings."—*(Ib.)*

The *Sactis*, or *energies*, of the three great powers ought, perhaps, in strictness of arrangement, to follow our superficial relation of their respective Lords. But before those divine helpmates, SARASWATI, LAKSHMI, and PARVATI, be more particularly introduced, I am desirous of clearing the way by a consideration of some allegorical or historical personages; of great importance, doubtless, in mythological investigations, but not so immediately executive, or brought so often under our notice as the said *Sactis*. The next division of our work will, therefore, be devoted to some account of those allegorical personages.

In addition to what occurs in former pages, respecting the lower half of PLATE 20. I will here note, that it is taken from a tolerably well executed picture that I purchased at *Poona*. The body of the picture is white, with lotos flowers scattered about, denoting water to be understood, in which the leafy cradle of NARAYANA must be supposed floating. The deity is of a uniform dark blue colour; his fingers, and soles, and lips, are tinted red; the ornaments in his ears, round his arms, legs, waist, and neck, are of gold and pearls; his only clothing is a sash, flowing from his neck, as represented in the plate, which, as before noticed, differs in the position of the naked figure, the original being a front fore-shortened view. The plate has also more anatomical expression and accuracy; in the original, indeed, the left uplifted foot is turned the wrong way, the great and little toes having changed places. There is, I think, a peculiarity in the hair that I have not observed in any other pictures of VISHNU, in either of his *Avataras*, or of any deity, except BUDDHA: on the top of the head it is thick and woolly, as is usually given to the last named personage: the style in which it flows, or curls, on the shoulders, in PLATE 20. is also unusual. No other subject selected for this work has the forehead marked like this of

NARAYANA; but I have several pictures of VISHNU, in his *Avataras* of KRISHNA and RAMA, and in other characters, with the forehead similarly marked. Another singularity is observable in this subject: he has a nose-jewel, worn commonly by females, but rarely, I believe, by male divinities: I have, however, some pictures of NAUTHJI, KRISHNA or VISHNU, as worshipped in *Hardwar*, that have the nose-jewel. On the picture is written, in *Sanskrit*, *Vat patra Sayi* BHAGAVAN; which is, BHAGAVAN reposing on a *Vat* leaf: *Vat* is the *Ficus Indicus*, commonly called the *Banian* tree.

OF VIRAJ—the MENUS—the BRAHMADICAS, or PRAJAPATIS—the RISHIS—the MUNIS—the PANDUS—the RUDRAS—the ADITYAS—the VASUS—the MARUTS—the PITRIS—the DANAVAS—the SURS and ASURS—the DEVARSHIS, BRAHMARSHIS, MAHARSHIS, and RAJARSHIS—RAKSHAS—YAKSHAS—APSARAS—and other ALLEGORICAL BEINGS of the INVISIBLE WORLD.

FREQUENT mention is made in the course of this work, and, indeed, in all *Hindu* writings and conversations, whether historical, scientific, or poetical, of certain mythological persons under the above designations; and in view to a ready reference to some general information respecting such beings, when their names or characters may come before us in the progress of our work, I shall here take the opportunity of introducing them to the reader's notice, explaining briefly, and as clearly as I am able, who they were.

It is said, in the *Ins.* of MENU, (Chap. I. v. 32.) that the Mighty Power, having divided his own substance, became male and female; and from that female produced VIRAJ. VIRAJ produced the first MENU, named SWAYAMBHUVA:* he, the ten *Brahmadicas*, or *Prajapatis*, whom he calls ten lords of created beings. They produced *seven other Menus*, whose names were SWAYAMBHUVA, SWAROCHESHA, UTTAMA, TAMASA, RAIVATA, CHACSHUSHA, and SATYAVRATA. These *Menus* are, by some authorities, said to have produced the seven *Rishis*; but others state the seven *Rishis* to have sprang immediately from BRAHMA: their names are KASYAPA, ATRI, VASISHTA, VISWAMITRA, GAUTAMA, JAMADAGNI, and BHARADWAJA.—WILFORD. *As. Res.* Vol. V. p. 246.

I will introduce the texts, from the *Institutes* of MENU, above adverted to, comprising the names of the ten *Brahmadicas*, or *Prajapatis*; descriptive also of VIRAJ; and from which it is likely that the *Hindu* sculptors and painters have derived their idea of the half male, half female, figure, seen in the cave on *Gharipuri (Elephanta)*, that I will presently notice, and of the subjects represented in PLATES 7. and 24. called *Ardha Nari.*

* Here the seven *Menus* will appear to be the grand-sons of SWAYAMBHUVA; who, however, is himself one of the seven.

Chap. I. v. 32.—" Having divided his own substance, the Mighty Power became half male, half female, *or nature active and passive*; and from that female he produced VIRAJ.

" 33. Know me,* O most excellent of *Brahmans*, to be that person whom the male *power*, VIRAJ, having performed austere devotion, produced by himself: Me, the *secondary* framer of all this *visible* world.

" 34. It was I who, desirous of giving birth to a race of men, performed very difficult religious duties, and first produced ten lords of created beings, eminent in holiness:

" 35. MARICHI, ATRI, ANGERAS, PULASTYA, PULAHA, CRITU, PARCHETAS or DACSHA, VASISHTA, BHRIGU, and NARADA.

" 36. They, abundant in glory, produced seven other MENUS, together with deities, and mansions of deities, and *Maharshis*, or great sages, unlimited in power;

" 37. Benevolent genii and fierce giants; blood-thirsty savages; heavenly quiristers; nymphs and demons; huge serpents, and snakes of smaller size; birds of mighty wing; and separate companies of *Pitris*, or progenitors of mankind."

Before we return to the *Brahmadicas*, &c. it may be expedient to give a farther account of VIRAJ, as translated by *Mr.* COLEBROKE, from the White *Yajur Veda*, and his judicious observations connected with the perplexing subjects now under our consideration.

" He," (the primeval being) " felt not delight; therefore man delights not when alone. He wished the existence of another; and instantly he became such as is man and woman in mutual embrace. He caused this, his own self, to fall in twain; and thus became a husband and wife: therefore was this body so separated as it were an imperfect moiety of himself. This blank, therefore, is completed by woman: he approached her, and thence were human beings produced.

" She reflected, doubtingly, ' How can he, having produced me from himself, incestuously approach me? I will now assume a disguise.' She became a cow, and the other became a bull, and approached her; and the issue were kine. She was changed into a mare, and he into a stallion; one was turned into a female ass, and the other into a male one: thus did he again approach her; and

* The first MENU, SWAYAMBHUVA, is speaking. *Note*: The words in *Italics* in this quotation are not in the original text of MENU, but form, by interpolation, a concise gloss of his commentator.

the one-hoofed kind was the offspring. She became a female goat, and he a male one; she was an ewe, and he a ram: thus he approached her; and goats and sheep were the progeny. In this manner did he create every existing pair whatsoever, even to the ants and minutest insect."

"The sequel of this passage," Mr. COLEBROKE says, "is also curious; but is too long to be here inserted. The notion of VIRAJ dividing his own substance into male and female occurs in more than one *Purana*; so does that of an incestuous marriage and intercourse of the first MENU and his daughter SATARUPA: and the commentators on the *Upanishad* understand that legend to be alluded to in this place. But the *Institutes*, ascribed to MENU, make VIRAJ to be the issue of such a separation of persons, and MENU himself to be the offspring. There is, indeed, as the reader may observe from the passages cited in the present essay, much disagreement and consequent confusion in the gradation of persons interposed by *Hindu* theology between the supreme Being and the created world."—*As. Res.* Vol. VIII. p. 442.

Ten *Brahmadicas* have been noticed and named; but the *Puranas* do not agree as to their number. Although the *Ins.* of MENU, and the *Bhagavata*, enumerate ten, there are but nine noticed in other passages of the *Puranas*: in the *Scanda Purana* it is declared there were no more than seven; nor are authorities wanting to reduce them to three: namely, the three sons * of SWAYAMBHUVA, who was BRAHMA himself in a human shape.

Mr. WILFORD,† to whom I am obliged for the information contained in the preceding paragraph, thinks it likely that the seven *Menus*,‡ the seven *Brahmadicas*, and the seven *Rishis*, to be the same, and to make only seven individual persons; first called *Brahmadicas*, or children of BRAHMA, and created for the purpose of supplying the world with inhabitants. Having fulfilled this mission, they became sovereigns, or *Menus*; who, when far advanced in years, withdrew from the world to solitary places to prepare for death, as, according to the *Puranas*, was the general practice of mankind in former ages; and became *Rishis*, or holy penitents, who, by their salutary counsels, and the example of their austerities, discovered the paths of virtue and rectitude to mankind.

This seems the most probable mode of reconciling the many contradictions that appear from a consideration of the *Menus*; but there is still much confusion

* Meaning, I imagine, DAKSHA, NAREDA, and BHRIGU.

† *As. Res.* Vol. V. p. 246.

‡ In the *Gita*, Lecture X. "the *four* MENUS" are spoken of. In the *Sivpurana* fourteen are mentioned.

in their persons and characters. It is, indeed, the first and last only that are usually heard of: and we may here generally notice, that the first, named SWAYAMBHUVA, or *son of the Self Existent*, is he who is supposed to have revealed the *Institutes*, known by the title of MENU's; and that, in the time of the seventh MENU, surnamed SATYAVRATA, (called also VAIVASWATA, or *child of the Sun,*) the general deluge occurred. The first *Sir* WILLIAM JONES * judged to be the same with ADAM; the other NOAH, " the great progenitor and restorer of our species."

It may, perhaps, tend to give a clearer idea of these personages, if their names were placed together: they are here recapitulated.

Brahmadicas, or *Prajapatis*; that is, lords of *prajas*, or creatures.	*Menus*.	*Rishis*.
MARICHI	SWAYAMBHUVA	CASYAPA
ATRI	SWAROCHESHA	ATRI
ANGIRAS	UTTAMA	VASISHTA
PULASTYA	TAMASA	VISWAMITRA
PULAHA	RAIVATA	GAUTAMA
CRITU	CHACSHUSHA	JAMADAGNI
VASISHTA †	SATYAVRATA	BHARADWAJA

These two lists on the authority of *Mr.* WILFORD.—*As. Res.* Vol. V. p. 246.

In these lists we find the names of ATRI and VASISHTA both as *Brahmadicas* and *Rishis*, but no other name common to any two lists. The contradictions, however, that are discoverable in the above account are numerous and perplexing.

The *Rishis*, be they who they may, have had the honour of becoming the seven bright stars in the great bear; and they are fabled to be married to the *Pleiades*. There being now but six of the latter, farther fables became necessary to reconcile the difference. I know not whether this circumstance is most in favour of, or against, the antiquity of *Hindu* astronomy; it would not, perhaps, be easy to prove the existence of the fable before the disappearance of the seventh bright star, that formerly shone with the existing six *Pleiades*.

* *As. Res.* Vol. II. p. 119.

† From the *Scanda Purana*; which omits the names of DAKSHA, BRIGHU, and NAREDA, who are included both in the *Ins.* of MENU, and in the *Bhagavata*.

Mr. WILFORD, in the ninth volume of the *As. Res.* gives many circumstances relating to the *Rishis* and *Pleiades.* I shall presently notice one or two, premising that "the names of the seven *Rishis,* shining in the wain," (p. 85.) are (not those in our list of *Rishis* in page 86, but precisely) those contained in the first list of *Brahmadicas,* or *Prajapatis:* exactly corresponding to which list of *Brahmadicas, Mr.* COLEBROKE in the same volume also names the *Rishis.*—(P. 355.) The ninth volume of the *As. Res.* has come into my hands since this article was in a great measure prepared for the press, but does not enable me to remove the difficulties that stood in the way of a clear understanding of the distinction, if there be any, between the *Rishis, Brahmadicas,* &c. or, if there be none, to prove their identity.

Near VASISHTA (who is in lat. 60° N.) is a small star, representing his wife ARUNDHATI. Astrologers watch carefully their motions, because their influences are variously modified; and whatever new-married couple see them in an auspicious conjunction or position, they are surely to live happy together for a hundred years.—Page 85.

Before I notice an article of scandal respecting these brilliant ladies, I will mention that other legends speak favourably of Madam ANISUYA, (otherwise ANISUMYA*) spouse of ATRI, and of AHILYA, wife of GOTAMA; but, from being in bad company, their characters have suffered, and I am apprehensive that the latter cannot, as the sequel will show, be wholly exculpated.

It is related that AGNI, the ardent deity of Fire, was charitably disposed to communicate a portion of his warmth to these ladies; and situated as they were, in the arctic circle, we cannot much wonder at their complacency to such a comfortable suitor. But it is said that, in fact, he had not complete success; for that his wife, (I suppose SWAHA,) dreading the résentment of the holy *Rishis,* successively assumed the shape and countenance of each of their desirable wives, and thus personifying them, satisfied her husband's ardour. ARUNDHATI, however, having always been exemplary as to holiness and sanctity, was not suspected on this unlucky occasion; but the other six *Rishis,* in consequence of scandalous reports, not only dismissed their sparkling spouses, but, like great bears, drove them out of the arctic circle; and they now shine the *Pleiades.* It would appear, as will be noticed under a future article, that they had qualified themselves for wet nurses, and accordingly nursed young CARTICEYA; or were entrusted with his education, and were placed by him in the Zodiac.

* She is sometimes called "ANASUYA, the virtuous wife of AGASTYA."—*Ramayana.* Sect. I. p. 9. AGASTYA is the star *Canopus.*

"The *Pleiades*, according to mythologists in the west, were entrusted likewise with the education of BACCHUS, (who, according to MACROBIUS, was the same with MARS, or KARTICEYA) and on that account he translated them into heaven. According to those writers they suffered a real bodily pollution; and the seventh, says HYGINUS, (*Poet. Astro.* p. 471.) left her sisters, and fled to the regions of the heavens within the arctic circle: and this is the ARUNDHATI of the *Hindus*."—P. 86.

In *Mr.* COLEBROKE's Dissertation on the *Indian* Zodiac, *As. Res.* Vol. IX. the *Rishis* are called, from the *Puranas*, "the *Munis*;" "the virtuous sages, who delight in protecting the people;" "the mighty sages."—P. 358.

There is a cavern near *Gaya*, in *Bengal*, called the grot of the seven *Rishis*; from which an inscription has been copied, and a translation is given of it by *Mr.* WILKINS in the second volume of the *As. Res.* art. 10. But it has no immediate reference to *Ursa Major*, or to the *Rishis* under any designation; perhaps it may have been used for the especial contemplation of that constellation, so very striking and beautiful in those latitudes.

BRAHMA is sometimes said to be SWAYAMBHU, (or the Self Existent,) an appellation that I have been taught to apply to BRAHM, or the Supreme Being. Sometimes BRAHMA is called SWAYAMBHUVA, or son of the Self Existent, the name of the first MENU; who by some accounts is made BRAHMA's son, by others his grandson. The *Menus*, the first of whom is SWAYAMBHUVA, are the offspring of the *Brahmadicas*, who are the production of SWAYAMBHUVA, who was produced by VIRAJ, who proceeded from the male portion of the divided Mighty Power. I cannot reconcile this; for it makes SWAYAMBHUVA his own grandson, progenitor of *seven other* MENUS, and a distinct person from the first MENU, which there is none but this contradictory and confused authority for considering him. By the *Saivas* SWAYAMBHU is identified with SIVA, as will be shown presently. The first and last MENUS are also sometimes confounded with each other, and with other characters, as will appear from the extracts that I shall proceed to make from the papers of *Sir* WILLIAM JONES and *Mr.* WILFORD, and *Mr.* COLEBROKE; on which, as occasion may invite, I shall offer what occurs to me in the form of notes and remarks.

"In the present* day of BRAHMA the first MENU was surnamed SWAYAMBHUVA, or *son of the Self Existent*; and it is he by whom the *Institutes of civil and religious duties* are supposed to have been delivered. In his time the deity,

* This passage will be explained by a subsequent extract.

descended at a *sacrifice*; and by his wife SATARUPA he had two distinguished sons, and three daughters. This pair were created for the multiplication of the human species after that new creation of the world which the *Brahmans* call *Padmacalpiya*, or the *lotos* creation.

Of the five MENUS who succeeded him I have seen little more than the names; but the *Hindu* writings are very diffuse on the life and posterity of the seventh MENU, surnamed VAIVASWATA, or *child of the Sun.* He is supposed to have had ten sons, of whom the eldest was ICSHWACU; and to have been accompanied by seven *Rishis*, or holy persons, whose names were" (as given precedingly): "an account of which explains the opening of the 4th chapter of the *Gita.* 'This immutable system of devotion,' says CRISHNA, 'I revealed to VIVASWAT, or *the Sun*; VIVASWAT declared it to his son MENU; MENU explained it to ICSHWACU: thus the chief *Rishis* know this sublime doctrine, delivered from one to another.'"—*As. Res.* Vol. II. p. 117. JONES on the *Chron.* of the *Hindus.* See also *Ins.* of MENU, ch. i. v. 58. *Gita*, ch. iv.

"From this seventh MENU the whole race of men is believed to have descended; for the seven *Rishis*, who were preserved with him in the ark, are not mentioned as fathers of human families. But since his daughter ILA was married, as the *Indians* tell us, to the first BUDDHA, or MERCURY, the son of CHANDRA, or the Moon, a male deity, whose father was ATRI, son of BRAHMA, (an allegory purely astronomical, or poetical) his posterity are divided into two great branches; called the *Children of the Sun*, from his own supposed father, and the *Children of the Moon*, from the parent of his daughter's husband."—*Ib.* p. 127.

In the page preceding that whence the above passage is quoted, *Sir* WILLIAM JONES states VIVASWATA to be the son of SURYA, the son of CASYAPA, or URANUS, the son of MARICHI, or *Light*, the son of BRAHMA.

VIVASWATA means the son of VIVASWAT, which is one of the names of SURYA, or the Sun; which deity will hereafter come particularly under our notice.

From what precedes, the following lists of succession may be deduced; but I fear the perplexities of this article will be rather concentrated than removed by them, and that little else will be in my power.

1.	2.	3.
VIRAJ. SWAYAMBHUVA. — First MENU. *Brahmadicas.* — Among them, MARICHI and ATRI. *Menus.* — Among them, SWAYMBHUVA and SATYAVRATA. *Rishis.* — Among them, KASYAPA and ATRI.	BRAHMA, father of MARICHI, father of KASYAPA, father of SURYA, father of VIVASWATA, or SATYAVRATA, seventh MENU.	BRAHMA, father of KASYAPA, father of SURYA, father of VIVASWATA, or SATYAVRATA, the seventh MENU.

An inspection of these lists offers the following among other difficulties: SWAYAMBHUVA is declared to be BRAHMA in a human shape, and the first MENU: he appears again his own grandson, as the first of the seven MENUS. SWAYAMBHUVA and ATRI stand in the relationship of father and son, whether the first named be considered as father of the *Brahmadicas,* or as father of the *Rishis*; but the first SWAYAMBHUVA is great grandfather of the last ATRI, as per list the first.

In the same list the seventh MENU, SATYAVRATA, is among the ancestors, and may be called the father of KASYAPA, one of the *Rishis*; and in the other lists KASYAPA is the grandfather of SATYAVRATA, SURYA being his immediate father, although his name doth not appear among the *Brahmadicas,* from whom the seven MENUS are said to have proceeded: on the contrary, he (SURYA) is by the second list the grandson of MARICHI, one of those *Brahmadicas.*

Other incongruities might be pointed out, and are easily discoverable by the inquisitive reader; but these will suffice to show the difficulties attending the attempt at reconciling the contradictions so evident in the mixed history and mythology of the *Hindus.* *Mr.* WILFORD's suggestion, that the *Brahmadicas, Menus,* and *Rishis,* were the same individuals, seems very probable; and we may farther imagine a confusion among the legends referring to the first and seventh MENUS, and to the two persons who bear the surname of the first. Both these MENUS had ten sons; both had a wife named SATARUPA, who will appear presently as the wife also of BRAHMA when under the same name of SWAYAMBHUVA, whose offspring she is also said to be.

In the genealogical section of the *Ramayana* the following passage occurs; but the succession does not agree with either of the lists given in the preceding pages: it agrees best with the second of the last three.

"Indescribable is the origin of BRAHMA—eternal, imperishable, ever the same. From him was produced MARICHI; the son of MARICHI was KASYAPA: from the descendant of MARICHI was produced ANGIRA; his son was PRACHETA:* the son of PRACHETA was MENU; and IKSHWAKU, the first sovereign of AYODHA,† was the son of MENU."—Sect. 57. p. 395.

The reader will begin to be aware of the endless diversity of theogonical legends; or of those referring to the early animated productions of the different *Hindu* deities. One taken generally, though not literally, as I have altered the spelling, &c. from the curious work of ANQUETIL DUPERRON, called by him *Oupnekhat*, may be introduced appropriately in this place, as bearing immediately on the subjects discussed under this head; and, if not illustrating them, exhibiting at least another instance of their wildness, and perhaps inconsistency.

BRAHM said, "Rise up, O RUDRA! and form man to govern the world."

RUDRA immediately obeyed: he began the work; but the men he made were fiercer than tigers, having nothing but the destructive quality in their composition: and they soon destroyed one another; for anger was their only passion. BRAHMA, VISHNU, and RUDRA, then joined their different powers, and created ten men, whose names were NAREDA, DAKSHA, VASISHTA, BHRIGU, CRITU, PULAHA, PULASTYA, ANGIRA, ATRI, and MARICHI; (that is, Reason, Ingenuity, Emulation, Humility, Piety, Pride, Patience, Charity, Deceit, Morality): the general name of whom is the *Munis*. BRAHMA then produced DHERMA, Justice, from his breast; ADHERMA, Injustice, from his back; LABHA, Appetite, or Passion, from his lips; and KAMA, Love, or Desire, from his heart. The last was a beautiful female, and BRAHMA looked upon her with amorous emotions; but the *Munis* telling him she was his own daughter, he shrunk back, and LADJA, Shame, a blushing virgin, sprung from him. BRAHMA, deeming his body defiled by its emotions towards KAMA, purified himself by partially changing it into ten females, who were respectively espoused by the *Munis*.

In the above legend we find the ten "lords of created beings," that MENU describes as produced by himself, ascribed to the joint powers of the three great personified attributes of the Deity. Here they are called *Munis*; in other passages they are considered as *Brahmadicas*, or *Prajapatis*, and as *Rishis*. This may

* Alias DAKSHA, by some authorities. † *Oude*.

serve as a farther specimen of the endless allegories in which the poetical fabulists have veiled the moral, scientific, and theological knowledge of the *Hindus*: all of which, as well as history, and even arts, if not buried in, are obscured by, and intimately connected with their wild and bold mythology. Thus, again, the *Mahabarat* is a continued allegory between man's virtues and his vices: the former personified under the names of the five sons of PANDU; of whom BHIMA, YUDISHTIRA, and ARJUN, said to represent Justice, Fortitude, and Prudence, were by one mother, KOONTI; two, NAKAL and SAHADEVA, personifications of Temperance and Wisdom, by MADERI. Other legends attribute the virtues of Modesty and Tenderness to YUDISHTIRA; Strength to BHIMA; and Skill, or Courage, to ARJUN. To NAKAL Beauty, or Harmony; and to SAHADEVA Wisdom and Penetration. The two last brothers are by some said to be the twin virtues of Temperance and Chastity.

Man's manifold vices are personated by the hundred sons of KURU, the brother of PANDU: hence a near relationship exists between Vice and Virtue.

I will here introduce other texts from the *Ins.* of MENU, with the like view of recording and giving some explanation of names of common occurrence, and that we may hereafter have occasion to refer to.

Ch. XI. v. 222.—"The eleven *Rudras*; the twelve *Adityas*; the eight *Vasus*; the *Maruts*, or genii of the winds; and the seven great *Rishis*, have peformed this lunar penance* as a security from all evil."

The names of the eleven *Rudras* I do not know, nor their occupations, nor the reason of their peculiar number: they are distinctions of SIVA in his character of Fate, or Destiny. SANCARA is one, and the principal of them; and that name also appertains to other characters: SIVA himself is sometimes so called.

The twelve *Adityas* are said to be the offspring of ADITI, who is called the mother of the gods. They are emblems of the sun for each month of the year; and are themselves called suns: their names are VARUNA, SURYA, VEDANGA, BHANU, INDRA, RAVI, GABHASTI, YAMA, SWARNARETA, DIVAKARA, MITRA, and VISHNU.—(*Gita*, p. 144.) Of these VISHNU seems to be considered as the

* The *penance* thus named is called *Chandrayana*, and consists in the sinner, or devotee, "eating for a whole month no more than thrice eighty mouthfuls of wild grains, as he happens to meet with them, keeping his organs in subjection."—*Ib.* v. 221. The reward is attaining the same abode as CHANDRA, the regent of the Moon; and it absolves a *Brahman* from the sin of slaughtering a thousand small animals which have bones, or of boneless animals enow to fill a cast; and it is also the common penance for killing a *Sudra*, a *Hindu* of the fourth or servile class.

first; for Crishna, describing his own pre-eminence, says, "Among the *Adityas* I am Vishnu."—(*Ib.* p. 85.)

A *Vasu* is one of the eight divinities who form a *Gana*, or *assemblage* of gods; and there are nine of those *Ganas*, (*As. Res.* Vol. III. p. 40.): which nine *Ganas*, or companies of deities, are enumerated in the *Amarcosh*. Ganesa is said to derive his name *(Gan·Isa, Lord* of the *Ganas,)* from his supposed situation as the principal or president of those assemblages; although Agni, the god of Fire, is generally deemed the chief of the *Vasus*, eight of whom were among the earliest productions of Brahma.

The *Maruts*, or genii of the winds, have Pavan as their chief deity: of whom we shall take farther notice when speaking of his son Hanuman.* Marichi is also ranked as a chief among the *Maruts*.†

Ins. of Menu, ch. iii. v. 192.—"The *Pitris*, or great progenitors, are free from wrath; intent on purity; ever exempt from sexual passions; endued with exalted qualities: they are primeval deities who have laid arms aside.

"193. Hear now completely from whom they sprung; who they are; by whom, and by what ceremonies, they are to be honoured.

"194. The sons of Marichi, and of all the other‡ *Rishis*, who were the offspring of Menu, son of Brahma, are companies of *Pitris*, or forefathers."

Many tribes of *Pitris* are enumerated in following texts.

"200. Of these just enumerated, who are generally reputed the principal tribes of *Pitris*, the sons and grandsons, indefinitely, are also in this world considered as great progenitors.

"201. From the *Rishis* come the *Pitris*, or patriarchs; from the *Pitris* both *Devas* and *Danavas*; from the *Devas* this whole world of animals and vegetables in due order."

Many other verses in this chapter refer to ceremonials in honour of the *Pitris*: the above will suffice here. The following text, however, introduces them to us in another character.

Ch. i. v. 66.—"A month of mortals is a day and a night of the *Pitris*, or patriarchs, inhabiting the Moon: the half, beginning with the full moon, is their

* They are seen together, with Agni, in plate 80.

† The poets sometimes speak of "the thirty-three gods," comprising the eight *Vasus*, the eleven *Rudras*, the twelve *Adityas*, and Aswini and Kumara. See *Ramayana*, p. 257.

‡ This text seems to speak of Marichi as a *Rishi*: preceding passages have taught us to consider him a *Brahmadica*, and even as a *Marut*.

day for action; and that, beginning from the new moon, is their night for slumber."

The time most peculiarly sacred to the *manes* of the *Pitris* is the dark half of each month; and the day of conjunction is the fittest day.—*As. Res.* Vol. III. p. 258.

Yama, or Pluto, is the sovereign of the *Pitris:* of him we shall speak particularly in another page.

From the *Pitris* both *Devas* and *Danavas* are above said to have sprung.

The title *Deva* is very comprehensive, meaning generally a deity; *Devi* is its feminine, but is applied mostly to Bhavani, consort of Mahadeva, which name of Siva is literally *Great God.* But as the title of *Deva* is given to other gods, superior and inferior, so that of *Devi* is, as hath been before stated, occasionally bestowed similarly on other goddesses. *Devata* is the plural of *Deva*; by some writers spelled *Dewtah.*

Danava is the plural of Danu, the individual whence proceeded this race of evil spirits, or fallen angels. *Asura* means nearly the same, generally, as *Danava,* although there may be different legendary accounts of their origin. *Daitya* and *Raksha* are names of evil beings—spirits in other worlds, or malignantly incarnate in this.

There are also good angels, *Surs.* These words, *Sur* and *Asur*, or *Sura* and *Asura,* are commonly spelled *Soor* and *Asoor*; and the *Hindu* writings abound in allusions to their state of continued warfare. And it seems probable, that such fables are of an astronomical nature, and relate to the rising and setting, and other phenomena, of stars in the two hemispheres.

The terms *Devarshi, Rajarshi, Maharshi,* are nearly synonimous with *Rishi*; meaning saint, deified saint, great saint, or great sage. There are differences, doubtless; for Nareda is reckoned the chief of the *Devarshis,* and he appears among the *Brahmadicas*—not as a *Rishi.* Crishna (in the *Gita*, p. 82.) speaks of his "holy servants, the *Brahmans* and the *Rajarshis*;" and says, "I am Brigu among the *Maharshis*:" "and of all the *Devarshis* I am Narad."—P. 86. Narada, Dacsha, and Bhrigu, are among the *Brahmadicas* of Menu; and are generally and more especially termed sons of Brahma.

By the recent publication of the *Ramayan* I am enabled to make some explanatory additions to this head of my work; but not, I doubt, to clear it of its difficulties or perplexities. What precedes was written before this curious publication reached me, and I have not seen occasion to make any alteration in it.

The term *Mahàrshi* occurring in the sixth section of the *Ramayana*, the learned translators subjoin the following note.—"There are four kinds of sages, or *Rishis*: the *Rajarshi*, or royal sage; the *Maharshi*, or great sage; the *Brahmarshi*, or sacred sage; and the *Devarshi*, or divine sage: of these the first is esteemed the lowest, and the last the highest."—P. 64. 8vo. edition.

According to the translators of the *Ramayana*, *Sura* means any fermented liquor; and *Asura*, rejecting spirituous liquors.—(P. 287.) Describing the well known allegory of churning the ocean, that will be particularly noticed hereafter, "the daughter of VARUNA, VARUNI," (is produced; and said, in a note, to be spirituous liquors) "seeking for acceptance. The sons of DITI did not receive the daughter of VARUNA; upon which the sons of ADITI accepted the inestimable damsel. On this occasion, therefore, are the descendants of DITI called *Asuras*, while the descendants of ADITI are termed *Suras*. By the reception of VARUNI the glad *Suras* were filled with pleasure."—*Ib.*

When, in the course of this churning process, the *Amrita*, the beverage of the gods, the water of immortality, was produced, the *Suras* and *Asuras* contended for its possession; and a tremendous combat ensued between them. "When all were exhausted, VISHNU, the mighty, assuming by illusion the form of a captivating damsel, speedily stole the *Amrita*," and afterwards crushed the *Asuras*, or sons of DITI; who are said, however, (*Ramayana*, p. 289.) to have "been slain by the heroic sons of ADITI." "In this most dreadful conflict between the *Dityas* and the celestials, the former being subdued, PURANDARA received the kingdom." PURANDARA is a name of INDRA.

Let us, however, dwell a while longer on the offspring of this all-prolific mother DITI, who, with her productive spouse, KASYAPA, seems, in *Hindu* theogonies, to be ever at hand to answer in all cases of perplexing parentage.

The 37th section of the *Ramayana* details how this distressed goddess, thus bereft of her children, implored her husband KASYAPA (the son of MARICHI) to bestow on her "an INDRA-destroying son," to retaliate her injuries on that deity, and the rest of KASYAPA's sons, who had destroyed her's. Her request was complied with, on the condition that she should remain pure in the performance of sacred austerities for a thousand years. The time was nearly expired, when the crafty INDRA, who had all along insidiously, with affected filial respect, ministered to her conveniences, contrived to lead her into impurity, in as far that she slept indecorously "with her head in place of her feet; and became impure through the locks of her head touching her feet."—(*Ramayana*, p. 293.) INDRA thereby having power over her, treated her in a very indelicate and barbarous manner, dividing with his tremendous weapon, *Vajra*, the fœtus, with which she was quick, into *forty-nine* pieces; which, at the request of the afflicted DITI, were transformed by INDRA into the *Maruts*, or winds. And this is the legendary account of their origin and number; and it is not uncommon to hear the winds so spoken of: "The *forty-nine* regents of the winds."—*Ramayana*, p. 121. But we shall have occasion to notice these allegorical beings when we arrive at the consideration of their principals, PAVANA, or VAYU, HANUMAN, &c. INDRA and DITI, to conclude their tale in this place, mutually forgave each other: she had endeavoured to beguile and destroy him, by the process and produce of her impregnation; and he had, by craft and cruelty, counteracted her. INDRA must be reintroduced at some length hereafter: it may suffice here to say, that he is the reputed son of KASYAPA, but not by DITI. He is, indeed, said (in the *Ramayana*, p. 144.) to be the son of ADITI, who, though, like DITI, she is, in poetical theogonies, the ever-ready mother of the gods, is herself stated to be the daughter of DAKSHA.

Many other benevolent and malevolent races of spiritual beings are enumerated, and occur, generically and specifically, in the *Ramayana*, and other *Hindu* authorities. The *Sidhas*, of whom there were eight only: the *Gandbarbas*, *Kinniras*, *Dundhubis*, &c. who are numerous, and appear to be choristers, dancers, flower-showerers (*Pushpa-vrishta*), and other pleasant companions: and the *Rakshas*, *Yakshas*, (*Rakshni*, and *Yakshni*, in the feminine; and *Rakshasa*, and *Yakshasa*, in the plural,) are generally engaged in malignant combinations: not, however, always; for as the great gods themselves, as well as the subordinate deities, are occasionally employed in divers and contradictory occupations, so these good and evil genii appear to change characters. For instance: sometimes *Yakshas* are benevolent, or at least classed with good beings, (*Ramayana*, p. 122.): sometimes malignant, (*ib.* p. 185.): *Danavas* are also (p. 122,) good, and (p. 166.) at other times, "evil genii; at enmity with the gods." Their goodness is, however, very equivocal.

Another race of angelic creatures, although most ungallantly neglected in mythologic fable, we must not pass by unnoticed. These are the interesting, the beautiful, *Apsaras*: they are proverbially elegant and graceful; but, alas! not so for virtue or morals. DASARAT'HA, the heroic monarch of *Ayodha (Oude)*, the happy father of the renowned RAMACHANDRA, to whom many of our future pages must be devoted, had three queens, who "in elegance of form rivalled the *Apsaras*."—(*Ramayana*, p. 142.)

These fair maids were produced when the ocean was churned in the time of the *Kurmávatara*; in number no less than six hundred millions! of resplendent and celestial form; adorned with glorious ornaments, and endowed with beauty, youth, sweetness, and every grace." Their female attendants were innumerable; but "not having undergone the legal purification, none of the gods, or *Danavas*, received these damsels in marriage: hence they all remained without a lord."—*Ramayana*, p. 287.

Thus we find the *Hindu* invisible world well peopled; but there are several other tribes of mythological beings introduced into the complicated machinery of *Hindu* poetics. There is a race of pigmies, no bigger than a man's thumb, called *Balakilya*, of whom sixty thousand were produced from the hairs of BRAHMA's body; and another race of Lilliputian sages, produced from his nails. —See *Ramayana*, p. 316.

All of these beings are by name, birth, parentage, and education; life, death, and burial, &c. &c. &c. especially chronicled in the *Puranas*, and other sacred and prophane books; and one's brain is almost bewildered in endeavouring, as they ever and anon recur, to trace their genealogy, character, connexions, and a long train of *etceteras*, combined with their allegorical origin, progress, and termination.

The colossal figure, before adverted to, in the *Elephanta* cave, that I fancy to bear reference to the division and reunion of VIRAJ, I will notice in the words that I find used in a little description of that celebrated excavation, written mostly in the cave, and afterwards corrected on the spot by a farther inspection of its mythological wonders.

"Fronting the centre of the entrance is the well known bust of the grand triad of powers; respecting which I shall here notice only, that the vindictive ferocity of SIVA's countenance is finely contrasted with the mild serenity of VISHNU's. On the right of the bust, (the spectator's left when looking at it,) having a colossal figure leaning on a dwarf between, forming the front of a pilaster, is a grand compartment, containing, among a variety of groups and single figures, a gigantic four-handed form of MAHADEVA, conjoined with PARVATI. One of his right hands rests on the head of a bull, well executed; another holds a shield; a third a *cobra de capela*, the hooded serpent. On the right is BRAHMA on the lotos, with swans, in the usual style;* and on the other side, corresponding, is VISHNU mounted on GARUDA, also in his usual style, which, it must be confessed, is here somewhat ridiculous; for VISHNU is gene-

* This refers to compartments described in earlier paragraphs of the account.

rally seated on and bestriding GARUDA's shoulders* with his legs in front, GARUDA holding VISHNU on by the ankles. GARUDA throughout the cave wears just such a wig as *Sir* JOSHUA REYNOLDS has given in his portrait of *Doctor* JOHNSON: he has always a snake round his neck, the head and tail joined in front.

"Near BRAHMA is INDRA on IRAVATI, the elephant, sitting in a good posture. In the lower corner, nearest the grand bust, is a standing female, bearing a small box on the palm of her hand, her fingers pointing horizontally behind her: the arm is broken off. Above her a wigged boy, holding a *chawrie*: above him a wigged woman: above and near her several other figures with peruques.

"On each side of the great figure of MAHADEVA is a handsome pair, male and female; seen also in almost every compartment; sometimes, as in this instance, on the side next the bust, holding garlands of flowers: on the other side the male wears a dirk.†

"The grand figure of MAHADEVA in this compartment is fourteen feet high, an inch or two more or less. In this character he is called ARDHA NARI, or *half woman*: the one left breast is very prominent and conspicuous, and has given rise to various surmises of its having reference to the story of the *Amazons*. This compartment is well filled with groups and single figures; many with wigs. The fine figure of the emaciated *Brahman* is again seen with admiration."

The pictures of MAHADEVA and PARVATI conjoined, that in a former page I have supposed to bear reference, as well as the sculptured figure in the *Elephanta* cave, to the male and female moities of VIRAJ, are engraved in PLATES 7. and *figures* 1. 2. of 24: the former from a well executed picture in *Colonel* STUART's collection; the latter from two pictures, pretty well done, but inferior, in mine. Being coloured, the blue skin of MAHADEVA, and the yellow skin of PARVATI; the difference of their dresses, hair, collar of skulls and flowers, ornaments, attributes, &c. is very strikingly contrasted; and cannot of course be represented in an outline engraving. The only point they have in

* In the mode of which PLATE 18. exhibits an example.

† The beautiful and graceful couple here noticed occur frequently in this cave, and also in that of *Amboly*, on *Salsette*. They are seen likewise in good preservation, and in superior beauty, at the entrance, on each side of the door, of a smaller cave, on the island of *Elephanta*: this latter cave has never been described, nor, perhaps, five years ago, was ever seen by ten *Europeans*. It is nearly choked up with rubbish; but will, I trust, through the efforts of the *Bombay Literary Society*, be restored, with the many other mythological treasures within their reach, to the light of day, and the admiration of the world.

common is, in PLATE 24. the sectarial hieroglyphic on the forehead; but in PLATE 7. each moiety has its own peculiar mark: his, half the crescent, and half the eye; her's, half that mystical symbol the *Yoni*, adopted by her exclusive worshippers, the *Sactas*, or *Yonijas*: on which some extracts and remarks will be made in a future article.

In the following particulars the three pictures agree.—Being four-handed: having the *Trisula*, and *Damaru*, or *Dindima* ("a drum to be sounded by the destroying angel."—*Hitopadesa*, p. 312.): the river *Ganga* flowing from SIVA's portion of the head, (but not the goddess personally in his hair, nor the *Nag* over her, as in PLATE 7. where the river flows over PARVATI's shoulder; in PLATE 24. over SIVA's): the *Nandi* of each deity; the bull properly so called, and the tiger, called *Vyaghra*, (but differing in position, the bull being in PLATE 7. on PARVATI's side, and the tiger on SIVA's; and the reverse in PLATE 24.): the *mund-mala*, collar of heads, and *pushpa mala*, collar of flowers, joined in the middle: the glory encircling their heads: in these points, and in others less important, the three pictures agree. A *dindima* in a right and left hand, with the others joined in a posture of adoration; and the figure sitting on a lotos, and having no snakes round the arms and neck; with some other points, are peculiar to PLATE 7. where the *Ganga* is seen issuing through a cleft in the rock on which the figure is seated.

The two pictures engraved in PLATE 24. I purchased at *Poona*: they are exactly of the same description in size, style, &c. and were most likely painted by the same artist, and meant to be the counterpart of each other. Excepting the distinctions that necessarily arise from difference of positions, I perceive only that the standing figure wears the tiger's skin over the thigh, and the other sits on it: the shape of the sword differs also; and the sitting figure has a snake round the wrist of the inferior right arm, which the other has not. In both the *Ganga* issues from SIVA's dusky braided hair: his ear has a brown wooden ring, such as *Saniyasis*, and other enthusiastic individuals, are now seen with: a snake protrudes its head over his shoulder; others form his arm and wrist-bands: his hands hold a silver *trisula* and a deep red *damaru*: the *mund-mala*, collar of heads, terminates at half its length, where commences PARVATI's *pushpa mala*, or collar of red flowers: in like manner the other necklaces differ in description and colour; her side being chiefly of pearl, his of black beads: her hair is black; and she holds the *pasha*, or cord, to bind victims, and the *kardgha*, or sword, to destroy or sacrifice them: the sacrificial knife, used at sanguinary offerings, is also called by that name. The glories encircling the heads are of bright green; and the back-ground of the picture is formed of the dark green *Malura*, or *Bilva*, a shrub sacred to SIVA, as is noticed in page 55.

The mark on the forehead, being common to both deities, is continued to both their foreheads. The eye that the crescent encircles is that of SIVA; but some say that it is the symbol also of the sacred *Yoni*, PARVATI's especial hieroglyphic: three yellow lines spring on each side from the demi crescent.

On the pictures are written, in *Sanskrit* and *Mahraty*—SEW PARVATI.

Deeming the subject of these plates curious and important, I have described them with, I fear, tiresome prolixity, which the reader will, I hope, excuse.

SWAYAMBHUVA.

In addition to what occurs in the preceding article respecting this important personage, I shall here introduce some farther particulars of him, and other mythological characters.

"Swayambhuva, or the son of the self-existing, was the first Menu, and the father of mankind: his consort's name was Satarupa. In the second *Veda* the Supreme Being is introduced thus speaking: 'From me Brahma was born: he is above all; he is *pitama*, or the father of all men: he is Aja and Swayambhu, or self-existing.' From him proceeded Swayambhuva, who is the first Menu: they call him Adima (or the first, or Protogonus): he is the first of men; and Parama-purusha, or the first male. His help-mate, Pracriti, is called also Satarupa:* she is Adima,† or the first: she is Visva-jenni, or the mother of the world: she is Iva, or like *I*, the female energy of nature; or she is a form of, or descended from, *I*: she is Para, or the greatest: both are like Mahadeva, and his *Sacti* (the female energy of nature), whose names are also Isa and Isi.

"Swayambhuva is Brahma in a human shape, or the first Brahma; for Brahma is man individually, and also, collectively, mankind: hence Brahma is said to be born and to die every day. Collectively, he dies every hundred years; this being the utmost limits of a life in the *Cali-yug*, according to the *Puranas*: at the end of the world Brahma, or mankind, is said to die also at the end of a hundred divine years. Swayambhuva in the present *Calpa* is Vishnu, in the character of Brahma *rupi* Janardana, or the Vishnu with the countenance of Brahma. To understand this it is necessary to premise, that it has

* Satarupa is here the wife of Brahma, (or the first Menu, or Swayambhuva,) and is declared to be the same with Pracriti, or *Nature*; a title generally given, not to Saraswati, the consort or *Sacti* of Brahma, but to Devi, *Sacti* of Mahadeva.

† "Adimi is the feminine gender; from *Adima* or *Adimas*."

been revealed to the *Hindus*, that, from the beginning to the end of things, when the whole creation will be annihilated and absorbed into the Supreme Being, there will be five great *Calpas*, or periods. We are now in the middle of the fourth *Calpa*, fifty years of BRAHMA being elapsed; and of the remainder the first *Calpa* is begun. These five great *Calpas* include 500 years of BRAHMA; at the end of which, nothing will remain but the self-existing. Every *Calpa*, except the first, is preceded by a renovation of the world, and a general flood.

"These five *Calpas* have five deities, who rule by turns; and from whom the five *Calpas* are denominated. These five deities are DEVI, SURYA, or the Sun, GÁNESA, VISHNU, and ISWARA. BRAHMA has no particular *Calpa*: he is intimate to every one of them. Every deity in his own period is CALSVA-RUPI, or CHRONUS: we are now under the reign of the fourth CHRONUS: the western mythologists mention several ruling deities of that name. CALSVA-RUPI signifies he who has the countenance of CALA, CHRONUS, or TIME: this is now the *Calpa* of VISHNU; who, to create, thought on BRAHMA, and became BRAHMA-RUPI-JANARDANA. He preserves and fosters the whole creation in his own character, and will ultimately destroy it through ISWARA, or RUDRA: the *Calpa* of VISHNU is called also the *Padma*, or *Lotos-period*. It is declared in the *Puranas*, that all animals and plants are the *Ling*, or *Phallus* of the CALSVA-RUPI deity; and that, at the end of his own *Calpa*, he is deprived of his *Ling* by his successor, who attracts the whole creation to himself, to swallow it up, or devour it, according to the western mythologists; and at the end of his *Calpa* he disgorges the whole creation. Such is the origin of CHRONUS devouring his own offspring; of JUPITER disgorging it through a potion administered to him by METIS; and of CHRONUS castrating his own father. According to this, SWAYAMBHUVA is, conjointly and individually, BRAHMA, VISHNU, and ISA, or MAHADEVA. To SWAYAMBHUVA were born three daughters, ACUTI, DEVASRUTI, and VISRUTRI, or PRASRUTI. BRAHMA created three great *Rajapatis* to be their husbands: CARDAMA, DACSHA, (the same who was also a *Brahmadica*,) and RUCHI. CARDAMA is acknowledged to be a form of SIVA, or SIVA himself; and DACSHA to be BRAHMA: hence he is often called DACSHA-BRAHMA; and we may reasonably conclude, that the benevolent RUCHI was equally a form of VISHNU. It is said in the *Puranas*, as I am assured by learned *Pandits*, that these three gods sprang in a mortal shape from the body of ADIMA; that DACSHA-BRAHMA issued mystically from his navel; VISHNU from his left, and SIVA from his right, side. It is declared in the *Puranas*, that ISWARA cut off one of the heads of BRAHMA; who, being immortal, was only maimed."—From WILFORD's learned Essay on the Chronology of the *Hindus*. *As. Res.* Vol. V. Art. 18.

Anecdotes of DACSHA will be found under that head: one, similar to those there given, relative to his losing his head from the violence of MAHADEVA, follows, in the Essay, the extract just concluded.

The figure of VISHNU, as it is generally denominated, reposing on SESH-NAGA,* with BRAHMA issuing in a lotos from his navel, is the popular mode, I imagine, by which the *Vaishnavas* represent the Supreme Being contemplating, or willing the renovation of the world, at the conclusion of one *Calpa*; or between such conclusion, and the commencement of another: in which interregnum "nothing will remain but the self-existing."

Another mode of exhibiting this subject is a picture of VISHNU, otherwise called, as before noticed in this character, NARAYANA, with his toe in his mouth, reposing on a floating lotos leaf: this seems puerile; and, indeed, what *popular exhibition* of such subjects doth not? and may, perhaps mean to represent a circle. The toe in the mouth, like the tail of a snake in its mouth, in mythological language, is interpreted *Endless*: applied to time, *Eternity*: to a being, *Eternal.*—See PLATE 20. which, by the way, I will here notice, is somewhat altered in regard to position, but not at all in any other respect, by the artist who made the drawing from the original picture for the engraver: the original being *nude*, he has given the figure a less indelicate posture. SONNERAT gives a plate of this subject; and alludes to it in these terms, in which the reader will see the outline, received with tolerable accuracy from verbal communications, of the legend more fully and classically detailed in *Mr.* WILFORD's valuable chronological essay, above extracted from.

"On the death of BROUMA all the worlds will suffer a deluge; all the *Andons* be broken; and the *Cailasson*, and the *Vaicondon*," (*Kailasa*, and *Vaikont'ha,*) "will only remain. At that time VICHENOU, taking a leaf of the tree called *Allemaron*,† will place himself on the leaf, under the figure of a very little child, and thus float on the sea of milk, sucking the toe of his right foot. He will remain in this posture till BROUMA, anew, comes forth from his navel in a tama-

* See PLATE 7.

† "The *Ficus admirabilis* of LINNÆUS: the great fig-tree of the *Pagodas*: the *Banian* tree." I imagine, however, the leaf on which the deity reclines is intended for the lotos, as well as that which springs from his navel, called by SONNERAT a tamarind. Some affirm that the floating cradle is a leaf of *betel*.

rind flower. It is thus that the ages and worlds succeed each other, and are perpetually renewed."—Vol. I. p. 226.

The following legend explains the origin of SATARUPA, as well as of BRAHMA's four faces.

"According to the *Matsya Purana* BRAHMA, in the north-west part of *India*, about *Cashmir*, assumed a mortal shape; and one half of his body springing out, without his suffering any diminution whatever, he framed out of it SATARUPA. She was so beautiful that he fell in love with her; but having sprang from his body, he considered her as his daughter, and was ashamed. During this conflict between shame and love he remained motionless, with his eyes fixed upon her: SATARUPA, perceiving his situation, and to avoid his looks, stepped aside: BRAHMA, unable to move, but still desirous to see her, caused a face to spring out in the direction to which she moved: she shifted her place four times; and as many faces, corresponding with the four corners of the world, grew out of his head. Having recovered his intellects, the other half of his body sprang from him, and became SWAYAMBHUVA."—WILFORD: on Mount *Caucasus*. *As. Res.* Vol. VI. p. 472.

SWAYAMBHUVA is the *son* of the Self Existent, the latter epithet being generally and appropriately applied to the One Supreme Being; but, as we have had, and shall have, such frequent occasion to notice, sectaries will exalt the deity of their own exclusive adoration into the almighty seat, and of course magnify him in mistaken terms.

From an inscription on a stone, found in the district of *Adoni*, and communicated to the *Asiatic Society* by *Major* MACKENZIE, (*As. Res.* Vol. IX. p. 425.) I shall quote several stanzas; containing other mythological matter, and giving the epithet SWAYAMBHU to SIVA. SAMBHU is a name by which he is frequently addressed; and it looks like an abbreviation of the other.

"ADORATION *be to the Auspicious* SWAYAMBHU NAT'HA, *or* SELF EXISTENT PROTECTOR.

"1. I prostrate myself before SAMBHU, whose glorious head is adorned with the resplendent moon; and who is the chief prop of the foundation of the three worlds.

"2. May SWAYAMBHU be propitious; he who won immortal renown; who grants the wishes of those that earnestly entreat him; who pervades the universe; the Sovereign Lord of deities; who destroyed the state and arrogance of the demons; who enjoyed the delightful embraces of PARVATI; to whom the learned prostrate themselves: the God above all gods.

"3. I prostrate myself before SAMBHU, whose unquenchable blaze consumed the magnificent TRIPURA; whose food is the nectar dripping from the beams of the moon; who rejoiced in the sacrifice of heads by the lord of *Racshasas*;* whose face is adorned with smiles when he enjoys the embraces of GAURI.

"5. By the consort of DEVI, whose divinity is adored; the spouse of PARVATI, resplendent, with the glorious light of gems reflected from the crowns of the lords of gods and demons, whose heads lay prostrate at his feet; with a face ever lighted up with smiles; he is the Self Existent Deity. May the wealth and stations of his saints be ever granted to us.

"6. The beams of whose light, like the frequent waving of the lotos flower, flashes, reflected, from the numerous crowns of glorious kings, of the chief of gods, of the king of kings, and of the lord of demons; who exists in all things; in all elements—in water, air, earth, ether, and fire; in the sun and moon; the renowned deity manifested in eight forms: SAMBHU. May he grant our ardent prayers.

"7. Cheerfully I bow to SAMBHU in the lotos of the heart; to him who increases and gives delight to all; who holds supreme command over all; who through his three divine attributes created and animated fourteen worlds; who ever resides in the minds of his saints."—*As. Res.* Vol. IX. p. 426.

The date of this inscription corresponds with 1173, A. D.

"The god SWAYAMBHU DEVI" occurs in the same volume, p. 430.

* RAVANA.

DAKSHA.

THE name of DAKSHA occurs several times in the course of my work; and, as a good deal of mythological legend is attached to it, I shall collect in this place what I have extracted from the *Asiatic Researches* relative to that character.

" ISWARA attempted to kill his brother BRAHMA, who, being immortal, was only maimed; but ISWARA finding him afterwards in a mortal shape, in the character of DAKSHA, killed him as he was performing a sacrifice." *Mr.* WILFORD discovers in this the story of the death of Abel; and offers very learned and ingenious reasons for his belief: the following is a continuation of the legend from *Hindu* sacred books.—

There had subsisted for a long time some animosity between BRAHMA and MAHADEVA in their mortal shapes; and the latter, on account of his bad conduct, which is fully described in the *Puranas*, had, it appears, given much uneasiness to SWAYAMBHUVA and SATARUPA: for he was libidinous, going about with a large club in his hand. MAHADEVA was the eldest, and was indignant at seeing his claim as such disregarded in favour of BRAHMA, which the latter supported by such lies as provoked MAHADEVA to such a point, that he cut off one of his heads in his divine form. In his human shape, we find DAKSHA boasting that he ruled over mankind. One day, in the assembly of the gods, DAKSHA coming in, they all respectfully arose except MAHADEVA, who kept his seat, and looked gloomy, which DAKSHA resented; and reviled and cursed MAHADEVA in his human shape, wishing he might ever remain a vagabond on the face of the earth; and ordered that he should be avoided, and deprived of his share of the sacrifices and offerings. MAHADEVA, irritated, in his turn, cursed DAKSHA; and a dreadful conflict took place between them: the three worlds trembled, and the gods were alarmed. BRAHMA, VISHNU, and the whole assembly, interfered, and separated the combatants; and, at length, even effected a reconciliation. In consequence of which, DAKSHA gave one of his daughters, named SATI,* in marriage to MAHADEVA: SATI was an incarnation of DEVI; for SRIDEVI, the wife of DAKSHA, and daughter of ADIMA and IVA, entreated the goddess to give her one daughter exactly like herself. Her request was granted; and DEVI was incarnated in her womb, and was born as SATI. SRIDEVI had besides a hundred daughters, but no son, which she and DAKSHA deeply lamented; and agreed to make a solemn sacrifice to obtain one. On this occasion DAKSHA convened gods and men, omitting, however, MAHADEVA, who took but little notice of the neglect; for he is represented in all his *Avataras* as indifferent to praise or abuse. But his wife SATI insisted on going, and could not be dissuaded; and was treated so contemptuously by her father, DAKSHA, that she flung herself into the fire, and thereby spoiled the sacrifice. MAHADEVA hearing this, blamed her for her rash conduct, in thus spoiling a religious sacrifice, and cursed her; and she consequently was doomed to a transmigration of a thousand years, into an inferior being. Thus she became a *Pica*, (a sort of bird of the *Cuckoo* tribe); and MAHADEVA, to please her, assumed the form of a *Picas*, under the title of PICESWARA, or PICESA-MAHADEVA.

MAHADEVA afterwards went up to BRAHMA, in the character of DAKSHA, and after much abuse began to beat him: the confusion became general in the assembly, who all took the part of DAKSHA; but SIVA, striking the ground with the locks of his *Jatta*, produced two heroes, and an army of demons came to his assistance: the battle raged, and in the general conflict MAHADEVA cut off DAKSHA's † head: several of the gods were wounded, particularly the Sun and Moon: heaven, hell, and the earth, trembled.

The gods at last humbled themselves before MAHADEVA, who was appeased, and order was restored. At their request he promised to restore DAKSHA to life; but the head could not be found: during the fray it fell into the fire, and was burnt. A he goat was then brought, and his head was struck off and placed on the lifeless body of DAKSHA, who instantly revived; but he remained weak and powerless, till he was again born a son of NOAH.

MAHADEVA taking up the body of his beloved SATI, carried it seven times round the word, bewailing his misfortune. "Here I shall remark," continues *Mr.* WILFORD, "that when any accident happens to any of the gods, they

* In the octavo edition of the *Asiatic Researches* this name is often misspelled SITA: the error is important, and may cause confusion and trouble.

† The story of DAKSHA losing his head in a similar way is again related by *Mr.* WILFORD in the *Asiatic Researches*, Vol. V. p. 249.

generally set off at full speed, going seven times round the world, howling all the way most woefully."

"The gods whom SATI contained in her womb burst out; her limbs were scattered all over the world; and the places where they fell are become sacred. Her breasts fell near *Jalander* in the *Panjab*; the *Yoni* into *Asam*; and the *Guhya** into *Nepal*; where they are most devoutly worshipped to this day: the latter is a small cleft in a rock, with an intermitting spring; it is called *Gubya-st'han*." —WILFORD: on Mount *Caucasus*. *As. Res.* Vol. VI. p. 477.

To the foregoing may be added some farther particulars, though somewhat differing, relating to DAKSHA, and to the subject of some of my plates, of which my information was very scanty, from *Mr.* PATERSON'S Essay on the Origin of the *Hindu* Religion.

He thinks the fable refers to an unsuccessful attempt to abolish the worship of the male and female symbols; and invented by the *Saivas* to show the imbecility of their opponents, and to exalt their own doctrines: the gods themselves being introduced as actors instead of their votaries.

DAKSHA, celebrating a *yajnya,* invited all the *Devatas* except his son-in-law, SIVA. His consort, the goddess, hurt at this exclusion, went to the assembly, and after vain remonstrances, expired with vexation on the spot. SIVA, on hearing this, throws his *Jeta*, or plaited hair, upon the ground, and from that produced BIR BHADR, a furious being armed with a trident, who attacks and disperses the whole assembly; puts a stop to the sacrifice; and cuts off the head of DAKSHA † SIVA took up the body of his deceased consort, and placing it upon his head, in a fit of madness danced up ‡ and down the earth, threatening all things with destruction. VISHNU, at the request of the other *Devatas*, with his *chakra* cut the body into fifty-one pieces, which SIVA, in his frantic dancing, scattered in different parts of the earth. Each place where a part fell became a place of worship of the female power; and the frenzy of SIVA subsiding, he ordained that the *Linga* should likewise be worshipped at each of these places. And DAKSHA, on condition of embracing the doctrine of SIVA, was restored to life, degraded with the head of a goat instead of his own.—*As. Res.* Vol. VIII. p. 80.

* *Podex.* The servants of CUVERA, the deformed deity of riches, are called *Guhyacas*; and into such beings the dark souls of men, addicted in this world to selfish gratifications, transmigrate.

† The decapitation of BRAHMA, of whom DAKSHA is an earthly form, or *Avatara,* is touched on under NARAYANA.

‡ SIVA is frequently seen in a dancing attitude.—See PLATES 14. and 32.

It appears to me that PLATE 25. and the same subject in PLATE 26. *fig.* 1. refer to the story of DAKSHA, whose name, however, doth not occur in my very insufficient memoranda on the last named subject. All I find, indeed, is, exclusive of a description of the image, the following memoranda, taken, I recollect, from the information of a *Poona Brahman.*—" VIRA BHADRA, son of MAHADEVA; not by PARVATI: has temples in the *Carnatic*; not about *Poona*: a warlike character: his history is detailed in the *Cassi-kand*, and in the *Siv-purana*." This appears to have been merely hints for intended future inquiries, that I had no opportunity of making.

It would appear, *Mr.* BENTLY says, that DAKSHA was cotemporary with BHRIGU; that he was an astronomer, and formed the twenty-seven lunar mansions, and other constellations, of which he is allegorically called the father.—*Mr.* BENTLY (*As. Res.* Vol. VIII. p. 230.) gives a *Sanskrit* verse from the *Calica Purana*, which he translates thus: " In the early part of the *Treta yug* the daughters of DAKSHA were born: of these daughters he gave twenty-seven to the Moon."

" DAKSHA, in some respects, bears a strong resemblance to ATLAS; who, according to heathen mythology, was the father of the *Pleiades* and *Hyades*, the CRITICA and ROHINI of DAKSHA."—*Ib.* p. 231.

I do not find the names of all DAKSHA's daughters, nor are they so important as to demand much research: the names of some occur incidentally. Two others I will notice as the mothers of extraordinary progeny: these are JAYA, and VIJAYA, " of slender waist," who brought forth a hundred weapons, " missive and manual," wherewith to arm RAMA for his war of *Lanka*. *

In the *Ins.* of MENU, ch. i. v. 35. DAKSHA and BRIGHU are named among the *Brahmadicas*; or the ten lords of created beings, produced by the first MENU: DAKSHA is there otherways called PRACHETAS. Those ten beings, " eminent in holiness," are said, in the next verse, to have produced " deities, and mansions of deities." The lunar mansions are also attributed to " KASYAPA, the first production of BRAHMA's head."

" In MENU's *Institutes* the twenty-seven lunar asterisms are called the daughters of DAKSHA, and the consorts of SOMA, or the Moon."—*Sir* WILLIAM JONES. *As. Res.* Vol. II. p. 305.

Having introduced, perhaps rather heterogeneously, a number of deities, more or less connected with each other, I shall, before I proceed to the consi-

* *Ramayana.*

deration of the characters of the consorts, or *Sacti*, of the three great powers, devote another page or two to the notice of some other mythological personages; who if, peradventure, not particularly in place here, may not hereafter offer themselves more appropriately.

Of Bhrigu and Nareda, who seem to be considered more immediately as the brethren of Daksha than the rest of the *Brahmadicas*, or sons of Brahma, of whom some notice has been taken in a former page, we may perhaps have occasion to make casual mention in a future article. They are, indeed, mythological personages of no small importance; and apprehended want of room prevents me, in this place, from a farther relation of their character and actions.

PRIT'HU AND PRIT'HIVI, AND VISWACARMA.

PRIT'HIVI is the goddess of the Earth. VISWACARMA, the artificer of the universe, that is the lord of creation assuming that character, moulded the earth, and it became *prithivi*—conspicuous; and therefore is that name, PRITHIVI, assigned to the earth.—*As. Res.* Vol. VIII. p. 452.

PRIT'HU is her husband: he was an incarnation of VISHNU; as related in the following fable, from WILFORD'S Chronology of the *Hindus*.—*As. Res.* Vol. V. p. 253.

VENA, being an impious and tyrannical prince, was cursed by the *Brahmans*; and in consequence died without issue. To remedy this, his left arm was opened, and churned with a stick till it produced a son; who, proving as wicked as his father, was set aside; and the right arm was in like manner churned, which also produced a boy, who proved to be a form of VISHNU under the name of PRIT'HU.

Gods and men came to make obeisance to him, and to celebrate his appearance on earth. He married a form of the goddess LAKSHMI, who was thence named PRIT'HIVI, or PRIT'HWI, and was in fact the earth; and at this time refused so obstinately to give her wonted supplies to mankind, that PRIT'HU was forced to beat and wound her; when she (the earth), assuming the form of a cow, ascended to *Meru* to complain to the gods; who, on learning that she refused the common necessaries of life, not only to mankind in general, but to PRIT'HU, her husband, rejected her complaint. PRIT'HU and his descendants were allowed to beat and wound her in cases of noncompliance, and the earth reluctantly submitted; and since that time mankind are continually wounding her with ploughs and other implements of husbandry.

PRIT'HU was fond of agriculture, became a husbandman, cut down forests, levelled the earth, &c.; which is to be understood by his quarrel with the earth.

In the form of a cow PRIT'HIVI was milked by SWAYAMBHUVA, or ADAM, grand ancestor of PRIT'HU, who so employed him: perhaps the old sire took delight in attending the dairies and fields of his beloved PRIT'HU.—*Ib.* p. 256.

Mr. WILFORD thinks this PRIT'HU to be the same with SATYAVRATA, or NOAH. His heavenly father was the Sun; and SATYAVRATA is also declared to be an incarnation of VISHNU. Here it must be observed, that at night, and in the west, the Sun is VISHNU: he is BRAHMA in the east, and in the morning: from noon to evening he is SIVA.—*Ib.* p. 254.

In another place, (*As. Res.* Vol. VIII. p. 299.) *Mr.* WILFORD finds ILA, a name of the daughter of King BHARATA, the fifth from SWAYAMBHUVA, or ADAM.—" Her name was ILA, or the earth: this was also the name of the daughter of SATYAVRATA, or PRIT'HU; for though the earth was his wife, she also became his daughter."—And in page 318, we find " ILA to signify the earth: ILA, or ILAS, was the son of MENU, or NOAH; called also MITRA VARUNA in the *Puranas*, or the friendly VARUNA, or NEPTUNE." *Sir* W. JONES also mentions ILA as the daughter of the seventh MENU, or SATYAVRATA: he married her to the first BUDDHA, or MERCURY, who was the son of CHANDRA, the Moon; whose father was ATRI, son of BRAHMA.—*As. Res.* Vol. II. p. 127.

Unless ILA be a name appertaining to more persons than one, it is here applied to the wife, daughter, and son, of PRIT'HU, or NOAH; or the seventh MENU, surnamed SATYAVRATA and VAIVASWATA.—(See of MENU, under VIRAJ.)

In the third volume of the *Asiatic Researches*, p. 374. *Mr.* WILFORD gives this passage.- - " DEVI, or *the goddess,* and ISI, or the *sovereign queen*, is the ISIS of *Egypt*; and represents *Nature* in general—but in particular the earth: which the *Indians* call PRIT'HIVI; while water, and humidity of all kinds, is supposed to proceed from VISHNU, as they were by the *Egyptians* to proceed from OSIRIS."

In the *Institutes* of MENU a king is described as a being formed of the qualities of various deities: among them PRIT'HIVI.—

" As PRIT'HIVI supports all creatures equally, thus a king, sustaining all subjects, resembles in his office the goddess of earth."—Ch. IX. v. 311.

PRIT'HIVI is one of the deities to whom daily sacrifices, *Sradha*, are offered by *Brahmans*, to the manes of deceased ancestors. They are enumerated in the *Ins.* of MENU, Ch. III. v. 85, 86. The latter runs thus.—

"To CUHU, goddess of the day, when the new moon is discernible; to ANUMATI, goddess of the day, after the opposition; to PRAJAPATI, or the lord of creatures; to DYAVA and PRIT'HIVI, goddesses of sky and earth; and, lastly, to the fire of the good sacrifice."

We find the habitable earth also called VASTA; and a ceremony, called *Vasta-puja*, is performed in honour of this personification, both by *Saivas* and *Vaishnavas*: the former offering a sheep to the earth; the other, a bloodless oblation to fire: these offerings are chiefly, on this occasion, made by land-holders. And *Mr.* PATERSON (*As. Res.* Vol. VIII. p. 79.) thinks, that in the name of the ceremony, and in the object of worship, there may be traced the goddess VESTA of the *Romans*: the goddess of nature, under whose name they worshipped the earth and fire. But *Mr.* COLEBROKE, in a note on this passage, (*ib.* p. 87.) says, that *Vasta-puja*, as a ceremony, is peculiar to *Dhacca*, and districts contiguous to that province, and is not practised in the western parts of *Bengal*; and seems altogether unknown in other parts of *India*. The word *Vasta*, he says, signifies, not the habitable earth in general, but the site of a house, or other edifices, in particular.

PRIT'HIVI, as a personification of the earth, also represents Patience: the *Hindus* refer to the earth, or PRIT'HIVI, proverbially, as an example of patience, or forbearance; permitting her bowels to be ripped open, her surface lacerated, and suffering every indignity without resentment or murmuring. She is quoted also as an example of correctness; as returning good for evil. PRIT'HIVI PATI, i. e. Lord of the Earth, is a title conferred on terrestrial, or real, as well as mythological, sovereigns.

Having introduced the name of VISWACARMA, I will here add what I have chiefly to say referring to that person.

Sir W. JONES thinks VISWACARMA to be the VULCAN of the *Greeks* and *Romans*; being, like VULCAN, the forger of arms for the gods, and inventor of the *Agnyastra*, or *firey shaft*, in the war between them and the *Daityas*, or Titans. —*As. Res.* Vol. I. 264.

He is deemed the architect of the universe, and chief engineer of the gods. He revealed the fourth *Upaveda* in various treatises on sixty-four mechanical arts, for the improvement of such as exercise them; and he is the inspector of all manual labours and mechanical arts.

His name is of some celebrity in mythological legends. In *Mr.* COLE-

BROKE's Dissertation on the *Vedas*, in the eighth volume of the *As. Res.* an account is given of the rites and ceremonies attendant on the inauguration of INDRA, when elected by the gods to be their king; and a list is there given of many persons who, in the heroic history of *India*, obtained universal monarchy by the successful practice of similar rites: among them VISWACARMA, son of BHUVANA, who was consecrated by KASYAPA. On this occasion the earth, as sages relate, thus addressed him: "No mortal has a right to give me away; yet thou, O VISWACARMA! son of BHUVANA, dost wish to do so. I will sink in the midst of the waters; and vain has been thy promise to CASYAPA."

So great was the efficacy of consecration, observes the commentator in this place, that the submersion of the earth was thereby prevented, notwithstanding this declaration.—P. 412.

VISWACARMA seems to have some reference to the *Varahavatara*, and, of course, to be also an *Avatara* of VISHNU. The *Vabara* gives a name to one of the astronomical periods called *Calpa*, or renovations of the universe, denominated the *Vahara-calpa*. The following passage, translated from the Black *Yajurveda*, occurs in *Mr.* COLEBROKE's Dissertation on the *Vedas*.—*As. Res.* Vol. VIII. p. 452.

"Waters (alone) there were: this world originally was water. In it the lord of creation moved, having become air: he saw this (earth), and upheld it, assuming the form of a boar, *(vahara)*; and then moulded that (earth), becoming VISWACARMA, the artificer of the universe. It became celebrated *(aprathata)*, and conspicuous *(prit'hivi)*; and therefore is that name (PRIT'HIVI) assigned to the earth."—See PRIT'HIVI.

By most accounts he was employed by CRISHNA to build for him the present city of *Dwarka*,* in *Gujarat*, when forced to quit his beloved *Matra*; but others (*As. Res.* Vol. IX. p. 197.) relate, that "TWASHTI, the chief engineer of the gods," built it. TWASHTI is a name of the Sun; and if also of VISWACARMA, it in a manner identifies this mythological personage with the Sun. I should rather have expected the name to have been applied to CRISHNA.

In the *Ramayana* (p. 201.) a catalogue of weapons, with which RAMA was armed, occurs; and this passage: "Also the weapon of SOMA, called *Shishira*; and the pain-inflicting weapon, *Twashtra*." And the learned translators sub-

* Of which city, so important in the history of CRISHNA, a good account is much wanted.

join in a note, "Possessing the power of TWASHTRA, the architect of the gods." This seems to identify TWASHTRA (or TWASHTI; for they are doubtless the same) with VISWACARMA. He had a daughter, named BARHISMATI; but I know nothing of her, and introduce her name merely as a clue to inquiry, should any one have occasion to pursue it.

The name or title VISWACARMA means, I believe, the all-performing—*factotum*.

OF the SACTI:

CONSORTS, or ENERGIES of MALE DEITIES.

It has been noticed, that the principal attributes of the Deity, Brahma, Vishnu, and Siva, have consorts assigned them; which consorts are personifications respectively of the active energies of their lords, and are called *Sacti*. Saraswati is the *Sacti* of Brahma, Lakshmi of Vishnu, and Parvati of Siva: hence those, of whatever sect, who worship exclusively the female power—Parvati (i. e. Devi), however, more especially, are called *Sactas*. Not only are the three great powers so accommodated; the inferior deities in their own persons, and the *Avataras* of the superior, are likewise mated in fable, and have their wills executed by active helpmates; each of whom, except in sex, exactly resembles the deity whose partner she is: from whose bodies, indeed, as Eve from Adam's, they are, in some theogonies, supposed to have proceeded; and whose powers and attributes they are armed with.

Eight of these *Sactis* are more particularly recorded: their names are the following.—

Maheswari,	the *Sacti* of Mahesa, or Siva.
Brahmi, or Brahmani,	the *Sacti* of Brahma.
Narayani,	the *Sacti* of Narayana.
Aindri,	the *Sacti* of Indra.
Kaumari,	the *Sacti* of Karticeya.
Varahi,	the *Sacti* of Vishnu in the *Vaharavatara*.
Narasinhi,	the *Sacti* of Vishnu in the *Narasing Avatara*.

Aparajita, a form of Bhavani; the female principle.

This list is taken from *Mr.* Paterson's Essay on the Origin of the *Hindu* Religion, in the eighth volume of the *As. Res.* p. 68. The last, *Mr.* Paterson remarks, may be the Aphrodite of the *Greeks*; and Maheswari, or a female Siva, riding on a white bull, may have given rise to the story of Europa's rape; while BRAHMI, or the female BRAHMA, with the swan, may, in like manner, have occasioned the fable of JUPITER and LEDA. These explanations were, perhaps, invented by the *Greeks*, to account for symbols, of the meaning of which they were ignorant.

On the foregoing passage *Mr.* COLEBROKE gives a note, containing the following information.—

The eight *Sactis*, or energies of as many deities, are also called *Matris*, or mothers. They are called BRAHMI, &c. because they sprung from the bodies of BRAHMA and the other gods respectively.*

In some places they are thus enumerated: BRAHMI, MAHESWARI, AINDRI, VARAHI, VAISHNAVI, CAUMARI, CHAMUNDA, and CHARCHICA. Some reduce the number to seven; omitting the two latter, and adding CAUVERI.

Prayers are addressed to the *Matris* on various occasions, especially in the *Cavachas*, or defensive incantations: I shall cite two by way of example, and subjoin extracts, from the *Marcandeya Purana*, descriptive of these goddesses.

"May BRAHMANI, conferring the benefit of all benedictions, protect me on the east; and NARAYANI on the south-east, for the sake of realizing every wish: MAHESWARI too on the south, rendering every thing auspicious; CHAMUNDA on the south-west, discomfiting all enemies; and, on the west, CAUMARI, armed with her lance, and slayer of foes: on the north-west APARAJITA, the beauteous giver of victory; on the north VARAHI, granter of boons; and, on the north-east, NARASINHI, the banisher of terror. May these mothers, being eight deities and active powers, defend me."

Another incantation simply enumerates the same eight goddesses, and proceeds thus: "May these, and all *Matris*, guard me with their respective weapons on all quarters, and on every point."

In the *Devi mahatmya* the assembling of the *Matris* to combat the demons is thus described.—"The energy of each god, exactly like him, with the same form, the same decoration, and the same vehicle, came to fight against the demons. The *Sacti* of BRAHMA, girt with a white gourd, arrived on a car yoked with swans: her title is BRAHMANI. MAHESWARI came riding on a bull, and bearing a trident, with a vast serpent for a ring, and a crescent for a gem. CAUMARI, bearing a lance in her hand, and riding on a peacock, being AMBICA, in the form of CARTICEYA, came to make war on the children of DITI. The *Sacti* named VAISHNAVI also arrived, sitting on an eagle, and bearing a

* RAYA MUCUTA, on the *Ameracosha*.

conch, a discus, a club, and a bow, and a sword in her several hands. The energy of HARI, who assumed the unrivalled form of the holy boar, likewise came there, assuming the body of VARAHI. NARASINHI too arrived there, embodied in a form precisely similar to that of NRISINHI, with an erect mane reaching to the host of stars. AINDRI, came, bearing the thunder-bolt in her hand, and riding on the king of elephants, and in every respect like INDRA, with a hundred eyes. Lastly came the dreadful energy named CHANDICA, who sprung from the body of DEVI, horrible, howling like a hundred shakals: she, surnamed APARAJITA, the unconquered goddess, thus addressed ISANI,* whose head is encircled with his dusky braided locks."

The story, which is too long for insertion in this place, closes with these words: "Thus did the wrathful host of *Matris* slay the demons."

In the *Uttara Calpa*, of the same *Purana*, the *Matris* are thus described.—"CHAMUNDA standing on a corpse; VARAHI sitting on a buffalo; AINDRI mounted on an elephant; VAISHNAVI borne by an eagle; MAHESWARI riding on a bull; CAUMARI conveyed by a peacock; BRAHMI carried by a swan; and APARAJITA revered by the universe; are all *Matris* endowed with every faculty."

It may be proper to notice, that CHAMUNDA, CHARCHICA, and CHANDICA, are all forms of PARVATI According to one legend, CHAMUNDA sprung from the frown of PARVATI to slay the demons CHANDA and MUNDA: according to another, the mild portion of PARVATI issued from her side, leaving the wrathful portion, which constitutes CALI, or the black goddess.

CAUVERI is the energy of CUVERA, the deformed god of Riches. NARAYANI, mentioned by *Mr.* PATERSON, and also in the prayers or incantations above cited, is the same with VAISHNAVI.—See *As. Res.* Vol. VIII. p. 85.

Mr. COLEBROKE, however, in other places, identifies NARAYANA with BRAHMA.—See instances under NARAYANA, p. 80.

In the thirteenth section of the *Ramayana* the company assembled at an *Aswamedha*, or sacrifice of a horse, is enumerated; and the following passage occurs, a line of which I have had occasion to quote in a former page.—"Thither were previously collected the gods, the sages, &c. for the sake of receiving their respective shares. BRAHMA too, the sovereign of the gods, with ST'HANU, and NARAYANA, chief of beings, and the four supporters of the universe, and

* ISANI is a name of SIVA, also ISA: hence, as before, MAHESA. Under this denomination his *Sacti's* name is ISI.

the divine mothers of all the celestials, met together there."—P. 120. A note on this passage informs us, that the "four supporters of the universe" are "INDRA, regent of the east; YAMA, of the south; VARUNA, of the west; and CUVERA, of the north." "The divine mothers of the celestials" are stated to "be seven: BRAHMI, MAHESWARI, RUDRI, KOMARI, VISHNUVI, VARAHI, INDRANI." The supporters of the universe are considered in future pages; and I will here enumerate, or recapitulate, the names of the *Sactis*, or *Matris*, of the different deities that occur to me as being so mated; adding, also, the *vahan* or *vehicle* by which such power, male or female, is conveyed.

1. BRAHMA	BRAHMI, or SARASWATI,	the swan, or goose.
2. VISHNU	VAISHNAVI, or LAKSHMI,	(generally) GARUDA.
In his character or *Avatara* of	LAKSHMI, under her several names of	
VARAHA	VARAHI,	a buffalo, or a boar.
NARASINGA	NRISINHI	
NARAYANA	NARAYANI	
3. RUDRA MAHESWARA	RUDRI, MAHESWARI,	a bull; the *Sacti* sometimes on a tiger.
And several other names of SIVA and	BHAVANI.	
4. INDRA	INDRANI,	the elephant IRAVATI.
5. KUMARA, or KARTIKYA,	KUMARI,	a peacock.
6. CUVERA	CAUVERI.	

I, therefore, make out but *six* separate *Sactis*, or *Matris*; and as one of them, KUMARI, is understood to be the same with AMBICA, a name or form of DEVI, (or BHAVANI, or PARVATI, the reputed mother of KARTICKYA, or KUMARA,) they may be reduced to five; and, indeed, as all the gods are resolvable into three, and ultimately into one, so, similarly, are their *Sactis* or consorts.

I have hitherto made, and found, no distinction between *Sacti* and *Matri*; but I am of opinion that there is some difference, although I do not know what it is. Several deities have *Sactis* as well as those above enumerated, whose names there are no authorities for adding to the list as *Matris*: SITA, for instance, is called the *Sacti* of RAMA; RADHA of KRISHNA; CHANDRI of CHANDRA; SWAHA of AGNI; PRIT'HIVI of PRIT'HU; NIRITI of NIRUT; VARUNI of VARUNA; and although their names do not occur in any of the foregoing lists, they are considered, generally, as the *Sactis*, or the subordinate powers, or energies, of their respective Lords.

SECTS of HINDUS.

Mr. Colebroke, in different volumes of the *Asiatic Researches,* has given several most interesting and instructive essays "on the religious ceremonies of the *Hindus.*" From a note to the ninth article, in the seventh volume, I extract the whole of the matter that, with the trifling exception of the note below, I give under this head of Sects.

"That *Hindus* belong to various sects is universally known; but their characteristic differences are not perhaps so generally understood. Five great sects exclusively worship a single * deity: one recognises the five divinities which are

* These are.—1. The *Saivas*; who, however, worship Siva and Bhavani conjointly.
2. The *Vaishnavas,* who worship Vishnu.
3. The *Suras,* who worship Surya, or the *Sun.*
4. The *Ganapatyas,* who worship Ganesa.
5. The *Sactas,* who exclusively worship Bhavani, the *Sacti,* or female energy, of Siva.

But if we closely examine the relation they respectively bear to each other, we shall find the 4th and 5th to be subdivisions, or ramifications of the 1st, or *Saiva*: of which may be traced these distinctions.—1. *Saiva* itself meaning the worshippers of Siva, or of Siva and Parvati conjointly. 2. *Lingi,* the adorers of Siva, or his *Phallic* type, separately. 3. *Sacta,* the adorers of the *Yoni* of Bhavani, or her symbol, separately. 4. The *Ganapatyas,* the exclusive worshippers of Ganesa, the first-born of Mahadeva and Parvati.

The second grand sect of *Vaishnavas* is variously divided and subdivided.

First, or division of *Gocalast'ha,* or worshippers of Gocal, or Krishna, is subdivided into three.—

1. Exclusively worship Krishna as Vishnu himself: this is generally deemed the true and orthodox *Vaishnava.*
2. Exclusively worship Radha as the *Sacti* of Krishna or Vishnu: this sect is called *Radha-ballabhi.*
3. Worship Krishna and Radha conjointly.

Second, or division of *Ramanuj,* or worshippers of Ramachandra, is, in like manner, subdivided into three.—

1. Worship Rama only.
2. Worship Sita only as his *Sacti.*
3. Worship both Rama and Sita conjointly.

adored by the other sects respectively; but the followers of this comprehensive scheme mostly select one object of daily devotion, and pay adoration to other deities on particular occasions. Even they deny the charge of polytheism, and repel the imputation of idolatry: they justify the practice of adoring the images of celestial spirits by arguments similar to those which have been elsewhere employed in defence of image worship. If the doctrines of the *Veda*, and even those of the *Puranas*, be closely examined, the *Hindu* theology will be found consistent monotheism, though it contains the seeds of polytheism and idolatry. I shall take some future occasion of enlarging on this topic; I have here only to remark, that modern *Hindus* seem to misunderstand the numerous texts which declare the unity of the Godhead, and the identity of VISHNU, SIVA, the Sun, &c. Their theologists have entered into vain disputes on the question, Which, among the attributes of GOD, shall be deemed characteristic and pre-eminent? SANCARA ACHARYA, the celebrated commentator on the *Veda*, contended for the attributes of SIVA; and founded, or confirmed, the sect of *Saivas*, who worship MAHADEVA as the Supreme Being, and deny the independent existence of VISHNU and other deities. MADHAVA ACHARYA, and VALLABHA ACHARYA, have, in like manner, established the sect of *Vaishnavas*, who adore VISHNU as God. The *Suras* (less numerous than the sects above mentioned) worship the Sun, and acknowledge no other divinity. The *Ganapatyas* adore GANESA as uniting in his person all the attributes of the Deity.

"Before I notice the fifth sect, I must remind the reader that the *Hindu* mythology has personified the abstract and attractive powers of the Divinity, and has ascribed sexes to these mythological personages. The *Sacti*, or energy, of an attribute of God is female, and is fabled as the consort of that personified attribute. The *Sacti* of SIVA, whose emblem is the *Phallus*, is herself typified by the female organ: this the *Sactas* worship, some figuratively, others literally.

"VOPADEVA, the real author of the *Sri Bhagavata*, has endeavoured to reconcile all the sects of *Hindus* by reviving the doctrines of VYASA. He recognises all the deities, but as subordinate to the Supreme Being, or rather as

As the *Saiva* has a fourth undivided sect in the *Ganapatyas*, so the *Vaishnava* has a fourth undivided sect in the *Bhagavatas*. And, indeed, we find the sects melting into each other; for, in consequence of the interposition of VISHNU to appease a physiological difference between MAHADEVA and PARVATI, or the worshippers of the *Linga* and *Yoni*, his (VISHNU'S) navel, or rather *os tincæ*, came to be considered as the same with the *Yoni*; confounding the *Yonijas* with the *Vaishnavas*. In addition to the divisions of *Vaishnavas*, might be named the *Bauddhists*, or followers of the doctrines of BUDDHA; and these form three sects, named after their respective founders, BUDDHA, JINA, and MAHIMAN: the two last appear schisms of *Buddhism*. In future articles the subjects of this note will be farther noticed.

attributes or manifestations of God. A new sect has been thus formed, and is denominated from that modern *Purana*; but the numerous followers of it do not seem to have well apprehended the doctrines they profess. They incline much to real polytheism; but do at least reject the derogatory notions of the Divinity, which the other sects seem to have adopted.

"The *Vaishnavas*, though nominally worshippers of VISHNU, are, in fact, votaries of deified heroes. The *Goculast'has* * (one branch of this sect) adore KRISHNA, while the *Ramanuj* worship RAMACHANDRA. Both have again branched into three sects: one consists in the exclusive worshippers of KRISHNA; and these only are deemed true and orthodox *Vaishnavas*: another joins his favourite RADHA with the hero: a third, called *Radha-ballabhi*, adores RADHA only, considering her as the active power of VISHNU. The followers of these last mentioned sects have adopted the singular practice of presenting to their own wives the oblations intended for the goddess; and those among them who follow the left-handed path (there is in most sects a right-handed, or decent path, and a left-handed, or indecent mode of worship) require their wives to be naked when attending them at their devotions.

"Among the *Ramanuj* some worship RAMA only, and others both RAMA and SITA: none of them practise any indecent mode of worship. And they all, like the *Goculast'has*, as well as the followers of the *Bhagavata*, delineate on their foreheads a double upright line with chalk, or with sandal-wood, and a red circlet with red sanders, or with turmeric and lime; but the *Ramanuj* add an upright red line in the middle of the double white one.

"The *Saivas* are all worshippers of SIVA and BHAVANI conjointly; and they adore the *Linga*, or compound type of this god and goddess, as the *Vaishnavas* do the image of LAKSHMI-NARAYANA. There are no exclusive worshippers of SIVA besides the sect of naked gymnosophists, called *Lingis*; and the exclusive adorers of the goddess are the *Sactas*. In this last mentioned sect, as in most others, there is a right-handed and decent path, and a left-handed and indecent mode of worship; but the indecent worship of this sect is most grossly so, and consists of unbridled debauchery with wine and women. This profligate sect is supposed to be numerous, though unavowed. In most parts of *India*, if not in all, they are held in deserved detestation; and even the decent *Sactas* do not make public profession of their tenets, nor wear on their foreheads the marks of their sect, lest they should be suspected of belonging to the other branch of it.

* GOCAL; a name of CRISHNA, the cowherd.

"The *Saivas* and *Sactas* delineate on their foreheads three horizontal lines with ashes obtained, if possible, from the hearth on which a consecrated fire has been maintained: they add a red circlet, which the *Saivas* make of red sanders, and which the *Sactas*, when they avow themselves, mark either with saffron, or with turmeric and borax.

"The *Sauras* are true worshippers of the Sun; and some of them, it seems, adore the dormant and active energies of the planet conjointly. This sect, which is not very numerous, is distinguished by the use of red sanders for the horizontal triple line, as well as for the circlet on their foreheads.

"The *Ganapatyas* have not, so far as I can learn, branched into different sects; nor can I add any information, respecting their peculiar tenets, further, than that Ganesa is exclusively worshipped by them. This sect is distinguished by the use of red minium for the circlet on their foreheads.

"The left-handed path, or indecent mode of worship, of the several sects, especially that of the *Sactas*, is founded on the *Tantras*, which are, for this reason, held in disesteem. I was misinformed, when I described them (*As. Res.* Vol. V. p. 54. *Cal. edit.*) as constituting a branch of literature highly esteemed, though much neglected: the reverse would have been more exact."

Mr. Colebroke concludes this very instructive note by observing, that the information it contained rests chiefly on the authority of verbal communications.

We now proceed to introduce more particularly the consorts, or *Sactis*, of the three great personified powers, who are respectively seen together in plate 23.

SARASWATI.

In the *Asiatic Miscellany*, Vol. I. and in *Sir* W. Jones's Works, Vol. XIII. will be found a spirited hymn, addressed to this goddess.—

> "Sweet grace of Brahma's bed."
> "Whose sigh is music, and each tear a pearl."

From the argument prefixed to it I extract the following passages.—

"The *Hindu* goddesses are uniformly represented as the subordinate *powers* of their respective lords: thus Lakshmi, the consort of Vishnu the *Preserver*, is the goddess of *abundance* and *prosperity*; Bhavani, the wife of Mahadeva, is the genial power of *fecundity*; and Saraswati, whose husband was the *Creator* Brahma, possesses the powers of Imagination and Invention, which may justly be termed *creative*. She is, therefore, adored as the patroness of the fine arts, especially of Music and Rhetoric; as the inventress of the *Sanskrit* language, of the *Devanagry* characters, and of the sciences which writing perpetuates: so that her attributes correspond with those of Minerva *Musica*, in *Greece* or *Italy*, who invented the flute, and presided over literature. In this character she is addressed in the ode; and particularly as the *Goddess* of *Harmony*, since the *Italians* usually paint her with a musical instrument in her hand. The seven notes, an artful combination of which constitutes *Music*, and variously affect the passions, are feigned to be her earliest production. And the greatest part of the hymn exhibits a correct delineation of the *Ragmala*, or *Necklace* of *Musical Modes*, which may be considered as the most pleasing invention of the ancient *Hindus*, and the most beautiful union of painting with poetical mythology and the genuine theory of music."

I omit the curious outline, that next follows, of this theory: the argument proceeds thus.—

"A full discussion of so copious a subject would require a separate dissertation;* but here it will be sufficient to say, that almost every allusion and every epithet in the poem, as well as the names, are selected from approved treatises, either originally *Persian*, or translated from the *Sanskrit*, which contain as lively a display of genius as human imagination ever exhibited."

"We thirst, VACDEVI, for thy balmy lore,
Drawn from that rubied cave
Where meek-eyed pilgrims hail the triple wave."

The name SARASWATI means flowing; applicable both to the river, and the goddess of eloquence. VACHI, LEPITA, have meanings chiefly referrible to *speech*, or *speaking*. She is also called VANI, BRAHMI or BRAHMANI, and by several other names.

The last line alludes to the celebrated place of pilgrimage, at the confluence of the *Ganga* and *Yamuna*, which the *Saraswati*, the third sacred river, is supposed to join underground.†

"The *unarmed* MINERVA of the *Romans* apparently corresponds, as patroness of science and genius, with SARASWATI. Both goddesses have given their names to celebrated grammatical works; but the *Sareswata* of SARUPACHARYA is far more concise, as well as more useful, than the MINERVA of SANCTIUS.

"The MINERVA of *Italy* invented the *flute*; and SARASWATI presides over Melody: the protectress of *Athens* was even, on the same account, surnamed MUSICE."—JONES. *As. Res.* Vol. I. p. 253.

The last watch of the night is peculiarly sacred to SARASWATI.

"Let the housekeeper wake in the time sacred to BRAHMI, the goddess of speech, that is in the last watch of the night; let him then reflect on virtue and virtuous emoluments, and on the whole meaning and very essence of the *Veda*." —MENU, Ch. IV. v. 92.

The fifth day of the month *Magha* is called *Sri-punjemi*, on which SARASWATI, or SRI, the goddess of arts and eloquence, is worshipped with offerings of perfumes, flowers, and dressed rice: even the implements of writing, and books, are treated with respect, and are not used on this holiday. The following meditation on this goddess will furnish a description of her person and attributes.

* Which, fortunately, the indefatigable author found time to give in the third volume of the *Asiatic Researches*: Art. IV. "On the Musical Modes of the *Hindus*." And on that subject see also *As. Res.* Vol. IX. Art. XI. by *Mr.* PATERSON.

† PLATE 75. *fig.* 2. is a personification of this Triad of Rivers.

"May the goddess of speech* enable us to attain all possible felicity: she who wears on her locks a young moon; who shines with exquisite lustre; whose body bends with the weight of her full breasts; who sits reclined on a white lotos; and from the crimson lotos of her hands pours radiance on the implements of writing, and on the books produced by her favour."—*As. Res.* Vol. III. p. 273.

SARASWATI is, among other deities, especially propitiated in the marriage-ceremonies of the *Brahmans*: the following hymn is chanted in her honour.—"Charming SARASWATI! swift as a mare, whom I celebrate in the face of this universe, protect this solemn rite. O thou! in whom the elements were produced, in whom this universe was framed, I will now sing that hymn," (the nuptial text) "which constitutes the highest glory of women."—COLEBROKE. *As. Res.* Vol. VII. p. 303.

Whatever deity a *Hindu* may have occasion to invoke, or rather whichever be the object of his adoration, whether god or goddess, superior or inferior, he will array his patron in the attributes of the Almighty himself. The ardent imagination of a poet knows no restraint; but we must recollect that a female deity is actually her lord: SARASWATI is the active energy or power of her consort BRAHḾA—his *Sacti*; she is therefore endowed with his attribute of creation. And, in the preceding and following extracts, we see her, not unappropriately, invoked as the being "in whom the elements were produced, in whom this universe was framed;" and also gifted with the peculiar powers and attributes of other deities.

In the following extract from COLEBROKE's Essay on the *Vedas*, *As. Res.* Vol. VIII. p. 402. the origin and attributes of this beneficent deity will more fully appear.

"Near the close of the tenth chapter" (of the tenth book of the *Rigveda*), "a hymn is spoken by VACH, daughter of AMBHRINA, in praise of herself as the supreme universal soul.† VACH signifies *speech*; and she is the active power of BRAHMA, proceeding from him. The following is a literal version of this hymn,

* Here SARASWATI, who, from the latter part of the quotation, is evidently invoked, is (as BHAVANI is in page 45,) addressed as the goddess of speech; which, indeed, as appears in the preceding quotation from MENU, is her peculiar character. Sitting reclined on a white lotos is rather indicative, as well as the name SRI, of LAKSHMI; while wearing on her locks a crescent, or young moon, approaches her to the consort of SIVA.

† "In another place VACH is mentioned as receiving a revelation from AMBHINI, who obtained it from the Sun: but here she herself bears the almost similar patronymic, AMBHRINI."

which is expounded by the commentator consistently with the theological doctrines of the *Vedas.*

"I range with the *Rudras,* with the *Vasus,* with the *Adityas,* and with the *Viswadevas.** I uphold both the sun and the ocean, (MITRA † and VARUNA,) the firmament (INDRA) and fire, and both the ASWINS. I support the moon, (SOMA) destroyer (of foes), and (the sun entitled) TWASHTI, PUSHAN, or BHAGA.‡ I grant wealth to the honest votary who performs sacrifices, offers oblations, and satisfies (the deities). Me, who am the queen, the conferrer of wealth, the possessor of knowledge, and first of such as merit worship, the gods render, universally, present every where, and pervader of all beings. He who eats food through me, as he who sees, or who breathes, or who hears, through me, yet knows me not, is lost; hear then the faith which I pronounce. Even I declare this self, who is worshipped by gods and men: I make strong whom I choose; I make him BRAHMA, holy and wise: for RUDRA I bend the bow, to slay the demon, foe of BRAHMA; for the people I make war (on their foes); and I pervade heaven and earth. I bore the father on the head of this (universal mind), and my origin is in the midst of the ocean;|| and therefore do I pervade all beings, and touch this heaven with my form. Originating all beings, I pass like the breeze; I am above this heaven, beyond this earth; and what is the great one, that am I."

In another page I have hinted my opinion, that more sects of *Hindus* (classes, I mean, who exclusively adore one deity, in person or through his *Sacti,*) exist than we are at present aware of: at any rate, if they do not now exist, such passages as that last quoted almost prove that they have prevailed heretofore. No sect, or perhaps individual, now exclusively worships either BRAHMA or SARASWATI; but, surely, the passage in question must have been penned or conceived by a sectarist of that deity. Many legends do, indeed, assert the fact of

* *Viswadeva,* like *Serva-deva,* means the gods collectively: all the gods: the *Pantheon.* See MENU, Ch. III. v. 121.—"One oblation to the assembled gods, thence named *Vaiswadeva,* both for evening and morning."

† The words between brackets are in this, as well as in other instances, interpolated by the commentator to illustrate the text, which would in many cases be obscure, and scarcely intelligible without it.

‡ Names of SIVA; also of the Sun.

|| "Heaven, or the sky, is the father; and the sky is produced from mind, according to a passage of the *Veda*: its birth is therefore placed on the head of the supreme mind. The commentator suggests three interpretations of the sequel of this stanza: 'my parent, the holy AMBHRINA, is in the midst of the ocean;' or 'my origin, the sentient deity, is in waters, which constitute the bodies of the gods;' or 'the sentient god, who is in the midst of the waters, which pervade intellect, is my origin.'"

BRAHMA's coequality, in the points of temples and adoration, with his brother members of the Triad: the above hymn we may, therefore, (if we admit the historical fact) infer is, in respect of age, anterior to the overthrow of BRAHMA's temples, the dispersion of his sectarists, and the abolition of his worship.

In cases where a *Hindu* have lied, or given false evidence, the sin is expiated by an easy oblation to the goddess of speech.

It has been extensively remarked, that the *Hindus* are more than usually prone to falsehood; nor can it be denied, that the discouragement of this offence is too little pointed, both in regard to the trifling degree of disgrace that attaches to a man's character on detection, and to the too great qualification of the prohibitory clauses of the law against lying. Falsehood is not only tolerated in some cases of evidence, but is declared, in special affairs, to be even preferable to truth: a few texts from MENU will evince this.

Ch. VIII. v. 103.—" In some cases a giver of false evidence, from a pious motive, even though he know the truth, shall not lose a seat in heaven: such evidence wise men call the speech of the gods.

" 104. Whenever the death of a man, *who had not been a grievous offender*, either of the servile, the commercial, the military, or the sacerdotal class, would be occasioned by true evidence, *from the known rigour of the king, even though the fault arose from inadvertence or error*, falsehood may be spoken: it is even preferable to truth.

" 105. Such witnesses must offer, as oblations to SARASWATI, cakes of rice and milk addressed to the goddess of speech: and thus will they fully expiate the venial sin of benevolent falsehood."

The words in *Italics* are not in the original code, but are the interpolated gloss of CULLUCCA. If the text be read, omitting the words in *Italics*, it will not materially tend to the greater discouragement of falsehood.

Another reason that, among the *Hindus*, deviation from truth is not held in deserved abhorrence, may be found, perhaps, in this circumstance: that, in their mythological legends, their gods are frequently represented as liars. One can scarcely help suspecting, that imbibing such notions in early youth must necessarily produce a pernicious influence on the principles and conduct of men.

Images of SARASWATI are seldom seen: I have not one among my images; nor do I immediately recollect having ever seen one. Of pictures I have several; and some representations of her are given in our plates, of which I will now give some description.

She is usually drawn either two or four-handed: in PLATES 4. 23. she is the immediate two-handed helpmate and associate of her husband BRAHMA; and has, of her own, no distinguishing attributes. In PLATE 24. *fig.* 4. she is four-handed, holding her *Vina*, or lyre, a lotos, a cup, and a scroll: which being noticed, with such other particulars as seemed to require it, in a preceding page (59), we shall not dwell longer on in this place. In PLATE 45. she is also four-handed, playing on her *Vina* with two hands; the others empty: she is here riding a peacock, and not, as one would expect, a swan, the *Vahan* of her consort; which, indeed, I never saw her mounted on.—(See page 59.) Riding a peacock, the immediate vehicle of KARTIKYA, a son, or reputed son, of PARVATI, and addressing GANESA, (as she is in the upper part of PLATE 45.) another of her sons, seems to connect SARASWATI with the *Sacti* of the destroying power: holding the cup, *pan-patra,* in PLATE 24. farther indicates the relationship between these goddesses, corresponding with that so often remarked between their divine partners.

PLATE 45. is engraved from two pictures drawn by an artist in my employ in *Bombay,* superintended by a *Pandit,* as will be noticed on a future occasion. I recollect no particular mythological reason assigned for associating the goddess of eloquence, harmony, and the arts, with the god of prudence and policy: it is, however, rational enough.

SARASWATI in both pictures is dressed in a red *Sari*; in one a red, the other a green, *Chuli*; the peacock is blueish, with a green tail.

Some of the early catholic missionaries, who attempted to explore and explain the religious doctrines and opinions of the *Indians,* discovered in their zeal, if not in their judgment, the history of the patriarch ABRAHAM, and his wife SARAH, veiled under that of BRAHMA and SARASWATI: which names may, by those ignorant of the power of *Sanskrit* letters, be spelled BRAHAM, or BRAHAMA, and SARAH-SWATI. To an etymologist, transposing the final vowel is but a trifling liberty; and in the case of BRAHAMA, making it initial, the required name is at once produced: and in the second name, say the missionaries, the termination SWATI is merely an epithet, equivalent to goddess or mistress. I know not if the zealous fathers found much coincidence in the respective histories of the compared personages, for I have not the books, in which I read the account, to refer to.

It would assuredly be a very curious catalogue, were some competent scholar to make one of *Sanskrit* words, having synonims in *European* languages: two or three instances, that at once occur, I will here note; and, without laying any particular stress on them, would ask, if it be likely that such, among hundreds of others, and many doubtless more striking coincidences, can be entirely accidental?

The name of the goddess, the subject of our next article, is LAKSHMI: it is often, and I so find it among my notes, spelled LUXMI, which is the usual mode of pronouncing it in the western parts of *India*. She is the goddess of fortune, and queen of beauty; and every thing grand and splendid is attributed to her by her votaries. The word *Laksh*, in *Sanskrit*, whence her name is derived, has the meaning of *lux*, as well as of luck, luxury, &c.

ASWA, and BASWA, are horse and bull, *bos*, and pronounced not very unlike those words. *Aksha* is ox; *Gow*, a cow.

LAKSHMI.

LAKSHMI is the consort of VISHNU; the *Sacti*, or active energy, of the personified preservative power. She is considered as the goddess of riches, and would be invoked for increase of wealth by a desiring *Hindu* rather than CUVERA, the PLUTUS of their Pantheon: she might, therefore, be naturally considered as the appropriate consort of the deity of wealth, but I do not recollect her immediately in that capacity; and should, indeed, be grieved to see the queen of beauty, as under the name of REMBHA she must be considered, in the penurious arms of the deformed and sordid god. Descending from mythology to man, from the Pantheon to the world, it is a sacrifice too often contemplated.

The followers of VISHNU esteem LAKSHMI as the mother of the world, and then call her ADA MAYA; and such *Vaishnavas* as are *Sactas*, that is adorers of the female energy or nature-active, worship her exclusively as the symbol of the Eternal Being.—(See *Sects* and *Sacti.*)

As REMBHA, the sea-born goddess of beauty, she sprang one of the fourteen gems from the ocean, when churned by the good and evil beings for the *amrita*, or immortal beverage. She then assumes the character of VENUS APHRODITES, of the *Greeks*; who, as HESIOD and HOMER sing, arose from the sea, ascended to *Olympus*, and captivated all the gods.

In the 36th section of the *Ramayana*, describing the *Kurmavatara*, the production of LAKSHMI is thus painted.—" The gods, the *Asuras*, and the *Gandharvas*, again agitating the sea," (as is represented in PLATE 49.) after a long time, appeared the great goddess, inhabiting the lotos, clothed with superlative beauty, in the first bloom of youth, covered with ornaments, and bearing every auspicious sign; adorned with a crown, with bracelets on her arms, her jetty locks flowing in ringlets, and her body, which resembled burning gold, adorned with ornaments of pearl. This great goddess appeared with four arms, holding a lotos in her hand; her countenance incomparable in beauty. Thus was produced the goddess PADMA, or SRI, adored by the whole universe; PADMA by

name. She took up her abode in the bosom of PADMA-NABHA, even of HERI."
—P. 289.

Although in this passage LAKSHMI, or, as she is called, PADMA, or SRI, is very respectfully and gloriously depicted, yet considered, which, as the offspring of the sea, she generally is, in the character of REMBHA, corresponding with our popular VENUS, it is not always that she is deserving of such encomiums. It is not, of course, to be supposed, that under this character she is always strictly correct; on the contrary, she is, somewhat inconsistently, considered as an *Apsara*, (see page 96.) and is occasionally employed by the celestials on no very creditable missions. For example: when the ascetic VISWAMITRA, after his debasement through the wiles of the fascinating MENAKA, (as will be related under the head of INDRA,) had learned wisdom by his fall, and was again engaged in a course of most severe austerities, INDRA, who dreaded rivalship from their effects, thus addressed the *Apsara* REMBHA.—"O thou of most engaging mien, celebrated among all the *Apsaras*; O REMBHA, able to perceive and accommodate thyself to the disposition of every lover, accomplish this work of the gods: by the riches of thy beauty entice the son of KASHEKA, engaged in sacred austerities."—*Ramayana*, sect. 51.

REMBHA's only objection was the irascibility of the sage; but INDRA encouraged her by promising to assume the form of the heart-ravishing KOKILA,* and to be at hand, accompanied by KANDARPA (KAMA, the god of love), to second the witchery of her beauty by a concord of sweet sounds, cooling zephyrs, and perfumed odours; "rendering the captivating REMBHA still more charming by the power of song." The sage, however, seeing, by the eye of contemplation, through the subtilty of the depraved PURENDARA (INDRA), and remembering his former fall, cursed the unlucky REMBHA into a stone; to remain a petrean statue for ten thousand years, and to be relievable only by a *Brahman* perfected by sacred austerities.—*Ib.* p. 369.

As the goddess of fortune, the epithet *fickle* is sometimes applied to LAKSHMI, in contradistinction to PARVATI, or SATI, who is called the *constant*, or *faithful*. In this fickle character she is called LOCKI, a mere shortening, or rapid pronunciation, I imagine, of her common name.

But, excepting figuratively, as the goddess of fortune, I do not see why she should be deemed fickle; for she is always seen with her Lord: when reposing on SESHNAGA (see PLATES 7. 8.) she is *shampooing* his feet. In VISHNU's *Avatara*

* A black bird, very common in *India*, which sings in the night: in notes as various and melodious as the nightingale, but louder.

of RAMA, LAKSHMI was incarnated in the person of the adopted daughter of RAJA JANEKA, and became SITA, the most faithful spouse of her heroic lord. In the *Avatara* of KRISHNA she was ROKMENY, the most beloved of the amorous deity. In all the other incarnations of VISHNU, whether *Avatara* or *Avantara*, i. e. superior or inferior, she appears, if he had a wife, to have been with him; and mostly under her own name of LAKSHMI.

As mother of KAMADEVA, by KRISHNA, we shall notice her under the article KAMA by the perplexing appellation of MAYA. And as spouse of NARAYANA (see that article) she is called NARAYANI, as well as LAKSHMI.

It was not without a good reason that the *Hindus*, and after them the imitative *Greeks*, feigned the goddess of beauty to have sprang from the sea: health is the parent of beauty; and the fable teaches us to seek it in those fresh from the wave; an allusion especially salutary in the warm poetical latitudes of *Hindustan* and *Greece*. Nor, to digress a little, is it unmeaning, when DIANA, patroness of the chase, is the goddess presiding also over chastity, and necessarily the foe of VENUS: violent exercises, particularly on horseback—I do not, however, mean to say that DIANA is oftenest so seen, are, as is well and popularly known, of a tendency highly anti-*aphrodisiac*; and restoration from their lassitude can nowhere be so profitably sought as, whence beauty sprung, in the health-bestowing wave.

The *Hindu* women, in imitation and in honour of LAKSHMI, bathe with particular ceremonies on certain days: such ceremonies, piously performed on the third day of the light half of the moon *Jaish'ta*, which day is called REMBHA *tritiya*, are peculiarly auspicious to female beauty.—REMBHA bathed on that day.

I will here notice some other days on which LAKSHMI is propitiated, under auspices more than commonly favourable. These are taken from the *As. Res.* Vol. III. art. 12. On the Lunar Year of the *Hindus*: by *Sir* W. JONES.

On the third day after that before mentioned, that is the sixth day of the moon's age, which is called *Aranya-shashti*, "women walk in the forests, with a fan in one hand, and eat certain vegetables, in hope of beautiful children. See the account given by PLINY of the *Druidical* misletoe, or *viscum*, which was to be gathered when the moon was *six* days old, as a preservative from *sterility*."—Page 284.

Although not particularly so mentioned by the learned author of the essay under our notice, I have ascribed the honours of this *sixth* day to LAKSHMI; for she is the goddess who presides over marriage, and as the deity of prosperity is invoked also for increase of children, and especially male children. Nothing is more lamented or deprecated by *Hindus,* male and female, than being unfruitful: with many sects, a woman proving so affords the unhappy husband unobjectionable grounds of seeking in a second wife the chance of so desirable and essential a blessing.

On the dark last day of the moon, *Aswina,* ceremonies of a peculiar and two-fold nature are performed in honour of both LAKSHMI and BHAVANI.

"A fast all day, and a great festival at night, in honour of LAKSHMI; with illuminations on trees and houses. Invocations are made at the same time to CUVERA."—P. 264. Here appears a greater connexion between these ill-assorted personages than is seen on other occasions. Riches or prosperity is the object of the invocations; and the presiding deities are of course conjoined.

"On this night, when the gods, having been delivered by KESAVA, were slumbering on the rocks that bounded the sea of milk, LAKSHMI, no longer fearing the *Daityas,* slept apart on a lotos."—*Ib.*

I do not know to what legend this passage alludes.

"Flowers are also offered on this day to SYAMA, or the *black,* an epithet of BHAVANI, who appears in the *Caliyug* as a damsel twelve years old; and torches and flaming brands are kindled and consecrated to burn the bodies of kinsmen, who may be dead in battle or in a foreign country, and to light them through the shades of death to the mansions of YAMA: these rites bear a striking resemblance to those of CERES and PROSERPINE."—P. 264. This day is called LAKSHMI-*puja,* and SYAMA-*puja,* and the dark day preceding, is marked by "bathing and libations to YAMA, regent of the south, or lower world, and judge of departed spirits."—*Ib.*

I extract a passage from the first volume of the *Asiatic Researches,* by the same learned and lamented author, descriptive of LAKSHMI.

"It having been occasionally observed, that CERES was the poetical daughter of SATURN, we cannot close this head without adding, that the *Hindus* have also their *Goddess* of *Abundance,* whom they usually call LAKSHMI; and whom they consider as the daughter (not of MENU, but) of BHRIGU, by whom the first code of sacred ordinances was promulgated. She is also named PEDMA and CAMALA, from the sacred lotos, or *Nymphæa;* but her most remarkable name is SRI, or, in the first case, SRIS, which has a resemblance to the *Latin,* and means *fortune,* or *prosperity.*"

Sir WILLIAM JONES was too cautious to lay much stress on the fallacious ground of etymological resemblance; and although, among his earliest researches into *Hindu* mythology, he discovered this similarity of names and characters, he would not pronounce on the identity of the subjects. He has not, however, escaped the strictures of continental writers, who find fault with him on this very point; in which, in fact, he, above almost all writers, is comparatively faultless.

"It may be contended," he continues, "that although LAKSHMI may be figuratively called the CERES of *Hindustan*, yet any two, or more, idolatrous nations, who subsisted by agriculture, might naturally conceive a deity to preside over their labours, without having the least intercourse with each other; but no reason appears, why two nations should concur in supposing that deity to be a female: one, at least, of them would be more likely to imagine that the *earth* was a goddess,* and that the god of abundance rendered her fertile. Besides, in very ancient temples, near *Gaya*, we see images of LAKSHMI with full breasts, and a *cord* twisted under her arm, like a *horn of plenty*, which looks very much like the old *Grecian* and *Roman* figures of CERES."—P. 240.

The epithet of SRI is not, however, exclusively applied to LAKSHMI, but to several other gods and goddesses: SRI GANESA I have frequently heard; and have read of SRI DEVI, as applicable to PARVATI: it is sometimes also given to men. The *Brahmanical* head of the *Poona* government is generally, in the third person, styled SRI MANT: it may, perhaps, have been personally assumed by the present *Peshwa* BAAJY RAO, and not in use by his predecessors.

Sir WILLIAM JONES has addressed a hymn to LAKSHMI, "the world's great mother," that cannot be perused by an oriental student without great profit; nor by any one without unqualified admiration.—See Works, Vol. XIII. In the argument he calls her "LAKSHMI, or SRI, the CERES of *India*, the *preserving power* of nature; or, in the language of allegory, the consort of VISHNU, or HERI, a personification of the divine goodness. Some represent her as the daughter of BHRIGU, a son of BRAHMA; but, in the *Mercandeya Puran*, the *Indian* ISIS, or *Nature*, is said to have assumed three transcendent forms, according to her three *gunas*, or qualities, and each of them to have produced a pair of divinities: BRAHMA and LAKSHMI, MAHESA and SARASWATI, VISHNU and CALI. After whose intermarriage, BRAHMA and SARASWATI formed the mundane egg, which MAHESA and CALI divided into halves; and VISHNU, together with LAKSHMI, preserved it from destruction. A third story supposes her to have sprung from the *sea of milk*, when it was churned on the second incarnation of

* As, indeed, is the case with the *Hindus*, in the instance of PRIT'HIVI.—See that article, page 111.

HERI, who is often painted reclining on the serpent ANANTA, the emblem of eternity; and this fable, whatever may be the meaning of it, has been chosen as the most poetical. The other names of SRI, or *Prosperity*, are HERIPRIYA, PEDMALAYA, or PEDMA, and CAMALA: the first implying the wife of VISHNU, and the rest derived from the names of the lotos."

"Not long inswath'd the sacred infant lay,
(Celestial forms full soon their prime attain):
Her eyes, oft darted o'er the liquid way,
With golden light emblaz'd the darkling main;
And those firm breasts, whence all our comforts well,
Rose with enchanting swell;
Her loose hair with the bounding billows play'd,
And caught in charming toils each pearly shell
That, idling, through the surgy forest stray'd;
When ocean suffer'd a-portentous change,
Toss'd with convulsion strange:
For lofty *Mandar* from his base was torn,
With streams, rocks, woods—by gods and demons whirl'd,
While round his craggy sides the mad spray curl'd—
Huge mountain! by the passive tortoise borne.
Then sole, but not forlorn,
Shipp'd in a flower, that balmy sweets exhal'd,
O'er dulcet waves of cream PED-MALA sail'd:
So name the Goddess, from her lotos blue,
Or CAMALA, if more auspicious deem'd;
With many-petal'd wings the blossom flew,
And from the mount a flutt'ring sea-bird seem'd,
Till on the shore it stopp'd—the heav'n-lov'd shore,
"Bright with unvalu'd store
Of gems marine, by mirthful INDRA wore;
But she, (what brighter gem had shone before?)
No bride for old MARICHA's frolic son,
On azure HERI fix'd her prosp'ring eyes.
"Love bade the bridegroom rise;
Straight o'er the deep, then dimpling smooth, he rush'd,
And tow'rd th' unmeasur'd snake—stupendous bed!
The world's great mother, not reluctant, led:
All nature glow'd whene'er she smil'd or blush'd;
"The king of serpents hush'd
His thousand heads, where diamond mirrors blaz'd,
That multiply'd her image as he gaz'd." V. 4.

PLATE 49. represents the scene described in the first part of this verse: PLATES 7. and 8. that of the last.

It may be in place to remark here, that I have been taught by *Brahmans* to give the name of DEVI sometimes to LAKSHMI. They tell me, that when DEVI has the *Chank* and *Chakra* she is then called VISHNU DEVI, or an *Avatara* of LAKSHMI: *fig.* 3. of PLATE 6. (see page 25.) is an instance of this. The *trisula* and *damru* especially mark BHAVANI.

In the *Srad'ha*, or obsequies in honour of deceased ancestors, LAKSHMI is, among most other deities, earnestly invoked; particularly when a votary, by gifts to *Brahmans*, is "desirous of obtaining celestial bliss for the defunct." A donation of a milch cow is attended by many appropriate ceremonies, finishing with the following prayers, the accepter holding during the recital the sacred animal by the tail.

"1. May the goddess, who is the LAKSHMI of all beings, and resides among the gods, assume the shape of a milch cow, and procure me comfort.

"2. May the goddess, who is RUDRANI in a corporeal form, and who is the beloved of SIVA, assume the shape of a milch cow, and procure me comfort.

"3. May she, who is LAKSHMI reposing on the bosom of VISHNU; she, who is the LAKSHMI of the regent of riches; she, who is the LAKSHMI of kings, be a boon-granting cow to me.

"4. May she, who is the LAKSHMI of BRAHMA; she, who is SWAHA, the wife of fire; she, who is the exerted power of the sun, moon, and stars, assume the shape of a milch cow for my prosperity.

"5. Since thou art *Swadha*, the food of them who are the chief among the manes of ancestors, and SWAHA,* the consuming power of them who eat solemn sacrifices, therefore, being the cow that expiates every sin, procure me comfort.

"6. I invoke the goddess, who is endowed with the attributes of all the gods, who confers all happiness, who bestows abodes in all the worlds, for the sake of all people.

"7. I pray to that auspicious goddess for immortality and happiness."—COLEBROKE: on the Religious Ceremonies of the *Hindus*. *As. Res.* Vol. VII. page 263.

The boon-granting cow, so honoured in the preceding extract, is called SURABHI; and her descendants are much revered by all classes of *Hindus* above those that may be denominated base. It is common for *Brahmans*, and others,

* SWAHA is usually understood to be the goddess of fire, the consort or *Sacti* of AGNI. She will, with her ardent spouse, come under our notice hereafter.

to feed a cow before they take their own breakfast, ejaculating, as they present her food, "Daughter of SURABHI, framed of five elements, auspicious, pure, holy—sprung from the sun, accept this food given by me: salutation unto thee!" Or, if he conduct the kine to grass, "May cows, who are mothers of the three worlds, and daughters of SURABHI, and who are beneficent, pure, and holy, accept the food given by me."—COLEBROKE. *As. Res.* Vol. VII. page 276.

The *Hindus* hope to obtain the favour of the boon-granting cow by shewing kindness to her offspring: and adoration of a cow is not uncommon; such as presenting flowers to her, washing her feet, &c. Many instances of affectionate tenderness for cows and calves have come under my notice, on the part especially of *Brahmans* and *Banias*; and many stories are beautifully told in *Hindu* poetics, of boons obtained by those means. Of VASISHTA's cow, NANDINI, attended by the king DILIPA, for the sake of obtaining a boon through her means, a pretty fable is given, by CALIDASA, in the *Raghuvansa*: another of the cow BAHULA, whose expostulation with a tiger, pleading for her life, is referred to by *Mr.* COLEBROKE as an admired passage in the *Itahasas*, a collection of stories, supposed to be related by BHIMASENA while he lay wounded at the point of death. Images of her and of her calf are worshipped; and the extract from the *Itahasas* is read on a particular day, sacred to BAHULA, with great solemnity. —*Ib.* *Fig.* 2. PLATE 34. may, perhaps, be a rude image of this description.

In marriage ceremonies a cow is one of the actors.—"The hospitable rites are then concluded by letting loose a cow at the intercession of the guest: a barber, who attends for that purpose, exclaims, 'The cow! the cow!' Upon which the guest pronounces this text: 'Release the cow from the fetters of VARUNA. May she subdue my foe; may she destroy the enemies of both him (the host) and me. Dismiss the cow, that she may eat grass and drink water.' When the cow has been released, the guest thus addresses her: 'I have earnestly entreated this prudent person, saying, kill not the innocent harmless cow, who is mother of RUDRAS, daughter of VASUS, sister of ADITYAS, and the source of ambrosia,' &c. It is evident," continues *Mr.* COLEBROKE, "that the guest's intercessions imply a practice, now become obsolete, of slaying a cow for the purposes of hospitality."—*Ib.* p. 293.

The essay above referred to, by *Mr.* COLEBROKE, is very curious throughout; as, indeed, are all the papers of this learned gentleman, with which the *Asiatic Researches* are enriched.

A cow, the reader will perceive, is no unimportant mythological personage, nor is the bull: the latter has been spoken of, in another place, as the *Nandi* of MAHADEVA, and the symbol of divine justice. NANDINI has just been noticed as the cow of VASISHTHA the sage, or *Rishi*; and I have no doubt but these two names and persons, as they may be called, have relationship and connexion in the legendary fables of the *Puranas*.

In the *Ramayana* this all-yielding animal is called SHABALA, as well as NANDINI.—(P. p. 320. 322). The 41st section details an entertainment given by "VASHISHT'HA, chief of ascetics," to VISWAMITRA and his pupil RAMA. The royal sage and his whole army, "composed of plump well-fed men," were filled with whatever they desired, rained down from SHABALA. But VISWAMITRA, not contented with his entertainment, coveted also the donor; and after endeavouring in vain to purchase the cow, took her from VASHISHT'HA by violence: hence ensued curses and battles between these two sages and their adherents, as detailed at tiresome length in the 42d and following sections of the *Ramayana*. The cow produced many kings and armies in aid of her legal lord, and at length destroyed the forces of the covetous VISWAMITRA; who, as is usual in all cases of distress, betook himself to austerities, and was enabled by MAHADEVA to renew hostilities, which, after various revilings and reverses, terminate in the discomfiture and conversion of the greedy king, who was not of course a *Brahman*, as VASHISHT'HA was. The 43d section offers several priestly reflections on *Brahmanical* potencies, while the subsequent sections evince that these are all astronomical legends, strung together on wild fictions of mythological poetry.

The time is not, perhaps, very remote, when the original inhabitants of *Hindustan* had less abhorrence of killing kine than many sects now feel on that point. Ancient books prescribe the slaying of kine, as well as other animals. The extreme utility of the cow and bullock in well peopled and agricultural countries* will almost necessarily give rise to a repugnance at slaying them, which will in time grow to stronger prohibitory feelings, and at length be stamped with the sanction of holiness. Here we see, what we may in many cases suppose, that

* It is a curious fact, that the *Chinese* make no use of milk, either crude, nor in the shape of curds, butter, or cheese: the young animals are allowed the whole produce of their mothers; and the *Chinese* have of course no repugnance at killing cows, nor indeed to killing and eating any thing else. And I will just notice, though altogether irrelevant, that among the dainties of a *Chinese* market I have noticed horseflesh, dogs, cats, hawks, crows, owls, &c. offered as edibles: the small animals are sold alive, and by weight, as is fish generally. Nor is it very uncommon to see a *Chinese* pick the lice off his garments and eat them: this I saw but once; and on my silently beckoning one of the gentlemen of the *English* factory at *Canton* to come and behold so strange a thing, he assured me that it was not novel to him.

mythology and religion inculcate principles grounded originally on the conveniences or wants of mankind.

SURABHI,* the cow of plenty, was, as well as LAKSHMI, one of the *Chawda Ratna*, or *fourteen gems*, produced by the ocean when churned for the *Amrita*; and as these "two gems" seem to be strung together in a former quotation in this article, I will include in it some farther particulars of this important quadruped.

She is also called KAMA-DHOK, and KAMA-DENO, the granter of desires. Under the latter name, SONNERAT describes her as being white, having a woman's head, three tails, and giving suck to a little calf; but I never saw her so delineated. A cow suckling a calf is a very favourite subject of *Hindu* artists, in paint, ivory, brass, mortar, &c.: *fig.* 2. of PLATE 34. is so very rude as to be almost as much like elephants and young ones as cows and calves; but I suppose it to be intended for the latter. It is a cast in brass, about the size of the plate; and in my memoranda I find it noted, that this kind of thing is made to invoke a lucky calving-time: and that adoration is paid to this domestic idol called *Gaw-puja*, or cow-worship. Such images may, however, have some reference to SURABHI, and have adoration paid to them more extensive than a looked-for calf would excite; which, by the way, is a matter of moment to a family whose chief luxuries are lacteal.

Many writers have noticed the superstitious veneration that some sects of *Hindus* have for cows and calves: the custom, so universal in *India*, of using cow-dung for covering for floors and walls, can, however, scarcely be considered as a superstition; for it is used for floors by all sects, as well as *Hindus*, as the most cool and cleanly article. Once a week, perhaps, it is common to rub over earthern floors with fresh cow-dung, mixed up with as much water as will render it easy to spread: this is done, not only in tents and temporary houses of gentlemen, but sometimes over the best apartments of splendid habitations of *Europeans* as well as natives. The smell, which is not at first unpleasant, quickly goes off; and no floor is so cool and comfortable, nor so obnoxious to fleas and vermin. This pleasant and salutary article is falling into disuse with the *English*, who, in their habitations and habits, are departing more and more from the sober dictates of nature, and the obedient usages of the natives. We now, for instance, build lofty rooms, admitting insufferable glare and heat through long

* In the *Hitopadesa*, p. 110. the earth is called SURABHI; and the learned translator (WILKINS) notes the name to be not usually so applied, although the earth may well be called the cow of plenty.

glazed windows fronting the sun, reflected by marble or polished floors: domestic comfort is sacrificed to exterior decoration. No man of taste would now build a low sun-excluding viranda, nor mitigate the intensity of the heat by a cow-dung flooring. In *Bombay* the delectable light that, twenty or thirty years ago, was so commonly admitted through thin semi-transparent panes, composed of oyster-shells, is no longer known among the *English*, except in the church; and these, perhaps, will, when the present worthy clergyman shall vacate his cure, give way to the superior transparency of glass. The church will then be, like our new houses, insufferably hot; and the adaptation of *Pankhas*, monstrous fans, ten, twenty, thirty, or more, feet long, suspended from the ceiling of sitting-rooms, and moved to and fro by men outside by means of ropes and pullies, will be necessary. These *Pankhas*, it must be admitted, are articles of great luxury in warm weather: the idea is taken from the natives. I have mythological pictures where persons are seated under them. In *Calcutta* they are articles also of elegance and expense; some of them being curiously painted, and so shaped or scooped as to admit their vibratory motion without deranging the economy of the chandeliers suspended in the same line with the *Pankha*, and when at rest occupying the space scooped out.

But to return to the *Hindus*. Cow-dung is plastered over the cooking-place before the meal of a person of a high class be cooked: in camps, or on journies, a space of ten or twelve square feet is so purified, and is easily polluted by the approach of impure persons or things; in which vexatious case the food becomes unholy. The ashes of cow-dung are also of a very purifying nature; and *Hindus*, of almost all ranks and degrees, men and women, occasionally, or frequently, use them, mixed sometimes with other ingredients, to mark their foreheads, necks, arms, &c. Sometimes men, especially holy beggars or penitents, or those having some claims to sanctity, are rubbed all over with these ashen mixtures, and make a curious sky-blue appearance. MAHADEVA is frequently painted blue, or rather of an ashey colour, and the gentry just noticed perhaps imitate that deity; or KRISHNA, also a deity of a blue or black hue.

Cow-dung is a great purifier on several occasions. It is related in the *Agni Purana*, that a most wicked person, named CHANYACA, had exceeded every known possibility of salvation. At the court of INDRA were assembled gods and holy men; and as they were discoursing on such enormities, INDRA, in answer to a pointed question, said, that nothing certainly could expiate them except the *Carshagni*. It happened that a crow, named, from her friendly disposition, MITRA-CACA, was present, and immediately flew and imparted the welcome news to the despairing sinner, who immediately performed the *Carshagni*, and went to heaven. This expiation consists in the victim covering his whole body with a thick coat of cow-dung, which, when dry, is set on fire, and consumes both sin and sinner. Until revealed by the crow, this potent expiation was unknown; and it has since been occasionally resorted to, particularly by the famous SANCHARA-CHARYA. The friendly crow was punished for her indiscretion; and was forbidden and all her tribe to ascend to heaven, and were doomed on earth to live on carrion.*—See WILFORD. *As. Res.* Vol. IX. page 98.

But the greatest, or, at any rate, the most convenient, of all purifiers is the urine of a cow: the catholic devil himself cannot, as the proverb runs, hate holy water more than the *Hindu* spirits of impurity abhor this sin-expelling sanctifying liquid. Images are sprinkled with it: no man of any pretensions to piety or cleanliness would pass a cow in the act of staling without receiving the holy stream in his palm, sipping a few drops; and, with his bedewed fingers, marking and crossing his forehead, shoulders, and breasts, in the same manner as papists do, and as I, though no papist, have in their countries often done, with the pure contents of the holy water vessel, on entering a temple. I never had, however, sufficient curiosity to use the *Hindu* holy water after their manner.

To strangers it is diverting enough to witness this spiritual sip; and it may be seen at the *Bazaar* gate, in *Bombay*, almost any morning at sunrise: cows and buffaloes are daily brought, and people resort, thither, for milk. The buffalo is, however, in all points, held in far less estimation by *Hindus* than the cow; and the ingredient in question is by no means equally revered when proceeding from the buffalo. If the animal be retentive, a pious expectant will impatiently apply his finger, and by judicious tickling excite the grateful flow; if heedless, however, he may perhaps, by super excitation, receive a greater boon than the "descendant of SURABHI" was implored to yield. I shall not readily forget a contingency of this description, that was witnessed also by a group of happy sailors returning at early day, by the *Bazaar* gate, from *Dungaree*,† to their ship. Their eager but silent curiosity, while contemplating the ridiculous posture and

* The crow is reckoned a bird of ill omen in *India*; still *Malabar* females are sometimes named KAKA, the name in that dialect, as well as in *Sanskrit*, for the crow. The females of *Malabar* are, I think, more than others, called after animals: *Mani*, the alligator, is a name among them.

† A very populous village, adjoining the esplanade of *Bombay* fort. The proper name is perhaps *Dundgiri*: *dund*, or *dun*, or *dunger*, is, in several dialects, derived from the *Sanskrit*—a hill, or mountain; as it was also in some of the old languages of *Europe*.

countenance of the patient animal, looking backwards at the pious *Bania*, who, with serious air, had removed her tail, and, " with well-curved palm," was tickling under it—all expectancy: this, I say, was ludicrous enough. But their extatic vociferation, when the *lucky* banker gaped, while he hastily shook out the unlooked-for handful, is not to be conceived or described: their bursts were so excessive that they must have been well nigh in the same state of excitement, though differently caused, with poor " SURABHI, the boon-granter," before they became sufficiently collected to crack their jokes on the grinning thankless object of her bounty. I must drop the curtain, remarking, however, that it was a scene *bien comique*—the most so I ever beheld: had HOGARTH felt it, the cow would be immortalized beyond the bounds of *Hindustan*.

Images and pictures of LAKSHMI, both in her own person, and in her various forms or *Avataras*, are very common. PLATES 6. to 12. inclusive, contain some representations of her; in PLATE 23. she is seen with her lord: all of which subjects have been described in former pages. She will appear again frequently, in her *Avataras*, as SITA, spouse of RAMA, and in other characters.

PARVATI.

Of the many names of the goddess that we are about to introduce more particularly, those of Parvati, Bhavani, Durga, Kali, and Devi, or the *Goddess*, are the most common: they are, indeed, used almost indiscriminately in this work, as well as in the writings and conversation of the *Hindus*.

Although, in the present age, human sacrifices are perhaps no longer made, there can be no doubt of the existence of the practice formerly. To Bhavani, in her character of Kali, it would appear they were chiefly offered; and no religious rite can be more minutely ordained and detailed than this is in the *Calica Purana*: the sanguinary chapter of which has been translated by *Mr.* Blaquiere, and given in the fifth volume of the *Asiatic Researches*, Art. XXIII.—As well as the ceremonies, the implements, prayers, &c. used on these horrid occasions, are minutely described and recited. I shall make some extracts from this article, premising that Siva is supposed to address his sons, the Bhairavas, initiating them in these terrible mysteries.

"The flesh of the antelope and the rhinoceros give my beloved" (i. e. the goddess Kali,) "delight for five hundred years.

"By a human sacrifice, attended by the forms laid down, Devi is pleased one thousand years; and by a sacrifice of three men, one hundred thousand years. By human flesh Camachya, Chandica, and Bhairava who assumes my shape, are pleased one thousand years. An oblation of blood, which has been rendered pure by holy texts, is equal to ambrosia: the head and flesh also afford much delight to the goddess Chandica.

"Blood drawn from the offerer's own body is looked upon as a proper oblation to the goddess Chandica.

"Let the sacrificer repeat the word Kali twice, then the words Devi-Bajreswari, then *Lawba Dandayai, Namah!* which words may be rendered—*Hail,* Kali! Kali! *hail,* Devi! goddess of thunder; *hail, iron-sceptred* goddess! Let him then take the axe in his hand, and again invoke the same by the *Calratriya* text as follows.—

"Let the sacrificer say *Hrang, Hring!* KALI, KALI! O horrid-toothed goddess! eat, cut, destroy all the malignant—cut with this axe; bind, bind; seize, seize; drink blood; *spheng, spheng!* secure, secure. Salutation to KALI.—Thus ends the *Calratriya Mantra*.

"The *Charga* (the axe) being invoked by this text, called the *Calratriya Mantra*, CALRATRI (the goddess of darkness) herself presides over the axe, uplifted, for the destruction of the sacrificer's enemies."

Different *Mantras* are used, in reference to the description of the victim to be immolated: if a lion, this—

"O HERI! who, in the shape of a lion, bearest CHANDICA, bear my evils, and avert my misfortunes. Thy shape, O lion! was assumed by HERI to punish the wicked part of the human race;* and under that form, by truth, the tyrant HIRANYA-CASIPU was destroyed."

Females are not to be immolated, except on very particular occasions: the human female never.

"Let princes, ministers of state, counsellors, and venders of spirituous liquors, make human sacrifices, for the purpose of attaining prosperity and wealth."

"Let the victim offered to DEVI, if a buffalo, be five years old; and if human, twenty-five."

The following is the *Cawsici Mantra*, to be uttered at a particular part of the ceremony.

"Hail, CAWSICI! three-eyed goddess, of most terrifying appearance, around whose neck a string of human skulls is pendent; who art the destroyer of evil spirits; who art armed with an axe, the foot of a bed,† and a spear—*Rhing* CAWSICI! Salutation to thee with this blood."

An enemy may be immolated by proxy, substituting a buffalo or a goat, and calling the victim by the name of the enemy through the whole ceremony, thereby "infusing, by holy texts, the soul of the enemy into the body of the victim: which will, when immolated, deprive the foe of life also." On this occasion—

"Let the sacrificer say, O goddess, of horrid form! O CHANDICA! eat,

* Alluding to the *Narasingavatara*: the former part of this verse seems to indicate that the lion, on which BHAVANI sometimes rides, is VISHNU in that form.

† This is a curious piece of armour; and, if there be no ambiguity, or error, in the translation, has doubtless a legend accounting for it. In one character (PLATE 40. *fig.* 1.) DEVI is called PALYANGHA BHAVANI: *Palang*, in common language, is a litter; hence, perhaps, *Palki*, or, as we call it, palankeen.

devour, such a one, my enemy. O consort of Fire! salutation to fire. This is the enemy who has done me mischief, now personated by an animal—destroy him, O MAHAMARI! *spheng*, *spheng!* eat, devour!"

A great variety of regulations and invocations, rites, &c. are minutely laid down, in this curious article, for the performance of sanguinary offerings; whether the immolation of a victim, or an offering of the sacrificer's own blood, or burning his flesh, &c. &c.

Let the reader picture to himself these wild declamations, accompanied by the potencies of scenic delusions; representing this "goddess of horrid form," as in PLATES 27. 28. for instance, of gigantic proportions, smeared with blood, among the ravings of bedlamites and the outrageous clangour of discordant instruments; and imagine what an effect it must have on the timid minds of the trembling affrighted multitude, and what a hold such a religion must have on the sensibilities of its votaries.

Although it must appear evident, that human sacrifices were formerly legal, they are still most pointedly prohibited in very ancient books: such prohibition is, indeed, a farther proof of the existence of the practice. In the *Brahma-Purana* every *neramedha*, or *man-sacrifice*, is expressly forbidden; and, in the fifth book of the *Bhagavat*, Sir WILLIAM JONES has pointed out the following emphatical words.—"Whatever men in this world sacrifice human victims, and whatever women eat the flesh of male cattle, those men and those women shall the animals here slain torment in the mansions of YAMA; and, like slaughtering giants, having cleaved their limbs with axes, shall quaff their blood." See, for comments on this passage by the learned translator, *As. Res.* Vol. III. p. 260.

Considering KALI, PARVATI, BHAVANI, and DEVI, as names of the same goddess (or *Sacti*, or personization of an energy) in different characters, I sometimes use the names indiscriminately; and it may be not always accurately: for instance, were I to give the name of MAHADEVA KALI, or MAHADEVA BHAVANI, or MAHADEVA DURGA, to the subject of the principal figures of PLATE 16. or to PLATES 17. 18. instead of MAHADEVA PARVATI, or SIV-PARVATI, a *Brahman* would correct it: the latter name, PARVATI, is that borne by the goddess as the immediate companion or associate of her divine partner. Were she, when seen in the act of transfixing the demon MAHESHASUR, (PLATES 34. 35.) to be called PARVATI, or BHAVANI, or perhaps any name but DURGA, or DEVI, it would not be appropriate; and, of these two names, DURGA is the most correct. Again, neither of these epithets are usually applied to her as seen in PLATES 28. 29. where she is KALI, the *Sacti*, or active energy of all-renewing Time.

MA is a name of BHAVANI as a personification of nature: so it was among the *Greeks*, who represented her, as the goddess is represented in *India*, in a car drawn by lions, holding a drum, and having a towered coronet on her head.—I have several pictures of DEVI answering to this description. Under her name of BHAVANI she is said to designate the general power of fecundity.

Among the *Greeks* and *Romans* DIANA was invoked, under the name of LUCINA, as the goddess presiding over childbirth: so, with the *Hindus*, BHAVANI, being the *Sacti* of the power of reproduction, is invoked, with an appropriate burnt-offering of certain perfumes, by women in labour. On this occasion she is named IDITA, or ILITA: RUDRA, her lord, is the deity of pregnant women. ILYTHIA is a title of LUCINA, or of DIANA in that character.—See BELL's *Pantheon*.

IDITA and ILITA, in *Sanskrit*, are words implying praise, and applied to the goddess because she is *praised* by women invoking her assistance; and was invoked and praised by the assembled gods, imploring her aid on an occasion of difficult parturition. As the story comprises other points of mythology, to which I may have occasion to advert in other places, I shall give it, on the authority of *Mr.* WILFORD, and nearly in his words.

VISHNU had two warders of his ethereal palace, who carried the pride of office to such a length that they insulted the seven *Maharshis*, who had come, with SANACA at their head, to present their adorations. The offended *Rishis* pronounced an imprecation on the insolent warders, condemning them to be *adhoyoni*, or *born below*, thrice in mortal forms, before they could be readmitted into the divine presence. In consequence of this imprecation they appeared in their first birth as HIRANYACASHA, or *golden-eyed*, and HIRANYA-CASIPU, or *clad in gold*;* secondly, as RAVANA and KUMBHACARNA; and lastly, as KANSA and SISUPALA.

In their first appearance they were the twin sons of KASYAPA and DITI. Before their birth the body of their mother blazed like the sun, and the *Devatas*, unable to bear its excessive heat and light, retired to the banks of the *Cali*, resolving to lie concealed until she was delivered; but the time of her gestation was so long, and her labour so difficult, that they remained a thousand years near the holy river, employed in acts of devotion. At length DEVI appeared, and assisted DITI; and the twin *Daityas* were born. She then assured mankind, that whatever woman should, in a similar situation, fervently implore her, should

* In another place the name of HIRANYA-CASIPU, the blaspheming giant, (who, denying his omnipresence, VISHNU, became incarnate as NARSINGA, to destroy,) is translated, "*with a golden axe.*"

have immediate relief; and she is accordingly invoked under the name of ILITA DEVI. See *As. Res.* Vol. III. p. 393.

Fra PAOLINO says, that "SHIVA and PARVADI produced GANESHA, KARTIGUNA, or SCANDA, HANUMAN, and BHAGAVADI," page 332; and, in page 87, says "the BHAGAVADI is a gold coin, with the figure of that goddess, called by the *Europeans*, very improperly, *Pagodi*, or *Pagoda*." This is a derivation of that name which I never before saw; nor do I find such a goddess as the offspring of SIVA and PARVATI.

To BHAGAVADI, he says, page 221, the house-cock is dedicated, and presented at the door of her temple as an offering. In the time of infectious diseases, which the *Indians* ascribe to this goddess, their priests and fortune-tellers sometimes slaughter a cock, and mutter over certain forms of prayer: such, for example, as "O'M *badracali nama!*" that is, "Adoration to thee, O goddess! thou who art black and good." Other prayers he translates: "Thou offended angry deity:" "O woman! with the five visages:" "O goddess! who art formed like a wild swine."

Hence it is pretty clear, that BHAGAVADI, supposed by the worthy priest to be the daughter of SIVA and PARVATI, is the goddess herself under the name of BADRACALI, by which she is known, in a particular character, in most parts of *India*: in *Malabar* she appears to be called BHAGAVADI. I never saw her, however, with five visages; but as her lord has, when he is called PANCHA-MUKI-PARAMESWARA, (see PLATES 15. 16. 19.) she may, as his double, be also styled PANCHA-MUKI, or five faced. Neither have I ever seen her described as a wild swine.

I have attended ceremonies and sacrifices in *Malabar*, where a cock was the victim immolated. Women at certain periods, but whether monthly, or after delivery, or miscarriage, I do not recollect, are purified by such a procedure. Young *Malabar* females, especially of the *Tiya* (or *Teah*) sect, who are called *Teahti*, or *Tiviti*, have visitations of the devil, as they term it, and are not to be cleansed but by public exorcism. I have been invited to this process, which, in common language, was termed "beating the devil out;" but it is many years ago—when I was very young, and attended but little to mythology: what remains in my recollection is, that the ceremonies were long, tiresome, and clamorous from drums, trumpets, and shouting. The possessed girl sat quietly, perhaps several hours, with dishevelled hair, surrounded by her relations, supporting in both palms a pan (or *patra*), said to contain blood. At length, exhausted by fatigue, or roused into *hysteria* by the noise and tumult, she went into a fit, when a cock's head was cut off close by her. The struggles of the evil spirit in resisting the exorcism are supposed to cause the convulsive agonies of the possessed, in the excess of which it passes into the cock, and is dismissed by his decapitation. These matters are always performed in the night, and are attended with considerable expense for priests, music, &c.

It was once my misfortune to live in *Bombay*, in the immediate neighbourhood of an exorciser, who planted himself near my garden-wall; and by the horrid yells and music, the necessary accompaniments of his craft, so disturbed my repose, that, failing by remonstrance and threats, I was forced to apply to the police for its restoration and security. This man must, from the number of his patients, have been of some note, or the possessed numerous; for every full moon he was occupied the whole night. I believe women are mostly, if not exclusively, possessed; but I did not, lest my appearance should seem to sanction the annoyance, attend, to observe my noisy neighbour's exorcisms.

SIVA, as the consort of KALI, is KAL, or KALA; sometimes, however, we see KAL as a distinct personage, and the devourer of SIVA, as well as of BRAHMA and VISHNU. PLATE 10.* is of KAL, or Time; and in *Colonel* STUART's picture he is black, as I have always seen him represented: the word, indeed, in *Sanskrit*, implies blackness, darkness, and ideas connected with it: MAHADEVA, or SIVA, as the spouse immediately of PARVATI, is, as hath been noticed, painted white. *Mr.* PATERSON, *As. Res.* Vol. VIII. page 56, says, that KAL is painted white. "The contemplation," he says, "of the distinctions of day and night; of the light and dark divisions of the month; of the six months night, and six months day, of the gods, (occasioned by the obliquity of the sun's path); and lastly, the contrast of the visible creation with eternal night, suggested the idea of painting KAL white, and KALI black.

"MAHA KALI, black and dreadful, is encompassed by symbols of destruction: two of her hands seem employed in the work of death; of the other two, one appears pointing downwards, alluding to the universal havoc which surrounds her, while the other, pointing upwards, seems to promise the regeneration of nature by a new creation.

"MAHA KALI is represented without a crescent, (the artificial measure of

* On a late inspection of the original of PLATE 10. I find occasion to add, that round the black neck of KAL the beads are white and green: round his arms white. It is not clear, whether he holds a roll of paper or a cup; it is of gold: his sword is silver; his eye red. SIVA is white; VISHNU blue; BRAHMA red: the latter holds a staff, the *Veda*, and a vase; his beards are white. SIVA and VISHNU have golden glories: BRAHMA has none.

of time,) because it is unnecessary to her character as the hieroglyphic of eternity; but the belief of the *Hindus* in successive destruction and renovations of the universe accounts for her wearing a *Mund Mala*, or necklace of skulls, as emblems of those revolutions."—PATERSON. *Ib.*

When KAL, or TIME, shall have devoured all things, the three personified powers will likewise cease to exist; and KAL, devouring himself, will then also cease to be. Descending into such depths of abstract metaphysics, some confusion of ideas and persons must arise; but this does not deter the *Hindu* from endless personizations.

In a former passage, as well as in PLATE 10. of *Maha Pralaya*, or the grand consummation of all things, we see all creation falling, and BRAHMA, VISHNU, and SIVA, about to fall into the "jaws of inexistence." One would have imagined that INEXISTENCE might have remained unpersonified: here, however, we see it embodied. The poet, at a loss for words to express so recondite a conception, has necessarily recourse to metaphor for illustration: the painter, at no loss, pursues the allegory, and fills up the ideal outline of the poet.

Sir W. JONES has addressed hymns to DURGA and BHAVANI, two names of PRAKRITI, or created nature, (*As. Mis.* and Works, Vol. XIII.); and the argument prefixed is replete with mythologic lore. ISWARA, or ISA, and ISANI, or ISI, are, he says, unquestionably, the OSIRIS and ISIS of *Egypt*. ISWARA, SIVA, or HARA, (for these are his names among nearly a thousand more,) united with ISI, represent the *secondary causes*, whatever they may be, of natural phenomena; and principally those of temporary *destruction* and *regeneration*. But the *Indian* ISIS, in her many characters, appears in those of PARVATI, KALI, DURGA, and BHAVANI, which bear a strong resemblance to the JUNO of HOMER, to HECATE, to the armed PALLAS, and to the *Lucretian* VENUS.

The name PARVATI took its rise from a wild poetical fiction. *Himalaya*, or the mansion of snow, is the name of the vast chain of mountains that limit *India* to the north, and embraces it with its eastern and western arms, both extending to the ocean: one named *Chandra-sechara*, or the moon's rock; and the other, which reaches westward to the mouths of the *Indus*, was called by the ancients *Montes Parveti*. The mountain *Himalaya*, being personified, is represented as a powerful monarch, whose wife was MENA: their daughter is named PARVATI, or mountain-born, and DURGA, or of difficult access. She is said to have been married to SIVA in a pre-existing state, when she was named SATI; but we are informed by this illustrious author, in another place, (*As. Res.* Vol. VI. p. 144.) that she bore no children till she became regenerate in the person of PARVATI.

The daughter of *Himalaya* had two sons: GANESA, the wisest of deities, always invoked at the beginning of every literary work; and CARTICEYA, commander of the celestial armies.

The following is the last stanza of the hymn.—See PLATES 34. 35.

"O DURGA! thou hast deign'd to shield
Man's feeble virtue with celestial might,
Gliding from yon jasper field;
And, on a lion borne, has brav'd the fight:
For when the demon Vice thy realms defy'd,
And arm'd with death each arched horn,
Thy golden lance, O goddess! mountain-born,
Touch'd but the pest—he roar'd, and died!"

The last stanza refers to a transfiguration of BHAVANI, very commonly met with in pictures and casts. Among mine I have, besides those given in this work,* upwards of a dozen different casts of it in metal, in which the goddess has from two to thirty-two arms, filled with a variety of weapons. I have also several pictures of this subject: they generally agree in the time, which is the moment when the armed monster issues from the neck of the buffalo, whence the head is just severed by the sword of the goddess; who, planting her foot on its body, is transfixing the monster with her golden lance.

In the first volume of the *As. Res.* is an inscription, found in a cave near *Gya*, in *Bengal*, of which a translation is given by *Mr.* WILKINS: the first lines are thus rendered—

"When the foot of the goddess was, with its tinkling ornaments, planted upon the head of MAHISHASUR, all the blossoms of the new-blown flower of the fountain were dispersed with disgrace by its superior beauty. May that foot, radiant with a fringe of refulgent beams issuing from its pure bright nails, endue you with a steady and an unexampled devotion, offered up with fruits, and shew you the way to dignity and wealth."

In *Mr.* WILKINS's introductory letter is the following passage, describing the combat between the monster and DURGA, as well as the birth or origin of that form of the goddess.

"The first lines of the first verse allude to the story of BHAVANI's killing the evil spirit MAHISHASUR, who, in the disguise of a buffalo, as the name imports, had fought with INDRA and his celestial bands for a hundred years, defeated him, and usurped his throne: the story is to be found at length in a

* And they, each differing from the other, are numerous: viz. PLATES 33. 34. 35. 37. (*fig.* 2.) 101. (*fig.* 8.)

little book called *Chandi.* The vanquished spirits, being banished the heavens, and doomed to wander the earth, after a while assemble, and resolve to lay their grievances before VISHNU and SIVA. Conducted by BRAHMA, they repaired into the presence of those deities, who heard their complaint with compassion; and their anger was so violent against MAHISHASUR, that a kind of flame issued from their mouths, and from the mouths of the rest of the principal gods: of which was formed a goddess, of inexpressible beauty, with ten arms, and each hand holding a different weapon. This was a transfiguration of BHAVANI, the consort of SIVA: under which she is generally called DURGA. She is sent against the usurper: she mounts her lion, the gift of the mountain *Himalaya,* (snowy,) and attacks the monster, who shifts his form repeatedly; till at length the goddess *planteth her foot upon his head,* and cuts it off with a single stroke of her sword. Immediately the upper part of a human body issues through the neck of the headless buffalo, and aims a stroke, which being warded off by the lion with his right paw, DURGA puts an end to the combat by piercing him through the heart with a spear."

The book, whence the preceding passage and story are taken, must indeed be a most valuable deposit of mythological wealth. *Sir* W. JONES (*As. Res.* Vol. III. p. 14.) says, that "the learned works of SELDEN and JABLONSKI, on the gods of *Syria* and *Egypt,* would derive more illustration from the little *Sanskrit* book entitled *Chandi* than from all the fragments of oriental mythology that are dispersed in the whole compass of *Grecian, Roman,* and *Hebrew,* literature." If published with notes, in the style of the *Gita* or *Hitopadesa,* it must greatly extend our information on the copious subject it embraces. The work is, I know, in England, and in the best hands; but they are unluckily too much occupied in larger, and perhaps more important, but less interesting, works.

PARVATI, we find, means *mountain-born*; DURGA, *of difficult access.* The former word, in the *Mahrata* countries pronounced *Parbat,* or *Parvat,* is used as a name for hills: one near *Poona,* commonly called *Parbati,* on which is a temple of the goddess, is spoken of in another part of this work. In the other name of DURGA we trace the origin of the names of hill-forts, in *Mysore,* and other countries of the *Dekkan*: such as *Chitteldroog, Rai Droog, Doori Droog,* &c. In the *Tamal* dialects this termination is, as is usual with them, changed into *Durgam,* as I had occasion to explain at large in my NARRATIVE; wherein I also pointed out the proper mode of spelling and pronouncing the names of hill-forts terminating in *Droog,* or *Durga.*

The following texts from MENU are conclusive on this point.—

Ch. VII. v. 71.—"With all possible care let a king secure a fortress of mountains; for it has many transcendent properties."

"73. As enemies hurt them * not in the shelter of their several abodes, thus foes hurt not a king who has taken refuge in his *durga*; or (says the gloss of CULLUCA) '*place of difficult access.*'"

"The attributes of DURGA, or *difficult of access*, are conspicuous in the festival called by her name, *Durgotsava*; and in this character she resembles MINERVA—not the peaceful inventress of the fine and useful arts, but PALLAS, armed with a helmet and spear: both represent heroic *virtue*, or valour united with wisdom. Both slew demons and giants with their own hands; and both protected the wise and virtuous, who paid them due adoration."—JONES. *As. Res.* Vol. I. p. 252.

In her multiplicity of names, a distinction by which the consort of MAHADEVA is more eminently marked than any other goddess, she is found to resemble the ISIS *Myrionimos*. Many of her names occur incidentally in our pages; and, without attempting any thing like a complete list, the following appellations may be noted as her's.

HARI, the feminine, as the consort of HARA: in like manner sometimes SIVA, which is considered the feminine of SIV, as her lord is called. SRI, and PEDMADEVI; the latter meaning the lotos goddess, or the goddess in the lotos, she shares with LAKSHMI. ANTARGATI is an epithet under which she is invoked as the goddess of victory, referring to her possession of the breast or heart; thereby giving strength and courage. KATYAYANI, KIRTI, MAHAMAYI, SHASHTI, GHIRJA, UMA, are other names of DEVI: GAWRI is another, meaning fair or young; as does SUDURGA. HAR-GAWRI, like SIV-PARVATI, is a title given to the joined deities represented in PLATES 7. and 24.

"As the mountain-born goddess, or PARVATI, she has many properties of the *Olympian* JUNO: her majestic deportment, high spirit, and general attributes, are the same; and we find her on mount *Cailasa*, and at the banquets of the deities, uniformly the companion of her husband."—JONES. *As. Res.* Vol. I. p. 251.—See PLATES 17. 18.

The river *Kali*, or *Nile*, in *Egypt*, is said, by *Mr.* WILFORD, to have derived its name from MAHAKALI; who is stated, in the *Puranas*, to have made her first appearance on its banks in the character of RAJARAJESWARI: called also ISANI, or ISI; and in the character of SATI she was transformed into the river itself.

* Speaking of wild beasts, vermin, &c. inhabitants of different places.

The word *Cala*, or *Kala*, signifying *black*, means also, from its root, *Kal*, *devouring*: whence it is applied to Time, and, in both senses in the feminine, to the goddess in her destructive capacity. In her character of MAHACALI she has many other epithets, all implying different shades of *black* or *dark azure*: viz. CALI, or CALA, NILA, ASITA, SHYAMA, or SHYAMALA, MEKARA, ANJANABHA, KRISHNA. The same river is also called *Nahushi*, from the celebrated warrior and conqueror DEVA NAHUSHA; called, in the spoken dialects, DEONAUSH, the DIONYSIUS, probably, of the ancient *Europeans*. See *As. Res.* Vol. III. p. 304.

ASHTARA-DEVI: hence the ASHTAROTH of the *Hebrews*; and the *Astara*, or *Sittara*, of the *Persians*, is a name derived from spikes or points.—See a legend accounting for it, *ib.* p. 390.

AMBA, or UMA, the consort of BHAVA, the author of existence: ARANYA-DEVI, or goddess of the forest.—*Ib.* p. 388. PRABHA, meaning light: ASWINI, a mare, the first of the lunar mansions; assuming this name and shape, the Sun approached her in the form of a horse, and, on their nostrils touching, she instantly conceived the twins; who are called ASWINI-KUMARI, the two sons of ASWINI.—*Ib.* p. 391. SATWA-DEVI refers to her as the author, or the consort of the author, of existence: PRACRITI, that from whence all things were made —Nature personified: SARVA-MANGALA, presiding over the welfare of all nature.

This catalogue might be greatly extended; but the reader will probably deem it long enough.

In the character of BHANANI *Sir* WILLIAM JONES (*As. Res.* Vol. I. p. 254.) supposes the wife of MAHADEVA to be, as well the JUNO *Cinxia*, or LUCINA of the *Romans*, (called also by them DIANA *Solvizona*, and by the *Greeks*, ILLITHYIA,) as VENUS herself: not the *Italian* queen of laughter and jollity, who, with her nymphs and graces, was the beautiful child of poetical imagination, and answers to the *Indian* REMBHA, with her train of *Apsaras*, or damsels of Paradise; but VENUS *Urania*, so luxuriously painted by LUCRETIUS, and so properly invoked by him at the opening of a poem on Nature.—"VENUS presiding over *generation*, and on that account exhibited sometimes of both sexes (an union very common in the *Indian* sculptures), as in her bearded statue at *Rome*; and, perhaps, in the images called *Herma-thena*, and in those figures of her which had a conical form: 'for the reason of which figure we are left' (says TACITUS) 'in the dark.' The reason," continues our author, "appears too clearly in the temples and paintings of *Hindustan*, where it never seems to have entered the heads of the legislators, or people, that any thing natural could be offensively obscene; a singularity which pervades all their writings and conversation, but is no proof of depravity in their morals."

In a former work I had occasion to quote part of the preceding passage, and, apprehending no evil, took the opportunity of introducing some remarks on the subjects it embraces; but received in consequence so rude, and I may say unmerited, a castigation from some critics of that, and, for ought I know, of the present, day, as, in this place, may well deter me from a similar indulgence of such propensity, if it still exist.

The author, continuing the subject, identifies the *Stygian*, or the *Tauric*, DIANA, otherwise named HECATE; and often confounded with PROSERPINE, with KALI, or the wife of SIVA, in his character of the *Stygian* JOVE. Human victims, as well as the sacrifice of horses and bulls, enjoined by the *Vedas*, being in the present age absolutely prohibited, kids are now offered to this black goddess; and, to palliate the cruelty of the slaughter, which gave such offence to BUDHA, the *Brahmans* inculcate a belief that the poor victims rise in the heaven of INDRA, and become the musicians of his band.—*Ib.*

The feasts, fasts, and ceremonies, of various sorts, observed in honour of this deity, under her different names and characters, are very numerous.

The bright half of the month *Aswina*, the first of the *Hindu* lunar year, seems peculiarly devoted to DURGA. The first nine nights, called *Navaratricam*, are, with appropriate names, allotted to her decoration: the fifth is for the preparation of her dress: on the sixth she is awakened: on the seventh she is invited to a bower formed of the leaves of nine plants, of which the *Bilwa** is the chief. The seventh, eighth, and ninth, are the great days: on the last of which the victims immolated to her honour must be slain, as particularly directed in the *Calica Purana.*—"The sacrificed beasts must be killed by one blow, with a broad sword or sharp axe." The next day the goddess is reverently dismissed, and her image is cast into the river, which finishes the festival called *Durgotsava* and *Dasera*. On the fifteenth day, that of the full moon, her devotees pass the night in sports and merriment, and games of various sorts: it is unlucky to sleep; for on this night the fiend NICUMBHA led his army against DURGA, and LAKSHMI descended, promising wealth to those who were awake. On this night CUVERA and INDRA are also worshipped.

The festival of *Durgotsava*, and that of *Huli*, Sir W. JONES decided to relate to the autumnal and vernal equinoxes; and the sleep and rise of VISHNU to the

* *Bilwa*, or *Bilva*: the *Crateva Marmelos* of LINNÆUS.

solstices, (*As. Res.* Vol. III. Art. XII. p. 258.); but *Mr.* COLEBROKE (*Ib.* Vol. VIII. p. 87.) thinks, that the *Huli* had not in its origin any connexion with the vernal equinox, or with the close of the year, but with the close of winter, and the beginning of *Vasanta*, or the *Indian* spring.

The *Huli*, among the *Hindus*, reminds one strongly of the *Saturnalia* with the *Romans*: people of low condition take liberties with their superiors in a manner not admissible on other occasions. The chief fun in public is throwing coloured powders on the clothes of persons passing in the streets, and squirting about tinted waters. Dignified personages avoid, as much as they can, appearing abroad while these jocularities are passing, unless with the view of gaining popularity they condescend to partake in them: in general they confine themselves to their houses, and sport with their women. I have several pictures, belonging to series illustrating the domestic occupations of the *Indians*, in which the diversions of the *Huli* appear like those more publicly exhibited: scattering yellow and red powders, and squirting coloured water. Sending simpletons on idle errands contributes also to the delights of the *Huli*: this is performed exactly similar to our ceremony of making April-fools on the first of that month, and is common to all ranks of *Hindus*; and *Mahomedans*, indeed, join in this, as well as in other items of *Huli* fun and humour. Another opportunity of merriment, similar to our May-day gambols, is afforded to the *Hindus* in a festival in honour of BHAVANI, that always falls on, or near, that day. The *Huli* seems a festival in honour more especially of KRISHNA.

It has been noticed (in page 30), that one of BHAVANI's numerous forms is that of ANNA-PURNA DEVI, meaning the goddess who fills with food. She is a very common household deity, most families in the *Mahrata* country, and other parts on the western side of *India*, including her among their *Dii Penates*: in shortness her name is generally pronounced ANPURNA.

Among my images I have ten of her single, and several others in groupes, or *ganas*. PLATE 9. contains a representation of four, with but little variation, either in character, attributes, or position: they are two-handed—indeed I have but one with four arms, which, in addition to the ladle that all her images bear, hold the *Kardgha*, or sacrificial sword, and the *Dahl*, or shield.

Several of my images are less than an inch, and no one more than three inches in height; nor are any of them at all well executed: some have the appearance of having been buried.

Fig. 4. of PLATE 9. is from a subject in bronze, or zinc, or some dark metal, two inches high: her ladle is empty. *Fig.* 5. is of brass, less than two inches high, and is, I think, the neatest of my casts of this deity: her ladle is here heaped up, looking, indeed, more like a fruit, or some other roundish article, than a heap of rice: some images have four or five round balls *(pinda)* of rice. *Fig.* 6. and 7. are also of brass, with empty ladles: the former sits on something peculiar, but I know not what. Two of these images (5. and 7.) have the mark on their foreheads that forms of BHAVANI usually have: not unlike, in this plate, the mark that VISHNU is distinguished by. All the rest of my images of ANNA PURNA either have no mark, or it has been obliterated by time.

It cannot be doubted that the ANNA PERENNA of the *Romans* was the same deity: several authorities are adduced in proof, by *Mr.* PATERSON and *Mr.* COLEBROKE, in the eighth volume of the *As. Res.* p. p. 69. 85. The crescent on her forehead is mentioned as a characteristic mark of ANNA PURNA, as well as of DIANA; but I never saw her so distinguished. She is, *Mr.* PATERSON says, represented sitting on a throne, giving food with a golden ladle to an infant SIVA, who stretches out his little hand to receive it; strikingly resembling AMALTHEA nursing the infant JUPITER: none of my images are so employed. In PLATE 83. *fig.* 5. is represented a *Gana*, or company of deities, comprising GANESA, lord of *Ganas*, with the *Linga* and *Nandi* of SIVA before him; on his right PARVATI and BALKRISHNA; on his left ANNA PURNA and *Naga*: it is taken from a modern cast in brass, to which *Brahmanis* offer daily adoration. The goddess, now under our notice, is sitting, as usual, with her ladle in her two hands, as she is in several other similar *Ganas* in my possession. In a congress of this sort it is, perhaps, that she is seen employed in the act noticed by *Mr.* PATERSON, who farther describes her in the following terms, from the *Anada cripa*.

"She is of a ruddy complexion; her robe of various dyes; a crescent on her forehead; she is bent by the weight of her full breasts. BHAVA, or SIVA, (as a child) is playing before her, with a crescent on his forehead; she looks at him with pleasure, and, seated on a throne, relieves his hunger—all good is united in her: her names are ANNADA, ANNA-PURNA DEVI, BHAVANI, and BHAGAVATI."

Mr. COLEBROKE informs us, that this beneficent form of BHAVANI is described, and her worship inculcated, in the *Tantras*, but not, he thinks, in the *Puranas*, except in the *Siva Purana*; nor are the legends concerning her numerous. She has a temple at *Benares*, situated near that of VISWESWARA. He thinks the *Roman* deity ANNONA may bear affinity to ANNA PURNA; the *Sanskrit* word *anna, food,* being a more likely origin of her name, than its supposed root, *annus*, a *year*.—See *As. Res.* Vol. VIII. p. 85. SPENCE's *Polymetis,* Dial. 10. BELL's *Pantheon,* Vol. I. p. 67.

Sir CHARLES MALET notices a figure of this goddess, grouped with many others, among the magnificent sculptures at *Ellora.*—*As. Res.* Vol. VI. p. 410.

Of ANNA PURNA, the beneficent form of DEVI, or BHAVANI, this notice must suffice. A glance at our plates will show in what a variety of other forms we have still to consider her, as we will now proceed to do; describing, as briefly as may be, the plates allotted to this portion of our work, recommencing with PLATE 27. as those of earlier occurrence, that contain representations of this goddess, have already been noticed.

PLATE 27. is taken from a cast, as mentioned in p. 55. It is eighteen inches high, including the pedestal, which is about a foot in diameter, six inches deep, and hollow, as if intended to be fixed on something; and I was told that such images are occasionally fastened on the top of the *Rat'h*, or carriage, dragged about the streets on certain festivals. KALI is said to assume this form to frighten sinners into repentance and virtue: her attitude seems a chasing one, put on to cause immediate terror; her limbs bend; her hands are open, fingers lengthened into points, stretched out; a serpent forms her girdle; she is naked, except a scanty cloth, called *Pira*, round her middle; her belly is empty, thin, and shrivelled; her breasts pendent, with long disgusting nipples; a serpent convolves round her neck, and, twining on her bosom, projects its head to support her protruded long rough tongue; her chin is peaked; immense teeth and tusks are fixed in her lipless gums; her nostrils and goggle eyes are distended and bloated; snakes form appropriate rings for her nasty ears, being knotted in the pendent lobes, with their heads raised and their hoods expanded; her hair is stiffened out, forming a frightful glory round her head, diverging to meet a wider glory that rises from a flower on each side, forming a support to the figure. The cast, however disgusting to the eye, is far from being devoid of merit: our engraving is taken from an exact portrait, and exhibits considerable expression.

PLATE 28. is from a very fine bronze image, about a foot high, cast, I was informed, in the *Carnatic.* It was presented to me by a *Brahman*, and is, I think, on the whole, the most elegant and best finished figure in my possession. She is in this form called BHADRA-KALI, MAHA-KALI, and by other names; also, being eight-handed, *ashta-buja*: two of her hands are empty, pointing upward and downward, in the position before noticed: one of her right hands holds something not unlike a caduceus, which the original resembles more nearly than the plate; its corresponding left hand, the *patra*, or cup: the next right and left hands, a singular crooked sword, and a shield with an embossed flower or fruit: the superior right hand has an agricultural implement, called *Nangar*; the left, the cord, *pas*, or *pash*, to catch or strangle sinners with. Her fine person is full-dressed, with a profusion of ornaments; between her full breasts a five-headed serpent uprears itself; she has a necklace of human heads; her ear-drops are elephants; and a row of snakes' heads peep over her coronet. Her forehead is marked either with SIVA's third eye, or her own hieroglyphic; and her open mouth shows her teeth and tusks, giving her a fierce and threatening aspect. On the pedestal the broken remains of what I imagine was a surrounding exterior glory are perceptible.

PLATE 29. is from a sketch in ink, representing the goddess, four-handed, or *chatar-buja*, seated in a temple, with *Brahmans* adoring her: their rosaries have been before alluded to. *Sir* WILLIAM JONES noticed it as a very singular circumstance, that the peacock was sometimes seen depicted about the temples of this goddess: we see the bird here: the *Linga* of her consort is placed also in small temples above. The plate is a *fac-simile* of my sketch, except in the position and drapery of the females, which are more easy and elegant than can be looked for from the hand of an ordinary artist.

PLATE 30. is from a well executed marble, that was sent to me from *Indore*, the capital of the HOLKAR family. It is about two feet high, and half as broad; representing the goddess seated on the calyx of the lotos, whence several of those flowers branch in different stages of blossom; two of them forming pedestals for two males, who fan the goddess with *chawries*, and hold *loti* in their other hands: above them are elephants, in the act of pouring from vessels some liquid over the shoulders of DEVI; two of whose hands are also furnished with budding lotoses; the other two appear to hold scrolls of paper.

The sculpture of this subject is in bold relief, the spaces above and below the hands of DEVI, and several other parts, being entirely cut out: it has been painted and gilt, but in most parts such ornamental work is worn off. At the time I describe this plate I have not the original before me; but I have compared it with the plate, and found the latter correct, with the exception of giving a greater effect to the attitudes than the marble in strictness warrants; it has too a greater air of neatness and elegance.

The legend that this subject may bear allusion to I do not know: from the number of *loti* introduced, the epithet of PEDMA-DEVI, one of her names, meaning the goddess of the lotos, might be applied to it. From among my pictures and casts I have selected one of each description for this work: the upper part of PLATE 33. is from a tinted picture: *fig.* 4. of PLATE 39. from a cast in bronze, in which the characteristic elephants are conspicuous, evincing the identity of the subjects, although they be somewhat differently handled. The umbrella, in PLATE 30. indicates imperial or pre-eminent dignity in the person it overspreads.

Whatever may be the story that this subject alludes to, it is of long standing, and is still in currency: for the ancient grant of land, dug up on *Salsette*, bearing date A. D. 1018, (*As. Res.* Vol. I. art. 19.) has, as I found on a late examination, the copper plates, on which it is engraved, connected by a ring, having an impression of DEVI, and two elephants with their trunks joined over her head. Another similar instrument, engraved on two brass plates, joined by a ring bearing a similar impression, was dug out of an old wall, in 1801, at *Benares*: this grant is so ancient as A. D. 192.—See *As. Res.* Vol. IX. p. 108. *Sir* CHARLES MALET (*Ib.* Vol. VI.) noticed it among the sculptures at *Ellora*; the elephants' trunks joined, as if fighting: an appearance that I have frequently seen them assume in old and imperfect subjects. *Colonel* STUART has one in small brass, with four elephants joining their trunks over DEVI's head: I never elsewhere saw it with more than two.

PLATE 31. is taken from a sketch in ink, made by an artist in my employ, superintended by my *Pandit*. The drawing of the sketch, from which the plate is engraved, differs in no essential point from its original; only, indeed, in the omission of some trees and animals, and in making the figures more correct and graceful: in nowise, however, altering their postures or character.

We here see DEVI seated in her temple, on the summit of a hill, and the three great powers, her consort the first, ascending it, to approach and adore her: these persons are each four-handed. SIVA is marked by his hair, *Dhurjati*, with GANGA enfolded, as has been sufficiently described. Behind the goddess are three other persons ascending in like manner: the first of these is AGNI, the regent of fire, distinguished by two faces, three legs, and seven arms; the meaning of which I shall endeavour to unfold when we discuss the character and attributes of that deity. Next to him is INDRA, king of the firmament, known by his eye-bespangled skin: being so important a personage he must necessarily be introduced more particularly in his place. The person beneath him I do not know. Above are seen SURYA and CHANDRA, (PHŒBUS and LUNUS) in their chariots: the former driven by ARUNA, or the dawn personified, (AURORA,) drawn by his seven-headed horse, indicative of the prismatic divisibility of a ray of light. The crescent and antelope distinguishes CHANDRA, or the Moon.

We must not quit PLATE 31. without some notice of the ascetics seen about the hill, propitiating, by their austerities, the favour of DEVI: one has his left arm held up, with the fingers clenched till the nails have grown through the back of his hand. Near him sits another penitent, also on the skin of a tiger, with both hands similarly uplifted over his head; a disciple near him is about to give him drink: when both hands are thus upheld the person is called *Urdba-bahu.* A very celebrated *Saniyasi* of this description, named PURANA-PURI, lately died at *Benares*; who had made a vow to continue in that position four and twenty years, but died before their expiration. Of this person, and his extraordinary travels, a very interesting account is given, by the *Hon. Mr.* DUNCAN, in the fifth volume of the *As. Res.* art. 2. where is also a print of him. I have met, and several times conversed with, this interesting man: his arms had fallen, quite shrivelled, on his elbows; the upper arms being perpendicular, the fore-arms horizontal; his clenched fingers falling on the opposite elbow; thus, his fore and upper arms being nearly at right angles, forming three sides of a square over his head. When I saw him he had, I think, been twelve years in this position, and his arms were of course immoveably fixed; but he told me that, at the expiration of his vow, he expected to restore their functions by friction, accompanied by the superior potencies of ceremonies and sacrifices.

He was attended by several disciples and servants, and travelled very respectably in a palky, with suitable attendants; and was, of course, treated every where with great attention, all pious persons feeling happy to contribute to his conveniences. His nails were very long, and crooked, or spirally curved; his hair and beard were also very long, and were plaited and bound up together on his head: he wore no clothing but a slight cloth round his middle; nor did his disciples, who were mostly very stout handsome young men.

On the left of our *Urdha-bahu* is another worthy, standing on one leg, with uplifted hands, and his eyes fixed on the sun: a very powerful method of obtaining favour or forgiveness. Below are two others, with their legs raised over their heads. I once saw a man who had been in this attitude many years: his shrivelled legs had fallen on his neck; his posteriors, if now properly so called, were in front, under his chin; and he sat on his curved spine. These, and other self-inflicted austerities, are called *Tapeswa*: eleven different species are enumerated in p. 51.—Some books describe eighteen varieties.

PLATE 32. is taken from a tinted picture of DEVI, eight-handed, *ashta-buja*, seated in her temple on a lotos, with MAHADEVA dancing before her: VISHNU, BRAHMA, GANESA, and INDRA, are in respectful attendance. BRAHMA is playing on a long-drum, called *pakaos*, and GANESA on the *vina*. MAHADEVA is white, VISHNU blue, and the rest of the same copper colour. The *Linga* and *Nandi* of SIVA are seen in small temples above, and in the picture trees form a back-ground. Although no alteration whatever has been allowed in attributes, character, or attitude, still the plate exhibits much more ease and elegance than its original.

The upper part of PLATE 33. has been noticed in the account of PLATE 30. It is from a coloured picture, in which the elephants are unequivocally pouring water on the shoulders of DEVI.

DURGA slaying the demon MAHISHASUR, as described in an earlier page of this article, occupies the lower part of PLATE 33. It is from a coloured picture, representing DEVI, eight-handed, spearing the crimson monster, who is in the act of springing offensively from the neck of the buffalo, just decapitated by the pursuing and avenging goddess.

PLATE 34. has the same subject, from a cast in brass, seven inches high. She has here seized the monster by the hair, and is spearing him with the *trisula* of SIVA: a sword and shield fill the other hands of DURGA.

Fig. 2. of this plate has been before noticed, under LAKSHMI.—P. 139. 141.

Fig. 3. called *Saptapsara*, or the seven *Apsaras*, is from a thin piece of embossed copper of the same size: it is of very rude execution, to suit the lower classes. And I find it mentioned in my memoranda, that these seven *Apsaras*, whose names I have not noted, preside particularly over water, and are much invoked for supplies to rivers, tanks, and wells: on which occasions sheep are sometimes sacrificed to them. By the *Mahratas* these *Naiads* are in shortness called *Satasra*; and the buffalo, seen with them in the subject under consideration, they call *Mahsuba*. There is some accuracy of allusion in making a buffalo the companion of water-nymphs; for it is an animal that delights peculiarly in water, and is often used for raising it for purposes of irrigation, &c. from tanks, wells, or rivers, by wheels or leathern bags.

PLATE 35. is from two brass casts, about seven inches high, of DURGA in the act before described: that four-handed is old, and a very spirited composition, as the plate indicates. The eight-handed subject is modern, and clumsy: her right hands hold a sword, an arrow, and two tridents; her left, a double-headed hand drum, a bow, a shield, and the hair of the armed demon, who is here seen issuing, not, as usual, from the severed neck, but from the mouth, of the buffalo; or rather of a bull, or bullock, for it has a hump on its shoulders. DURGA has no lion or tiger in the action; and this subject may, perhaps, represent some other exploit of the goddess.

PLATE 36. exhibits BHAVANI, in five different characters, all from casts in brass. *Fig.* 1. is three inches high, somewhat ancient: three of her four hands hold the lotos, and other flowers; one three-leaved, to represent the *trisula*. *Fig.* 2. is a modern eight-handed figure, six inches high, of very little merit: a sword, a crooked *kris*, or dagger, and the *pan-patra*, occupy three of her right hands; the fourth is empty. Her left hands hold a *chakra*, drum, and lotos; the fourth once had, I imagine, the *trisula*, a hole or niche to receive it being near her left knee, just under her hand, which is in a posture for receiving it.

Fig. 3. is the goddess lion-borne, ten-handed, from an ill finished cast, the size of the plate: it is not easy to define what she holds; a sword, bow and arrow, and shield, can be distinguished, and a human head.

Fig. 4. is from an old rude subject, more so than the plate indicates: the goddess is here only two-handed, holding a *linga*, and a *mala* and *patra*, rosary and cup. *Fig.* 5. is nearly the same, more ancient, and better cast. The goddess, when two-handed, is mostly called PARVATI; and I find it noticed, that the *linga*, held by these two figures, is of that sort called *partha linga*, made, for daily or temporary purposes, by *Brahmans*, or by women themselves, of earth, and offered in SIVA's temples, as directed in the *Sivpuran*.

PLATE 37. is from old subjects, in metal, of the size represented. *Fig.* 1. DEVI, mounted on a quadruped, holding the *Chank* and *Chakra* of VISHNU, a sort of sword, and the sacrificial axe, called, when in this shape, *Charga*. *Fig.* 2. is very old and rude, of DEVI, on a tiger, six-handed, spearing an infant with a *trisula*: she holds a sword, shield, and cup. *Fig.* 3. is not so old as the others, and is rather of a singular description: the camels, and the appearances below, I could get no account of: the head, as my *Brahman* determined it to be, is less conspicuous in the cast than in the plate. DEVI has a rosary in a right hand: others hold the lotos, and a ball of food perhaps. *Fig.* 4. is from a very old and tolerably good cast: the goddess has a curious coronet (less perfect, as is her face, than the plate), with a *linga* on her head, overspread by a five-headed snake, tied in a club on her shoulders. She holds the *lawha-dandayai*, or iron sceptre, (called, shortly, by the *Poona Brahmans, lu-dand,*) a shield, a cup, and perhaps some fruit, or flower.

PLATE 38. contains six more casts of this endless divinity: the first four are of the size of the engraving. *Fig.* 1. is old, in an easy attitude, with a crooked *kris*. *Fig.* 2. is ten-handed, modern, and clumsily cast, the weapons, &c. being scarcely discernible: a trident, cup, and shield, can be made out. The falling collar of heads, with one in her hand and under her foot, indicate that this image represents the goddess in a particular and avenging character. We may indeed assert, that every variety of image has its own legend, and represents some leading fact in the history of BHAVANI under some one or other of her forms and characters. *Fig.* 3. is of modern brass, tolerably well executed: the *naga*, that overspreads the *linga* on the head of DEVI, is curled curiously round her clubed hair behind: something conical, therefore alluding to SIVA, is in one hand; the cup, *patra*, or perhaps *argha*, of which hereafter, in another: the other two have a mace and shield. The animal beside her is called *Singha*; at *Poona*, corrupted into *Siwn*, or *Seewn*, which generally means a lion, but in mythological tales has a fabulous and marvellous history: I have separate casts of it, but have not an engraving in this work. *Fig.* 4. holds the conical subject, and something equivocal in the right hand, looking as much like a roll of paper as any thing else. This is a tolerably good cast, and may be of almost any other goddess, with whom the conical lotos-bud is a common attribute, as well as of PARVATI: the hair is neatly arranged.

Fig. 5. of PLATE 38. is a singular and curious subject in brass, modern, and pretty well cast, about seven inches high. The hooded serpent, overspreading PARVATI's coronet, is seen behind winding round her head, although neither the plate, nor the front view of the image, exhibit that appearance: the third eye in the forehead, snakes for earrings, and round the arms, waist, and ankles, are conspicuous. Whether or not the circle, surrounded by dots, on her palms and soles, on the throat of the snakes, and on her left, not on her right, arm, have any particular allusions, I am ignorant.

Fig. 6. of PLATE 38. is of DEVI, from an old and pretty good cast, nine inches high: she holds some of her common attributes, and on her forehead a ruby forms her mark.

PLATE 39. contains six more representations of DEVI, in different forms, from casts about the same size as the engraving. *Fig.* 1. is old, and rather clumsy; holding the double drum of the destroying spirit, the sacrificial knife, the cup to receive the blood, and the head of a victim. *Fig.* 2. is very rude and confused, much more so than the plate: a prostrate human figure at her feet marks the avenging character of the goddess. *Fig.* 3. is a modern and not very good cast in brass, of the same subject I apprehend as PLATE 30. although, in this instance, the elephants have not their trunks joined as usual; nor are they pouring any liquid over the head of the goddess, who is two-handed, holding, I believe, lotoses. *Fig.* 4. is noticed in the account of PLATE 30. it is from a very good bronze cast of the same subject, apparently ancient, but in good preservation: what the elephants stand on appear to be lotoses. *Fig.* 5. is an old image, whether male or female not clear, holding the double drum and trident. *Fig.* 6. I find called, in my memoranda, VISHNU DEVI, having been taught by *Brahmans* to apply that appellation to the goddess when distinguished by the *Chank* and *Chakra*. Although this cast be unlike any other that I have seen of that subject, I am disposed to refer it to the same as PLATE 35. It is of modern brass, and tolerably fair.

For the accommodation and comfort of the poorer class of *Hindus*, who may be unable to indulge in the expensive possession of an image, impressions of deities are taken off on thin plates of copper from iron or steel dies: I have many of these, old and new, as well as some dies; of the latter, both sunk and raised. The impression thus taken can be purchased, of a small size, for a few pence, being of course very common and rude. Nine of them are represented in PLATE 40. of the size of the originals, of which they are, as nearly as possible, exact copies. *Fig.* 1. sitting on a bed, or litter, is thence called *Palanga*, or, more correctly, *Palyanga* BHAVANI. At *Tuljapur*, a respectable town in the *Mahrata* country, between *Poona* and *Hydrabad*, the goddess in this form has, I am told, a temple, and is much worshipped in the neighbourhood: whence the name of the town is sometimes given to her as an epithet, and she is called *Tuljapury*. An ear of corn is said to be in one of her hands. *Fig.* 2. is of YENKUBA and GANESA: the latter often called GANPATI; the former is a deity, or saint, of local celebrity, not being chronicled in sacred or ancient books; and I have no legend respecting him. *Fig.* 3. is of DEVI, tiger-mounted, thence named VYAGHRA YAHI. *Fig.* 4. is of HANUMAN. *Fig.* 5. DEVI, or RUDRANI, in a form named NAWLAHI: in which she also holds an ear of corn, and is invoked by the *Corambis*, or *Mahrata* cultivators. *Fig.* 6. GARUDA. *Fig.* 7. another form of DEVI, named MAHISHA-SAYI, from being mounted on a buffalo. *Fig.* 8. two heads of BHAVANI, (but one has mustachoes) called YEHSAHI-MEHSAHI; why,

I know not. *Fig.* 9. DEVI in her character of MEHSAHI. Of the next PLATE, (41.) *fig.* 5. is called SATWA DEVI, representing her as the author of existence: *Satwa* means also truth, or purity. When a child is five years old, *Mahrata* families invoke the goddess under this name for health and prosperity. The larger of the subjects given in PLATE 40. have the same description of exterior ornament, or finish: the part beyond that is often folded flat back, to strengthen the plate, and sometimes over a second flat piece of copper, or brass, with the space between filled up with *lak*, to prevent injury by pressure, or blows on the impression.

PLATE 41. The trident and cup mark this very old rude cast (*fig.* 1.) to be of DEVI: two ill formed animals are beside her, two feet in front, with balls, and other undefinable attributes, that doubtless have allusion to some legend of the goddess. *Fig.* 2. is very old and ugly, much more so than the plate: a supplicating figure holds DEVI's sword-arm, and seems anxious to hinder the perpetration of some threatened act of vengeance. *Fig.* 3. looks like a skeleton: it is apparently extremely old. Of this description of image I have some scores, most of which appear to have been buried. They are generally said to be of BHAIRAVA: among the *Mahratas*, called BHEROBA, an appellation derived from *Bheru*; meaning *terrific, tremendous*, and hence applied to SIVA, his *Sacti*, and their offspring. It is generally given to a reputed son, or *Avatara*, of SIVA; and as such we will notice it again presently. *Fig.* 4. although classed with DEVI, is very equivocal: it is modern, and ill executed in brass. The articles like the *chank* and *chakra*, as well as the mark in the forehead, indicate VISHNU, or LAKSHMI: the club appertains to DEVI. The originals of this plate are of the size represented: also of PLATE 42. *figures* 1. 2. and 3. of which are referrible to BHAIRAVA. *Fig.* 4. is an old brass cast of DEVI, denoted by some of her usual attributes, as well as by the *Linga*: the lion and scorpion may excite speculation, but in the original it is not so clearly a scorpion as in the plate.

Of PLATE 43. *figures* 1. and 4. are of BHAIRAVA; and I shall here notice only *figures* 2. and 3. The former of which is of DEVI, holding a *Linga*, and what I judge to be a lotos, although in the engraving it may look more like a head: her inferior two hands seem to rest on the heads of dwarfs, but in the cast, which is of modern brass, the size of the engraving, they do not touch: the characters on the pedestal are on the original, but I know not what they are. Nor do I know to what legend *fig.* 3. may relate, or scarcely what deities it represents: I deem it a curious subject; it is ancient, but in good preservation, and well cast in some brassy composition. The turreted coronets, one expanded, the other closed, will remind the classical reader of descriptions of CYBELE, and of ISIS and DIANA: in the hand of the male the *Chank* of VISHNU is evident; in the inferior left hand of the female it is equivocal, more so in the cast than in the plate. The diamond, or lozenge, in the hand of both, I know nothing of; and the flowers seen in their hands, and about them, may refer to the characters and tenets of both *Saivas* and *Vaishnavas*. One under the influence of ignorance is prone to see mysteries: hence it is, perhaps, that I fancy profundity of allusion in several points of this subject.

Of Ganesa, Kartikya, Vira Bhadra, and Bhairava, the offspring of Mahadeva and Parvati.

Ganesa is the *Hindu* god of prudence and policy: he is the reputed eldest son of Siva and Parvati, and is represented with an elephant's head, an emblem of sagacity; and is frequently attended by a rat, sometimes riding on one, the conduct of that animal being esteemed by the *Hindus* as peculiarly marked by wisdom and foresight: he has generally four hands, but sometimes six, or eight, or only two. He is invoked by a *Hindu*, I believe of all sects, in the outset of any business: if he build a house, an image of Ganesa is previously propitiated, and set up on or near the spot: if he write a book, Ganesa is saluted at its commencement, as he is also at the top of a letter: beginning a journey, Ganfsa is implored to protect him, and, for the accommodation of travellers, his image is occasionally seen on the road-side, especially where two roads cross; but sometimes it is little else than a stone, rudely chiselled into something like an elephant's head, with oil and red ochre daubed over it, decorated, perhaps, with a chaplet of flowers by some pious neighbour or traveller. It is common to see a figure of the god of prudence in or over bankers' and other shops; and, upon the whole, there is perhaps no deity in the *Hindu* Pantheon so often seen and addressed.

I have of course given a figure of Ganesa as a frontispiece to this my humble undertaking, invoking his auspicious aid to my design, and my mode of executing it: how far his attributes of *Wisdom* and *Prudence* may have been successfully propitiated remains to be manifested by the discerning public, and felt by the author, unassumingly endeavouring to contribute to their amusement.

In the *Voyage to India*, by Paolino *de San* Bartolomeo, the author says, that "statues which supply the place of mile-stones, and serve to guide strangers, are found every where erected along the high roads. As the *Greeks* and *Romans* employed for this purpose the god Terminus, the *Hindus* use their deity Ganesha, who by the common people, not well acquainted with the *Samscred* language, is called Poleyar." – P. 70.

The learned *Carmelite* proceeds to describe the elephant-headed GANESA; as holding in one of his hands a key in the form of a hook, like those used in the earlier ages when doors had no iron-work; as having always under him a mouse, an animal held in the utmost abhorrence by the elephant, and, according to the *Indians*, representing the wicked demon, the enemy of wisdom, or, in other words, the devil. *Indian* women, he says, who are married, wear an image of GANESA, which they call *Taly*, suspended from the neck by a string, serving as a love pledge, and as a token of their chastity and conjugal fidelity.

I will in this place take the liberty of offering some remarks, general and particular, that were suggested by the above account of GANESA.

Europeans, visiting *India*, are apt, when they communicate their observations, to say, that the "*Indians* do so and so;" implying, that the immense population of *India* have similar and uniform habits: whereas, no inference can be more erroneous. Travelling through *India*—say from *Ceylon*, centrally, up the *Carnatic*, the *Dekkan*, and *Bengal*, to *Kashmir*, an extent of about thirty degrees of latitude, an observer would notice as great a variety of habits, languages, religious observances, &c. as in travelling through a like space through *Europe*—say between *Russia* and the *Mediterranean*.

It is said, in the preceding extract, that "statues which supply the place of mile-stones, and serve to guide travellers, are erected *every where* along the high road." The author, whose abode, however, seems to have been confined to the southern parts of the peninsula, and chiefly to the provinces of *Malabar* and *Canara*, has doubtless seen statues placed as direction-posts, and at regular distances, on the roads; but they are not every where so placed. For I have lived more than twenty years in that part of *India* which we call the peninsula, and for months, nay years, in *Malabar* and *Canara*, and have travelled some hundreds, I may say thousands, of miles in those provinces, and never, to the best of my recollection, saw one instance of a statue, or any thing else, placed by natives either as a direction-post, or to mark the termination of distance.

What PAOLINO calls a *key*, in the form of a hook, I understand to be intended for the instrument with which elephants are guided, called *Ankas*, which sometimes is scarcely distinguishable from a sort of fan occasionally seen in the hands of GANESA. But the good friar may be right; for this deity is found to be JANUS, in whose hands the *Romans* placed a key.

GANESA has not *always* a mouse under him, as the learned *Carmelite* states: sometimes he has a mouse, or a rat, as I have been taught to call it, under or near him, but is oftener seen without. Besides those given in this work, I have fourteen images in metal, and many pictures of him alone, and in groups; and his rat or mouse appears in a very small proportion of them. I never before heard that the mouse was "held by the elephant in the utmost abhorrence;" and if it is, the mouse is not, therefore, appropriately selected as its companion: nor did I know that it was in this case meant to "represent the wicked demon, the enemy of wisdom, or, in other words, the devil." I do not either recollect ever to have seen, as the good brother has, "married females wear an image of GANESA, suspended from their necks by a string:" nor should I, if I had, have at once seen, admitting he was originally hung there as a "love pledge," how it particularly "serves as a token of chastity and conjugal fidelity."

PAOLINO further informs us, that the cocoa-nut is dedicated to GANESA, "because it makes a whole without any joining," p. 260: a mysticism praised both by the author and his translator and commentator. But I should have expected a more appropriate reason for dedicating such a fruit, admitting the fact, particularly to the god of prudence and policy: the reason given would apply equally well to an egg, or to an apple, or almost any other fruit.

The same author says, that, in *Ceylon*, GANESA is represented with goat's feet: I never saw his image or picture so designated.

SONNERAT calls GANESA, POLLEAR: by which name, it would appear, he is known in the *Carnatic*. He says, "that images of the gods may be made of stone, copper, or gold, but never of silver, or other metals: that of POLLEAR must be always of stone." There may perhaps, but I never heard so, be some restrictive rules in the *Carnatic* for the composition of images; in other parts there are none. I have gilt images of silver, with gold rings; some with rubies in the eyes and other parts. I have images, made in the *Carnatic*, of different compositions, of copper and brass; nor do I think there is generally any objection to making GANESA of different metals. My *Pandit*, in *Bombay*, had him and KRISHNA, and ANNA PURNA, and others, in silver: they were, I believe, made in *Bombay*. Idols are also made of crystal and gems; of which I have seen several: BUDHAS are more common in crystal, I think, than any other deity.

Although GANESA be almost always considered, and called, the son of MAHADEVA and PARVATI, there is yet a legend in the *Sivpuran* of his origin, that would exclude his reputed father from any share in the honour of his existence: I will give the legend as briefly as I can, as it contains other points of mythological fable.

GANESA is sometimes represented with but one tusk: to account for which, it is related in the *Purana*, that he was formed of fair proportions by PARVATI, from the excrementitious particles and impurities of her own body, at which MAHADEVA was jealous and displeased. GANESA was his mother's champion, vindicating her honour and rights on all occasions, even against the infringements of VISHNU and his mother's lord. On one occasion VISHNU and GANESA fought, and the latter would have been victor but for the interposition of SIVA, who cut off GANESA's head.

PARVATI was greatly displeased and distressed at this event, and proceeded in revenge to austerities that threatened to derange the destinies of the universe, from which nothing could divert her but the restoration of her son; which, on the earnest application of the congregated deities, SIVA consented to. But the severed head could not be found; and it was determined to fix on his trunk the head of the first animal that should make its appearance, which happened to be an elephant with but one tooth. SIVA adopted GANESA; and all the deities, to appease and console PARVATI, consented that he should on all occasions be first invoked,

Another legend states, that, in a desperate combat, GANESA, having exhausted all means of offence, plucked out one of his tusks, and hurled it at his adversary.

In a picture of mine, GANESA is represented with two wives (I recollect, however, my *Pandit* telling me they were not actually his wives; but I do not retain sufficient of the story to impeach the morality of the deity of policy on that point), whose names were SIDDI and BUDDHI, daughters of VISHWARUPA: who were sought also by GANESA's brother, KARTIKYA; and it was agreed, that whichever of them could first traverse the earth should win and have the damsels. GANESA, in a disputation, proved, by his logical talents and aptness at quotation of divine texts, that he had so done, and obtained the prize long before his brother's return from his weary pilgrimage; to the great disquiet of both families, when the sophistry of GANESA was exposed.

GANESA is not so correct a character as one might hope and expect from the deity of policy and sagacity: I do not think the *Hindus* have that excellent though homely adage, connecting honesty and policy; although they may mean, perhaps, by GANESA's peccadillos, to inculcate how insufficient are all worldly acquirements without morals. On one occasion, of a conspiracy among six of the *Rishis* and their wives, against their brother GOTAMA and his wife AHILYA, they prevailed on GANESA to assume the shape of a cow, animated by the most minute spark of life, and to appear before GOTAMA in such a manner as to provoke him to strike her: which, however, was done by the temperate saint, merely with a blade of grass; but it was sufficient to kill the feeble cow, and poor GOTAMA and his family were of course involved in deep distress at the unhappy accident. On their contrition, SIVA pardoned him; and, to purify him of his offence, let loose the *Ganga* from his head.

Some points of astronomy are connected with this allegory, and perhaps also with that of KARTIKYA going round the earth. The popular moral inculcates the ill effects of passion, and the merit of forbearance, especially toward kine.

As well as the character of wisdom being ascribed by the *Romans* to JANUS, they considered him as "the god who presided over the beginning of all undertakings: the first libations of wine and wheat were offered to him, and the preface to all prayers was addressed to him."—BELL's *Pantheon.*

These and many other coincidences seem to establish the identity of JANUS and GANESA as *initial* deities; nor would a keen etymologist want matter on which to ground a conjecture of similarity in names. The final letter of the *Hindu* name is seldom used in conversation: their deity is generally called GANES, or GUNNIS, or GONEISH. The hard *G* might easily have been changed in passing through *Egypt* to *Rome,* and the soft *G,* or *J,* substituted, which would give nearly the same sound to the name in *Italy* as in *India*: this may be deemed the more likely, as this deity was not received into the *Roman Pantheon* through the *Greeks,* who did not know of JANUS.

GANESA is not, I believe, ever seen like JANUS *bifrons*; nor is his temple subject to the ceremony of opening and shutting in times of war and peace, as JANUS's was at *Rome* where, indeed, the ceremony appears to have had an origin more accidental than characteristic.

Under the head of *Sects,* p. 121. is an account of the five grand divisions of *Hindus* who exclusively worship a single divinity, uniting in its person all the attributes of BRAHM himself: one of these divinities is GANESA, and the sectaries who thus worship him are called *Ganapatyas.* GANPATI, in conversation, more correctly spelled GANAPATI, is the name commonly given to this deity about *Poona, Bombay,* &c. places on the western side of *India.*

A singular instance of superstition, in this sect of *Ganapatyas,* has been described in the "Account of a hereditary living deity at *Chichur,* near *Poona,*" to whom adoration is paid by the *Brahmans,* and others, in that neighbourhood, published in the seventh volume of the *As. Res.* The story is there given at length by me: it is briefly this—GANESA, gratified at the persevering piety and devotion of a *Gussayn*, named MURABA, rewarded him by incarnating himself in his person, and covenanting that the divinity should descend in his children to the seventh generation; empowering the incumbent to work miracles, and in a limited degree to look into futurity: with this divine patrimony is inherited the guardianship of a sacred stone, a type of the deity. At the period of my visit to this holy person, five generations had passed away; the sixth inheritor, GABAJI-DEVA, has since died; and it is agreed by the *Brahmans*, that the *Avatara* will end with the life of the present inspired portion of carnality, unless perpetuated or renewed by a farther miraculous expression of the divine will.

Great respect, indeed adoration, is paid by the *Peshwa*, and of course all other *Brahmans* about *Poona*, to this sanctified inheritor of the gifts of prophecy and miracle, as related at length in the article above referred to.

His *Highness* SRI MANT, the *Peshwa*, I should hence suppose to be of the sect of *Ganapatyas*. He has a very magnificent room in his palace at *Poona*, called the *Ganes* room, in which, on particular festivals in honour of GANESA, he receives numerous visitors: I have seen more than a hundred dancing girls in it at one time. At one end, in a recess, is a fine gilt figure, I believe in marble, of this deity, and many other mythological decorations around it: the other end of the room, bounded by a narrow strip of water in which fountains play, is open to a garden of fragrant flowers, which, combined with the murmuring of the fountains, has a very pleasing effect. This room is well designed in *Mr.* DANIEL'S fine picture of the *Poona Durbar*, unrivalled perhaps in oriental grouping, character, and costume; but it has more mythological ornaments than are actually in the room. This picture* was painted for *Sir* CHARLES MALET, from sketches by the late *Mr.* WALES; and the artist has chosen the time when *Sir* CHARLES, then our ambassador at the Court of *Poona*, attended by his suite, delivered to his *Highness* the *Peshwa*, in full *Durbar*, the treaty of alliance, ratified by his *Majesty*, between *Great Britain* and his *Highness*; made, preparatory to the war between the triple allied powers and TIPPOO, in 1790.

Images and pictures of GANESA are very common; such as have been selected for this work I will proceed to notice. PLATE 44. is taken from five casts in copper, of nearly the size there represented. *Fig.* 1. is modern, and tolerably good: holding a hook and fan. *Fig.* 2. is not before me at this moment: it is rather ancient, and well cast; and I may, perhaps, see occasion to notice it again. *Fig.* 3. is a modern figure, clumsily executed: he holds VISHNU'S

* It is exceedingly well engraved, and published by CRIBB, in *Holborn*.

Chank, a club, something to eat, and a broken tooth; the legend relating to which has been mentioned: here his tooth appears broken off, not pulled out. *Fig*. 4. is from a modern good cast, similar in most points to *fig*. 1. *Fig*. 5. is GANESA mounted on his rat: it is from an old cast, holding the same things as *fig*. 3. except that, instead of the tooth, in one of his hands there is something equivocal.

The upper part of PLATE 45. represents GANESA and SARASWATI, as hath been before mentioned. It is from a tinted picture: GANESA, profusely decorated with chaplets of flowers, &c. has a yellow robe over his loins, and sits on a red lotos expanded on a stool or throne: a mark of the *Saivas* is traced on his forehead, and a flower-crowned *naga* projects its head above it.

Of KARTIKYA, brother to GANESA, mention has been made in a former article, (page 52); and a legend is there given, accounting for his six faces. In the *Ramayana*, sect. 30. the origin of KARTIKYA, and other mythological points, are detailed: of which, here follows a rapid sketch.—The great mountain *Haimavat*, sovereign of mountains, the grand magazine of metallic substances, had two daughters, of unparalleled beauty, by his spouse MERA, daughter of MERU. Their names were GANGA and UMA: the former was yielded in marriage to all the celestials at their earnest solicitation. UMA remained a virgin, and became a devotee of extraordinary rigidity; but was at length espoused by the incomparable RUDRA, otherways denominated SHITAKOONT'HA, (the blue-throated, similar to NILAKOONT'HA,) who devoted himself to connubial enjoyment, but without any issue. All the gods, to whom the production of a son was of great moment, addressed HUTASHANA (AGNI), saying, "Accompanied by VAYU, combine thyself with the *Rudrian* energy:" which being poured forth, was pervaded by AGNI, for the purpose of producing the puissant KARTIKYA, resplendent as the god of fire himself. UMA (a name and form of DEVI), enraged at this promised offspring, in which she was not participant, laid her maledictions on all the celestials for soliciting such a solitary production, and on the earth for receiving it.—"Never," she imprecated, "may ye obtain offspring from your own spouses, since ye have debarred me, desirous of offspring, from nuptial rites." This curse RUDRA declared to be irrevocable, but promised that a son should, by the influence of AGNI, be produced by GANGA; which son would be acknowledged by UMA, her younger sister. GANGA, receiving the influence of AGNI, thus addressed him who precedes all the celestials—"O divine one! filled with inexpressible pain, I am unable to bear thy influence; I am burning by this fire." He, who consumes the oblations made to all the gods, (AGNI, or Fire,) replied: "O sinless one! deposit thy burden here, on the side of *Haimavat*;" and she produced KUMARA from her side. (A close consideration of this legend would induce a belief, that the discovery and obtaining of gold is veiled in this wild allegory.)

The gods, with INDRA and the *Maruts*, now delivered this son to the six *Krittikas* (the *Pleiades*), to be nourished by them; and they offering their breasts, the six-headed was nurtured, and named KARTIKYA, the descendant of the *Krittikas*.

He is, notwithstanding, generally esteemed the second son of SIVA and PARVATI, the god of war, and commander of the celestial armies. *Sir* W. JONES (*As. Res.* Vol. I. p. 252.) notices his numerous eyes as bearing some resemblance to ARGUS, whom JUNO employs; but, in other points, he is deemed to be clearly the ORUS of *Egypt*, and the MARS of *Italy*. And *Sir* WILLIAM was persuaded, that the name SKANDA, by which he is called in the *Puranas*, has some connexion with the old SEKANDER of *Persia*, whom the poets ridiculously confound with the *Macedonian*.

MANGALA, the MARS of the *Hindu Pantheon*, is in some accounts stated to be the offspring of PRIT'HU, an incarnation of VISHNU: above we find him the son of SIVA.

SUBRAMANI is another name for the subject of this article, used both on the *Bombay* and the *Madras* side of *India*, especially the latter. SONNERAT relates a *Carnatic* legend of his having sprang from SIVA's central eye, to destroy the giant SOURAPARPMA, whom he cut in two, and the severed monster assumed the shapes of a peacock and a cock; the former of which the victor determined to use as a vehicle, and the latter to be borne in his standard.—Vol. I. p. 56.

I have no image of this hero, nor any picture wherein he is riding on a peacock, nor where he has twelve arms; but he is, I know, sometimes so represented. In PLATES 18. 19. we see him six-faced, six-armed, with his father, mother, and brother. In PLATE 46. he is again seen with his reputed parents; and PARVATI seems to be addressing him in a spirited style—more spirited and elegant in her person than the picture whence it is taken.

We may suppose that the number six is often found appertaining to this six-headed, six-armed, six-mothered, personage. The sixth day, severally, of the months *Margasirsha* and *Chaitra*, are sacred to the god of arms and war.—*As. Res.* Vol. III. p. 268.

If the reader be desirous of farther intelligence of this deity, I beg to refer him to MAURICE's *Ancient History*, where (Vol. I. p. 207. Vol. II. p. 108.) my learned friend discusses the astronomical and other points connected with KARTIKYA in his usual style of eloquence and elegance.

VIRA BHADRA, a heroic personage, now demands our notice: he is sometimes called a son, sometimes an *Avatara*, of SIVA. In PLATE 25. he is represented with the attributes of his prototype, the *Linga* and *Nandi*, and armed with bow and arrow, sword and shield. It is related in the *Ramayana*, sect. 53. p. 379. that the famous bow of VISHNU, named *Danush*, was used by SANKARA (SIVA) with great effect at the destruction of DAKSHA's sacrifice; and I imagine the ram-headed figure in PLATE 25. to be DAKSHA himself, or BRAHMA in a human shape after his decapitation by SIVA: a legend of such frequent occurrence, and so difficult to explain.—See DAKSHA, p. 107. This plate is taken from a curious embossed shield, in very good preservation, belonging to *Lord* VALENTIA: it is fourteen inches high, of copper, with a brass border, fixed by pitch to a wooden back, in which is a hole for the hand. Our plate is an exact copy of it, with, perhaps, a little addition of general neatness, especially in the person of the elegant lotos-bearing female, who is, I apprehend, SRIDEVI, wife of DAKSHA.—See p. 107.

Fig. 3. of PLATE 26. is the same subject, handled in a ruder style: it is from a brass cast nine inches high, in very bold relief, the principal figure projecting considerably. There is very little difference in the two subjects: the *nag*, or serpent, in PLATE 26. the cross on the cap (or *mukut*) of VIRA BHADRA, and the marks on the foreheads, are the chief varieties observable. The large ears in one, and the rather singular cones over the ears of the other, may attract notice: large ears, in male or female, are generally esteemed in *India*: if the cones, as is likely, have any meaning, I am ignorant of it.

VIRA BHADRA is a personage of extensive celebrity, and his exploits are recorded in ancient and sacred books. SONNERAT (vol. I. p. 58.) mentions him in the *Carnatic* under the name of VIRAPATRIN, as the fourth son of SIVA, produced, with a thousand heads and a thousand arms, by the sweat of his body, to avert the effects of a sacrifice. In the *Sivpuran* it is mentioned, that he was produced from a drop of SIVA's sweat.

BHAIRAVA is another of SIVA's sons; sometimes, like VIRA BHADRA, spoken of as an *Avatara*: the name being derived from *Bheru*, meaning *terrific*, *tremendous*, &c. is, as hath been before said, applied also to SIVA, his spouse, and their offspring.

It is, I believe, chiefly among the *Mahratas* that this form of SIVA is worshipped: with them it is called BHEROBA; and his spouse is named YUGASIRI, pronounced Jogasery. Their images are met with more commonly than that of any other deity: of different descriptions, separately and together, I have, I imagine, nearly a hundred in copper and brass; mostly old and rude, with an appearance of having been buried. Several of them are represented in the plates that have already come descriptively under our notice, and I will now give such farther account of them as they in this place require.

Plate 12. has Bhairava four-handed, holding, as is mentioned in page 33, the commonest attributes of Vishnu, the *Chank* and *Chakra*; while most of the other distinctions appertain to Siva, the cup, *linga*, and bull, especially. The ram's or goat's head refers, I conjecture, to Daksha's substitute; for some legends attribute the decapitation of Brahma in that form to Bhairava: the horse, five balls, sun, and moon, are very commonly seen with this and with other characters. The original of the portion of plate 12. under our consideration, is of the size represented; old and rude, but in good preservation.

Fig. 3. of plate 24. is from a coloured picture, where Bhairava holds the ghastly head of Brahma, and a cup of his blood: two dogs attend, in apparent expectation of sharing in the horrid banquet. The figure has a dark blue skin; palms, soles, and lips, tinged red; clothed only with short red breeches, and a white scarf: the collar of blanched skulls, crescent and eye in the forehead, trident, and blood-coloured cup, mark his parentage and relations.

Fig. 3. of plate 41. is of Bhairava, and has been noticed in the description of that plate, under the article Parvati, p. 167. *Fig.* 1. of plate 42. is from an old copper cast: the figure is thin and emaciated, holding the *pasha*, or cord of punishment; the other points, such as sun, moon, balls, goat's head, human feet, &c. are usual. *Fig.* 2. of this plate I should at once have called Mahadeva and Parvati; and, from the horse, should, perhaps, have imagined it to represent them in their *Avatara* of Kandeh Rao and Malsara: but my *Brahman* determined it to be Bhairava and Yugasiri. It is from an old cast in brass, and both persons appear to hold the same things; sword, trident, double drum, and cup: her inferior left hand is, indeed, broken off. *Fig.* 3. of plate 42. is the same subject; whether male or female is, however, equivocal: it is of brass, very old and rude, and has the usual, and some unusual, points, or attributes.

Of plate 43. *fig.* 4. remains to be noticed: it is from a cast in brass, larger than the engraving, and, although old, is in tolerable preservation. It is said to be Bhairava and his consort: they appear as skeletons; a bull and *linga* are beneath them; the things at their feet are not easily made out.

PLATE 47. is from two coloured pictures of BHAIRAVA: above he is represented on a buffalo, the beast and himself of the same dark blue colour: below he is, like the other figures, copper-coloured; the head and the dog blue; the serpent white. What he holds in his superior right hand appears like a cutting instrument, or it may be meant for SIVA's double hand-drum: the adoring female with her child may be supposed in supplication, to avert apprehended injury from this terrific and avenging character.

SONNERAT notices this deity as honoured in the *Carnatic*: he calls him VAIREVERT, third son of SIVA; produced from his breath to humble the arrogance of BRAHMA, one of whose heads he wrenched off, and used the skull to receive the blood of his other antagonists. He is described pretty much as represented in PLATE 24. but said to be *mounted* on a dog, a position that I never saw him in.

The *Mahratas*, and most likely many other classes of *Hindus*, have the habit of making images in honour of deceased ancestors, and of their *guru*, or spiritual instructors: *Brahmans* are said to discourage this idolatrous propensity. These *Lares*, or *Penates*, or *Lemures*, for the household gods of the *Hindus* partake of the characters assigned by the *European* heathens to those different descriptions of departed spirits, are easily confounded with the variety of forms in which BHAIRAVA appears. *Nat* and *Vira* are epithets that I have heard *Brahmans* apply to such domestic images, which others have called of BHAIRAVA; while, to many other subjects in my possession, they seemed altogether at a loss what epithet to apply. Some of these are represented in PLATES 99. 100. and 101.

Vira and *Virata*, imply *heroism*, or victory. VIRATA-RUPA is a name of VISHNU, and given also to RAMA; and perhaps others of his *Avataras*: meaning universal monarchy, or an all-conquering form.

AVATARAS.

ALLUSIONS and references to the *Avataras* occur so perpetually in all researches into the mythology of the *Hindus*; and, indeed, nearly all of their history and literature is replete with mythological fables; that it seems necessary, in a work of this sort, to give some connected view of the subject, including a notice of such legends as are generally considered as descriptive of the leading events in the fabulous relations connected with the *Avataras*.

The word itself, in strictness, means a *descent:* in which sense it is still retained in several dialects of *India*. But in its more extended signification, and in the sense now under consideration, it means an *incarnation* of a deity in the person generally of a human being (see page 13): such incarnations have been innumerable. The three principal powers of the Deity, their consorts and offspring, the inferior deities, and almost the whole host of mythological personages, have had their *Avataras,* or *descents* on earth, for various purposes, of punishing tyrants and sinners, rewarding the good, or reclaiming the wicked.

When, however, speaking of *the Avataras,* it is generally meant to be confined to the *ten incarnations* of VISHNU, *das Avatara,* as pre-eminently distinguishing them from others of a less important, or less potent nature.

The *das Avatara* are usually thus arranged and named.—1. MATSYA, or *Fish.*—2. KURMA, or *Tortoise.*—3. VARAHA, or *Boar.*—4. NARASINGHA, or *Man lion.*—5. VAMANA, or *Dwarf.*—6. PARASU RAMA, the name of the favoured person in whom the deity became incarnate.—7. RAMA, the same.—8. KRISHNA, the same.—9. BUDHA, the same.—10. KALKI, or *Horse.* Of these, nine are past; the tenth is yet to come.

When we hear that *the Hindus* speak of the Deity having been thus incarnated, we must understand it with some qualification; for, in fact, there is, perhaps, scarcely one point in their mythological religion that the whole race of *Hindus* have faith in. There are sectaries and schismatics without end, who will believe only certain points that others abjure: individuals of those sects dissent from the doctrines believed by the majority; other philosophical sceptics will scarcely believe any thing, in opposition to their easy-faithed brethren, who disbelieve nothing. Thus some *Saivas,* or followers of SIVA, admit the sacredness of the *Avataras* of VISHNU, but in different degrees of potency and sanctity: they generally admit the personified interposition of the preserving attribute of the Deity in the affairs of the world, without yielding the point of supremacy in the prototype. And some zealous *Vaishnavas*, or followers of VISHNU, giving themselves up to his adoration in some incarnation—KRISHNA, or RAMA, for instance, reject with indignation, commensurate with their zeal or bigotry, all farther application of divine terms. Hence may, in part, be discerned the liability under which inquirers labour, of being misled by sectaries into receiving schism as orthodoxy, and of forming general conclusions from individual or partial information. But, in fact, there is no general orthodoxy among *Hindus*, any more than among *Christians*; nor can it be expected: in the restlessness and diversity of men's minds such a thing is not in nature or reason. All religions profess alike belief in the Deity, and array him in nearly similar attributes; but when the idea of interposing incarnations be received, faith and reason are let loose in contest, and it is admitted or rejected, or modified, according to the feelings, or unhappily, in many cases, according to the interests, of individuals.

1.—The MATSYA, or FISH.

This *Avatara* has been demonstrated to have immediate reference to the general deluge, and to be the same history, disguised in oriental fiction, of that event, as is related in our scriptures. *Sir* W. JONES (*As. Res.* Vol. I.) assents to the opinion of BOCHART, that the fable of SATURN was raised on the true history of NOAH: he shows that the seventh MENU, SATYAVRATA, corresponds in station and character. In his reign, the *Hindus* believe the whole earth to have been destroyed by a flood, including all mankind, who had become corrupt, except the pious prince himself, the seven *Rishis*, and their several wives; who, by command of VISHNU, entered a *babitra*, or spacious vessel, accompanied by pairs of all animals. VISHNU, assuming the form of a *fish*, commanded the ark to be fastened by a cable, formed of a vast serpent, to his stupendous horn, secured thereby until the flood subsided; when he and BRAHMA slew a monster, named HYAGRIVA, who, while BRAHMA was reposing at the end of a *Kalpa*, stole the *Vedas*, and mankind had consequently fallen into the depths of ignorance and impiety. This mighty demon is called the prince of *Danavas:* his name means *Horse-necked*. The *Vedas* having been recovered, the world was progressively repeopled with pious inhabitants, descendants of the devout SATYAVRATA and his favoured companions. As NUH, the true name of our patriarch NOAH, may be easily deduced from MENU, so ADAM may from *Adim*, in *Sanskrit* meaning the *first*; tending, as is evidently *Sir* W. JONES's opinion, to the conclusion that the first and last of the seven MENUS can be no other than the great progenitor and restorer of our species. The history of this *Avatara* is the subject of the first *Purana*, or sacred poem, consisting of 14,000 stanzas, and is concisely told in the eighth book of the *Sri Bhagavata*, or life of KRISHNA.

2.—KURMA, or the TORTOISE.

The second grand *Avatara* of VISHNU, in the form of a tortoise, evidently refers also to the flood. In that of the *Matsya*, or *Fish*, we find the necessity of a deluge to cleanse the world from its sinful taints. By the demon HYAGRIVA having stolen the *Vedas* while BRAHMA was dosing, we must understand the dereliction of mankind from the doctrines and conduct laid down in the scriptures, and the criminal indifference of their pastors. The preserving attribute of the Deity interposed, saved a remnant of creatures from destruction, and, by recovering the scriptures, reclaimed mankind to purity of faith and conduct.

For the purpose of restoring to man some of the comforts and conveniences that were lost in the flood, VISHNU is fabled to have become incarnate again in the form of a tortoise: in which shape he sustained the mountain *Mandara*, placed on his back to serve as an axis, whereon the gods and demons, the vast serpent VASOKY serving as a rope, churned the ocean for the recovery of the *Amrita*, or beverage of immortality. PLATE 49. exhibits this process, where VISHNU is seen in his place, with the two other great powers opposed to the *Asuras*, and again on the summit of the mountain, and again in the form of the tortoise. The history of this *Avatara* forms an episode in the *Mahabarat*; and *Mr*. WILKINS has introduced a fine translation of it into his elegant version of the *Gita*, where, however, the metamorphosis of VISHNU into the tortoise is not directly mentioned. But such is the usual mode of telling and receiving the story, which is one of the most popular, both in recitation and painting, among the monstrous mass of subjects derived from the copious *Pantheon* of the *Hindus*.

KURMA, or KOORMA, is the *Sanskrit* appellation of the *Avatara*. Among the *Mahratas*, and others in the western parts of *India*, it is more commonly called *Katch*; that word, or *Katchwa*, meaning, like *Kurma*, a tortoise or turtle. The

Matsya Avatara is by such people in like manner called *Match*, or *Mutch*; *matchi* being the common name for a fish, as *matsya* is in more refined language.

The result of the operation that chiefly distinguished this *Avatara* was the obtainment of fourteen articles, usually called fourteen gems, or *chaterdesa ratana*; in common language *chowda ratny*. These fourteen jewels are thus enumerated: 1. The Moon, CHANDRA.—2. SRI, or LAKSHMI, the goddess of fortune and beauty.—3. SURA, wine; or SURADEVI, the goddess of wine.—4. *Oochisrava*, an eight-headed horse.—5. *Kustubha*, a jewel of inestimable value.—6. *Parijata*, a tree that spontaneously yielded every thing desired.—7. *Surabhi*, a cow similarly bountiful.—8. DHANWANTARA, a physician.—9. *Iravat*, the elephant of INDRA, with three *probosci*.—10. *Shank*, a shell conferring victory on whoever should sound it.—11. *Danusha*, an unerring bow.—12. *Bikh*, poison, or drugs.—13. RHEMBA, the *Apsara*, a beautiful and amiable woman.—14. *Amrita*, the beverage of immortality.

No better occasion may perhaps offer for noticing that the *Hindu* deity of wine, SURADEVI, thus obtained among the earliest blessings of the renovated world, is a female. In page 95, VARUNI, the daughter of VARUNA, the regent of the sea, is said to be spirituous liquors, and is called "an inestimable damsel, by whose reception the glad *Suras* were filled with pleasure." These two females are most likely the same, under different names and characters; and their fabulous existence and origin seems to indicate that the ancient *Hindus* considered exhilarating beverages a blessing, though the effects of intemperance induced their early legislators to prohibit the dangerous indulgence.

The eight-headed horse, the all-yielding tree, and the three-trunked elephant, are supposed to be possessed by INDRA. Of RHEMBA, notice has been taken in page 132; and of SURABHI, in page 141. The *Amrita*, or water of life, is generally understood as the primary object of this churning process: the other *gems* appear to have been obtained incidentally.

3.—VARAHA, or the BOAR.

In this *Avatara* VISHNU is generally represented four-handed, armed as usual, and with the head of a boar, on whose tusks rests a crescent, containing in its concavity an epitome of the earth, which had been immerged in the ocean as a punishment for its iniquities. So that this, as well as the two former *Avataras*, seems to be a repetition of the story of the deluge: the second combines with it a portion of astronomical allegory; and none of the other of the ten *Avataras* have any apparent reference to the universal catastrophe, so pointedly indicated by the three first, which are understood to have occurred in the earliest ages of *Hindu* history, if such a chaotic mass as their fabulous records may be dignified by such a term.

There are many fables accounting for the shape thus assumed by VISHNU on this occasion; and the boar is in *Hindu* legends, as well as in the mythological romances of *Greece* and *Egypt*, an animal very frequently introduced.

It is related in one fable, that a *Daitya*, named HIRANAYAKSHA, or the golden-eyed, (see p. 148.) passed a long life in practising religious austerities in honour of BRAHMA, and was requited by the appearance of the deity, with a promise of granting any boon he should ask. He required, as usual in these idle stories, to become universal monarch, and to be exempt from hurt by noxious animals, which he enumerated, but omitted the hog. The ambitious *Daitya*, after obtaining his wishes, became excessively wicked and presumptuous; to such a degree as to seize on the earth, and carry it with him into the depths of the ocean. The interposition of the preserving power of the Deity now became necessary, and VISHNU, assuming the form of a boar, a symbol of strength, dived into the abyss; and after a dreadful contest of a thousand years, slew the wicked monster, and restored the earth on the point of his tusks. Another legend says, that VISHNU emanated from BRAHMA's nostrils in the shape of a pig, and grew naturally to a boar.

PLATE 48. represents these three first incarnations, from *Mr.* WILKINS' casts: the images are about eight inches high, bearing VISHNU's usual emblems, as hath been already sufficiently described. *Fig.* 2. of PLATE 6. is from a small cast of VISHNU and LAKSHMI, in the third *Avatara*, then called VARAHA and VARAHI. The subjects of PLATE 48. as well as those of PLATE 51. and the others given in this work from *Mr.* WILKINS' fine series, are beautifully cast in a composition, called *biddery*, which I have occasionally, but perhaps not in strict accurrcy, denominated zinc.

4.—NARA SINGHA, or MAN-LION.

Under the head of PARVATI, (p. 148.) it is related how two etherial warders of VISHNU's palace were cursed with banishment from his presence, for insolence to SANAKA, who, attended by the seven *Rishis*, was approaching to reverence the deity. It is related, that LAKSHMI was desirous of witnessing a battle, and that VISHNU, to gratify her curiosity, willed this insolence on the part of his servants, seeing presciently all its consequences. The sentence of eternal exile on earth was mitigated to seven transmigrations; during which, if they performed their duty of sincere *Vaishnavas* faithfully, their crime would be expiated: or, if they preferred to seven faithful transmigrations, three as *Daityas*, and enemies of VISHNU, taking the consequences, they might be restored to *Vaikont'ha* at the end of their third unholy lives. The latter, as was foreseen, they determined on, and first became the *Daityas* of the third and fourth *Avataras*; and in the character of HIRANYAKASIPU, one of them was slain by VISHNU, incarnated for that purpose in the form of half-man, half-lion: to account for which, the following legend is current.

The *Daitya* performed for ten thousand years the most rigorous austerities in honour of BRAHMA, and, as usual, obtained the boon he sought; which, in addition to universal monarchy, was an exemption from death by the means either of god or man, or of any animal; either by night or day; within doors, or without; on earth, or in heaven.

His arrogance now became so great, that his impiety was insufferable; and VISHNU proceeded to the farther gratification of his inquisitive consort, by exhibiting a conflict, short, but extremely fierce, in variation of that she had before been spectatress of, in the *Varahavatara*, which lasted, as related, a thousand years. He accordingly inspired the *Daitya's* virtuous son, PARALADHA, to a commencement of a controversy with his impious father, involving the perplexing question of omnipresence, which is ingeniously enforced by the virtuous youth. "Is then the deity here?" vociferated the father, pointing to a pillar that stood just on the threshold of the house; and on being answered affirmatively, he in blasphemous defiance smote the pillar with his sword. It was now evening, and the pillar, rent asunder, exhibited the terrific spectacle of the deity in the monstrous shape of half-man, half-lion, NARASINGHA; who issuing forth, attacked HIRANYAKASIPU, and after a severe conflict of an hour, seized his devoted opponent by the hair, and at the moment when the day ends, dragged him to the severed pillar, and rent him in pieces.

PLATE 50. represents this moment, when the avenging deity, evading the covenant that BRAHMA made, sent the soul of his victim to its third and final transmigration. It is taken from a fine cast of *Mr.* WILKINS'; and although the plate exactly represents the character and attitudes of the original, it is certainly superior in point of anatomical accuracy and expression.

The upper part of PLATE 21. refers to a story something similar of SIVA, who burst from a *Linga* to avenge an insult offered to it by an impious monster.

Fig. 1. of PLATE 26. is from a small cast of VISHNU and LAKSHMI in this *Avatara*, or NARSINGHA and NRISINHI.

5.—VAMANA, or the DWARF.

The four first *Avataras* are said to have occurred in the earliest, or *Satya*, age of the *Hindus*; corresponding in character with the golden or virtuous age of the fabulists of other regions. The fifth happened in the second, or *Tirtya yug*.

MAHA BELI, a monarch reasonably virtuous, was still so elated by his grandeur, that he omitted the essential ceremonies and offerings to the deities; and VISHNU finding it necessary to check the influence of such an example, resolved to mortify and punish the arrogant *Raja*. He therefore condescended to become the son of KASYAPA and ADITI, and the younger brother of INDRA, and assumed the form of a wretched *Brahman* dwarf; and appearing before the king, asked a boon, which being promised, he demanded as much as he could pace in three steps: nor would he desire farther, although urged by BELI to demand something more worthy of him to give.

Whenever a *Hindu* historian have occasion to mention the magnificence of any monarch, a ready source of aggrandizement is offered in the trite legend of religious austerity, by which some deity, generally BRAHMA, is so irresistibly propitiated, as to yield compliance in the request, for the obtainment of which, the rigorous penance is self-inflicted.

It was so in this instance; and the boon asked and yielded, was, as usual, the sovereignty of the universe, which includes the three regions of the earth, heaven, and hell.

VISHNU, on obtaining the king's promise, required a ratification of it, which is performed by pouring water on the hand of the applicant. This BELI proceeded to do, although warned of the consequences; for he scorned not to ratify that for which his royal word stood pledged.

As the water fell into his hand, the dwarf's form expanded till it filled the world; and VISHNU now manifesting himself, deprived BELI at two steps of heaven and earth, but, he being on the whole a virtuous monarch, left *Patala*, or Hell, still in his dominion. In this character VISHNU is sometimes called TRIVIKRAMA, the three-step-taker. BELI, as king of the infernal regions, is, we may hence suppose, the same with YAMA, who corresponds also with SRADHADEVA, or god of obsequies; a title and character likewise of the seventh *Menu*, SATYAVRATA.

It is maintained by some *Vaishnavas*, that the ratifying stream, poured on the hand of VISHNU in this *Avatara*, was the river *Ganga*; which, falling from the hand of the miraculous dwarf, descended thence upon his, now VISHNU's, foot, whence, gushing as a mighty river, it was received on the head of SIVA. In *M. le* GENTIL's *Voyage aux Indes*, a rough map or plan is given, from a native original, of the course of the *Ganges*; in which it issues from the foot of VISHNU, and falling on the head of SIVA, flows in the style commonly seen through the cow's mouth.—See PLATES 17. 18. Except in this instance, I do not recollect having seen the source of the river delineated, as proceeding directly from VISHNU.—See p. p. 37. 41.

The pictures of this *Avatara*, of which I have many, but have not engraved any for this work, usually represent BELI in the act of pouring the water into the dwarf's hand, through a spouted vessel. In some, the evil counsellor, SAKRA, otherwise called SUKRA, is represented with one eye, or holding his hand before the other. SAKRA is, in fact, the same with INDRA; and as VRIHASPATI, the regent of the planet JUPITER, is the counsellor or preceptor to the gods and *Suras*, so SAKRA is adviser of the demons and *Asuras*, and is constantly employed in counteracting the divine beings and their endeavours for the good of man. To prevent the preserving power in this *Avatara* from accomplishing the projected end, in the punishment of pride and arrogance personified in BELI, SAKRA apprised him of the deceit under which he was promising the universe away; but as the monarch had too much pride to recant his royal word, the evil counsellor assumed the form of a muskito, and insinuating himself into the spout of the vessel, through which the ratifying stream was to pass, arrested its passage; when the dwarf, taking a straw to clear it, thrust out the eye of the gnat, a defect ever after retained by SAKRA in all shapes: it is said to indicate the half-enlightenment of evil counsellors. Why the thousand-eyed god, in the character of INDRA, should be the one-eyed SAKRA, I cannot explain.

6. PARASU RAMA. 7.—RAMA CHANDRA. 8.—KRISHNA. 9.—BUDDHA.

Having introduced a number of plates illustrative of the history of these incarnations, they will be considered and described separately in the next divisions of our work.

10.—KALKI, the HORSE.

This incarnation is yet to come. VISHNU, mounted on a white horse, with a drawn scimitar, blazing like a comet, will, as minutely prophesied as to place, time, &c. end the present, or *Kali* age, and renovate the creation with an era of purity. I give no plate of this subject, which is represented in pictures by an armed man leading a winged white horse.

The whole of these *Avataras* have been amply and ingeniously discussed by *Mr.* MAURICE, in his antiquities and ancient history; to which the reader is referred, if desirous of more particular information.

Kalki, or *Calci*, (with the *C* hard) is otherwise called *Kalenki*, and *Aswah*; all said to mean a *horse*. But as *Kal* is *Time*, and in several dialects means both yesterday and to-morrow; or, more extensively, the past and future, may not the name *Kalki*, of this ender and renovator of ages, have some allusion to that idea, rather than be confined to the form in which it is to be manifested?

The *Hindus*, like most other people, have thus a prophetic tradition of the coming of a punisher and redeemer. The *Sybilline* and *Delphic* oracles foretold it. The *Chinese, Japanese, Siamese*, and other eastern nations, have been taught to expect such an event; an idea that seems to prevail so generally among people so distinct, as to be deducible only from a common source.

It has been said, that the fourth and fifth *Avataras, Narsingha* and *Vamana*, are probably allegorical stories of the two presumptuous and impious monarchs, NIMROD and BELUS, under the names of HIRANYAKASIPU and BELI; the former meaning *with a golden axe*, or, according to other authorities, *clad in gold:* that the three RAMAS, two of whom were invincible warriors, and the third not only valiant in war, but the patron of agriculture and wine, which derives an epithet from his name, are different representations of the *Grecian* BACCHUS, and either the RAMA of scripture, or the Sun, first adored by his idolatrous family.—See *As. Res.* Vol. II. p. p. 132. 401. Vol. III. p. 486.

Kircher, in his *China Illustrata*, folio edit. *Amsterdam*, 1660: gives plates of the ten *Avataras*, very similar—exactly, indeed, in all material points, to the pictures of the present day. He has given *Sanskrit* characters over his plates; but they seem to have been merely copied from a *Sanskrit* alphabet, to give an effect to the plates, having no reference to their subjects, nor indeed any meaning whatever. The titles or names of the *Avataras*, as given in *European* characters, are in most instances misapplied.

I have a well executed set, that I purchased at *Poona*, from which PLATE 49. is taken, very like that of Kircher's. That given by Baldeus, an author I believe, but have not his works to refer to, still anterior to Kircher, is also the same with the drawings commonly offered for sale in different parts of *India*. This I notice, to show how little, in the lapse of a century and a half, the *Hindu* artists alter their designs of sacred subjects; they are, indeed, in a measure restricted from so doing. I had for some time an artist in my employ, a man of some genius, who had, with thousands of others, taken refuge in *Bombay* from the distresses and persecutions of *Poona*, who would, I believe, have improved himself, if let alone; but as I wanted from him accuracy, rather than invention, his performances were scrutinized by my *Pandit:* and if at any time the painter's imagination was too prurient, the *Brahman*, by a *shloka* from a *Veda* or a *Purana*, immediately restored him to orthodox sobriety.

RAMA.

Among the *Avataras* of Vishnu are recorded three favoured personages, in whom the deity became incarnate, all named Rama. They are distinguished by the names of Bala Rama, usually called Balram, Parasu Rama, or Parasram, and Rama Chandra, and are all famed as great warriors, and as youths of perfect beauty.

The first named Bala Rama, was elder brother to Krishna, (see p. 29.) and greatly assisted him in his wars; so that, in this instance, Vishnu seems to have duplicated himself, as indeed may be also said of the other Ramas; for Parasu Rama, and Rama Chandra, otherwise called, patronimically, Dasrat Rama, were cotemporaries. But it has been made a question, whether they be not three representations of one person, or three different ways of relating the same history: and, whether any, or all of them, mean Rama, the son of Cush, *Sir* W. Jones (*As. Res.* Vol. II. p. 132.) says he leaves others to determine. He deems Rama to be the same as the *Grecian* Dionysos, who is said to have conquered *India* with an army of *Satyrs*, commanded by Pan; and Rama was also a mighty conqueror, and had an army of large monkeys, or *Satyrs*, the general or prince of whom was Hanuman, a name said by this author to mean *with high cheek-bones*; others translate it, *with bloated cheeks*, alluding to his fabled origin from Pavan, regent of the wind. Rama is also found to resemble the *Indian* Bacchus; he is a descendant of the Sun, and the husband of Sita; and it is very remarkable, that the *Peruvians*, whose *Incas* boasted of the same descent, styled their greatest festival *Ramasitoa*.—See, on this subject, *As. Res.* Vol. I. p. 426. Vol. III. p. 68. Krishna, describing himself to Arjun as the first of all things, says, "Among those who carry arms, I am Rama."—*Gita*, p. 86.

Of Parasu Rama it is related, that he was born near *Agra*, in the *Tirtya Zug*, or second age. His parents were Jamadagni, whose name appears as one of the *Rishis*, and Runeka. Jamadagni, in his pious retirement, was intrusted by Indra with the charge of the wonderful boon-granting cow, Kamadenu, or Surabhi; and on one occasion, regaled the *Raja* Diruj, who was on a hunting party, in so magnificent a manner, as to excite his astonishment, until he learned the secret of the inestimable animal possessed by his host. Impelled by avarice, or rather heart-hardened by the gods, who willed the *Raja's* punishment should appear to be the immediate result of that base passion, the cow was demanded from the holy *Brahman*; and on refusal, force and stratagem were employed, which ended in the death of JAMADAGNI, but without success as to the acquisition of the desired animal, which disappeared. RUNEKA became a *Sati*, that is, burnt herself with her husband's corpse, charging the *Raja* with the guilt of the double murder, imprecating curses on his head, and enjoining their valorous son RAMA to avenge the death of his parents by the condign puuishment of the impious *Raja*, whose measure of iniquity and oppression was completed by this final attrocity.

The prayers or imprecations of a *Sati* are never inefficiently uttered; the great gods themselves cannot listen to them unmoved. VISHNU accordingly inspired RAMA, who appears to have been previously educated by MAHADEVA, on *Kailasa*, with a portion of his divinity, and sent him forth to combat the *Raja*; who, after twenty battles, was slain, the military race of KHETTRI annihilated, and his usurped kingdoms were relieved from oppréssion.

The pictures of this *Avatara* generally represent the combat between PARASU RAMA and the *Raja* with his twenty arms, some of which are scattered about, severed by the weapon of his semi-divine opponent. The miraculous cow, the immediate source of the contention, is sometimes seen taking her flight in the air.

After a life spent in mighty and holy deeds, RAMA gave his whole property in alms, and retired to the *Kokan*, (the low country between *Surat* and the southern cape, although not the whole extent of this tract,) where he is said to be still living.

On the occasion of the self-immolation of RUNEKA, it is related, that, to strengthen the potency of her imprecations on the head of the murderous *Raja*, she, in addition to her own immolation, performed also the ceremony of *Naramedha*, or the sacrifice of a man, thereby rendering her solicitation to the avenging deities absolutely irresistible; and that so lasting is the effect of the wrath felt and transmitted by the vindictive *Sati* and its attendant sacrifice and incantations, that nothing can avert its severity, continued even to the present day, but a counteracting *Naramedha:* and that, with the permission of PARASU RAMA, a man is accordingly sacrificed to appease the wrath of RUNEKA DEVI, in every generation, by the tribe of *Carhara*, settled in the *Kokan*, or *Concan*.

Mr. WILFORD (*As. Res.* Vol. III. p. 388.) observes, that although human victims, *Naramedha*, allowed by ancient authorities, are now prohibited under pain of the severest torments in the next world, the prohibition is said to be disregarded by the *Pamaras*, or *Pariar* races in different parts of *India*. But he cannot imagine, he says, that any *Brahman* would now officiate at so horrid a ceremony, denounced as it is, in the *Brahma* and *Aditya Puranas*, and in the *Bhagavat* itself.

The *Ramayana* contains the heroic description of the battles and life of all three RAMAS, although it more particularly details the exploits of RAMA CHANDRA, or DASRAT RAMA, so distinguished from his royal father, DASARAT'HA. The name of this heroic monarch means, *whose car had borne him to ten regions*; that is, to the eight cardinal and intermediate points, the zenith, and nadir. He was a descendant from SURYA, or HELI, which is a name of the Sun in *Greek* and *Sanskrit*; and one of his ancestors, the great RAGHU, had conquered the seven *dwipas*, or the whole earth. But I cannot explain, why a *Suryavansa*, or *descendant of the Sun*, should be styled RAMA CHANDRA, the latter patronimic referring contradistinguishingly to the *descendant of the Moon*, CHANDRAVANSA. In the *Hindu* mythology, however, as I have so often had occasion to observe, every thing seems, directly or indirectly, to merge in, radiate from, or amalgagate with, the Sun, or SURYA, in one or other of his names, or prototypes.

All sects and tribes of *Vaishnavas* (bating such deistical philosophers as sceptically deny the personal existence of inferior deities, attributes, or *Avataras*,) agree in stating, that, with the exception of KRISHNA, the potentiality of the preserving power of the Deity was never exhibited in such plenitude as in this *Avatara* of RAMA. In popularity, and in dramatic, historic, and poetic, shapes, it rivals the *Avatara* of KRISHNA. And as the sect of *Gocalasthas* adore KRISHNA as the Deity himself, and draw rules for their religious and moral conduct from the *Sri Bhagavata*, so the sect called *Ramanuj* (see p. 121.) similarly clothe RAMA in almighty attributes, and deem the *Ramayana* a complete body of ethics and morality.

Since my plates, illustrative of this *Avatara*, were engraved, the first volume of a translation of the *Ramayana* has been published in *Calcutta* and *London*. I had prepared a long article, collected from the communications of *Brahmans*, comprising an abstract of the *Ramayana*, as far as relates to the history and adventures of DASARAT'HA, his three wives, and their offspring; RAMA's contest for, and acquisition of, SITA; her origin, seizure, and escape from RAVANA; and many particulars of HANUMAN, and other mythological persons. Some of which may be introduced incidentally in this work; but the publication of the *Ramayana* will give them in a form so much more full, authentic, and correct, that

I shall altogether omit the article alluded to. The learned will now be able to estimate the assertion of *Sir* WILLIAM JONES, that VALMIKI's great epic poem (the *Ramayana*), in unity of action, magnificence of imagery, and elegance of diction, far surpasses the elaborate work of NONNUS, in forty-eight books, intitled *Dionysiaca*; and how far the heroes of the two poems, RAMA and DIONYSOS, be the same. The *Ramayana* is so highly venerated, that the fourth class of *Hindus*, the *Sudra*, is not permitted to read it. At the end of the first section, a promise is made of great benefit to any individual of the three first tribes who shall duly *read* that sacred poem: "a *Brahman* reading it, acquires learning and eloquence; a *Kshettria* will become a monarch; a *Vaisya* will obtain vast commercial profits; and a *Sudra hearing* it, will become great."

Among my pictures are many from the *Ramayana*, from which I have selected several for this work, as specimens of the scenery of that fine poem. In PLATE 52. the reader will perceive the discomfiture of RAWAN, or RAVANA, in his attempt to bend the divine bow, *Danush*; and RAMA's successful effort, when contending for the hand of the divine SITA. PLATE 53. represents the construction of RAMA's bridge, from the continent of *India* to *Ceylon*, by HANUMAN and his associate brethren, for the passage of RAMA's army, when proceeding to attack RAVANA, and to rescue from his treachery and power the captive SITA. The rocks with which it was constructed, being marked RA, or MA, adapted themselves, by the magic potency of these syllables, to the precise spot destined for them, HANUMAN having merely to receive and place them. HANUMAN, in PLATE 54. is carrying RAMA and SITA: as the offspring of SIVA, HANUMAN is drawn five-headed. In the lower compartment he is admitted to an audience of the ten-headed, twenty-handed, tyrant of *Ceylon*. On this occasion, it is related, that HANUMAN's tail, on which he was seated, spontaneously elongated itself, and by reduplicating its folds, exalted his head above that of RAVANA. PLATE 55. exhibits SITA receiving from her husband RAMA an intimation of the necessity of her undergoing the fire ordeal, to satisfy, not himself, for he had no suspicions, but the world, of her chaste escape from the hands of RAVANA: it was not sufficient that RAMA's wife be pure—she must not be suspected. In the upper compartment she is shown in the flames, protected and consoled by the presence of AGNI, the god of fire. Her miraculous incombustibility, and safe deliverance thence, is raptuously hailed by the associates of HANUMAN, who communicates to RAMA the joyful tidings, as seen in PLATE 56. And in PLATE 57. RAMA is reunited to his incomparable SITA, around whose neck he throws the *mala* of flowers, the chaplet of marriage, to the great delight of HANUMAN and his brethren; who express their satisfaction in awkward gambols, while angels are showering flowers on the heads of the happy pair: these heavenly beings are ever ready, in the machinery of *Hindu* epics, to perform their pleasing office on every important occasion; they are called *Pushpa-vrishti*, or flower-rainers.

PLATE 51. is taken from *Mr.* WILKINS' set of casts, about eight inches in height. *Fig.* 2. is of BALA RAMA, who, although a warrior, may, from his attributes, be esteemed a benefactor to mankind; for he bears a plough, and a pestle for beating rice; and he has epithets derived from the names of these implements—viz. HALAYUDHA, meaning *plough-armed*; and MUSALI, as bearing the *musal*, or rice-beater. His name, BALA, means strength; and the beneficent attributes, here noticed, are by some called a ploughshare, for hooking his enemies; and a club, for destroying them: and being sometimes seen with a lion's skin over his shoulders such statues have been thought to resemble, and allude to, those of the *Theban* HERCULES, and their legends.* *Fig.* 3. is of RAMA CHANDRA, distinguished by *Danusha*, the famous bow of VISHNU, with which he won the peerless SITA, or LAKSHMI incarnate in that character. It was ordained, that he only who could bend this bow, and with it shoot a fish,

* The *pestle* and mortar is with *Hindu* families a very important domestic implement, and few are without it. The mortar is generally a log of wood, the lower part shaped into a sort of foot, and in the upper is a conical cavity of the contents of about two gallons. The pestle is of hard wood, about four feet long, and two inches in diameter, with the ends tipped or ferrelled with iron, to prevent their splitting or wearing. It is usual for two females, to whose lot beating rice out of the husks, and similar domestic operations, generally fall, to work together: the pestle is raised perpendicularly by the right hand of one, and as it falls is caught by the right hand of the other, she who raised it quitting it in its fall: when tired with the right hands, the left relieve them—a song is frequently chanted during the work.

In one of the following verses, from the *Ins.* of MENU, it will be seen, that this article of furniture is introduced on grave occasions: the other verses will serve to show the detail of daily domestic offerings demanded of a *Hindu* housekeeper, and refer to deities and beings noticed in other parts of our work.

Chap. III. v. 87. (verse 86. is extracted under PRIT'HU, p. 112).—"Having thus, with fixed attention, offered clarified butter in all quarters, proceeding from the east in a southern direction, to INDRA, YAMA, VARUNA, and the god SOMA, let him offer his gift to animated creatures:

"88. Saying, 'I salute the *Maruts*,' or winds; let him throw dressed rice near the door, saying, 'I salute the water gods,' in water; and on his pestle and mortar, saying, 'I salute the gods of large trees.'

"89. Let him do the like in the north east, or near his pillow, to SRI, the goddess of abundance; in the south-west, or at the foot of his bed, to the propitious goddess BHADRAKALI; in the centre of his mansion, to BRAHMA, and his household god:

"90. To all the gods assembled, let him throw up his oblation in the open air; by day, to those spirits who walk in light, and by night, to those who walk in darkness."

while revolving on a pole, through the left eye, not seeing the fish, but its reflection in a pan of oil, should espouse SITA. PLATE 52. represents this contest, in which RAMA was of course successful. Above, is the discomfiture of RAVANA, witnessed by RAMA, his brother LAKSHIMAN, their *guru*, VISWAMITRA, and the anxious SITA. *Fig*. 4. of PLATE 51. is of PARASU RAMA, with VISHNU's usual attribute, the lotos, and the battle-axe with which he is often seen in pictures combatting his many-armed foe DIRUJ, whose tribe, the *Khettri*, or military, the potent RAMA annihilated. The epithet PARASU, distinguishingly prefixed to the name of this RAMA, means a *sword*. He is also sometimes called by his father's name, JAMADAGNI, who is said to have descended from BHRIGU.

It is RAMA CHANDRA, however, who is the favourite subject of heroic and amatory poetics: he is described "of ample shoulders; brawny arms, extending to the knee; neck, shell-formed; chest, circular and full, with auspicious marks; body, hyacinthine; with eyes and lips of sanguine hue; the lord of the world; a moiety of VISHNU himself; the source of joy to IKSHWAKU's race." He is also called RAGHUVA, or the descendant of RAGHU; and SHYAMULA, or *blue-bodied*, an appellation of KRISHNA, as well as of the prototype of both—VISHNU. The epithet of KAKA-PAKSHADARA, or *crow-winged*, is given to RAMA and to other warriors, from a certain mode of shaving the head, leaving the hair over the ears only, resembling wings as is fancied.

SITA is said to have been so named, from SET, a *field*, or *furrow*, she having been found in a field, apparently about five years old, enclosed in a box, by a *Brahman* at plough; and was presented to the childless *Raja* JANEKA, after whom she is called JANEKI. SITA, however, means fair, or white, and may be thence derived.—"Endued with youth, beauty, sweetness, goodness, and prudence; an inseparable attendant on her lord, as the light on the moon; the beloved spouse of RAMA, dear as his own soul, formed by the illusion of the *Deva*; amiable, adorned with every charm." SITA is also a favourite in descriptive poetry, and is held forth as an example of conjugal affection. Several incidents in the *Ramayana*, and in the *Sri Bhagavata*, told similarly of their several heroes, seem to mix the characters of RAMA and KRISHNA: each won a wife by bending an unyielding bow—not, indeed, very unlike the story of ULYSSES; each is described as overcoming the malignant KUMBHAKARNA: KRISHNA descended into hell, and so did SITA, the *Sacti* or energy of RAMA. But we must close our hasty account of this *Avatara*, and proceed to another still more popular and important; noticing, however, at parting, that the name of RAMA is used, beyond the pale of his own sectarists, in supplication and praise. *Rám-Rám* is a usual salutation, like our good morrow, between friends at meeting or passing, and is used by both *Vaishnavas* and *Saivas*; but I know not, if the latter, like the former, reverently reiterate it in times, and in aid, of abstraction, and in moments of enthusiasm or distress.

The author of the *Ramayana*, in the vanity of playful egotism, that, from its frequency with oriental poets, has ceased to seem assuming, calls on his readers to "salute VALMIKY, the *kukila (cuckoo)*, who, mounted on the branch of poesy, sounds the delightful note of *Rám-Rám-Rám*."

KRISHNA.

In this *Avatara* Vishnu is said, by his sectaries, to have manifested himself in a degree of power and glory far exceeding any other of his forms: in which he assumed only an *ansa*, or *portion* of his divinity, while Krishna was Vishnu himself in mortal mould. Other tribes of *Hindus* call Krishna an impious wretch, a merciless tyrant, an incarnate demon, now expiating his crimes in hell: his mortal parents were Vasudeva (meaning the *giver of wealth)* and Devaky. In plate 58. the miraculous escape of the infant over the *Yamuna* is represented, conveyed by his father, and protected by *Sesha*, or immortality; the guards placed by Kansa over his pregnant sister having failed in their vigilance. Kansa, enraged, ordered all newly born infants to be slain; but Krishna escaped his various snares: one of which was sending a woman, named Patnia, with a poisoned nipple, to nurse him. He was fostered by an honest herdsman, named Ananda, or *Happy*, and his amiable wife, Yasuda, or the *giver of honour*; and passed the gay hours of youth, dancing, sporting, and piping, among a multitude of young *Gopas*, or cow-herds, and *Gopias*, or milk-maids, from whom he selected *nine* as favourites.

Plate 59. from a beautiful and highly finished picture, may easily remind us of the representations by Papists of Mary and the infant Jesus. The plate is an exact outline of the picture, without any addition or alteration whatever, save, perhaps, some portion of ease and elegance in the position of the females. From the glory that encircles her head, which, as well as that of the infant, is of green, edged with gold, I imagine the nurse to be also the mother of Krishna; but I find her otherwise described as Yesuda, his foster mother, to whose care Vasudeva is conveying him in plate 58. Krishna, in the picture, is of a dark brown colour, and not, as his name indicates, and as he is generally seen painted, dark azure. The tray and stands bearing fruits, animals, &c. one would imagine to be merely what they represent; but with enthusiastic *Hindus* every thing is mysterious: and they will affirm, that the dominion of Krishna over the animal and vegetable worlds are here typified; nor are legends wanted in the fabulous history of this extraordinary person, applicable to, and accounting for, each of the animals that are seen in the dish,

The low table, on the right of the nurse, is similarly said to hold food, poison, and *Amrita*, symbolical of life, death, and immortality; adverting, of course, to KRISHNA's potency; while the triangular die, denoting trinity in unity, marks his coequality with the grand powers of the Triad conjoined.

With the exception of the last figure, which is from a picture, PLATE 60. is taken from casts of KRISHNA. The first six, representing him in playful pastimes, are called *Bal* KRISHNA, or the *infant*; or KRISHNA *Krira*, the *playful*. A child is called *Bala* till it attain the age of fifteen years; from which period, till he be fifty, he is *Yavana*, (hence, perhaps, the *Persian* جوان and the *Latin Juvenis*), that is, in a state of youth; but both periods are much varied, and the terms are not strictly applied. This description of image is very common, and some of them have considerable merit: they are generally small, about the size represented in the plate, which exhibits exact portraits of the originals: the style in which the hair is done up, in *figures* 1. and 2. is singular: the little ball, held in the right hand of many of these images, is by some said to be a symbol of the earth, denoting this deity's supremacy, or dominion over it; while others, less mystical, describe it as a plaything, or a cake of *jughrât*, a sort of sweetmeat with which the divine child was wont to be delighted. On one occasion, as is related in the *Bhagavat*, the *Gopia*, his playfellows, (that is the Muses, for KRISHNA is APOLLO,) complained to YASUDA, that he had pilfered and ate their curds; and being reproved by his foster mother, he desired her to examine his mouth, in which, to her just amazement, she beheld the whole universe in all its plenitude of magnificence.

Fig. 7. represents him, while yet a boy, destroying the terrible serpent *Kaliya*. *Fig*. 8. is his character of MURLIDUR, or the *Tuneful*, a personification of ethereal harmony. And *fig*. 9. from a tinted picture, in which KRISHNA is of a dark azure colour, seems to combine both characters; identifying him with APOLLO, the slayer of the serpent PYTHON, and the deity presiding over music. Under the name of GOPALA, or the herdsman, he is the pastoral APOLLO, who fed the herds of ADMETUS, surnamed NOMIOS by the *Greeks*. I will here notice, that the figure of KRISHNA, in PLATE 13. (occupying a space found not large enough for the subject originally intended for it,) is taken from the same cast as *fig*. 7. of PLATE 60. the ingenious gentleman, who made the beautiful drawings for my plates, having there availed himself of my permission to throw a grace and ease into the figure not possessed by the original, as faithfully pourtrayed in *fig*. 7. of PLATE 60. I have many pictures and casts of him in the character of MURLIDUR, piping to the damsels and herds of

MATRA, or GOVERDHEN. The dancing and singing girls, attached to the temple of *Jejury*, of whom it was said, when I visited it in 1792, there were more than two hundred, are called *Murly*; a term most likely of similar allusion, of which I was not aware, when I gave some account of that temple in a former work.

At the age of seven, his historians relate, that he uplifted, on the tip of his little finger, the mountain *Goverdhen*, the *Hindu Parnassus*, to shelter the *Gopa* and *Gopia* from the wrath of INDRA, the JUPITER *Pluvius* of the *Hindu Pantheon*; who, enraged with jealousy at the diminution of his votaries and sacrifices, consequent to the adoration of KRISHNA, attempted to destroy them by a partial deluge. This story is represented in PLATE 61. from the *Matsya Purana*, whence *Sir* W. JONES has thus poetically introduced it in his hymn to INDRA. The bard

———— "Smil'd, and, warbling in a softer mode,
Sang the red lightning, hail, and whelming rain
O'er *Gocal* green, and *Vraja's* nymph-lov'd plain,
By INDRA hurl'd, whose altars ne'er had glow'd,
Since infant KRISHNA rul'd the rustic train—
Now thrill'd with terror. Them the heavenly child
Call'd, and with looks ambrosial smil'd:
Then, with one finger rear'd the vast *Goverdhen*,
Beneath whose rocky burden,
On pastures dry, the maids and herdsmen trod:—
The lord of thunder felt a mightier god."

I have several pictures of this miracle, in which KRISHNA is always represented as a man, attended by his favourite mistress, RADHA, and sometimes by a multitude of shepherds and shepherdesses; the former with poles, steadying the uplifted sheltering mountain, as seen in PLATE 61. a shower of rain and fire falling vainly on its summit.

The destruction of *Kaliya* by KRISHNA is more elaborately represented in PLATE 62. taken from a sketch. The upper and lower portions (the scene of one being on land, and the other in the *Yamuna*,) relate, I imagine, to the same event, although I do not know sufficient of the story to connect them. It has been surmised by respectable writers, that the subject here represented has reference to an awful event, figuratively related in our scripture; and KRISHNA is not only painted, as seen also in the preceding plate, bruising the head of the serpent, but the latter is made to retort by biting his heal. Among my images and pictures of this deity (and they are very numerous, for he is enthusiastically and extensively adored, and his history affords great scope for the imagination,) I have not one original, nor did I ever see one, in which the snake is biting KRISHNA's foot; and I have been hence led to suspect, that the plates engraved in *Europe* of that action are not solely of *Hindu* invention or origin. I may easily err in this instance, but I am farther strengthened in the suspicion, from never having heard the fact alluded to in the many conversations that I have held with *Brahmans* and others on the history of this *Avatara*.

SONNERAT was, I believe, the first who has exhibited KRISHNA crushing a snake: how, otherwise, would he, or any man, kill it so easily and obviously, as by stamping on its head? nor can the reptile in any mode retort but by biting the foot of its assailant. Zeal sometimes has in its results the same effect as infidelity; and one cannot help lamenting, that a superstructure requiring so little support should be encumbered by awkward buttresses, so ill applied, that they would, if it were possible, diminish the stability of the building that they were intended to uphold. Of this description were the zealous researches of some missionaries, who, in BRAHMA and SARASWATI, as noticed in page 130. easily found ABRAHAM and SARAH; and the *Christian* Trinity is as readily discovered in the monstrous Triad of the *Hindus*. Of this description also, I am disposed to think, are the attempts at bending so many of the events of KRISHNA's life to tally with those, real or typical, of JESUS CHRIST. That KRISHNA, according to his historians, passed a life of a most extraordinary and incomprehensible nature, may be admitted; and that his name, and the general outline of his story, were long anterior to the birth of our Saviour, is very certain, and probably to the time of HOMER. His miracles are amazing, but ridiculous; a term that may, perhaps, be applied to a majority of the legends detailed with such prolixity in the modern poem, the *Sri Bhagavata*, which is esteemed as the eighteenth *Purana*. He is represented as the meekest, tenderest, and most benevolent, of beings; still, however, he fomented the terrible war described in the *Mahabarat*: he washed the feet of the *Brahmans*: he exhibited an appearance of excessive libertinism; but it was all *Maya*, or *delusion*; for he was pure and chaste in reality: he uplifted mountains, raised the dead, descended into hell, and performed such motley exploits, as induced *Sir* WILLIAM JONES (*As. Res.* Vol. I. p. 274.) to think that "the spurious Gospels, which abounded in the first ages of Christianity, were carried to *India*, and the wildest parts of them repeated to the *Hindus*, who engrafted on them the old fable of KESAVA, the APOLLO of *Greece*."

The subject so beautifully represented in PLATE 63. is said to be KRISHNA and his *Gopia*, as well in their characters of APOLLO and the Muses, as in those of the Sun, and the planets in harmonious movements round him; and was formerly adduced in support of the idea, that the *Hindus* had a knowledge of the true solar system, a point that no longer requires proof. A legend is popularly related, accounting for the multiplied appearance of KRISHNA in this *Ras mandala*, or *circular dance.* A number of virgins having assembled to celebrate in mirth and sport the descent of KRISHNA, the god himself appeared among them, and proposed a dance; and to remove the deficiency of partners, he divided himself into as many portions as there were damsels, which number differs in different pictures. HOLWEL gives a rude sketch of this subject.—*Hist. Ev.* Part II. p. 132. And MAURICE (*An. Hist.* Vol. I. p. 103. II. p. 356.) relates the story with appropriateremarks.

On certain holidays, most towns exhibit sets of these nocturnal dancers; all, however, males: ten, fifteen, or more, in a set, with a short stick in each hand, moving slowly in the direction of the sun; singing, and keeping time with awkward movements and stamping of the feet, and as awkwardly by turning to the persons before and behind; and alternately striking each other's sticks, as represented in the plate, to the subject of which such dances may perhaps allude. I have, however, seen a dance something like it, but much more animated with hand and foot, among the *Maplas*, a sect of *Mahomedans*, in *Malabar*.

The comparison between KRISHNA and APOLLO runs parallel in a great many instances. The destruction of PYTHON by APOLLO, the commentators tell us, means the purification of the atmosphere by the sun from the mephitic exhalations consequent to the deluge; and KRISHNA's victory over the noxious *Kaliya naga*, may, by those who, allegorizing all poetical extravagance deprive poetry of half its beauties, be explained in the same manner. In honour of KRISHNA's triumph, games and sports are annually held in *India*, as the *Pythic* games were at stated times exhibited in *Greece*. Like the *Pythian* serpent in the temples of APOLLO, *Kaliya naga* enjoys also his apotheosis in those dedicated to the worship of KRISHNA; nor are arguments wanted toward identifying *Serpentarius*, on our sphere, with his formidable foe, and the theatre of the warfare, the river *Yamuna*, with the *via lactea.* So the variety of demons, sent to annoy KRISHNA, are perhaps the allegorical monsters of the sky, attempting in vain to obstruct his apparent progress through the heavens, where other constellations are fabled as so many beautiful nymphs ready to receive him, and have given rise to allegories of his inconstancy. The well-known story of NAREDA's visit to the numerous chambers of KRISHNA's seraglio, and finding the ardent deity in them all, may refer to the universality of the sun's presence at the equinoxes. APOLLO and KRISHNA are both inventors of the flute. One was disappointed by DAPHNE, who was turned into the *Laurus*, hence sacred to APOLLO; KRISHNA's coy nymph was transformed into the *Tulasi*, alike sacred to him.

The *Tulasi* is the black *Ocymum:* to this azure deity several animals and vegetables, of a black or blue colour, are sacred. The metamorphosis of his fleet nymph into this lovely shrub, is related in a style perfectly *Ovidian* in the *Puranas*. *Tulsy*, as it is called in speech, forms a pretty feminine appellation at this day; for, among *Hindustani* females, the beautiful, warlike, and amorous KRISHNA, is the most popular deity.

Before we quit PLATE 63. I must notice, that, with the exception of the male and female figures piping in the centre, which are exact portraits, the artist, who made the drawing for the engraver from the sketch by my native painter, has, with my permission, given considerable grace and elegance to the subject, not possessed by the original: he has not, however, in any wise, deviated from it in points at all affecting the character of the composition, but merely improved on the attitudes and outline. Some pictures exhibit seven females making measured movements around a central deity; I have others with four: these we may, as our fancies suggest, suppose to refer to the planetary orbs, or to the seasons and their source.

PLATE 64. represents the frolicsome deity receiving in marriage the hand of a bear, tinted in the picture, whence the engraving is made, of the same azure hue as the bridegroom. This was a left-handed marriage; and the name of this sylvan lass, JAMBAVANTI, is not found in the muster-roll of KRISHNA's regular wives: of her, something more hereafter. In the lower part of the plate is another of his miracles: being, on one occasion, in great jeopardy, from the wrath of some of his numerous enemies, he produced an immense snake, which received and sheltered in its capacious stomach his flock, herds, himself, and fellow shepherds. In the variety of histories extant of the life and actions of the preserving power in this *Avatara*, legends abound popularly detailing these events, which refer most likely to some astronomical phenomena.

PLATE 65. exhibits whimsical combinations of KRISHNA and his damsels, the latter forming for him a *palky* and an elephant; and in PLATE 66. they are formed into a peacock and horse. The originals of the *palky* and horse are tinted pictures; the peacock and elephant from outline sketches. No stress can be laid on the number of the nymphs thus employed, as they differ in different subjects. I have had models in wax and in clay of the elephant similarly formed, in which the number nine was uniformly preserved. Many years back, at *Oxford*, I obtained a sketch of a picture of a *palky* similarly formed, copied from a book, marked LAUD. A. 181. in the *Bodleian* library. It is better imagined than that from which my plate is taken: one of the seven women, in rather a curious posture, forms the arch over the head of the deity—if, in that instance, it be meant for KRISHNA, which I rather doubt, as it seems in the style of a *Mahomedan* work, and his features and dress correspond. The book contains illuminated specimens of *Arabic* and *Persian* penmanship, with pictures.

PLATE 67. is taken from a very pretty coloured picture, given to me by my old friend *Major* JOHNSON, of the *Bombay* engineers. KRISHNA is seldom drawn unattended by females, and where seen with but one, she is always said to be RADHA, his favourite mistress, or divine spouse, who I imagine to be the same with RUKMENI; but the latter is sometimes distinguished as his legal worldly wife, and the former as a personification of religion. RUKMENI had a mortal father, *Raja* BHISHMAKA; and I have an abridged MS. life of the "*all-conquering* HERI," in which mention is made of his loves with "RADHA, wife of ANEYAH:" she is also called KANTAMATI. The winged figure in PLATE 67. pouring from the sky a golden glory on the head of KRISHNA, is singular. We have here seven damsels in attendance on the favoured deity, although the number of his regular wives is said to have been eight: viz. 1. RUKMENI, an incarnation of LAKSHMI.—2. YAMUMINTI.—3. KALENDIRI, a water nymph, daughter of the Sun.—4. SATYAVAMA.—5. LAKSHMENI.—6. MITRAVINDA.—7. SATYA.—8. VRUNDI. Perhaps PLATE 67. may exhibit them all, his divine spouse being in the clouds, and, by a heavenly emanation, spiritualizing his seemingly mortal and carnal enjoyments. Besides these, he attached to him sixteen thousand women that he found virgins in the ample seraglio of BHUM, a five-headed *asura*, who, for his manifold crimes, KRISHNA slew. The legendary tales, descriptive of these events, are of great length and variety. Each of these sixteen thousand and eight women bore him ten sons, and each supposed herself the exclusive favourite of her lord. KAMA, the god of love, is said to have been the offspring of his first wife, RUKMENI; and in this birth he was named PRADYAMNA: stripped of its allegory, it means, I suppose, that they had a lovely son. On the death of KRISHNA, RUKMENI became a *Sati*, and, with several other of his wives, burned herself, in view to an immediate re-union with her lord in *Vaikont'ha.*

In musical legends it is said, that there were, in the days of KRISHNA, sixteen thousand *Ragas*, or musical modes; or rather *passions*, or *affections* of the mind; and each of his *Ragnis*, or musical nymphs, selected one of these *Ragas*, in which to modulate her strains for affecting and securing the heart of the amorous and harmonious deity. This may perhaps mean, that KRISHNA, devoted to music, receives and enjoys every variety of modulation, multiplied to the number of 16,000, and fancifully personified in the form of nymphs, derived from the five-headed BHUM, (a five-stringed or five-stopped instrument) KRISHNA similarly multiplying himself into as many persons, or *Ragas*, as were requisite to espouse, or adapting himself to receive, the many-noted *Raginis*.

As a specimen of the tales related of this sportive deity, I here give, as I find it in my memoranda, that of NAREDA's visit to the numerous chambers of KRISHNA's *haram*, allusive, as it is thought, to the universality of the sun's equinoctial influence, or, more mystically, to the attribute of omnipresence.

It happened in *Dwarka*, a splendid city built by VISWAKARMA, by command of KRISHNA, on the sea-shore, in the province of *Guzerat*, that his musical associate, NAREDA, had no wife or substitute, and he hinted to his friend the decency of sparing him one from his long catalogue of ladies. KRISHNA generously told him to win and wear any one he choose, not immediately in requisition for himself. NAREDA accordingly went wooing to one house, but found his master there; to a second—he was again forestalled; a third, the same; to a fourth, fifth, the same: in fine, after the round of 16,008 of these domiciliary visits, he was still forced to sigh and keep single; for KRISHNA was in every house, variously employed, and so domesticated, that each lady congratulated herself on her exclusive and uninterrupted possession of the ardent deity.

NAREDA, the mythological offspring of SARASWATI, patroness of music, is famed for his talents in that science—so great were they, that he became presumptuous; and emulating the divine strains of KRISHNA, he was punished by having his *Vina* placed in the paws of a bear, whence it emitted sounds far sweeter than the minstrelsy of the mortified musician. I have a picture of this joke, in which KRISHNA is forcing his reluctant friend to attend to his rough-visaged rival, who is ridiculously touching the chords of poor NARDEA's *Vina*, accompanied by a brother bruin on the cymbals. KRISHNA passed several practical jokes on his humble and affectionate friend: he metamorphosed him once into a woman; at another time, into a bear. But volumes, instead of pages, would be necessary to contain the thousandth part of the fables connected with the romantic history of KRISHNA.

It must not, however, be supposed, that NAREDA is altogether, or generally, a subject for ridicule or jokes; on the contrary, he is a very distinguished personage: son of BRAHMA and SARASWATI; a wise legislator; great in arms, arts, and eloquence; and, indeed, of such historical celebrity, that his actions are the subject of a *Purana*, named after him: he was an astronomer, and an exquisite musician. He invented the *Vina*, a sort of lute, which, as remarked by *Sir* W. JONES as a singular fact, is otherwise called *Katchapi*, which has the same meaning as *Testudo*; and being also a frequent messenger of the gods to one another, or to favoured mortals, his character, in these and other points, resembles that of HERMES, or MERCURY. In the histories of KRISHNA, NAREDA is very frequently introduced; and, on one occasion, is expressly said to be only another form of KRISHNA himself.

KRISHNA's names are, like other deified personages, numerous. He being VISHNU, they enjoy several in common: MURARI, HERI, MADHAVA, (VISHNU destroyed the giant MADHU,) BHAGAVAN, are among them.—GOVINDA, GOPALA, GOKALA, are derived from his occupation of herdsman.—GOPINAT'HA, the *Gopi's* god.—MURLIDER, the Tuneful.—KESSU, KESAVA, or KESAVI, refer to the fineness of his hair; VANIMALI, to his pendent garland; YADAVA, VARSHNEYA, and VASUDEVA, to his tribe and family.

The loves of KRISHNA and RAD'HA, which, in the writings and conversation of the *Hindus*, are as constantly adverted to as those of LEELI and MAJNUN, by *Mahommedans*, are said to mean, in their emblematical theology, the reciprocal attraction between the divine goodness and the human soul; and are told at large in the tenth book of the *Bhagavat*; and are the subject of the beautiful pastoral drama, entitled *Gita Govinda*, by JAYADEVA, who wrote before our era. On some other occasions, I have acknowledged my obligations to the translator of that exquisite poem, and am about to make from it copious extracts, descriptive of the person and appearance of KRISHNA, who, or GOVINDA, or HERI, is the immediate hero of the piece; as well as illustrative of the mystical style of *Hindu* theology, and of mythological allusions, that I can in no other mode so pleasingly introduce. The reader will occasionally call to mind, that some of the effusions must be received, not literally, but emblematically, as in the mystical poetry of other people.

The following tender lamentation of RAD'HA, for the absence of her lord, I commence my extracts with.—

"Though he takes recreation in my absence, and smiles on all around him, yet my soul remembers him, whose languishing reed modulates an air, sweetened by the nectar of his quivering lips, while his ear sparkles with gems, and his eye darts amorous glances;—him, whose locks are decked with the plumes of peacocks, resplendent with many-coloured moons, and whose mantle gleams like a dark-blue cloud illumined with rainbows;—him, whose graceful smile gives new lustre to his lips, brilliant, and soft as a dewy leaf—sweet and ruddy as the blossoms of *Bandhujiva*, while they tremble with eagerness to kiss the daughters of the herdsman;—him, who disperses the gloom with beams from the jewels which decorate his bosom, his wrists, and his ancles—on whose forehead shines a circlet of sandal wood, which makes even the moon contemptible, when it moves through irradiated clouds;—him, whose earrings are formed of entire gems, in the shape of the fish *makara* * on the banners of love—even the yellow-robed god, whose attendants are the chief of deities, of holy men, and of demons;—him, who reclines under a gay *kadamba* tree, who formerly delighted me while he gracefully moved in the dance, and all his soul sparkled in his eyes. My weak mind thus enumerates his qualities; and though offended, strives to banish his offence. What else can it do? It cannot part with its affection for KRISHNA, whose love is excited by other damsels, and who sports in the absence of RAD'HA. Bring, O my sweet friend! that vanquisher of the demon KESI,† to sport with me, who am repairing to a secret bower; who look timidly on all sides, who meditate with amorous fancy on his divine transfiguration. Bring him, whose discourse was once composed of the sweetest words, to converse with me, who am bashful on his first approach, and express my thoughts with a smile sweet as honey. Bring him, who formerly slept on my bosom, to recline with me on a green bed of leaves just gathered, while his lips shed dew, and my arms enfold him. Bring him, who has attained the perfection of skill in love's art, whose hand used to press these firm and delicate spheres, to play with me; whose voice rivals that of the *Kocila*,‡ and whose tresses are bound with waving blossoms. Bring him, who formerly drew me by the locks to his embrace, to repose with me; whose feet tinkle as they move with rings of gold

* KAMA, the god of love, bears on his banner the fish *Makara*.

† A monster, slain by VISHNU.

‡ An admired singing bird, with green plumage, red beak and feet: sometimes said to be the cuckoo.

and gems, whose loosened zone sounds as it falls, and whose limbs are as slender and flexible as the creeping plant. That god, whose cheeks are beautified by the nectar of his smiles, whose pipe drops in ecstasy from his hand, I saw in the grove encircled by damsels of *Vraja*;* who gazed on him askaunce from the corner of their eyes. I saw him in the grove with happier damsels, yet the sight of him delighted me. Soft is the gale that blows over yon clear pool, and extends the clustering blossoms of the voluble †*asoca*; soft, yet grievous to me in the absence of the foe of MADHU. Delightful are the flowers of the ‡*Amra*, on the mountain top, while the murmuring bees pursue their voluptuous toil; delightful, yet afflicting to me, O friend! in the absence of the youthful KESAVA."

An officious female friend thus describes KRISHNA to the forsaken and afflicted RAD'HA.

"With a garland of wild flowers, descending even to his yellow mantle that girds his azure limbs; distinguished by smiling cheeks, and by earrings that sparkle as he plays, HERI exults in the assemblage of amorous damsels. One of them presses him with her swelling breasts, while she warbles with exquisite melody; another, affected by a glance from his eye, stands meditating on the lotos of his face; a third, on pretence of whispering a secret in his ear, approaches his temples, and kisses them with ardour. One seizes his mantle, and draws him towards her, pointing to the bower on the banks of the *Yamuna*, where elegant *Vanjulas* interweave their branches. He applauds another, who dances in the sportive circle, whilst her bracelets ring as she beats time with her palms. Now he caresses one, and kisses another, smiling on a third with complacency; and now he chases her whose beauty has most allured him. Thus the wanton HERI frolics in the season of sweets, among the maids of *Vraja*, who rush to his embraces, as if he were Pleasure itself assuming a human form; and one ‖ of them, under a pretext of hymning his divine perfections, whispers in his ears—'Thy lips, my beloved, are nectar!'"

KRISHNA, afflicted by the jealous anger of RAD'HA, exclaims—

"Grant me but a sight of thee, O lovely RADHICA! for my passion tor-

* A country between *Agra* and *Dehli*, intersected by the *Jumna*, and including the city of *Mat'hura*.

† A species of beech.—See p. 55.

‡ The *Mango*: with which flower, one of the five arrows of the god of love is tipped.

‖ It may be accidental; but still there are few things in *Hindu* mythology of incidental occurrence: almost every thing, however trivial, is intended, and has its allusion. It may yet, I say, be accident, but RADHA's officious friend describes KRISHNA in distinct dalliance with *nine* damsels.

ments me. I am not the terrible MAHESA: a garland of water lilies, with subtile threads, decks my shoulders—not serpents with twisted folds: the blue petals * of the lotos glitter on my neck—not the azure gleam of poison: powdered sandal wood is sprinkled on my limbs—not pale ashes. O, god of love! mistake me not, for MAHADEVA; wound me not again; approach me not in anger; hold not in thy hand the shaft barbed with an *amra* flower. My heart is already pierced by arrows from RADHA's eyes, black and keen as those of an antelope; yet mine eyes are not gratified by her presence. Her's are full of shafts; her eyebrows are bows, and the tips of her ears are silken strings: thus armed by ANANGA, the god of desire, she marches, herself a goddess, to ensure his triumph over the vanquished universe. I meditate on her delightful embrace; on the ravishing glances darted from the fragrant lotos of her mouth; on her nectar-dropping speech; on her lips, ruddy as the berries of the *Bimba*."

RADHA, half pacified, thus tenderly reproaches him.—

"Alas! alas!—Go MADHAVA—depart KESAVI; speak not the language of guile: follow her, O lotos-eyed god—follow her, who dispels thy care. Look at his eyes, half opened, red with waking through the pleasurable night—yet smiling still with affection for my rival. Thy teeth, O cerulean youth! are as azure as thy complexion, from the kisses which thou hast imprinted on the beautiful eyes of thy darling, graced with dark blue † powder; and thy limbs, marked with punctures in love's warfare, exhibit a letter of conquest, written in polished sapphire with liquid gold. That broad bosom, stained by the bright lotos of her ‡ foot, displays a vesture of ruddy leaves over the tree of thy heart, which trembles within it. The pressure of her lips on thine, wound me to the soul. Ah! how canst thou assert, that we are one; since our sensations differ thus widely?—Thy soul, O dark-limbed god! shows its blackness externally; even thy childish heart was malignant, and thou gavest death to the nurse who would have given thee milk."

* Written in the north of *India*; the lotos in the southern parts, *Bengal*, and the *Dekhan*, having only white and red flowers. Hence the *Hindu* poets feign that the lotos was dyed red by the blood of SIVA, that flowed from the wound made by the arrow of KAMA.

† RADHA feigns that the pigment of powdered antimony, with which the *belles* of *India* trace, at the insertion of the eyelashes, a black animating line, has been rubbed off the eyes of her rival by the ardent salutations of KRISHNA.

‡ *Hindustani* women dye the soles of their feet, and nails, of a bright red.—See p. 64. RADHA, in her frenzied jealousy, fancies she sees a print of her rival's foot on KRISHNA's breast; observing, perhaps, the indelible impression of the foot of BRIGHU, received on his breast by VISHNU, as related in another place. —See PLATE 11. *fig.* 6.

Krishna is thus farther described, in the same poem:—

"His azure breast glittered with pearls of unblemished lustre, like the full bed of the cerulean *Yamuna*, interspersed with curls of white foam. From his graceful waist flowed a pale yellow robe, which resembled the golden dust of the water lily, scattered over its blue petals. His passion was inflamed by the glances of her eyes, which played like a pair of water birds with azure plumage, that sport near a full blown lotos on a pool, in the season of dew. Bright ear-rings, like two suns, displayed, in full expansion, the flowers of his cheeks and lips, which glistened with the liquid radiance of smiles. His locks, interwoven with blossoms, were like a cloud variegated with moon-beams; and on his fore-head shone a circle of odorous oils, extracted from the sandal of *Malaya*—like the moon just appearing on the dusky horizon; while his whole body seemed in a flame, from the blaze of unnumbered gems."

In the following animated apostrophe, Krishna is immediately identified, not only with Vishnu, "who reclinest on the bosom of Kamala," and "sittest on the plumage of Garuda," and in the *Kurma* and Ram *Avataras*, but with the Sun, "from whom the day star derives his effulgence;" and to Brahma, "who calledst three worlds into existence;" and to Mahadeva, "sipping nectar from the radiant lips of Pedma:"—

"Oh thou, who reclinest on the bosom of Kamala, whose ears flame with gems, and whose locks are embellished with sylvan flowers—thou, from whom the day star derived his effulgence; who slew the venom-breathing *Kaliya*; who beamedst, like a sun, on the tribe of Yadu, that flourished like a lotos—thou, who sittest on the plumage of Garuda; who, by subduing demons, gavest exquisite joy to the assembly of immortals—thou, for whom the daughter of Janaca was decked in gay apparel—thou, whose eye sparkles like the water lily—who calledst three worlds into existence—thou, by whom the rocks of *Mandar* were easily supported; who sippest nectar from the radiant lips of Pedma, as the fluttering *Chacora* drinks the moon-beams;—be victorious, O Heri, lord of conquest!"

I must indulge myself with one more extract from the *Gita Govinda*, painting the emotions of the lovers in the morning after the night of reconciliation, "when affliction ceased, and ecstasy drowned the recollection of past sorrows."

"In the morning she arose, disarrayed, and her eyes betrayed a night without slumber; when the yellow-robed god, who gazed on her with transport, thus meditated on her charms in his heavenly mind:—'Though her locks be diffused at random; though the lustre of her lips be faded; though her garland and zone be fallen from their enchanting stations, and though she hides their places with her hands, looking toward me with bashful silence; yet, even thus disarrayed, she fills me with ecstatic delight.' But RADHA, preparing to array herself, before the company of nymphs could see her confusion, spake thus with exultation to her obsequious lover:—

"'Place, O son of YADU! with fingers cooler than sandal wood—place a circlet of musk on this breast, which resembles a vase of consecrated water, crowned with fresh leaves, and fixed near a vernal bower to propitiate the god of love. Place, my darling! the glossy powder, which would make the blackest bee envious, on this eye, whose arrows are keener than arrows darted by the husband of RETI. Fix, O accomplished youth! the two gems, which form part of love's chain, in these ears, whence the antelopes of thine eyes may run downwards, and sport at pleasure. Place now a fresh circle of musk, black as the lunar spots, on the moon of my forehead; and mix gay flowers on my tresses with peacocks' feathers, in graceful order, that they may wave like the banners of KAMA. Now replace, O tender-hearted! the loose ornaments of my vesture; and refix the golden bells of my girdle on their destined station, which resembles those hills where the god with five shafts, who destroyed SAMBAR, keeps his elephant ready for battle.'

"While she spake, the heart of YADAVA triumphed; and obeying her sportive behests, he placed musky spots on her bosom and forehead; dyed her temples with radiant hues; embellished her eyes with additional blackness; decked her braided hair, and her neck, with fresh garlands; and tied on her wrists the loosened bracelets, on her ankles the beamy rings, and round her waist the zone of bells, that sounded with ravishing melody."

But we must recollect. that the seemingly amorous conflicts of these ardent lovers are mere mystical descriptions of "the reciprocal attraction between the divine goodness and the human soul."—This is the emblematical theology that PYTHAGORAS admired and adopted; that the *Sufi* poets, HAFEZ, SADI, and others among the *Persians*, and SOLOMON also, in his fine song, so beautifully inculcate. Like our *quietists* and *enthusiasts*, and *saints*, in a mode not easily comprehended by the sinful and unenlightened; or, at any rate, not believed by them to be very permanent, however innocent its institution; "they profess eager desire, but without carnal affection; and circulate the cup, but no material goblet: in their sect, all things are spiritual—all is mystery within mystery."

—See *Sir* WILLIAM JONES's admirable Essay on the Mystical Poetry of the *Persians* and *Hindus*, in the third volume of the *Asiatic Researches:* in which a translation of the *Gita Govinda* of JAYADEVA is introduced.

Quitting these mystical rhapsodists, let us turn to a work of a different description, and observe the terms in which KRISHNA is described in the *Bhagavat Gita*. It will not be easy to exceed them in sublimity, divesting them of their local and mythological allusions, even in genuine theological language.

ARJUN, the son of PANDU, addresses KRISHNA (*Gita*, p. 86.) as "The Supreme BRAHM: the most holy; the most high God; the Divine Being before all other Gods; without birth; the mighty Lord; God of Gods; the universal Lord." In different parts of the *Gita*, he says of himself—"I am, of things transient, the beginning, the middle, and the end: the whole world was spread abroad by me in my invisible form. At the end of the period *Kalp*, all things return into my primordial source; and, at the beginning of another *Kalp*, I create them all again.—I am the creator of mankind; uncreated, and without decay.—There is not any thing greater than I; and all things hang on me, even as precious gems on a string.—I am the understanding of the wise, the glory of the proud, the strength of the strong; I am the eternal seed of all nature; I am the father and mother of this world, the grandsire, and the preserver; I am death and immortality; I am entity and nonentity; I am never-failing time; I am all-grasping death; and I am the resurrection."—

"The great BRAHM is my womb; in it I place my fœtus; and from it is the production of all nature.—The great BRAHM is the womb of all those various forms which are conceived in every natural womb; and I am the father that soweth the seed."—Page 107. "I am the emblem of the immortal, and of the incorruptible; of the eternal, of justice, and of endless bliss."—Page 110. "Neither the Sun, nor the Moon, nor the Fire, enlighteneth that place from whence there is no return; and which is the supreme mansion of my abode."—Page 112.

SANJAY, one of the interlocutors of the *Gita*, describes KRISHNA, as he revealed his "million forms divine" to ARJUN, "Covered with every marvellous thing—the eternal God, whose countenance is turned on every side. The glory and amazing splendour of this mighty being may be likened to the Sun, rising at once into the heavens with a thousand times more than usual brightness.—The son of PANDU then beheld, within the body of the God of Gods, standing together, the whole universe divided forth into its vast variety."—Page 90.

ARJUN, terrified at this wonderous exhibition, exclaims: "Thou art the

Supreme Being! I see thee without beginning, without middle, and without end; of valour infinite, of arms innumerable; the Sun and Moon thy eyes; thy mouth a flaming fire; and the whole world shining with thy reflected glory. Having beholden thy dreadful teeth, and gazed on thy countenance, emblems of Time's last fire, I know not which way I turn; I find no peace.—Have mercy then, O God of Gods! thou mansion of the universe! and show me thy celestial form; with the diadem on thy head, and thy hands, armed with the club and *chakra*.—Assume then, O God of a thousand arms! image of the universe! thy four-armed form."—Page 91.

Under the head PARVATI, p. 156, mention is made of the festival of *Huli*, more classically called *Hulica*; otherwise *Phalgutsava*, meaning the festival of *Phalguna*, it occurring in the month of that name, commencing about the full moon, at the approach of the vernal equinox. It is one of the greatest festivals among the *Hindus*, and almost all sects seem to partake in its festivities; and all ranks, from kings downward, appear animated by the season, which is peculiarly dedicated to KRISHNA. Images of the deity are carried about in *palkeys*, and on elephants, horses, &c. attended by music and singing, and various antics. People of condition receive numerous visitors, who are entertained with dancing girls, music, singing, betle, and rose-water. I have had the honour of visiting his *Highness* the present *Peshwa*, and divers other great men of the court of *Poona*, on the occasion of this festival. I find in my memoranda, an estimate of upwards of two hundred dancing girls being at the *Peshwa's* palace: the songs are exclusively in honour of KRISHNA, and hailing the return of the season, personified under the name of VASANTA—pronounced BESSANT at *Poona*. Although the songs be exclusively in honour of KRISHNA, the subject affords a very extensive range for poetical effusion. As well as BESSANT, his friend KAMA, the god of love, who is, as we have seen, KRISHNA's son, and a host of allegorical personages, can easily be introduced.

Besides the *Huli*, several other holidays,* especially in honour of KRISHNA, occur: on one, gifts of water and grain, particularly of *barley*, with oblations of perfumes, and other religious rites, produce fruit without end in the next world. On another, the festival is called *Rat'ha jattra*, or the festival of the chariot, in which the images of KRISHNA and BALA RAMA are borne about in a car by day: on this occasion KRISHNA is worshipped as JAGANAT'HA, or lord

* A punster, as he ought to be called, rather than an etymologist; or, perhaps, he was ridiculing the strained application of a pliant etymology; derived our holiday from *huli* day.

of the universe. At the temple of that name, the concourse of people is very great: the rising of the moon is the sign for the commencement of the feast, which must end when it sets. There is, doubtless, some astronomical allegory connected with these ceremonies, as well, more especially, with another, of which a legend is given, of KRISHNA having hid himself in the moon, in consequence of a false accusation of stealing a gem from PRASENA, who had been killed by a lion. To see the moon on the fourth day after full, and the fourth day after new, of the month *Bhadra*, is hence deemed inauspicious; and is consequently avoided by pious *Vaishnavas*.

It is related in the *Padma Purana*, and in the *Bhagavat*, that the wife of KASYA, the *Guru*, or spiritual preceptor to KRISHNA, complained to the incarnate deity, that the ocean had swallowed up her children on the coast of *Gurjura*, or *Gujerat*, and she supplicated KRISHNA for their restoration. Arriving at the ocean, VARUNA, its regent, assured KRISHNA, that not he, but the sea-monster, SANKASURA,* had stolen the children. KRISHNA sought, and after a violent conflict slew, the demon, and tore him from his shell, named *Panchajanya*, which he bore away in memorial of his victory, and used afterwards in battle by way of a trumpet. Not finding the children in the dominions of VARUNA, he descended to the infernal city, *Yamapuri*, and sounding his tremendous shell, struck such terror into YAMA, that he ran forth to make his prostrations, and restored the children of KASYA, with whom he returned to their rejoicing mother.

SONNERAT notices two *basso-relievos*, placed at the entrance of the choir of *Bordeaux* cathedral: one represents the ascension of our Saviour to heaven on an eagle; the other his descent, where he is stopped by *Cerberus* at the gates of hell, and PLUTO is seen at a distance armed with a trident.

In *Hindu* pictures, VISHNU, who is identified with KRISHNA, is often seen mounted on the eagle GARUDA, sometimes with, as well as without, his consort LAKSHMI.—(See PLATE 10.) And were a *Hindu* artist to handle the subject of

* SANKASURA means demon of the *Shank*, or *Conch*; and it seems likely, that our generic term may be derived from that of the *Hindus*, with whom *Shank*, or *Chank*, is generally a shell. Early continental travellers would spell it *Chanch*; and in exotic words, a hard is easily substituted for a soft initial, giving *Kank*, or *Conch*. Shells, as arousing implements of war, were much used in former times among the *Indians*, as trumpets are with us. In the terrible civil war between the *Pandus* and their kinsmen, the *Kurus*, as *Homerically* described in the *Mahabharat*, KRISHNA used the shell *Panchajanya*, obtained as above: each chief also sounded a shell, to which, like the swords of our chivalrous knights, distinct and significant names are given.—See *Gita*, p. 29.

KRISHNA's descent to hell, which I never saw, he would most likely introduce *Cerbura*, the infernal three-headed dog of their legends, and YAMA, their PLUTO, with the *trisula*, or trident: a farther presumption of early intercommunication between the pagans of the eastern and western hemispheres.

KRISHNA fought eighteen bloody battles with DEVA-CALA-YAVANA, in common language called DEO-CALYUN, whence the *Greeks* easily made DEUCALION. He is represented in the *Puranas* as a most powerful prince, who lived in the western parts of *India*; and is called an incarnate demon, because he opposed KRISHNA, and was very near defeating his ambitious projects: indeed KRISHNA was worsted in the seventeen first battles, and, according to the express words of the *Puranas*, was forced to have recourse to treachery, by which CALYUN was totally defeated in the eighteenth. The title of *Deva* is not of course given to CALYUN in the *Puranas*, but would probably have been given him by his descendants and followers, and by the numerous tribes of *Hindus*, who, to this day, call KRISHNA an impious wretch, a merciless tyrant, an implacable and most rancourous enemy; in short, those *Hindus* who consider KRISHNA as an incarnate demon, now expiating his crimes in the firey dungeons of the lowest hell, consider CALYUN in a very different light, and would have no objection to his being called DEO CALYUN. This legend is taken from WILFORD's Essay on the Chronology of the *Hindus*.—*As. Res.* Vol. V. page 289.

The act of treachery to which KRISHNA was forced to have recourse, to destroy CALYUN, was this:—

MUCHU-KUNDA, son of king MANDATA, having defeated and humbled the *Daityas*, obtained from INDRA, and the grateful gods, a boon; permitting him, being sorely fatigued, to sleep till the coming of KRISHNA, denouncing instant destruction from the fire of his eye, should it open on any arousing intruder. KRISHNA, aware of this, fled, pursued by his potent foe, toward the cave wherein slept MUCHU-KUNDA, and placing himself near his pillow, (some accounts say he threw his yellow mantle over the person of the sleeper,) awaited the pursuit of CALYUN; who arriving, and finding a man asleep, or mistaking him for his yellow-robed adversary, struck him several times, and awoke him, and was instantly reduced to ashes by a flame that issued from the opening eye of the aroused sleeper.—See WILFORD on *Mount Caucasus*.—*As. Res.* Vol. VI. p. 509.

I have, in my possession, a summary of the life and actions of the "All-conquering HERI," translated by my old and valued friend *Colonel* BODEN, of the *Bombay* establishment, from the work, comprised in thirty-six chapters, of

SRIDHARA SWAMI. It details many escapes of the infant from the machinations of his devoted uncle, KANSA: among them, and not noticed heretofore, that he sent TRAMBAT *asur* in the shape of a whirlwind, which, in the vain effort to carry off KRISHNA, injured very severely the city of *Gokal.* This may, perhaps, have foundation in some historical fact. Another attempt, of crushing him by the oversetting of a waggon, was equally fruitless. Eleven thousand malevolent genii then essay his destruction, but meet their fate through the agency of a host of *Gandharvas,* (celestial choristers). On another occasion, HANUMAN complied with KRISHNA'S requisition, and destroyed some of the base emissaries of KANSA. The *asuras,* DEVANTEKA and NERANTEKA, assumed the shape of lions, and attacked KRISHNA and his brother BALI BHADRA, but were themselves destroyed: other *asuras* took the form of snakes, birds, &c. equally in vain. BRAHMA himself attempted fruitlessly to interrupt the happy pastimes of KRISHNA and his companions, who had retired with their herds into a forest; and he is, in the sequel, forced to recognize the supremacy of the pastoral god.

In recompense for a rigorous course of meritorious penance, a *Raja* obtained possession of the inestimable solar gem, called *Srimantak Aditya,* which he rather disdainfully refused to relinquish at the desire of KRISHNA: it was afterwards purloined by the *Raja's* son, who was slain on a hunting party by a great bear, named JAMBAVANTA, who carried off the brilliant booty to his den. This bear had borne an important part in some of the exploits of RAMA, in the preceding *Avatara.* KRISHNA, in pursuit of the gem, overcomes the bear, and obtains, not only the object of his enterprise, but the beautiful daughter of his rude adversary. In my series of pictures, illustrative of KRISHNA'S adventures, no peculiar beauties, or graces, are observable in KRISHNA'S four-footed bride: she is as rough and uncouth as her papa and kindred. At one of the festivals incident to this curious wedding, it was, that NAREDA witnessed the mortifying superiority of the sylvan musicians, as noticed in another place. KRISHNA having thus obtained the *Srimantaka,* returned to *Dwarka,* and presented it to *Raja* SETRA JETA, who in return gave the victor his lovely daughter, SATYAVAMA; but having thereby violated his pledge to a prior suitor, the exasperated lover struck off his head, and seized the solar jewel, but was forced again to forego it, and to flee for safety.

If the legends alluded to in the preceding paragraph were examined, they would, I think, resolve themselves into a connected astronomical allegory of KRISHNA'S (or the Sun's) approach to, and receding from, the northern tropic.

The offspring of the great bear espousing KRISHNA, (or receiving the solar influence,) may be the Pleiades, or some other stars, fabled, as noticed in another place, as having formerly glittered in the more northern and beautiful constellation, *ursa major*. The *Srimantak Aditya*, or solar jewel, I apprehend to mean the adoration paid to the Sun, or SURYA, by the *Sauras*, who (see p. 124.) exclusively worship him. It is a historical fact, that the Sun was among the earliest objects of idolatrous adoration, to which succeeded the *Sabian* superstition, or the worship of the stars.* If SURYA could dread the transfer of his rites to any rival, he might well be jealous of the attractive loveliness of JAMBAVANTA, supposing this personification of the great bear, which in tropical latitudes shines with a beauty scarcely to be imagined by mere neighbours of the arctic circle. I am, however, no impartial umpire, as the greater bear is to me a constellation of especial interest, having been forced, under circumstances of extraordinary distress and pain, to watch its rising and setting night after night, and week after week: as a wavering *Saura*, I should, therefore, not long hesitate as to what luminary should succeed in receiving my votive offerings.

But, to return to KRISHNA: his possessing himself of the *Srimantaka* may historically mean, that the reformation introduced by him, transferred the solar and stellar sacrifices to his own altars. The fabled resentment of INDRA (the JOVE of the *Hindu* Pantheon), and other deserted deities,

> ——— "Whose altars ne'er had glow'd
> Since infant KRISHNA rul'd the rustic train,"

is noticed in former pages, and depicted in PLATE 61.

The MS. proceeds to relate KRISHNA's adventures and marriages.—He espoused the incomparable KALENDERI, daughter of SURYA; another wife he won, by mastering seven unruly *oxen* yoked together, the only condition exacted by her royal parent; and LAKSHIMANY he gained, by bending a certain *bow*, and piercing the eye of a *fish*, an achievement attributed also to RAMA, as pourtrayed in PLATE 52. An examination of these, and similar allegories, might induce an opinion of their being astronomical; and that the figures on our celestial globe might be recognised as bearing evidence of a common origin: but this is not the place for such examination.

* It would appear, that these follies were *relapses* on the part of the *Hindus*, whose earlier religion, as founded on the *Vedas*, was the unity of the Deity. There are some portions of the *Vedas*, but they are reasonably suspected to be more modern interpolations, inculcating the worship of the stars, planets, elements, and deified heroes; which polytheistic superstitions are posterior to the institutions of the unsuspected parts of the *India* scripture. This subject may perhaps be resumed.

It is scarcely to be expected that KRISHNA's multitude of wives, although something more than mortals, could long live in peace and harmony: jealousies arose. NAREDA having given KRISHNA a flower of the *Parijat*, or *Pariyataka*, INDRA's all-yielding tree, he gallantly presented it to RUKMENY, to the great annoyance of SATYAVAMA, who could be appeased only by the promised possession of the whole tree, which KRISHNA, on a visit to INDRA's capital, made free with, but not without exciting some feelings of resentment on the part of the god of showers; but seeing who was his spoliator, he was fain to be silent. The gift of this desirable tree to SATYAVAMA offended the rest of his wives; and to prevent farther domestic bickerings, he thought it best to separate them, and accordingly built for them distinct habitations, and multiplied his person to the extent of his uxorious plurality. By the fable of obtainingand communicating this tree, that "yields all the heart can desire," may perhaps be understood, that NAREDA, who, in many particulars corresponding with MERCURY, partakes in some of the light and roguish parts of his character, instructed KRISHNA in some novel mode of entertaining his spouses; and that, although RUKMENY claimed the first, or flower, it was SATYAVAMA who in fact monopolized the fruit or tree of his affection. In this part of his work, the author, SRIDHARA, alluding particularly to the ubiquity of his hero, desires his readers to exercise their own judgment as to the literal or typical sense in which such relations ought to be understood; affirming, however, that "KRISHNA's only and attached wife was RUKMENY, or *Religion*."

He then proceeds to relate how RUKMENY bore a son to KRISHNA, who was named MAKADAMA, or MADAMAT; and was, indeed, no other than KAMA, the god of love, thus incarnated: how he was stolen by SAMBARA, chief, or *Raja*, of the *Daityas*, cast into the sea, and swallowed by a fish; which being caught, and presented to the *Raja*, was opened by his cook, or purveyor, RETI, (a personification of affection or pleasure, and KAMA's wife in a pre-existent state,) who discovered and preserved the child. NAREDA gives her a *mantra*, or talisman, rendering the child invisible at pleasure: he is nurtured by KAMDENU, (see p. 141.) attains manhood, and delusion *(maya)* being removed from their intellects, they reunite; and SAMBARA, in consequence of her pregnancy treating RETI with indignity, is destroyed by PRADYAMNA, as KAMA is named in this *Avatara*, who is restored to his delighted mother, RUKMENI.

As KRISHNA's son, KAMA, in this *Avatara*, is also called ANIRUDHA, which latter name is given sometimes to the son of PRADYAMNA; indeed SRIDHARA expressly states him to be one and the same person with his father KRISHNA, who fights several battles in aid of his son, particularly in the achievement of USHA, daughter of *Raja* BHIMA, who had worsted and taken ANIRUDHA prisoner; but is in the sequel overcome by KRISHNA, and bestows his daughter on the conqueror's son.

SATYAVAMA, in the excess of her love, evinces a jealous disposition, and is punished by the temporary deprivation of her lord's attentions; and in revenge, is induced, at the instigation of NAREDA, to sacrifice, or yield up, KRISHNA to him, in a way not easily made out. His loving wives, agonized at this separation, importune the unbending NAREDA to restore their lord; and he at length consents to accommodate them, on condition of receiving an equal weight in gold, which affords the widowed mourners an opportunity of dispossessing themselves of their ornaments and property. But all would not suffice; KRISHNA's scale still kept down; till RUKMENY, throwing the flower *Tulasi* (perhaps the golden ornament so called) into the other scale, caused it to preponderate: NAREDA is satisfied, the amorous deity is restored, and his wives are rendered happy.

HANUMAN visits DWARKA; meets SUPERNA (or GARUDA); they fight, (see PLATE 90.) and SUPERNA is chastised, he having been banished for arrogance; as was also KRISHNA's son, who is likewise beaten by HANUMAN. The prowess of this "son of the wind" is so great, as to disturb KRISHNA; who, by the advice of NAREDA, assumes the form of RAMA, RUKMENY that of SITA, (PARVATI once did the like on another occasion,) and the counsellor that of LAKSHIMAN; and SUPERNA is sent to invite HANUMAN to visit them, which ends in a reconciliation of all parties; and HANUMAN returns to his favourite *Tirt'ha*, or place of pilgrimage, *Ram Iswara*, at the southern point of the promontory, or peninsula.

NAREDA becomes presumptuous, and is metamorphosed into a woman, (RHEMBA; but I know not, if the same with the *Apsara.—Vide* p. 133.) and bears several children; but is restored to manhood on due contrition. This motley character, NAREDA, is on some occasions said to be the same with KRISHNA:* some miracles of his are related; among them, the transformation of a *Gopa*, named NAL KUBAL, and his wife, into two sandal trees, in a manner reminding one of BAUCIS and PHILEMON.

* In the *Ramayana* he is very respectfully chronicled, as a person "who, in the universe, is transcendent in excellence; versed in all the duties of life; attached to truth; steady in his course; exuberant in virtues; a sage acquainted with the past, the present, and the future."---Page 4.

JAMBAVANTI, the daughter of the bear, brings KRISHNA several children: one of them, SAMBA, steals a daughter of a *Kuru Raja*, which gives rise to battles, in which SAMBA is made prisoner: these differences are at this time healed, but appear to have laid the foundation of the future war, described in the *Mahabarat*.

A *Brahman* anchoret having lost his life in punition of some liquorish propensities, incompatible with his abstemious vows, NAREDA wickedly cast the corpse near a spot where extensive preparations were making for a potent sacrifice, patronised by KRISHNA; who, to avert the impurity and consequent distress of the parties interested, restored the dead body to life: this miraculous event is detailed at length in a book called *Jamava-bharat*.

The last chapter of SRIDHARA's work relates the prediction of KANSA's destruction by a child of his sister DEVAKY, and of the terrified tyrant having caused six of them to be put to death: they were reanimated by KRISHNA, and restored to their overjoyed mother; or, as it is expressed, returned at his desire by YAMA. In this chapter is also an account of a peccadillo of a *Raja* MRUGA being punished by transformation into a scorpion.

Of most of the incidents, mentioned in this hasty account of KRISHNA, I have, among many others, images and pictures. But it is more than time to put an end to this division of my work, in which, however difficult to perceive, I have studied brevity; and we now proceed to another, not, perhaps, of fewer difficulties, though they differ in description, but which haply will not, in point of length, be so great a tax on the patience of my readers.

BUDDHA.

Such *Hindus* as admit Buddha to be an incarnation of Vishnu, agree in his being the last important appearance of the deity on earth; but many among the *Brahmans*, and other tribes, deny their identity; and the *Buddhists*, countenanced by the *Rahans*, their priests, do, in general, likewise assert the independent existence, and of course paramount character, of the deity of their exclusive worship. As most of Vishnu's *Avataras* were apparently destined for the accomplishment of some especial object, so this of Buddha seems to have been for the purpose of reclaiming the *Hindus* from their proneness to animal sacrifice, and their prodigality even of human blood. A people having once satisfied themselves, that the fat of bulls, and kids and goats, is acceptable to their deities, and a priesthood having gained such a triumph as to persuade their deluded flock into a belief of the meritorious immolation of their brethren or themselves, cannot but with great difficulty be diverted from practices, and divested of feelings, so repugnant to humanity; their continued existence evincing their strength and tenacity. The mild heresy preached by Buddha, a leading tenet of which is the *sin of depriving any animal of life*, would naturally alarm the orthodox priesthood, whose coffers overflowed from the donations of affrighted sinners, and whose hierarchy was threated by the dawn of reason and the diffusion of philosophy. It cannot therefore be supposed, that such an innovation, condemning the prescribed doctrines of their most sacred books, and the practices founded on them of the most sacred sect, in its consequences deeply involving the supposed sanctity of both, could be contemplated by the *Brahmans* without considerable jealousy, or its progress witnessed without opposition. And we are accordingly informed, that *Buddhism* having in time so encroached on the respect antecedently shown to the *Brahmans*, and caused a great diminution of their flock, the latter were roused, not only to the exercise of legitimate and reasonable means of resistance, but at length to the excesses of invective, and the terrible resource of civil and religious persecution. Whatever rivalrous enmity might anciently have been excited, it seems now happily extinct: rivalry is no longer, and enmity died with it. The orthodox supremacy of the *Brahmans*, in almost all parts of the hither peninsula, views with pity, and perhaps with contempt, the heretical insignificance of the fallen *Rahans*, or priests of BUDDHA.

I am not sufficiently informed of the tenets or usages of the *Buddhists*, to say in what particulars especially consist the difference between them and the tenets and usages of the *Brahmans*. A continuance of many centuries will perhaps have widened those sectarial differences; but whatever they may now be, a very great dissonance in doctrine and superstition is not, I think, discoverable in times remote.

ABU'L FAZEL, in the *Ayin Akbery*, speaking of the *Jainas*, a subdivision of the general schism of *Buddhism*, has a striking passage evincing the mutual malignity existing in his day between that sect and the *Brahmans*, which is not I think now any where observable.

"From the most ancient times," he says, "down to the present, the learning and wisdom of *Hindustan* has been confined to the *Brahmans* and the followers of JAINA; but, ignorant of each other's merits, they have a mutual aversion: KRISHNA, whom the *Brahmans* * worship as God, these consider as an infernal slave; and the *Brahmans* carry their aversion so far as to say, that it is better to encounter a mad elephant, than to meet a man of this persuasion."

On the question of less dissimilarity having formerly existed between the followers of BUDDHA and the adherents of BRAHMA, if such a term be in strictness admissible, than is now supposed to be discoverable, a strong evidence is offered in an inscription on a stone, found at *Buddha Gaya*, a town of *Bengal*, in which the *Buddhism* of *Hindustan* seems formerly to have had its principal central seat, as it had at *Buddha Bamiyan*, the northern metropolis of the sect. *Ceylon* appears its present refuge, from the supposed persecutions of *Hindustan* and the *Dekkan*.

If the inscription be admitted as genuine, on which I never heard a question, it may be received, supposing it to speak the language of the sect, as conclusive on the controverted point, of the identity of the person worshipped by the followers of BUDDHA, and the *Avatara* of VISHNU so denominated. In the *Avataras* of RAMA and of KRISHNA, we have seen those deified heroes iden-

* This industrious and liberal writer has in this place fallen into the frequent error of supposing an unity of precept or practice among the *Brahmans* or *Hindus*; and of speaking of a sectarial deity as one universally worshipped. It has been shown in another place, that it is the *Gokalast'has* only who adore KRISHNA as the Deity; and that the anathematizing of KRISHNA is not confined to the *Buddhists*, but is common to other sects of *Hindus*, equally hostile to his claims to deification. ABU'L FAZEL wrote the *Ayin Akbery* about A.D. 1600.

tified with the great *Powers*, and addressed by their sectaries immediately as the Deity: in this of BUDDHA we shall find the same. Substituting the name of any other deity, exclusively worshipped by any other sect of *Vaishnavas*, KRISHNA more especially, the invocatory parts of the inscription will apply to such deity, being in the usual style of sectarial hyperbole, as well as to BUDDHA.

"In the midst of a wild and dreary forest, flourishing with trees of sweet-scented flowers, and abounding in fruits and roots, infested with lions and tigers, destitute of human society, and frequented by the *Munis*,* resided BUDDHA, the author of happiness, and a portion of NARAYANA. This deity, HARI, who is the lord HARISA, the possessor of all, appeared in this ocean of natural beings at the close of the *Dwapara*, and beginning of the *Kali yug*. He who is omnipresent, and everlastingly to be contemplated; the Supreme Being, the Eternal One, the Divinity worthy to be adored by the most praiseworthy of mankind, appeared here with a portion of his divine nature.

"Once upon a time the illustrious AMARA, renowned amongst men, coming here, discovered the place of the Supreme Being in the great forest. One night he had a vision, and heard a voice, saying: 'Name whatever boon thou wantest.' AMARA DEVA, astonished, with due reverence, replied: 'First give me a visitation, and then grant me such a boon.' He had another dream, and the voice said: 'How can there be an apparition in the *Kali yug*? The same reward may be obtained from the sight of an image, or from the worship of an image, as from the immediate visitation of a Deity.' Having heard this, he caused an image of the Supreme Spirit, BUDDHA, to be made; and he worshipped it, according to the law, with perfumes, incenses, and the like; and he thus glorified the name of that Supreme Being, the incarnation of a portion of VISHNU: 'Reverence be unto thee, in the form of BUDDHA: reverence be unto the Lord of the earth: reverence be unto thee, an incarnation of the Deity, and the Eternal One: reverence be unto thee, O God! in the form of the God of Mercy: the dispeller of pain and trouble; the Lord of all things; the Deity who overcomest the sins of the *Kali yug*; the guardian of the universe; the emblem of mercy toward those who serve thee—O'M! the possessor of all things in vital form. Thou art BRAHMA, VISHNU, and MAHESA; thou art the Lord of the universe; thou art the proper form of all things, moveable and im-

* Of *Munis*, see p. p. 88. 91: Some authorities enumerate twenty of these personages; who are called *inspired writers*, as well as virtuous and mighty sages.

moveable; the possessor of the whole; and thus I adore thee:—Reverence be unto the bestower of salvation; reverence be unto thee (KESAVA), the destroyer of the evil spirit, KESI.—O DAMORDARA! shew me favour. Thou art he, who resteth upon the face of the milky ocean, and who lieth upon the serpent SESHA; thou art TRIVIKRAMA,* who, at three strides, encompassed the earth. I adore thee, who art celebrated by a thousand names, and under various forms, in the shape of BUDDHA, the God of mercy.—Be propitious, O Most High God!'

"Having thus worshipped the guardian of mankind, he became like one of the just. He joyfully caused a holy temple to be built, of a wonderful construction, and therein were set up the divine foot of VISHNU, for ever purifier of the sins of mankind, the images of the *Pandus*,† and of the descents of VISHNU; and in like manner of BRAHMA, and the rest of the divinities.

"This place is renowned; and it is celebrated by the name of *Buddha Gaya*. The forefathers of him, who shall perform a *Srad'ha* at this place, shall obtain salvation. The great virtue of the *Srad'ha* performed here, is to be found in the book called *Vayu-purana*. AMARA-DEVA built this holy temple in the country of *Bharata*,‡ and the province of *Kikata*, where the place of BUDDHA, purifier of the sinful, is renowned: a crime of a hundred fold shall undoubtedly be expiated by a sight thereof; of a thousand fold, by a touch thereof; and of a hundred thousand fold, from worshipping thereof. But where is the use of saying so much of the great virtues of this place? even the hosts of heaven worship with joyful service both day and night."

The above is from *Mr.* WILKINS' translation of the inscription, (*As. Res.* Vol. I. Art. 11.) which concludes with a minute record of its date, being the era of VIKRAMADITYA, 1005; whereof the 1864th year, (reckoning from his

* In the *Vamanavatara*.—See p. 187.

† I do not recollect ever having seen any images of the *Pandus* as objects of adoration. The divine foot of VISHNU, connected with the reverence paid by some *Hindus* to the impressions, or forms of feet, is intended to be noticed hereafter.

‡ *Bharata*, or *Bharata versha*, is the only name formerly used by the natives for the countries that we included in the term *India*. *Hindu*, for the people, and *Hindustan*, for their country, now generally applied by natives and foreigners, are probably of *Persian* origin. BHARATA was an ancient king of *India*, and hence *Mr.* WILKINS derives its name; rejecting of course the supposition, that the river *Indus* (properly *Sindhu*, vulgarly pronounced *Sindh*,) either gave a name to the country, or received one from it: also of *Indu*, a name of the moon, being the origin of *Hindu* and *Hindustan*, the *Sanskrit* having no such words.—See *Hetopadesa*, p. 333.

death at *Oojein*, about 57 years before CHRIST,) commenced on the 20th of October, 1808, giving to the above inscription an age of 859 years.

The preceding extract will serve to show how little difference there really was in the manner of addressing the Deity in former times, by the sectaries of BUDDHA, and by those of any other *Avatara* of VISHNU, or, indeed, of any other deity. On *Ceylon*, the *Singhalese*, as its inhabitants are denominated, have traditions respecting BUDDHA, that, like the legends of KRISHNA, identify him with his prototype, VISHNU. Although *Buddhism* is suppressed, or banished from most parts of the hither peninsula of *India*, it appears to have had a triumph on *Ceylon* over its more generally successful opponent; for *there* are found ruined *Brahmanical* temples converted into those of BUDDHA, and the towns, villages, rivers, &c. retain names derivable from the mythology of the *Brahmans*, satisfactorily indicating its anterior sway.

Major MAHONY, in the seventh volume of the *As. Res.* gives a very interesting article "on *Singhala*, or *Ceylon*, and the doctrines of BUDDHA, from the books of the *Singhalais*," which exhibits many doctrinal points similar with those of other *Vaishnavas*. Twenty-two BUDDHAS are stated to have appeared, at different periods, for the government of the world. The principal descents of VISHNU, as enumerated in the third chapter of the *Bhagavat Purana*,* are twenty-two in all; they conclude thus:—"19. and 20. He appeared as RAMA and KRISHNA, of the race of VRISTI. 21. In the beginning of the *Kali Yug*, *he will* appear,† for the confusion of the enemies of the gods, in the person of BUDDHA, in the land of *Kikata*. 22. In the evening twilight of the *Kali Yug*, when sovereigns will be little preferable to robbers, he will appear in the form of KALKI. These twenty-two are the principal of the innumerable descents of the Deity."

"Few persons," continues the *Edinburgh* reviewers, "will, we believe, after comparing the information furnished by *Major* MAHONY with the preceding quotation, dissent from our conclusion, that each descent of the Deity, named

* As given in the *Edinburgh Review*, for October, 1806, under their notice of *Major* MAHONY's article.

† From this quotation it would appear, that the *Sri Bhagavat* affects to be prospective, or prophetic, in reference to *Avataras* and times subsequent to KRISHNA; whose life and actions comprise a great proportion of it. This is an artifice resorted to, I imagine, to give the work an antique and genuine appearance: with those disposed to receive scriptural doctrines on such authorities, this artifice will succeed, and must be conclusive. The relative age of the *Bhagavat* is ascertained; viz. between the appearance on earth of KRISHNA and BUDDHA, a portion of time not exceeding, it is believed, two centuries.

Avatara by the *Brahmans*, is termed a *Buddha* by the *Buddhists*; and that the twenty-two BUDDHAS of the *Singhalese* are the twenty-two incarnations above specified." The reviewers notice other striking points of similarity, and express their opinion on the question in these terms:—"Many circumstances, indeed, had induced us to imagine, that the *Buddhists* were a sect whose opinions were not materially different from those of other *Hindus*; and the paper before us, composed by an officer who has no hypothesis to support, completely confirms the justice of our conjectures, and proves that, notwithstanding their rejection of the *Veda*, the *Buddhists* are genuine *Vaishnavas*, or adorers of VISHNU."

From *Major* MAHONY's paper we learn the opinions of the *Singhalese*, that "BUDDHA, before his appearance as a man, was a god, and the supreme of all the gods. At the solicitation of many of the gods, he descended on earth, and was frequently born as a man; in which character he exercised every possible virtue, by extraordinary instances of self-denial and piety." If the name of VISHNU, or SIVA, were substituted in the above passage for that of BUDDHA, it would express equally well the doctrine of either of those sects; still the *Singhalese* will not allow their BUDDHA to be the *Avatara* of VISHNU.

"He was at length," continued *Major* MAHONY, "born of MAHAMAYA DEVI, after a pregnancy of ten months, and had for his father SOODDOODENEH RAJA. He lived happily with his queen, YASSODERA, and 40,000 concubines, for thirty-one years." This is in the style of KRISHNA's habits, and is not in keeping with the other feature of BUDDHA's portrait, where, as just quoted, he is praised for "the practice of every possible virtue, and for extraordinary instances of self-denial." But the *Hindus* can reconcile the extremes of libertinism and chastity in their deities, the former being all *Maya*, or *illusion*.

The most striking dissonance that the *Edinburgh* reviewers could discover in the systems of the *Buddbists* and the *Brahmans*, is the celibacy enjoined to the priests of the former, and the permission or practice of eating animal food.—"With respect to the slaughter of animals, it remains to be known," says the *Edinburgh Review*, "whether it be practised in contradiction to precept, or whether the law allows it." Under another article, if I have room and time, I think I shall bring forward sufficient evidence to remove the last-expressed doubt of the learned gentlemen: on the important question of clerical celibacy there is a pointed disagreement.

Mr. JOINVILLE* notices other dissonances in the practices of the *Buddhists*

* On the Religion and Manners of the People of *Ceylon*.—*As. Res.* Vol. VII. Art. 15.

and the *Brahmans*. He informs us, "that the *Brahmans* respect fire—the *Buddhists* do not. The former eat of no animal; the latter are prohibited from nine only, of which the ox is the principal." These dissonances are not, I think, so manifest as my ingenious and industrious friend was disposed to conclude.

The *Singhalese*, although denying the identity of their BUDDHA and the ninth *Avatara* of VISHNU, have, nevertheless, the same legends of the birth and birth-place of their god, as the *Brahmanical* books relate of the *Avatara*. SADUDHANA is the mortal father of both: he was, by both accounts, a *Raja* of a country that corresponds with the neighbourhood of *Oude*; and an annotator on the *Bhagavata* mentions *Gaya* as a city in the province of *Kikata*, where most *Hindu* accounts agree in placing the birth of BUDDHA. It has been remarked, that some of the *Puranic* genealogies make SAKYA, who is generally understood to be BUDDHA under another name, the father, and not the son, of SADUDHANA; but the near relationship in which they stand to each other, is a farther proof of their identity.

The *Singhalese*, we have seen, make BUDDHA the son of SADUDHANA RAJA and MAHAMAH DEVI, who went with him ten months; and give him YASADERA as a wife.

Let us compare with such belief the following items, extracted from an inscription, engraved in the *Magha* language, on a silver plate, found in a cave or pit near *Islamabad* (on the eastern side, but very far north, or high up, in the bay of *Bengal)*; premising, that the pit appears to have been dug for the purpose of receiving "one hundred and twenty brazen images, of small dimensions, denominated *Tahmudas*;* also twenty brazen images, of a larger size, called *Languda*;* and one large image of stone, called *Langudagari*,* with a vessel of brass, containing two of the bones of T'HACUR:" which articles would render more holy the temple intended to have been built over the pit.—

——— "When BUDDHA *Avatar* descended from the region of souls, and entered the body of MAHAMAYA, the wife of SOOTAH DANNAH,† *Raja* of *Kailas*, her womb suddenly assumed the appearance of clear transparent crystal, in which BUDDHA appeared, beautiful as a flower, kneeling, and reclining on his hands." After ten months and ten days of her pregnancy had elapsed, MAHAMAYA, travelling to see her father, was suddenly seized in a garden with the

* I know not what these words mean: many images in my collection have evidently been buried. T'HAKUR is a name applied to several deities by their sectaries.

† Clearly another mode of spelling the name SADUDHANA, or SUDODHANA, &c.

pains of labour, and taking hold of the trees for support, they instantly declined their boughs to conceal her person during her delivery; at which juncture, BRAHMA himself attended with a golden vessel, on which he laid the child, and delivered it to INDRA: the child walked seven paces. At this time, TAPISWA MUNI, who, residing in the woods, devoted his time to the worship of the deity, learned by inspiration, that BUDDHA was come to life, flew through the air to the *Raja's* residence; and being introduced to the child, predicted, from observing two feet on his head, something both of good and bad, and began to weep and laugh alternately. After five days, four *Pandits* were assembled to calculate the destiny of the child; three of whom divined, that as he had marks on his hands resembling a wheel, he would at length become a *Raja Chacraverti*; another divined that he would arrive at the dignity of *Avatar*.

"He was now named SACYA, and attaining the age of sixteen years, gained in marriage VASUTARA, the daughter of *Raja* CHUHIDAN, by bracing a certain bow which many *Rajas* had in vain attempted: such feat the *Raja* having insisted on from the winner of his daughter. SACYA succeeded: they had a son, named RAGHU."

On a subsequent occasion, "BRAHMA descended, and held a canopy over the head of SACYA; INDRA also, with a large fan, and NAGA, the *Raja* of serpents, with shoes in his hands, together with the four tutelar deities of the four corners of the universe,* who all attended to do him service and reverence. At this time, likewise, the chief of *Assurs* came with his forces, riding on an elephant, to give battle to SACYA; upon which BRAHMA, INDRA, and the other deities, deserted him, and vanished. SACYA, observing that he was left alone, invoked the assistance of the earth; who, attending at his summons, brought an inundation over the ground, whereby the *Assur* and his forces were vanquished, and compelled to retire."—*As. Res.* Vol. II. Art. 16.

On the foregoing inscription I have to note, that miraculous conceptions are not uncommon in the legends of the *Hindus*; and, indeed, may be found among most eastern nations, when wishing to dignify the origin of a deity or a hero. The two feet which BUDDHA had on his head when born, I do not recollect ever seeing on any image of him, or in any other relation. The marks on BUDDHA's hand are said to resemble a *wheel:* hence the term *Chacra-*

* These are, I imagine, INDRA, YAMA, VARUNA, and KUVERA; respectively the regents of the East, South, West, and North points: as, with the intermediate regents, will be noticed hereafter.

*verti**—*Chakra* generally meaning a wheel, but particularly the missile discus, frequently spoken of, and pourtrayed in this work, as a usual attribute of VISHNU. I had supposed such marks, occasionally seen on the images of BUDDHA, (see PLATES 68. 69. *fig.* 5. of 70. *fig.* 3. of 75.) were meant to represent flowers, and to allude perhaps to the innocent nature of the offerings made at his shrine, distinguished from the sanguinary sacrifices, as enjoined by the *Vedas*, at those of his rival deities.

Obtaining a wife by bending a bow, stubborn to the efforts of other potent candidates, is not unusual in the legends of *Hindu* heroic history: RAMA won SITA by such superiority; and KRISHNA obtained one of his wives by accomplishing a similar parental stipulation. It has been noted in a former page, that one of RAMA's ancestors was named RAGHU.

I shall not expressly enter any farther into the question of the identity of the deity, exclusively worshipped by an extensive sect, under the name of BUDDHA, and of the *Avatara* of VISHNU so denominated: the case I deem clearly made out. Farther passages, both in favour of and against such questions, may perhaps appear in the extracts made in other pages. We will return for a moment to the account of *Buddhism* on *Ceylon*, by my old and valuable friend *Major* MAHONY.

"The religion of BUDDHA," he says, "seems, as far as I have had any insight into it, to be founded on a mild and simple morality. He has taken for his principles Wisdom, Justice, and Benevolence:† from which principles emanate ten commandments, held by his followers as the true and only rule of their conduct. He placed them under three heads—Thought, Word, and Deed; and it may be said, that the spirit of them is becoming, and well suited to, him whose mild nature was first shocked at the sacrifice of cattle."

"A priest is bound to celibacy, but may quit the priesthood without disgrace; being ejected thence for ill behaviour is, however, deemed very ignominious. Various are the modes by which they incur guilt: among them may be principally noted, killing—even a fly; connexion, or a desire for it, with women; the use of strong liquor; theft, or a lie, if of ever so trifling a kind. They may eat but once a day, between sunrise and eleven A. M.; may drink oftener and later. They live on charity, and may eat any food so offered; but

* Since this article was written, I find, by the ninth volume of the *As. Res.* Art. 4. that *Chakravarti* is a distinction, or surname, of many eminent persons in the legends of the *Jainas*.

† In *Singhalese*—*Buddha, Derma, Sangeh.*

must not have any thing killed purposely for their repast, as the law of BUDDHA forbids the killing of any animal. The *Buddhists* of *Ceylon* eat no beef; but, unlike other *Hindus*, do not object to seeing or touching cow's-flesh, and are not shocked at the use made of it by *Europeans*."

During the authority of the *Portuguese* on *Ceylon*, *Buddhism* was much persecuted; and became in consequence neglected, and almost unknown. When the *Dutch* possessed themselves of *Ceylon*, greater licence of religion was allowed, and that of BUDDHA revived; and, by the assistance of some learned men, sent from *Siam*, began again to flourish.

"Before the birth of BUDDHA, according to a *Singbalese* MS. the island of *Ceylon* was known by the name of *Sri Lankaweh*. In former times there was a mighty war on this island, termed RAWENA *Joodé*, after which it continued void of population for a term of 1845 years, being entirely overrun with malignant spirits. BUDDHA was then born, and in due time took on himself his holy character."

Mr. JOINVILLE, in his valuable dissertation on the religion and manners of the people of *Ceylon*, informs us, that the priests are all dressed in yellow: their garment is large, and folded back, as in the image of BUDDHA, on the left shoulder, leaving the right breast and shoulder uncovered. They are forbidden to marry, or to have concubines, or to eat meat; eggs and vegetables being their sole diet: they are not to eat after noon. The temples of BUDDHA have no certain form, being generally built in the caves of rocks; and the form of the cave determines the attitude of the image, whether it be standing, sitting, or lying. The statue is invariably yellow, from the head to the feet; the body covered, except the right breast, by a large yellow garment, lined with red, no part of the lining being seen, save that folded and thrown over the left shoulder. BUDDHA has bracelets like other *Indian* figures; his head is naked; his hair neatly plaited from the fore to the hind part of his head, which at the top has a flame rising—in a figure of eighteen cubits, two or three inches: the images are made of any kind of materials.

On *Ceylon*, BUDDHA appears every where the prevailing deity. *Major* MACKENZIE, in his "Remarks on Antiquities on the S. W. coast of *Ceylon*," (*As. Res.* Vol. VI.) describes several temples and statues of BUDDHA. One statue, in a reclining position, eighteen feet in length; his head on a pillow, supported by one hand, the other extended on his body; covered from the neck to the heels; with a plain belt across the body: the countenance was mild and full, and the top of the head painted to represent hair in several small curls, of black colour. Another smaller figure, in a corner of the same room, was seated, cross-legged, on a coiled snake, and shaded by its expanded head. In a third corner, the second being occupied by a graceful female holding a lamp, was another figure, said by the priests to be of VISHNU, and in the fourth RAMA. But BUDDHA was the grand idol, before which were several lamps, and a profusion of flowers. In the temple were also several paintings, referring to the history of BUDDHA: one appeared to represent the birth of the divine child; others, his youthful adventures—akin seemingly to the sportive amusements of KRISHNA.

As a supplement to *Major* MACKENZIE's account, *Mr.* HARRINGTON has added a note, descriptive of some temples, images, and usages, of BUDDHA and his adherents, on *Ceylon*; from which it farther appears, that they do not look with any abhorrence on the polytheistic worship of the *Brahmans*, but that figures of other *Hindu* deities are found in their temples. In a temple at *Kalani*, near *Columbo*, images of stone were noticed nearly the same as one well known at *Budd'ha gaya:* being a man sitting cross-legged, his arms resting on his legs; the right arm and breast uncovered; the left side and the waist covered with a folding vest, the end of which hangs down before. The complexion fair; but *Mr.* HARRINGTON draws no conclusion from this, nor from the features, as two images in different temples, at *Kalani*, differ in those points; one having a fair round face, the other darker and more oval: both have long pendent earrings, and crisp hair; but instead of a knot of the latter, as apparently represented on the image at *Budd'ha gaya*, the heads of all the *Kalani* BUDDHAS are crowned with a sort of *tiara*, somewhat resembling a hand, or rather five fingers joined to each other. In front of a glass-case, containing three images, which *Mr.* HARRINGTON was allowed to approach and inspect, a table is placed, on which offerings are made at noon, and usually consist of flowers, fruits, and money, no animals being here sacrificed. As well as of BUDDHA, which, however, are the most frequent, figures of HANUMAN, BRAHMA, and VISHNU, are painted on the walls.

Mr. HARRINGTON proceeds to notice the reclining figure, described by *Major* MACKENZIE, as composed of earth and cement; with the same *tiara*, earrings, and curled hair, as on all the other images of BUDDHA that had come under his observation: the complexion is azure brown, whilst other images in the same temple are of a dusky yellow colour: before the figure were placed flowers of several sorts, and above a dozen small brass images of BUDDHA;

one of which the chief priest presented to *Mr.* HARRINGTON, although not without an evident struggle with his feelings, which was overcome by the persuasions of his brethren present.*

Two figures to the right and left of an image of BUDDHA, with *chawries* in their hands, were said to be of VISHNU in attendance, but *Mr.* HARRINGTON had doubts of the accuracy of the information; for an image, evidently of VISHNU, of a black hue, with a high *tiara*, is placed near another of BUDDHA in a different part of the temple, bearing no emblem of attendance: but the priests, while they acknowledged VISHNU to be a *Deva*, maintained his inferiority to BUDDHA, in whose temples he was an attendant worshipper.† "It may," continues *Mr.* HARRINGTON, "be of use to observe, that on my pointing out the uniformity of the head-dress, in respect to the crisped hair, and asking, whether it meant to represent the hair of an *Abyssinian*, the priests, four of whom were present, answered in the negative, with apparent abhorrence; and one of them repeated his previous information of BUDDHA being the son of SODUDHANA *Raja*, and born in *Muggud deish (Bahar)*; adding, in explanation of the hair being short and crisp, that BUDDHA had, on a certain occasion, cut his hair with a golden sword, and its appearance in consequence was meant to be represented on his images."

Some statues of BUDDHA certainly exhibit thick *Ethiopian* lips; but all, with woolly hair: there is something mysterious, and still unexplained, connected with the hair of this, and only ‡ of this, *Indian* deity. The fact of so many different tales having been invented to account for his crisped woolly head, is alone

* Of this image *Mr.* HARRINGTON has given a print. It seems very similar to that from which *fig.* 5. of PLATE 70. of this work is taken, which *Lord* VALENTIA obtained on *Ceylon:* the mark on the forehead appears also to have been on *Mr.* HARRINGTON's image, but it is not carefully preserved. What this mark may particularly allude to I do not know; or whether it be intended for any thing beyond a lock of hair affectedly waved on the forehead, in aversion of the unpleasing inferences derivable from the woolly curly rigidity exhibited on the frizzled scalp of all images of this deified personage.

† Figures, male and female, with *chawries* and lotoses in their hands, are very common in temples of BUDDHA; and the people who show them, if *Buddhists*, will, in view to the aggrandizement of their deity, inform the inquirer that they are of VISHNU, &c. in attendance. A figure of VISHNU, to be unequivocal, should be four armed, with his usual attributes, as before described: the shell is, at any rate, indispensable. But should such be seen in attendance on BUDDHA, no positive superiority is thence to be deduced, but merely an argument in proof of sectarial arrogance, which is sufficiently common to all the various tribes of *Hindus*.

‡ In PLATE 59. as well as in its original, the hair of the infant KRISHNA approaches more to a woolly appearance than I recollect to have elsewhere seen on his head, or that of any other deity, BUDDHA excepted.

sufficient to excite suspicion that there is something to conceal—something to be ashamed of: more exists than meets the eye. One authority asserts that he was born without hair: this is not peculiar, and, unless something extraordinary was connected with the hair of BUDDHA, need not to have been noticed.

Major MACKENZIE, in his account of the *Jains*, (*As. Res.* Vol. IX. p. 249.) relates that they have three sects of ascetics; one of which must not shave the head with a razor, but must employ the disciples of his sect to pull out the hair by the roots; and to the effect of this operation the *Jainas* attribute the appearance on the heads of the images of their *gurus*, which *Europeans* suppose to represent woolly hair. But a reference to the plates of BUDDHA, from PLATE 68. to 74. will exhibit such decidedly woolly heads on statues so distant in situation and origin, (*China*, *Pegu*, *Ceylon*, *Kanara*, and different parts of *Hindustan*,) as no sophisticated legends, or sectarial assurances, can straighten, or reconcile to similarity with the lank smooth hair of all the other deities of *Indian* superstition. We cannot wonder that devotees should desire to conceal a disagreeable fact, or to divert inquiry from investigating it, when we find so ingenuous a writer as my respected friend, *Mr.* JOINVILLE, describing the hair of BUDDHA as "neatly plaited from the fore to the hind part."—(See p. 229.) The truth must surely be, that living long among these people, pleased with their mildness and benevolence, and grateful for their extension of it toward himself, he was unwilling to see what they were desirous to conceal; and permitted himself to doubt what his habitual keenness, unobstructed by amiable feelings, could not but at once reveal.

An author may reasonably be thought somewhat favourably prejudiced toward the people, on whose history or doctrines he employs much of his thoughts and time: hence we find local historians generally claiming for their own subject a superiority on points not readily conceded by writers who view it more distantly, or treat it more at large. Thus *Mr.* JOINVILLE deems the religion of BUDDHA more ancient than that of the *Brahmans*, and anterior to the doctrine of the *Vedas*; and *Dr.* F. BUCHANAN, (*As. Res.* Vol. VI.) hostile to the claims of the *Brahmans*, to either antiquity, literature, or science, ably, but not conclusively, contends in favour of the superiority, on these and other points, of the *Rahans*, or priests of BUDDHA. But if the question of antiquity were confined to *Ceylon*, there are, I think, so many facts, as well as arguments, tending to impress a contrary belief, as force themselves almost irresistibly on our conviction. Without entering into the difficult subject of *Indian* chronology, it may be remarked, that the books of the *Ceylonese* admit the appearance of BUDDHA, as we are informed by *Major* MAHONY, to have been 1845 years subsequent to the war of RAVAN; and however difficult it may be to fix the exact period of that war, the comparative existence of these two personages is sufficient to determine the question of mere priority; for it can scarcely be disputed, that the superstition of the *Brahman* had obtained anterior to the theme of the *Ramayana*, itself manifestly posterior to the days of RAVAN. The *Buddha Sarsa*, the era of the *Ceylonese*, as reckoned from the death of BUDDHA, has now (1809) reached its 2351st year, marking the 542d before ours for that event, and the 2387th for the war of RAVAN and RAMA—carrying us back 4196 years from the present time: the *Singhalese*, we thus see, reckon 542 years before our era for that of BUDDHA. *Sir* W. JONES, (*As. Res.* Vol. II. Art. 7.) after investigating the subject with his usual acuteness, thinks about 1000 years to have elapsed between them, agreeing nearly with the *Chinese* historians; while those of *Japan*, according to KÆMPFER, and the *Siamese*, according to LOUBERE, reckoned the first year of BUDDHA to correspond with the 544th before CHRIST—agreeing almost exactly with the *Singhalese*; so that they have apparently taken their dates from a common origin, or borrowed one from the other. We will recapitulate the different computations of the era of BUDDHA, as made and admitted by different calculators and people.—ABU'L FAZEL, in the *Ayin Akbery*, 1366 years before CHRIST.—The *Chinese*, when receiving a new religion from *India*, in the first century of our era, made particular inquiries concerning the age of BUDDHA, whom, having no *B* in their alphabet, they call FO, or FO-HI, and they place his birth in the 1036th year before CHRIST: other *Chinese* historians, according to *M. de* GUIGNES, say he was born about 1027 years before CHRIST, in the kingdom of *Kashmir*.—The *Tibetians*, according to GIORGI, 959; the *Siamese* and *Japanese*, 544; and the *Ceylonese*, 542 years, anterior to the same period.—*M.* BAILLY, 1031; and *Sir* W. JONES, *about* 1000. An attempt has been made to reconcile these, and greater differences, in respect to the epoch and history of BUDDHA, by supposing two important personages to have existed in times wide of each other, bearing the same name: the first corresponding with the *Gothic* WODEN; and the second, the founder of the new religion which has given so much offence in *India*, and which was introduced into *China* in the first century of our era.

Sir W. JONES supposes *Buddha* to have been only a general word for a philosopher. AMARAKOSHA,* the celebrated philologist, who was himself a

* The same, I imagine, who built the temple, noticed in the inscription on a stone, in a former page of this article.

Bauddha, as the adherents of BUDDHA are properly denominated, has, in his famous *Sanskrit* dictionary, one head containing eighteen general names of *a Buddha*; including MUNI, SASTRI, DHERMARAJA, SUGATA, &c. significative of *excellence, wisdom, virtue,* and *sanctity:* another, containing the name of a particular BUDDHA-MUNI, *who descended in the family of* SAKYA (the words of the original); such as SAKYAMUNI, SAKYASINHA, SAUDHODANI, GAUTAMA, ARKABANDHU, or kinsman of the Sun, and MAYA-DEVI-SUTA, or child of MAYA; the first being general epithets, and the second proper names, or patronymics of one and the same person. The epithet of *Buddha* has been similarly supposed to be a generic word, like *Deva*, but applicable to a sage or philosopher—a mere wise man without supernatural powers.

JAYADEVA, in the *Gita Govinda*, the whole tenor of which bespeaks him a *Gokalaust'ha*,* thus addresses BUDDHA (or rather VISHNU, or KRISHNA so incarnated,) in his series of eulogy on each of the *Avataras*.

"9. Thou blamest (O wonderful!) the whole *Veda*, when thou seest, O kind-hearted! the slaughter of cattle prescribed for sacrifice—O KESAVA! assuming the body of BUDDHA.—Be victorious, O HERI! lord of the universe."

Sir W. JONES thinks it highly probable, that the BUDDHA thus celebrated was the SAKYA *Sinha*, or *lion* SAKYA, who, though he forbade the sacrifices of cattle which the *Vedas* enjoin, is believed by the most orthodox *Brahmans* to be VISHNU himself in a human form; and that another BUDDHA, one perhaps of his followers in a later age, assuming his name and character, attempted to overset the whole system of the *Brahmans*, and was the cause of that persecution from which the *Bauddhas* are known to have fled into very distant regions. The difference of opinion among the *Hindus*, as to the time of BUDDHA's appearance, may be reconciled on the supposition that they have confounded the two BUDDHAS.

* But KRISHNA is not included in the series of the invoked *Avataras*; because, as I imagine, the whole poem being in praise of KRISHNA as VISHNU, or *The Deity*, he is not addressed in his place in the subordinate form of an *Avatara*. In lieu of KRISHNA, his elder brother, "BALA RAMA, with a furrowing ploughshare," is invoked as the eighth incarnation; RAMA CHANDRA, and PARASU RAMA, being the seventh and sixth. Although rather out of place, it may be here observed, that the above quotation, from an author who wrote in the century before CHRIST, and not many centuries, probably, after the time of BUDDHA, is nearly conclusive in respect to the relative antiquity of the doctrines of that person, and of the *Vedas*, directly censured by those doctrines; the *Vedas* themselves making no mention of them or of their founder, but containing, among others, a system of philosophy, the apparent origin of that of BUDDHA.

A text of the *Bhagavat*, prophesying the appearance as to time of "VISHNU, in the form of BUDDHA the son of JINA, at *Kikata*,"* leads to an obvious inference, that the founder of the sect of *Jinas*, or *Jainas*, was anterior to BUDDHA; and his sectaries do not fail to avail themselves of the opportunity of claiming for themselves superiority on that point, as well as on others referring to literature and science: specimens of their skill on the latter I shall presently exhibit. Their situation in the scale of sectarial precedence I cannot determine; but it is generally understood to be a schism from the general faith of *Buddhism*.

SANKARA CHARYA, a bigotted *Saiva*, from his vindictive intolerance believed indeed to have been an *avantara* of MAHADEVA, has the accursed fame of having been the greatest persecutor and enemy of the heretical *Jainas* that their history records. To account for this supposed incarnation, and the historical fact connected with it, a legend is related by *Brahmans*, of which the following is a brief outline:—

At a period of great distress, from continued drought, a pious prince, surnamed DIVODASA, or *servant of heaven*, was called by the gods to the government of *Kasi*, that he might collect and instruct the scattered remains of the human race: an office he accepted, on the condition of enjoying exclusively the glory to be thence acquired; and that no *Deva* should remain in his capital. BRAHMA and SIVA accordingly quitted their favourite abode; and the prince became so great and powerful, and made his subjects so happy, that the deities were jealous; and, impatient to revisit their beloved city, determined to pervert the mind of DIVODASA, and thus, rendering him unworthy of his exalted situation, to deprive him of his dominion. DEVI first assailed him in the alluring forms of sixty-four *yoginis*, or female anchorets, but without success: the twelve *Adityas* also failed. GANESA was next deputed by his father, MAHADEVA; and in the garb of an astronomer, assisted by thirty-six *Ganesis*, his female offspring, began to change the disposition of the people, and to prepare them for the coming of the principal deities.

VISHNU now appeared in the character of JINA, inveighing against sacrifices and the ceremonies prescribed by the *Vedas*; asserting that all true religion consisted in *killing no creature that had life*: his consort, JAYADEVI, preached the new doctrine to her own sex; and the inhabitants of *Kasi* were perplexed with doubts. They were seconded by MAHADEVA, in the form of ARHAN, or

* I am not quite sure how this word ought to be pronounced: it is generally spelled *Cicata*.

MAHIMAN, and his wife MAHAMANYA, and the heresy gained ground. And at length appeared BRAHMA, as BUDDHA, who, with his consort VIJNYA, confirmed the principles inculcated by his predecessors; and finding the people seduced, soon succeeded, in the capacity of a *Brahman*, in corrupting the mind of the king: who consequently lost his empire, and MAHADEVA returned to his former residence.

The new doctrines had, however, gained so much ground, that MAHADEVA, having in vain contended with their obstinate and numerous adherents, resolved to exterminate them; and for that purpose assumed the shape of SANKARA, surnamed ACHARYA, who explained the *Vedas* to the people, destroyed the temples of the *Jainas*, caused their books to be burned, and massacred all who opposed him.

The above legend is taken from *Mr.* WILFORD's Dissertation on *Egypt* and the *Nile.—As. Res.* Vol. III. Art. 13. He says, that few of this persecuted race now remain in the *Gangetic* provinces; and that they are divided into three sects: the followers of JINA, who are chiefly dispersed on the borders of *India*; those of BUDDHA, in *Tibet*; and those of ARHAN, who are said to have been anciently the most numerous of the three, now chiefly reside in *Siam*, and in other kingdoms of the eastern peninsula.

The above-named SANKAR ACHARYA, whose excellent theological works, in prose and verse, are still extant, and are sedulously studied by a particular school, tarnished the brilliancy of his reputation by the persecution that he fomented. To the compunctious visitings of his conscience may, perhaps, be attributed the mode of his departure from this world, which was by the expiatory process of a meritorious species of suicide, called *Karshagni*, as noticed in page 142.

In the above tale BUDDHA appears as an *Avatara* of BRAHMA, a character that I never elsewhere saw him in. While many *Brahmans* insist that the BUDDHA who perverted DIVODASA was not the ninth incarnation of VISHNU, others, who, from the nature of the evidence, are found, though reluctantly, to admit it, contrive to throw odium on his doctrines by extravagant relations of the causes of the deity's interposition. It was, they say, at the intercession of the *Devas*, alarmed at the power likely to be obtained by certain *Daityas*, who, instructed by the malignant INDRA, had made preparations for potent sacrifices, accompanied by oblations, as prescribed by the *Veda*. VISHNU accordingly assumed the form of a *Sanniyasi*, named BUDDHA, with his hair braided in a knot on the crown of his head; wrapped in a squalid mantle;

and with a broom in his hand to sweep before him, lest he should chance to tread on some innocent reptile: he therefore, on the same account, never bathed, or washed his clothes. He preached the cruelty and sin of depriving any animal of life with such eloquence, that the affected *Daityas*, admitting his precepts, and following his example, abandoned their intended sacrifice, and its sin-expelling accompaniments. This *maya*, or delusive appearance of VISHNU, frustrating the ambitious projects of the *Daityas*, one of BUDDHA's titles is the son of MAYA. "Whether," continues *Mr.* WILFORD, from whose Essay (*As. Res.* Vol. III.) the above tale is borrowed, "BUDDHA was a sage or a hero, (another of his names, SAKYA *Sinha*, or the *Lion* SAKYA, intimating that he was a warrior as well as a philosopher,) the leader of a colony, or a whole colony personified; whether he was black or fair, his hair curled or straight—if, indeed, he had any, which some deny; whether he appeared ten or two hundred, or a thousand, years after KRISHNA, it is very certain that he was not of the true *Indian* race. In all his images, and in the statues of *Bauddhas*, male and female, in many parts of the *Bengal* provinces, and in both peninsulas, there is an appearance of something *Egyptian* or *Ethiopian*; both in features, and in dress, differing from the ancient *Hindu* figures of heroes and demi-gods. The three sects of JINA, MAHIMAN, and BUDDHA, whatever may be the difference between them, are all named *Bauddhas*;* and as the chief law, in which, as the *Brahmans* assert, they make virtue and religion consist, is *to preserve the lives of all animated beings*, we cannot but suppose that the founder of their sect was BUDDHA, in the ninth *Avatara*; who in the *Agni puran* has the title of SAKRIPA,

* In *Guzrat* and the *Dekkan* a distinction is usually made: there is, in the former province, a numerous race, called *Maheman*, or, in conversation, *Mehman*; the same sect, I imagine, but may be mistaken, as *Mr.* WILFORD makes known to us. Many families of this sect, some hundreds perhaps, live in *Bombay*, and are very useful, hard-working, trusty people: I never heard them called either *Bauddhas* or *Jainas*. In *Kanara* are many families, and towns, and temples, of JAINA: of which sect very few individuals live in *Bombay*, perhaps none permanently; and these people are not termed *Bauddhas*, or *Mahimans*. On *Ceylon* the *Bauddhas* are seldom, I believe, called *Jainas*, or *Mahemans*: how far their tenets differ, is a subject of interesting inquiry; and has, I understand, attracted the investigation of a very intelligent member of the *Bombay* Literary Society. I have had *Mehmans* in my service several years in *Bombay*, and have fancied they looked somewhat disdainfully on *Jaina* priests, with whom I occasionally conversed, but always found them very reserved; imputable partly, perhaps, to a want of a common language, their knowledge having been, as far as I could judge, confined to *Kanarese* and *Malabar*, to which mine did not sufficiently extend. Since this was written, the ninth volume of the *Asiatic Researches* has reached me, in which is *Major* MACKENZIE's full and curious account of these sects, with much original and valuable information annexed, by *Mr.* COLEBROKE.

or *benevolent*; and in the *Gita Govinda*, that of *Sadaya-hridaya*, or *tender-hearted*, where it is said by JAYADEVA, that he 'censured the whole *Veda* because it prescribed the immolation of cattle.' This alone, we see, has not destroyed their veneration for him; but they contend that atheistical doctrines have been propagated by modern *Bauddhas*, who were either his disciples, or those of a younger BUDDHA; or so named from *buddhi*, because they admit no supreme divinity but intellect: and they add, that the old *Jainas*, or *Jyanas*, acknowledged no gods but JYA, or *earth*, and VISHNU, or *water*.—But," *Mr.* WILFORD concludes, after some comparison of this tenet with one similar among another people, "a complete account of BUDDHA can be given only by some studious man, who shall collect all that relates to him in the *Sanskrit* books, particularly in the *Vayupuran*, and compare it with the testimonies drawn from other sources by KÆMPFER, GIORGI, TACHARD, LOUBERE, and by such as have access to the literature of *China*, *Siam*, and *Japan*."—*As. Res.* Vol. III. p. 417.

Thus we find the modern *Brahmans*, almost every where, speaking contemptuously of the origin of BUDDHA and his doctrines, but no where acting malignantly toward his adherents: on the other hand, the *Rahans*, or *Bauddha* priests, retort the contempt on the *Brahmans* and their practices. In *Ava*, where *Bauddhism* is orthodoxy, the idea is upheld that it was equally prevalent, in the same form, throughout *India*, till about the second century before CHRIST, when the *Brahmans* are stated to have introduced themselves and their rites, and, by their superior knowledge and address, to have excluded the *Rabans* from almost every part of *India*; substituting their own dogmas, but retaining many of the scientific and historical facts of the ejected party: whose monuments of antiquity are also said to have been destroyed by the artful *Brahmans*, with the view of concealing their own foreign origin, and the novelty of their doctrines. The *Rahans* farther insist that the *Brahmans* came with their religion from *Egypt*; while, by others, it is conversely maintained, that the *Egyptians* derived their doctrines and science from *India*. But such are the legends of *Ava*, whose priests are naturally jealous and envious of the *Brahmanical* hierarchy—if it may be so called, of the hither peninsula, and of *Hindustan*, where the religion of BUDDHA was heretofore, and probably about the era of *Christianity*, indisputably of extensive prevalence, as is evinced by many stupendous monuments; some of which will be noticed in the sequel of this article. In his history of *Kashmir*, ABU'L FAZEL states, that it was in the reign of *Raja* NERKA that the worshippers of BUDDHA were proscribed, and their temples destroyed, in that country. This *Raja*, it is said, is known to have reigned anterior to our era; although it has been contended, that the overthrow of *Buddhism* in *Kashmir* did not take place until about the middle of the fourth century.

The people of the extensive empires on the eastern side of the bay of *Bengal*, seem generally to have received and retained the doctrines of BUDDHA. Among the *Burmas* (according to *Dr.* F. BUCHANNAN, *As. Res.* Vol. VI. Art. 8.) his name of GODAMA prevails; and in statues, he is there represented as a young man of a placid countenance, with strongly characterized *Burma* features, and generally in the dress of a *Rahan*, or priest. His postures are various, and he has different epithets derived from, or connected with, them: one is *Ananda*, signifying *plenty*, from its supposed virtues. The most common is that of sitting cross-legged on a throne, with his left hand resting on his left leg, and holding a book; his right hand hanging over his knee.—(See PLATE 71. *fig.* 3.) In some images he is standing, in four postures, the difference being in the position of his hands; in others, he is reclining on a couch, with his head supported by pillows. His images are of various materials—clay, copper, silver, and alabaster; some wholly, others in part, gilded, and ornamented with paintings of flowers: in size they are equally various, some not six inches in height, others colossal. *Dr.* BUCHANNAN saw a sitting image in old *Ava* of one solid block of pure white alabaster: he had no opportunity of measuring it, but its fingers appeared to be about the length of a man's thigh and leg; whence a conjecture may be formed of the immensity of the whole figure.

Most oriental people seem to have prided themselves on distinguishing their deities by a great many names: instances of it have been seen in this work, and in the case of BUDDHA we have another. Several of his *Hindustany* names have occurred, which I shall not recapitulate, nor shall I study to add to the number. It may be well, however, to observe, that BUDDHA, BOODA, BUTTA, and others of nearly similar sound, are mere varieties, in different parts of *India*, in orthography and pronunciation; and so, perhaps, is the BUD, or WUD, of the ancient pagan *Arabs.*—POUT, in *Siam*; POTT, or POTI, in *Tibet*; and BUT, in *Cochin China*, are the same. The *Chinese*, having, it is said, no *B* or *D* in their alphabet, and their language being monosyllabic, softened his name into FO, FO-E, or FO-HI: they also call him XA-KA, a variation, perhaps, of the *Hindu* SAKYA. That the TOTH of the *Egyptians*, and the WODEN of the *Scandinavians*, and other northern *Europeans*, is the same name and deity, is upheld by some; but the supposition is derided by others—some, indeed, will not recognise him in the FO of *China*. *A* BUDDHA, whether the ninth *Avatara* or not may be doubted, has been deemed to answer in character with MERCURY—so has the *Gothic* WODEN; each respectively gives his name to the same planet, and to the same day of the week: *Budhvar*, all over *India*, I believe, whether among *Bauddhas*, *Saivas*, or *Vaishnavas*, being the same with *Dies Mercurii*, or WODEN's day, whence our *Wednesday*.

In respect to the numbers of its followers, and the extent over which they have spread, the doctrines of BUDDHA have probably obtained greater dominion than those of any other religious persuasion. Although now comparatively trifling on the continent of hither *India*, his doctrines are still retained, differing in externals, and divided into sects, throughout *China* and its tributary nations; in the great empires and states of *Cochin China*, *Cambodia*, *Siam*, *Pegu*, *Ava*, *Asam*, *Tibet*, *Budtan*; many of the *Tatar* tribes; and generally all parts east of the *Ganges*; including many of those vast and numerous islands in the seas eastward and southward of the farther *Indian* promontory, whose inhabitants have not been converted to *Islamism*. In these great and distant parts of the globe the tenets of BUDDHA, distinguished of course by various appellations, may be recognised as forming the religion of the people; an extent exceeding that either of the *Mahomedan* or *Brahmanical* superstition, and outnumbering, perhaps, the followers of the religion of JESUS CHRIST.

In a country civilized to a considerable degree of intellectual refinement, where the imagination has room for expansion, and where the exuberance of writers is not chastened by criticism, or restrained by the dread of exposure through the press, every manuscript becomes equally a volume of historical record, yielding abundance of materials for the collating or inventive faculties of commentators. Hence, perhaps, the uncertainty of how or where the heresy or reformation of BUDDHA was introduced and promulgated; but most likely in a mild and temperate manner, operating chiefly by its reasonableness and humanity. We are told, and may perhaps occasionally witness, that the followers of BUDDHA are held in abhorrence by *Brahmans* and other zealous individuals of more orthodox sects; but, in fact, those sects and tribes, if we include therein the whole *Brahmanical* flock as opposed to the heresy of BUDDHA, are so numerous, and their tenets, although so different, so little understood or noticed by each other, that there seems no proof, or evidence, to conclude that the introduction or promulgation of this heresy was attended on its part with any violence: jealousy of its success, it is believed, induced opposition—opposition, resistance; and so on, to persecution, war, and the dire catalogue of calamities incident to the effervescence of popular passion; scorning the restraints of reason or humanity, provoked, perhaps, by an intolerant priesthood, and unrestrained by the correcting hand of government.

A *Saiva*, or a *Vaishnava*, of another sect, becoming a *Bauddha*, need not, I think, unless intemperately zealous, so far depart from his usual habits as to be an object of hatred or jealousy to his own sect or family. If but reasonably attached to his new faith—rather, perhaps, grafted on his old stock of superstition, than eradicating it, he may endow his new type of the deity with the symbols that distinguished the objects of his former adoration: he may, as in PLATE 69. adorn it with the attribute of SURYA, and worship BUDDHA and the Sun together: he may shadow him with SESHA, and recognise in BUDDHA half the mythological personages of his scarcely-rejected *Pantheism*.—In short, in a rational and temperate spirit, and no convert is so likely to be mild and temperate as a *Hindu*, he may, I think, embrace all the advantages of this heresy without becoming an object of contempt with his own tribe or family, or materially departing from his polytheistic idolatry, or his superstitious practices,

Buddhism, like other distinctions of faith among *Hindus*, is divided into sects. If it be reckoned the grand generic schism, we may deem those of JINA and MAHIMAN specific varieties; and there seems no good reason why they should not all be classed, with the other sects who adore exclusively one of the *Avataras* of VISHNU, under the comprehensive denomination of *Vaishnavas*.

In very ancient sculptures and excavations we find the image of BUDDHA among the other deities of *Brahmanical* superstition. The cave on *Gharipuri*, called by us *Elephanta*, an island in *Bombay* harbour, is an instance of this; and this temple in itself may be called a complete *Pantheon:* for among the hundreds, I may, perhaps, say thousands, of figures there sculptured, every principal deity is found. Many deified heroes, in the more modern mythological romances, contained in some of the *Puranas* and *Tantras*, will have been exalted since the excavation of this wonderful cavern; but I strongly believe that all the gods of the *Vedas*, or, if I may so term them, all the legitimate *Hindu* deities, will be found in its different compartments—if not, indeed, too much defaced for recognition. In a little account, written and corrected by me in the cavern, I find the following noticed:—BRAHMA, VISHNU, SIVA, BUDDHA, GANESA, and INDRA; and these are, in fact, all that are, by their forms or attributes, or vehicles, unequivocally distinguishable. PARVATI, and other females, are seen with their lords; but being all mere one-headed two-handed beings, without peculiar attributes,* will answer to any given appellation. In one compartment a woman is suckling a child, which a *Gokalast'ha* would perhaps say is DEVAKY, or VASUDEVA, with KRISHNA (see PLATE 59.); but, otherwise, I do not observe any notice in my memoranda of KRISHNA, RAMA, or any of the *Avataras*, or minor deities, introduced into this work, as forming the monstrous objects of the existing polytheism; or, if one were allowed to coin a word, as it might be called, *myriotheism*. I have noticed beings *like* SURYA and CHANDRA at an apparent wedding, at which BRAHMA is seen kneeling, and VISHNU can be fancied; but their identity is not positive: the head of one is encircled by a crescent, and the other has a disk near his.—(See PLATE 89.) This wedding group fills a large compartment; as may be supposed, when it be stated, that many of the figures are as large as men of the present day, and that the four-handed bridegroom is ten feet, and the finely-formed diffident and bashful bride eight feet high.

The figure of BUDDHA, in the temple of *Gharipuri*, is immediately on your left at entering, opposite to a similar compartment on the right, fifty-five feet distant, containing a spirited eight-armed colossal statue of SIVA, in the act of drawing a sword. I will revert descriptively to BUDDHA presently, having here to observe, that he is evidently, from his size and situation, a principal personage; yet not He to whom the temple seems peculiarly dedicated, which I apprehend to be the One Supreme Being. But as no representations are ever made of that Being, his three principal powers, or attributes, (viz. according as they be contemplated—mythologically, ethically, metaphysically, or philosophically:—

BRAHMA	POWER	CREATION	MATTER	The PAST	EARTH
VISHNU	WISDOM	PRESERVATION	SPIRIT	— PRESENT	WATER
SIVA	JUSTICE	DESTRUCTION	TIME	— FUTURE	FIRE)

are united in the most conspicuous place, immediately fronting the entrance, and forming that gigantic triune bust, of which NEIBUHR and others have given plates; but not, I think, a good one, and I have compared all that I know of with the archetype. Symbols of the powers of nature are seen in the form

* Similar females and males abound in temples of BUDDHA, where we seldom, I had almost said never, see any sculptures of other deities as objects of adoration, or any but mere men and women; frequently, indeed, of colossal dimensions, but seldom any thing emblematical in their hands, save the lotos, which, whatever it mean, and in the eye of mystics it means a great deal, is very common: sometimes the figures hold a scarf.

of monstrous *Lingas*, necessarily coeval with the formation of the temple; for, exclusive of their size precluding the idea of introduction, the floor, pillars, pilasters, walls, roof, and all the figures, were once one undistinguished mass of granite, which, excavated, chiselled, and polished, produced the fine cavern and forms that we now contemplate with so much admiration and surprise. Of the three-faced bust, PLATE 81. exhibits a tolerable outline; taken, as will be noticed in another place, from a similar bust in miniature, dug by me from the ruins of a demolished temple on the island of *Bombay*.

In the magnificent excavations near *Ellora*, in the neighbourhood of the city of *Aurungabad*, the image of BUDDHA is also seen, as well as the images of other deities; and although he is there likewise very respectably situated, he is not the paramount deity to whom the temples are in general dedicated. One, of a superb description that will presently be more particularly noticed, seems exclusively his, as are similar temples on *Salsette*, and near the village of *Karly*, between *Bombay* and *Poona*. Others on *Salsette* are said to exhibit BUDDHA as the paramount deity, as well also as the deities that may be more immediately denominated *Brahmanical*: at *Amboly*, for instance. But, although I have more than once visited this curious and singular excavation, the figures are so much injured by time, and, from the friable nature of the subterraneous rock, out of which it is dug, hastened so to decay, that I am not certain that I recognised other *unequivocal Hindu* deities: more accurate observers say they have.

Neither the grand cave, nor those inferior, at *Kenereh*, on *Salsette*, have, to the best of my recollection, any sculptures of the images of *Brahmanical* superstition. I made no written description of what I saw on and in that excavated mountain or city, honeycombed with caves. Of the colossal figures at each side of the entrance to the grand arched temple, *Mr.* DANIEL has given accurate representations, in his unrivalled publications of oriental scenery, and ancient *Hindu* architecture. These colossal figures have the thick lips and woolly heads, common to statues that are usually called of BUDDHA; but probably we are apt to confound the statues of BUDDHA, JINA, and MAHIMAN, or of their disciples or martyrs, as well as their doctrines. And although these heresies may, in principle, be pretty much alike, yet distinctions will, on our farther researches into the subject, be found sufficiently varied on particular points, to mark their followers; if not as a separate people, yet as *sectarially* different, both in doctrine and practice.

The principal arched temple of *Kenereh* is exactly on the same plan of that near *Karly*, and the principal object is alike in both; consisting of a vast hemisphere of stone, resting on a round pedestal of greater diameter, having its convexity surmounted by a sort of canopy or umbrella, of peculiar construction. The ground-plan of an arched temple of BUDDHA at *Ellora* is exactly similar; but the principal object is different, being BUDDHA himself, with the semi-globe on the round pedestal behind him. In neither of these three arched caves will, I think, be found any sculptures referring to the gods of the *Brahmans*; and these three are the only caves that I ever saw, or heard of, constructed with an arched roof. And I presume to hazard an opinion, that they are of modern origin, relatively with other excavations at *Ellora* and on *Elephanta*, containing, with and without BUDDHA, many of the deities now worshipped by the *Brahmans*.

What I would hence infer is, that in the older sculptures we find BUDDHA mixed with the other *Hindu* gods: *Elephanta*, and the flat-roofed *Pantheistic* temples at *Ellora*, I reckon among the oldest. In sculptures more modern, BUDDHA, as a deity, is often seen exclusively pourtrayed: the arched caves of *Ellora*, *Karly*, and *Kenereh*, I judge to be of later date; and as to form and proportion, of more refined and elegant construction. May we be allowed, from these premises, to deduce a farther confirmation of the idea, that the BUDDHA incarnation of VISHNU, and the sectarial deity of that name, exclusively worshipped by so many different nations under different forms and designations, are one and the same person? and that such exclusive worship, and its accompanying ceremonies and privations, is a heresy or reformation, or whatever it may be termed, of the more ancient *Brahmanical* religion? Among *European*, as well as *Indian* inquirers, this opinion will find the most numerous, but, like other majorities, not the most zealous, supporters.

Sir CHARLES MALET's description (*As. Res.* Vol. VI.) of the arched temple of *Ellora*, above alluded to, will furnish us with some applicable information, although not exactly such, perhaps, as may be required in support of the opinion just offered; but I have no particular hypothesis that I care to uphold.

It is there called VISWAKARMA *ka jumpri*, or *the hovel of* VISWAKARMA; or, as *Sir* CHARLES observes in a note, "the Creator of the world, but allegorically artificer of RAMA."* "According to the legend, VISWAKARMA was the artist

* It may be noted in passing, that this explanation was probably derived from an individual of the sect of *Ramanuj*. A *Gokalast'ha* would have called him the *artificer of* GOKAL, or KRISHNA. A more general *Vaishnava*, or a *Saiva*, would have generally called him *artificer of the gods*.—See p. 113.

who fabricated the whole of these wonderful works in a night of six months; but the cock crowing before they were finished, they remained imperfect, and he retired, having wounded his finger, to this his hovel;* in which state, the figure, in front of the entrance of this beautiful excavation, is said to be a representation of him holding the wounded finger; but I rather think, with due respect to the legend, that the figure is in the act of devout meditation, as many figures with similar positions of the hands occur. But quitting the fable for the fact, this excavation is in beauty inferior to no one: in form it is unique, and in design elegant, having the appearance of a chapel with an arched roof; and is exactly in the style of a similar excavation at *Ekverah*,† near the top of the *Bbore ghaut*, first explored by *Mr.* WALES. But the two latter caves are not inhabited by VISWAKARMA, they having only a very high altar; the top of which is circular, and situated, as represented in the plate, at the back of VISWAKARMA."

The plate, referred to by *Sir* CHARLES, gives exactly a representation of the temples of *Karly* and *Kenereh*, as far as regards ground plan and general design; and they must certainly have originated in the same person, or one have been taken from the other. The capitals of the interior pillars, from which the arched roofs spring, are different: at *Ellora* they appear, from the plates accompanying the interesting description of my greatly-respected friend, *Sir* CHARLES MALET, to be men in the act of adoration: at *Karly* the entablatures are elegantly formed of figures of men and women, seated on kneeling elephants, whose *probosci*, joining at the angles, form, in graceful curves, the volutes of the capitals.

The following is the memoranda made in the *Elephanta* cave, descriptive of the compartment containing BUDDHA:—

On the left, immediately entering the cave, is BUDDHA sitting on an expanded lotos; the stem of which is supported by two much-mutilated males. On BUDDHA's left is a well-executed plantain tree; the trunk, with several leaves, pretty perfect: over the tree is GARUDA carrying VISHNU; GARUDA's beak and face damaged; and two of VISHNU's arms broken off—in one of them he held a lotos: over VISHNU is a male figure, mounted in a spirited style

* This magnificent cavern is hyperbolically called a *hovel (jumpri):* which word, *hovel*, may not unaptly be derived from *havelly*, or *hovelly*, pronounced the same; among *Mahratas*, and other *Hindus*, and probably a *Sanskrit* word, signifying a house—not, however, particularly a mean one.

† That near *Karly*.

on a quadruped of equivocal species; its hoofs are discernible, and it may be a horse. On Buddha's right, in the superior corner, is Brahma sitting on a lotos; on the calyx of which are three or four well-embossed swans: in the opposite corner is an emaciated *Brahman*; seen also in several other compartments, and in most admirably executed: beneath Brahma is Indra; his elephant but faintly discernible. On the right of Buddha the remains of Ganesa may be fancied: on the right of Ganesa a man, as large as life, is sitting on a step; and on the other side of Buddha, a corresponding figure, holding a chaplet of beads. The remains of an animal, like a lion, may be traced near the males who hold the stem of the lotos supporting Buddha: several groups of figures, in bold relief, overspread him; some hold *chawries:* Buddha's head-dress is finely ornamented; several crescents are among its ornaments; and a large rose projects on each side, behind his head, as if confining his hair. If Buddha were standing, he would be about fifteen feet high: the whole compartment, or niche, is about eleven feet square: the niche is indented four feet into the rock; and the most prominent parts of the figures are not advanced toward the exterior (or framing, shall we call it, of the picture or niche,) nearer than three feet: the lower part of the niche is two feet from the floor; thus forming a sort of shelf, or table, under the figures that support the lotos.

The reader is requested to compare this account of the Buddha compartment, in the *Elephanta* cave, with plate 72. (keeping in mind, that it was written before I ever saw the drawing from which that plate was made; and although I have seen the original of the drawing, it has entirely escaped my recollection,) and he will find a unity of design in regard to the primary idea of Buddha being seated on the expanded lotos, issuing from its similarly-supported stem. The precise attitude or action of Buddha at *Elephanta* is not noticed if discernible: in the plate, just referred to, he is in the same attitude and act described, at *Ellora*, by *Sir* Charles Malet in a preceding quotation. The subject of plate 72. is on the right of the entrance into the arched cave at *Karly*, and is taken from a sketch, made on the spot, by *Mr.* Salt,* who obligingly per-

* This gentleman has had the advantage of seeing, with an artist's eye, more of the remains of *Hindu* architecture than perhaps any *European*. The interesting points of *Rameswara*, *Karly*, *Elephanta*, and *Kenereh*, be has visited at his leisure, and made many sketches of. A valuable collection of these sketches, more particularly, I understand, of images of Buddha, a subject *Mr.* Salt has particularly attended to, is, with a descriptive memoir, in the possession of the *Bombay* Literary Society, who will doubtless make the best use of them. I will take this occasion to notice, that as well as the subjects for the plates of *Lore*

mitted me to copy it for this work. I have several times visited this magnificent excavation at *Karly*, or *Ekverah*, as the mountain, out of which it is scooped, is more accurately called; but so transiently, as not to admit of my making any description of it. The visitor, on such occasions, is so struck with the grandeur of the whole, that it is some time before he can condescend to particulars.

The city of *Bamiyan* was considered at a very early period as the metropolis of the sect of BUDDHA; and was hence called *Buddha Bamiyan*. It is a place of great antiquity, situated about eight days journey north-westerly from *Kabul*. The account given of it, from the relations of native travellers, by *Mr.* WILFORD, in his Essay on Mount *Caucasus*, (*As. Res.* Vol. VI.) reminds us strikingly of the excavated mountain *Kenereh*, on *Salsette*; and the colossal figures seem also very similar, identifying their authors with the indefatigable race of workmen who, at such a distance as the *Dekkan*, constructed the gigantic statues in the cave at *Kenereh*, as well as those in the open air in the province of *Kanara*, of which plates are given in this work (73. 74.) and of which some notice will be taken presently.

Like *Thebes*, in *Egypt*, *Bamiyan* is cut out of an insulated mountain, and consists of a vast number of apartments, scooped out of the rock; some of which, on account of their extraordinary dimensions, are supposed to have been temples. Some of them are adorned with niches and carved work; and the remains are seen of figures in *relievo*, mutilated by the *Mussulmans*, and of paintings on the walls: but the latter are nearly obliterated by smoke and dirt. The *Ayin Akbery* says there were twelve thousand of these apartments, or recesses; and the report of native travellers tend to confirm it. In some apartments very remote, and inconvenient for the residence of *Mussulmans*, the paintings with which they are adorned look quite fresh.

What chiefly attract the notice of travellers are two colossal statues, in a sort of niche; the depth of which is equal to the thickness of the statue, erect, and adhering to the mountain in which they are cut. Accounts differ as to their height—from eighty ells to fifty cubits: their origin, name, and sex, are also variously related. The few *Hindus* who live in that neighbourhood say they are of BHIM and his consort: the followers of BUDDHA, that they are of SHAHAMA and his consort, SALSALA: the *Mussulmans* call them ADAM and EVE;

VALENTIA's great work, *Mr.* SALT has availed himself of every opportunity of taking views on *Ceylon*, in the *Bengal*, *Carnatic*, *Dekkan*, and other provinces of *India*; in *Arabia*, *Abyssinia*, *Egypt*, and other oriental and interesting countries. Select subjects will soon be offered to the public.

and a third statue, half a mile distant, about twenty feet high, they say is of SEISH, or SETH, their son. The author of the *Farhang Jehangiry* says they existed in the time of NOAH; but gives them other names.—P. 466.

PURANA PURI, the celebrated *Urdba bahu*, of whom mention is made in page 162. noticed two figures of VISHNU at *Basra*, on the banks of the *Euphrates:* they are called GOVINDA RAYA, and KALYANA RAYA; or, as commonly pronounced, GOBIND ROW, and KALYAN ROW: they are said to be carefully concealed from the sight of *Mussulmans.* In the city of *Cambay* there is a subterraneous *Hindu* temple that is said to be also concealed from the *Mussulmans.* I have never been in this city; but from the accounts that I have heard of the temple, I conclude it to be of *Buddhaic* origin: it is said to contain many images; among them, some of crystal. Being immediately within our reach at *Bombay*, an expectation may reasonably be indulged, that this, and the many other interesting objects of antiquity or curiosity, so lavishly scattered in its neighbourhood, and hitherto undescribed, will not remain much longer strangers to the literary public.

We will now proceed to notice more particularly the plates illustrative of this portion of our work, which I regret to find has already in length exceeded my expectation, and I fear my reader's wishes or patience.

PLATE 68. is from a fine statue in black marble, of the size of an ordinary man; sent to me from *Goa* by my worthy friend *Major* JOHNSON, and is deposited in his name in the Museum at the *India* house. The statue is well proportioned, but, like almost all *Hindu* sculptures, is deficient in anatomical expression. A reason has been assigned for this inaccuracy in oriental artists, on the supposition that the soft effeminate exterior of *Asiatics* offers no model of muscular symmetry. This is in a certain degree true; for the individuals of the higher classes of society are, from their indolent and luxurious style of living, the use of baths and unguents, very round and smooth in their contour; and from these models we may reasonably expect more of the APOLLO than the HERCULES in the works of the artists: among the labouring classes may, however, be found men exceedingly athletic, with strongly-marked muscles. I apprehend the statue now under our notice is of *Jaina* origin: the plate is a very good representation of it, except that I think it has rather too old and rigid a countenance. The original seems more placid, as well as younger; and I should imagine, but it did not occur to me to examine particularly when within reach of it, has elongated lobes of the ear, instead of rings in them, as indicated by the plate: I think too it has a more downcast meek look, of devout contemplation. The mark in the palm has been noticed in a former page as referring to a *Jaina* epithet, CHAKRAVERTI. I must not forget that the nose of this statue, otherwise in perfect preservation, has suffered from the pious zeal of some *Portuguese* zealot; but I did not choose to represent a favourite subject defective in that article, and requested my ingenious draughtsman to act the part of TALIACOTIUS on this occasion, which he has done very skilfully. An admirer of the remains of *Hindu* superstition will follow with regret the course of the former possessions of the *Portuguese*, marked with destruction to their finest monuments: scarcely a figure is seen unmutilated in the cavern of *Elephanta*. The furious bigotry of this semi-christian people, let us hope, is sufficiently punished in the wretchedness and contempt of their present miserable existence: let us farther hope that it will serve as a beacon, warning the *English* from following such a vile example, and from deserving such a signal chastisement.

The original of PLATE 69. is also in the museum at the *India* house: it is about fourteen inches high, of a whitish, and I think a calcareous, sort of stone: an inscription is on the pedestal, under the crescent, but is not easily to be made out or copied, and it has therefore been omitted. This image is, I think, of a very singular and curious description: its curly hair, thick lips, and position, mark it decidedly of *Buddhaic* origin, while its seven heads refer it to a sect of *Sauras:* hence the appellation of SURYA BUDDHA, appropriately applied to it. But of the existence of a sect of *Saura-bauddhas* no information has hitherto been obtained; and as I never saw or heard of any other seven-headed BUDDHA, am disposed to think that this is an unauthorised innovation on the mere human form in which this deity is mostly elsewhere depicted: the offspring possibly of an individual, but half converted from a *Saura* to a *Bauddha*. —(See p. 124.) The quadrated lozenge, on the breast and in the palm of this image, is also unaccounted for, and singular.

The four figures in the upper part of PLATE 70. are from images of the same size: *figures* 1. and 3. of copper or bronze, 2. and 4. of brass; and although I have called them all *Jain* figures, I am not sure of being correct, for their identity is by no means certain. *Fig.* 1. I decidedly think is not of BUDDHA, in any of his forms, but referable rather to that class of idols mentioned in page 179, and seen in various shapes in PLATES 99. 100. and 101.: it is very old, and less perfect in features than in the plate, and seems to hold a staff and bag, like many others in my collection, and as is seen in *fig.* 2. of PLATE 99. It has the mystical string, *zennaar*, not usually, I believe very seldom, seen on images of BUDDHA, and has the hair clubbed behind, with no appearance of any on the top or upper parts of the head.

Fig. 2. of PLATE 70. is noted in my memoranda as a *Jain* figure of BUDDHA, and like *fig.* 3. neither respected nor recognized by *Brahmans:* they are in an attitude of adoration; and *fig.* 2. has the soles upward, which neither 1. nor 3. have: it has a staff as is now commonly seen in the hands of *Jaina* priests; and, on minute inspection, marks are observable on its arms, similar to PLATES 73. and 74. but it has also the *zennaar*, not visible in a front view, and a lock of hair behind neatly clubbed, both, I think, irreconcilable to a *Jaina* figure; nor are its hands in any of the usual peculiar positions. *Fig.* 3. is still more doubtful; as neither its hands or feet are in a regular *Jaina* attitude, although the implement at its right shoulder has been supposed to be a broom; and its want of hair has farther referred it to a *Jaina* source. *Fig.* 4. is not very old, or, if old, has been furbished up, giving it a rough modern appearance, but ruder than the plate represents. This I do not hesitate to class with the *genus* of BUDDHA idolatry: its hands and feet correspond, and the pedestal is a semi-circle, a plan not often seen under images. *Fig.* 5. of this plate has a pedestal rounded at the ends, &c. to the rear, and indented or concave in front: *fig.* 4. is straight in front, with sharp corners. The five-headed *naga*, or snake, overshadowing *fig.* 4. and concealing its hair or its want of it, hangs straight down the back, and its tail approaching the front, there terminates. The ears of the first four figures of PLATE 70. are large and long, but not so particularly conspicuous as on many *Jaina* images: these four I obtained in and about *Poona*.

Fig. 5. of PLATE 70. is from a very fine cast in brass, entirely and well gilt, save, however, the woolly hair, which is black: it was procured on *Ceylon* by *Lord* VALENTIA, who obligingly favoured me with the loan of it for this work. *Fig.* 5. gives a very good front and back view, exhibiting the peculiar position and marks of hands and feet; the vestment, or wrapper, and shoulder-band; ears, with long pierced lobes, woolly hair, and on the head what *Mr.* HARRINGTON (see p. 230.) calls a *tiara*, or something resembling a hand, or five fingers touching each other—a similitude that would not have occurred to me on examining my plate or its original, or his: touching the mark on the forehead, I, in page 231, confessed my ignorance. *Lord* VALENTIA's image is nearly seven inches high, and is solid, but the pedestal is hollow.

The three little BUDDHAS below are taken from a number of similar casts in lak, that were dug up at different times at *Buddha gaya*, in *Bengal*, and belonged to the collection of the late *Mr.* RICHARD JOHNSON; now, I believe, they are in the museum at the *India* house. The originals are of the size and form represented; and the whole, a score perhaps, or more, are, I think, in the same position, and have all frizzled heads, and some lines of inscription under the figures; but as it is difficult to copy, and more so to translate them accurately, I have altogether omitted them—desirous to avoid the risk of misleading, where I am unable to instruct.

Fig. 1. of PLATE 71. is the BUDDHA of *Mr.* WILKINS' set of *Avataras*, cast at *Benares*; it is of *biddery*, or *zinc*, six inches high: the position of the hands and feet, and the woolly head, are in the usual style; but being a *Brahmanical* BUDDHA, we here see long hair braided in a neat knot on the top of the head; and he has not the pendent ears common to the BUDDHAS of *Ava*, the *Dekkan*, and *Ceylon:* neither has it, although *Brahmanical*, the *zennaar*.

The original of *fig*. 2. of PLATE 71. I met with, among many others exactly similar, in a shop in *Bombay:* a box full of them had been brought from *China* as toys, or pretty things for children. I purchased several of them at two rupees (five shillings) each, glad of the opportunity of enriching the cabinets of my collecting friends with so curious a subject. The image is of alabaster, about six inches high, delicately sculptured: the cone on the head, and the band over the left shoulder, are gilt. The similarity of this figure in attitude, hair, ears, conical coronet, and band, with the other images of BUDDHA, clearly identifies the BUDDHA, or the FO-HI, as I should expect this idol to be named, of *China*, with his *Indian* archetype. PLATE 69. and others, have a conical termination to the heads; and I have seen drawings of *Dekkan* images, with the quadrangular like this of *China*.

Fig. 3. of PLATE 71. is the same deity from *Ava*, where, as well as in *Siam*, he is, among other names, called SRAMANA, or SRAVANA GAUTAMA: the epithet, which means *holy*, is sometimes pronounced *Samana*; and in the name a *d* is sounded for the *t*, giving the SOMMONACADOM of former inquirers into *Siamese* and *Japanese* theology. It is of silver, eleven inches high, and neatly cast. Here we see him in one of the postures described in a former page, and as seen in the three *Gaya* BUDDHAS in PLATE 70. with the conical coronet like his brother of *China*, and the shoulder-belt similar to that, as well as to *fig*. 5. of PLATE 70. from a *Ceylon* subject. It has also the long ears and thick lips, so often noticed in others; a woolly head of course.

PLATE 72. has been noticed before.—(See page 246.) It is a *fac-simile* of *Mr.* SALT's sketch, and I presume is a faithful copy of its original, in the grand cave at *Ekvera*, or *Karly*. I should not, however, have expected to see BUDDHA seated on a plane throne, nor such throne supported by dogs: the other points are not uncommon in other sculptures: the superior figures in light attitudes, the arc springing from monsters' mouths, beings supporting a crown or mitre, others with *chawries* and lotoses, and those supporting the stem of the lotos on which BUDDHA sits, are seen in the caves of *Elephanta* and *Kenereh*. The attitude is the same as is described of VISWAKARMA, by *Sir* CHARLES MALET, in the *Ellorá* cave; and the woolly head and thick lips are almost universal: the long ears, and raised head, here scarcely conical, may be noticed in passing.

Before we proceed to a different style of statuary, as exhibited in the two next plates, I will refer the reader to a *Bengal* image of BUDDHA, in PLATE 75. *fig.* 3. taken from an inked drawing, in the collection of my liberal friend *Colonel* STUART: it appears to be from a carved original, and is the only one I ever saw with such a many-headed fan-like overhanging snake. This I imagine to be, as well as *fig.* 1. of PLATE 71. the acknowledged BUDDHA *Avatara* of the *Brahmans*; for the hair is straight on the crown, and the woolly portion is so managed as to resemble a fillet of beads round the temple. The mark in the breast and palms, as well as the style of head, is nearly similar to that of SURYA BUDDHA in PLATE 69. the heads too are raised conically on the crown: it has no *zennaar*.

The lower part of PLATE 76. is also a *fac-simile* of a sketch of *Mr.* SALT's, from a ruined temple, called SIVA *Samudra*, or the *Sea* of SIVA, on an island in the river *Caveri*. *Mr.* SALT determined the figure to be of BUDDHA; and although it has some appearance of it, both in itself and in the attendants, yet it is so unlike any other that I have ever seen, that I cannot decide upon it: the termination in folds, snake-like, is not in character for BUDDHA. It reminds one of RAHU and KETU, of whom some notice must be taken in their place.

Although none of my plates exhibit BUDDHA four-handed, he is sometimes so painted: I have several sets of the *Avataras* in which he is so represented, and others where he has but two hands, placed in the usual manner, palms upwards. Where he has four hands, they are in one picture empty; in another he holds lotoses and books; and in several instances, where he is both two and four-handed, he has an umbrella over his head, an insignia of royalty. Under the authority of *Brahmans* he is generally painted white, and as a handsome youth, with attendants fanning him with *chawries*. One picture, in a set of *Avataras*, has a mark in the forehead similar to that which distinguishes generally the sect of *Vaishnavas*, viz. a black circlet between two upright red lines; and in this instance too his long hair is evident, similar to that of other *Avataras:* but he has no *zennaar* in any of my pictures.

Fig. 1. of PLATE 73. is taken from a sketch that *Sir* ARTHUR WELLESLEY obtained in *Kanara*; and we are informed by *Dr*. BUCHANAN, who, in his curious and valuable "Journey through *Mysore* and *Kanara*," gives a print of this subject, that the Right Honourable *General* thought the *Colossus* less clumsy than the sketch.—Vol. III. p. 410.* On my sketch, copied from that of my gallant friend, the height of the statue is noted to be sixty feet three inches; but *Dr*. BUCHANAN states it at seventy feet three inches. It is situated on a hill, called *Indra Giri*, near the village of *Bellegola*, or *Belgula*, surnamed *Sravana*, or *holy*, from being a very revered place of worship of the *Jainas:* the town and fort of *Chinraypattam*,† as it is commonly called, is only four miles distant. This *colossal* statue is called GOMATA RAYA, or GOMAT ISWARA, with the epithet *Swamy*, or *divine:* it is also called JAINESWARA, and JAINADEVA. A strong wall, with several temples and other buildings, surround the statue, and contained formerly seventy-two well-shaped images, of which only forty-two now remain. The great image is, of course, too lofty to be covered; and to a distance of eight *kos*,‡ in all directions, appears, *Dr*. BUCHANAN says, like a column. *Sir* ARTHUR WELLESLEY thinks the mountain was formerly much higher than it is now, and that it has been cut away, leaving only the image: it is, indeed, difficult to conceive how, in any other mode, such a mass of stone could have been so situated, its magnitude precluding the supposition of conveyance and erection.

Fig. 2. of PLATE 73. is taken from a drawing made for me by my old friend *Captain* BRUTTON, then of the 75th regiment. The drawing is of a dark blue, approaching to a black colour, and is entitled "BUD'HA, at *Yennoor*, carved in one solid piece of rock, and measuring in height thirty-five feet." *Yennoor* is more correctly spelled *Einuru*. I have no farther information, except a passage that will be given presently, respecting this image, which is evidently of GOMAT RAYA. *Dr*. BUCHANAN does, indeed, mention it in these terms: "At *Einuru* is an immense colossal image of one of the gods worshipped by the *Jainas*, formed of one solid piece of granite, and standing in the open air."—*Journey*,

* See also his account of the *Jains*.—*As. Res.* Vol. IX.

† *Jaina* images are, in *Kanara*, vulgarly called CHINDEO; a corruption of JAINADEVA: hence the name of this fort, *Chinraypatan*, may be, perhaps, in correcter orthography, *Jaina-raya-patana*.

‡ In this part of *Kanara* a *kos* may be estimated at two miles at least. Of GOMAT RAYA, an account is given in a book entitled GOMUTA RAYA *Charitra*.

Vol. III. p. 73. There is something peculiar in the lips of *fig.* 2. but nothing very *Ethiopic*. The woolly heads of both figures are sufficiently conspicuous, and the pierced elongated ears are characteristic: the attitude, ornaments, and general style of carving, sufficiently identify the object honoured by these gigantic monuments.

The sketch from which PLATE 74. is taken, I must, I think, have obtained from the same source as that of *fig.* 1. of the last plate; but having omitted to mark it, I am not certain. The plate is an exact copy, and is very similar to one given by *Dr.* BUCHANAN in his *Journey*; a work published since my plate was engraved: on my sketch the height of the statue is noted at thirty-eight feet. *Dr.* BUCHANAN says it is of one piece of granite, and gives the following dimensions: height, above ground, thirty-eight feet; breadth, ten feet and a half; thickness, ten feet: he thinks it must be at least three feet in the ground, it having no lateral support; and says that, according to an inscription on the stone itself, it was made by VIRA PANDIA, son of BHAIRAVA INDRA, 369 years ago.—Vol. III. p. 83.

Major JOHNSON has, among many other curious subjects in its neighbourhood, a drawing and measurement of this statue of GOMUT RAYA: he favoured me with the following dimensions; and I regret that I was not able to avail myself farther of his friendly offer of access to his valuable materials. "Height, from heel to crown, thirty-six feet six inches; length of the head, six feet six inches—of the arms, eighteen feet six inches; breadth at the shoulders, eleven feet six inches—at the little fingers, eleven feet; length of the nose, one foot six inches—of the ears, three feet—of the feet, four feet six inches. It stands on a stone platform, four feet and a half high; and its pedestal is said to be inserted in the rock beneath the platform." It is readily seen that the sketch, from which my plate is taken, does not accord in its proportions with these accurate dimensions.

The beautiful drawing from which PLATE 77. is engraved, was made for me by my ingenious young friend *Lieutenant* DICKENSON, of the *Bombay* engineers. Standing in front of the entrance to a *Jain* temple, we may conclude it to be the workmanship of an individual of that sect; and highly creditable, it must be acknowledged, it is to him and his brotherhood. The colour of the obelisk is dark blue, or brownish: the inferior portion of the shaft is square; its sides nearly alike as to ornaments: it is then, for a few feet, sexagonal; and at this elevation is a figure—whether on more sides than one I am not informed; and I have never had an opportunity of examining this fine specimen of *Jaina* architectural skill. In the PLATE, and in *Mr.* DICKENSON's drawing, the position of the figure is equivocal. In another view of the pillar, made for me by *Captain* BRUTTON, it is much more like the usual sitting figure of BUDDHA, and has a sort of cap, or something bell-shaped, suspended over his head; and he is encircled by a border of flowers, or leaves. Higher, the shaft has more angles; and approaching the capital, very many sides, so as, indeed, to be nearly round. The architrave is supported at its four corners by animals that appear like lions, from whose paws chains drop, with bells at their extremities; other animals, with human figures, are seen at higher angles of the entablature; and the whole is crowned with a spire in *Mr.* DICKENSON's drawing, but in *Captain* BRUTTON's by a flame tri-forked: these differences may have arisen from the difference of situation whence the views were respectively taken. The shaft is of one stone, and has no inscriptions; the pedestal is composed. This is altogether the most elegant column hitherto noticed in *Kanara:* but I have accounts of others, in that rich and interesting province, very similar; some of which, instead of the flame, are surmounted by the figure of a cow: such may be seen at the towns of *Wurrup*, or *Woorp*, and *Batkula*, or *Batcola*, where there are elegant temples.

The *Jain* temple at *Mudubidry*, commonly called *Moorbidry*, is, however, the most elegant in the province: it is of large dimensions, having an interior cupola, supported by many columns, of great diversity in respect of design and ornament: GANESA, VISHNU, and SIVA, are said to be conspicuously carved throughout. The roof, over the body of the building, is composed of brass plates: there is an exterior viranda, supported by plain pillars, with a stone roof. One of my *Kanara* correspondents says, that the sacred image of the temple is tri-form, "exhibiting their Trinity in three brass figures grouped, burnished like gold; all quite naked, with curly heads like the colossal statues in the neighbourhood, but without the leaves twined round them." He adds, in another part, that the *Jainas* of *Mudubidry*, *Eimuru*, and *Karkulla*, particularly venerate flame. These three towns are about thirty miles north-easterly from *Mangalore:* the former the principal *Jaina* town, but of late years considerably decreased in population and importance: in its neighbouring plains are many tombs of great antiquity and magnitude. The natives are very reserved on matters of religion.

From another correspondent, travelling in *Kanara*, I received the following items, descriptive of the temple at *Mudubidry*. It is of three stories, and very magnificent both within and without: there are, we were told, a thousand pillars in and about it, and no two are alike: the sculpture is certainly fine, both in design and execution. Entering an inner apartment, on the ground-floor, is a large tablet, apparently of marble, on each side, covered with inscriptions in the *Kanarese* character, but hitherto not translated or copied: all the images of the gods on this floor are of brass, highly polished. On the second are some of marble. In the third, which is the most beautiful and worthy of observation, some are of brass, some of crystal, and others of marble and different stone: one in particular, of a reddish stone, was noticed, very large and handsome, which our conductors said was brought from *Europe*. The figures, on the whole, are very numerous. The roofs of the body of the temple have a curious appearance externally: they rise one over the other, three or four deep: some are covered with wood, some with copper, in pieces not unlike *English* bricks: the roof of the lower story is composed of massive slabs of granite, three or more inches in thickness, two or three feet broad, and from four to eight feet long. Many of the pillars in the interior have inscriptions and sculptures: on four principal corner ones we observed respectively an elephant, a monkey, a bird, and a conical figure: on many is the *cobra de capella*, or hooded snake. The exterior pillars are of elegant forms, light and airy in their appearance: the doom is grand and rich, composed of large flat stones, resting angularly on each other, and narrowing from the base; the top being of a slab nearly circular, and beautifully carved: on the door, at the entrance, are several elephants.

My correspondent now proceeded to *Karkula*, about twelve miles from *Mudubidry*, where is another *Jaina* temple, on a plan nearly similar, this being square; but smaller, although but little less striking and beautiful. Its pillars are very massive, and finely sculptured: it has four entrances exactly alike, and at each, on the inner side, are three figures of the god MINISWARA,* in highly-polished stone, with a number of smaller images placed around him. Opposite one entrance stands, exteriorly, a column, similar to that at *Mudubidry*, but smaller and less ornamented: at the latter place are, indeed, many such columns near temples; all of which are surmounted by a tablet, bearing a cone more or less perfect: at *Karkula* it is of an undulating form, like flame. Near the temple, whence is a good view of it, on a high rocky hill, is a colossal image of MINISWARA of one stone, and, it is said, nearly forty feet high; but mis-

* This name for GOMAT RAYA, or GOMAT ISWARA, occurs several times as that of the principal deity worshipped at the temples of *Karkula* and *Mudubidry*. I do not recollect ever having heard it, or seen it, except in the descriptions of this correspondent: MUNISWARA could be traced to historical authorities.

shapen as to proportions, and ill wrought. MINISWARA is again noticed at *Einuru*, as of smaller dimensions than his colossal brother at *Karkulla*, being estimated at but thirty feet in height: its feet are thirty-seven inches long, by twenty inches in breadth.

At *Mudubidry* is a palace of a curious structure, having a number of doors and pillars with sculptures of deities: one of these pillars, singularly and not inelegantly formed of wood, is represented in PLATE 78. from a drawing of *Lieutenant* DICKENSON; who was so good as to send me also a descriptive account of it, and other curiosities in *Kanara*, which unluckily has eluded my recent research. Another correspondent, as before mentioned, noticed "the Trinity in three figures grouped:" perhaps the unaccountable figure, or figures, in the upper part of this pillar may bear some reference to the same idea. For in different parts of *India* the *Hindu* Trinity is represented differently compounded: sometimes by a three-faced bust, as in *Elephanta*, and in PLATE 81. or three heads on one body, as in PLATE 82. Sometimes three heads and bodies on one leg, as in the magnificent *choultry* of TRIMAL NAIG, at *Madura*, in the *Carnatic*. —(See KINDERSLEY'S *Specimens* of *Hindu Literature*.) But these are all of *Brahmanical* origin; and I know of no representation of the *Trimurti*, or *three-formed* deity, as an object of worship or superstition among *Bauddhas* of any sect. If really existing in *Kanara*, it is a point of curious inquiry. Returning to PLATE 78. I should judge that the right and left leg of the central body answer in the original for the left and right legs of the side ones; and the arms the same, although not exactly so represented in my plate or drawing; nor are the birds on the exterior fists so clear in the drawing as in the plate. The elephant formed of women one would not expect to find in a *Jaina* palace: in this I have allowed of a little alteration: *Mr.* DICKENSON'S grouping is confused: I have in the plate rendered it clearer, improving the attitudes of the women from another picture, whence PLATE 65. is taken. The woman driving the elephant, and seated on its neck, should have borne, instead of the *ankasa*, or goading-hook, a banner, as she does in the drawing; and as is mentioned in a description of this pillar by another correspondent, who notices the men with bows and arrows on the animal's back.

In one part of the palace that contains this wooden pillar lives the former *Raja* of *Mudubidry*—I know not, though, if that was his exact title; and another square of it is appropriated to our Collector of the district. The only mention made of this poor man, I mean the *Raja*, by any of my correspondents, is coupled with the following anecdote:—During his meals a bell is rung close to him, in prevention of the possibility of his hearing a dog bark; which unpropitious event must be immediately followed by the unavoidable rejection of whatever food he might be about partaking of: whether this be an individual whim, or any sectarial rule in dietetics, I am not informed.

Having thus rapidly and superficially discussed the principal deities, powers, *Avataras*, &c. of the long catalogue of *Hindu* immortals, we proceed now to another description of demigods; and, eventually, to a more miscellaneous consideration of less important characters, whose influences, however, are supposed to be in constant operation, affecting the comforts and destinies of mankind; and whose names frequently occur in the endless ceremonies of the *Brahmans*, and in all writings and conversation, mythological or poetical.—Of these beings INDRA is generally deemed the chief.

Of INDRA,

And GENII subordinate to him.

Sir William Jones has addressed a hymn to Indra, replete with mythological allusions, and embellished with all the charms of poetry. The extracts that I am about to offer from it and its argument, will form a favourable introduction to my account of this important personage, and others of less note, directly or remotely connected with him.

"Indra, or the king of immortals, corresponds with one of the ancient Jupiters, for several of that name were worshipped in *Europe*; and particularly with Jupiter the *conductor*, whose attributes are so nobly described by the *Platonic* philosophers. One of his numerous names is Dyupeti, or, in the nominative case, before certain letters, Dyupetir; which means the *Lord of Heaven*, and seems a more probable origin of the *Hetruscan* word, than *Juvans Pater*; as Diespeter was probably not the *Father*, but the *Lord*, of Day.

"He may be considered as the Jove of Ennius, in his memorable line,

'Aspice hoc sublime candens, quem invocant omnes Jovem;'

where the poet clearly means the firmament, of which Indra is the personification. He is the God of Thunder, and of nature's elements, with inferior genii under his command; and is conceived to govern the eastern quarter of the world, but to preside, like the *Genius*, or *Agathodæmon*, of the ancients, over the celestial bands, which are stationed on the summit of *Meru*, or the north pole, where he solaces the gods with nectar and heavenly music. Hence, perhaps, the *Hindus*, when giving evidence, and the magistrate who receives it, are directed to stand fronting the east or north.

"The *genii*, named *Cinnara*, are the male dancers in *Swerga*, the heaven of Indra; and the *Apsara* are his dancing girls, answering to the fairies of the *Persians*, and to the damsels, called in the *Koran*, *hhuruluyun*, or *with antelope's eyes*."—Jones's *Works*, Vol. XIII.

Indra resides in the celestial city of *Amravati*, where his palace, *Vaijayanta*, is situated, in the garden *Nandana*, which contains the all-yielding trees *Pariyataka*,* *Kalpadruma*, and three others similarly bountiful. Although these, or even

* I have a sketch of a tree yielding, if not all sorts, a curious sort of fruit, viz. *men*; with a man of larger mould climbing up its stem: a second, with a bow at his back, is looking on, encouraging him. The picture is marked merely with the name Bhima; but I have no knowledge of the legend to which it alludes. Fifteen men are hanging on the boughs like fruit.

one of them, might suffice, and qualify its owner for the title which INDRA bears of *Lord of wealth*, he is sometimes represented to possess likewise the all-prolific cow, KAMDENU, as well as OOCHISRAVA, the eight-headed horse, that arose with the cow and first-named tree from the churned ocean, as related in another place. His consort is INDRANI: he rides the elephant IRAVATY, driven by his charioteer MATALI; and he holds the weapon *Vajra*, or the thunder-bolt, and is hence named VAJRAPANI. His chief musician is named CHITRARAT'HA, who rides in a painted car, which on one occasion was burned by ARJUN, the confidential friend and agent of KRISHNA, or the Sun. INDRA is more especially the regent of winds and showers: the water-spout is said to be the trunk of his elephant; and the *iris* is appropriately called his bow, which it is not deemed auspicious to point out.*

INDRA, as well as the deity presiding over the firmament, and over atmospheric or meteoric phenomena, is himself, as are most of the minor deities, a star, or a constellation: his name is among the twelve *Adityas*, or Suns. He is fabled to have lost for a while his kingdom to the *Asuras*, which are in fact the stars of the southern hemisphere, under the dominion of YAMA; who holds his court in the antarctic circle, and is at frequent war with INDRA and the *Suras*, in the northern hemisphere: the metropolis of which is *Meru*, the *Olympus* of INDRA, the celestial north pole, allegorically represented as a mountain of gold and gems. Deeming the *Suras* and *Asuras* to be the stars in the two hemispheres, I apprehend that some astronomical fact is veiled in the allegory of INDRA's dethronement: the precession of the equinoxes, perhaps, or annual motion of the stars from east to west, by which INDRA has his stellar locality usurped by some other luminary, and is hence fabled to have been dethroned in warfare with YAMA's legion of *Asuras*, or malignant spirits.

SONNERAT mentions that " INDRA, king of the demigods, and supporter of the east part of the universe, has had many wars to sustain against giants, enemies of the gods; alternately conqueror and conquered, he has several times been driven out of *Sorgon (Swerga)*; and it was only by the protection of the three superior gods that he destroyed his enemies, and recovered and retained possession of his celestial abode."—Vol. I. p. 61.

These contests of INDRA relate possibly to a cycle, depending on some periodical alteration in the state or places of the heavenly bodies: he loses his

* " Let not him, who knows right from wrong, and sees in the sky the bow of INDRA, show it to any man."—*Ins.* of MENU, chap. iv. v. 59.

dominion; that is, some other constellation succeeds to his or his subjects' place for a period; when, by the favour of the superior gods, or, in other words, by the harmony of the spheres, or the regular movements of the celestial bodies, INDRA and his sidereal host, at the recommencement of the cycle, resume their stations in the heavens.

In his wars he employs many elephants, which, in reality, are clouds, and have names derived from that source of metaphor; such as the *lightning sender*, similar to the برک انداز *berk andàs*, of the *Persians*; *thunder bearer*, *black*, *white*, *blue*, *rumbler*, *growler*, &c. &c. The chief of all is IRAVAT, it being his *vahan*, or vehicle: the name means *watery*, the aqueous property of clouds being that most apparent. IRAVAT, as INDRA's vehicle, is frequently painted with three trunks; but some of my pictures have other deities, especially RAMA and KRISHNA, mounted on this favoured animal.

The *Hindus* have assigned regents to each cardinal and intermediate point of the compass. INDRA being esteemed the first of firmamental deities, and especially the ruler of the east, that point is reckoned first, and the others are thus ruled: AGNI, south-east; YAMA, south; NIRIT, south-west; VARUNA, west; VAYU, north-west; KUVERA, north; ISANI, north-east. To which are sometimes added three other quarters, or points, viz. *above*, governed by BRAHMA; *below*, by NAGA, or SESHNAGA, the king of serpents, otherwise named VASUKY; and the *centre*, ruled by RUDRA, or SIVA.

Here we find BRAHMA and SIVA in situations apparently subordinate to INDRA: SIVA, indeed, holds two offices, being as ISA, or ISANI, governor of the north-east region; and as RUDRA, of the central district. But they are both confessedly superior to INDRA, who is generally esteemed prince of the beneficent *genii*; and is, like his betters, an extraordinary and equivocal character, as will appear in the sequel. He is poetically described as

> "Mounted on the Sun's bright beam"—
> "Darter of the swift blue bolt"—
> "Sprinkler of genial dews and fruitful rains
> O'er hills and thirsty plains"—

and is called *Lord of wealth*, for which a good reason has been already given; *beautiful*, *with a thousand eyes*; and the *destroyer of towns*. We have before noticed his fruitless attempt to destroy *Mat'hura*, saved by the miraculous interposition of KRISHNA (see PLATE 61. and page 199); but the name is more appropriate in reference to the destruction of the classical city of *Ujjaini*, or *Oogeen*, the present capital of DOWLUT ROW SINDEA: of which extraordinary event, some account is given in the note below.* It is not likely, however, that this event, which occurred about 1900 years ago, was the origin of his name of "destroyer of towns;" similar visitations, of earlier date, are probably related in the *Puranas*.

* The city of *Ujjaini*, called also *Avanti*, boasts of very high antiquity, and is considered as the first meridian by *Hindu* geographers and astronomers. *Mr.* HUNTER, in the sixth volume of the *Asiatic Researches*, ("Journey from *Agra* to *Ougein*,") gives a description of the modern city, which, by repeated observations, he determined to be in long. 75° 51′ E. lat. 23° 11′ N. The ancient city was about a mile farther south, and now lies buried in the earth to the depth of from fifteen to eighteen feet: on digging, its walls are said to be found entire, pillars unbroken, &c. Tradition imputes its destruction to a shower of earth; an idea likely to have originated in superficial observation: for although *Mr.* HUNTER observed no traces of volcanic hills, nor *scoria*, in the neighbourhood, and thinks the style of the walls militates against the supposition of an earthquake having effected the submersion of the city, it is still difficult to impute it to any other than a volcanic cause, operating, perhaps, with less violence and convulsion than usually attend such a phenomenon. It may be remarked, that the neighbourhood of *Oojein* is particularly subject to inundation from the alluvion of the river *Sippara*, near which the city is situated: this, combined with the soft sinking nature of the soil, may afford *data* for a *Neptunist* to uphold a different hypothesis, accounting for the submersion of the ancient city. Whatever may have been the real cause of the catastrophe that befel this metropolis, it cannot be supposed that the wild fancies of *Hindu* historians would suffer the fact, in itself highly poetical and romantic, to be simply told: it must be dressed up in a mythological allegory; and the intervention of the gods cannot be dispensed with. The following story is accordingly related; and I have borrowed it from the interesting "Journey from *Agra* to *Ougein*," of my learned friend, before mentioned.

A certain deity, named GUNDRUSEIN, was condemned, for an affront to INDRA, to be born on earth in the shape of an ass; but, on entreaty, the sentence was mitigated, and he was allowed at night to re-assume the form and functions of a man. This incarnation took place at *Oujein*, in the reign of *Raja* SUNDERSEIN, whose daughter was demanded in marriage by the ass; and his consent was obtained, on learning the divine origin of his intended son-in-law, confirmed, as he witnessed, by certain prodigies. All day he lived in the stables like an ass; at night, secretly slipping out of his skin, and assuming the appearance of a handsome and accomplished young prince, he repaired to the palace, and enjoyed the conversation of his beauteous bride.

In due time the princess became pregnant; and her chastity being suspected, she revealed to her inquisitive parent the mystery of her husband's happy nocturnal metamorphosis: which the *Raja*, being conveniently concealed, himself beheld; and unwilling that his son should return to his uncouth disguise, set fire to, and consumed, the vacant ass's skin.

Although rejoiced at his release, the incarnate deity foresaw the resentment of INDRA, disappointed of his vengeance; and warned his wife to quit the city, about to be overwhelmed with a shower of earth. She fled to a village at a safe distance, and brought forth a son, named VIKRAMADITYA; and a shower of cold earth, poured down by INDRA, buried the city and its inhabitants.—See *As. Res.* Vol. VI.

This legend gives a date to the catastrophe; for the prince, so renowned in his origin and birth, was not less so as a monarch and an astronomer; and his name marks an era much used all over *India*: of which the 1865th year, as noticed in page 223, corresponds with 1809, of ours. Several monarchs of this name are recorded; and disputes exist on some chronological questions connected with this era.—See

On one occasion INDRA assumed the form of a shepherd's boy, that he might the easier steal from a garden some pomegranate blossoms, to deck the dark tresses of his charming consort INDRANI. The story, which is borrowed from the popular mythology of *Nepal* and *Tibet*, is told by *Sir* W. JONES in his hymn; and I shall extract the passage, as well for the purpose of relieving a little the prosaic dulness of description by the enlivening intervention of poetry, as that it again introduces some of the minor deities, or agents of INDRA, of whom some farther account must be given.

"The reckless peasant, who these glowing flowers,
Hopeful of rubied fruit, had foster'd long,
Seiz'd, and with cordage strong,
Shackl'd the god who gave him showers.
Straight from seven winds immortal genii flew—
VARUNA green, whom foamy waves obey;
Bright VAHNI, flaming like the lamp of day;
KUVERA, sought by all, enjoy'd by few;
MARUT, who bids the winged breezes play;
Stern YAMA, ruthless judge! and ISA cold;
With NAIRRIT, mildly bold:
They, with the ruddy flash that points his thunder,
Rend his vain bands asunder.
Th' exulting god resumes his thousand eyes,
Four arms divine, and robes of changing dyes."

His "robes of changing dyes" are the evanescent and variable clouds, with which he (the firmament personified) is clad as with a garment, bespangled with a thousand eyes, or stars.

Great and glorious as INDRA is, he could not resist temptation; and is described as prone to indulge his propensities in a manner much more criminal than his attempt at ornamenting the beauteous tresses of his wife: which description, if taken literally, would transform his distinction of *thousand-eyed* from glory to disgrace; for he is fabled to have been once covered with, instead of eyes,

WILFORD on the Eras of VIKRAMADITYA and SALIVAHANA, *As. Res.* Vol. IX. where the legend of the ass is differently told.

In our late war with the *Mahrata* confederates, the *Bombay* army, under my good and respected friend *General* JOHN MURRAY, possessed itself of *Ougein*, the capital of SINDEA's hereditary possessions, as well as its neighbouring city, *Indore*, the capital of HOLKAR: and although we retained the former some time in our hands, I have not heard of any literary result from our possessing so curious and interesting a spot— the *Herculaneum* or *Pompeii* of *India*. The subject represented in PLATE 30. and described in page 160, was sent to me at that time from *Indore*, by a friend.

marks of a different sort, indicating, among other unworthinesses, his being undeserving of the faithful and virtuous PULOMAYA, as his consort INDRANI is sometimes called; or more correctly, perhaps, POWLAMYA.

AHILYA, the handsome wife of the pious *Rishi* GOTAMA, has been mentioned on a former occasion.—(See p. p. 87. 172.) Her beauty attracted the depraved INDRA; and he was well nigh succeeding in his adulterous pursuit, but for the unseasonable, or I should rather say seasonable, intrusion of the holy man, who imprecated this curse upon INDRA—that he should be covered with the mark of what had been the object of his lawless desires; which took immediate effect. On the repentance and entreaties of the detected deity, the good man relented, and mitigated the curse by changing the marks of his shame to as many eyes.

This moderation, on the part of the temperate sage, had not, however, its effect on the persevering deity, who, disguising himself in the semblance of the venerable man, succeeded in seducing the austere AHILYA, under circumstances of peculiar indelicacy, as related in the 38th chapter of the *Ramayana*. —"This depraved one, knowing SAKRA in the disguise of a sage, through wantonness consented, he being king of the gods."—P. 301. GOTAMA again intruded, too late, indeed, but *malapropos* for the frail ones, and thus cursed his unlucky wife: "For an innumerable series of years, O sinful wretch, of depraved heart! lie in ashes in a certain forest, enduring excessive pain, and invisible, until the coming of RAMA: beholding of whom, without selfish views, thou, cleansed from sin, and filled with joy, shalt again approach GOTAMA without fear."—P. 302. INDRA, "the profligate lord of the gods," by the malediction of the sage, became an eunuch, and was overcome with shame and sorrow; but at the intercession of all the gods and the *Maruts*, with AGNI at their head, he was restored to manhood by the *Pitris*, at the expense of a ram: and from that time, and in memory of this renewal, the *Pitris* (see p. 93.) have been propitiated by the sacrifice of an imperfect sheep, entire animals of that class being now never offered to them. Poor AHILYA, a name still given to *Hindu* females, was also released from the curse of her husband, by RAMA entering her sorrowful abode: she viewing him, although so handsome, without impure desires, became visible; and "GOTAMA, with his divine eye, beholding his consort purified by severe sufferings, was reunited to her, and with her again engaged—in sacred austerities."

From such instances of frailty, INDRA became, among the saints and sages, proverbial for profligacy. When the sanctified ascetic, VISWAMITRA, (see page 133.) who had for thousands of years been engaged in the most rigid mortification, beheld MENAKA, the *Apsara** sent by INDRA to debauch him, "bathing, of surprising form, unparalleled in beauty, in appearance resembling SRI—her clothes, wetted by the stream, exhibiting her fascinating symmetry of frame; he, subdued by the arrows of KANDARPA, approached her: and five times five years, spent in dalliance with this seducing female, passed away like a moment." —"What!" exclaimed, at length, the reflecting sage, "my wisdom, my austerities, my firm resolution, all destroyed at once by a woman! Seduced by the crime in which INDRA delights, am I stripped of the advantages arising from all my austerities!"—*Ram.* sect. 50.

We have before noticed INDRA as an evil counsellor, aiding by his advice the malignant *asuras*, or any ill-disposed human beings, in counteracting the beneficent intentions of the gods, and thwarting the piety of men. Covetous of sacrifices, he sees not without envy and jealousy offerings made to other deities; and when not especially or exclusively dedicated to himself, has been known to steal the victim, or some essential sacrificial utensil. At an *aswamedha*, or in the ceremonies preparatory to it, he will steal the horse, which is let loose to wander whither it pleases, properly attended, for the whole year previous to its immolation. In the 48th section of the *Ramayana* it is related how INDRA stole from the sacred pile the victim of the king, AMBARISHI, of *Ayodha (Oude)*; who, resolving on a *Naramedha*, or human sacrifice, had consecrated a man, bearing the characteristic marks, and appointed for the immolation. The search after another victim affords opportunities of introducing some pathetic passages. And in the 23d section it is stated how INDRA, in a rage, occasioned by hunger, killed his friend and companion NAMUKI.

INDRA, however, if not unreasonable, might well be satisfied with his allowed portion of sacrificial propitiation; for he is very frequently, and, in point of precedence, honourably, invoked in many *Brahmanical* ceremonies. At the *Srad'ha*, or obsequies in honour of deceased ancestors, in this form: the priest, meditating the *Gayatri*, says, "May INDRA and VARUNA accept our oblations, and grant us happiness: may INDRA and the cherishing Sun grant us happiness in the distribution of food: may INDRA and the Moon grant us the happiness of attaining the road of celestial bliss, and the association of good offices."— COLEBROKE. *As. Res.* Vol. VII. Art. viii.

And in the eighth volume, the same learned gentleman, in his most valuable Essay on the *Vedas*, Art. viii. describes from that fruitful source a supposed

* *Apsara* is derived from *ap, water,* in one case *apsu,* and *rasa,* the sensation of *taste.*

consecration of INDRA, when elected by the gods to be their king. I extract the concluding paragraph—the whole is curious.

"Thus consecrated by that great inauguration, INDRA subdued all conquerable earths, and won all worlds: he obtained over all the gods supremacy, transcendant rank, and pre-eminence. Conquering in this world below, equitable dominion, separate authority, attainment of the supreme abode, mighty power, and superior rule; becoming a self-existent being, and independent ruler, exempt from early dissolution; and reaching all his wishes in that celestial world, he became immortal; he became immortal."*

In the *Ins.* of MENU, the component parts of a king are enumerated; among which INDRA obtains a place.

Chap. V. v. 96.—"The corporeal frame of a king is composed of particles from SOMA, AGNI, SURYA, PAVANA, INDRA, KUVERA, VARUNA, and YAMA, the eight guardian deities of the world."

In another similar text, the deities, although the same, are differently placed; for the sake, perhaps, of a metrical arrangement of their names.

Chap. VII. v. 3.—"If the world had no king, it would quake on all sides through fear: the ruler of the universe, therefore, created a king for the maintenance of this system, both religious and civil;

"4. Forming him of eternal particles, drawn from the substance of [1] INDRA, [2] PAVANA, [3] YAMA, [4] SURYA, of [5] AGNI and [6] VARUNA, of [7] CHANDRA and [8] KUVERA:

"5. And since a king was composed of particles drawn from these chief guardian deities, he consequently surpasses all mortals in glory.—

"6. He is [5] fire and [2] air; he both [4] sun and [7] moon; he the god of [3] criminal justice; he the genius [8] of wealth; he the regent of [6] waters; he the lord of the [1] firmament." †

C. IX. v. 301.—"All the ages called *Satya, Treta, Dwapara,* and *Kali,* depend on the conduct of a king who is declared in turn to represent each of those ages:

"302. Sleeping, he is the *Kali* age; waking, the *Dwapara*; exerting himself in action, the *Treta*; living virtuously, the *Satya*.

"303. Of INDRA, of SURYA, of PAVANA, of YAMA, of VARUNA, of CHANDRA, of AGNI, and of PRIT'HIVI, let the king emulate the power and attributes.

* "In the didactic portion of the *Veda*, the last term in every chapter is repeated, to indicate its conclusion."

† The figures of reference are not in the *Institutes*: I have added them to assist the reader in connecting the names and characters of the deities enumerated.

"304. As INDRA sheds plentiful showers during the four rainy months, thus let him, acting like the regent of clouds, rain just gratifications over his kingdom:

"305. As SURYA with strong rays draws up the water during eight months, thus let him, performing the functions of the Sun, gradually draw from his realm the legal revenue:

"306. As PAVAN, when he moves, pervades all creatures, thus let him, imitating the regent of wind, pervade all places by his concealed emissaries:

"307. As YAMA, at the appointed time, punishes friends and foes, or those who revere and those who contemn him, thus let the king, resembling the judge of departed spirits, punish offending subjects:

"308. As VARUNA most assuredly binds the guilty in fatal cords, thus let him, representing the genius of water, keep offenders in close confinement.

"309. When the people, no less delighted on seeing the king, than on seeing the full moon, he appears in the character of CHANDRA.

"310. Against criminals let him be ever ardent in wrath; let him be splendid in glory; let him consume wicked ministers; thus imitating the functions of AGNI, god of fire.

"311. As PRIT'HIVI supports all creatures equally, thus a king, sustaining all subjects, resembles in his office the goddess of earth."

Intending, under this head, to notice some characters subordinate to INDRA, I shall introduce them, among others, by a quotation from *Mr.* COLEBROKE's Essay on the *Religious Ceremonies of the Brahmans*, to which, on so many occasions, I am indebted; adding, occasionally, a note of illustration In the marriage ceremony, after previous details, "eighteen oblations are offered, while as many texts are meditated: they differ only in the name of the deity invoked.

"1. May AGNI, lord of (living) beings, protect me in respect of holiness, valour, and prayer, and in regard to ancient privileges, to this solemn rite, and to this invocation to deities.—2. May INDRA, lord, or regent, of the eldest (that is, of the best of beings), protect me, &c.—3. May YAMA, lord of the earth, &c.—4. Air, lord of the sky.—5. The Sun, lord of heaven.—6. The Moon, lord of stars.—7. VRIHASPATI,* lord (that is, preceptor) of BRAHMA

* VRIHASPATI, the regent of the planet JUPITER, is called Preceptor of the gods, as he is frequently found giving them good advice; and, as well as NAREDA, is often represented as their orator, or messenger, when any intercourse is carried on between the three superior powers.

(and other deities).—8. MITRA (the Sun), lord of true beings.—9. VARUNA, lord of waters.—10. The Ocean, lord of rivers.—11. Food, lord of tributary powers.—12. SOMA (the Moon), lord of plants.—13. SAVITRI (the generative Sun), lord of pregnant females.—14. RUDRA (SIVA), lord of (deities that bear the shape of) cattle.—15. The fabricator * of the universe, lord of forms.—16. VISHNU,† lord of mountains.—17. *Maruts* (winds), lord of *Ganas* (sets of divinities).—18. Fathers, grandfathers, remoter ancestors, more distant progenitors, their parents, and grandsires."‡

The eight guardian deities of the eight points of the heavens, with INDRA at their head, are sometimes called the *winds*, and almost confounded with the *Maruts*; of whom, however, are reckoned forty-nine, as noticed in page 96, where their parentage is given. In pages 92, 93, the eight *Vasus*, and the *Maruts*, or genii of the winds, are spoken of as distinct personages; a *Vasu* being one of the eight divinities who form a *gana*, or *assemblage* of the gods; and there being nine of those *ganas*, and AGNI being reckoned the chief of the *Vasus*; and VAYU, or PAVAN, the chief of the *Maruts*. In the above quotation the *Maruts* (winds) are termed lords of *ganas*. INDRA and his *gana*, or *assemblage*, are not, perhaps, easily, identified with the *Vasus*, whose discriminative names I do not recollect to have seen enumerated. The names of the regents of the eight winds, or points, as first given in this article, I noted from the information of my *Pandit*, viz. INDRA, ruler of the east; AGNI, south-east; YAMA, south; NIRIT, south-west; VARUNA, west; VAYU, north-west; KUVERA, north; ISANI, north-east. The next enumeration of them, in *Sir* W. JONES's poem, runs thus: INDRA, VARUNA, VAHNI, KUVERA, MARUT, YAMA, ISA, or ISANI, NAIRIT, or NIRIT; omitting AGNI and VAYU, and introducing VAHNI and MARUT: the latter may, indeed, be deemed the same with VAYU; but VAHNI, whom I should judge to be SARASWATI, (see p. p. 57. 126.) I never, in any instance, saw elsewhere introduced into this *gana*, or *assemblage*, with INDRA and the male genii—among the female guardians we shall see her presently. The order of their arrangement I, in this case, lay no stress on, as being in a poetical dress, the names may have been transposed, in view to a more metrical

* BRAHMA, I suppose.

† I should rather have expected the application of this title to SIVA, as the consort of PARVATI, daughter of HIMALAYA.—See p. 151.

‡ The reader will allow me to remind him, that the words within brackets in the above, and in similar quotations, are interpolated by the commentator, whose gloss the translator has followed, to illustrate the text, which would otherwise be often obscure.

arrangement. A third list, from the *Ins.* of MENU, as given in a back page, alluding, I imagine, to the same *gana*, differs from both the preceding; and a fourth list, in the same code, also given under this article, differs from all three. A fifth, taken from the *Brahmanda Purana*, as will be presently stated, differs from the first only in this instance; substituting "the lord of the *Zodiac*," MAHODAYA, for KUVERA; of whom it may, indeed, be another name, although I do not know it as such, nor its meaning: it may possibly be the name of his *Sabha*, or court, and not the lord's.*

* *Mr.* WILFORD, in the eighth volume of the *As. Res.* gives, as a specimen of the geographical style of the *Hindus*, a translation, in the very words of the *Brahmanda Purana*, descriptive of the fabulous mountain *Meru*. I here extract part of it, this mountain being often mythologically alluded to in this work, and its distinguished inhabitants the immediate subject in discussion. The style of this *Purana* indicates a sectarial superiority on the part of BRAHMA, similar to what we have seen applied by their respective sectarists to his coequal powers, VISHNU and SIVA.

"The great God; the great, omnipotent, omniscient one; the greatest in the world; the great Lord, who goes through all the worlds, incapable of decay, and without body, is born a moulded body, of flesh and bones, *made*, whilst himself *was not made*. His wisdom and power pervade all hearts; from his heart sprang the *Padma Lotos-like* world in times of old. It was *then* in this, that appeared, *when* born, the God of gods, with four faces; the Lord of the lords of mankind, who rules over all; the Lord of the world. *When* this flower was produced by VISHNU, then from his navel sprang the worldly *Lotos*, abounding with trees and plants.

"Round it are four great islands, or countries: in the middle, like the germ, is *Meru* thus called; a great mountain of various colours all round."—(Here follow its appearance, shape, measurements, &c. it being throughout likened to a lotos.)—"Every *Riski* represents this lord of mountains as it appears to him from his station: BRAHMA, INDRA, and all the gods, declare that this largest of all mountains is a form consisting of jewels of numberless colours; the abode of various tribes; like gold; like the dawning morn, resplendent, with a thousand petals; like a thousand water-pots, with a thousand leaves.

"Within it is adorned with the self-moving cars of the gods, all beautiful; in its petals are the abodes of the gods, like heaven; in its thousand petals they dwell with their consorts. There resides above, BRAHMA, God of gods, with four faces, the greatest of those who know the *Vedas*; the greatest of the great gods, also of the inferior ones. There is the court of BRAHMA, consisting of the whole earth, of all those who grant the object of our wishes; thousands of great gods are in this beautiful court: there the *Brahmarishis* dwell: it is called by all the world *Manovati*. There, in the east, is INDRA for ever to be praised; the god sitting upon a *vimana*, resplendent, like a thousand suns. There the gods, and tribes of *Rishis*, are always sitting in the presence of the four-faced god: these the god makes happy with his resplendence: there the gods are singing praises to him. There is the lord of wealth, beautiful, with a thousand eyes; the destroyer of towns: the *Indra-locas* enjoy all the wealth of the three worlds. In the second interval, between the east and the south, is the great *vimana* of AGNI, or *fire*, with a great resplendence, variegated with a hundred sorts of metals, resplendent; and from whom sprang the *Vedas*: there is his court; he does good to all; and his name is JIVANI: in the mouth of whom the sacred elements of the *homa* are put.

Perhaps my readers may not be displeased at seeing these eight personages again enumerated, as in the preceding lists. I prefix the points of the compass to that of my *Pandit*, and annex them to that from the *Brahmanda Purana:* in the others, the points, respectively governed by the regents, are not stated.

"On the third side, in this very same manner, know there is the court of VAIVASWATA YAMA, called by mankind SU-SANYAMA. Thus, in the next, or fourth, is the court *Sabha* of the lord of the corner, or country, of *Nairita:* his court is called *Crishnangana:* his name is VIRUPACSHA, *with a disagreeable countenance.* On the west know there is the court of VARUNA, called *Subhavati:* now, toward the north, in the north-west, is the court of VAYU, called *Gand'haviti.* In the seventh corner is the *Sabha* of the lord of the *Zodiac,* called MAHODAYA; his seat, most beautiful, is of *Vaidurya,* or *lapis lazuli.* In the eighth corner is the seat of ISANI, or SIVA; its colour is of fervid gold, and it is called *Yasovati.* These are the great and beautiful *Vimanas,* in the eight corners, of the eight most benevolent gods, called *Indra-muc'hyas.* There dwells on the summit the God of gods, with four faces: there is the beautiful court of BRAHMA, served by tribes of *Rishis:* it is called *Manovati* by mankind. There the *Rishis,* the gods, and *Gand'harvas,* the *Apsarasas,* the great snakes, are the attendants, most fortunate, and constantly lifting up their hands."—P. 350.

"The *nymphæa,* or lotos floating on the water, is an emblem of the world: the whole plant signifies both the earth and its two principles of fecundation. The stalk originates from the navel of VISHNU, sleeping at the bottom of the ocean, (see PLATES 7. 8.) and the flower is the cradle of BRAHMA, or mankind. The germ is both *Meru* and the *Linga:* the plants and filaments are the mountains which encircle *Meru,* and are also the type of the *Yoni:* the four leaves of the *Calyx* are the four vast *dwipas,* or countries, toward the four cardinal points. Eight external leaves, placed two by two in the intervals, are eight subordinate *dwipas,* or countries."—*Ib.* p. 308.

At the end of this essay, a map of the world is given, fancifully shaped like a lotos; the *calyx* forming *Meru,* like a bell, mouth upwards, or like an inverted *linga.* Here, on one of its three peaks, is *Kailasa,* the Olympus of SIVA; and on another, the *Swerga,* or paradise of INDRA: but his terrestrial abode is otherwise described as placed in the mountains of *Sitanta,* "skirted by a most delightful country, well watered, enlivened with the harmonious noise of the black bee, and frogs. There, among immense caves, is the *Cridavana,* or place of dalliance of MAHENDRA; where knowledge, and the completion of our wishes, is fully accomplished. There is the great forest of the *Parajita* tree, of the king of the gods, known through the three worlds; and the whole world sings his praise from the *Vedas.* Such is the place of dalliance of him with a thousand eyes, or INDRA. In this charming grove of SAKRA, or INDRA, the gods, the *Danavas,* the snakes, *Yakshas, Rakshasas, Guhya,* or *Kuveras, Gand'harvas,* live happy; as well as numerous tribes of *Apsarasas,* fond of sport."—P. 366.

	1.	2.	3.	4.	5.	
E.	INDRA	INDRA	INDRA	INDRA	INDRA	E.
S.E.	AGNI	VAHNI	AGNI	AGNI	AGNI	S.E.
S.	YAMA	YAMA	YAMA	YAMA	YAMA	S.
S.W.	NIRUT	NIRIT	SURYA	SURYA	NIRIT	S.W.
W.	VARUNA	VARUNA	VARUNA	VARUNA	VARUNA	W.
N.W.	VAYU	MARUT	PAVAN	PAVAN	VAYU	N.W.
N.	KUVERA	KUVERA	KUVERA	CHANDRA	MAHODAYA	N.
N.E.	ISANI	ISA	CHANDRA	PRIT'HIVI	ISANI	N.E.

Female guardian angels are also supposed to protect the eight points, or quarters of the universe; but they do not accord as the *Sacti,* or energies, or consorts, of the above gods. They are as follow: BRAHMANI, or SARASWATI, protectress of the east; NARAYANI, or LAKSHMI, of the south-east; MAHESWARI, or DEVI, or PARVATI, of the south; CHAMUNDA, or DEVI, of the south-west; KAUMARI, consort of KARTIKYA, of the west; APARAJITA, another form of PARVATI, or BHAVANI, of the north-west; VARAHI, *Sacti* of VARAHA, or VISHNU in that *Avatara,* of the north; and NARASINHI, his *Sacti* in the *Narsinghavatara,* is protectress of the north-east. AINDRI, or INDRANI, is sometimes included among them; so is KAUVERI, the *Sacti* of KUVERA; and two of DEVI's forms are then omitted.—See p. 117.

INDRA is generally represented on his elephant, as noticed in other places: he is so seen in the *Elephanta* cavern, and in the excavations at *Ellora.* Sir CHARLES MALET gives, with his description of those excavations, some drawings; one of them representing INDRA on an elephant, and his lovely wife, INDRANI, with a child on her lap, seated on a lion: she is a beautiful figure, and has, what I should not have expected, a skull and bones in her girdle.—*As. Res.* Vol. VI. This is the only figure I ever saw of INDRANI; and I have some doubt if it was really intended for her. I do not think I have any casts of INDRA: a rather curious one in my collection, of a man on an elephant, so contrived as to be moveable like a child's rocking-horse, but sidewise, I am disposed to fancy is of INDRA; but I have not given it in this work. The man, by a hinge, can be dismounted and remounted at will; and this may possibly allude to his astreal depositions and restorations: I have several pictures of INDRA. In PLATES 31. and 32. we see him, with other deities, reverencing DEVI. PLATE 79. is from two tinted pictures, where he is painted covered with eyes, and of the usual copper colour. Above he is mounted on his famous elephant, IRAVATY; in the picture white, with a crimson outline, trunks, and hair.

Like the other *Hindu* deities, INDRA is distinguished by several names: SAKRA is that by which he is generally called in his capacity of the adviser of evil. SHATUKRATU, or SHATKRATU, means him to whom is made a *hundred sacrifices:* VRITRAHAN, the *slayer* of the demon VRITRA. HERI is sometimes applied to him, as well as to VISHNU and KRISHNA: and HARI, a name of both SIVA and VISHNU; and the latter is, in the *Ramayana*, sect. 1. called UPENDRA, *(up* is equivalent to our *sub,)* inferring subordination to INDRA, who is sometimes named MAHENDRA, or the *great* INDRA: also PURENDRA, and VASAVA, and PAKA-SHASANA. VAJRA-PANI means *grasper of the thunder-bolt,* reminding us of the JUPITER *Fulminator,* or *Tonans*; as doubtless adverted to by *Sir* WILLIAM JONES, when describing him as "darter of the swift blue bolt," or as JUPITER *Fulgurator*; as well as to JUPITER *Pluvius,* when he calls him

> "Sprinkler of genial dews and fruitful rains
> O'er hills and thirsty plains."
>
> Hymn to INDRA.—Works, Vol. XIII.

His consort, INDRANI, or AINDRI, is also named POWLAMYA, or PULOMAYA, sometimes POWLUMI, and SAKI; and as she is, as far as I know of her, very virtuous, as well as beautiful, I am unwilling to dismiss her without some farther notice; and will, therefore, introduce a legend in which her fidelity was tried.

The virtuous NAHUSHA was elevated to the heavenly mansions by the title of DEVA NAHUSHA, or, as he is in shortness called, DEONAUSH, whence, as before observed, is easily made DIONYSIUS; and, notwithstanding his virtue, fell in love with PULOMAYA, who, resisting his assiduities, and resolved on fidelity to her lord, was advised by VRIHASPATI, he presciently seeing the consequences, to pretend to favour the lover's addresses, if he would visit her in a *palky* carried by four holy and learned *Brahmans,* which he had influence enough to procure. Their movements not according with the lover's eagerness, he impatiently exclaimed to the chief bearer—"*Serpe! Serpe!*" which has precisely the same signification in *Sanskrit* and in *Latin.* The holy sage, unused to such an imperative address, replied—"Be thyself a serpent;" and, such is the power of divine learning, the king, from the force of the imprecation, instantly fell to the earth in the shape of that large serpent called, in *Sanskrit, ajagara,* and *boa* by naturalists. In this state of humiliation he wandered to the banks of the *Kali,* and once attempting to swallow a *Brahman,* deeply learned in the *Vedas,* his throat was so scorched that he was forced to disgorge the sage; by contact with whom, his own intellects became irradiated, and he remembered with penitence his crime and its punishment. He ceased to devour human beings, and recovering his understanding and speech, he sought some holy *Brahmans* who might predict the termination of his misery; and learned, at length, that he would be restored to his pristine shape by the sons of PANDU. He, therefore, patiently visited holy places of pilgrimage, founded by himself in happier days, and waited with resignation the coming of the *Pandavas*, whose adventures are the subject of VYASA's great epic poem, the *Mahabarat*.—(From WILFORD's Essay on the *Nile*. *As. Res.* Vol. III.)

Strictness of arrangement not being easily attainable in a work of this sort, I shall, in the next head or division, notice, with other deities, some of those subordinate to INDRA as chief of the demigods, and immediately connected with him as regents of quarters, or points, or winds; and some of them that do not demand any lengthened discussion, we will notice here, viz. VARUNA, KUVERA, and NIRRIT.

The former is the regent of the ocean, and generally of large masses of water. As light is thought to be excluded from the depths of water, VARUNA is also deemed the governor of the night, or of darkness: still he is one of the *Adityas*, or Suns, (see p. 92). He is likewise styled the lord of punishment; and in this character the wealth of criminals is directed to be offered to him, or, in other words, thrown into the waters; or it may, instead, be bestowed on a learned priest: the latter, we may suppose, is likely to outshare the deity.

Ins. of MENU, Chap. IX. v. 243.—" Let no virtuous prince appropriate the wealth of a criminal in the highest degree; for he who appropriates it through covetousness, is contaminated with the same guilt.

" 244. Having thrown such a fine into the waters, let him offer it to VARUNA; or let him bestow it on some priest of eminent learning in the scriptures.

" 245. VARUNA is the lord of punishment; he holds a rod even over kings; and a priest who has gone through the whole *Veda* is equal to a sovereign of the world."

In a former quotation from MENU, this passage occurs: " VARUNA most assuredly binds the guilty in fatal cords."—Chap. IX. v. 308. And the *cord* of VARUNA, called *pasa*, or *pasha*, or *Varunapasha*, is frequently spoken of, which he is supposed to hold in his hand; but I have no image or picture of this deity that I know of. In the first volume of the *Asiatic Researches*, Sir W. JONES gives a plate of him, empty-handed, bestriding a monstrous fish: he is drawn merely as a man, without any attributes. And it is there said of him, that "he is the genius of waters; but, like the rest, is far inferior to MAHESA, and even to INDRA, who is the prince of the beneficent genii."—P. 251. SONNERAT, (Vol. I. p. 62.) calls him, after the *Carnatic* pronunciation, VAROUNIN; and says he is represented mounted on a crocodile, and holding a whip in his hand.

The *pasha*, which in his hand has been surmised to be emblematical of the sea encircling the earth, is often seen in the hand of other deities: in that of SIVA, (see PLATE 13.) of DEVI, or KALI, PLATES 24. 28. of HANUMAN, PLATE 92. of GANESA, PLATE 102. and sometimes with BHAIRAVA; all, it may be remarked, connected in family with SIVA, who bearing the trident, *trisula*, in that and other points participates with VARUNA in the character of NEPTUNE.

A long catalogue of weapons presented to RAMA, armed by VISWAMITRA for the war of *Lanka*, occurs in the 26th section of the *Ramayana:* they have particular names, generally derived from some deity, either from being the appropriate weapon used by those deities, or from partaking in some way of their power. There is "the *Dherma* weapon, scarcely less fatal than YAMA himself;" this is religion, justice, or virtue: "the KALA weapon, insupportable to enemies:" "the divine *Chakra* of VISHNU, and the terrible discus *(Vajra)* of INDRA; the huge *Shivean* spear; the DHERMA *pasha*; the dreadful KALA *pasha*; and the highly valued VARUNA *pasha:*" severally the cords of *Justice*, of *Death*, and of VARUNA, or NEPTUNE. There is also the *Agniya*, having the property of flame or fire, and many others of allegorical names; such as *joy-producing*, *folly*, *intoxication*, *infallible*, *hot*, *fiery*, *quaking*, *foe-seizing*, *flesh-devouring*, *energetic*, *invisible*, &c. &c. &c. All, or any of these, come, when called for by appropriate *mantras*, or magical words, made known to the favoured person thus divinely gifted.—See page 109.

In the black *Yajurveda*, an *upanishad* is named after VARUNA: he is there made the father of BHRIGU,* and is introduced as instructing his son in the mysteries of religious science, particularly as to the nature of BRAHM; who is, he says, "That, whence all beings are produced; that, by which they live when born; that, toward which they tend; and that, unto which they pass."

BHRIGU, after meditating in devout contemplation, recognised food (or body) to be BRAHM: "for all beings are indeed produced from food; when born they live by food; toward food they tend; and they pass into food."

* Who, in p. 78 appears as the offspring of BRAHMA; and in p. 84. of MENU.—See also pages 86. 91. 94. and *Ins.* of MENU, Chap. I. verses 35. 59.

Unsatisfied, however, he, again deeply meditating, discovered breath (or life) to be BRAHM: "for all beings are indeed produced from breath; when born they live by breath; toward breath they tend; they pass into breath."

Again desired to seek BRAHM in profound meditation, he discovered intellect to be BRAHM: "for all these beings are produced from intellect; when born they live by intellect; toward intellect they tend; and they pass into intellect."—This he understood; (but) again coming to his father VARUNA, saying, "Venerable (father), make known to me BRAHM"—VARUNA replied, "Inquire by devout contemplation; profound meditation is BRAHM."

He thought deeply; and having thus meditated (with) devout contemplation, he knew *ananda* (or felicity) to be BRAHM: "for all these beings are indeed produced from pleasure; when born they live by joy; they tend toward happiness; they pass into felicity."—"Such is the science which was attained by BHRIGU, taught by VARUNA, and founded on the supreme ethereal spirit: he who knows this, rests on the same support; is endowed with (abundant) food, and becomes (a blazing fire) which consumes food: great is he by progeny, by cattle, and by holy perfections; and great by propitious celebrity."—COLEBROKE on the *Vedas*. *As. Res.* Vol. VIII. p. 456.

VARUNA, it will be recollected, is the especial protector of the west point of the heavens: he has a *Sacti*, or consort, named VARUNI.—See p. 120. She is sometimes called his daughter.—See p. 95. He is one of the *Adityas*, or Suns, the offspring of ADITI.—See p. 92. And in p. 112. the appellation of *Mitra* VARUNA, or the *friendly* VARUNA, is applied to MENU. But, although he is one of the many deities invoked and propitiated in the daily ceremonies of the *Brahmans*, his name does not very often occur in *Hindu* writings or conversation.

KUVERA, the regent of wealth, for a moment demands our attention; and although few people seek the favour of this deity with greater avidity than the *Hindus*, yet I find but little mention of him in my mythological memoranda; nor have I any image or picture of him. Let us hope that the *Indian* PLUTUS will not, by for ever withholding his favour, resent my brief notice of him, compared with the more extended account of more social or more amiable deities. On KAMA, LAKSHMI, or SARASWATI, poets and historians dwell with complacency and delight; but the gloomy, selfish, and deformed KUVERA, claims not, nor deserves, so much of our attention.

He is, we have seen, the guardian of the northern region; described, in respect of externals, as a mere man, but as a magnificent deity residing in the splendid city *Alaka*, otherwise called *Chitrarat'ha*; or borne through the sky in a gorgeous car, called *pushpaka*. He is also called VITTESSA; and PAULASTYA, a name of one of the *Brahmadicas*, (see p. 84); also VISRAVANA, or VAISRAVA, and DHANADA. He is said to be son of a sage name VISRAVA, or VISWASRAVA; the father also of RAVANA, who, as well as KUVERA, is hence called VISRAVANA. KUVERA and RAVANA are thus half-brothers, having different mothers: both are occasionally named PULASTYA.

His servants and companions are the *Yakshas* and *Guhyakas*, into whose forms transmigrate the souls of those men who in this life are addicted to sordid and base passions, or absorbed in worldly prosperity. The term *Guhyaka* is derived from *Guh (ordure)*, a word retained in several dialects: hence *Guhya (podex)*.—See p. 108. We happily do not find that the regent of wealth is related in marriage or otherwise with LAKSHMI, the goddess of riches, to whom a *Hindu*, as mentioned in page 132, would address himself for that boon, and not to KUVERA: he has, however, a *Sacti*, or consort, named KAUVERI, (see p. 119,) whence, I conjecture, the river of that name, in *Mysore*, derives its appellation.

NIRRIT, otherwise called NAIRITA and NIRUT; and sometimes, as noticed in page 57, VIRUPAKSHA, meaning, it is said, *with three eyes*; but, according to *Mr.* WILFORD, in page 270, *with a disagreeable countenance*; is the last of the eight guardian regents that we shall notice in this article. His name occurs but seldom in writing or conversation; and I have no image or picture of him, nor did I ever see one. His consort is NIRRITI, who seems to share with him the honour of his government; and a man becoming criminal on certain points, it is incumbent on him to "sacrifice a black or a one-eyed ass, by way of a meat offering to NIRRITI, patroness of the south-west, by night, in a place where four ways meet."—"Let him daily offer to her in fire the fat of that ass; and, at the close of the ceremony, let him offer clarified butter, with the holy text *Sem*, and so forth, to PAVANA, to INDRA, to VRIHASPATI, and to AGNI, regent of wind, clouds, a planet, and fire."—*Ins.* of MENU, Chap. XI. verses 119, 120.

This expiation is for the sin of *Onanism:* on incurring of which, the manipulist is termed *avacirna.*—"To the four deities of purification, MARUTA, INDRA, VRIHASPATI, and AGNI, goes all the divine light, which the *Veda* had imparted, from the student who commits the foul sin *avacirna.*"—*Ib.* v. 122.

Of SURYA, CHANDRA, *and* AGNI,

The REGENTS of the SUN, the MOON, and of FIRE; and of some less important Characters.

PLATE 87. of SURYA, is taken from a fine cast in zinc; one of *Mr.* WILKINS' set, made at *Benares*, where, in a temple dedicated to MAHADEVA, in his character of VISWESWARA, (see p. 58,) is a spirited sculpture, the original of this subject. The cast is nine inches in height, representing the glorious god of day holding the attributes of VISHNU, seated on a seven-headed serpent; his car drawn by a seven-headed horse, driven by the legless ARUN, a personification of the dawn, or AURORA. SURYA's distinguishing attributes will come more particularly under discussion in a future page.

So grand a symbol of the Deity, as the Sun "looking from his sole dominion like the god of this world," which, to ignorant people, must be his most glorious and natural type, will of course have attracted the earliest adoration; and where revelation was withheld, will almost necessarily have been the primary fount of idolatry and superstition. The investigators of ancient mythology accordingly trace to this prolific source, wherein they are melted and lost, almost every other mythological personage; who, like his own light, diverge and radiate from his most glorious centre.

"We must not," says *Sir* WILLIAM JONES, "be surprised at finding, on a close examination, that the characters of all the *pagan* deities, male and female, melt into each other, and at last into one or two; for it seems a well-founded opinion, that the whole crowd of gods and goddesses, in ancient *Rome* and modern *Varanes*,* mean only the powers of nature, and principally those of the *Sun*, expressed in a variety of ways, and by a multitude of fanciful names."—*As. Res.* Vol. I. p. 267.

The following passages are extracted from the argument to the hymn, addressed by the same author to SURYA; and some extracts will follow from the

* The proper name for *Benares*, otherwise called *Kassi*: the most classical name is, perhaps, *Vara'nasi*, so called from two rivers that form a junction of waters and names near its site.

hymn, as affording more information than I can otherwise furnish; enlivened too by the graces of eloquence and poetry. The hymn will be found in the *Asiatic Miscellany*, Vol. II. and *Works*, Vol. XIII.

"A plausible opinion has been entertained by learned men, that the principal source of idolatry among the ancients, was their enthusiastic admiration of the sun; and that when the primitive religion of mankind was lost amid the distractions of establishing regal governments, or neglected amid the allurements of vice, they ascribed to the great visible luminary, or to the wonderful fluid of which it is the general reservoir, those powers of pervading all space, and animating all nature, which their wiser ancestors had attributed to one eternal Mind, by whom the substance of fire had been created as an inanimate and secondary cause of natural phenomena. The mythology of the east confirms this opinion; and it is possible, that the *triple divinity* of the *Hindus* was originally no more than a personification of the sun, whom they call *Treyitenu*, or *three-bodied*, in his triple capacity of *producing* forms by his genial heat, *preserving* them by his light, or *destroying* them by the concentrated force of his *igneous* matter: this, with the wilder conceit of a *female power* united with the *Godhead*, and ruling nature by his authority, will account for nearly the whole system of *Egyptian*, *Indian*, and *Grecian* polytheism, distinguished from the sublime theology of the philosophers, whose understandings were too strong to admit the popular belief, but whose influence was too weak to reform it.

"It will be necessary to explain a few other particulars of the *Hindu* mythology, to which allusions are made in the poem. Soma, or the Moon, is a *male* deity in the *Indian* system, as Mona was, I believe, among the *Saxons*, and Lunus among some of the nations who settled in *Italy*. Most of the *Lunar mansions* are believed to be the daughters of Kasyapa,* the first production of Brahma's head; and from their names are derived those of the twelve months, who are here feigned to have married as many constellations: this primeval *Brahman*, and Vinata, are supposed to have been the parents of Arun, the charioteer of the Sun, and of the bird Garuda, the eagle of the great *Indian* Jove; one of whose epithets is Madhava."

After an exordium, deeply scientific and profound, the hymn proceeds—

"Lord of the lotos, father, friend, and king,
Surya, thy powers I sing:

* In other legends they are said to be the daughters of Daksha.—(See Daksha, p. 109.) He was, however, an *Avatara*, or son of Brahma; and Kasayapa was also produced by him.

Thy substance, INDRA, with his heavenly bands,
Nor sings, nor understands;
Nor e'en the *Vedas* three to man explain
Thy mystic orb triform, tho' BRAHMA tun'd the strain."—Verse 1.

" First o'er blue hills appear,
With many an agate hoof,
And pasterns fring'd with pearl, seven coursers green;
Nor boasts yon arched woof,
That girds the show'ry sphere,
Such heav'n-spun threads of colour'd light serene,
As tinge the reins which ARUN guides—
Glowing with immortal grace,
Young ARUN, loveliest of *Vinatian* race;
Though younger he, whom MADHAVA bestrides,
When high on eagle-plumes he rides.
But, Oh! what pencil of a living star
Could paint that gorgeous car,
In which, as in an ark, supremely bright,
The lord of boundless light,
Ascending calm o'er the empyrean sails,
And with ten thousand beams his awful beauty veils!"---Verse 7.

Under the article AGNI, I shall endeavour to explain farther why the regents of the Sun and of Fire, so intimately connected as their primary properties apparently are, should be distinguished by common or similar attributes. SURYA'S "mystic orb triform," and AGNI'S triplicate of legs, are deducible from the three descriptions of sacred fire venerated by the *Hindus*; and proceeding from the Sun, as the three great powers of nature proceed from the Eternal Mind, we can easily discern how the Sun and BRAHM came to be identified. Though the Sun be invoked in the *Gayatri*, it is only, they say, as the symbol of the Deity: its *creative* heat, *preserving* light, and *destroying* fire, are personified in BRAHMA, VISHNU, and SIVA. SURYA'S "*seven* coursers green," and AGNI'S seven arms, are appropriate allusions, especially the former, to the prismatic divisibility of SURYA'S preceding ray. In PLATES 87. 88. 89. will be seen the seven precursors of his glorious car.

" SURYA is believed to have descended frequently from his car in a human shape, and to have left a race on earth, who are equally renowned in the *Indian* stories with the *Heliades* of *Greece*. It is very singular that his two sons, called ASWINA, or ASWINI-CUMARA in the dual, should be considered as twin brothers, and painted like CASTOR and POLLUX; but they have each the character of

ESCULAPIUS among the gods, and are believed to have been born of a nymph, who, in the form of a mare, was impregnated with sunbeams. I suspect the whole fable of KASYAPA and his progeny to be astronomical; and cannot but imagine that the *Greek* name CASSIOPEIA* has a relation to it."—JONES. *Asiatic Researches*, Vol. I. p. 263.

An indifferent print is given, with the above account, of SURYA in his car, drawn by seven horses, driven by ARUN, or the *dawn*; and he is described as followed by thousands of genii, worshipping him, and modulating his praises. "He has a multitude of names, and among them twelve epithets, or titles, which denote his distinct *powers* in each of the twelve months; those *powers* are called *Adityas*, or sons of ADITI, by KASYAPA, the *Indian* URANUS; and one of them has, according to some authorities, the name of VISHNU, or *Pervader*."—*Ib.*

VISHNU is doubtless (see p. 92,) one of the epithets of the Sun, in whom will be found to merge all the idolatrous machinery of all systems of mythology.—"Here it must be observed," as quoted in another place, "that at night, and in the west, the Sun is VISHNU: he is BRAHMA in the east, and in the morning: from noon to evening he is SIVA."—WILFORD. *As. Res.* Vol. V. p. 254.

General VALLANCEY, whose learned inquiries into the ancient literature of *Ireland* were considered by *Sir* WILLIAM JONES as highly interesting, finds that KRISHNA, in *Irish*, is the Sun, as well as in *Sanskrit*. In his curious little book, "On the Primitive Inhabitants of *Great Britain* and *Ireland*," the only one of the learned gentleman's works that I am fortunate enough to possess, is given an *Irish* ode to the Sun, which I should, untaught, have judged of *Hindu* origin: the opening especially, "Auspiciate my lays, O Sun! thou mighty Lord of the *seven* heavens; who swayest the universe through the immensity of space and matter;" and the close, "Thou art the only glorious and sovereign object of universal love, praise, and adoration;" are in the language precisely of a *Saura*, be he of *Hindustan* or *Hibernia*.

Again: In the mythology of *Ireland*, SOM is the deity presiding over plants: he is the same in *India*; for the final in "SOMA, lord of plants," (see p. 268,) is merely a grammatical termination, and not radical. Again: ARUN is the forerunner of the Sun, the dawn, AURORA, both in *Irish* and *Hindu* mythology.—Other curious analogies are traced in the learned *General's* work.

This interesting and lamented author, *Sir* W. JONES, not altogether agreeing with NEWTON, that ancient mythology is nothing but historical truth in a poeti-

* As is fully proved by *Mr.* WILFORD's subsequent investigations.

cal dress; nor with BACON, that it consisted in moral and metaphysical allegories; nor with BRYANT, that all the heathen deities are only different attributes and representations of the Sun, or of deceased progenitors; conceived that the whole system of religious fables rose, like the *Nile*, from several distinct sources: and inclined to the opinion, that one great spring and fountain of all idolatry, in the four quarters of the globe, was the veneration paid by men to the Sun; and another, the immoderate respect shewn to the memory of powerful or virtuous ancestors, especially the founders of kingdoms, legislators, and warriors, of whom the Sun or Moon were wildly supposed to be the parents.—*Ib.* Vol. I. p. 427.

PLATE 88. represents the *Hindu* zodiac and solar system, called *Rasi Chakra*, or *revolutionary dance:* it is taken from a handsome picture of *Colonel* STUART's, which will be more particularly described. Here we see SURYA in the centre, surrounded in the first circle by the planetary orbs, viz. CHANDRA, (*fig.* 7.) —MANGALA, or MARS, (6.) BUDDHA, or MERCURY, (5.)—VRIHASPATI, or JUPITER, (2.)—SUKRA, or VENUS, (9.)—SANI, or SATURN, (8.)—RAHU and KETU, (4. and 3.) the ascending and descending nodes.

Mr. COLEBROKE, in his Essays on the Religious Ceremonies of the *Hindus*, (*As. Res.* Vol. V. and VII.) shows us how unceasingly the mythological persons of their Pantheon are brought to the contemplation of the pious; and, indeed, obtruded on all descriptions of persons, at almost all times, in the endless series of ceremonials that they are, one way or other, called on to perform, or to participate in. From the seventh volume I will here extract the sacrificial prayers to the nine characters named in the preceding paragraph, introduced into the rites of the oblation to Fire; part of the worship offered to the gods, and one of the five daily sacraments of a *Brahman:* with each prayer an oblation of *ghee* (clarified butter) is made.—

" 1. The Divine Sun approaches with his golden car, returning alternately with the shades of night; rousing mortal and immortal beings, and surveying worlds.—May this oblation to SURYA be efficacious.

" 2. Gods! produce that (MOON) which has no foe, which is the son of the solar orb, and became the offering of space, for the benefit of this world;* produce it for the advancement of knowledge, for protection from danger, for vast

* " According to one legend, a ray of the Sun, called *sushumna*, became the Moon; according to another, a flash of light from the eye of ATRI was received by *Space*, a goddess---the *via-lactea* personified: she conceived, and bore SOMA, or CHANDRA, who is, therefore, called a son of ATRI."

supremacy, for empire, and for the sake of INDRA's organs of sense.—May this oblation to CHANDRA be efficacious.

"3. This gem of the sky, whose head resembles fire, is the lord of waters, and replenishes the seeds of the earth.—May this oblation to (MANGALA) the planet MARS be efficacious.

"4. Be roused, O FIRE! and thou (O BUDHA)! perfect this sacrificial rite, and associate with us; let this votary, and all the gods, sit in this most excellent assembly.—May this oblation to the planet MERCURY be efficacious.

"5. O VRIHASPATI! sprung from eternal truth, confer on us abundantly that various wealth * which the most venerable of beings may revere; which shines glorious among all people, which serves to defray sacrifices, which is preserved by strength.—May this oblation to the planet JUPITER be efficacious.

"6. The lord of creatures drank the invigorating essence distilled from food; he drank milk and the juice of the moon-plant.† By means of scripture, which is truth itself, the beverage thus quaffed became a prolific essence, the eternal organ of universal perception, INDRA's organs of sense, the milk of immortality, and honey to the *manes* of ancestors.—May this oblation to (SUKRA) the planet VENUS be efficacious.

"7. May divine waters be auspicious to us for accumulation, for gain, and for refreshing draughts; may they listen to us, that we may be associated with good auspices.—May this oblation to (SANI) the planet SATURN be efficacious.

"8. O *Durva!* ‡ which doth germinate at every knot, at every joint, multiply us through a hundred, through a thousand, descents.—May this oblation to (RAHU ||) the planet of the ascending node be efficacious.

* Probably intellectual wealth, VRIHASPATI being preceptor to the gods; the most venerable of beings.

† *Somalata*; the *Asclepias acida*. ‡ *Durva*, the *Agrostis linearis*.

|| RAHU was the son of KASYAPA and DITI, according to some authorities; but others represent SINHICA (perhaps the *sphinx*) as his natural mother. He had four arms; his lower parts ended in a tail like that of a dragon; and his aspect was grim and gloomy, like the *darkness* of the chaos; whence he had also the name of TAMAS. He was the adviser of all mischief among the *Daityas*, who had a regard for him; but among the *Devatas* it was his chief delight to sow dissension. And when the gods had produced the *amrit*, by churning the ocean, he disguised himself like one of them, and received a portion of it; but the Sun and Moon having discovered his fraud, VISHNU severed his head, and two of his arms, from the rest of his monstrous body. That part of the nectareous fluid that he had time to swallow secured his immortality: his trunk and dragon-like tail fell on the mountain of *Malaya*, where MINI, a *Brahman*, carefully preserved them by the name of KETU; and, as if a complete body had been formed from them, like a dis-

"9. Be thou produced by dwellers in this world to give knowledge to ignorant mortals, and wealth to the indigent, or beauty to the ugly.—May this oblation to (KETU) the planet o. the descending node be efficacious."—P. 238.

The great family, called "*children of the Moon,*" is so named in contradistinction from another race, called "*children of the Sun,*"—See RAMA, p. 192. They are severally called *Surya-vans*, and *Chandra-vans*; but both families are, in the theogony of the *Hindus,* deducible from BRAHMA.

In a note, in a preceding page, CHANDRA is made the offspring of ATRI, who was a son of BRAHMA. CHANDRA's son, BUDHA, or MERCURY, married ILA, daughter of MENU, or NOAH: hence originate the *Chandra-vans.*

The *Surya-vans,* or offspring of the Sun, also proceed from this seventh MENU, who is fabled to be the son of SURYA: one of whose names is VAIVASWAT; thence named VAIVASWATA. SURYA is the son of KASYAPA (or URANUS), the son of MARICHI (or *light*), the son of BRAHMA.—See p. 89.

Another astronomical allegory marries the Moon to the Sun—CHANDRA to SURYA-SAVITRI; the Sun being in his turn a female.

In the *Gayatri*, a subject remaining for discussion, the Sun is called SAVITRI; as he is also in an invocation to divers deities in marriage ceremonies, as extracted under INDRA, (page 268,) but not apparently as a female: indeed, in the latter instance, decidedly not, as he is especially styled "SAVITRI, the generative Sun, *lord of pregnant females.*" And in the Essay on the Lunar Year of the *Hindus, (As. Res.* Vol. III. p. 282.) *Sir* WILLIAM JONES marks a day in the Ca-

membered polype, he is even said to have adopted KETU as his own child. The head, with two arms, fell on the sands of *Barbara,* where PIT'HENAS was then walking with SINHICA, by some called his wife: they carried the *Daitya* to their palace, and adopted him as their son. This extravagant fable is, no doubt, astronomical; RAHU and KETU being the *nodes,* or what astrologers call the head and tail of the dragon. It is added, that they appeased VISHNU, and obtained readmission to the firmament, but were no longer visible from the earth, their enlightened sides being turned from it; that RAHU strives, during eclipses, to wreak vengeance on the Sun and Moon who detected him; and that KETU often appears as a comet, a whirlwind, a fiery meteor, a water-spout, or a column of sand. Fifty-six comets are said, in the *Chintamani,* to have sprung from KETU; and RAHU had a numerous progeny of *Grahas,* or crocodiles."—WILFORD. *As. Res.* Vol. III. p. 419.

PLATE 88. exhibits RAHU and KETU; but the latter is merely a head, as he is also in *Sir* W. JONES's plate: in the above quotation, two of RAHU's arms are said to have shared the fate of his head. In p. 252, I have hinted the possibility that the lower portion of PLATE 76. may refer to this legend, rather than to BUDDHA: RAHU's lower parts do not, in the zodiacal pictures, end in a tail, as they do in the figure in PLATE 76. and as he is described above. As the adviser of evil with the *Daityas,* and sower of dissension among the *Devas,* he partakes of the malignant part of INDRA's character. NARAYANA is sometimes (JONES's *Works,* Vol. XIII. p. p. 280. 282.) spoken of as the decapitator of RAHU.

lendar, called "SAVITRI *vratam,*" as "a fast, with ceremonies by women at the roots of the *Indian* fig-tree, to preserve them from widowhood."

Mr. COLEBROKE (*As. Res.* Vol. VIII. p. 402.) says, "the seventh chapter of the tenth book of the *Rig Veda* opens with a hymn, in which SURYA, surnamed SAVITRI, the wife of the Moon, is made the speaker, as DAKSHINI, daughter of PRAJAPATI, and JUHU, daughter of BRAHMA, are in subsequent chapters." To this passage, *Mr.* COLEBROKE subjoins the following note: "This marriage is noticed in the *Aitareya Brahmana,* where the second lecture of the fourth book opens in this manner: 'PRAJAPATI gave his daughter SURYA SAVITRI to SOMA the king.' The well-known legend, in the *Puranas,* concerning the marriage of SOMA with the daughters of DAKSHA, seems to be founded on this story in the *Veda.*"

PRAJAPATI means the *lord* of *prajas,* or *creatures*; and although mostly applied to BRĀHMA, is a name or title sometimes given to his sons, and other persons.—(See p. p. 83. 86.) SOMA, or CHANDRA, we have seen in a former page (109), married twenty-seven of DAKSHA's daughters, of whom SURYA SAVITRI appears to be one; above said to be the daughter of PRAJAPATI, a name applicable to DAKSHA, as well as to BRAHMA.

I will now describe *Colonel* STUART's picture, from which PLATE 88. is taken. By its style I should judge it to be the production of a *Jeypoor* artist: the names of the zodiacal signs, and of the planets, are given in *Sanskrit,* as well as *Persian*; but I have copied the names of the latter only, and in the latter language.

SURYA, in the *Persian* spelled سورج *Surj:* his car and horses are enveloped in a blaze of gold, terminating in a radiated glory: he is of gold, bearing the usual attributes of VISHNU, with an umbrella over his head, and with streamers at each corner of his car. ARUN, his charioteer, is of deep red: the horses are green, with black manes, and red legs. VRIHASPATI, or JUPITER, (*fig.* 2.) in the *Persian* spelled برهسپت BERHESPET, is also of gold, with red clothes, bearing a lotos, green and white, and a staff. KETU, (*fig.* 3.—I have heedlessly numbered these figures without adverting to their relative importance, for RAHU and KETU should have been noticed last,) in the *Persian* spelled کیت KIT, or KEET, is like his body, RAHU, black. The headless RAHU, (*fig.* 4.) راو RAO in *Persian,* is black, with red clothes; mounted on a brown owl, and holding the *gadda,* and a lotos, red and white. BUDDHA, or MERCURY, (*fig.* 5.) بده BUDDHA in *Persian,* is green, with green clothing, and a *gadda,* and a blue and white lotos: a chaplet of white flowers, and a cup and saucer, are beside him. MANGALA, or MARS, (*fig.* 6.) منگل MANGAL in *Persian,* is deep red, with pink *chulna,* or breeches; mounted on a white ram, with red legs: he bears a lotos, white and green, and a sort of staff. CHANDRA, the Moon, (*fig.* 7.) جندر CHANDER in *Persian*, has, like SURYA, the attributes of VISHNU, (none of the others are four-handed,) and is mounted on a pied antelope. SANI, or SATURN, (*fig.* 8.) سنیچر SANICHER in *Persian*, (he is sometimes named SANICHARA, or SANAISCHARA, in *Sanskrit*,) is blue, with a yellow *pitamber*; holding a bow and arrow, and riding a light brown raven, with yellow legs. SUKRA, or VENUS, (*fig.* 9.) سکر SUKER in *Persian*, is white, with blue clothes; mounted on an equivocal sort of animal, something like a rat, and holds a red lotos and a staff: the *Hindus* make SUKRA a male, and he is otherwise called USANAS. The heads of all these beings, except of course poor RAHU, have golden glories; and so has VIRGO, among the zodiacal signs, but none of the others.

In the oriental zodiac, given by *Sir* W. JONES in the second volume of the *Asiatic Researches*, the planets are accommodated with vehicles differing from those in PLATE 88. SURYA is on a lion; and ARUN is beneath him, driving the seven-headed horse yoked to the empty car: CHANDRA is riding an antelope: SURYA and CHANDRA, but none of the rest, have glories: MANGALA is on a horse, with a huge sabre in his hand: BUDDHA rides an eagle: VRIHASPATI, a boar, and holds apparently a book: SUKRA holds a disk, and rides a camel: SANI is mounted on an elephant: the headless RAHU holds a spear, and stands on a tortoise; and KETU, his head, is borne by a frog.

The antiquity, and other controverted points, of the *Indian* zodiac, having rendered it a subject of interesting discussion, I will here subjoin the instances enumerated, in which my plate (88,) and the zodiac given by *Sir* W. JONES, (the only ones that I know of hitherto published,) agree or disagree, as far as relate to the planetary spheres. The zodiacal signs, properly so called, I shall leave unnoticed; and premise that, in regard to the Sun, so appropriately situated in PLATE 88. it is, in *Sir* W. JONES's plate, at top; the centre being fancifully occupied by the earth, with *Meru* conspicuously placed: indicating that such an arrangement was the production rather of a disciple of the *Ptolemaic* school, than of one possessing a competent knowledge of the true system of COPERNICUS, as exhibited in PLATE 88.

Names of Planets, &c.		Days, over which they respectively preside.		Vehicles, or Seats.	
English.	*Hindu.*	*English.*	*Hindu.*	*Sir* W. Jones's plate.	*Col.* Stuart's picture, and plate 88.
Sun	Surya	Sunday	*Aditvar*	Lion	Chariot
Moon	Chandra	Monday	*Somvar*	Antelope	Antelope
Mars	Mangala	Tuesday	*Mangalvar*	Horse	Ram
Mercury	Buddha	Wednesday	*Budvar*	Eagle	Carpet
Jupiter	Vrihaspati	Thursday	*Vrihaspetvar*	Boar	Ditto
Venus	Sukra	Friday	*Sukervar*	Camel	Rat?
Saturn	Sani	Saturday	*Sanivar*	Elephant	Raven
Dragon's head	Ketu			Frog	Carpet
Dragon's tail	Rahu			Tortoise?	Owl

The arrangement of these beings in the two plates differs in several instances, as well as necessarily in the position of Surya; but the general order of arrangement is alike in *India* and in *Europe*, as is evinced in the above *table*; and as appears by the series of invocation given in a preceding page.

On the above table it may be well to observe, that Soma is a name of the Moon almost as common as Chandra; and the day *Monday, Somvar*, has received its designation from the former name. The tortoise, as the equipage of Rahu, I have noted as doubtful in *Sir* W. Jones's plate, where it is equivocal; but in Maurice's *Ancient History*, where (vol. I.) the subject is re-engraved, it is decidedly a tortoise.

On the subject of the *Hindu* zodiacal signs, I shall not say any thing; it would lead us into a lengthened disquisition. Begging, therefore, to refer the reader, desirous of information on that interesting point of *Hindu* science, to *Sir* William Jones's Dissertation, in the second volume of the *Asiatic Researches*; to *Mr.* Colebroke's, in the ninth—both expressly on the *Hindu* zodiac; and to the labours of my learned friend, *Mr.* Maurice, in his *Ancient History*, and *Indian Antiquities*; I here quit the subject.

The names of Surya are numerous, as are also the designations of the Sun in the mythological romances of *Greece* and *Rome*. I will give here some of the *Hindu* names, that etymologists may trace resemblances in the nomenclature of these distant people.

ARYAMA, VIVASWAT, MARTUNDA, SURA, RAVI, MIHIRA, BHANU, ARKA, HERIDASWA, CARMASACSHI SAVITRI, PUSHAN, BHASCARA, TAPANA, TWASHTI, BHAGA, MIT'HRA, HELI, VARUNA, VEDANGA, INDRA, GABHASTI, YAMA, DIVAKARA, VISHNU, KRISHNA.

SURYA, or the Sun, is exclusively worshipped by a sect, hence called *Suras*, or *Sauras*, who acknowledge no other deity; but this sect is not so numerous as those of the *Saivas* and the *Vaishnavas*, of which latter, indeed, they may perhaps be, in strictness, termed a branch.—See p. 124.

It will be presently noticed, that PRABHA, or *Brightness*, is the consort of the glorious luminary SURYA; and that, unable to sustain the pressure of his intensity, she once assumed a form named CHAYA, or *Shade*, and was impregnated by him: this personification of shade is sometimes called the wife of SURYA. I shall extract a verse, wherein she is so called, from an inscription engraved on copper, conveying the town of *Harihara*,* on the banks of the *Tunga-bhadra (Toombadra)*; which, while it serves as a specimen of oriental adulation, will introduce to us some other mythological personages.

(The father of the royal granter has just been mentioned.)

———"GAURAMBHICA became his queen; a princess respectable for her virtues, as RAMA,† the beloved wife of KRISHNA; as GAURI,‡ of SIVA; as SARASWATI, of BRAHMA; as CHAYA, of SURYA. By the charms of her graceful gaiety she obscured ‖TILOTTAMA; by her happy fidelity to her husband she excited the envy of ANASUYA."§—*As. Res.* Vol. IX. p. 416.

The date of this inscription corresponds with 1359, A. D.

A fine picture of SURYA, in *Colonel* STUART's collection, in which the gorgeous deity is enveloped, with his car drawn by "seven coursers green," in a golden blaze of splendour, preceded by hosts of persons chaunting his praises, has, behind his car, a black ill-favoured figure; a personification of the dark-

* In the fort of this town, where I have passed many a chequered day, are two immense upright stones, covered with inscriptions in the *Canarese* character: there is also, in front of its respectable temple, one of the handsomest columns, of a single stone, that I ever saw. If I might take the liberty, I would suggest that they may be within the reach, and deserving of the attention, of the active and intelligent gentleman *(Major* MACKENZIE), from whose exertions the *Asiatic Researches* are so much enriched, by communications, among others, of ancient inscriptions.

† Probably meant for RADHA. ‡ A name of PARVATI.

‖ A nymph celebrated for her beauty.—See p. 65.

§ ANASUYA (sometimes spelled ANASUMYA,) is the wife of ATRI, the *Rishi*, and distinguished for conjugal affections: the name signifies *unenvious*.—See p. 87.

ness that the god of day is dispelling, or leaving behind him. I know no name of this person, but perhaps he has several: TAMASA probably among them.

"In the *Uttara-charitra*, and other ancient books, we find many stories concerning SURYA; some of which have a mixture of astrological allegory. Once, it seems, he was performing acts of austere devotion in the character of TAPANA, or the *Inflamer*, when his consort, PRABHA, or *Brightness*, unable to bear his intense heat, assumed the form of CH'HAYA, or *Shade*, and was impregnated by him. After a hundred years, when gods and men, expecting a terrible offspring, were in the utmost consternation, she was delivered of a male child in a remote place; afterwards called *Arki-st'han*, or *Sauri-st'han*, from *Arci* and *Sauri*, the patronymics of ARCA and SURYA. He was the genius of the planet which the *Latians* called SATURN; and acquired, among the *Hindus*, the epithet of SANI; and SANAISCHARA, or *slow-moving*."—WILFORD. *As. Res.* Vol. III. p. 379.

Enthusiastic devotees are encouraged to penances in honour of different deities, by stories in their sacred books of boons having been heretofore obtained, through the kindness of the deities so propitiated. Gazing on the Sun, a mode of moving SURYA's favour, must be exceedingly hurtful and distressing: it is not a very uncommon penance in these days, (see pages 51, and 162); and has its reward, as we learn, by the following tale, from the *Bhascara mahatmya.* —I abridge it.

A careless and voluptuous king—I omit names, having been expelled his dominions, retired to the banks of the *Cali*; and having bathed in the sacred river, he performed penance for his former dissolute life, by standing twelve days on one leg, without ever tasting water, with his eyes fixed on the Sun; the regent of which, SURYA-ISWARA, appeared to him, and, granting his required boon, restored him to virtue and his empire; and ordered him to raise a temple to SURYAESWARA on that very spot; promising to efface the sins of all pilgrims who should visit it with devotion; and fixed a day for a yearly festival, to be there celebrated by his votaries.—*Ib.* p. 398.

The *dawn*, the precursor of SURYA, or the Sun, is personified in ARUN, who may be styled the AURORA of the *Hindus*. ARUN, or ARUNA, is the charioteer of SURYA. His parents are the prolific KASYAPA, and VINATA: hence he is, in the hymn, called—"glowing with immortal grace, young ARUN, loveliest of *Vinatian* race." GARUDA is his younger brother; and hence, from the incomparable swiftness of GARUDA, may the idea of ARUN's lameness, or rather want of legs, have possibly arisen: for he is painted as perfect to his knees only.—See PLATE 87. I find no legend immediately explanatory of ARUN being thus "curtailed of his fair proportions." VINATA appears sometimes as the father of ARUN and GARUDA.

In *Mr.* COLEBROKE's Essay on the *Vedas*, is a passage that seems to have some reference to it: if so, ARUN, or ARUNA, I presume on the identity, is there seen in a character apparently unconnected with that of SURYA's charioteer. ARUNA is noticed as the grandfather of SWETACETU, and father to UDDACALA: the latter, a theologian, was referred to by a number of pious persons, "deeply conversant with holy writ, and possessed of great dwellings; who, meeting together, engaged in this disquisition: 'What is our soul? And who is BRAHM?'"

UDDACALA, son of ARUNA, being "well acquainted with the universal soul," was applied to without immediate success. On this question being put to him, 'Whom dost thou worship as the soul, O descendant of GOTAMA?' he replyed, 'The earth.' On which he was thus admonished:—'Whoever worship this for the universal soul, shares like enjoyments, and views as beloved an object, and has religious occupations in his family: but this forms only the feet of the soul.' —'Thy feet had been lame,' said the king, 'hadst thou not come to me."—*As. Res.* Vol. VIII. p. 467.

A story is related in the *Sivpuran*, of the birth of a being who sprang from BRAHMA, that deity having been most violently, and, indeed, indelicately, enraptured and agitated at the sight merely of PARVATI's fascinating foot, at her marriage with MAHADEVA. This being, the offspring of his amorous effusion, was named VITUKY; and is said to have been first the pupil, and then the precursor of SURYA's car: but I know not if he be the same with ARUN.

CHANDRA, the regent of the Moon, appears in a car drawn by pied antelopes; his head encircled by a crescent, and sometimes with a rabbit on his banner. Although in most of my pictures of this personage, he has one or more of the usual emblems of VISHNU, he seems still, in a greater degree, in respect to legends allusive to parentage and family, connected with SIVA, who is often seen *moon-crowned*; and has hence the epithet of CHANDRA-SEKRA: he is also frequently seen with CHANDRA's emblem, the antelope.—See PLATES 5. 14. 15. 23, and p. p. 39. 48. A crescent on his forehead, and on the foreheads of his consort and offspring, is also a distinguishing family bearing. ISA is, indeed, in one of his forms, expressly called the Moon; and his consort ISI is then LUNA, agreeing still with the *Grecian* DIANA in one of her manifold characters. The idea of a male and female moon has given birth to many legends and allegories. ISA and ISI, under their names of CHANDRA and CHANDRI, undergo several sexual and other changes. CHANDRA, or *Deus* LUNUS, is the moon when in opposition to the sun; and CHANDRI, or *Dea* LUNA, when in conjunction. The origin of this idea may, perhaps, be successfully sought in the notion, that the lunar influences are more powerfully exerted on men at one of the lunar periods, and on women at the other: in high latitudes such influences are scarcely perceptible; but near the tropics, especially in situations where the tide of the sea has a great rise and fall, no individual scarcely—certainly no one at all affected with feverish or nervous symptoms—is exempted from extraordinary periodical sensations (I will not say *caused* by the changes of the moon, for I could never fully convince myself, however plausible the theory, that the coincident phenomena of spring-tides, and full and change of the moon, were cause and effect,) at the conjunction and opposition, or, what amounts to the same, at the periods of spring-tides.

In the sol-lunar legends of the *Hindus*, the Sun is, as we have seen, sometimes male and sometimes female; and both wife and husband of LUNUS and LUNA, under their names of SURYA, SAVITRI, CHANDRA, and CHANDRI. Although this may relate merely to sol-lunar phenomena, it must of course be veiled in sexual allegory; and we are accordingly amused with legends in which CHANDRA lost his virility, and became CHANDRI; who, concealing herself in the mountains, was there visited by SURYA: from which conjunction arose a numerous family, called *Pulinda*. The following is a poetical narrative of this lunarian progeny.

The god SOMA, or CHANDRA, was traversing the earth with his favourite consort ROHINI; and arriving at the southern mountain, *Sahyadri*, they unwarily entered the forest of GAURI, where some men having surprised MAHADEVA caressing that goddess, had been formerly punished by a change of their sex, and the forest had retained a power of effecting a like change on all males who should enter it. CHANDRA, instantly becoming a female, was so afflicted and ashamed, that she hastened *far to the west*, sending ROHINI to her seat in the sky; and concealed herself in a mountain, afterwards named *Soma-giri*, where she performed acts of the most rigorous devotion. Darkness then covered the world each night; the fruits of the earth were destroyed; and the universe was in such dismay, that the *Devas*, with BRAHMA at their head, implored the assistance of MAHADEVA, who no sooner placed CHANDRI on his forehead, than she became male again; and hence he acquired the title of CHANDRASEKARA.

This fable is taken from the *Puranas*, and was thus explained to *Mr.* WILFORD by an ingenious *Pandit.*—

"To the inhabitants of the countries near the source of the *Kali*, the moon, being in the mansion of ROHINI, or the *Pleiades*, seemed to vanish behind the southern mountains. Now, when the Moon is in opposition to the Sun, it is the god CHANDRA; but when in conjunction with it, the goddess CHANDRI, who was in that state feigned to have conceived the *Pulindas* before mentioned. The moon is believed by the *Hindu* naturalists to have a powerful influence on vegetation, especially on certain plants; and, above all, on the *Somalata*, or *Moon-plant*.* This mode of interpretation may serve as a clue for the intricate labyrinth of the *Puranas*, which contain all the history, phisiology, and science, of the *Indians* and *Egyptians*, disguised under similar fables. It may be added, that the *Pulindas* consider the *female* moon as a *form* of the celestial ISI, or ISIS, which may seem to be incompatible with the mythological system of *India:* but the *Hindus* have, in truth, an ISIS with *three forms*, called SWARDEVI in heaven, BHU-DEVI on earth, and PATALA-DEVI in the infernal regions. The consort of the terrestrial goddess is named BHU-DEVA, who resides on *Sumeru*, and is a vicegerent on earth of the three principal deities."—*As. Res.* Vol. III. p. 384.

Deus LUNUS was common among several people of the ancient world.—See BRYANT's Analysis, (Vol. III. p. 62. On the Deluge. Octavo edition.) where several symbolical figures of this deity are given.

As well as a solar, the *Hindus* have a lunar, zodiac, divided into twenty-eight mansions, called *Nakshatra*; and believed to have been so divided, or invented, by DAKSHA, a mythological son of BRAHMA: hence their poetical astronomy feign these *Nakshatras* to be the offspring or daughters of DAKSHA, and, as diurnally receiving the moon in his ethereal journey, to be the wives of CHANDRA. Of these wives, CHANDRA is fabled to have the greatest affection for ROHINI, the fourth daughter of DAKSHA, who, on the complaint of the majority, of this pointed partiality, cursed CHANDRA with a consumption that continued fifteen days; but on his due repentance, his strength and splendour were gradually restored: the meaning of this story, which is detailed in the *Siv-purana*, is obvious. CHANDRA, like the western LUNUS, is somewhat proverbial for inconstancy; and tales are related of his adulterous communication of his influences to the radiant spouses of others of the heavenly host.

ROHINI is the bright star in the bull's eye, and although generally, and even proverbially, the favourite of CHANDRA, is not always so; for the lovely PURNA-VASU, DAKSHA's seventh daughter, sometimes rivals her elder sister in the affec-

* *Somalata, Asclepias Acida*, or *Cynanchum viminale.*

tions and attentions of their horned lord. PURNAVASU is the seventh *Nakshatra*, or asterism, marking the moon's path; and is the star, marked on our globes β *Geminorum:* ROHINI being α of the constellation, whose name دبران *Deberán*, we have, with many others, borrowed from the *Arabians*; or with the article prefixed, الدبران *Aldeberán*; and the fourth lunar asterism.

We have seen, in former pages, that the Moon, as well as being the husband and wife, is also the offspring, of the Sun; his ray being personified under the name of SUSHUMNA, and applied to the Moon. Another legend makes the Moon proceed from a flash of light emitted from the eye of ATRI, the *Rishi*, which impregnated SPACE, a goddess, the *via lactea* personified, under what name I know not: CHANDRA, or SOMA, was the offspring of this extravagant amour. A son of SOMA's, BUD'DHA OR MERCURY, espoused ILA; herself a very equivocal damsel, sometimes called a daughter of MENU. On some misdemeanor, PARVATI * cursed her, and she became alternately one month a man, and a month a woman; but by the efficacy of devotions paid to a *part'h*, or *linga*, was restored to her permanency of sex through the favour of MAHADEVA. Some notice of ILA is taken in pages 89, and 112.

I find, in the *Hitopadesa*, the rabbit mentioned as an emblem of CHANDRA.—"Then I will declare what are the commands of the god CHANDRA.—He bade me say, that in driving away and destroying the rabbits, who are appointed to guard the fountain which is consecrated to that deity, you have done ill: 'for,' said he, 'they are my guards; and it is notorious that the figure of a rabbit is my emblem."—P. 177.

On this passage, *Mr.* WILKINS says, in a note, that "the *Hindu* poets have imagined the Moon as a deity drawn by two antelopes, holding in his right hand a rabbit."—P. 320.

I have no picture of CHANDRA with a rabbit as an attendant: his car is always drawn by an antelope—one, or more; and the rabbit, being a nocturnal and swift animal, may refer to the season, and, as well as the antelope, to the apparent celerity of CHANDRA.

Sir WILLIAM JONES, in his hymn to SURYA, addresses a verse to the Moon, illustrative of its attributes.—

* PARVATI, under one of her forms, and when exerting her energies, as in the instance of the unlucky ILA, is named PATALA, or PATELI DEVI; which is said to mean the *thin* goddess. *Patela* is *thin* in some *Hindu* dialects, and is applicable enough to the goddess presiding, as she does, over atrophy and wasting. But the name is farther deducible, from *Patála*, or hell; PARVATI, as spouse of YAMA, corresponding with HECATE, consort of PLUTO. Of these characters, more will occur presently.

"Thou nectar-beaming Moon,
Regent of dewy night—
From yon bright roe that in thy bosom sleeps
Fawn-spotted, SASIN hight—
Wilt thou desert so soon
Thy night flowers pale, whom liquid odour steeps,
And OSHADHI's transcendent beam,
Burning in the darkest glade?
Will no lov'd name thy gentle mind persuade
Yet one short hour to shed thy cooling stream?
But, ah! we court a passing dream:
Our prayers nor INDU, nor HIMANSU hears—
He fades, he disappears;
E'en KASYAPA's gay daughters twinkling die,
And silence lulls the sky,
Till *chatacs* twitter from the moving brake,
And sandal-breathing gales on beds of ether wake."—Verse 2.

"KASYAPA's gay daughters" are, I imagine, the same with DAKSHA's: the brothers are sometimes confounded with each other.

SASI, or SASIN, is rendered a *roe* by some *Sanskrit* scholars; by others, a *hare:* both these animals are, we find, among the attributes of CHANDRA, and are said to have been allotted to him from a fancied resemblance of their spots to the shades of light on the moon's surface. This would answer very well, as far as regards the roe, or antelope, which is pied, or marked, like the moon, light and dark in abrupt terminations; but the hare is not so, as far as I ever noticed: tame rabbits (which, in a preceding page, we have seen are also consecrated to CHANDRA,) are so pied. But I suspect the allusion is of a phisiological nature, and refers to certain secretions in the female hare, or rabbit, the only quadrupeds, perhaps, that have them: supposed, as in the case of the human female, to be regulated by lunar influences.

A grant of land, engraven on copper, about 600 years old, found lately in the district of *Tipura*, contains a verse alluding to the subject under discussion.

"2. From him sprung the happy chief of ministers, who exhibits the joys of unsullied glory; a spotless moon among mortals, and at sight of whom, the hare-spotted luminary appears swoln (with envy,) and distempered with alternate increase and wane."

On this verse, *Mr.* COLEBROKE says, in a note, (*As. Res.* Vol. IX. p. 403.)

"The Moon is named SASIN, from a fancied resemblance of its spots to a leveret."

Since I wrote this article, I have met with *Sir* W. JONES's translation of the *Hitopadesa*, (*Works*, Vol. XIII.) in which the passage, quoted in page 292, is rendered somewhat differently. An antelope speaks:—"In driving away the antelopes, who are appointed keepers of the pool sacred to CHANDRA, thou hast acted improperly: we antelopes are its guardians. Hence also the god is named SAGANCA, or fawn-spotted."—P. 125. 8vo. edit.

In the portion of this article allotted to the consideration of SURYA, several passages occur descriptive of CHANDRA, and allusive to his history and family.

The two brilliant deities are seen together in PLATE 89. taken from tinted pictures, in which we see both deities four-armed, bearing the *Chank* and *Chakra* of VISHNU. And I will here observe, that, although all the *Hindu* deities partake more or less remotely of the nature and character of SURYA, or the Sun, and all more or less directly radiate from, or merge in, him, yet no one is, I think, so intimately identified with him as VISHNU; whether considered in his own person, or in the character of his most glorious *Avatara* of KRISHNA.

But, to return to PLATE 89. Both deities are marked with VISHNU's sectarial hieroglyphic, viz. two perpendicular red lines over the nose, with a black spot between them: both are copper-coloured, and their cars and banners are alike; the latter deep red; which colour, and yellow, are mixed on their cars. Their ornaments are similar, and their dress, save that the scarf of SURYA is yellow—of CHANDRA, blue, fringed with yellow: the waist-cloth of both is red. SURYA's car is drawn by his seven headed horse, driven by the legless ARUN; and his glory is white, with golden *radii*. CHANDRA is drawn by a pied antelope, and his crescent is of silver.

I have several pictures of these deities, but most of SURYA. CHANDRA appears in this work only, I think, in PLATES 88. 89. and 31. in company, in both instances, with SURYA.

I do not find, in my memoranda, so many names of this fickle deity as one might expect: CHANDRA and SOMA are the commonest. INDU, HIMANSU, SASIN, SAGANKA, and ANUMATI, are the only varieties of his designations that I find noted; and the latter is equivocal, it being CHANDRA when wanting a digit of his full orb; and is applied also to the "goddess of the day" at a particular period, (see p. 113): as CHANDRI, or LUNA, perhaps; and then the name of CUHU, or KUHU, may be also *Lunarian*. BHADRA is likewise among lunar appellations; and is found as such in *Hebrew' Arabic*, *Persian*, and other languages, as well as in *Sanskrit:* it is applied generally to the full moon. BHADRA KALI is, we have seen, a name of PARVATI, and is sometimes translated the *beautiful* or *fair* KALI: the moon is a common symbol of female beauty: SU-KALI has the same meaning. But BHADRA is also an appellation referable to the Sun, and is one of his mansions in his zodiacal journey; and thus, if the idea were pursued, we should, as usual, lose our subject and ourselves in the all-absorbing all-pervading SURYA.

AGNI is the *Hindu* regent or personification of Fire. In all my tinted pictures (and, except my own, I never saw any picture of him,) he is painted a deep red. He has two faces, three legs, and seven arms: when mounted, he has a ram as his *vahan* or vehicle, and his banner bears that animal: from each mouth a forked tongue or flame is seen to issue.—See PLATE 80. All these distinguishing and singular characteristics have doubtless a meaning; and we will endeavour, perhaps not successfully, to trace and explain it.

His two faces, I imagine, allude to the two fires, solar and terrestrial, or to creative heat and destructive fire: three legs, to the three sacred terrestrial fires of the *Brahmans*—the *nuptial*, the *ceremonial*, or funereal, and the *sacrificial*, which will be farther explained presently; or to the influence of fire in and over the three regions of the universe: his seven arms, like the seven heads of SURYA's horse, or the seven horses of his car, were originally derived from the prismatic divisibility of a ray of light; light or heat, and fire, being so immediately connected, we may expect to find a common attribute derived from the same source. We shall, however, see presently, that more familiar allusions, and his seven arms, have mutual reference to each other.

The sacred triad of fires that determined his number of legs are thus enumerated in the *Ins.* of MENU. Chap. II. v. 229.—"Due reverence to those three (the parents and preceptor) is considered as the highest devotion; and without their approbation, no man must perform any other duty.

"230. Since they alone are held equal to the three worlds; they alone, to the three principal orders; they alone, to the three *Vedas*; they alone, to the three fires;

"231. The natural father is considered as the *garhapatra*, or nuptial fire; the mother, as the *dacshina*, or ceremonial; the spiritual guide, as the *ahavaniya*, or sacrificial: this triad of fires is most venerable.

"232. By honouring his mother, he gains this terrestrial world; by honouring his father, the intermediate, or ethereal; and by assiduous attention to his preceptor, even the celestial world of BRAHMA."

In the ceremony called *Viswadeva*, or *all the gods*, which is a comprehensive one, including the essentials of the whole detail of daily sacrifice, and practised therefore by *Brahmans* engaged in worldly occupations, and by some even who follow the regular vocation of the sacerdotal tribe, the mystical number of *seven* frequently occurs; in this prayer, for instance, addressed to AGNI:—

"Fire! seven are thy fuels; seven thy tongues; seven thy holy sages; seven thy beloved abodes; seven ways do seven sacrificers worship thee; thy sources are seven. Be content with this clarified butter: may this oblation be efficacious."

"The seven tongues of fire," a commentator observes, "are *Pravaha, Avaha, Udvaha, Samvaha, Vivaha, Parivaha, Nivaba,* (or *Anuvaha)*; all of which imply the power of conveying oblations to the deities to whom offerings are made. The seven holy sages and sacrificers are the *Hotri, Maitravaruna,** *Brahmanachandasi, Ack'havac, Potri, Neshtri,* and *Agnid'hra*; that is, the seven officiating priests at very solemn sacrifices. They worship fire seven ways; by the *Agnishtoma*, and other sacrifices. The seven abodes are the names of the seven worlds; and fire is called in the *Veda, saptachitica,* which seems to allude to seven consecrated hearths. In the sixteen verses, called *Purusha*, the names of the seven worlds, thrice repeated, are understood to be meant by the thrice seven fuels; and the seven oceans are the seven moats surrounding the altar. Fire, like the sun itself, is supposed to emit seven rays: this may, perhaps, account for the number seven being so often repeated."—COLEBROKE. *As. Res.* Vol. VII. page 274.

The following note by *Mr.* COLEBROKE refers to the same subject, and contains also a description of a *bull*, or justice personified, that applies, in respect to heads, hands, and legs, to AGNI. "I omit the very tedious detail respecting sins expiated by a set number of repetitions; but in one instance, as an atonement for unwarily eating or drinking what is forbidden, it is directed that eight hundred repetitions of the *Gayatri* should be preceded by three suppressions of the breath, touching water during the recital of the following text: "The bull roars; he has four horns, three feet, two heads, seven hands, and is bound by a threefold ligature: he is the mighty resplendent being, and pervades mortal

* MAITRA VARUNA is probably the same as MITRA VARUNA, or the friendly VARUNA; an epithet of MENU, as noticed in page 275.

men.' The bull," *Mr.* Colebroke continues, "is justice personified: his four horns are the *Brahman*, or superintending priest; the *Udgatri*, or chanter of the *Samaveda*; the *Hotri*, or reader of the *Rigveda*, who performs the essential part of a religious ceremony; and the *Adhwarin*, who sits in the sacred close, and chants the *Yajurveda*: his three feet are the three *Vedas*: oblations and sacrifice are his two heads, roaring stupendously: his seven hands are the *Hotri*, *Maitravaruna*, *Brahmanach'handasi*, *Gravastata*, *Achhavac*, *Nishtri*, and *Potri*; names by which officiating priests are designed at certain solemn rites: the threefold ligature by which he is bound, is worshipped in the morning, at noon, and in the evening."—*As. Res.* Vol. V. p. 356.

The names given in this note, as the seven hands of the bull, are the same, with the exception of one, (*Gravastata*, substituted for *Agnidhra*,) as those in the preceding extract, from the seventh volume of the *Asiatic Researches*; both lists said to designate officiating priests.

The sixteen verses, called *Purusha*, are given entire in another place, (p. 75); but I will here quote that alluded to above, and its antecedent.—

"14. In that solemn sacrifice, which the gods performed with him, a victim, (with Purusha, the primeval being,) spring was the butter, summer the fuel, and sultry weather the oblation:

"15. Seven were the moats (surrounding the altar); thrice seven were the logs of holy fuel at that sacrifice which the gods performed, immolating (or binding, or consecrating) this being as the victim."

The thrice seven fuels, or thrice seven holy logs, may, perhaps, refer to the thrice seven hells of the infernal machinery of the *Hindus*, they reckoning that number of receptacles for sinners, as will be shown presently; and I should expect that just one-third of the twenty-one are of fire in different forms, and thence more especially applicable to the attributes of Agni.*

* Referring, however, to *Mr.* Wilkins, I did not find my expectations verified. The names of the thrice seven hells are the following, taken from the *Ins.* of Menu, Chap. IV. verses 88, 89, 90. I add the meaning of such of the epithets as I am acquainted with.—1. *Tàmisra*, darkness; 2. *Andha támisra*, utter darkness; 3. *Mahá-raurauva*, most dreadful; 4. *Raurava*, dreadful; 5. *Naraka*, the region of serpents; 6. *Kala surra*; 7. *Maha-naraka*; 8. *Sanjivana*; 9. *Mahávichi*; 10. *Tapana*, heating; 11. *Sampratapana*, over-heating; 12. *Sangháta*; 13. *Sakakola*, ordure; 14. *Kudmala*; 15. *Putimrittika*, stinking dirt; 16. *Loha sanku*, iron-pointed; 17. *Rijisha*; 18. *Panthána*; 19. *Salmali*, a river; 20. *Asi-patra-vana*, sword-leaved forest; 21. *Lóhángáraka*, hot-iron coals. One, perhaps *No.* 2. is placed in the bowels of the earth; and unfortunate souls go in succession through them all; and this lengthened *gauntlet* is to be run on some occasions that one would not deem so very sinful.—See *Ins.* of Menu, Ch. IV. v. 87.

Numerous instances could easily be adduced of the mysterious import of the number *seven* among the *Hindus*, as well as among *Jews*, *Mahommedans*, and *Christians*. *Three*, *eight*, and *nine*, are also favourite numbers with different sects: *eight* among the followers of BUDDHA chiefly.

AGNI's seven arms, therefore, may be concluded to denote the universal power of the all-pervading element of fire; as may his three legs, its extension similarly over the three portions of the universe—the celestial, terrestrial, and infernal regions.

The *Vedas* are variously subdivided, and certain portions are variously attributed to certain gods and men. To AGNI is assigned seven *Kandas*, or books, of the *Yajur Veda*.—*As. Res.* Vol. VIII. p. 452. One of the *Puranas* is called the AGNI *Purana*. He is named "JIVANI: he does good to all; from whom sprung the *Vedas*."

AGNI had seven brothers, whose names signify *flame*. By one wife he had three sons—UTTAMA, TAMASA, RAIVATA; they became *Menus*, and their names have, I imagine, some allusions, direct or inverse, to fire, or heat, or light: TAMASA, for instance, is *darkness:* their names occur in the list of *Menus* in page 86. By another wife, AGNI* had nine sons: one of his wives was named SWAHA; and she is called the goddess of fire, and is invoked on some occasions.—See LAKSHMI, p. 138, where SWAHA is called "the consuming power of those who eat solemn sacrifices;" that is Fire, she being the *Sacti* or energy of AGNI.

PAVAKA, and AGNIDHRA, are other names of AGNI: PAVAKA signifies the *Purifier*. He is also called ANALA.

KRISHNA, describing his own pre-eminence among all things and creatures, says to ARJUN, "Among the *Vasus* I am PAVAK."—*Gita*, p. 86.

He is a guardian regent of one of the magnetic points: he rules the south-east.

It is noted above, that three of AGNI's sons are found among the *Menus*; who, on divers occasions, are called sons of BRAHMA.—See p. 86. Between BRAHMA and AGNI may hence be traced something of identity: both are likewise painted red. It must be in reference to his creative heat that he is connected with BRAHMA: his igneous property connects him with the destructive SIVA; and his light, so intimately related to fire, with VISHNU, the conservator. This triple connection between the deity of heat and the great powers, is similar

* See *As. Res.* Vol. V. p. 250.

to what is remarked of the Sun, under the article SURYA. When so contemplated, he is called TRITNU, or the three-bodied; as *producing* forms by his genial heat, *preserving* them by his light, and *destroying* them by his igneous property.

The following extract from *Sir* WILLIAM JONES's Dissertation on the Gods of *Greece*, *Italy*, and *India*, will explain various points referring to AGNI and SURYA.

"The worship of solar or vestal fire may be ascribed, like that of OSIRIS and ISIS, to the second source of mythology, or an enthusiastic admiration of nature's wonderful powers; and it seems, as far as I can yet understand the *Vedas*, to be the principal worship recommended in them. We have seen that MAHADEVA himself is personified by fire; but subordinate to him is the god AGNI, often called PAVACA, or the *Purifier*, who answers to the VULCAN of *Egypt*, where he was a deity of high rank: and AGNI's wife, SWAHA, resembles the younger VESTA, or VESTIA, as the *Eolians* pronounced the *Greek* word for a *hearth*. BHAVANI, or VENUS, is the consort of the Supreme Destructive and Generative Power; but the *Greeks* and *Romans*, whose systems are less regular than that of the *Indians*, married her to their *divine artist*, whom they also named HEPHIASTOS, and VULCAN, and who seems to be the *Indian* VISWACARMAN, the *forger of arms* for the gods, and inventor of the *Agniyaster*,* or *fiery shaft*, in the war between them and the *Daityas*, or Titans."—*As. Res.* Vol. I. p. 264.

Again, speaking of some reform among the ancient *Persians*, in the eighth or ninth century before CHRIST, he says, that "while they rejected the complex polytheism of their predecessors, they retained the laws of *Mahabad*, with a superstitious veneration for the sun, the planets, and fire; thus resembling the *Hindu* sects called *Sauras*, and *Sagnicas*; the second of which is very numerous at *Benares*, where many *Agnihotras* are continually burning, and where the *Sagnicas*,

* This *fiery shaft* has been supposed to be the *rocket*, formerly so much, but of late years less, used in the armies in *India* as a missile weapon. I have often seen them applied, but never with any great destruction, against bodies of horse and foot: the former are much terrified by their noise. I have known them do considerable mischief; for, wherever they pitch, their violence is not easily resisted: one striking a tumbril, or a slight magazine, would imminently endanger its exploding: it would kill an elephant; but their irregularity is so great, no certain direction can be given them. For the purpose of burning or terrifying towns, or collected shipping, they appear well adapted: *Col.* CONGREVE's rockets I believe to be very similar to those used immemorially in *India*, where the iron-work of one has been found to weigh thirty pounds. Another description of fiery engines of destruction, called *Shatagni*, is mentioned in the *Puranas*, and in the *Ramayana*; and it is thought to have been a sort of cannon: the word means a *hundred fires*, or a fire capable of destroying a hundred men.

when they enter on their sacerdotal office, kindle, with two pieces of the hard wood *Semi*, a fire, which they keep lighted through their lives—for their nuptial ceremony, the performance of solemn sacrifices, and the obsequies of departed ancestors, and their own funeral pile. This remarkable rite was continued by ZERATUSHT, who reformed the old religion by the addition of *genii*, or angels, presiding over months and days; of new ceremonies in the veneration shewn to fire; of a new work which he pretended to have received from heaven; and, above all, by establishing the actual adoration of one Supreme Being."—Discourse on the *Persians*.—*Ib.* Vol. II. p. 60.

"AURVA was a son of SURYA, who expelling SANI, another of his sons, to whom he had resigned his realm, appointed AURVA in his stead: AURVA purified the land, recalled the holy men, and restored his subjects to the happiness that the baneful reign of SANI had deprived them of. On one occasion he gave a dreadful proof of his power: as ARAMA, the son of SATYAVRATA, (and consequently the ARAM of scripture,) was hunting in that country *(Aurvast'han,)* with his who learmy, near a spot where DURVASAS, a choleric saint and a supposed *Avatara* of MAHADEVA, was sitting, wrapt in deep meditation, he inadvertently shot an arrow, which wounded the foot of DURVASAS; who no sooner opened his eyes, than AURVA sprung from them in the shape of a flame, which consumed ARAMA and his party, together with all the animals and vegetables of *Cusha-dwip*. It appears to me," continues *Mr.* WILFORD, "that AURVA is VULCAN, or the god of fire, who reigned, according to the *Egyptian* priests, *after the Sun*; though some have pretended, says DIODORUS, that he had existed before that luminary; as the *Hindus* allege that AGNI, or Fire, had existence, in an elementary state, before the formation of the Sun, but could not be said to have dominion till its force was concentrated."—WILFORD. *As. Res.* Vol. III. p. 380.

It is probable that the legend of AURVA, or Fire, reigning after SANI and SURYA, or the Sun, is merely an allegorical mode of communicating the historical fact alluded to, in a preceding quotation, by *Sir* WILLIAM JONES; namely, that the worship of Fire succeeded that of the planets and the Sun.

I know not if the *Hindus* ever possessed the art of concentrating the sun's rays by a lens, so as to obtain fire by that process: that used by *Brahmans* for cooking, and for religious ceremonies, is produced by the friction of two pieces of hard wood; one about five inches diameter, with a small conical hole, or socket, in the upper part, into which the other, shaped like a pin, is introduced, and whirled about backward and forward by a bow; the pin and socket fitting, the great attrition soon produces fire. This machine, which every *Brahman* ought to possess, is called *Arani,* and should be made of the *Sami* * tree, it being sacred to DEVI in the character of SAMI DEVI; or if that be not procurable, of the *Pipala,*† resembling in appearance and name some species of our *poplar.* A particular day is set apart for the festival of SAMI DEVI, when fires are lighted in the evening under the *Sami* tree: offerings are made of rice and flowers, and sometimes of spirits: the votaries sing her praise, and in praise of the tree; some of the leaves of which, and some earth, are carried home, and kept till the festival of the ensuing year.—See *As. Res.* Vol. IV. p. 382. and Vol. VIII. p. 256.

Few, perhaps none, of the almost innumerable ceremonies of the *Brahmans,* are complete without invocatory oblations to the all-pervading element of fire, or to AGNI, its personification: his name perpetually occurs: all other deities, superior and inferior, come in also, of course, for a portion of adoration; including BRAHMA, VISHNU, SIVA, INDRA, SURYA, CHANDRA, YAMA, DEVI, in a variety of characters, LAKSHMI, SARASWATI, ADITI, VRIHASPATI, VARUNA, &c. &c.—See *Mr.* COLEBROKE's curious and interesting Essays on the Religious Ceremonies of the *Hindus,* in the fifth and seventh volumes of the *Asiatic Researches.*

In sacrificial ceremonies, as ordained by MENU, AGNI is the deity of primary invocation.

A *Brahman* is directed, in his domestic fire for dressing the food of all the gods, (see page 281,) each day to make an oblation:

"First, to AGNI, god of fire, and to the lunar god, severally; then to both of them at once."—Chap. III. v. 85.

Again, in offerings to the *Dii Manes*:—

Chap III. v. 207.—"The divine *manes* are always pleased with an oblation in empty glades, naturally clean, on the banks of rivers, and in solitary spots."

"211. First, as it is ordained, having satisfied AGNI, SOMA, and YAMA, with clarified butter, let him proceed to satisfy the *manes* of his progenitors."

AGNI also holds a foremost place in the composition of a king, according to a verse extracted in INDRA, page 266, where, indeed, the name SOMA appears first; but, in the original, AGNI is first named, SOMA being interpolated by CULLUCA, whose gloss on MENU *Sir* WILLIAM JONES has preserved, ingeniously interwoven with the text.

The name and characteristics of this important deity have occurred fre-

* The *Sami* tree is the *Adenanthera aculeata,* or *Prosopis aculeata.*

† *Ficus Indica,* or *Ficus Bengalensis;* otherwise *Ficus religiosa,* or commonly *Banyan* tree.

quently in former pages, under different articles, as pointed at by the *Index*. In page 87, a legend is given of his supposed inconstancy to his consort SWAHA, a lady that I find no particular mention of: her name has occasionally occurred, and will again, probably, in a future article. In page 52, is a relation of a successful embassy, executed by the regent of Fire, to the frigid SIVA, with whom he participates in the honour of KARTIKYA's origin.

AGNI appears in several of our plates: PLATE 31. represents him, with other deities, propitiating DEVI: in PLATE 55. he is in his own element, supporting and comforting the incombustible SITA. He is uniformly, in all my tinted pictures, of a dead fiery red colour, with a yellow *pitamba*, or waist-cloth; and with two faces, three legs, and seven arms, a forked flame issuing from his mouths: on his head-piece, two horns rise over each forehead. In PLATE 80. he is seen mounted on his *vahan*, or vehicle, the ardent ram, which, in the picture, is of deep azure hue, with red horns; as it is also in the upper red banner: in the yellow banner, below, the ram is also yellow. What he holds in his hands I cannot make out, beyond the fan and flower.

Of YAMA, SANI, *and* VRIHASPATI,

The REGENTS of HELL, and the PLANETS SATURN and JUPITER.

YAMA is a very important deity: his name occurs frequently in the sacrificial ceremonies of the *Hindus*; oblations and invocations to him, forming a portion of several of those ceremonies. He is regent of the south, or lower world, in which the *Hindus* place the infernal regions; thus corresponding, as the judge of departed souls, with the *Grecian* PLUTO, or MINOS. MINOS has before been supposed the same with MENU; with whom, especially with the seventh, SATYAVRATA, YAMA also agrees in character, as well as in name; both being called VAIVASWATA, or offspring of the Sun, and SRAD'HADEVA, or lord of the *Srad'ha*. *Srad'ha*, as will be more particularly explained presently, is the ceremonial oblation in honour of deceased ancestors; which obsequies to the *dii manes* are attended with feasting, and various observances of a curious and singular description. YAMA has many names; and, in his character and functions, is related to many important personages of sacred and profane history. Among his names are DHERMA-RAJA, or king of justice; PITRIPETI, or lord of the *Pitris*, or patriarchs; MRITU, or MRITYU, or *Death*, a title also of SIVA, or KALA. SUSANYAMA, and VAIVASWATA YAMA, are derivatives: the first from a word implying comeliness, or beauty; the other from his solar origin. KRITANTA is another name; and *Kritamala* being the name of a river connected with the history of SATYAVRATA, the epithets may have a common origin. AUDHUMBARA is a name derived from a species of wood, by the attrition of which fire is produced, wherewith to light the pile on which funereal obsequies are performed to YAMA. ANTEKA, or *Death*, or the *Destroyer*: thus KALANTAKA YAMA is YAMA, the destroyer of KAL, or TIME; a personification of great boldness and extent; and KAL is a name also of YAMA. This epithet, *anteka*, is frequently applied in composition for forming names; in earlier pages we have met with TRIPURANTIKA SIVA, or SIVA, the destroyer of the *Asura*, TRIPURA.—See PLATE 14. NERANTEKA, and DEVANTEKA, are spoken of, under the article KRISHNA, as two *Asuras*, sent, in the shape of lions, by his malignant uncle to kill him: their names mean the destroyer of men, and of gods; and

NAGANTEKA is a name of GARUDA, the destroyer of serpents. YAMA has other names compounded of words, meaning the slayer of all beings; king of deities; reducer of all things to ashes; the dark-blue deity; of wolf-like belly; the variegated being; the wonderful inflictor of pains.—See *As. Res.* Vol. V. p. 366. where, in the ceremonies of oblation to the manes of deceased ancestors, fourteen different titles of YAMA are enumerated, being considered as so many distinct forms of that deity; to whom the priest offers, from the hollow of both hands joined, three oblations of water mixed with *tila (Sesamum Indicum)*, fourteen times repeated with the different titles of YAMA.

His abode is in the infernal city of *Yamapur*, whither the *Hindus* believe that a departed soul immediately repairs; and receiving a just sentence from YAMA, ascends to *'Swerga*, the first heaven, or descends to *Naraka*, the snaky hell; or assumes on earth the form of some animal, unless its offences had been such as deserved condemnation to a vegetable, or even to a mineral, prison.—See *Asiatic Researches*, Vol. I. p. 239.

Mr. WILFORD believes YAMA, or PLUTO, to be the same with SERAPIS; deriving the latter name from a compound *Sanskrit* word, implying *thirst of blood.* "The sun, in *Bhadra*, had the title of YAMA; but the *Egyptians* gave that of PLUTO, says PORPHYRY, to the great luminary near the winter solstice.—YAMA, the regent of hell, has two dogs, according to the *Puranas*: one of them named CERBURA, or *varied*; the other, SYAMA, or *black*: the first is also called TRISIRAS, or *with three heads*; and has several other epithets, signifying *stained*, or *spotted*: CERBURA is indubitably the CERBERUS of the *Greeks*. The dragon of SERAPIS I suppose to be the SESHNAGA, which is described as in the infernal regions by the author of the *Bhagavat*."—*As. Res.* Vol. III. p. 409.

We are farther informed, by the same learned gentleman, that "DHERMA RAJA, or the king of justice, has two countenances: one called his *divine countenance*, mild, and full of benevolence; and those only see it who abound in virtue. His servant is named KARMALA, who brings the righteous on celestial self-moving cars to DHERMA RAJA, the sovereign of the *Pitris*. His other countenance, or form, is called YAMA; this the wicked alone can see: it has large teeth, and a monstrous body. YAMA is lord of *Patala*, or the infernal regions: there he orders some to be beaten, some to be cut to pieces, some to be devoured by monsters, &c. His servant is named KASHMALA, who drags the wicked, with ropes round their necks, over rugged paths, and throws them headlong into hell: he is unmerciful, and hard is his heart; every body trembles at his sight." —*Ib.* Vol. V. p. 298.

The following dirge, called the song of YAMA, is chanted by a priest at the funeral of children dying under two years of age, whose bodies are not then burned, but, decked with wreaths of fragrant flowers, are buried by their relations in a clean spot; they saying, *Namo! Namah!*

"The offspring of the Sun, day after day, fetching cows, horses, human beings, and cattle, is no more satiated therewith than is a drunkard with wine." —COLEBROKE. *Ib.* Vol. VII. p. 243.

The fourteenth day of the dark half of the month *Aswini* is called *Yamaterpanam*, and is sacred to YAMA: bathing and libations are auspicious on that day; and on the following, torches and flaming brands are kindled, and consecrated to burn the bodies of kinsmen who may be dead in battle, or in a foreign country, and to light them through the shades of death to the mansions of YAMA. "These rites," says *Sir* WILLIAM JONES, combining them with some others, (see p. 135,) "bear a striking resemblance to those of CERES and PROSERPINE."—*Ib.* Vol. III. p. 264.

The second day of the following month, *Kartika*, is also sacred to YAMA, conjointly with his youngest sister, the river goddess YAMUNA, (or the *Jumna,*) she having entertained her brother on that day: in imitation of which, sisters give entertainments to, and receive presents from, their brothers.—*Ib.* p. 266.

But, in the tenth book of the *Rig Veda*, YAMUNA is called the *twin* sister of YAMA; and a dialogue is given, in which he endeavours to seduce her, but his base offers are rejected by her with virtuous expostulation.—*Ib.* Vol. VIII. page 402.

YAMUNA, or, as the name is commonly pronounced, JUMNA, is a favourite feminine appellation in many parts of *India*; particularly with that class of women with whom the example of their virtuous namesake is the least regarded.

KRISHNA, in the *Gita*, p. 86. describing his own pre-eminence, says to ARJUN, "Among all those who rule I am YAMA;" implying a superiority on the part of YAMA, who is certainly a most important personage. But this priority has reference probably to the lower regions only; for among the *dii minores*, as enumerated under INDRA, the latter deity is almost universally esteemed the first.

PLUTO is mated by western mythologists: his consort, PROSERPINE, is but a form of DIANA; and YAMA, king of *Patala*, or hell, enjoys the society of BHAVANI in her character of PATALADEVI: in heaven she is SWARDEVI, and BHU-

DEVI on earth. Thus DIANA, with the *Greeks*, is the earthly name of the goddess; LUNA, in heaven; and PROSERPINE, or HECATE, in hell.

In a preceding passage we have seen YAMA identified with SIVA. *Mr.* WILFORD *(As. Res.* Vol. V. page 299.) says, "PLUTO, or YAMA, is but a form of VISHNU;" and in page 246, of the same volume, and in page 101, of this work, we find SWAYAMBHUVA, (as a MENU closely allied to YAMA,) expressly mentioned as "BRAHMA himself in a human shape:" and BRAHMA is farther said to direct the motions of SANI, or SATURN, who, in his character of Time, is, as well as the MENUS, intimately connected with NOAH. SANI, like MENU and YAMA, is the offspring of the Sun: SANI, or SATURN, is KRONOS, or TIME, or KALA; so are YAMA and SIVA. NOAH, or NUH, as his name is spelled in *Hebrew,* is the same with MENU; which, in the nominative case, is MENUS, who bears etymological and historical and mythological affinity with MINOS, like him a great lawgiver, and a reputed son of JOVE. MINOS, as the judge of departed souls, corresponds with YAMA, himself the same with MENU: hence YAMA, KALA, SANI, SATURN, TIME, devouring or destroying their own offspring and all created things, will, if their allegories and allusions be examined, be found to run into the same train of ancestry and character, and mixing identically with the history of the MENUS, of NOAH, and MINOS. Indeed a different line of personification may be connected with the above characters: PRIT'HIVI is the Earth, the mother of MANGALA, or MARS; and also the same with SATYAVRATA, or NOAH: her husband, PRIT'HU, is an incarnation of VISHNU: BRAHMA is also the Earth; and like PRIT'HU, or PRIT'HIVI, for mythological beings change sexes as well as names, may be brought to coalesce in family and functions with TELLUS, TERRA, CŒLUS, or URANUS, (the latter, like SIVA, the patron of astronomy,) TITAN, VESTA, ATLAS, RHEA, and a whole host of *Grecian* deified personages.

The above names, both of *Grecian* and *Indian* originals, might be considerably extended, and a family connection still traced throughout them: all will be found melting into each other primarily, and ultimately into the Sun—

> —— "Fountain of living Light;
> But far more glorious HE, who said serene,
> BE! and THOU WAST—Himself unform'd, unchang'd, unseen!"
>
> JONES's Hymn to SURYA.

Thus would BRYANT's solar hypothesis derive considerable strength from the mythology of a people whose name, as theologians, was scarcely known to that ingenious and learned gentleman.

That very interesting and affecting ceremony, called *Srad'ha*, is an oblation of daily recurrence with individuals who rigidly adhere to the ritual. It is offered in honour of deceased ancestors—but not merely in honour of them, but for their comfort; as the *Manes*, as well as the gods connected with them, enjoy, like the gods of the *Greeks*, the incense of such offerings: which are farther of an expiatory nature, similar, I imagine, in their potencies, as well as in the motives that induce them, with the masses of the *Romish* church. Over these ceremonials of *Srad'ha* presides YAMA, in his character of SRAD'HA-DEVA, or lord of the obsequies: what I deem necessary to say on that subject will, therefore, be appropriately introduced here.

Mr. COLEBROKE (*As. Res.* Vol. VII. p. 249.) tells us, that the priests, in the performance of the *Sradha*, meditate the *Gayatri*, and thrice repeat—"Salutation to the gods, to the manes of ancestors, and to mighty saints; to SWAHA (goddess of fire); to SWADHA (the food of the manes). Salutation to them for ever and ever."

M. le GENTIL found a strong resemblance between the funeral rites of the *Chinese* and the *Srad'ha* of the *Hindus*. On which *Sir* W. JONES (*As. Res.* Vol. II. p. 378.) says, "that all the circumstances which have been mentioned under the two heads of literature and religion, seem collectively to prove (as far as such question will admit proof,) that the *Chinese* and *Hindus* were originally the same people; but having been separated near four thousand years, have retained few strong features of their ancient consanguinity; especially as the *Hindus* have preserved their old language and ritual, while the *Chinese* very soon lost both. And the *Hindus* have constantly intermarried among themselves, while the *Chinese*, by a mixture of *Tartarian* blood from the time of their first establishment, have at length formed a race distinct in appearance from both *Indians* and *Tartars*."

In the third chapter of the *Ins.* of MENU, the rules for the performance of the *Sradha* are detailed with prolixity. I shall quote some texts explanatory of its rites, premising that *Brahmans* only ought to be invited; and such men should be of holy and learned habits: a *Sudra*, one of the fourth, or servile class, it will be seen, is urgently prohibited as a guest.

Chap. III. v. 82.—"Let the house-keeper who knows his duty perform each day a *Sradha* with boiled rice and the like, or with water, or with milk, roots, and fruit; for thus he obtains favour from departed progenitors."

"123. Sages have distinguished the monthly *Sradha* by the title of *anwa-*

harya, or *after-eaten*; that is, eaten after the *pinda*, or ball of rice: and it must be performed with extreme care, and with flesh meat in the best condition."

"125. At the *Sradha* of the gods, he may entertain two *Brahmans*; at that of his father, paternal grandfather, and paternal great-grandfather, three; or only one at that of the gods, and one at that of his paternal ancestors. Though he abound in wealth, let him not be solicitous to entertain a large company."

"133. As many mouthfuls as an unlearned man shall swallow at an oblation to the gods and to ancestors, so many red-hot iron balls must the giver of the *Sradha* swallow in the next world."

"176. The foolish giver of a *Sradha* loses, in a future life, the fruit of as many admissible guests, as a thief, or the like person, inadmissible into company, might be able to see."

"178. Of the gift at a *Sradha*, to as many *Brahmans* as a sacrificer for a *Sudra* might be able to touch on the body, the fruit is lost to the giver if he invite such a wretch."

"191. He who caresses a *Sudra* woman after he has been invited to sacred obsequies, takes on himself all the sin that has been committed by the giver of the repast."

"250. Should the eater of a *Sradha* enter on the same day the bed of a seducing woman, his ancestors would sleep for that month on her excrement.

"251. Having, by the word *Swaditam*, asked the *Brahmans* if they have eaten well, let him give them, being satisfied, water for an ablution.

"252. Then let the *Brahmans* address him, saying *Swadha*; for in all ceremonies relating to deceased ancestors, the word *Swadha* is the highest benison."

Here we find the word *Swadha* used as a benediction, or grace after meat; but the *Edinburgh* reviewers say that SWADHA is the goddess of funeral obsequies. In a former extract *Swadha* is said, on the authority of *Mr.* COLEBROKE, to be the food of the *Manes:* the word *Swadha* is, in fact, of a very mystical nature; and authorities, however respectable, may well differ in expounding it. Sometimes it is used as equivalent to *Maya*, or illusion, or the world of ideas.—(See *As. Res.* Vol. VIII. p. 405.) In page 138, the word bears the same import as above; namely, the food of the *Manes*.

The following is the passage alluded to, in the *Edinburgh Review*, for January, 1807.

"SWADHA is a goddess, whose adventures are very poetically narrated in the *Brahma-vaivartica-purana*, originally a nymph of *Golaca*, the paradise of VISHNU. Her celestial charms excited the jealousy of RADHA, who perfectly represents the *Grecian* JUNO in her caprices, her jealousy, and her fury. Hurled by the goddess from the *Empyrean*, VISHNU, to console her under her banishment, gave her in marriage to the *Dii Manes*. She is the goddess of funeral obsequies; conveying to the manes the offerings of men, and rewarding the latter for their piety to ancestors."

In the preceding extract RADHA is called the wife of VISHNU. In his *Avatara* of KRISHNA she was his wife; but not otherwise, under that name, in his character of VISHNU. VISHNU's paradise is *Vaikont'ha*. As a cowherd deity, KRISHNA is called *Gowly*, and GOKALA; and *Golaka*, as a residence, is a derivative similarly from *Go*, a cow.

I will here subjoin some elegant elegiac verses, as connected with the *manes* to whom the *Sradha* is offered; prefixing a slight account of the last ceremonies attendant on the expiring *Hindu*. It is taken from COLEBROKE's Dissertation on the Religious Ceremonies of the *Hindus*, (*As. Res.* Vol. VII. Art. 8.) where the reader, among much valuable matter, will find many curious particulars descriptive of the *Sradha*.

"A dying man, when no hopes of his surviving remain, should be laid on a bed of *Kusa** grass in the open air, his head sprinkled with water drawn from the *Ganges*, and smeared with clay brought from the same river. A *Salagrama*†

* *Poa Cynosuroides.*

† This sacred stone is essential in many rites and ceremonies of the *Brahmans*: it is used in propitiatory oblations to VISHNU, as well as in funereal and other ceremonies. The *Salagrama* is not, I believe, ever considered as a type of MAHADEVA, as some other holy, particularly conical, stones are.

Mr. COLEBROKE, whose authority on every point connected with *Hindu* and *Sanskrit* history and literature is of the first respectability, informs us (*As. Res.* Vol. VII. p. 240.) that the *Salagramas* are found in a part of the *Gandaci* river, within the limits of *Nepal*. They are black, mostly round, and are commonly perforated in one or more places by worms, or, as the *Hindus* believe, by VISHNU, in the shape of a reptile. According to the number of perforations, and of spiral curves, in each, the stone is supposed to contain VISHNU in various characters. For example: such a stone perforated in one place only, with four spiral curves in the perforation, and with marks resembling a cow's foot, and a wreath of flowers, contains LAKSHMI-NARAYANA. The stones called *Ban-ling*, found in the *Nermada*, are, in like manner, considered as types of SIVA. The *Salagrama* is found upon trial not to be calcareous: it strikes fire with steel, and scarcely at all effervesces with acids.

SONNERAT describes the *Salagrama* as a petrified shell, of the species *cornes d'ammon*; very heavy, commonly black, but sometimes violet; oval, or round; a little flat, nearly resembling a touchstone, and

stone should be placed near him, holy strains from the *Veda* should be chaunted aloud, and leaves of holy basil scattered over his head.

"When he expire, the corpse must be washed, perfumed, and decked with wreaths of flowers, and carried by the nearest relations to some spot in the forest, or near water: the funeral-pile is lighted from the consecrated fire maintained by the deceased: the nearest relation applies the flaming brand to the pile, hung round with flowers, and the attendant priests recite the appropriate invocations.—'Fire! thou wast lighted by him; may he, therefore, be reproduced from thee, that he may attain the regions of celestial bliss. May this offering be auspicious.' All who followed the corpse walk round the pile, but may not view the fire: they then proceed to the river, and after bathing, present oblations of water from the joined palms of their hands to the manes of the deceased, saying, 'May this oblation reach thee.' Elegiac verses, such as the following, are then recited.—

"1. Foolish is he who seek for permanence in the human state; insolid, like the stem of the plantain tree; transient, like the foam of the sea.

"2. When a body, formed of five elements, to receive the reward of deeds done in its own former person, reverts to its five original principles, what room is there for regret?

"3. The earth is perishable; the ocean, the gods themselves, pass away.—How should not that bubble, mortal man, meet destruction?

hollow, (how can it then be very heavy?) with only one small aperture: within, he says, it is almost concave, with spiral lines terminating towards the middle. Some are supposed to represent the gracious incarnations of VISHNU, and are then highly prized; but when they border a little on the violet, they denote a vindictive *Avatara*, such as *Narasinga*, when no man of ordinary nerve dares keep them in his house. The possessor of a *Salagrama* preserves it in clean cloth: it is frequently perfumed and bathed; and the water thereby acquiring virtue, is drank, and prized for its sin-expelling property.

The *Brahmans*, and *Hindus* in general, look on this stone with much reverence: it is not exceedingly scarce, but certainly not common; for I never had an opportunity of possessing one; which, indeed, I never particularly sought. *Colonel* STUART, of *Soho Square*, has had many, and has now two: I know of no other in *England*. They are less than a small billiard-ball, nearly round, with the appearance of a common smooth pebble soaked in oil, and thereby blackened: they are solid, without perforation or aperture.

Veneration for stones may be traced among almost all nations: the following instance from our scripture reminds one strongly of *Hindu* simplicity—

"And JACOB rose up early in the morning, and took the stone he had put for his pillow, and set it up for a pillar, and poured oil on the top of it."—*Gen.* chap. xxviii. v. 18.

"4. All that is low must finally perish; all that is elevated must ultimately fall; all compounded bodies must end in dissolution; and life be concluded with death."

Of SANI and VRIHASPATI, SATURN and JUPITER, a few words remain to be said: the former is described in some passages of the *Puranas* as clad in a black mantle, with a dark turban loosely wrapped round his head; his aspect hideous, and his brows knit with anger; a trident in one of his four hands, a cimeter in a second, and in the other two, a bow and shafts. In PLATE 88. (*fig.* 8.) he is two-handed, with the bow and arrow, and mounted on a raven. In the other *Hindu* zodiac, which has been given to the public, he is, as noticed in page 285, riding an elephant, and has but two hands, and they are empty.

The elephant has been thought an appropriate vehicle for the sluggish "slow-moving son of SURYA," as referring to the immense scope of SATURN's orbit, and the apparent slowness of his motion. And SANI being, among the astrologers of *India*, as well as with their sapient brethren of *Europe*, a planet of malignant aspects, the ill-omened raven may also be deemed a fit *vahan* for such a dreaded being. But this is not, I think, a sufficient reason for the conspicuous introduction of the raven into the mythological machinery of the *Hindu* system, so accurate, so connected, and so complete in all its parts; although the investigations that it hath hitherto undergone have not fully developed or reached such points of perfection. Now let me ask the reason, why, both in *England* and in *India*, the raven is so rare a bird? It breeds every year, like the crow, and is much longer lived; and while the latter bird abounds every where to a degree bordering on nuisance, a pair of ravens, for they are seldom seen singly or in trios, are not found duplicated in any place. Perhaps, take *England* or *India* over, two pair of ravens will not be found on an average extent of five hundred or a thousand acres. I know not, for I write where I have no access to books, if our naturalists have sought the theory of this; or whether it may have first occurred to me, which it did while contemplating the character and attributes of SANI, that the raven destroys its young; and if this notion be well founded, and on no other can I account for the rareness of the annual-breeding long-lived raven, we shall at once see the propriety of symbolizing it with SATURN, or KRONOS, or TIME, devouring or destroying his own offspring.

The following astrological allegory will exhibit a specimen of the mythological veil through which even scientific facts must be viewed in the relations of *Hindu* writers.

In the reign of DASARAT'HA, the mortal father of RAMACHANDRA, in whose person VISHNU, as has been related, became incarnate, it happened that SANI, in his celestial journey, threatened a most inauspicious conjunction; and it was foretold to the king, by the sage VASISHT'HA, that unless he attacked the regent of the planet, neither INDRA, nor BRAHMA himself, could avert the continuance of the distressing drought, consequent to such aspects, for twelve years. DASARAT'HA attacked, and after a violent battle subdued, SANI, extorting from him a promise that he would never again, by a similar passage, (entering the *Hyads*, the *Rohini* of the *Hindus*, from the lunar mansion *Krittica*, their *Pleiades*; and this passage of SANI is called *Sakata-beda*, or the *section of the wane*,) threaten so unhappy a conjunction: a promise that he would keep until about our year 1796, which the *Hindu* astrologers have long predicted would be peculiarly inauspicious, as the noxious planet would then again approach the wain of ROHINI. And in this age we cannot, they say, look for a hero, like DASARAT'HA, in a miraculous car of pure gold, to place himself at the entrance of the wain, blazing like his progenitor the Sun, and drawing his bow, armed with the tremendous arrow *Sanharastra*, which attracts all things with irresistible violence—even SANI, "the slow-moving son of SURYA, dressed in a blue robe, crowned with a diadem; having four arms, holding a bow, a spiked weapon, and a cimeter:" thus, according to *Mr.* WILFORD, (*As. Res.* Vol. III. p. 461.) he is described in the *Brahmanda Puran*. The astrologers add, that MANGALA, or MARS, the child of PRIT'HIVI, has also been prevented from traversing the waggon of ROHINI; but that VRIHASPATI, SUKRA, and BUDDHA, or JUPITER, VENUS, and MERCURY, pass it freely and innocently; while it is the constant path of SOMA, or the Moon, of whom the beautiful ROHINI, or *α Aldeberan*, is the favourite consort.*—*Ib.*

Of VRIHASPATI, the regent of the planet JUPITER, we shall say but little, although he is in fact an important person, especially in astronomical calculations; giving his name to a cycle, and being, as with us, the hinge on which turns many interesting scientifical deductions: while, in mere mythology, I have only to notice him as the preceptor to the gods, and their occasional mes-

* This astronomical fable may, perhaps, be too loosely noticed in the *Puranas* to admit of any scientific calculus being grounded on it; otherwise, as it relates to a particular position of certain celestial bodies, in the reign of DASARAT'HA, that did not occur again until the year 1796, the times of these coincidences might possibly point to nearly the era of RAMACHANDRA: a very important point in respect both to the history and chronology of the *Hindus*.

senger from one to another. VRIHASPATI is supposed to have been also a legislator and a philosopher, and thus to have given his name and character to the planet, in which SIVA himself is said also to shine, while the Sun is the peculiar station of VISHNU; and SANI of BRAHMA, who hence became an object of abhorrence with the *Egyptians*, they not daring even to pronounce his true name, and abominating all animals with red hair, because it was his colour.—*Ib*. p. 382. Some enthusiastic individuals among the *Hindus* will not eat carrots, which appear to be indigenous all over *India*, because, I have been told, they look like beef; but possibly the objection may have a more remote origin.

Of HANUMAN, and his *Sire* PAVANA;

Of RAVANA; of GARUDA, and other *Characters* of less note.

THE honour of being father to HANUMAN is claimed by SIVA, and by PAVANA: the latter is the regent of winds, and, as we have seen in a former page, lord, or governor, more especially of the north-west quarter of the heavens. To explain this joint concern in the paternity of HANUMAN, I will briefly relate a legend from, as I understand, the *Ramayan*; it having been detailed to me by narrators of that extraordinary poem. For the reason given in page 192, I shall make my story as short as I can; but must premise that DASARAT'HA had three wives, KAHUNSILYA, or KAOSALYA, SUMITRA, and KAHIKEYA, but was childless; and after many fruitless efforts of piety, &c. betook himself, almost in despair, to the jungles, or forests—that is, to a life of abstinence and devotion. It happened that a *Brahman*, named SHRAVANA, was at this time resorting, with his aged and infirm parents, to a *jatra*, or holy fair; and the old people being faint with thirst, SHRAVANA went in search of water to a *Baburi*, (or *Bowrie*,*) near to which DASARAT'HA had taken his secret stand, expecting game. Hear-

* A *Bahuri* is a well with steps sloping down to the water, frequently met with in arid places, the grateful gift of pious *Hindus*: often have I, when nearly in the state of SHRAVANA's parents, offered up a prayer for the eternal welfare of the benevolent founders of this excellent species of charity. And here let me be allowed to notice, without giving offence, how much better it would be, if useful monuments were constructed by our grateful nation to the memory and honour of characters worthy of remembrance and celebrity, instead of useless triumphal arches, or pillars, or similar trophies. A naval asylum, for instance, to be called the NELSON, would, in my humble judgment, have a better effect in all desirable relations than all the idle obelisks the admiring nation can elevate, or than all the personal honours or wealth it can force into conspicuity; and surely a jet of water, so easily and cheaply attainable, in an ill supplied neighbourhood, or in the place of his nativity, would be an offering more grateful to the *manes* of departed heroism, than a useless inaccessible sepulchral stone. The citizens of *Dublin*, I have heard, erected, in a part of the city where water was most wanted, a public fountain, and, dedicating it to the memory of a just and benevolent ruler, called it RUTLAND; an act truly *Christian*, or *Hindu*-like. In the *Sivpuran*, it is promised, that he who, at *Benares*, makes a well, or tank, ensures to himself *muksh* (or beatitude); and restoring them when fallen to decay, obtains pardon for all crimes.

ing the gurgling of the water into SHRAVANA's vessel *(lota)*, he let fly his arrow, and hastening to his supposed game, discovered his unhappy error, and that he had wounded a *Brahman*. This he lamented deeply, but was consoled by the forgiving SHRAVANA, who desired that he might be left to die; directing DASARAT'HA to carry the *lota* of water to his infirm parents, who were perishing with thirst; cautioning him, at the same time, to present it in silence, lest his parents, who were blind from age, should, by his voice, discover the absence of their son, and refusing drink from any other hand, thus surely perish. He did as desired; but the affectionate parents, though so distressed, refused refreshment until cheered by their son's loved voice; and so afflicting was their anxiety, that DASARAT'HA, alarmed for their safety, was unable to withhold the fatal truth. The agonized parents sunk under the calamity, and, rejecting all aid or consolation, gave themselves up to grief and death; calling, in their last moments, on their son's loved name, and imprecating, in prophetic agony, a fate like their's on the unknown homicide, the wretched DASARAT'HA. Miserable, in thus having destroyed a *Brahman* and his parents, superadded to his constant affliction of being childless, he did not deprecate the fate they threatened; but declared that could he once behold the face of a son, now, from the sensations excited by the recent scene, more than ever desired, he would die contented.

DASARAT'HA, distracted by his trying situation, repaired, for advice and consolation, to a learned *Guru*, named VASISHT'HA, who directed him how to perform the funereal rites, and what sacrifices were necessary to be made in expiation of the enormous sin of slaying a *Brahman:* among them, that called *howm*, or *homa*, otherwise *yadnika*. All this was done with due extent of charitable distribution; and he was farther desired to take from the remains of the *homa* a portion of certain articles, such as rice, ghee, sugar, &c. and to make them into three cakes,* or balls; and, with pious devotion, repairing home, to give, after certain ceremonies, one cake to each of his three wives. He did so: one to the first named, one to the second, and to the third, named KAHIKEYA; but the latter, knowing herself the youngest and favourite wife, was pettish, and chagrined that she had not been the first complimented by her lord on his return from his expiatory absence; and looking disdainfully on it, as she held the *pind* of promise in her hand, a kite made a stoop, and carried it off. Grievously

* These balls are generally termed *pinda*, but have particular names according to the ceremonies in which they are offered, and to the object supplicated. An oblation, in view to progeny, of a *pinda* of rice, &c. to a *Linga*, is called *charu*; meaning, I believe, an offering of *hope*.

afflicted at this, and apprehensive that the ceremonies being incomplete, her chance of pregnancy was thereby forfeited, she gave way to grief and lamentation, which moved her two kind sharers in their lord's benevolence to give her each half of their better-guarded cakes; and those respective proportions were accordingly, with due anxiety and hope, severally eaten; and with due effect, for they soon all proved "as women wish to be, who love their lords."

KAHUNSILYA produced a son, the great RAMACHANDRA; SUMITRA a son also, the renowned LAKSHIMANA: the first being, indeed, an *Avatara* of VISHNU; and the second, of SHESHNAGA, the mighty thousand-headed serpent, on whom VISHNU reposes in *Vaikont'ha.*—(See page 29.) KAHIKEYA, having eaten a double portion of *pinda*, produced twins,* named BHARATA and SHATRUGNA.

Returning to the ravished cake, to the results of which all this is introductory, it is related, that a married *Brahmany*, named ANJENI, being childless, had piously performed divers acts leading to fecundity: such as supplication and sacrifice to MAHADEVA; daily prayers and offerings to a *part'ha*, or *linga*; the ceremony of *pradakshna*, or daily walking a certain number of times, with appropriate abstraction and prayers, round and round the *pipala*, or *Banian* tree; *jap*,† or, with silent devotion, counting the rosarial beads; abstinence, &c. &c. and had, by these powerful means, so extorted the favour of the generative deity, RUDRA, that he promised her an incomparable offspring; and directed her to fix her eyes in profound attention on the Sun, holding upwards the palms of her hands, (in the posture of suppliant expectancy, called *anjli*,) and to eat directly up any substance that might, heaven-directed, fall therein—calling on his name. The cake that the kite had borne off from KAHIKEYA fell in, and she ate it as ordered, and became pregnant; and in due season, (on the 15th day of the dark half of the lunar month *Chaitra*,) was delivered of a son, of such surpassing prowess, that at his birth he ground to powder a large stone that happened to be near, nor could his mother restrain him. This child was HANUMAN.

* SUMITRA, a name meaning *fair friend*, is, by some manuscripts, made the mother of the twins, instead of KAHIKEYA, or KIKEYI; but, in narratives, SUMITRA is the mother of LAKSHIMAN, who is, indeed, often called by her name. He espoused URMILA, daughter of JANEKA; and the twins, his half-brothers, married the *Rajas'* nieces. RAMA's wife, JANEKY, or SITA, is also called JANEKA's daughter, by adoption, she having, as noticed in p. 195, been produced out of the ordinary course of nature; being, indeed, an *Avatara* of LAKSHMI. She bore RAMA two sons, KUSHI and LAVA, great orators and minstrels.

† Hence *jap mala* is a rosary adapted for silent and abstracted worship.—See PLATE 22. and page 68.

The surprising boy, the immediate offspring of MAHADEVA's favour—rather, indeed, the DEVA himself, incarnate, became immediately hungry; and his desires—he already spoke, were commensurate with the magnificence of his origin: for he longed for the rosy radiance of the then rising sun, in lieu of the ordinary nourishment provided for him by nature and his mother; and the demur incident to the demand for this uncommon food, induced the vigorous boy himself to seek it: and he accordingly flew, like the wind, to seize the glory of SURYA, who, affrighted at the bold attempt, fled with his complaint, pursued by HANUMAN, to the abode of INDRA. The god of thunder, placing SURYA safely near him, launched his ever-ready *vajra*,* and smote the audacious chacer in the mouth, and felled him almost lifeless to the earth.

The share that PAVANA had in the production of HANUMAN appears to be confined to this: that he, PAVANA, commissioned a *Marut*, one of his subjects, to guard the dubious cake falling from the kite's beak, and to convey it with happy exactness into the hands of ANJENI; a task duly performed by the obedient well-directed zephyr, or *Marut:* and hence HANUMAN is called MARUTY, the offspring of MARUT, a name of PAVAN, or VAYU; all meaning wind: HANUMAN signifies, with puffed or *bloated cheeks*. I have heard MARUTY derived from MAHARUDRA,† the name of HANUMAN's other father; but MARUT is its obvious source, and such claim to the child, slight as it seems, is generally admitted; and the name, character, and actions of HANUMAN, confirm his windy or boisterous origin. In PLATE 80. PAVANA, or MARUT, is seen with the young HANUMAN, or MARUTY, in his arms.

PAVANA, afflicted and offended at his son's mishap, revenged himself by

* The *vajra* of INDRA is in fact lightning, as noticed in page 272; but it is sometimes described as similar to the *chakra* of VISHNU, being a *discus*, with a hole in the middle like our quoit, but the circle is larger, and the hole smaller for the introduction of the fore-finger. They are now seen occasionally in the hands of *Saniyasis*, and other holy people; about a foot in diameter, sharp at the edge, and thickening toward the central hole; on which it is quickly turned round the finger, and launched whirling at its devoted object. In pictures, fire is sometimes seen flaming from its periphery, as if from the vehemence of its centrifugal energy.—See p. 24.

† And, indeed, it may be so derived; for *ruda* and *rudra* mean *lamentation, tears:* and SIVA, as the lord of punishment, is, under his name of RUDRA, the god of tears and lamentation. When INDRA, dreading the progeny of the pregnant DITI, mangled with his *vajra* the fœtus in her womb, (see page 95,) and divided it into seven times seven pieces, he said to the weeping fœtus *ma ruda, weep not:* thus the parts were named. And having, at the request of the afflicted mother, been transformed by INDRA into the forty-nine immortal winds, they retained the general name of *Maruty*, time having effected a little alteration in it.—See *Ramayana*, Book I. Sect. 37.

giving INDRA and all the gods the colic: he inflated them to their fullest stretch, and closed their breathing orifices to a most painful pitch; and obstinately persisted in retaining the central position he had assumed, until the *Devas* consented to the restoration of MARUTY: to whom INDRA granted immortality, SURYA glory, CHANDRA celerity, KUVERA wealth, &c. &c. happy in being emptied and relieved of his troublesome sire, PAVANA. MARUTY, however, retained the cleft in his face, given him by INDRA's never-failing *vajra*; receiving as an atonement a magical *languti*, or girdle, rendering him invisible at will, and other benefits, in unity with the story of the *Ramayana*, in which all these incidents have a connected tendency to the *denouëment* and catastrophe of the work.

The husband of HANUMAN's mother was named VANYERA; and although the mother, ANJENI, is described as a *Brahmany*, yet by some casual anecdotes that help to diversify the narrative, they appear, like their son, to partake much of the monkey; their posterior appendage animating the witty narrator to some sly strokes of merriment, cordially enjoyed and returned by the audience.—(See note at the end of this account of HANUMAN.)

In the article of RAMA mention has been made of the simian hero now under our notice. It does not readily appear, why the offspring of such exalted parentage should have been a monkey; but as a popular idea is entertained on the continent of *India*, that *Ceylon* is still peopled by monkeys and demons, the priests and poets of the days of RAMA, or rather those who chronicled and sung his exploits, may have found a like impression then existing, and have constructed their epic machinery for the *Ramayana* in conformity to the public prejudices or taste.

As in the *Trojan* war the deities of the combatants personally interposed, so in that of *Lanka* did the divinities of *India:* many of them, by command of VISHNU, condescended to an immediate interference. "From the bodies," said he to all the gods, "of the chief *Apsaras*, the *Gand'harvas*, the daughters of the *Yakshas*, and the *Hydras*; from the Bears, the *Vidyadbaris*, the *Kinnaris*, and the female monkeys,— procreate sons, monkey-formed, in power equal to yourselves. From the mouth of me, wide gaping, has JAMBUVAN, the mighty bear, been already produced."—*Ramayana*, Sect. 16. The celestials produced accordingly a progeny of sylvan heroes, monkey-formed. "TAPANA," (the Sun; the name means the *Inflamer*,) "supremely fervid, begat SUGRIVA: INDRA gave birth to VALI, sovereign of the simian tribes, in splendour equalling his illustrious sire: VRIHASPATI produced the wise, the peerless TARA, the mighty ape, chief in renown amidst the monkey tribe: the son of DHANADA (KUVERA) was the fortunate GANDHA-MADANA: VISHWAKARMA begat the mighty ape, by name NALA: the son of PAVAKA," (AGNI; the word means the *purifier*,) "was NILA, the fortunate; resplendent as the fire; the hero surpassing in energy, fame, and valour: VARUNA was the parent of the monkey SUSHENA: the son of MARUT was HANUMAN, the fortunate; destructive as the thunderbolt, as swift as VINATEYA (GARUDA); excelling in wisdom amidst the chief monkeys."—*Ib.* "Thus were produced, by millions, monkeys able to assume any form: the great leaders of the simian tribes begat also a race of heroic monkey chiefs; a numerous host, ready to destroy the ten-headed" (RAVANA); "heroes of boundless energy, in size equal to elephants or mountains; incarnate; in haughtiness and might equalling the tiger and the lion; able to wield in combat rocks and mountains, and tremendously annoy the enemy with their tails and teeth: skilled in every kind of weapon they would remove the greatest mountains, pierce the stoutest trees, and in swiftness put to shame SAMUDRA,* the lord of rivers, causing him to overflow his bounds; and mounting in the air, seize the very clouds: they could seize inebriated elephants, and with their shout cause the feathered songsters to fall to the ground. For the sake of assisting RAMA was the earth covered with these mighty simian chiefs; in appearance resembling the assembled clouds, and in size appalling all with terror."—*Ib.*

Of the contests that ensued between these strange beings, and hordes of others equally strange who sided with RAVANA, and generally illustrative of the *Ramayana*, I have some scores of pictures: some of them are given in PLATES 52. to 57. Others refer to divers of the exploits of RAMA, LAKSHIMAN, HANUMAN, SUGRIVA, and their associate heroes, against the devoted RAVANA and his abettors. Among them is depicted the death of a very malignant *Yakshi*, named TAREKA, who it seems was the daughter of a virtuous *Yaksha*, named SUKETU; obtained through the propitiated favour of BRAHMA, and endowed by him with the strength of a thousand elephants. This blooming maid, famous, beautiful, and young, married to SUNDA, the son of JAMBHA, produced a son, MARICHA, scarcely to be conquered. SUNDA being killed, the widow and her son seized, and endeavoured to devour, AGASTYA, the divine sage, who cursed TAREKA into the form of a "*Yakshi*, a cannibal, deformed, with misshapen countenance, and terrific appearance;" and it became

* The Sea, which some *Hindu* writers assert flows with a swiftness exceeding any river.

necessary that RAMA should destroy her. But his humanity revolted against killing one "protected by her female nature," and he cut off her hands, then her ears and nose; but was urged by his *Mentor*, VISWAMITTRA, "for the sake of the bovine race and the *Brahmans*, to destroy this impious, horrid, and tremendous *Yakshi:* there being, in the three worlds, no man but thou, joy of RAGHU's race, who dares to destroy this accursed one."—*Ib.* Sect. 24. And was reminded, that DIRGA JIHWA (or *Long-tongue*) was killed by INDRA; and that the wife of BHRIGU, and mother of KAVYA, devoted to her husband, desiring the heaven of INDRA, was killed by VISHNU. These arguments and precedents, added to the incorrigible malignity of TARKA, overcame RAMA's scruples, and he killed her with an "arrow capable of perforating even a sound."—*Ib.*

The resemblance of the histories of RAMA and DIONYSOS has been noticed in page 190. The latter is said to have conquered *India* with an army of *Satyrs*, commanded by PAN: RAMA's army of *Satyrs* was commanded by the son of PAVAN, the all-pervading *Wind*. PAN improved the pipe by adding his reeds, making the instrument called by his name, and of late so much in use; and was an exquisite musician. HANUMAN was also a musical genius; and one of the four *matas*, or systems of *Hindu* music, is named after him.

It may, perhaps, have been in honourable remembrance of HANUMAN, that the large species of ape has been, and is, so much venerated by certain individuals and sects of *Hindus*. It is very ridiculous to watch their antics in the neighbourhood of some temples where they are protected and fed: hundreds of them may be seen together waiting for their food, and a stranger coming upon them unawares will put them to the rout; and it is highly diverting to see their agility in running up the neighbouring trees, and scampering over the fields and hedges—some with a young one under the arm, and a second clinging to their neck; and when in safety, their chattering and grinning.

The most numerous bodies of monkeys that I ever saw were on the banks of *Jyghur* river, between *Bombay* and *Goa*; and near the source of that river is a strong hill-fort, the capital of the *Raja* of *Panella*, called *Pavangher*; meaning the abode of PAVAN, or the *Winds*. In *Guzerat* apes also abound; and in that province is another strong hill-fort, likewise *Pavangher:* it otherwise, or, perhaps, the town rather, is called *Shampanir*, or *Champanir*; a name that I fancied might have been of *Mahummedan* origin, and derivable from شاہپنیر *Shah-panir*, the *refuge of kings*; but I find (in the ninth volume of the *As. Res.* p. 187.) that it was so called from a market-man who built it, named CHAMPA. This fort and town* were taken by the *Bombay* army, under my old and gallant friend *Colonel* WOODINGTON, in our late contest with the *Mahrata* confederates.

Of PAVAN, or VAYU, what I have to say, may be said here: he is, as often mentioned, also called MARUT, all names meaning the *Wind*, of which he is the personification, or regent: he is likewise called ANILA, and is sometimes represented mounted on an antelope, to mark his aerial celerity, with a sabre in his hand, denoting his energy and acuteness. I have no such picture of him, and he appears but in one of the plates of this work, (80.) where he is represented as a mere man, with his son HANUMAN in his arms. The lower part of PLATE 80. is from one picture; but I know of no relationship between the regents of Fire and Wind, or reason for their being drawn together: it may have been merely the whim or convenience of the person who painted the picture; or the connection may have some mythological or philosophical authority.

Considering the mythological machinery of the *Hindus*, as we are warranted in doing, as the invention of poets, it is not easy to account for their having chosen to represent their deities as immoral characters, when they might as well, so far as is apparent to common observation, have described them as patterns for imitation rather than as examples to deter: the observation, however, applies with equal force to the gods of the *Greeks*. Anecdotes related in former pages, and they might have been increased, have placed several of the deities in a discreditable light; and, in reference to PAVANA, we find him as wanton as his celestial brethren. We cannot, at the same time, deny, that, although such legends appear, in our present state of knowledge, to be merely whimsical and voluntary jocularity, there may still be physical facts concealed in the wildness of allegorical narration.

Of the regent of the wind it is related, that, unable to seduce the hundred peerless daughters of KUSHNABHA, "in beauty of form unparalleled through the earth," begat on GHIBATCHI, a celestial courtesan, he affected them by a curvature of the spine. "Seeing these damsels one day in the garden, appearing like the stars among clouds, endowed with youth and beauty, and possessed of every accomplishment; VAYU, pervading all, thus addressed them: 'I entreat you all be espoused to me; abandon the nature of man, and you shall obtain the blessing of longevity. Among mortals, youth is a transitory thing: possessed of unfading youth, you shall obtain immortality." Incensed at the decorous and

* Of which a good print has been lately published by CRIBB, in *Holborn*.

dutiful reply, which they concluded by saying, "Our father is our chief deity; to whomsoever he shall give us, him only will we espouse," the divine HARI, entering them, brake all their bodies. Thus broken by VAYU,* the damsels, overwhelmed with astonishment and shame, their eyes suffused with tears, entered the house of the king their father; saying, in reply to his anxious inquiries as to the cause of their deformity, touching his feet with their inclined foreheads,—"By VAYU, O king, who maintains the life of all, full of evil desire, and standing in an evil path; infatuated with this crime, and regardless of our words, have we been smitten in this dreadful manner." Their admiring father replied: "O daughters! you have acted nobly: forbearance is the great ornament of woman and of man; it is scarcely to be found even among the gods. O that forbearance like yours, O daughters! were possessed by all women: forbearance is generosity; forbearance is truth; forbearance is sacrifice: it is fame; it is virtue." The sequel of this tale shows the moral to be the efficacy of patience, and resignation to the will of heaven under any visitations, however distressing; for by such merits these forlorn damsels were successively espoused by a pious prince, named BRAHMA-DATA,† "by whose touch they became free from deformity, and shone refulgent in youth and prosperity."—*Ramayana*, Sect. 29. This event occurred at the city now called *Cannouj*, deriving its name, *Kanyakubja*, of which the former is a corruption, from *Kanya*, a damsel, and *Kubja*, a spinal curvature: so named, "because these damsels had there been made crooked by the power of VAYU;" from whose cruel exercise of his windy power they were thus happily released.

Some plates of HANUMAN remain to be described. In PLATE 90. he is represented, from a tinted picture, fighting with GARUDA; on the occasion, probably, noticed in page 218. *Fig.* 1. of PLATE 91. is from a curious cast in brass,

* HARI, a name of VISHNU, seems here applied to VAYU, who, in his windy form, so shamefully abused these good girls.

† This word means the *gift of* BRAHMA, *Deodand*. He was the gift of a holy *Rishi*, named CHULI, to his obsequious disciple, SOMADA, a *Gand'harva*; who, "acquainted with the graces of speech, in sweet accents said to the eloquent sage—'Conjoined with LAKSHMI, thou art an emanation of BRAHMA; thou art a great *Tapaswi*; thou art become BRAHMA himself. I am without a husband; may prosperity attend thee: I am the wife of no one; be pleased, by thy sacred power, to give thy humble suppliant a son." The sacred sage accordingly granted her a son, who was hence called the *gift of* BRAHMA, he having proceeded from the volition of CHULI; who, by *Tapas*, or intense devotion, reflecting on BRAHMA till fully possessed with the idea of identity with him, shared a portion of the deity's potentiality, or became, indeed, BRAHMA himself.—See *Ramayana*, Book I. Sect. 29.

in *Lord* VALENTIA's collection. It is of the size represented, and well cast; the parts that are white in the plate being perforations, in the style something of fillagree-work: the *chank* and *chakra* of VISHNU are seen in the exterior circle; the lotos flower, *pedma*, in HANUMAN's right hand: the other flourishing articles, in the central part of the plate, are his flowing robes. By the prostrate armed figure, at his feet, I conclude some warlike exploit of this simian hero is represented: the crushing, perhaps, of AKSHA, son of RAVANA. Near the extremity of his exalted tail is a little bell, this tinkling article being popularly gifted with the power of scaring evil spirits. But the most singular part of this subject is the figure of KRISHNA, in one of his infantine attitudes, as represented in PLATE 60. He is in PLATE 91. evidently a person of secondary importance; and here we see a mark of sectarial arrogance: one sect of *Vaishnavas*, that of *Ramanuj*, introducing the deity of another sect, the *Gokalast'ha*, in a situation of inferiority to a servant of their own deified hero, and that servant too a monkey—of no ordinary mould, it is true. The other five figures in PLATE 91. are from casts of the same size, and of some merit, *fig.* 2. especially, where HANUMAN is again seen in his warlike capacity: in the next three, (3. 4. and 5.) he is in a posture of prayer or supplication: *fig.* 6. is a cast of a mere monkey, of what description I cannot say; whether of any particular personage or not—it may answer for any one, and is introduced to fill up the plate.

Fig. 5. of PLATE 92. is the same subject as *fig.* 1. of PLATE 91: but handled in a very inferior style: in this KRISHNA does not appear. *Fig.* 1. of PLATE 92. is a part only of a cast, being made separate for the purpose of insertion into corresponding sockets, behind any figure of RAMA, who would then appear with HANUMAN surmounted by NAGA; in the same manner that HANUMAN is seen with KRISHNA so surmounted, in PLATE 91. where, however, the coronal ornament is fixed on the cast. I am not aware that NAGA, being five, seven, or single-headed, indicates any sectarial or characteristic distinction; but perhaps it may.

Fig. 2. of PLATE 92. is a *gant'ha*, or bell, used in the *puja*, or ceremonial offerings, of a *Ramanuj*; its handle being formed of HANUMAN, with his tail curled over his head. I have several similar bells: *fig.* 3. I imagine to have been also a bell; but, if so, its mouth is now covered over with a sheet of copper: the handle is formed of HANUMAN and GARUDA, back to back, reminding us a little of JANUS *bifrons*; but I do not know of any legends appertaining to either of those heroes, tending to approximate them in character to the GANESA of the *Roman* Pantheon.—See p. 173.

PLATE 93. is taken from two pretty coloured pictures, in *Colonel* STUART's collection, and is, perhaps, as being the most elaborate, the most difficult to explain of any in our work; and I am not at all confident of being able to explain them satisfactorily. In the upper part we see HANUMAN ten-armed: he is of a light copper colour, with a deep red face: the body in one of his right hands is of a dead-flesh colour, and more emaciated and corpse-like than the plate represents it. In view to the farther explanation of this subject, I will briefly relate the outline of the legend to which I apprehend a part of it refers.

During the war of *Lanka*, RAMA and a great part of his army were rendered insensible by the potency of certain magical weapons; the effects of which could be removed only by the application of a certain herb before the next rising of the moon. This herb was not a native of the southern parts of *India*—indeed it grew only on a particular hill in the north, whither HANUMAN repaired with inconceivable celerity; and arriving at the hill, called *Dun*, or *Dun-giri*, proceeded, as advised, to seek the shrub, which was to be particularised by a lamp under it: but HANUMAN was sorely perplexed at finding a lamp under every shrub and tree on the hill, placed there by the advice of the malignant INDRA. Enraged at being thus baffled, he indignantly tore up the whole mountain; and in PLATE 93. is seen poising it in one hand: the mountain is painted red. Passing over the city of *Ayodha (Oude)*, the rapidity of his movements caused much concussion in the air; and BHARATA, RAMA's half-brother, supposing it to proceed from some spirit of darkness, let fly an arrow, and brought HANUMAN and his ponderous burden to the ground; but seeing his mistake, offered, in view to the urgency of HANUMAN's speedy return, to launch him on an arrow in an instant to *Lanka:* which mode of conveyance was declined by HANUMAN, who proceeded on his journey as before; but some time having been lost by the accident of his fall, he perceived, from his elevation, the refracted rays of the rising moon; and to avert the fatal consequence of being so forestalled, he hid CHANDRA in his mouth: and thus arriving in time, revivified RAMA, LAKSHMAN, and their astounded associates.

I do not apprehend that the plate now under description relates exclusively to this, or to any one of HANUMAN's exploits, but to be a sort of epitome of his character or actions: thus the beings trodden under his feet I judge to relate to another of them, wherein it is stated that a woman, having, in consequence of a misdemeanor, been transformed into a fish by the imprecation of an offended *Muni*, she was fated to remain in that shape until the coming of RAMA;

and then it seems her restoration was to be effected by contact with HANUMAN, who, accidentally treading on the fish, would overcome, by his virtue and potency, the effects of sorcery. The exorcised, in gratitude, having informed her deliverer that some recent counsel, received from a pretended sage, was in fact given by a necromancer to impede his progress and the success of RAMA, HANUMAN trod also on and crushed the sorcerer; as is seen in PLATE 93. and perhaps *fig*. 1. of PLATE 91. and *fig*. 5. of PLATE 92. may likewise exhibit this latter fact. The woman so restored was then named MATSYA-DERY: *matsya*, a *fish*, and *dery*, a *step*, give the etymology of her name, and the nature of her metamorphosis. In the tinted picture the woman is copper-coloured, the man dark. But as the reader may be tired with any farther relation of supposed legends, I will conclude this account by briefly observing, that HANUMAN appears on this occasion full-gifted: he bears the *trisula* of his reputed father, SIVA, the sword of KAL, and a corpse emblematical of death; the *gadda* of VISHNU; the *pasba*, or cord, of VARUNA; the never-failing shield of LAKSHIMAN; the *ankas* (hook) of GANESA; the all-yielding tree *(parijata)* of INDRA; and the sacrificial vase of BRAHMA.

The four animals in HANUMAN's coronet are also somewhat perplexing: they relate, I imagine, to some victorious exploits of his, that I am not acquainted with, over these animals, or over demons who had assumed their forms. The animals are a horse, a boar, a lion, and a bird: the horse is a sort of armorial bearing of RAVANA, its head being often seen in pictures peeping over his crown; it is also seen similarly in pictures of *Raja* DIRUJ, slain by PARUSU RAMA, (see p. 190); sometimes, indeed, it is rather long-eared, and looks as much like an ass. There is something in the history of the RAMAS connected with the horse that has not been hitherto explained: the tenth-coming incarnation is to be on a white horse, and offers as much scope for ingenious speculation—which has, indeed, been amply bestowed upon it, as its fellow quadruped of our apocalypse. In the picture HANUMAN's horse is painted white: the boar's head is black. This animal is of much import in *Hindu* annals: it was, as we have seen, the shape assumed by VISHNU in one of his *Avataras:* it gives a name to a *kalpa*, or cycle, and is seen embossed on very ancient coins; some of which are in my possession, and will be given with this work, if the plate can be finished in time. The lion is *proper*, and may advert either to the *Narasingavatara*, to the vehicle of DEVI, or to some *Herculean* achievement: but the bird, which looks like a parrot, and is green, is, perhaps, the most puzzling. It is not, I think, intended for GARUDA, on whom RAMA in some of my pictures is riding, but referrable rather to a famous bird, called *Jettahi-paksha*, or *Jatayu*, otherwise called *Sampat*; and although he has an epithet equivalent to *king of the vultures*, he is sometimes painted more like a parrot, or peacock. I have a coloured picture representing the rape of SITA by RAVANA: he is bearing her through the air, with the parrot-like bird holding assailingly on his great toe. This bird, like RAVANA, was endued with topical prowess: shorn of this, he became like other birds. His attack on the giant was so vigorous, that the latter was fain to demand a parley, with the insidious view of ascertaining wherein the bird's *marran*, or supernatural strength, consisted; affecting first to communicate the secret respecting his own, which he said lay in the great toe of his right foot: deprived of this, he became like other men. The bird, however, suspecting treachery, made several evasive shifts; but on RAVANA's imprecating a dreadful curse on prevarication, and demanding an answer on the truth and purity of RAM himself, the bird was staggered; and previously demanding his adversary's secret, revealed his own: which was, that his *marran* was in the long feather of his tail. RAVANA, learning this, renewed the fight: SAMPAT tugged at his toe, but in vain: the giant had lied, and plucking out the potential feather, triumphed over poor SAMPAT, who, in a mode somewhat *Samsonian*, yielded the victory and his life; and had the honour of magnificent obsequies performed by RAMA, in whose cause, and in the act of invoking his name, he had lived and died. I should judge these animals to have particular allusions, rather than as general symbols of HANUMAN's character; giving him, as hath been suggested, the courage and ferocity of the lion, the strength of the boar (with the *Hindus*, a symbol of might), the energy of the horse, and the activity or celerity of the bird; or, perhaps, the drawing may have been made from a statue, in which the whole ten *Avataras* of VISHNU (or RAMA, according to his sectaries,) may be exhibited, with GARUDA; but not being at once in the eye of the draughtsman, he gave only what he saw. The *Hindus* feign that the four holy rivers of *Eden* flow through the mouths of as many animals; viz. the cow, lion, elephant, and horse: but these do not agree with those on HANUMAN's head—and if they did, the application is not evident.* After all, we leave the subject pretty much as we found it: an intelligent *Brahman* would at once explain every particular, even to the black tip of HANUMAN's tail; which, he would tell us, is indelible from an accident

* Nor do they agree with the *four beasts* of *Revelation*, iv. 7. the lion, calf, man-faced, and eagle.

that befel him in the war of *Lanka*; in revenge for which, he burnt and destroyed RAVANA's dwelling, servants, &c. and the whole country, save the garden, *Asoka*, where SITA was confined. The accident was, that, on an occasion not necessary to relate, he burnt his tail.

But there is no end to the legends that might be brought forward to the illustration of the curious subjects composing PLATE 93. which never, but in *Colonel* STUART's pictures, and that lately, came under my observation. The lower part of this plate is still more perplexing: it represents an extraordinary sort of *Hypogrif* that appeared to LAKSHIMAN; who, in astonishment at its non-descript appearance, is performing the respectful ceremony of *Pradakshna*, which consists in circumambulating several times the person, (parent, *guru*, or superior,) *linga*, image, temple, tree, or whatever object is to be reverenced, keeping, with closed palms, the right hand and the face towards it.

The subject now under our notice I have called VIRATARUPA, one of VISHNU's names; an epithet meaning an *universal monarch-form*, (see page 179,) and applied by *Vaishnava* sectarists, and perhaps by others, to the warlike hero of their exclusive adoration: in this case, I apprehend, it is intended to epitomize the achievements and attributes of RAMA or VISHNU; but, in a symbolical or hieroglyphical mode, not to be understood by the uninitiated. The neck and head of the bird are blue, and like a peacock's, and allude, I imagine, to the *Jettaya-paksha* before mentioned: it is swallowing a city, emblematical, like *Maha-pralaya*, in PLATE 10. of the consummation of all things. The uplifted man's hand holds the *gadda* of VISHNU, the club of *Fate*; the hand is copper-coloured: the mace of gold, with rubies and emeralds: the wrist is encircled by a serpent with its tail in its mouth, a happy emblem of eternity. The left fore-foot and shoulder are an elephant's; black, with gold chains: the hump on the shoulders is white, inserted in green feathers, or weeds: the body is yellow, and striped like a tiger's, to which the right hind-foot appertains: the four wings are green, fringed with gold; as the wings of *Kalki*, the white horse of VISHNU's expected advent, and the wings of GARUDA, are sometimes painted: the left hind-thigh and leg seem a horse's; brownish, with a gold ring over the hoof: the tail is formed of a black snake,* with a white throat and belly. Some birds, and a butterfly, with flowers, are the only decorations of the picture: LAKSHIMAN has nothing particular; his bow and shafts are grounded beside him.

* ——— "Their power is in their mouths, and in their tails; for their tails were like unto serpents, and had heads, and with them they do hurt."—*Rev.* ix. 19.

HANUMAN has appeared several times in former plates: in PLATE 53. he is seen, assisted by SUGRIVA (or *Fair-neck*), and their associates, building the bridge of rocks, from the continent to *Ceylon*, for the passage of RAMA's army, in the war of *Lanka*.* Some accounts make the mighty monkey, NALA, the son of

* In a note of the *Ayin Akbery*, (Vol. III. page 36. *Çalcutta* edit. apparently written by *Mr.* REUBEN BURROWES,) it is said that *Lanka* is not *Ceylon*, as hath been generally supposed, but a place determined by the intersection of the equator and the meridian of *Dehli*, answering to the southern extremity of the *Maldivey* islands.—" Indeed," the note continues, " there are many reasons for concluding *Lanka* to have been part of the *Taprobane* of the ancients; and that *Taprobane*, or, more properly, *Tapobon*, which, in *Sanskrit*, signifies the *wilderness of prayer*, was a very large island, including the whole, or the greater part, of the *Maldivey* islands, which have since been destroyed by inundations. This agrees very well with PTOLEMEY's description; and his island of monkeys seems to relate to those in the *Ramayan*."

The text in this part is avowedly obscure, and an error seems to have arisen somewhere: many arguments, if not proofs, may be adduced as to the identity of *Lanka* and *Ceylon*, and, perhaps, *Taprobane*. *Lanka* was the theatre of RAMA's exploits with its tyrannical sovereign, RAWAN; otherwise pronounced RAVAN, RABAN, RABON, RAVENA, RAWANA: the two latter are the most correct modes of spelling and pronunciation. Nor can there be much doubt of the island, that we now call *Ceylon*, having formed a part, at any rate, of that theatre, which might in former times have been of greater extent than that island is at present.

I have been informed, but am not certain if correctly, that, in *Sanskrit* books, *Ceylon* is called *Tapa-Rawan*: which may be equally correctly spelled and pronounced *Tapo-raban*; or, indeed, in common discourse, *Taprobana*, or *Taprobane*; as it is by PTOLEMEY. Much stress, under such a circumstance of doubt, is not to be laid on conjectural etymology: but, it may be observed, as tending to strengthen such conjecture, that the well-known traveller, PURANA PURI, (of whom an interesting account, and a picture, is given by *Mr.* DUNCAN in the fifth volume of the *As. Res.* Art 2.—See p. 162.) noticed a tank in *Ceylon*, called the " tank of RAVAN, or RABAN, (the *b* and *v* being pronounced indifferently in various parts of *India*,) from whom this *Tapu*, or island, may probably have received its ancient appellation of *Taprobane*, (i. e. the isle of RABAN): here also is a place, or pool, called *Sita-koond*, where RAMA placed his wife SITA on the occasion of the war with the ravisher RAVAN."

As the first meridian of the *Hindus* passed through *Ujayini (Oojein)* and *Lanka*, the latter cannot be *Ceylon*, if confined to its present extent. *Oojein* is in about 76°, and the westernmost part of *Ceylon*, in 80° east of *Greenwich*: the difficulty seems reconcilable only by supposing what is, indeed, asserted in *India*, that *Ceylon* was formerly of much greater extent than at present. And it is said, that appearances, between that island and the *Maldives*, justify a belief of their having been once joined.—See *As. Res.* Vol. III. p. 44.

In HAMILTON's account of the *East Indies*, (Vol. I. p. 142.) a map of the peninsula has one of the *Maldiva* islands marked *Hunnamandow*, and the southern part of the peninsula is marked RAM's *point*.—In page 348, he says, that in *Hunnamandow*, which lies in 7 degrees of latitude, he saw carving on some tombstones as ingeniously cut, with variety of figures, as ever he saw in *Europe* or *Asia*. The name of HUNUMAN occurring on the *Maldiva* islands affords farther room for suspecting a connection between those islands and the history of RAM, RAWAN, *Lanka*, &c.

of the divine architect, VISWAKARMA, the builder of this bridge. SUGRIVA, the son of SURYA, seems the next in rank to HANUMAN in this extraordinary * army: he is in great favour with RAMA. VALI, the son of INDRA, having usurped SUGRIVA's kingdom, they fought a desperate battle; and VALI was

RAMA's bridge, called in our maps, ADAM's bridge, an imaginary or poetical connection of the peninsula and *Ceylon*, is styled in *Hindu* writings, the *southern bridge*: it is now merely a series of rocks, some of which appear above water, whatever it may have been formerly. *Ceylon* very probably was, in ancient times, joined to the continent. In a royal grant of land, given in the third volume of the *As. Res.* Art. 3. the phrase, "from *Hemadri* to the southern bridge," is used as implying extent of dominion; "and the king became universally celebrated from the northern bank of the *Ganga* to *Lanka*, the equinoctial point:" again, "from the southern bridge to *Sumeru*," the north pole: it is also therein called "RAMA's bridge."

At the southern extremity of the peninsula stands the celebrated temple, sacred to VISHNU in his *Avatara* of RAMA, called *Ramiswara*; or, in its neighbourhood, *Ramisseram*, conformably with the *Tamul* and *Kanara* termination of names, ending with a vowel or a liquid. This temple, as well as *Ceylon*, has been recently visited by *Lord* VALENTIA, and will doubtless have attracted the particular attention of that inquisitive and observing traveller, with whose interesting work the literary world will shortly be gratified.

PTOLEMEY's island of monkeys, and the conspicuous part acted by those animals in the wars of the *Ramayana*, offer a farther mark of identity. Let it be noticed also, that, to this day, on the continent of *India*, *Ceylon* is spoken of as inhabited only by monkeys and monsters: and I was well acquainted with a very good man, and very intelligent also, who went to this island with my kind and greatly-respected friend *Mr*. F. NORTH, as *munshi* to his Excellency, and wrote what he called a history of *Ceylon*, in which he confirms the popular opinion; himself, no doubt, firmly believing that the interior, if not the coasts, which only he was personally acquainted with, was not inhabited by human beings of ordinary shapes. This historian, who was also a poet, is dead; and I would mention his name with regard, for he was one of the best *Mussulmans* I ever knew, but such an anecdote coupled with it might not, perhaps, add to the respectability of his memory.

* I am inclined to the opinion, that the *Ramayana*, like the *Mahabarat*, is allegorical, so far as relates to personal adventures; which, in both cases, are mere machinery for bringing forwards a concealed system of philosophy and ethics: in the first instance, the allegory is *physical*; in the latter, *moral*. The monkeys are winds, or gazeous metaphors: the *pandus* and *kurus* are, as before mentioned, (p. 92,) virtues and vices. In the *Ramayana* we find the machinery consisting of (personifications of) the Sun and planets, Fire, the Firmament, Wind, Water. It has been noticed in a former page, that the histories of KRISHNA and RAMA are similar in several instances.—(See page 195.) And, in addition, it may be observed, that both are the destroyers of the fiends KUMBA and NIKUMBA: both have adventures with the bear JAMBA, or JAMBAVANTI: both are the slayers of the *asuras*, NARANTEKA and DEVANTEKA.—See. p. 215. When these two fine poems, the *Mahabarat* and *Ramayana*, shall appear in *English*, and their allegories be more fully examined, it may, perhaps, be found, that not only the three RAMAS will melt into one, but that all will amalgamate with KRISHNA. The missionaries of *Serampore* have hitherto published only the first *Kanda*, or book, of the *Ramayana*, which, in the whole, comprises seven *Kandas*, viz.

afterwards killed by RAMA, who reinstated his friend. PLATE 54. exhibits HANUMAN (five-headed, a distinction inherited from his parent, SIVA,) conveying, on his extended arms, RAMA and SITA; and, in the lower compartment, he is seated on his spontaneously-elongated tail, at an audience with the ten-headed twenty-handed tyrant RAVANA, as is noticed in p. 193, where several other plates containing figures of this heroic character, are sufficiently described.

1. *Adi Kanda*	containing	64 Sections, and	2850 *Shlokas*, or metrical stanzas.
2. *Ayodhya Kandya*	———	80 ———	4170
3. *Aranyaka Kanda*	———	114 ———	4150
4. *Keshkindha Kanda*	———	64 ———	2925
5. *Sundara Kanda*	———	43 ———	2045
6. *Yudha Kanda*	———	105 ———	4500
7. *Uttara Kanda*	———	90 ———	3360
			24,000

NOTE.

In almost every part of *India* is met a description of persons who publicly narrate, to admiring audiences, stories or legends from the heroic and amatory histories. So much is this the general taste, that with many it is an accomplishment commenced in early life; and females are found to possess it in a degree adding greatly in the estimation of their admirers to their other fascinations. The extreme beauty of the moon-light nights in *India* peculiarly invites to this species of recreation: in towns, the buildings with opened terraced tops, secured from intrusive eyes, and in the country, enclosed gardens, are well adapted to the tranquil enjoyment of the refreshing coolness so delectable after the heat and tumult of the day. And in a country where, from frequent political changes and the general tendency of *Asiatic* governments, convivial or confidential intercourse forms so small a portion of the bliss of life, we may reasonably conclude that such nights, passed with beautiful women in listening to such tales, varied by interludes of music, dancing, singing, the *huka*, and betel, constitute the most exquisite recreative enjoyment that *Hindustany* gentlemen are in the habit of experiencing. Nor must we, although being denied admittance into the recesses of the *haram* we cannot be sure, too hastily conclude that SURADEVI (see p. 183,) is never invoked on these occasions by the *Hindu*: by *Brahmans*, and by individuals of the higher classes, it is likely that abstinence from intoxicating beverages is pretty strictly observed; but with the rest, and among *Mussulmans*, no species of indulgence is forbidden: pleasure and happiness are welcomed under whatever forms they may assume.

The tales recited on these occasions are as varied as the tastes, or as the imagination and ingenuity of man: portions of heroic history from the *Mahabarat* or *Râmayan*, or other similar works, are oftenest the subjects of public declaimers; who sometimes read, but more commonly recite from memory. In large towns they fix themselves in some open room, or, in fine weather, in the open air, the neighbours knowing where and when to seek them: in the country they travel from town to town, attended frequently by women, who play on some instrument as a kind of accompaniment to the drawling sort of nasal recitative of the principal performer, who sometimes exhibits in succession a series of pictures illustrating the history he recites. The loves and wars of KRISHNA, and of RAMA, rank the highest in popular estimation; and camps, above all places, abound in the gratification I am describing. Among *Mussulmans*, and, indeed, among *Hindus* likewise, tales from the *Arabian Nights* are much admired: I have heard several well told by *Hindu* females.

Nor must we omit to notice another description of itinerant orators, not, when uncompared in elegance, dissimilar to the *Improvisatori* of *Italy*, who, to a memory well stocked with chivalrous and mythologic lore, add the facility of spouting extemporaneous verses on the passing occurrences of the day. The operations of armies, or any thing that is attracting public attention, are taken as the subject; and the poet, by acquiring two or three leading events and the names of a dozen officers, can, by occasionally drawing on his memory for an often-told description, and varying it a little from the stores of his imagination, celebrate a battle or a campaign with reasonable accuracy and interest. A very inferior composer of this description was in the habit of resorting every evening for a considerable time to my house in *Bombay*, (to the day, indeed, of my departure thence,) to the great edification and delight of the children and servants, who would listen to him for an hour with attentive pleasure. This poor man was blind; and hence, if in no other point, could not fail of bringing to recollection, and, although himself the last and lowest, leading the imagination back to, the great-grandfather of his tribe.

To all these sources of popular instruction may be added another, not uncommon: which is a travelling puppet-show, dramatising interesting events, historical, civil, heroic, or religious. As most of these advantages, such as they are, can be easily and cheaply attained by all ranks of people, for no money is demanded (individuals give nothing, or as much or little as they please), it follows, that a great proportion of the citizens of *India* have some, and some a great, knowledge of its ancient and modern history; and as mythology is so plentifully blended with every thing that a *Hindu* can think or do or say, an individual above the class of a labourer is rarely met who has not some smattering in that species of *learning*.

In grateful return for such portion of the recreations here enumerated as have fallen to my lot to partake of, I have endeavoured to add to their number by constructing a magic-lanthorn; where, instead of the gambols of devils and saints, usually exhibited in our phantasmagoria, I have introduced the deities and heroes of the *Hindu* Pantheon; who, from their many-headed, many-armed, and other striking attributes, are peculiarly adapted to this description of *chiar'oscuro*. I please myself with the idea, that the exhibition of these figures, in addition to some holy and sacred hieroglyphics, will divert my old friends at my antipodes, and add to their common stock of innocent enjoyments.*

In such a country, where, with many, love (with which term, for want of a better, we must dignify the passion,) is more than half, and with others all, the business of life, it cannot be imagined that amatory topics are handled with the delicacy observed and admired in colder climes, where society is refined to elegance: generally speaking, the reverse is the case in *India*; and much that we should call grossness is listened to without offence by very decent individuals and audiences in *Hindustan*. In the common conversation incident to the usual occupations of life, expressions, that if given even in a dead language could not be written or read without a blush, perpetually occur. Parents in low, and in not very low, life,

* These magic-lanthorns and slides are well made by *Mr.* HARRIS, an ingenious optician in *Holborn*: some have been taken as articles of traffic to *India*, where it is probable they will have an extensive and profitable sale.

would not think of rebuking a child for applying in their presence terms that no *European* child, perhaps, ever was allowed, or, if he conceived them, dared, to use. In this, however, as in most other unpleasant things, an advantage may happily be discerned: blasphemy is unknown: with a tolerable knowledge of the common dialect, and a smattering of some others, I know of no expression bordering on blasphemy; nor could an epithet out of our copious vocabulary of such terms be put into the languages of *India*, otherwise than by a very circumlocutory process. Let it, however, be remembered, that indecency or grossness should be understood in reference to time and place: what is very gross in *England* may not be at all so in *India*; where, as *Sir* W. JONES has observed, that any thing natural can be offensively obscene seems never to have occurred either to the people or their legislators: a singularity pervading their writings and conversation, but no proof of moral depravity. And what at this time would, on the *English* stage, be disgusting and abominable, was not deemed indelicate in the days of ELIZABETH, and in times much more recent.

RAVANA, a name meaning *tyrant*, is also called DASAGRIVA, the *ten-necked*; and, as noticed before, (page 276,) PULASTYA; and VISRAVANA, as son of VISRAVA, the father also of KUVERA. His numerous heads, and his twenty hands, are the usual symbols of dominion and strength. It is said, in the *Ramayana*, that "where RAVANA remains, the Sun loses his force; the winds *(maruts)* cease to blow; the fire ceases to burn; the rolling ocean, seeing him, stills its waves." For his predestined destruction VISHNU became incarnate in the person of RAMA; and the events leading to it form the story of the *Ramayana*, wherein unity of action is said to be strictly observed. RAVANA is styled lord of *Rakshashas*, malignant beings; many specific varieties of which are enumerated in the first section of the first book of the poem, aiding him in defence of himself and his kingdom of *Lanka*. They are a marvellous ill-looking set; in many of my pictures painted green, blue, and red, and engaged in fierce contests with RAMA's monkeys. Several legions of these demons, each of 14,000, commanded by SURPANAKA, KHARA, DUSHANA, TRISHIRA, &c. were, with their leaders, destroyed by RAMA. RAVANA obtained his potency by the usual process of self-inflicted severities; and so ardent was he, that he offered to SIVA nine of his ten heads successively, and so extorted the favour of the condescending deity, that, pleased with such an important sacrifice, (see page 105,) he promised to grant, with some stipulations, whatever the rigid devotee should desire. The *Devatas*, alarmed, besought SIVA to recal his word; but such conduct is deemed unbecoming in deities, who, however, do not scruple to evade the performance of their promises by some deceit or prevarication; and SIVA deputed NAREDA to sound RAVANA as to what he would demand, which, as usual, was universal dominion, &c. NAREDA artfully persuaded RAVANA that MAHADEVA had been drunk, and had promised him what he could not perform: whereupon the vindictive giant tears up *Kailasa*, the *Paradise* of SIVA; which being contrary to the stipulations, releases SIVA from his promise, and he consents to the destruction of RAVANA: which is brought about by the *Avatara* of RAMA. From this story we may learn that all worldly affairs are the predestined ordainments of Providence; whose will that any event should take place on earth includes presciently all the routine and detail of its accomplishment, although we only see the links of a chain of causes leading naturally to its effect.

Respecting RAVANA I will notice but one tale, related to me by a *Brahman*, who, unable to make me feel the poetical beauties, or fully comprehend the morality of the *Ramayana*, blushed while he developed its follies; which, in conformity with popular tastes, or if taken separately, are apparently very numerous, although it must be confessed they are so contrived as to be intimately connected with the action of the poem. The following idle tale is of this description; but I shall not attempt to explain the causes that led to it, or the consequences that ensued.

RAVANA, by his power and infernal arts, had subjugated all the gods and demigods, and forced them to perform menial offices about his person and household. INDRA made garlands of flowers to adorn him withal: AGNI was his cook: SURYA supplied light by day, and CHANDRA by night: VARUNA purveyed water for the palace: KUVERA furnished cash: the whole *nava-graha* (the *nine planetary* spheres enumerated in page 281,) sometimes arranged themselves into a ladder, by which, they serving as steps, the tyrant ascended his throne: BRAHMA (for the great gods were there also; and I give this anecdote as I find it in my memoranda, without any improved arrangement—BRAHMA) was a herald, proclaiming the giant's titles, the day of the week, month, &c. daily in the palace—a sort of speaking almanac: MAHADEVA, in his *Avatara* of KANDEH-RAO, performed the office of barber, and trimmed the giant's beards: VISHNU had the honourable occupation of instructing and drilling the dancing and singing girls, and selecting the fairest for the royal bed: GANESA had the care of the cows, goats, and herds: VAYU swept the house: YAMA washed the linen; and in this manner were all the gods employed in the menial offices of RAVANA, who rebuked and flogged them in default of industry and attention. Nor were the female divinities exempted; for BHAVANI, in her name and form of SATWI, was head *Aya*, or nurse, to RAVANA's children: LAKSHMI and SARASWATI were also among them, but it does not appear in what capacity. Earthly kings and queens were likewise forced into the service of RAVANA, to the number of ninety-six royal families, as is said to be detailed in the *Ramayana*; but I have some doubt if such a relation be actually in this shape in that poem: this we shall see when its other books be translated and published. In my abstract of it, however, such a godly predicament seems essential to the main action, RAMA being thereby impelled by every consideration of piety and duty to immediate and energetic measures for the relief and liberation of the degraded divinities.

RAVANA is seen in PLATES 52. and 54. in situations sufficiently described in former pages; and we will now speak of GARUDA.

This animal, half-bird half-man, is the *vaban* or vehicle of VISHNU, and is very frequently introduced into the pictures of the *Vaishnavas* carrying the deity, with or without LAKSHMI: by their sectarists, KRISHNA and RAMA, identified with the preserving power, are sometimes mounted on this vehicle of their archetype. In PLATE 10. we see VISHNU and LAKSHMI, lotos-seated, on the back of GARUDA, whose celerity is proverbial, cleaving the air. From holding bows and shafts, attributes more particularly distinguishing RAMA, the picture that the lower part of PLATE 10. is taken from was perhaps painted by a *Ramanuj*, and RAMA and SITA will then be the persons represented; but the presence of HANUMAN is required to render it certain. In the picture GARUDA has a red comb and beak; his robe is red; his face, arms, legs, and pinions, green; the feathers of his wings and tail, green and blue. The sun is seen rising in a very beautiful style over a mountain forming the back-ground; beneath is a river with the lotos floating in it, and aquatic birds are sporting on its banks. Green, red, and blue, are the predominant colours in pictures of GARUDA, of which I have many; and there are some points in family and character of this cherub, or man-eagle, indicating that he is a personification of the Sky, the ethereal vehicle of VISHNU as the Sun.—See pages 16. 30.

In our series of plates GARUDA next appears in PLATE 18. where, as before noticed, (p. 64,) he is seen, in the original picture tinted nearly as above described, bestridden by VISHNU: in which style he appears in several compartments of the *Elephanta* cave, and somewhat ridiculously, as is noticed in p. 97. It is not pleasant to recur to invidious reflections, but I must here again notice the hellish bigotry of the *Portuguese* in wreaking destruction on this magnificent temple, especially on its most prominent features; and poor GARUDA's beak coming under this description, it has in no instance escaped. Were it not for their lamentable effects, these holy freaks of the *Portuguese Christians*, as they term themselves, would afford scope for ridicule; for they proceed *(risum teneatis)*, from their abhorrence of idolatry!*

* No one at all speculative can have examined the excavations on *Elephanta*, and in its neighbourhood, without occasionally recalling to his recollection the sensations they excited, and indulging probably some reflections on the origin and end of these extravagant works. It may have been with the ancient *Hindus* a love of seclusion that moved them to execute such stupendous labours in places not easily accessible; attaching, like the *Druids*, veneration to gloomy objects, or, at least, impressing that feeling on their trembling adherents. But I have, from a cursory geological examination of the neighbourhood of these caverns, persuaded myself that the island we call *Elephanta* was formerly not so insignificant in point of extent as we now see it: I think that, instead of being but five or six miles in circumference, it was formerly joined to its contiguous islands, and to the continent, from which it is now disjoined by a channel more than a mile in breadth. In the spacious harbour formed by the islands of *Caranja, Colaba, Bombay, Salsette,* and the continent, several smaller rocky islands are scattered, bearing of course different names, but which I deem formerly to have been but one, and probably under one designation; which might well have been that still retained by *Bombay*, or by *Elephanta*, or by a little island close to the latter that we call *Butcher's island.* Its *Hindu* name is *Deva-devy*, or the *Island of the Gods*, or *Holy Island:* it is low, less than a mile, I think, from *Elephanta*, in the direction of *Salsette.* With their usual sapience, the *English* have here built magnificent useless barracks, while in *Bombay*, where barracks are so severely wanted, we have none, or worse than none. And farther, to complete the system, a plan is now, or lately was, before the higher powers, for building docks on *Butcher's* island, where they will be useless, or worse than useless; while on *Bombay* we have, or may have, as many as our wants, extensive as they are, can require: the latter too are secure and accessible against all meditated mischief, and at all times; while the former must always be exposed to every mischief, and never easily, and sometimes not at all, accessible.—But this is irrelevant. The name of *Bombay* has been reasonably enough derived from the epithet so well bestowed upon its harbour by the *Portuguese*, after sailing up the bayless coasts of *Malabar* and *Kanara:* they are said to have called it *Buona-bahia*, the *good harbour.* And, perhaps, so they might; but a title nearly similar in sound was applied to it before the coming of the *Portuguese*, when it was, and still is, called *Maha-maha-deva*, or *Maha-maha-devy*; abbreviated to *Mamadevy*, the present name of the principal temple and tank on the island, which I have seen officially spelled MAHOMET DAVY's tank! From *Mamadevy, Mahomedan* natives made *Mumby devy*, (spelled, indeed, منبي *Munbi*, or *Munbai*, dropping the *devy*, which means an *island)*: and hence *Buona-bahia*, (*n* before *b* is almost necessarily sounded as *m*,) and our *Bombay*. *Maha*, as hath been before noticed, is an epithet of grandeur, and, as applied to a person, of pre-eminence: *Maha-maha devadevy* may, therefore, be interpreted the *Island* of MAHADEVA, or the *Great-great-God*, or SIVA; that deity being principally honoured in its chief temple, now on the little island of *Elephanta*, where monstrous *Lingas*, evidently, and, as before noticed, (p. 242,) necessarily, coeval with the excavation, and gigantic statues of him and his consort, indicate his paramount adoration. But such a long name being inconvenient and inharmonious, an epithet was dropped, and the name pronounced *Mahamadevy*. If this be objected to, let it be farther recollected, that MA is a name of DEVI, the consort of MAHADEVA, (page 148): which name of DEVI, the *goddess*, is pronounced exactly like *Devy*, an *island*; so that different modifications of these conjoined epithets, added, if necessary to that of *Deva*, a deity, will furnish several roots warranting the derivative I contend for; namely, of SIVA, under some one of his forms.

GARUDA next appears in PLATE 84. from a brass cast, larger than is represented in the plate. He is on one knee, in a posture of adoration, with a *naga*, or serpent, beside him; and supporting on his back a cup, or calyx, out of which spring the foliage of a *Kamal*, or lotos, holding in their concave expansion a dish,

Elephanta, I have before noticed, is called by the *Hindus*, *Gharipuri*; meaning, I am inclined to think, the *city* of *caves*: but this I ground on the supposition, that *Ghár* has, in *Sanskrit*, the same meaning as غار *Ghár* in *Arabic*; a *cave*, an *excavation*: which is not unlikely, for many words are synonimous in the two languages. Such name would, however, apply better to *Keneréh*, on *Salsette*; and, indeed, on my hypothesis of no disjunction of the islands, may have once belonged to the latter, or to both: for the direct distance between the caverns, having also others between, and, as it were, connecting them, is not so great as to exclude the supposition of one epithet serving generally for the whole.

The island that we, I know not why, call *Salsette*, is named *Shasta*, or *Shaster*, by natives. The name is supposed to be derived from *She-aster*; meaning, in *Mahraty*, *eighty-six*, it having formerly contained, it is said, that number of villages: it must, however, have had a name prior to such an advance of prosperity; and it is worth while to inquire what it was, and its meaning: neither is it likely that such a point would supersede any prior name, any more than originally give one. Any very grand object will soon give its own name to its neighbourhood, sinking the original appellative: *Saint* PAUL'S *Church-Yard*, for instance, most likely had a local designation before *St.* PAUL'S church was built there. This fine and interesting island of *Salsette* offers a rich harvest to mineralogical, botanical, or mythological inquiries: until lately, it has, in these, and in every other respect of policy and interest, been sadly neglected, or worse than neglected.

The largest island in *Bombay* harbour we call *Caranja*; the natives, *Uran*, or *Oran*. I do not know any meaning in either name, except, indeed, that the word in several dialects means *deserted*, *depopulated*, and may have had such application. *Hog* island, they call *Ghinal tikry*; meaning *harlot hill*: a modern name, most likely, originating from the immorality proverbially prevalent in the populous village in its neighbourhood.

To return for a moment to *Elephanta*.—It has been said in support of some hypothesis of its antiquity or *modernity*, or that of the *Vedas* and *Puranas*, (I, having no hypothesis to uphold, care not which,) that these books make no mention of its cavern-temple. But, let me ask, who has sufficiently examined those wonderful volumes to be enabled to say so? Several of our *Sanskrit* scholars have given us many surprising things that they do contain; but a knowledge of what they do not contain, or, in other words, of all that they do, will demand many more years of laborious examination. "Wherever we direct our attention to *Hindu* literature," said *Sir* W. JONES, "the notion of infinity presents itself; and the longest life would not be sufficient for the perusal of near five hundred thousand stanzas in the *Puranas*, with a million more, perhaps, in the other works before mentioned:" meaning the books on divine knowledge, called *Veda*, or what is *known*; and *Sruti*, or what has been *heard* from revelation.—See *Asiatic Researches*, Vol. I. Art. 18.

The cave of *Gharipuri* is not now in use as a temple: it has no establishment of *Brahmans*, or endowments, but neighbouring individuals make occasional offerings of prayers and oblations. I have seen the *lingas* adorned with recent flowers, with rice and money at the foot, or *yoni*. *Brahmans*, I have remarked, disregard imperfect images: the sad mutilations at *Gharipuri* may well, therefore, have caused their neglect of it.

called *patra*, or *argha-patra*, on which offerings of flowers are made to VISHNU in some of his forms: sometimes an image is placed on the *patra*, and duly propitiated by prayer and adoration. The *kamal* rises out of the cup by a screw, its female receptacle being in the stem of the cup: it thus can be contracted or expanded at will by a few turns. *Fig.* 4. of PLATE 83. shows one in a greater state of expansion: this is used in *puja*, or sacrificial oblations, to DEVI; and by taking out the *argha*, and turning back a few turns, the closing leaves sink into the cup, as seen in PLATE 85. *fig.* 5. which is a shut *kamal*, used in *puja* to VISHNU in the *Kurmavatara*, it being borne on the back of a *kurma*, or tortoise.

In PLATE 90. we see GARUDA and HANUMAN fighting, as noticed in a recent page; and below, he is seen bearing VISHNU in an upheld *argha*, the deity being about to reveal himself to VISWÁMITRA, the *guru*, or spiritual guide of RAMA, and to inspire that hero, or himself incarnate, to the accomplishment of his fated labours, as detailed in the *Ramayana*.

Images and pictures of GARUDA are very common: I have some scores. In PLATE 92. three are given, in his commonest posture of adoration: in *fig.* 3. he, conjoined with HANUMAN, forms the handle of a bell, used in *puja* to RAMA, (see page 69); *fig.* 4. represents him kneeling, with *naga* beside him; and *fig.* 6. standing with palms respectfully joined. A long nose and wings are what usually distinguish this important personage: sometimes, as seen in PLATE 10. he partakes more of the eagle, having its head and feet. On the handle of the beautiful vase, engraved in the last plate of our work, he looks like a griffin, or cherub: this vase will be more particularly noticed.

GARUDA, we have seen, is the son of VINATA; and hence called VINATEYA: VINATA, sometimes called VINAVA, is his mother, KASYAPA being his father. The all-prolific DITI is occasionally spoken of as GARUDA's mother; and he is brother to ARUNA, or AURORA.—See page 288. TARKSHA, GARUTWANTA, SUPERNA, and PUNAGRI, are other names of GARUDA, but I know not their meaning, or allusions: he has other epithets equivalent to *foe of serpents*, or their *destroyer*, NAG-ANTEKA; *favourite bird of* HARI; *lord of birds*; *swift as wind*; and he is generally spoken of, in a strain of praise, as being generous and merciful. The name SUPERNA is derived, I believe, from the beauty of his plumage.

He gives a name to a *Purana*, wherein his genealogy and exploits are detailed. He had a son of some note, named SUNABHA; and his sister, SUMATI, a maid of surpassing beauty, as her name implies, was espoused by SAGARA (a name of the Sea*), king of *Ayodha (Oude)*. Being childless, they engaged in sacred austerities; and BHRIGU, gratified thereby, gave her the choice of having one son, or sixty thousand sons: she preferred the latter, and brought forth a *gourd (Cucurbita lagenaria)*, whence issued that number of male children, who were carefully brought up by their nurses in jars filled with *ghee* (clarified butter). These nephews of GARUDA, attaining manhood, were sent by their pious father, SAGARA, about to perform an *aswamedha*, to seek the victim that had been stolen by a serpent assuming the form of ANANTA: they pierced the earth even to the lower regions, *Patala*, and sought the devoted horse so vehemently, that the universe was endangered by their energy. They at last found the horse feeding near "the wise VASUDEVA, the great MADHAVA, who claims the earth for his spouse; that divine one, residing in the form of KAPILA,"† predicted by BRAHMA as the destroyer of the numerous progeny of SUMATI, who rudely attempted to seize the sacred horse. But KAPILA, "filled with excessive anger, uttered from his nostrils a loud sound, and instantly by him, of immeasurable prowess, were all the sons of SAGARA reduced to ashes."

The long absence of his sons alarmed the king, and he sent his grandson, ANGSUMAN, from whose immediate care the sacred horse was stolen during its year of probationary wandering previous to its immolation, in quest of them and of intelligence. He at length found their heap of ashes, and, deeply afflicted, sought water wherewith to perform their funeral obsequies; but was informed by SUPERNA (the uncle of his deceased relatives), who now appeared "the sovereign of birds—in size, a mountain," that it was not proper to use common

* The word is, however, otherwise derived from *sa*, with, and *gara*, venom, or poison; and a legend, accounting for the name, is related of a king, named ASITA, leaving two pregnant widows, one of whom gave poison to the other, named KALENDI, to cause abortion. KALENDI, however, being very pious, was secured from its effects through the propitiated favour of the sage ascetic CHEVANA, a son of BHRIGU, and produced a son *with* the *poison*: which two words, joined, gave a name, SA-GARA, to her illustrious offspring.

† KAPILA is a very eminent literary character; founder of a philosophical theory, called *Sankya*, similar in many points to the *Italic* school: he thus corresponding in character and doctrines with PYTHAGORAS. His followers are numerous, and they pay him some divine honours under the name of VASUDEVA, affirming that one of VISHNU's secondary incarnations, sometimes said to be fifteen in number, was in the person of KAPILA. The *Saivas*, in like manner, honour a founder of one of their systems of theological doctrines, SANKARA CHARYA, with an apotheosis, (see p. 236.) maintaining that MAHADEVA incarnated himself in that furious person; and inspiring him with his intolerant spirit, sent him forth to coerce the unenlightened into conformity, or in default of faith, to smite them with his holy sword, and exterminate them in the name of the Lord.

water on this occasion; adding, "GANGA, O chief of men! is the eldest daughter of HAIMAVAT: with her sacred stream perform the funeral ceremonies for thine ancestors. If the purifier of the world flow on their ashes, the sixty thousand sons of thy grandfather will be received into heaven. Bring GANGA to the earth from the residence of the gods: take the horse, and go forth." He took home the horse, the sacrifice was completed, and his grandfather, SAGARA, died, after a reign of thirty thousand years, unable to devise any method of effecting the descent of GANGA from heaven. At length his great-grandson, BHAGIRAT'HA, (neither of the intermediate kings, ANGSUMAN, or his son DWILIPA, having been able to obtain the desired boon,) by a long course of austerities, gained the favour of BRAHMA; who, "completely won by austerities," propitiously yielded him the boon of a son, and of GANGA's descent to wet the ashes of his ancestors, that they might then ascend to the eternal heaven. "The venerable sire of all, the lord of creatures," said to him: "Engage HARA to receive in her descent GANGA, the eldest daughter of HAIMAVAT. The earth cannot sustain her fall; nor, beside SULA," (or SULI, or SHULI, from his dentated *trisula*, or *trident*,) "is any one able to receive her. Thus saying, the Creator, having spoken to GANGA, returned to heaven with the MARUTS and all the gods."

BHAGIRAT'HA, by farther austerities,* prevailed on BHARGA (SIVA), the lord of UMA (PARVATI), to receive the daughter of the mountain on his head. Ascending *Haimavat*, he exclaimed to the river flowing in the æther, "Descend, O GANGA!" "who, filled with anger at the irresistible command, assumed a form of amazing size, and, with insupportable celerity, fell from the air upon the auspicious head of SIVA," thinking with her weight to bear him down; but the "divine HARA, the three-eyed god," aware of her arrogance, determined to circumvent her, and receiving "the purifier on his sacred head, detained her in the recesses of the orb of his *Jata*, wherein, unable to obtain regress from its borders, she wandered for many series of years." BHAGIRAT'HA again betook himself to austerities; and SIVA, greatly pleased, discharged GANGA toward the lake *Vindu*, or *Bindu*, (see p. 41.) whence flowing in seven streams, she affords, by a variety of personifications, great scope for poetical exuberance

* Such as the *panshagni*, or *five fires:* that is, one toward each cardinal point, close to the devotee, and the sun, on which he constantly looks, over his head; standing, with uplifted arm, without aid or support, day and night feeding on air, immovable, on his right toe, upon the afflicted earth, &c.—See page 51, and 162.

in singing the wanderings, loves, adventures, &c. of the *joy-giving*, *purifying*, *water-abounding*, *beautiful-eyed*, *white*, (such are the meanings of their names,) pellucid heroes and heroines. The seventh followed the resplendent chariot of BHAGIRAT'HA; and her progress to the sea is magnificently described in the thirty-fifth section of the first book of the *Ramayana*, whence the quoted portions of this legend are borrowed. In the wondrous course, descending from the body of BHUVA (the *Existent*-SIVA), and tortuously rolling along the earth, celestial and terrestrial inhabitants were purified by her tact: those who through a curse had fallen from heaven, by ablution in her stream became free from sin. In this course she was interrupted; for having obtruded "on the sacrificial ground of the great JAHNU, of mighty works, who was then sacrificing, he, perceiving her pride, drank up the whole of the water of GANGA: a most astonishing deed!" But having been adored by the gods, &c. the great JAHNU, the most excellent of men, discharged GANGA from his ear;* and she again rushing forward, was led by BHAGIRAT'HA to the region of *Patala*, and watering the sacred ashes, sent the souls of the defunct to heaven.—See *Ramayana*, Book I. Sections 32. 33. 34. 35.

GARUDA has been before noticed as ARUN's younger brother: one being AURORA, or the dawn personified, there is a natural relationship between them, supposing the other to be the sky. He is sometimes described in the manner that our poets and painters describe a griffin, or a cherub; and he is placed at the entrance of the passes leading to the *Hindu* garden of *Eden*, and then appears in the character of a destroying angel, in as far as he resists the approach of serpents, which in most systems of poetical mythology appears to have been the beautiful, deceiving, insinuating, form that Sin originally assumed. GARUDA espoused a beautiful woman: the tribes of serpents alarmed thereat, lest his progeny should, inheriting his propensities, overpower them, waged fierce war against him; but he destroyed them all, save one, which he placed as an ornament about his neck. In the *Elephanta* cave GARUDA is often seen with this appendage; and I have several very old gold coins in which he has snakes or elephants in his talons and beaks—for he is sometimes spread, and double-headed, like the *Prussian* eagle, and one round his neck; but I do not recollect

* I have heard the discharge of this prodigious draught by the sage differently and less delicately related, accounting at the same time for the sea (which, though dug or hollowed before the descent of GANGA, had been till then empty,) being salt. The hollow or cavity for the sea is mysteriously contemplated, and is, by mystics, deemed the *Yoni* of the world: as mentioned in page 39, the *Ganga* is from this *embouchure*, named JAHNAVI, or the offspring of JAHNU.

seeing him so represented either in pictures or casts. Destroyer of serpents, NAG-ANTEKA, is one of his names.

He was of great use to KRISHNA in clearing the country round *Dwarka* (otherwise *Dravira*) from savages, ferocious animals, and noxious reptiles. VISHNU had granted to GARUDA the power of destroying his, as well as SIVA's, enemies; also generally those guilty of constant uncleanness, unbelievers, dealers in iniquity, ungrateful persons, those who slander their spiritual guides, or defiled their beds; but forbad him to touch a *Brahman*, whatever was his guilt, as the pain of disobedience would be a scorching flame in his throat, and any attack on a holy or pious person would be followed by a great diminution of strength. By mistake, however, GARUDA sometimes seized a priest, or a religious man, but was admonished and punished in the first case by the scorching flame, and was unable, even when he had bound him in his den, to hurt the man of piety.—See *As. Res.* Vol. V. page 514. To RAMA also, in the war of *Lanka*, GARUDA was eminently useful: in RAMA's last conflict with RAVANA, the latter was not overcome without the aid of GARUDA, sent by VISHNU to destroy the *serpent-arrows* of RAVANA. These arrows are called *Sarpa-vana*, (in the current dialect, *Sarpa*, a snake, is corrupted into *Saap*, or *Sámp*, and *vana*, an arrow, into *ban*,) and had the faculty of separating, between the bow and the object, into many parts, each becoming a serpent. VISWAMITRA conferred upon RAMA the power of transforming his arrows into *Garuda-vanas*, they similarly separating themselves into GARUDA's, the terror and destroyer of the *Sarpa*.

Some legends make GARUDA the offspring of KASYAPA and DITI. This all-prolific dame laid an egg, which, it was predicted, would produce her deliverer from some great affliction: after a lapse of five hundred years, GARUDA sprung from the egg, flew to the abode of INDRA, extinguished the fire that surrounded it, conquered its guards, the *devatas*, and bore off the *amrita (ambrosia)*, which enabled him to liberate his captive mother. A few drops of this immortal beverage falling on the species of grass called *Kusa*, (the *poa cynosuroides*,) it became eternally consecrated; and the serpents greedily licking it up, so lacerated their tongues with the sharp grass, that they have ever since remained forked; but the boon of eternity was ensured to them by their thus partaking of the immortal fluid. This cause of snakes having forked tongues is still popularly, in the tales of *India*, attributed to the above greediness; and their supposed immortality may have originated in some such stories as these: a small portion of *amrita*, as in the case of Rahu, (see page 282,) would ensure them this boon.

In all mythological language the snake is an emblem of immortality: its endless figure, when its tail is inserted in its mouth, and the annual renewal of its skin and vigour, afford symbols of continued youth and eternity; and its supposed medicinal or life-preserving qualities may also have contributed to the fabled honours of the serpent tribe. In *Hindu* mythology serpents are of universal occurrence and importance, and our plates* abound with them in some shape or other: the fabulous histories of *Egypt* and *Greece* are also decorated with serpentine machinery. Ingenious and learned authors attribute this universality of serpent forms to the early and all-pervading prevalence of sin, which in this identical shape, they tell us, and as, indeed, we all know, is as old as the days of our greatest grandmother: thus much as to its age, when there was but one woman; its prevalence, now there are so many, this is no place to discuss.

If such writers were to trace the allegories of Sin and Death, and the end of their empire, they might discover farther allusions to the *Christian* dispensation in the traditions of the *Hindus* than have hitherto been published.—Krishna crushing, but not destroying, the type of Sin, has already been touched on by me, and largely discussed by others. Garuda is also the proverbial, but not the utter, destroyer of serpents, for he spared one, they and their archetype being, in reference to created beings, eternal. His continual and destined state of warfare with the serpent, a shape mostly assumed by the enemies of the virtuous incarnations or deified heroes of the *Hindus*, is a continued allegory of the conflicts between Vice and Virtue, so infinitely personified. Garuda, at length, appears the coadjutor of all virtuous sin-subduing efforts, as the vehicle of the chastening and triumphant party, and conveys him, on the wings of the winds, to the regions of eternal day. Such specula-

* Images of snakes are common: I have many. The idea of their medicinal virtues is very old in *India:* a *Hindu* attacked by fever, or other diseases, makes a serpent of brass or clay, and performs certain ceremonies to its honour, in furtherance of his recovery. Such ceremonies are particularly efficacious when the moon is in the *nakshatra* (mansion, sign, or ásterism,) called *Sarpa*, or the *Serpent*; called also *Ashlesha*. I do not recollect that Dhanwantarà, the Esculapius of the *Hindus*, has an attendant serpent like his brother of *Greece:* the health-bestowing Dhanwantara arose from the sea when churned for the beverage of immortality. He is generally represented as a venerable man, with a book in his hand.—See plate 49. and pages 134. 183.

tions are not, however, pursued with safety by ignorant and profane pens—we, therefore, quit them.

The swan, or goose, the eagle, and the bull, it will be recollected, are the vehicles respectively allotted to the three great powers. The terrestrial sluggish nature of the first, I have supposed, pointed it out as an apt type of matter, personified in the creative power, and a contrast to VISHNU, or spirit, the preserving power, appropriately mounted on the buoyant eagle, the celestial GARUDA. SIVA, the destructive energy of the Deity, is Time, or Justice; and the *Hindus*, but I know no especial reason for it, deem the bull also its type, and give it to SIVA as his *vahan*, or mode of conveyance. These vehicles are supposed by *Mr.* PATERSON *(As. Res.* Vol. VIII. p. 48.) to have allusion to "*Purity*, *Truth*, and *Justice:* the first, typified by the *swan*, which, clothed with unspotted whiteness, swims, amidst the waters, as it were, distinct from, and unsullied by, them; as the truly pure mind remains untainted amidst the surrounding temptations of the world. GARUDA, brother to ARUNA, is remarkable for strength and swiftness; and the latter is described as imperfect, and, on account of his defects, destined to act as charioteer to the Sun, he being the dawn, the twilight preceding the sun. GARUDA is perfect light; the dazzling full blaze of day; the type of *Truth*; the celestial *vahan* of VISHNU.* *Justice*, typified in the sacred *bull*, is the *vahan* of SIVA: "the bull, whose body is PARAMESWARA, and whose every joint is a virtue; whose three horns are the three *Vedas*; whose tail ends where *ad'herma*, or injustice, begins."

* Perhaps the *Hindus* may, like western observers, have noticed the strong optic nerves of the eagle tribe; and have heard of the story of the parents destroying such of their brood as are unable to look steadily on the sun. I think I have seen the eagle called, in our poetry, bird of the Sun, as well as bird of JOVE: in both of which characters VISHNU particularly appears.

NOTE.

BARTOLOMEO says, that the vehicle of VISHNU is the sparrow-hawk; called *Garuda* in *Sanskrit*, and *Paranda* in the language of *Malabar*, where it is held in great veneration, particularly by women; and if one of these animals snatch a fish from their hand, they consider it as a most fortunate omen.—*Voyage to India*, p. 223. The term *sparrow-hawk* is, I apprehend, an error in the translation of the learned *Carmelite's* book; at any rate, the bird he describes is not of the species so called in *English*, but the kite, or falcon, or ospray. Some travellers call it the *Pondicherry* eagle, or *Malabar* eagle; LINNÆUS, after, BRISSON the *falco Ponticerianus*. In *India*, from its sacredness, it is commonly termed the *Brahmany* kite;

which, however, I do not think is specifically named *Garuda*, that being applied to the mixed animal when VISHNU's vehicle. And it is, moreover, the larger bird that the friar may so often have seen pouncing on the fish-baskets borne by the *Makatis* (females of the *Makwa*, or fishing, tribe,) on the coast of *Malabar*, or by the fishermen's wives and girls in *Bombay*.

The *Brahmany* kite is very useful in the populous towns of *India* in removing carrion and filth, and is never killed: in native towns and cities they, and unowned dogs, and jackals, and vultures, enjoy exclusively the office of scavenger. The usefulness of this bird was, perhaps, originally the cause of its obtaining, like the cow, a protecting legend in the popular superstition of the *Hindus*; and the veneration which, in different countries, we find paid to particular animals, may, perhaps, be traced to similar sources of utility: the *Ibis*, and *Ichneumon*, for instance, in *Egypt*, where filth and noxious animals abound as much as in *India*. It is happy where religious prejudices originate from, and promote, social conveniency.

Bombay, with its immense population, unequalled, perhaps, in reference to its extent, by any spot on the globe, is highly indebted to the kite, as well as to its numerous vultures: I do not join the unclaimed dogs in this commendation, for they are, in truth, a sad nuisance, being protected and fed, but not housed, by the *Parsi* inhabitants, as well as by *Hindus*. An expiring *Parsi* requires the presence of a dog, in furtherance of his departing soul, and to a banquet of the vultures the exposed body is speedily consigned: hence many of those voracious birds are attracted and retained, their sense of smell being acute to a wonderful degree; and their expedition in stripping a carcase to the bones is seen with surprise. Nor is the audacity of the *Brahmany* kite less admirable: I will mention but one instance, of which I was a witness, viz. stooping, and taking a chop off a gridiron standing over the fire that cooked it.

MISCELLANEOUS NOTICE

OF THE

BRAHMANS and HINDUS.

ALTHOUGH my work is avowedly and chiefly on mythology, it is not my intention, as the reader may early have perceived, to be confined exclusively to that subject: but, as hath been before observed, it is so blended with all points of religion, literature, and manners, that it is not easy to discuss one without touching on the other. So much has been published on the manners and customs of the inhabitants of *India,* that there seems no room, at any rate no call, for any thing farther to be said respecting them. It is certainly not my object to write professedly, or with any affectation of system or regularity, any strictures on a topic so apparently exhausted.—I say, apparently; for my real opinion is, that there is still a great deal for the *European* world to learn, and a great deal for it to unlearn, before a competent knowledge be obtained of the religion, mythology, manners, customs, prejudices, &c. of the many millions of our fellow subjects in *Hindustan.*

What I take the liberty of offering thereon, will be an incidental notice, here and there, either arising out of the subject in discussion, or introduced with the view of relieving the tædium that an uuvaried topic might excite; and in this place, as briefly as may be, to throw together two or three observations connected with the history of the extraordinary race of men who call themselves *Hindus.*

We are in the habit, more and more, of calling them *Hindus:* a few years ago the term *Gentoo* was commonly used in *Madras* and *Bombay* as synonimous with *Hindu,* but is getting, as intelligence spreads, into disuse. The latter is generally, as far as I can speak, indeed always, applied by the *Brahmans* and others in designation of their brethren; but the former never, except it be by ignorant persons at our seaports, who have derived it from *European* authorities; or if it be used by well-informed natives, it is in compliance with our habit, or as a term easiest comprehended. *Mr.* HALHED, it is to be lamented, has in some measure authorised the term *Gentoo*, by giving that appellation to his valuable code of laws.

Pagoda, in like manner, is a word altogether unknown beyond the corrupting influence of *European* colloquial example, whether used descriptively of a coin or of a temple: the former being called, generally by *Hindus*, *Hun*, or *Hoon*; the latter, *Deval*—from *Deva*, a deity, and *havely*, a house. About *Poona*, *Bombay*, and, perhaps, generally on the western side of *India*, the word, that in this work I write, *Deva*, (a deity,) is pronounced *Deo*, or *Dew*, or *Dev*; and the temple, *Dewal*.

The epithet *Deva* means a deity: BRAHMA, VISHNU, and SIVA, have each the common denomination of *Deva*. We frequently, in conversation, hear of BRAHMA DEVA, occasionally of VISHNU DEVA, and constantly of MAHA-DEVA, even from the mouth of a *Vaishnava*. SIVA DEVA I do not recollect ever to have heard; perhaps because the sound is unmusical: MAHADEVA, that is, the Great God, he is always styled by his votaries, and sometimes, as just noticed, by the *Vaishnavas*, who never apply the epithet to the object of their exclusive adoration; although it in fact seems an epithet of general superlative distinction, rather than as exclusively, either personally or characteristically, appertaining, except by courtesy, to SIVA. The word *Deva*, then, appears to be equivalent, as nearly as possible, to our God, or Lord; which names, as well as to the Supreme Being, we, like the *Hindus*, apply, certainly with seeming irreverence, to subordinate characters. We speak commonly of the god of war, the god of love, of wine, &c. &c. as do the *Hindus* of KAMADEVA, KRISHNA-DEVA, SURA-DEVI, &c. As to the word *Pagoda*, applied either to a coin or temple, to the latter especially, it ought, like *Gentoo*, to be dropped, as inaccurate and barbarous, and not at all used by the natives out of the reach of *European* tuition. I find an attempt to derive the word from *Mahommedan* authority, imagining that anti-idolatrous people to have called the temples of the *Hindus* by the debasing, but accurate, appellation of بت كده *but-gada:* from *but*, an *idol*, and *gada*, a *temple*. BARTOLOMEO says, the coin being impressed with the goddess BHAGAVADA, is, therefore, so called; *Pagoda* being a corruption, or abbreviation. But admitting BHAGAVADA to be a name of DEVI, and to be borne by some *huns*, it would apply to such only; whereas we give it to all gold coins of about the value of seven or eight shillings, be the impression what it may. And, indeed, I have lately seen a silver coin, worth about four shillings, with the word *pagoda*, or half *pagoda*, in *English*, with some oriental characters stamped on it; and a representation of a *Hindu* temple. This coin I imagine to be intended for the use of *Madras*, and cannot but lament that so miserable a specimen of our taste and talents should be suffered to go forth. In saying that the execution is worthy of the design, is stigmatizing both with deserved reprobation.

Here I will introduce a point somewhat connected with the foregoing, tending to account for what I deem erroneous impressions on the part of many earlier visitants of *India*; as well, indeed, (for the cause, although diminished, continues,) on the part also of those of later date.

A stranger landing, we will suppose at *Madras*, is speedily attended, I may almost say *beset*, by very intelligent individuals of rather, as I apprehend, a low *cast*; (this term *cast* is another word that they have learned from *Europeans*,) who will describe themselves as being of the *Gentoo cast*; another, as of the *Malabar cast*; how they attend at *Pagodas*, &c. &c. The stranger, unless more than usually inquisitive and discriminating, will scarcely discover that these are words unauthorised in, perhaps, any language in *India*, and that the ideas they convey, if they convey any, tend to error. By *Gentoo cast*, the *Dubash*, (another *Persian** compound word, although few *Dubashis* are aware of it,) means a high rank in the artificial scale of sectarial precedence. The *Dubashis* of *Madras* I imagine to be mostly of a low rank, of the tribe of *Bania*,† or *Banyan*, as they will call it: another word unintelligible to most *Hindus* distant from *Europeans*: which tribe is composed mostly of buyers and sellers of cattle, grain, cloths, &c. They are, in general, brokers and merchants: agriculture also appertains to this sect: admirably placid and shrewd in their conduct and dealings, and of primary use to all itinerant strangers. The *Seraf*, or *Shroff*, as it is most commonly pronounced in our towns, is a negociator of bills; dealer in money and valuable metals, and gems in general; and is also of the tribe or sect of *Bania*. Many subdivisions of which (I use the words sect, tribe, or subdivision, without much discrimination,) abstain from animal food; and the whole tribe, perhaps, from beef. I do not know that all the subdivisions of the tribe of *Bania* do so abstain; the higher certainly do very rigidly, and the lower profess

* *Dubashi*, an interpreter; one with two languages: دو *du, two*; باشي *bashi, language*.

† The *Ayin Akbery* says there are eighty-four subdivisions of the tribe or sect of *Bania*; itself but a subdivision of that of *Vaisya*. "There is a branch of the *Biess* tribe, called, in the *Hindu* language, *Bunnick*, or, more properly, *Bunnyek*, or grain merchants; and of these there are no less than eighty-four tribes: among whom are mendicants, men of learning, artists, magicians, handicrafts, and such expert jugglers, that their tricks pass for miracles with the vulgar, and impose even upon those who are wiser."—*Ay. Akb.* Vol. III. p. 89. *Cal.* 4to. edit.

to do so likewise: nor do I say that they act contrarily to their profession, but I am disposed to suspect they do. If, however, the whole tribe of *Bania** abstain from animal food, I am, I think, warranted in saying, that it is the only one that doth so among the whole race of *Hindus*. That the *Brahmans* do not will be shown presently; and, reasoning from analogy, one would not expect it in an inferior sect.

Be this as it may, into the hands of the *Dubash*, or *Seraf*, most visitants of *India* must primarily, and almost necessarily, fall; and from them, or their servants, as almost the only persons who speak intelligible *English*, or other foreign language, (for these *Dubashis* speak *French*, *Dutch*, *Portuguese*, *Arabic*, *Persian*, &c.) must be received the earliest impressions of the religion and manners of the wonderful race to which those individuals belong. They will teach naturally, and exclusively, the tenets and practices, duly magnified, by which themselves are guided. The inquirer will not often have opportunities of comparing different authorities, but will, by tongue or pen, fairly inform others what he has thus learned.

Of the four grand divisions of *Hindus*, that of *Vaisya*, and of the subdivisions of *Vaisya*, that of *Bania*, is the most intent on the good things of this world. Their selfish industry and economy is striking and universal; and were it a quality equally conspicuous, so would be their ignorance on superior points.

Hither may, I think, be traced upwards to its source, the stream of erroneous information; and thus may we account for the diffused use of certain unauthorised terms, as well as for the wide propagation of certain notions, that, with due deference to public and private opinions, I presume to think ungrounded.

The most prominent idea that arises in the mind of a *European*, coupled with *Hinduism*, is that of a characteristic and universal abstinence from eating flesh and shedding blood. From what information I may have gathered at our seaports I might probably have judged so too; but from observation, and information derived elsewhere, I do not think it at all a characteristic of that race. That a small sect, or part of a sect, or perhaps more sects than one, may be religiously prohibited the indulgence, I do not deny; but even that might be difficult to prove. Nothing is more certain than that many individuals of several sects do rigidly abstain from eating flesh, and many more profess to do

* From *Banyan*, or *Banian*, is, I suppose, derived the distinction, so universal, indeed official, in the navy, and generally at sea, of those days on which the ration includes no meat. On *Banian* days it is composed wholly of flour, plums, suet, cheese, and butter.

it; but my argument is, that it is but the act, and, as among *Christians*, the voluntary and fancied praiseworthy act, of individuals; and that a majority of sects or tribes, and the majority of the individuals of those sects, kill, and eat: not only a majority, but a very great majority—so great as to throw the minority comparatively out of sight. And, indeed, were it not for their local and foremost position, as just noticed, added, perhaps, to an ostentatious display of rigidity, they would scarcely have been at all observed.

All the inferior tribes, and they are vastly more numerous, in regard to individuals composing them, than the higher, eat, if not indiscriminately, for beef, with some forms an exception, any thing, and every thing: many do eat beef. What I am about to hazard, I do not expect to be entirely believed: all I ask is, that my readers will give me credit for being incapable of intentionally misleading them; and that I am persuaded the research of a few years will confirm my opinion, which is, that not one *Hindu* in ten thousand, taking the whole race, does actually, unless from necessity, abstain from animal food. It is not their common diet certainly, for it is not obtainable; but they may eat it if they please, and do when they can. I farther believe, that a great majority may legally eat beef; but they would not chuse it, perhaps, if they had the choice, any more than we would chuse horseflesh, and dogs and cats, that the *Chinese* and other people find so good. The *Brahmans* and *Banias* do not, I believe, ever eat beef; and it is, perhaps, forbidden them: pointed texts of a contrary tendency might, however, be quoted from their most sacred books. Wherever the influence of *Brahmans* extends, and among *Hindus* it would be difficult to define its bounds, (for *India*, like *Italy*, is a paradise for priests,) the killing and eating beef is discouraged. Under the *Brahmanical* government of *Poona*, killing oxen is in a great measure, though not entirely, prohibited: killing oxen to eat is, perhaps, to avoid the unnecessary diffusion of cruel spectacles, a sort of privilege restricted to particular towns; and butchers not so licensed, would probably be punished by fine, or certainly by popular clamour or contempt, for such an act. At *Poona* beef is never killed, or eaten, except by very base tribes of *Hindus*. Some towns in the *Mahrata* territory enjoy the privilege of killing beef for sale: *Kursi*, or *Koorsy*, on the river *Krishna*, is one; and *Wahi*, or *Wye*, about fifty miles to the southward of *Poona*, is another. The latter is the capital of the possessions, and principal residence of the rich and great *Brahman* family of *Rasta*, one of the five great independent feudal chiefs of the *Mahrata* empire, and nearly related to the *Peshwa*. The former is a respectable town on the right bank of the *Krishna*, where a *Mahummedan* saint, or *Pir* of renown, has a tomb: his shrine is much resorted to: I have visited it. The town is sometimes called *Kursia* MAH SAHEB; meaning, I believe, the *repose* of the saint so named. *Wye* is said to contain likewise a similar shrine.

The other *Mahrata* governments, such as HOLKAR, SINDIA, RAGOJI BHUN-SLA, &c. may likewise in imitation, or through the influence of their betters, (for none of these are *Brahmans*,) also prohibit or discourage the slaughter of kine: having *Brahmans* about them as ministers, &c. perhaps they do. But if so, it is a political, or personal, rather than a religious, regulation; although, from the continuance of the usage for a series of years, it may now be received by many as of prescriptive authority, or, by superstition or enthusiasm, even as of divine ordinance.*

The majority of *Brahmans* may, and do, eat animal food: priests, while officiating as such, perhaps, do not. The reader need not be told, that, although all priests are *Brahmans*, all *Brahmans* are not priests: as among the *Jews*, the tribe of LEVI furnished the priesthood, so among *Hindus*, it is furnished from that of *Brahman*.

The general and rigid abstinence of the *Poona Brahmans* I impute originally to an affectation, it may now have become a feeling, of purity, with the view of lessening the scandal that a *Brahman* government necessarily excites. To *reign*† is, indeed, forbidden to a *Brahman*; and the *Poona* government have a

* From an account, among my *memoranda*, of a reconciliatory public meeting, between the *Peshwa* and DOWLAT RAO SINDEA, after long political animosity, I extract a passage, written at the moment, that will show the prodigality of *Hindus* in blood, even at the capital. The meeting alluded to took place on the day of the festival, called *Dasra*, in honour of BHAVANI, or DURGA; it is also called DURGA *puja*. —"*Poona*, Sept. 30, 1797. As the astronomers in this part of *India* are not very accurate, schisms sometimes arise, as was the case this year, regarding which day is the first, or that of new moon, as most of their festivals are regulated by lunar calculations. The *Dasra* falls, as its name seems to imply, on the tenth day; and the usual mode is to reckon from the day on which the new moon is first seen. It is likely that this ceremony was one of gratitude for the past season, whence all necessaries are derived; for the rains may now be said to have closed, and the harvest in forwardness for reaping. On a general principle only, that festivals were chiefly of a grateful nature, can it be supposed that this was such; for no such idea can now be discovered among the *Mahratas*, who, on the contrary, rejoice at its arrival as the opening of the season for their rapine and plundering excursions. They wash all their horses, sacrificing to each a sheep, whose blood is scattered with some ceremony, and flesh eaten without any: few men, however poor, who possess a horse, omit this slaughter. SINDEA, this year, is said to have slaughtered twelve thousand. *Brahmans* give their servants money for the purpose, not, in this part, chusing to be the immediate cause of bloodshed."

† "With a slaughterer who employs ten thousand slaughter-houses, a king, not a soldier by birth, is declared to be on a level."—*Ins.* of MENU, chap. iv. v. 86.

little reserve, or salvo in the existence of a nominal legitimate *Raja* at *Sattara*. And the *Peshwa* professes, as the title implies, to be only his first servant; although he be, to all intents and purposes, a sovereign, as far as he can enforce its acknowledgment. But the *Poona* or *Kokan Brahmans* are, notwithstanding their sanctified abhorrence of eating meat, held in contempt by their carnivorous brethren of *Bengal*, and the northern countries. Some of the *Poona* and *Kokan Brahmans* object to eating carrots, as looking too much like beef: they do not use tobacco, except in the form of snuff. The *Brahmans* of *Bengal* and other parts eat flesh if they please, unless under some particular circumstances: it is likely, I think, that a majority of *Brahmans* eat animals, and that nine-tenths may, if they like it.*

BARTOLOMEO should not have accused DIODORUS SICULUS of "palpable falsehood," when he says, "that the *Brahmans* engaged in no public business, and accepted no dignified places." In his days they ostensibly, perhaps, did not; and the time is said to be comparatively recent, when they commenced their royal or ministerial career.

* "*Bengal Brahmans* live on fish to this day."—WILFORD. *As. Res.* Vol. IX. p. 63. (*Cal.* edit.) They eat flesh also. "*Brahmans* are by no means confined to a vegetable diet: like the *Jews* and *Mussulmans*, they are forbidden many kinds of flesh and fish."—WILKINS. *Hetopadesa*, p. 318.

Some curious particulars, connected with the pesent *Peshwa's* family, and other *Brahman* and *Mahrata* tribes, not very flattering to their pride of ancestry, are contained in *Mr.* WILFORD's chronological essay, in the ninth volume of the *As. Res.* Art. 3. whence I borrow the following.—

"According to the *Pauranics*, PARASU RAMA, having extirpated the *Cshettris*, and filled the earth with blood, wanted to perform a sacrifice, but could find no *Brahman* to assist, on account of his being defiled with the effusion of so much human blood. As he was standing on the summit of the mountains of *Kucan*, he spied fourteen dead bodies stranded on the adjacent shores below: these were the corpses of so many *Mlech'chas*, who had been flung into the sea by their enemies in distant countries in the west. They had been wafted by the winds, and were then in a high state of putrefaction. RAMA recalled them to life, imparted knowledge to them, and conferred on them the *Brahmanical* ordination; and bid them perform the sacrifice. From these fourteen dead men is descended the *Kucanastha* tribe of *Mahratas*: thus called, because, since that time, they have always *staid* and remained in the *Kucan*."

"There were three other individuals whose corpses were similarly stranded, more to the northward, toward the gulf of *Cambay*; and these were brought to life again by a magician. And from them are descended three tribes: one of which is the *Chitpawana*; and the *Ranas* of *Udayapur*, with the *Peshwa's* family, belong to it."—Page 239.

From the same authority we learn, that the *Karara* tribe of *Mahratas* are descended from men who were formed of the ribs of a dead camel, by a magician who could get no *Brahman* to assist at his nefarious rites. By his powerful spells he made men of the camel's ribs, and, moreover, conferred on them the *zenaar*.—*Ib.*

"The *Peshwa's* family of the *Chitpawana* wish very much to be considered as belonging to the *Kucanastha* tribe, since they reside also in *Kucan*."

"The *Mahratas* are called *Maha-rashtra* in *Sanskrit*: *Maha* is great and illustrious, and *Rashtra*,

I will go a step farther, and say, that not only do *Hindus*, even *Brahmans*, eat flesh, but that, at least, one sect eat *human* flesh. I know only of one sect, and that, I believe, few in numbers, that doth this; but there may, for aught I can say, be others, and more numerous. They do not, I conclude, (in our territory, assuredly not,) kill human subjects to eat; but they eat such as they find in or about the *Ganges*, and perhaps other rivers. The name of the sect that I allude to is, I think, *Paramahansa*, as I have commonly heard it named; and I have received authentic information of individuals of this sect being not very unusually seen about *Benares*, floating down the river on, and feeding on, a corpse. Nor is this a low despicable tribe, but, on the contrary, esteemed—by themselves, at any rate, a very high one. Whether the exaltation be legitimate, or assumed by individuals in consequence of penance, or holy and sanctified acts, I am not prepared to state, but I believe the latter; as I have known other instances where individuals of different sects, by persevering in extraordinary piety, or penance, have been deemed in a state incapable of sin.—The holiness of the actor sanctified the act, be it what it may; or, as we say, to the pure all things are pure: but I never heard of these voluptuous saints carrying their devotion or impudence to the disgusting extravagance under our consideration. They are still much respected; more, however, under all their shapes, by women than men.

I will finish my notice of the *Paramahansa** by observing, that my informa-

synonimous with *Raja-putra*, implies their royal descent; and their name also indicates that they were acknowledged to belong to the second class on their arrival in *India*, and, of course, that they were not *Brahmans*. When our new adventurers had obtained power and influence, they assumed the superior title of *Maha-Rashtras*; and by striking out such letters as become useless, when brought to the standard of the spoken dialects, we have *Maha-rata*, *Mahrata*, and sometimes *Mahrater*. Thus we have *Surat*, from *Surashtra*; and *Gujarat*, from *Gurja Rashtra*."—Page 241.

* Since this was written, I find the word used in the ninth volume of the *As. Res.* p. 318. (*Cal.* 4to. edit.) and applied to "ascetics of the orthodox sect in the last stage of exaltation: they disuse clothing. I have very seldom seen individuals *entirely* naked, except in *Poona*, where dozens sometimes of these brawny saints are seen lolling and sleeping in the streets, and on shop-boards, as naked as they were born. In other *Mahrata* towns, or travelling, I have occasionally seen one; always treated with great respect, especially by women, who will sometimes kiss the holy man in a mode that we should judge highly indecent. I have known one of these *nudes*, now and then, come to *Bombay*; but he has been speedily admonished by the officers of police of the necessity of a more decent appearance, or of immediate departure.

In the same volume a passage occurs, referring to the followers of the doctrines of BUDDHA, that countenances the idea that they are also cannibals; but it is so repugnant to the generally-received notions of the humanity of that sect, that I shall, without laying any stress on it, merely quote the passage.

" The *Jains* generally account modestly for all their tenets, and conduct themselves with propriety;

tion stated, that the human brain is judged by these epicurean cannibals as the most delicious morsel of their unsocial banquet.

It may be difficult for the *English* reader to believe this hitherto unrecorded story of the flesh-abhorring *Hindus*; as well, perhaps, as the now fully authenticated facts of their prodigality of human life. Not to mention the frequency of the self-immolation of widows, which is by no means confined to *Brahmans'* widows, on the contrary, of the five or six that I have attended, I do not think one was a *Brahmani*, but I have neglected to notice in every instancethe tribe of the victim, *Hindus* of all ranks in religion and life are in the habit of carrying their aged or diseased parents or friends to the *Ganges*, if within reach, if not, to some other holy stream, to perish by hunger, weather, or alligators. Mothers, incredible as it may seem, revolt not, as the reader must when he first hears it, at throwing their infants into the sea or river to be eaten alive by alligators and sharks. Whole tribes were in the habit of destroying, with but few exceptions, all their female children, (as is detailed, by a person of high distinction and respectability, in the fourth volume of the *As. Res.* Art. 22.) until they were reclaimed and reformed by the personal influence and persuasion of an *English* gentleman, whose name is respected and venerated by a greater number of *Hindus* than that, perhaps, of any other individual of whatever country or religion. In the account just alluded to, his name is unaccountably omitted, although whatever merit, and it cannot be trifling, may attach to the influence and perseverance necessary to effect so extraordinary a revolution in minds impelled by feelings stronger even than those of humanity and natural affection, attaches exclusively to one person, and that is the *Honourable* JONATHAN DUNCAN, now governor of *Bombay*.

Until lately, the horrid habitual practice of infanticide in *India* was supposed to have been confined to the tribes of *Rajkumar*, and *Rajvansa*, who inhabit districts in the neighbourhood of *Benares*; but our recent acquisitions of territory and influence in the fine province of *Guzarat* have disclosed the existence of a similar practice among several tribes in that extensive country. And here, again, the same indefatigable zeal, that never slackens in its exertions for the public good, not only added the resources of this garden of *India* to the stores of our national prosperity, but, awake to the stiller calls of humanity, discovered that here also existed the baneful practice of infanticide, and happily again suc-

and never assert that their bodies are eternal, and that there is *no God.* Nor do they, like the *Baudhists*, say, ' After death there is no pain in the flesh, or feeling: since it feels not pain, nor death, what harm is there in feeding upon it, when it is necessary to procure health or strength?"—Page 256.

ceeded in its effectual suppression. It cannot be imagined that coercion or prohibition, enforced by the severest penal denunciations, could abolish a custom existing in opposition to feelings of a nature beyond the reach of temporal considerations; and he would evince little knowledge of man who should so attempt it. Conciliation and reasoning have been the powerful instruments in effecting, by the same hand, so salutary a work, both in the east and west of *India*, in *Benares* and in *Guzarat*. In the latter province female infanticide was found to prevail among the tribe of *Jarejah*, of which are the principal chieftains of the peninsula: such as JAM of *Naggar*, otherwise *Nonagar*; the *Rajas* of *Wadwan*, of *Goundel*, and many others; all of whom have recently entered into voluntary engagements renouncing this unnatural practice—into the discovery, progress, and termination, of which, I had intended to enter somewhat more at large; but I learn that a full and authentic account thereof has been received lately by a gentleman likely to make the best use of it, and with which, I trust, the public will not long remain unacquainted. I, therefore, shall not dwell longer on the interesting subject.

Human victims were formerly immolated at the shrine of offended or avenging deities, as I have had occasion to notice in other places; but the practice is now, perhaps, entirely discontinued: in our settlements it is of course in that instance, as well as in every other of an atrocious nature, whether voluntary or otherwise.*

* But a few years have elapsed since a widow in *Bombay* wanted to become a *Sati*, (that is, to burn herself); which being of course prevented, she applied to the Governor, and on refusal, crossed the harbour to the *Mahrata* shore, and there received her crown of martyrdom.

Prodigality or carelessness of life has been, on another occasion, remarked as a conspicuous trait in the *Hindu* character: hence has arisen such an army of martyrs as no religion, perhaps, can outnumber. As well as meritorious suffering for religion's sake, suicide is in some cases legal, and even commendable: that, for instance, of the *Sati*, or the self-immolated widow; the only one that ever came under my notice, and to which sacrifice I have attended several victims. This triumph of priestcraft, the greatest, perhaps, it has to boast, occurs at *Poona*, in ordinary and quiet periods, annually about twelve times, on an average of as many years. I was lately a whole year at *Poona*, and I knew of its occurrence only six times; but it was a tumultuous and revolutionary period, and people were of course put out of their usual and ordinary routine of thought and deed. As this terrible ceremony is generally performed at *Poona*, at the junction of the *Moota* and *Moola* rivers, about a quarter of a mile from the skirts of the city, at which *junction* (thence called *Sangam*,) the *English* residency is situated; and as my habitation was as near as possible to the river, on the bank opposite to the spot of sacrifice, and not more distant than two hundred yards, I most likely knew of all that occurred, and, with the exception of one that took place at midnight, attended them all.

As this affecting sacrifice has been so often described, I shall not here enter on any detail of particu-

Well-authenticated anecdotes might easily be collected, to a considerable extent, of the sanguinary propensity of this people; such as would startle those who have imbibed certain opinions, from the relations of travellers, on the character and habits of the "abstinent and blood-abhorring *Hindus*," and "*Brahmans*, with souls unspotted as the robes they wear."

lars; it may be observed, however, that on no two occasions did the ceremonies, which sometimes are very numerous and striking, exactly coincide: they seemed prolonged or abridged in a degree corresponding to the fortitude or timidity of the victim.

The first that I attended was a young and interesting woman, about twenty-five years of age. From the time of her first coming on horseback to the river-side, attended by music, her friends, *Brahmans*, and spectators, to the period of her lighting the pile, two hours elapsed: she evinced great fortitude. On another occasion, an elderly, sickly, and frightened, woman was hurried into the pile in a quarter of an hour.

Of the first of these I took particular note. Soon after I arrived at the pile, then erecting, she saw me, and beckoned me to come to her: all persons immediately made way, and I was led by a *Brahman* close up to her; when I made an obeisance, which she returned, looking full in my face, and proceeded to present me with something that she held in her hand. A *Brahman* stopped her, and desired me to hold my hand out, that what she was about to give me might be dropped into it: to avoid pollution, I suppose, by touching any thing while in contact with an impure person. She accordingly held her hand over mine, and dropped a pomegranate, which I received in silence, and reverently retired. I was sorry that it was not something of an unperishable nature, that I might have preserved it: some ornament, for instance. My wife, who was in the house on the other side of the river, observing the ceremonies through a glass, was also disappointed, and, of course, curious to know what was the article presented in so interesting a manner at such an awful time.

After the *Sati* was seated in the hut of straw, built over the pile, with the corpse of her husband beside her, and just before the fire was applied, a venerable *Brahman* took me by the hand and led me close to the straw, through which he made an opening, and desired me to observe her, which I did attentively. She had a lighted wick in each hand, and seemed composed: I kept sight of her through the whole of her agony, as, until forced to retire from the intensity of the heat, which I did not, however, until a good deal scorched, I was within five feet of the pile.

When the victim is a person of consequence, the ashes are, it is said, collected and thrown into the *Ganges*: I do not imagine that such attention is paid to persons of inferior condition, but am, perhaps, mistaken. Of my interesting victim I was desirous to obtain some of the ashes, to preserve in lockets, &c. but was not able to obtain any. A military guard is generally placed over the spot of sacrifice, and my application was refused by an attendant *Brahman*; who, after some solicitation, told me, he could not imagine of what utility the ashes of the *Sati* could be of to me, unless for the purposes of sorcery. A firm belief in the power of witchcraft and necromancy exists very extensively among all ranks and religions in *India*; and some instances of its effects, both of a ridiculous and terrible nature, have come within my knowledge.

We are informed by *Mr*. COLEBROKE, that legal suicide was formerly common among the *Hindus*, and is not now very rare: among men, drowning themselves in holy rivers is oftener resorted to of late than burning. The blind father and mother of the young anchorite, whom DASARATHA slew by mistake, (see

I have hinted, that the example of one sect, or of an individual, may extensively influence the practice of another. Thus at *Poona*, on the *Mahomedan* fast in commemoration of the martyrdom of the sons of ALLY and FATIMA, it is usual among the faithful, as they call themselves, there, as well as at other places, to go about in mournful and frantic procession, preceded by an article slightly constructed of split-bamboo and paper, called *Tabut*, or *Taboot*, in imitation of a *Mahomedan* tomb. These *Tabuts* are of divers magnitudes and descriptions, generally surmounted by a dome, and frequently as grand as painting and gilding can make them; and, indeed, often not devoid of elegance and taste. Every family of distinction collects as many followers as they can, to grace the procession of the domestic *Tabut* to the sea or river, into which it is thrown. This ceremony one would imagine would be confined to *Mussulmans*; and so it is, wherever I have witnessed it, *Poona* excepted, where I have

page 515,) burnt themselves with the corpse of their son. The scholiast of the *Rhaghuvansa*, in which poem, as well as in the *Ramayana*, this story is beautifully told, quotes a text of law to prove that suicide is in such instances legal. Persons afflicted with loathsome and incurable diseases have not unfrequently caused themselves to be buried alive. And among the lowest tribes of the inhabitants of *Berar* and *Gondivana*, suicide is occasionally vowed by such persons in return for boons solicited from idols, and is fulfilled by the successful votary throwing himself from a precipice, named *Kala-bhairava*,* situated in the mountains between the *Tapti* and *Nermada* rivers. The annual fair, held near that spot at the beginning of spring, usually witnesses eight or ten victims of this superstition.—See *As. Res.* Vol. VII. p. 257.

The father of RHADACANT'HA, the *Pandit* so respectfully mentioned by *Sir* WILLIAM JONES in different parts of the *Asiatic Researches*, died a centenarian. His widow, who was fourscore, "became a *Sati*, and burnt herself to expiate sin."—Life of *Sir* W. JONES, Vol. II. p. 141.

In the *Mahrata* country, in *Benares*, and, I suppose, other parts of *India*, women, generally old women, are to be met with, I believe belonging to a particular tribe, who will devote themselves to death to attain certain ends, be it revenge or money, for themselves or their employers. But it does not often happen that the debtor, if it be on such an occasion, will venture, by refusing satisfaction, an imminent risque of the old heroine's actual self-murder. He is generally sufficiently terrified by the denunciations and execrations of the inexorable dun, who bitterly threatens the wretched defaulter with her present and eternal vengeance.

Sometimes the creditor takes a cow, or a calf, before the debtor's door, threatening, if his debt be not paid, to kill it; the sin of which will be on the head of the uncomplying party.

In the *Ayin Akbery* it is said that suicide is sometimes meritorious; and there are five modes of performing it preferable to others: 1. starving; 2. being covered with dry cow-dung, and consumed by fire; 3. being buried in snow; 4. going into the sea at the mouth of the *Ganges*, there praying and confessing sins until the alligators devour the penitent; 5. cutting one's throat at *Allahabad*, at the junction of the *Ganges* and *Jumna*.

* KALA, a name of SIVA, BHAIRAVA, his sons, &c.---See page 177.

seen the *Peshwa* BAAJY RAO, his brothers AMRIT RAO and CHIMNA APPA, NANA FIRNAVEES, and other personages of the highest distinction, imitate the *Mahomedans* in the procession and tumult of the *Tabut:* and come themselves on elephants, in magnificent state, preceded some of them by field-pieces to fire salutes, to the river to witness the immersion of the *Tabuts,* which is always performed at the junction of the *Moota* and *Moola* rivers, that join at the *English* residency; the habitations of which afford a fine view of this interesting and really magnificent spectacle. The *Tabuts,* however elegant and costly, are thrown into the water and demolished.

This is an instance of the *Brahmans,* and other *Hindus,* being less averse to imitate the customs of other people than the hitherto-received opinion would admit.

I will briefly mention a farther, a sort of *counter,* instance of imitation in an individual of another religion, or of the moral influence of example.

A *Mahomedan* butcher at *Poona,* who occasionally supplied our residency with meat, being asked—out of experimental curiosity of course, as no one there could have thought of seriously proposing such an act, if he would kill a calf, started back with horror at the proposal, ejaculating a prayer to be forgiven for having even heard it.*

A *Mahomedan* is forbidden to eat meat which has not been killed by one of the faithful; who is directed, among other easy ceremonies, to *hallal,* or sanctify, the animal by turning his face toward *Mecca,* and while the blood is ejected, to repeat their creed, or profession of faith—"There is no God but God, and MAHAMMED is the prophet of God." Many *Mahratas,* and other *Hindus,* pleased with the ceremony, bring their sheep, fowls, &c. to *Mahomedans* to be *hallalled,* and then eat them with increased satisfaction.

Another anecdote may be admissible, as tending to show how indifferent the extensive tribe of *Mahratas* are in their diet; premising, that the *Mahrata*

* Similar imitations are observed in other parts. "The *Mussulmans* of *India* do not scruple to borrow from the *Hindus,* superstitious ceremonies that are celebrated with festivity: they take an active part in the gambols of the *Huli,* and even solicit the favours of the *Indian* PLUTUS at the *Diwali.*† The bridal procession on the fourth day, with all the sports and gambols of the *Chaut'hi,* is evidently copied from the similar customs of the *Hindus.* In *Bengal* the *Mussulmans* have even adopted the premature marriage of infants."—COLEBROKE. *As. Res.* Vol. VII. p. 307.

† A festival in honour of KALI: called also KALI-*puja,* as the *Dasra* is, in honour of the same deity, under the name of DURGA; and called also DURGA-*puja,* and *Durgotsava*

belongs to the grand division *Ketri*, the second in rank of the four, immediately next to the *Brahman*. The tribe is very numerous: how the *Mahrata* may rank among its subdivisions I know not, but imagine low.

A *Mahrata*, much above a low station in life, a soldier of some rank, and it may be said, a gentleman, being on a visit to one of our officers at the Residency who was in the habit of rearing poultry, heard directions given to a servant to throw away a batch of eggs that had failed of hatching. The *Mahrata*, although aware of their condition, indicated a wish for the eggs; and on being asked what he could do with them—"could he eat them?" said, "perhaps not; but they would do for the children."

Mahratas eat almost indiscriminately; I know of nothing they object to, except beef and tame swine: wild hogs they will eat.

With the higher tribes, eating is a business of much ceremony and importance. Enough has been written on the particular caution observed not to partake of the same dish with an individual of an inferior *cast*; or cooked, or even touched, by an inferior. The temple of JAGA NATH, the famous resort for pilgrims of all sects, although KRISHNA be chiefly worshipped there, is a converging point, where all the contending parties unite in harmony with each other. It is commonly understood that here, and here only, do all casts, tribes, sects, or whatever terms may best include the whole race of *Hindus*, eat and drink together. I do not immediately recollect any good authority for this generally-received opinion: if correct, it is a curious subject for inquiry. It is well known that, in general, a *Brahman* will eat dressed victuals cooked only by a *Brahman*. I recollect much embarrassment being caused at *Poona*, by a *Brahman* of rank, who gave great dinners, discovering his favourite cook to be a *Mahomedan*. Considerable distress arose from this incident; less, however, I imagine, than if the impostor had been of a base tribe of *Hindu:* the impurity would be removed by expiatory fasting, washings, &c. penances; and, above all, alms to temples, and to *Brahmans*.

The *Brahmans* have great vanity on the point of cooking: they think that no other people know how to live. Many books are doubtless in their possession on this science; and a *Brahmanical Almanac de Gourmand* might perhaps rival its namesake. At an early period of our ambassador's residence at the court of *Poona*, it was usual for the *Peshwa*, and the ministers, and courtiers, to entertain him and suite at dinner; and it could be discovered that some of them supposed our party would never again tolerate the barbarous taste of our own national cookery; and while with reasonable hospitality urging us to partake of the good fare, insinuated, rather more plainly than is common to the artful refinement of *Brahmanical* politeness, that we might not, perhaps, soon meet again with such temptations to indulgence.*

It must be confessed, that both *Hindu* and *Mahomedan* cookery are in many instances excellent; still the politeness of an *English* guest is sometimes put to a severe test, when he feels it expedient to partake of a *syllakakabian* dish that his palate revolts at, rather than wound the harmless vanity of the host's or his cook's fancied acquirements in the sophistication of viands.

As well as in respect to their eating, the public opinion I think also erroneous as to the drinking of the *Hindus*. That their moral and religious books, like ours, recommend and ordain temperance and abstinence, is true enough; but the general practice is, I fear, different. All authors almost, from QUINTIUS CURTIUS to the existing race, tell us that the *Hindus* drink no intoxicating liquor. In that interesting and intelligent work, CRAUFURD'S *Sketches*, we are told, (Vol. I. p. 140.) that "no *Hindu*, of any of the four casts, is allowed by his religion to taste any intoxicating liquor: it is only drank by strangers, dancers, players, and *Chandalas*, or outcasts."

This is, I fear, distant from the truth: the lower orders of *Hindus*—of three out of the four tribes, are nearly as drunken a set as the lower classes of most other religions. It would be deemed very disgraceful in a *Brahman* to be seen drunk; and no instance of it occurs to my recollection: on the whole, the *Brahmans* are, I think, the most moral and best behaved race of men that I ever met with.

In the *Sri Bhagavata*, a life of KRISHNA, stories are given of drunken bouts, partaken of by himself, and his tribe of *Yadavas*, and others; which, however, he prohibited, in consequence of the disgraces and dilemmas in which the consequences involved the party.†

* The simplicity of the *Mahratas*, even of *Brahmans*, is sometimes amusing: I recollect hearing NANA FURNAVEESE, one of the wisest of men, ask some questions on nautical affairs of this description. On the occasion of a treaty, made with the *Poona* government in the year 1777, we gave some hostages from *Bombay* for its due performance. Passing a river, these gentlemen (W. G. FARMER, *Esq.* and *Captain* STUART,) asked permission to bathe: their request was duly considered by the chiefs, and negatived, lest, as the gentlemen afterwards learned, they might effect their escape; for the river running somewhere into the sea, the *Mahrata* officers could not be responsible for their charge if suffered to go into their *own element*, being *water people*, as they termed them.

† The following eloquent passage, applied by a popular author to the *Hindus*, does great credit to his heart, but must not, of course, be taken in reference to the whole race: to many individuals it may be haply extended.—"The most innocent and inoffensive people on earth; whose food is rice; whose simple

In the note below* are given some texts from the *Institutes* of MENU, and some other extracts, with remarks on the subject of the supposed abstinence of the *Hindus* from flesh meat; together with some of more general reference to the character and sanctity of *Brahmans*, that we next will proceed to the consideration of.

beverage is the water of the *Ganges*; whose bed is the luxuriant herbage of the ground; whose covering is the expanse of heaven: a people patient under suffering; hospitable in the highest degree to their own species, and overflowing with the most amiable benevolence even to the brute creation: a people, of which the first grand division is absorbed in the delightful researches of theology and philosophy; whose second tribe is distinguished by their wisdom in governing, and for fortitude in arms; while the third and fourth orders are equally eminent in the species of useful knowledge allotted for their acquisition, and distinguished by humility, honesty, and industry."

* Chap. III. v. 123.—"Sages have distinguished the monthly *Sradha* by the title of *anwaharya*, or after-eaten; that is, eaten after the *Pinda*, or ball of rice: and it must be performed with extreme care, and with flesh meat in the best condition.

"124. What *Brahmans* must be entertained at that ceremony, and who must be accepted; how many are to be fed, and with what sorts of food: on all those articles, without omission, I will fully discourse."

(And they are accordingly detailed.)

"227. Let him add spiced puddings, and milky messes of various sorts; roots of herbs, and ripe fruits; savoury meats, and sweet-smelling drinks."

"266. What sort of oblations, given duly to the *manes*, are capable of satisfying them for a long time, or for eternity, I will now declare, without omission—

"267. The ancestors of men are satisfied a whole month with rice, barley, black lentils, or vetches, water, roots, and fruit, given with prescribed ceremonies;

"268. Two months, with fish; three months, with venison; four, with mutton; five, with the flesh of such birds as the twice-born may eat;

"269. Six months, with the flesh of kids; seven, with that of spotted deer; eight, with that of the deer, or antelope, called *ena*; nine, with that of the *ruru*;

"270. Ten months are they satisfied with the flesh of wild boars and wild buffaloes †; eleven, with that of rabbits, or hares, and of tortoises;

† Buffaloes, although reckoned and eaten as beef by *Europeans*, seem of much less estimation than the cow or ox in the eye of a *Hindu*. I have known a *Brahman*, in the *Mahrata* country, during the war of 1790, against TIPPOO, supply a regiment of *Europeans* regularly with *buffaloes* for slaughter: I do not recollect whether or not any cows or oxen were among his supplies, but believe not. The *Brahman* seemed to have no sort of "compunctious visitings" on the occasion: beef was, perhaps inconsiderately, asked for, and he sent the *buffaloes*; had he sent sheep, which were abundant, they would have answered as well. The milk of the buffalo is much cleaner and better than that of the cow, and is in general preference either to eat or for tea, but not for butter. The young buffalo is, perhaps, the only animal that grows in comeliness as it grows in years: when very young, it is singularly ugly. While serving with PURSERAM BHOW's army in the war just mentioned, I, one very hot day on which we had a long march,

Enough, I think, has been offered, and on better authority than mine, to prove the fact that *Hindus*, even *Brahmans*, may legally eat meat. It has been

"271. A whole year, with the milk of cows, and food made of that milk; from the flesh of the long-eared white goat, their satisfaction endures twelve years.

"272. The potherb *calasaca*; the fish *mahasalca*, or the *diodon*; the flesh of a *rhinoceros*, or of an iron-coloured kid; honey; and all such forest grains as are eaten by hermits; are formed for their satisfaction without end."

Let it be remembered, that this entertainment of *Srad'ha*, in honour of deceased ancestors, is for *Brahmans* to partake of: it is laid down in verse 255, preceding, that "the liberal gifts of food, the due preparation for the repast, and the company of the most exalted *Brahmans*, are true riches in the obsequies to ancestors."

In v. 226. divers things are enumerated, as "wealth in the *Srad'ha* to the gods."

"227. Such wild grains as are eaten by hermits, milk, the juice of the moon-plant, meat untainted, and salt unprepared by art, are things fit in their own nature for the last-mentioned offering."

Chap. IV. v. 26.—"At the season when old grain is usually consumed, let a *Brahman* offer new grain for a plentiful harvest: at the solstices let him sacrifice cattle.

"27. Not having offered grain for the harvest, nor cattle at the time of the solstice, let no *Brahman* who keeps hallowed fire, and wishes for long life, taste rice or flesh;

"28. Since the holy fires, not being honoured with new grain and with a sacrifice of cattle, are greedy for rice and flesh, and seek to devour his vital spirits."

"112. Let not a *Brahman* read the *Vedas* lolling on a couch, nor with his thighs crossed; nor having lately swallowed meat, or other food, given on the birth or death of a relation."

"131. At noon, or at midnight, or having eaten flesh at a *Srad'ha*, or in either of the twilights, let not a *Brahman* tarry where four ways meet."

"205. Never let a priest eat part of a sacrifice not begun with the texts of the *Veda*; nor," &c. &c.

"213. Nor that which is given without due honour to honourable men; nor any flesh which has not been sacrificed."

"250. A bed, houses, blades of *Kusa* grass, perfumes, water, flowers, jewels, butter, milk, ground rice, fish, new milk, flesh meat, and great vegetables, let him not proudly reject."

Chap. V. v. 11.—"Let every twice-born man avoid carnivorous birds, and such as live in towns; and quadrupeds with uncloven hoofs, except those allowed by the *Veda*—

"12. The sparrow, the water-bird *plava*, the phenicopteros, the breed of the town-cock, the wood-pecker, the parrot, male and female;

"13. Birds that strike with their beak, web-footed birds, those who wound with strong talons, and those who dive to devour fish. Let him avoid meat kept at a slaughter-house, and dried meat;

---

took temporary shelter under a tree, where I saw a *dooly*, which is a *palky* of uncostly materials, many of which, with men to carry them, are always attached to our hospital department and corps, when in the field, for the accommodation of the sick and wounded; and supposing it might contain a wounded man, to whom some drink would be acceptable, I approached it, and to my great surprise and amusement found, as I drew aside the curtains, that it contained a buffalo! an ugly staring calf, of one of PURSERAM BHOW'S milch cows: but few persons, perhaps, ever saw a *buffalo* in a *Palankeen*.

asked, how, in former times of famine in *Bengal*, it happened that the *Gentoos*, as travellers relate, died in the streets rather than eat meat, or any food, proffered

" 14. The heron, the raven, all amphibious fish-eaters, tame hogs, and fish of every sort, but those expressly permitted.

" 15. He who eats the flesh of any animal is called the eater of that animal itself; and a fish-eater is an eater of all flesh: from fish, therefore, he must diligently abstain;

" 16. Yet the two fish, called *pathina* and *rohita*, may be eaten by the guests, when offered as a repast in honour of the gods, or the manes; and so may the *sasalka*, of every species."

Then follows a long list of permitted and prohibited animal food: among the former are the hedgehog, porcupine, lizard, tortoise, rabbit, hare.*—" These, among five-toed animals, wise legislators declare lawful food; and all quadrupeds, camels excepted, which have but one row of teeth:" the forbidden are solitary animals, unknown beasts or birds, though generally declared eatable, and all creatures with five claws.

" 19. The twice-born man who has intentionally eaten a mushroom, the flesh of a tame hog, or a town cock, or a leek, or an onion, or garlick, is degraded immediately."

(With a little alteration, the first part of JUVENAL's fifteenth satire, beginning *Quis nescit*, might be applied to the *Brahmans* as happily as to the *Egyptians*, the object of his severity. The following, with the necessary modification, is OWEN's paraphrase:—

Who knows not that there's nothing vile nor odd
Which brain-sick *Brahmans* turn not to a god?
Some of those blockheads bulls and cows adore;
Fish, reptiles, birds, and snakes, as many more.
A long-tail'd ape some suppliants admire,
Or man-like elephant—a god their sire:
One race a god half-man half-fish revere,
Others to beastly moities adhere:
Hosts to a stone's high deity bend down,
While others sticks with adoration crown;
Nay vegetables here hold rank divine—
On leeks or mushrooms 'tis prophane to dine.
Oh, holy nation! where the gardens bear
A crop of gods throughout the tedious year!)

The taint of illicit food is, however, easily expiated: the rules of expiation are given in this chapter.

" 22. Beasts and birds of excellent sort may be slain by *Brahmans* for sacrifice, or for the sustenance of those whom they are bound to support: AGASTYA † did this of old."

* Considering the superstitious notions of many ancient people, and of some among the moderns, I should have looked for the hare in the list of prohibited animals.

† AGASTYA was a diminutive but pious and learned *Brahman*; who, for his learning and virtue, was translated to the skies, and now shines *Canopus* in the constellation *Argo*. This sage is said to have been

by *Europeans*; and if rice or vegetables were not their only food, why substitutes of flesh were not resorted to? I have never been in *Bengal*, nor if I had, should I, perhaps, be able to account for the fact—admitting it to be one: it is, however, one thing to state, or to prove a fact, and another to account for

Other regulations follow for the eating or avoiding flesh meat; and so far from its being generally forbidden, the *Hindus* generally, even *Brahmans*, nay priests, are expressly enjoined to eat it, and are even cursed for refusing to eat flesh. Some few texts to this effect are here extracted, from the same most venerable and revered code extant among the *Hindus*, or, perhaps, among any existing people.

Chap. V. v. 28.—"For the sustenance of this vital spirit BRAHMA created all this animal and vegetable system; and all that is moveable or immoveable that spirit devours."

"30. He who eats according to law commits no sin, even though every day he taste the flesh of such animals as may lawfully be tasted; since both animals who may be eaten, and those who eat them, were equally created by BRAHMA."

"32. No sin is committed by him who, having honoured the deities and the *manes*, eats flesh meat which he has bought, or which he has himself acquired, or which has been given to him by another."

"34. The sin of him who kills deer for gain is not so heinous, with respect to the punishment in another life, as that of him who eats flesh meat in vain, or not previously offered as a sacrifice:

"35. But the man who, engaged in holy rites according to law, refuses to eat it, shall sink in another world, for twenty-one births, to the state of a beast."

"42. The twice-born man who, knowing the meaning and principles of the *Vedas*, slays cattle on the occasion above mentioned, conveys both himself and cattle to the summit of beatitude."

It would be superfluous to quote any more texts in proof that the *Hindus* in general, nay universally, may eat flesh meat; and my opinion is, that, with some, and, comparatively, not very many voluntary exceptions, they do eat it. There are, however, rules and recommendations of abstinence in this same venerable code whence I have extracted such contradictory indulgences. Verses 46. to 55. strongly enjoin, if they do not command, abstinence; and the very next runs thus:

Chap. V. v. 56.—"In lawfully tasting flesh meat, in drinking fermented liquor, in caressing women, there is no turpitude; for to such enjoyments men are naturally prone: but a virtuous abstinence from them produces a signal compensation."

I have been more tediously particular in my extracts from these sacred and holy *Institutes*, on the subject of the abstinence or non-abstinence of *Hindus*, and even *Brahmans*, from animal food, from a full persuasion that it is a point on which the general opinion of the *European* world is not more uniform than erroneous.

---

so learned and pious, that he overcame thereby the serpent SANCHANAGA, whose fiery breath was a poisonous wind, that burned and destroyed all animals and vegetables in his neighbourhood. AGASTYA reduced the serpent, and carried him about in an earthen vessel. There may be some astronomical fact concealed in this story; or it may refer to some mitigation of the effects of the *Samum*, or envenomed wind of *Abyssinia*, where this sage flourished. For farther notice of him, see *Asiatic Researches*, Vol. VIII. page 304.—MAURICE's *Ancient History*, Vol. I. p. 341. Vol. II. p. 38.

it.* But we may generally admit, that *Hindus* of the higher classes in each of the three first tribes would not receive any food so offered, be it of meat or vegetables: it is contrary to what they have been taught as pleasing to the gods. Hence the *Hindu* is the most indifferent of men in regard to life: he refuses food offered, as he is taught, unlawfully, and dies a martyr. If martyrdom were to be admitted, as it has been indiscreetly urged, in proof of religious truth, the *Hindu* cannot be outshone, either in the number or zeal of his "whole army of martyrs."

So stiff are even the lower orders of *Hindus* in the article of purity, that the inferiors of your menial servants will not only decline eating of your food, but *palky*-bearers, for instance, and some *mashalchis*, or link-boys, will not clean a knife, or touch a plate, because they have been in contact with meat—they would, if necessary, rather suffer martyrdom. But, if on a journey, they will

* The inutility of applying theoretical reasonings to cases where our feelings are paramount, however irrational such feelings may be, has been noticed with sufficient frequency. Although the incident that I am about to relate be not very creditable to my philosophy, I will nevertheless give it. I had left *Poona* about sunset on a journey to *Bombay*, and arriving at the top of the *Bhoor-ghaut* before sunrise next morning, quitted my horses and attendants, determining to descend the mountain alone, that I might uninterruptedly enjoy the tremendous scenery of this unrivalled region. Knowing the path so well, I did not judge it possible that I could lose it; but it so happened, that, wandering out of the regular road, I missed the well-known village of *Kapooly* at the *ghaut's* foot, where I was to have rejoined my retinue; and before I discovered my error, and could rectify it, found that I had proceeded several miles beyond the village: which distance was now to be retraced. It was the month of May, the hottest of the year; the road excessively stoney and dusty; the sun was high, and the inclining face of the mountain, looking to the westward, reflected his rays and heat full on mine; and before I again reached the foot of the hills, I was almost sinking with thirst and fatigue. I had arrived within a quarter of a mile of the fine tank of *Kapooly*, the bound, at that moment, of my earthly views; but impatient from such extreme thirst, entered a hovel, and requested water. A young woman immediately retired from a sort of front viranda, where a man was at work, and I listened to the gurgling of the liquid from a large into a portable vessel with feelings not to be described: she approached me with the water in her hand, and with benevolence in her face, and I most eagerly prepared to drink, and (as I thought) live. The man, looking at me, arrested the hand of his wife, and not seeing, perhaps, that I was a *Christian*, or not knowing our sources of impurity, told me, with distress and meekness, that I was in the house, and about to receive drink from the hand, of a *Chumár*, (that is, a cobbler, or leather-worker; among *Hindus*, a very base tribe). Can the reader believe that, in such a situation, I should on that account forego what on earth I most and alone required? But I certainly did—I hope with decent thanks by signs, for I could scarcely articulate them; and bent my miserable steps, directed by my anxious host, toward the town and tank, doubtful, near as they were, if I had energy or strength to reach them. Now this could not have been vanity; for in what point could I be vain-glorious before this kind cobbler and his benevolent wife? Nor could it have been hypocrisy; for I fancied myself almost on the threshold of another world. What the exciting feeling may have been I can scarcely tell; but it was not, I think, either of these.

remind you of the day being sacred to such a deity, and solicit a shilling* to buy a sheep, which they will kill and eat with all the *sang froid* and *gusto* of a *Christian.*

It has, perhaps, been a benevolent artifice of the priests to make the multitude contented, and even pleased, at abstaining from what such an immense population could not, under their bad, if under any, system of political and domestic economy, possibly obtain. Nor can such a population, or, indeed, perhaps, the population of any civilized nation, find in resorting to flesh any material relief from a dearth of vegetable food, where the latter, as it does almost every where, constitutes the chief ingredient of diet. In *Ireland* the peasantry abstain from animal food; and knowing no comparative superiority, scarcely repine: in *England* they abstain, and grumble: in *India* they abstain, and glory in it.

The authority of *Mr.* Colebroke, taken from his Dissertation on the Religious Ceremonies of the *Hindus, (As. Res.* Vol. VII. p. 271.) may be given as in point on the subject of eating animals, if it be not found to coincide exactly with my opinion.

" It should be observed," he says, " respecting the practice of giving food at these obsequies, that *Brahmans* generally give it to one or more of their own relations: a stranger, unless indigent, would be very unwilling to accept the food, or to attend at a *srad'ha,* for the purpose of eating it. The use of flesh meat is positively enjoined to *Hindus* at certain obsequies, (see *Ins.* of Menu, Chap. III. v. 124.) and recommended at all,† (Menu, Chap. III. v. 268. &c.) But the precepts of their lawgivers on the subject are, by some, deemed obsolete in the present age, and are evaded by others who acknowledge the cogency of these laws: these commonly make a vow of abstaining from flesh meat, and consider that vow as more binding than the precepts here alluded to. Others, again, not only eat meat at obsequies and solemn sacrifices, but make it their common diet, in direct breach of their religion."—(See *Ins.* of Menu, C. V. v. 31. &c.)

As well as in the *Institutes* of Menu, slaying and eating animals is allowed and enjoined in the *Vedas*; and one of the leading innovations of Buddha was the condemnation of such a practice. The abstinence from flesh—I apply the term to *Hindus* as I would to the fasts of *Christians,* may, perhaps, in some de-

* Half a *rupee,* or about a shilling, will buy a sheep in most of the interior parts of *India*; or where the quick interchange of money, introduced by *European* commerce, hath not rendered money cheaper.

† Exclusive of daily *srad'has,* formal obsequies are performed ninety-six times in every year, on fixed days; enumerated in the page preceding that whence the above passage is quoted.

gree, have arisen from the reforming mildness of BUDDHA and his doctrines. Such doctrines being evidently innocent, and gaining ground in the estimation of the people, would be a sufficient inducement for the leaders of the orthodox to tolerate and adopt them, and to emulate the approved practice of their heretical opponents. Some of our early missionaries observing the priests in *Malabar* to abstain from animal food, and the respect they consequently enjoyed, did so likewise, and called themselves *Christian Brahmans.*

The following passage is applicable to the topic under discussion, and elucidatory also of other parts of my work.

"The *Aswamed'ha*, and *Purushamed'ha*, celebrated in the manner directed by this *Veda*,* are not really sacrifices of horses and men. In the first-mentioned ceremony, six hundred and nine animals of various kinds, domestic and wild, including birds, fish, and reptiles, are made fast; the tame ones, to twenty-one posts, and the wild ones, in the intervals between the pillars; and after certain prayers have been recited, the victims are let loose without injury. In the other, a hundred and eighty-five men of various specified tribes, characters, and professions, are bound to eleven posts; and after the hymn, concerning the allegorical immolation† of NARAYANA, has been recited, these human victims are liberated unhurt; and oblations of butter are made on the sacrificial fire. This mode of performing the *Aswamed'ha* and *Purushamed'ha* as emblematic ceremonies, not as real sacrifices,‡ is taught in this *Veda*; and the interpretation is fully confirmed by the rituals, (particularly a separate ritual of the *Purushamed'ha*, by YAJNYADEVA,) and by commentators on the *Sanhita* and *Brahmana*: one of whom assigns as a reason, 'because the flesh of victims, which have been actually sacrificed at a *Yajnya*, must be eaten by the persons who offer the sacrifice: but a man cannot be allowed, much less required, to eat human flesh."—This passage is cited by *Mr.* COLEBROKE from memory: he adds, "It may be hence inferred, or conjectured at least, that human sacrifices were not authorised by the *Veda* itself; but were either then abrogated, and an emblematical ceremony substituted in their place, or they must have been introduced in later times on the authority of certain *Puranas*, or *Tantras*, fabricated by persons who, in this, as in other matters, established many unjustifiable practices, on the

* The White *Yajush*: the sacrifices are of a horse and a man.

† See NARAYANA, p. 75.

‡ Here seems to be a faint recognition of the doctrine of the *real presence*, and the *type* of the reformed religion among the different denominations of *Christians*.

foundation of emblems and allegories, which they misunderstood."*—COLEBROKE on the *Vedas*. *As. Res.* Vol. VIII. p. 438.

In a description of the species of cow called *Gayal*, in the eighth volume of the *Asiatic Researches*, are some passages that I will advert to, in evidence of the

* Although it will be abundantly proved, by various passages scattered through this work, that the philosophical or reasoning portion of the *Hindus* are not polytheists, as has, indeed, been asserted for many years by authors of different countries; still, as in the case of the *Romanists* of the *Christian* church, it will be difficult to acquit the lower and ignorant majority of idolatry and plurality of superior beings—differing in degree, but still sanctified and deified.

Image worship is very general among *Hindus* of all sects: there are, doubtless, some philosophic minds, and, perhaps, some in every sect, who have reasoned and rejected it; but I know of no such rejection by any whole tribe or description of men.

"It has now come to light," says ABU'L FAZIL, "that the generally-received opinion of the *Hindus* being polytheists has no foundation in truth; for although their tenets admit positions that are difficult to be defended, yet that they are worshippers of God, and only one God, are incontrovertible truths."—*Ayin Akbery*, Vol. III.

"They, one and all, believe in the unity of the Godhead," (this surely is too unqualified); "and although they hold images in high veneration, yet they are by no means idolaters, as the ignorant suppose. I have myself," continues ABU'L FAZIL, "frequently discoursed with many learned and upright men of this religion, and comprehend their doctrine: which is, that the images are only representations of celestial beings, to whom they turn themselves while at prayer to prevent their thoughts from wandering; and they think it an indispensable duty to address the Deity after that manner."

"In all their prayers they implore blessings from the sun. They consider the Supreme Being to be above all labour; believing BRAHMA to be the creator of the world; VISHNU, its providence and preserver; and RUDRA, (who is also called MAHADEVA,) its destroyer."

"One sect believes that God, who hath no equal, appeared on earth under those three forms, without having been thereby polluted in the smallest degree: in the same manner as the *Christians* speak of their MESSIAH.

"Others hold, that all three were only human beings, who, on account of their sanctity and righteousness, were raised to these high dignities."—*Ib.*

The respect in which images were very anciently held by the *Hindus*, appears in the following text of MENU. *Ins.* Chap. IV. v. 130.—"Let not a *Brahman* intentionally pass over the shadow of sacred images."

In the curious account of the *Hindu* trial by ordeal, in the *As. Res.* Vol. I. a process by images is thus detailed:

"The priest shall perform rites to the image of some tremendous deity; and, having bathed the idol, shall make the accused to drink three handfuls of the water that has dropped from it.

"If, in fourteen days after, he suffer no dreadful calamity from the act of the deity, or of the king, he must indubitably be acquitted."

The usage of having household gods is as old as history; but, perhaps, *Dii Lares*, or *Penates*, were never more common among any people than the *Hindus*. The gods of LABAN, which his daughter RACHEL,

Hindus of *Bengal*, and neighbouring provinces, killing and eating, not only animals, but the *Gayal*; which differs not much more from other species of kine than the *Hindu* does from the *European*. "By some sects the *Gayal* is hunted for the sake of the flesh and skins: the flesh of the *Gayal* is in the highest estimation

the wife of Jacob, was so strongly attached to, were, perhaps, similar to some in use among the *Hindus*: her's must have been small, as she carried them away and hid them under the harness of a camel. I have many so small, some scarcely an inch long, that several scores might be accommodated in one's hat. Others, again, of metal, will weigh many pounds: the subject of Plate 14. is the largest metallic idol that I brought from *India*. I have neglected to ascertain its weight; but it is equal I judge to thirty pounds, perhaps considerably more.

Mr. Colebroke, in his Dissertation on the *Vedas*, (*As. Res.* Vol. VIII.) offers some opinions on the histories of Krishna and Rama that invite investigation: the result of which, if the inquiry be pursued with the zeal and judgment that are displayed in his interesting essays, cannot fail of throwing much light on the real, as well as mythological, history of the *Hindus*. He suspects two of the *Upanishads*, or theological treatises, appertaining to the *Atharva Veda*, on the exploits of Krishna and Rama, to be of more modern date, and of less authenticity, than most other parts of the *Vedas*: these are the *Rama-tapaniya*, and part of the *Gopala-tapaniya*, which is called *Krishna Upanishad*. "The introduction to the first of these works contains a summary, which agrees in substance with the mythological history of the husband of Sita and conqueror of *Lanka*: the other exalts the hero of *Mat'hura*."

"Although the *Rama-tapaniya*," continues *Mr.* Colebroke, "be inserted in all the collections of *Upanishads* which I have seen, and the *Gopala-tapaniya* in some, yet I am inclined to doubt their genuineness, and to suspect that they have been written in times more modern, when compared with the remainder of the *Vedas*. This suspicion is chiefly grounded on the opinion, that the sects which now worship Rama and Krishna as incarnations of Vishnu are comparatively new: I have not found in any other part of the *Vedas* the least trace of such a worship. The real doctrine of the whole *Indian* scripture is the unity of the Deity, in whom the universe is comprehended; and the seeming polytheism which it exhibits, offers the elements and stars and planets as gods. The three principal manifestations of the Divinity, with other personified attributes and energies, and most of the other gods of *Hindu* mythology, are, indeed, mentioned, or at least indicated, in the *Vedas*. But the worship of deified heroes is no part of that system; nor are the incarnations of deities suggested in any other portion of the text which I have yet seen, though such are hinted at by the commentators."

"According to the notions which I entertain of the real history of the *Hindu* religion, the worship of Rama and Krishna by the *Vaishnavas*, and that of Mahadeva and Bhavani by the *Saivas* and *Sactas*, have been generally introduced since the persecutions of the *Baudd'has* and *Jainas*. The institutions of the *Veda* are anterior to Budd'ha, whose theology seems to have been borrowed from the system of Capila; whose most conspicuous practical doctrine is stated to have been the unlawfulness of killing animals, for the purpose of eating their flesh, under the pretence of performing a sacrifice, or *Yajnya*. The overthrow of the sect of Buddha, in *India*, has not effected the full revival of the religious system inculcated in the *Vedas*: most of what is there taught is now obsolete, and, in its stead, new orders of religious devotees have been instituted; and new forms of religious ceremonies have been established. Rituals, founded on the *Puranas*, and observances borrowed from a worse source, the *Tantras*, have, in great measure, anti-

among the *Cucis*, (a tribe of mountaineers); so much so, that no solemn festival is ever celebrated without slaughtering one or more *Gayals*, according to the importance of the occasion."—Page 517. "In some provinces the *Hindus* will not kill the *Gayal*, which they hold in equal veneration with the cow."—P. 519. "The *Raja* of *Cach'har*, who is a *Csbatriya** of the *Suryabansi* race, occasionally sends several *Gayals* to be sacrificed on certain hills in his country, in order to conciliate the *devata* of the place." "The *Gayal* is like a cow—consequently not a cow; a *Hindu*, therefore, commits no offence by killing one. But natives

quated the institutions of the *Vedas*: in particular, the sacrificing of animals before the idols of KALI) † has superseded the less sanguinary practices of the *Yajnya*; and the adoration of RAMA and of KRISHNA has succeeded to that of the elements and planets: If this opinion be well founded, it follows that the *Upanishads* in question have probably been composed in later times, since the introduction of those sects which hold RAMA and GOPALA in peculiar veneration."

"On the same ground every *Upanishad*, which strongly favours the doctrines of these sects, may be rejected, as liable to much suspicion. Such is the *Atmabhoda Upanishad*, in which KRISHNA is noticed by the title of MADHU-SUDANA, son of DEVACI; and such also is the *Sundaritapani*, which inculcates the worship of DEVI."—*As. Res.* Vol. VIII. p. 495.

In the ninth volume, (*As. Res.* p. 293.) *Mr.* COLEBROKE observes, in explanation of the above remark, that the mere mention of RAMA, or of KRISHNA, without any indication of peculiar reverence, would not authorise a presumption against the genuineness of that passage on his hypothesis, nor, admitting its authenticity, furnish an argument against that system. He supposes both heroes to have been known characters in ancient fabulous history, but conjectures that, on the same basis, new fables have been constructed, elevating those personages to the rank of gods.

Some of the above passages may be deemed irrelevant: they were not intended for this portion of my work, but for one that, considering to what an extent it has already reached, I fear I shall not find room or time for. I had attempted, and intended to offer, a brief Analysis of the *Vedas* and *Puranas*, together with the different systems of *Hindu* philosophy, in comparison with their probable offspring, the schools of *Greece* and *Italy*; and a notice of some of the more sacred and popular literary works of *India*. Intending to offer this in a connected form, I have, perhaps, in earlier parts of this work, left some points unexplained, in view to the explanation that I thus contemplated; but which, I fear, I must now altogether omit.

* The tribe next to the *Brahman*: *Cshatriya* is the classical mode of writing what is commonly called and written *Khetri*, or *Katri*. *Suryabansi*, or *Suryavansa*, is of the race of the Sun: called also *Helivansa*, of the same meaning.

† "In *Bengal*, and the contiguous provinces, thousands of kids and buffalo calves are sacrificed before the idol at every celebrated temple; and opulent persons make a similar destruction at their private chapels. The sect which has adopted this system is prevalent in *Bengal*, and in many other provinces of *India*; and the sanguinary chapter, translated from the *Kalica Purana*" (see p. 145.) "by *Mr.* BLAQUIERE, (*As. Res.* Vol. V.) is one among the authorities on which it relies. But the practice is not approved of by other sects of *Hindus*."

of *Bengal*, or of the mountains, who are *Hindus*, scruple to kill a *Gayal* themselves, because it is named *Gobay-gow*, or the *Gavaya cow*."—Page 523.

"*Methanas*, another name for the same animal, are sacrificed, especially by *Nagas* and *Cucis*, before the mountain gods, NAKHARAM and MAIRAM.* The *Cucis* and *Nagas* are fond of the meat, and therefore constantly keep such cattle, and eat their flesh; and often make presents of them to the *Raja* of *Cach'har*. The *Raja* preserves them, and sometimes offers *Methanas* in sacrifices to deities; or entertains with their flesh *Nagas* and *Cucis* who come to visit him. The mountaineers are much pleased with that compliment, and eat the meat with delight."†—Page 524.

In the sacred and other books of the *Hindus* this animal is classed with kine: its picture, as well as habits and conformation, clearly indicate its genus.

"The twenty-fourth chapter of the *Yajur Veda* enumerates the animals that should be consecrated to various deities at an *Aswamedha*. It is there directed, (verse 27.) that three *Risyas* (white-footed antelopes,) shall be consecrated to the deities named *Vasus*: in verse 28. that three buffaloes shall be presented to VARUNA;‡ as many *Gavayas*, to VRIHASPATI;‡ and the same number of camels, to TWASHTI.‡ The commentator on the *Veda*, (MAHIDHARA,) explains *Gavaya* as signifying 'wild cattle resembling kine.'—It is evident that this suits better with the *Gayal*,‖ than with any other animal known in *India*."—Page 525.

I find among my memoranda a note relating to the *Raja* of *Kooch-bahar*, (which may, perhaps, be another mode of spelling *Cach-bar*,) that was taken from the verbal communication of a gentleman who, I think, was present at the sanguinary ceremony it describes: the following is a copy of it—

"When the present (1804,) *Raja* of *Kooch-bahar*, in *Bengal*, succeeded to that title and station, one of the ceremonies of inauguration was marked by an extraordinary effusion of blood: fifteen hundred buffaloes were slaughtered in five days, and more than thrice that number of goats and kids. This bloodshed was in the presence, and under the direction, of *Brahmans*: the *Raja* himself killed

* I do not know these deities.

† This passage was written by a native—the *Vakil*, or agent, of the *Raja* of *Cach-har*; and, therefore, most likely a *Hindu*, if not a *Brahman*.

‡ Regents of Water, the planet JUPITER, and of the *Sun*, in the order in which they occur.

‖ A very strong fort, in the country of the *Raja* of *Berar*, is named *Gayal-gher*, or *Gher-gawail*, probably from this animal. It was taken by *Sir* ARTHUR WELLESLEY in our war with the *Mahrata* confederates; and the subject of *fig.* 1. of PLATE 12. was brought thence.—See p. 32.

with his own hand about thirty buffaloes, a *Brahman* making a mark with his finger, previously dipped into white paint, or lime and water, on the animal's neck, at the place proper for the *Raja* to strike: he struck the beasts with a short straight sword, or rather large knife. The *Raja* was a youth, and smote the first buffalo with considerable trepidation, but fortunately killed it."

The sacredness of the persons of *Brahmans*, and the veneration in which they are held, will appear in the verses, cited in the note below, from Menu.*

* Chap. I. v. 88.—"To *Brahmans*, the being supremely glorious, assigned the duties of reading the *Veda*, of teaching it, of sacrificing, of assisting others to sacrifice, of giving alms, if they be rich, and, if indigent, of receiving gifts."

" 93. Since the *Brahman* sprang from the most excellent part; since he was the first-born; and since he possesses the *Veda*; he is by right the chief of this whole creation.

" 94. Him, the being who exists of himself, produced in the beginning from his own mouth; that, having performed holy rites, he might present clarified butter to the gods, and cakes of rice to the progenitors of mankind, for the preservation of the world."

" 96. Of created things, the most excellent are those which are animated; of the animated, those which subsist by intelligence; of the intelligent, mankind; and of men, the sacerdotal class:

" 97. Of priests, those eminent in learning; of the learned, those who know their duty; of those who know it, such as perform it virtuously; and of the virtuous, those who seek beatitude from a perfect acquaintance with scriptural doctrine.

" 98. The very birth of a *Brahman* is a continued incarnation of Dherma, god of justice; for the *Brahman* is born to promote justice, and to procure ultimate happiness.

" 99. When a *Brahman* springs to light, he is born above the world, the chief of all creatures; assigned to guard the treasury of duties, religious and civil.

" 100. Whatever exists in the universe is in effect, though not in form, the wealth of the *Brahman*; since the *Brahman* is entitled to it by his primogeniture and eminence of birth.

" 101. The *Brahman* eats but his own food, wears but his own apparel, and bestows but his own in alms; through the benevolence of the *Brahman*, indeed, other mortals enjoy life."

Chap. IV. v. 142.—" Let no priest, unwashed after food, touch with his hand a cow, a *Brahman*, or fire."

" 165. A twice-born man who barely assaults a *Brahman* with intention to hurt him, shall be whirled about for a century in the hell called *Tamisra*."—(See p. 297.)

" 167. He who, through ignorance of the law, sheds blood from the body of a *Brahman*, not engaged in battle, shall feel excessive pain in his future life:

" 168. As many particles of dust as the blood shall roll up from the ground, for so many years shall the shedder of that blood be mangled by other animals in his next birth."

Chap. XI. v. 208. modifies the punishment for this crime: " So many thousand years shall the shedder of that blood be tormented in hell."

Chap. VIII. v. 380.—" Never shall the king slay a *Brahman*, though convicted of all possible crimes: let him banish the offender from his realm, but with all his property secure, and his body unhurt.

The violent death of one of these persons, "transcendently divine," as they are deemed by MENU, it may be supposed, rarely occurs. I have, however, known of three being put to death, and that too at *Poona*, the immediate seat of *Brahmanical* government; and where, of course, such an event is likely to be viewed in the extremest abhorrence: I will notice the three circumstances I allude to.

The first was the *Kutwal* of the city of *Poona:* the *Kutwal* is an officer of police, something similar, perhaps, to our active magistrate at the *Bow-street* office. It must be premised, that the police of *Poona* is, or at least, a few years back, was, spoken of as admirably regulated. At about nine o'clock in the evening a gun is fired from the village of *Bambora*, situated in front of the *English* Residency, on the side of the river opposite the city, toward which the gun is pointed; and being of very large calibre, it gives sufficient warning to all the citizens to retire to their homes; and after a reasonable time allowed for their so doing, the patrols take up and imprison every individual found in the

"381. No greater crime is known on earth than slaying a *Brahman*; and the king, therefore, must not even form in his mind the idea of killing a priest."

In the following verse, of which an explanation will be given in a future page, an expiation seems offered even for the slaughter of a *Brahman.*—

"Chap. XI. v. 249.—"Sixteen suppressions of the breath, while the holiest of texts is repeated, with the three mighty words, and the triliteral syllable, continued each day for a month, absolve even the slayer of a *Brahman* from his hidden faults."

But it is generally supposed that this offence is beyond the reach of expiation.—"The inviolability of a *Brahman* is a fixed principle of the *Hindus*; and to deprive him of life, either by direct violence, or by causing his death in any mode, is a crime which admits of no expiation."—*Lord* TEIGNMOUTH. *As. Res.* Vol. IV. Art. 22.

Chap. IX. v. 313.—"Let not a king, although in the greatest distress for money, provoke *Brahmans* to anger by taking their property; for they, once enraged, could immediately, by sacrifices and imprecations, destroy him, with his troops, elephants, horses, and cars.

"314. Who, without perishing, could provoke these holy men; by whom, that is, by whose ancestors, under BRAHMA, the all-devouring fire was created, the sea with waters not drinkable, and the moon with its wane and increase?

"315. What prince could gain wealth by oppressing those, who, if angry, could frame other worlds, and regents of worlds; could give being to new gods and mortals?

"316. What man, desirous of life, would injure those, by the aid of whom, that is, by whose ablutions, worlds and gods perpetually subsist; those who are rich in the learning of the *Veda?*

"317. A *Brahman*, whether learned or ignorant, is a powerful divinity; even as fire is a powerful divinity, whether consecrated or popular."

"319. Thus, though *Brahmans* employ themselves in all sorts of mean occupations, they must invariably be honoured; for they are something transcendently divine."

streets, who are carried before the *Kutwal* in the morning. A story is told of a former *Peshwa* having been taken up by the patrol for infringing, in this instance, the law, of the obedience to which he ought to have been an example: on particular occasions, however, the firing of the gun is delayed half an hour, or an hour, or perhaps more.

In the year 1791, a period when political parties had caused much animosity in the court and city of *Poona*, a *Brahman*, named GAHUNSA RAMA, commonly pronounced GAUNSARAM, a native of *Aurungabad*, of the tribe of *Gour*, warmly patronized by NANA FURNAVESE, the minister, held the office of *Kutwal*, and executed it with great ability, activity, and zeal. Toward the end of the month of August of that year, a large party of convivial *Brahmans* had separated rather late; and thirty-four of them remaining in the streets beyond the regular time after the firing of the *Bamboora* gun, were taken up by the police, and put in the place allotted for such defaulters; and in the morning twenty-one of them were found dead, and the rest scarcely alive. It did not appear that the *Kutwal* knew even of their imprisonment until the morning when the catastrophe was unhappily discovered—his officers had performed their usual duty in their usual way; still the clamour against GAUNSARAM was excessive, and at length rose to such a pitch, that the unfortunate *Kutwal* is said to have sought refuge in the *Peshwa's* palace. But even here, in a *Brahmanical* and royal sanctuary, he was not safe; and the *Peshwa*, yielding to his fears, gave up the unhappy man into the hands of the frantic mob, headed by a number of *Telingas:* of which tribe were the unfortunate sufferers. In his prosperity, the respectable GAUNSARAM had built a handsome temple, and dug a fine tank, close to the city, to which they are highly useful and ornamental; and hither was the victim dragged, with every species of indignity: he was bound, and the cord was held by a man of the tribe of *Bungi*, (the basest of the *Hindus*, being employed in moving carrion, night-soil, &c.) and thus, amid the revilings of infuriate devils, he was dragged, with every species of ignominy, and by the hands of *Brahmans*, of the *Telinga* sect, was stoned to death, hard by his own munificent donation. This sad event occurred on the 31st of August, 1791, and was seen in part by my deceased and lamented friend *Dr.* FINDLAY, surgeon to our legation at *Poona*; who also saw the mangled corpse. I was not there at the time, but have often passed the spot so suited to melancholy, although, perhaps, not unprofitable, sensations. *Sir* CHARLES MALET, and *Mr.* UHTHOFF, were at *Poona*, and were much affected by so deplorable an event; aggravated by the consideration, that it should have been effected by *Brahmans*; a *Brahman*, the sufferer, defiling almost the waters of a tank, and the holy shrine of a temple, of his own foundation; and this at the seat of government, and that government *Brahmanical*, thus forced to witness a degradation unheard of, perhaps, in the history of their sacred sect.

I have heard it said, and have, I think, seen it related, that on such an occasion (that, however, of popular insurrection, is very uncommon in *India*,) the victim has been put in a bag, and beaten, to avoid the denunciation against shedding a *Brahman's* blood.

The second instance of this aggravated offence was in the person of a *European*, and that too a woman.

In a former publication I gave an account of a female who had ingratiated herself into the favour of Nizam Ally-Khan at *Hydrabad*, and had received and exercised the command of a regiment in his *Highness's* service. My account left her departing from *Hydrabad*, intending to proceed to *Poona*.

This female was a native, I have been told, of *Florence*, and was the wife of the late James Hall, *Esq.* a respectable barrister in the supreme court of *Madras*. They had separated, and she sought her fortune in the military service of the native powers.

Arriving at *Poona*, she offered her services to several leading men in the military line, but did not receive what she deemed an eligible offer. She had in her employ a *Brahman*, who was very assiduous and useful to her; but unluckily, on a particular occasion, she discovered his cloven foot, and detected the holy man pilfering her goods and chattels, and otherwise acting contrary to her interests; and she ordered her servants to seize and flog him: which order was unhappily obeyed with such rigidity, that the *Brahman* died, either under, or in immediate consequence of, the inflicted punishment.

It is not easy to guess the uneasiness and distress that such an event must excite in a *Brahman* government. A member of their own sacred fraternity, whose life no law can reach, however deserved the forfeiture, thus treated under their eye, and in their own capital, a stranger would expect to call out their greatest severity of resentment, in punishment, or expiation, of a crime that a *Hindu* cannot reflect on without horror and dismay. But it was not so: had the offender been a native, the punishment would most likely have been capital; but for a stranger, and that stranger a female, the mild benevolent spirit of a *Hindu* made due consideration, and prevented any sanguinary exhibition of resentment. The lady was arrested, and confined in a hill-fort in the neighbourhood of *Poona*, where she remained for several years, and would probably have remained for life; but during the struggles and revolutions that occupied

Poona about the years 1795-6-7, an earnest application in her behalf was made to the minister, NANA FURNAVEESE, by *Monsieur* PERON, the officer who succeeded DU BOIGNE in the command of the *French* brigade in SINDEA's service. It was NANA's policy at that time, although, generally, he depended more on intrigue and influence than the army, to conciliate, and he yielded to PERON's request. The offender was liberated, and went to *Bombay*, where she died in 1798.

The military name, or title, assumed by this heroine, was جمال خان JAMAL KHAN. or جمال سردار JAMAL SERDAR: not an uncommon name among *Moghles*, (or *Moghuls*,) and meaning *Elegant Lord*, or *Elegant Commander*; but without the affectation or vanity that it seems to indicate in *English*. It will be seen that جمال JAMAL is a very good name for the wife of JAM. HALL.

Her dress at *Poona* was of a very warlike stamp, although still not entirely masculine. A long flowing *Jama*, in the style of the ordinary dress of the *Moghles*, with the loose *izar*, or trowsers; an enormous sabre, and a plumed helmet, graced the well-formed person of this daring *Amazonian*: and it may be supposed, that, had she taken the field with her corps while serving in the *Nizam's* army, her example would have been animating to his troops.

I have heard it related, that she was offered the command of the battalion of women that NIZAM ALLY KHAN raised for the interior duties of the *Mahl*, or ladies' apartments, or what we call the *Seraglio*. It consisted of five or six hundred women regularly dressed and disciplined, commanded by officers of their own sex, and armed with light fuzees: they mounted guard regularly over the ladies' apartments and vicinity, and are described as, on the whole, a very well set up corps. It actually took the field when the *Nizam* waged the disgraceful war of 1793, against the *Poona* government.

Although this corps may be thought of with levity, yet it is surely an improvement on the system of having eunuchs in attendance on the ladies in the *Mahl*. I know not if this battalion be still kept up, as I have not for some years had any intercourse with *Hydrabad*. Our martial dame is said to have declined the command of it.

The third instance of *Brahmanicide* occurred while I was at *Poona*; and I will transcribe it, without alteration, from my memoranda, premising that it happened during a period of great political convulsion and frequent revolution: *Poona*, indeed, was, at the same time, as revolutionary as *Paris*, but happily with infinitely less atrocity and bloodshed.—

"January 6, 1798. As RAKPAT-KANDHI RAO, a *Brahman*, *Duan*, or minister, of the HOLKAR chiefship, was returning to HOLKAR's camp last night, he was attacked and murdered in the quarter, called *Mangal** in *Poona*. Whether true or not, it will, in the present posture of affairs, be attributed to *Sindean* policy. The *Duan* was dragged from his *Palky*, and his head was severed from his body: one of his attendants was wounded—some say killed.

"January 12. The assassination of RAKPAT RAO on the 6th is without scruple now attributed to the instigation of KASSI RAO HOLKAR. No inquiry whatever has been made into the business, although the deceased was, as may be inferred from his official situation, a man, and a *Brahman*, of considerable consequence: so much so, that a few months back, on the celebration of some religious ceremonies in his family, he was visited by the *Peshwa*, AMRIT RAO, CHIMNA APPA, NANA, DOWLUT RAO SINDEA, KASSI RAO HOLKAR, and all the first people about *Poona*. The ceremonies cost him fifty thousand rupees, as he made great presents, and fed five thousand *Brahmans*."

Such a number of these "beings transcendently divine," as MENU describes them, as five thousand being assembled at a grand dinner, may, like the relation of five hundred female soldiers, sound strangely to an *English* ear; but if *India* be a *Paradise* of priests, *Poona* is their terrestrial heaven of heavens: and I have heard of forty thousand *Brahmans* having been assembled there. It was on the occasion of the *Datchna*, or alms-giving, and what I saw on that occasion, and noted at the time, I will, with the reader's indulgence, now relate, as I find it set down in my diary.—See note below.†

* The streets and places in *Poona* are named after mythological personages; adding the termination *warry*, equivalent to street, quarter, or place: *Mangalwarry*, the street of MANGALA, the regent of the planet MARS, and presiding over Tuesday: *Aetwar-barry*, (an abbreviation of *Aditya warry*; ADITYA being a name of SURYA, or the Sun: hence Sunday is usually called *Aetwar*.—See p. 286.) the street of ADITYA, or the Sun, &c. Mythology is farther brought to notice by paintings on the exterior of the houses: the history of the *Hindu* deities may, therefore, be read while traversing the streets of *Poona*.

† *Parvati*, generally called *Parbaty*, is a hill of considerable height at the southern end of the city of *Poona*; on the summit of which is a handsome, but not very elegant, temple in honour of PARVATI, consort of MAHADEVA. It is a very respectable temple, and much resorted to; and when lighted up on great occasions, it shows well; and from its top is a fine view of the city and environs. On the annual ceremony of *Datchna*, or alms-giving, great sums are given away at *Parbaty*. To this temple *Brahmans* come to share the loaves and fishes from considerable distances: it would not be worth the pains for the majority to come so far merely for what they get here; but as a gift on this day tells ten fold of an ordinary alms, others, as well as the *Peshwa*, make presents to some *Brahmans*, as do generous people on the road to and from this meritorious pilgrimage. The whole month is, indeed, very fit for the benefit of hospitality and alms-giving, so that the travelling *Brahmans* are fed, &c. all the way to *Poona* and home. Some come from

Many *Brahmans* are found in the military service of the *English*, as well as of the native powers. PURSARAM BHOW (as he is usually called; more correctly, perhaps, spelled PARASU RAMA BHAHU,) was a *Brahman*; so was HURRY PUNT, (HARI PANDIT): bearing arms is permitted on certain occasions to *Brahmans* by the law.

Surat, *Panderpoor*, and other more distant places; and it is confidently said, that forty thousand have been known to assemble on this occasion at *Parbaty*.

It is customary, on a few preceding days, for the *Peshwa*, and other great men, to entertain *Brahmans* of eminence, and to make them presents; and these favoured and learned persons do not crowd with the mob, if we may so designate so holy a congress, to *Parvati*. The *Peshwa*, it is said, gives some fifty, some a hundred, and even so far as a thousand, rupees, according, as my learned informant tells me, to their virtue and knowledge; but it is not likely that any examination or scrutiny can take place, or that the bounty can be bestowed otherwise than by favour and interest, tempered, perhaps, by the reputation or appearance of the receiver.

About *Parvati* are some inclosures: one square field has a high wall all about it, with four entrances through double gates. It is not usual for any but *Brahmans* to be admitted on the day of the *Datchna*; but, desirous of seeing what was going forward, *Captain* GARDNER and I, by the exercise of a little civility and patience, were let in, but not our attendants, as no *Brahman* was among them.

It appeared that at three of the four entrances *Brahmans* were admitted, and money given; and it was our intention to have observed them all; but, soon after our entrance, AMRIT RAO, the *Peshwa's* elder brother by adoption, who was superintending one of the gates, hearing there were gentlemen of the *English* Residency in the field, sent to invite us to visit him, an honour which we could not, of course, decline: and he detained us in conversation so long, that it was necessary to proceed immediately home, on account of the approaching night.

At this gate, where we heard the operation of weighing* and moving money, stood a cauldron of red liquid, from which a man, dipping his hand in, marked every candidate on some part of his garment, or, in default of garment, on his skin, with its expanded impression, and admitted him. It was now six in the evening, and the field was not half full—some thousands were waiting outside; but I should not, at a round guess, suppose that the field would contain many more than twenty thousand: to get money, how-

---

* Any large sum is not received by tale in *India*; it is weighed by persons, generally *Serafs*, whose business it is: their quickness and address are surprising. Some persons have a weight exactly of fifty rupees, against which they fill the other scale; but the usual way is for the *Seraf* to count first twenty-five rupees, then weigh twenty-five more against them, and, having counted the last twenty-five, put the fifty into one scale for the weight: he then, holding the scales in his left hand, fills and empties the other scale with his right as quickly as he can, from a heap of rupees placed near him. A skilful man will not, in perhaps twenty successive changes, drop into the scale one piece too many or too few, but, from his handful, exactly fifty rupees; which he places in lots to be taken by the receiver, who may, of course, count his money if he please; but such confidence is placed in the accuracy of the weigher, that it is seldom done. Gold, as well as silver, is issued and received in this manner by weight: when the weigher has finished his issue, he again counts his original fifty pieces; or, perhaps, if the issue be extensive, during the operation, while his assistant may be bringing fresh bags of coin.

Ins. of MENU, Chap. VIII. v. 348.—" The twice-born may take arms when their duty is obstructed by force; and when in some evil time a disaster has befallen the twice-born classes;

" 349. And in their own defence; and in a war for a just purpose; and in defence of a woman, or a priest, he who kills justly, commits no crime."

The term *twice-born*, that so often occurs in the *Hindu* sacred books, is applied to the three superior classes: their *second* birth is dated from assuming the thread called *Zennar*, of which I shall speak presently, and learning the *Gayatri*.

Ins. of MENU, Chap. X. v. 4.—" The three twice-born classes are the sacerdotal, the military, and the commercial; but the fourth, or servile, is once-

ever, a *Brahman* will make himself very small. We understand that until ten at night *Brahmans* were admitted; indeed, I suppose, no candidate is excluded. They are kept in the field until all are collected; but it is not clear to me whether the money is given at the entrance or exit: at any rate, it is expedient to keep them all together, or a cunning one might get two shares. If paid at entering, I see no use for the mark of the red hand; which would avail, if all were marked at entering, kept until the whole were collected, and, on showing the mark, paid, and let out. We observed no paying where we entered, and concluded that the money was given at quitting the field.

The usual dole I learned was from three to ten rupees, and I believe caprice or pleasure is the chief guide as to the amount. One pleasant jolly looking fellow, who was waiting with us on the outside, said he expected to get five, seven, or ten, rupees; but I could not gather from him what might ensure him a high share, or confine him to a low one: he said, indeed, that it was all fortune or fate. He had come from *Surat*; and on being asked how he found his account in coming so far on so slender an expectancy, he said he had nothing profitable to do at home, and was fed all the way out and home, received other hospitalities and alms on the road, and visited and met his friends, relations, and acquaintances; and paid his devotions also at other holy places near his route, which he contrived to make very pleasant by taking his own time: and farther, that there was reputation, as well as other benefits, allied to this sort of pilgrimage. He was gratified at my wishing, on taking leave, that he might this year receive a sum of rupees commensurate rather with his merit than his fortune, which I could not doubt would be three hundred at least. He had said that the last year his fate produced him but three rupees: this he volunteered, as I avoided putting the question, inferring, from his attributing a large sum to fortune, that his acquisition was but small.

The arrangement at the gates we understood to be this: the *Peshwa* at one; AMRIT RAO, CHIMNA APPA, (the *Peshwa's* youngest brother,) and NANA, at the other three. DOWLUT RAO SINDEA was likewise there, and we saw him go away on horseback about five o'clock. An immense crowd of people were assembled about *Parbaty*. The donations this year (1797) were greater than usual: BAAJY RAO, (the *Peshwa*,) perhaps, had a mind to be prodigal, to gain popularity; but NANA was said to have disapproved of it at such a time. The *Peshwa* was understood to have given away five *lak'hs* (500,000) of rupees: about sixty-two thousand pounds.

I note as rather an extraordinary thing, that a man, not, I think, a *Brahman*, who had been instrumental in obtaining us admission, refused to accept a rupee in return. I please myself by thinking he was not the man, nor our broad-faced friend of *Surat*, who took my topaz-pin; for some one had the address, while I was in the crowd, to convey a very handsome one from my shirt.

born: that is, has no second-birth from the *gayatri*, and wears no thread; nor is there a fifth pure class."

The *Zennar*, otherwise called *Janwi*, or *Janvi*, or *Jahnuvi*, (see page 40.) is regarded by the *Brahmans* as of highly mysterious and sacred import; and they do not consider an individual as fully a member of his class until he have assumed this holy emblem. A *Brahman* should be invested with it at the age of eight years, by the hands of his father, who, with his tutor, twists that first put on: a *Ketri* receives it at eleven, from a *Brahman*: a *Vaisya*, at twelve years of age.

The *Zennar* must be made by a *Brahman*: it is composed of three threads, each measuring ninety-six hands;* they are twisted together, and folded into three; then twisted again, making it to consist of nine threads; these are again folded into three, without twisting, and each end fastened with a knot. It is put over the left shoulder next the skin, and hangs down the right thigh as low as the fingers can reach: of these *Zennars*, a *Brahman* wears four; the other privileged tribes but three. Some writers call this the *Brahmanical*, or priestly, or sacerdotal, thread; but not, it would appear, in strict correctness, it not being confined even to the priestly tribe, but worn by three out of the four tribes of *Hindus*.

Ins. of MENU, Chap. II. v. 36.—"In the eighth year from the conception of a *Brahman*; in the eleventh, from that of a *Cshatriya*; and in the twelfth, from that of a *Vaisya*; let the father invest the child with the mark of his class."

The two next verses allow, on particular occasions, the assumption of the sacrificial thread in the fifth, sixth, or eighth years, respectively; or it may, in like manner, be delayed until the individual be double the age mentioned in verse 36.

"39. After that all youths of these three classes, who have not been in-

* A native of *India* is never in want of a measure: from his elbow to the tip of his middle-finger he reckons a *haut*, or *kovit*, of eighteen inches; and this is the usual measure for articles of ordinary value: the itinerant venders of which have frequently no other standard. *Haut* means *hand*.

The number of three threads, each measuring ninety-six hands, for the sacrificial string, may have some mystical allusion to the ninety-six fixed annual sacrifices, noticed in page 365, of this head.

The number three is mystical with almost all nations; and, with the *Hindus*, may refer to the same source as the three sacred fires, the three legs of AGNI, the triad of divine powers, &c. Ninety-six does not arise from any ordinary process of three, and seven, and two; the distinguishing numbers of AGNI's legs, arms, and faces: by some process of permutation, in which the *Hindus* are very curious and skilful, perhaps it may.

vested at the proper time, become *vratyas,* or outcasts, degraded from the *Gayatri,* and contemned by the virtuous."

I often use the term of *the four tribes,* or the *four grand divisions,* of *Hindus:* although the terms are pretty generally, they may not be universally, understood; and I will briefly mark the distinction, by quoting a text that will at once show their names, and their mythological origin.—

Ins. of Menu, Chap. I. v. 31.—"That the human race might be multiplied, He" (the Supreme Lord,) "caused the *Brahman,* the *Cshatriya,* the *Vaisya,* and the *Sudra,* (so named from the *scripture, protection, wealth,* and *labour,*) to proceed from his mouth, his arm, his thigh, and his foot."

I shall add a brief notice of the four tribes.

1. *Brahman:* written *Brahmana,* but the final is dropped in conversation.—From among this tribe the priests are chosen. I have said before, that all *Brahmans* are not priests.—"The natural duty of the *Brahman* is peace, self-restraint, zeal, purity, patience, rectitude, wisdom, learning, and theology."—*Gita,* p. 130. The word *Brahman* means a theologist, or divine: derived from Brahm, the Divinity. *Pandit* is a learned *Brahman;* a philosopher: *Panditya,* philosophy.

2. *Cshatriya,* commonly pronounced *Ketri,* comprises *Rajas,* or princes, and soldiers: all the other tribes, however, furnish soldiers; and, indeed, princes too, if the ambitious individual can effect it. "The natural duties of the *Kshettri* are bravery, glory, fortitude, rectitude, not to flee from the field, generosity, and princely conduct."—*Gita, ib.*

3. *Vaisya;* commonly called *Vais,* or *Bhyse:* merchants, traders, cultivators. In this tribe will also be found individuals of the three others; that is, practising the duties supposed to be exclusively allotted to the *Vaisya.* "The natural duty of the *Visya* is to cultivate the land, tend the cattle, and buy and sell."—*Ib.*

4. *Sudra;* otherwise *Soodra,* or *Sooder:* mechanics, artizans, and labourers, of every description. In the prosecution of the *Sudra's* avocations will be found persons of the second and third tribes, or classes, and, perhaps, also of the first; but of the first comparatively few. "The natural duty of the *Sudra* is servitude."—*Ib.*

The above are the four grand divisions, or tribes, or classes. The subdivisions are not to be enumerated with any accuracy; scarcely, perhaps, to be at all collected by name, even with the assistance of learned men, and to place them in their relative rank would be impossible: they consist certainly of some hundreds. The *Ayin Akbery*, Vol. III. p. 87. says, of the second tribe, or *Khetri*, are upwards of five hundred subdivisions; fifty-two of whom are in esteem, and twelve better than the rest. Of one of these subdivisions, that of *Rajputra*, or *Rajapoot*, the same authority says, there are upwards of one thousand different sects. In a former page I have noticed eighty-four sects of the *Bania*; itself only one sect, or subdivision, of *Vaisya*.

The four grand divisions are theologically reunited into two: the followers of VISHNU, called *Vaishnavas*, or commonly VISHNU-*bakbt*; and the followers of SIVA, called *Saivas*, or SIVA-*bakht*; and it is said they are to be distinguished externally by the line on their foreheads being drawn perpendicularly or horizontally—a point that I shall discuss in another place. This reunion of two is, as we have seen, again divided into five theological sects: *Saivas* and *Vaishnavas*, as above, and *Sauras*, *Ganipatyas*, and *Sactas*; the three latter the exclusive worshippers respectively of the Sun, GANESA, and a personification of the female energy of nature as paramount to the male. Of these some notice has been taken in former pages; and I doubt not but other sects exist whose peculiar doctrines and practices have not been hitherto developed. The worship supposed to be addressed to the male and female energies of nature, their symbols, and other particulars that may consistently be introduced into a work of this nature, I intend to make the subject of the next division of my volume.

LINGA.—YONI.

The mystery in which the real history of these emblems of nature is veiled, renders it extremely difficult to give a clear account of the origin or tendency of the rites by which we see their votaries honour them. That they had their origin in nature and innocence we may admit, without admitting likewise of the propriety of their continuance to a period when nature and innocence are no longer seen unsophisticated: knowing, however, so little of the genuine history of these rites and symbols, it is but a reasonable extension of charity to suppose that their origin was philosophical, though mysterious, and that their observance, although offensive, is not criminal.

It is some comparative and negative praise to the *Hindus*, that the emblems, under which they exhibit the elements and operations of nature, are not externally indecorous. Unlike the abominable realities of *Egypt* and *Greece*, we see the *phallic* emblem in the *Hindu* Pantheon without offence; and know not, until the information be extorted, that we are contemplating a symbol whose prototype is indelicate. The plates of my book may be turned and examined, over and over, and the uninformed observer will not be aware that in several of them he has viewed the typical representation of the generative organs or powers of humanity. The external decency of the symbols, and the difficulty with which their recondite allusions are discovered, both offer evidence favourable to the moral delicacy of the *Hindu* character.

I am not, however, prepared to deny the appearance, in many instances, of strong evidence to the contrary: the disgusting faithfulness of natural delineations, and the combinations so degrading to human nature, observable on some of the temples and sacred equipages of the *Hindus*, are, as I have had occasion to detail at some length in another work, deeply offensive to common delicacy and decency. And I continue of opinion, that such objects of depravity, continually offered to juvenile contemplation, cannot fail of exciting in such untutored, especially female, minds, ideas obnoxious to the innocence we love to think an inmate there.

It does not occur to me that I ever saw the obscenities I advert to in any place north of the river *Krishna*, nor, indeed, to the north of the *Tambadra*;* and I record with pleasure, that, among the hundreds—I may say thousands, of mythological subjects, in the form of images, pictures, &c. that have passed under my hand and eye within the few last years of my residence in *India*, not one was in any degree offensive to decency. Such images are never, I believe, seen in *India*; at any rate, they are very uncommon, or, among so many subjects as were brought or sent to me from almost every part of the country, some instances of their existence must have occurred. One subject, indeed, that I brought to *England*, may be adduced as a counter argument: it is, to be sure, rather of a civil or historical, than of a mythological, nature; and being a curiosity, may deserve more than this cursory attention: I shall, therefore, with due caution, describe it.

It is a stone, five feet high, and a foot and a half broad, and five inches thick: about a foot and a half of it appears to have been inserted in the ground, as it was evidently a *terminus*; although I do not find in the *Hindu* Pantheon an express personification similar to the *Deus* TERMINUS of the *Romans*. There is a long inscription covering the face of the stone, and about two feet in depth, comprising, perhaps, fifty or sixty lines; being a grant of land, including the names of donor, receiver, situation, with invocations, &c. and bearing date about 600 years back. At the top are a sun and moon, and beneath them, and over the inscription, are two figures that now more especially attract our notice. The inscription denounces the punishment there exhibited on all the females of the family of that man who shall do away the land-mark thus set up, or infringe the right thus granted in perpetuity; or, in oriental phraseology, while the sun and moon shall endure. Figuræ sunt, scilicet, asini cum fœminâ manibus pedibusque projectâ, more quadrupedis, rem fortiter habentis; illa retrorsa facie, labrisque prolatis, studio superincumbentem deosculandi, et plane confitendum, nihil exhibens dolore affectæ, minime punitæ—hunc lapidem apud Orientalis Societatis Indicæ museum deposuit auctor.

This stone I heard of near the village of *Viar*, or *Veear*, on the island of *Salsette*; and through the medium of a friend, the then collector and magistrate of that island, obtained possession of it: which, indeed, was a point of no difficulty, as the stone had lain immemorially disregarded and useless. Another of similar

* This river is more properly called *Tunga-badra*: *tunga* means *strong*, *fierce*. Of *badra*, or *bhadra*, see page 294.

tenor and date, but not quite so perfect in the *relievo* figures and inscription, was subsequently heard of in *Salsette*, and is now in the collection of a gentleman in *Bombay*. I will take this opportunity of observing or repeating, that the beautiful and interesting island of *Salsette* is as rich in mythological materials as any spot in *India*; and I trust that, in addition to what has already been done by *Mr.* SALT, with which the public will in due time be gratified, through the medium of the *Bombay* Literary Society, that this very respectable body will have its attention attracted to the preservation of the stupendous and beautiful remains of *Hindu* antiquities in their immediate neighbourhood.

I have some satisfaction in reflecting, that almost the last of my undertakings or acts in *India* was an effort to that effect; having in view also a scientific admeasurement and plan of the antiquities contained within the jurisdiction of the *Bombay* government, or within the reach of its research; together with accurate perspective views of the most striking and picturesque objects connected with them; and correct drawings of all the groups, figures, symbols, &c. contained in the interior of the temples, or excavations, or wherever found.

This plan was agreed on, and, in fact, arranged; but, I trust for a time only, frustrated by an accident: it will, I hope, be resumed by the Literary Society, under the auspices of its illustrious president and of the government of *Bombay*.

The subject of the *Linga* and *Yoni* being in itself very curious, and the difficulty of obtaining authentic information thereon evident, I shall take the liberty of borrowing at some length from the learned and ingenious Dissertation, by *Mr.* WILFORD, "On *Egypt* and the *Nile*, from the sacred books of the *Hindus*," in the third volume of the *Asiatic Researches*, an interesting portion, illustrating the dark subjects in question; or if not fully illustrating them, showing, at any rate, their mysteriousness, and the wildness of the allegories referring to them, which even his power of research seems scarcely competent to reach. The length of the extract will excuse my giving it in a note.*

* "*Yavana* is a regular participal form of the root *yu*, to *mix*; so that *yavana*, like *misra*, might have signified no more than a mixed people. But since *Yoni*, or the *female nature*, † is also derived from the

† *Linga*, the symbol of the *Regenerator*, SIVA, it will be recollected, is the *membrum virile*: the *Phallic* emblem of the *Greeks*. The symbol of the female power, SIVA's *Sacti*, or energy, PARVATI, who on this mystical occasion is more commonly called DEVI, is the *Yoni*; otherwise *Bhaga-pudendum muliebre*.

Speaking of BHAVANI, as distinguished by a variety of names implying nature, and, among others, using that of *Shakti*, a word that is generally, and in this work, spelled *Sacti*, PAOLINO, in his Voyage, p. 327, gives an account of the *Magna Mater* of the *Hindus*: he says, she changes and transforms herself

The *Linga*, the immediate type of the *Regenerator*, SIVA, is generally represented in mystical conjunction with both the *Yoni* and *Argha*; and perpetually offers itself to the investigator of *Hindu* mythology whenever he has occasion to contemplate the nature and attributes, or inspect images or pictures, of

same root, many *Pandits* insist that the *Yavanas* were so named from their obstinate assertion of a superior influence in the *female* over the *Linga*, or *male nature*, in producing a perfect offspring. It may seem strange that a question of mere phisiology should have occasioned, not only a vehement religious contest, but even a bloody war; yet the fact appears to be historically true, though the *Hindu* writers have dressed it up, as usual, in a veil of extravagant allegories and mysteries which we should call obscene, but which they consider as awfully sacred. They represent NARAYANA, *moving* (as his name implies) *on the waters*,* in the character of the *first male*, and the *principle* of all nature, which was wholly surrounded in the beginning by *Tamas*, or *darkness*: the *chaos*, or primordial night of the *Greek* mythologists, and, perhaps, the *Thaumaz*, or *Thamas*, of the ancient *Egyptians*. The *chaos* is also called PRACRITI, or crude nature; and the male deity has the name of PURUSHA,* from whom proceeded *Sacti*, or *power*, which, when it is ascribed to the earth, in contradistinction to the water, is called *Ahara-Sacti*, or the *power of containing*, or *conceiving*; but that power, in its first state, was rather a *tendency* or *aptitude*, and lay dormant, or inert, until it was excited by the *bija*, or vivifying principle, of the plastic ISWARA. This *power*, or aptitude of nature, is represented under the symbol of the *Yoni*, or *Bhaga*, while the animating principle is expressed by the *Linga*. Both are united by the creative power of BRAHMA; and the *Yoni* † have been called the navel of VISHNU—not identically, but nearly: for though it is held in the *Vedanta*, that the divine spirit penetrates or pervades all nature, and though the *Sacti* be considered as an emanation from that spirit, yet the emanation is never wholly detached from its source; and the penetration is never so perfect as to become a total union or identity. In another point of view, BRAHMA corresponds with the CHRONOS, or Time, of the *Greek* mythologists: for through him generations pass on successively; ages and periods are by him put in motion, terminated, and renewed; while he dies and springs to birth alternately; his exist-

* See NARAYANA, p. 72. Of PURUSHA, p. 75.

† Here is something obscure: it is, perhaps, a typographical error, but I have no opportunity of examining any other edition of the *As. Res.*

---

into a thousand shapes, and appears sometimes as a man and sometimes as a woman. I have introduced this author here to notice his observation, that on her forehead, as well as on their own, her votaries "paint the *Yoni*, or *Medhra*; which is represented by two side strokes, and a red one in the middle."

In page 341, he uses the word *Medhra* again: describing the marks on the forehead, &c. that *Hindus* distinguish their sect by, he says, that the mark of DEVI's sectaries is made of "three strokes; the lateral, white or yellow, the middle always red. This mark represents the *Medhra*, that is, the womb of BHAVANI, from which every thing existing was produced: it is much used by the *Shivanites* and *Vishnuvites*."

This word *Medhra* is new to me, and is, I suppose, a term used in *Malabar*; similar to *Yoni*.

As I intend to devote a page or two to the consideration of the sectarial and mysterious marks of the *Hindus*, I shall in this place say nothing farther thereon.

MAHADEVA. Among mine are numerous representations of the *Linga* so conjoined, in various forms, simple and compounded; many of which, as given in our plates, we will proceed to notice.

PLATE 83. *fig*. 1. represents a *Linga* supported by four heads, surrounded by

ence, or energy, continuing a hundred of *his* years, during which he produces and devours all things of less longevity. VISHNU represents *Water*, or the *humid principle*; and ISWARA, *Fire*, which re-creates or destroys as it is differently applied. PRIT'HIVI, or *Earth*, and RAVI, or the *Sun*, are severally *trimurtis*, or *forms*, of the three great *powers*, acting jointly and separately, but with different natures and energies; and by their mutual action, excite and expand the rudiments of material substances. The word *murti*, or *form*, is exactly synonimous with εἴδωλον, and, in a secondary sense, means an image; but, in its primary acceptation, it denotes any *shape* or *appearance* assumed by a celestial being. Our vital souls are, according to the *Vedanta*, no more than images, or εἴδωλα of the Supreme Spirit; and HOMER placed the *idol* of HERCULES in *Elysium*, with other deceased heroes, though the god himself was at the same time enjoying bliss in the heavenly mansions. Such a *murti*, say the *Hindus*, can by no means affect with any sensation, either pleasing or painful, the being from which it emanated; though it may give pleasure or pain from collateral emanations from the same source. Hence they offer no sacrifices to the Supreme Essence, of which our souls are *images*, but adore him with silent meditation; while they make frequent *homas*, or oblations, to fire, and perform acts of worship to the *Sun*, the *Stars*, the *Earth*, and the powers of *Nature*, which they consider as *murtis*, or images; the same in kind as ourselves, but transcendently higher in degree. The Moon is also a great object of their adoration; for though they consider the Sun and the Earth as the two grand agents in the system of the universe, yet they know their reciprocal action to be greatly affected by the influence of the lunar orb, according to their several aspects, and seem to have an idea of *attraction* through the whole extent of nature. This system was known to the ancient *Egyptians*; for, according to DIODORUS, Book I. their VULCAN, or *elemental fire*, was the great and powerful deity whose influence contributed chiefly towards the generation and perfection of natural bodies; while the *Ocean*, by which they meant water in a collective sense, afforded the nutriment that was necessary; and the earth was the capacious receptacle in which this grand operation was performed. Hence ORPHEUS described the earth as the *universal mother*; and this is the true meaning of the *Sanskrit* word *amba*. Such is the system of those *Hindus* who admit an equal concurrence of the two principles; but the declared followers of VISHNU profess very different opinions from those adopted by the votaries of ISWARA. Each sect is also subdivided according to the *degree* of influence which some of them allow to be possessed by that principle, which, on the whole, they depreciate: but the pure *Vaishnavas* are, in truth, the same with the *Yonijas*.

"This diversity of opinion seems to have occasioned the general war which is often mentioned in the *Puranas*, and was celebrated by the poets of the West as the basis of the *Grecian* mythology: I mean that between the gods, led by JUPITER, and the giants, or *sons of the earth*; or, in other words, between the followers of ISWARA and the *Yonijas*, or men produced, as they asserted, by PRIT'HIVI, a power or form of VISHNU; for NONNUS, *Dionys*. Book xxxiv. v. 241. expressly declares, that the war in question arose between the partizans of JUPITER and those *who acknowledged no other deities than Water and Earth*. According to both NONNUS and the *Hindu* mythologists, it began in *India*, whence it was spread over the whole globe; and all mankind appear to have borne a part in it.

"These religious and phisiological contests were disguised in *Egypt* and *India* under a veil of the wildest allegories and emblems. On the banks of the *Nile*, OSIRIS was torn in pieces; and on those of the *Ganges*, the limbs of his consort, ISI, or SATI, were scattered over the world, giving names to the places where they

the *Argha*, and the *Yoni* its rim: on which is a bull *couchant*, GANESA, and, opposite to him, another figure, standing in a sort of niche, but of whom, or of what sex, not determinable; for the subject, which is cast in brass of the size of the plate, is old and rude—more so than the engraving indicates: the faces

fell, and where they are still superstitiously worshipped. In the *Sanskrit* book, entitled *Maha Kala Sanhita*, we find the *Grecian* story concerning the wanderings of BACCHUS; for ISWARA, having been mutilated through the imprecations of some offended *Munis*, rambled over the whole earth bewailing his misfortune: while ISI wandered also through the world, singing mournful ditties in a state of distraction. There is a legend in the *Servarasa*, of which the figurative meaning is more obvious. When SATI, after the close of her existence as the daughter of DACSHA," (see p. 106.) "sprang again to life in the character of PARVATI, or *Mountain-born*, she was reunited in marriage to MAHADEVA. This divine pair had once a dispute on the comparative influence of sexes in producing animated beings; and each resolved, by mutual agreement, to create apart a new race of men. The race produced by MAHADEVA was very numerous, and devoted themselves exclusively to the worship of the male deity; but their intellects were dull, their bodies feeble, their limbs distorted, and their complexions of different hues. PARVATI had at the same time created a multitude of human beings, who adored the female power only; and were all well shaped, with sweet aspects and fine complexions. A furious contest ensued between the two races, and the *Lingajas* were defeated in battle. But MAHADEVA, enraged against the *Yonijas*, would have destroyed them with the fire of his eye, if PARVATI had not interposed, and appeased him: but he would spare them only on condition that they should instantly quit the country, to return no more. And from the *Yoni*, which they adored as the sole cause of their existence, they were named *Yavanas*.

"It is evident that the strange tale from the *Servarasa* was invented to establish the opinion of the *Yonyancitas*, or votaries of DEVI, that the good shape, strength, and courage, of animals depend on the superior influence of the female parent, whose powers are only excited, or put into action, by the male *aura*. But the *Linganeitas* maintain an opposite doctrine; and proofs in support of their opinion might be brought, from many examples in the animal and vegetable worlds. There is also a sect of *Hindus*, by far the most numerous of any, who, attempting to reconcile the two systems, tell us, in their allegorical style, that PARVATI and MAHADEVA found their concurrence essential to the perfection of their offspring; and that VISHNU, at the request of the goddess, effected a reconciliation between them: hence the *navel* of VISHNU, by which they mean the *os tincæ*, is worshipped as one and the same with the sacred *Yoni*."

Mr. WILFORD proceeds to show the identity of this with the *umbilical* mystery symbolized in the temple of JUPITER AMMON, combined with the *fossa navicularis*, or mystical boat, of ISIS.

"The mystical boat," he continues, "is called also, by *Greek* mythologists, the *cup* of the Sun; in which HERCULES, they say, traversed the ocean: and this HERCULES, according to them, was the son of JUPITER. But the *Greeks*, by whom the notion of an *Avatara*, or *descent* of a god in a human form, had not been generally adopted, considered those as the *sons* whom the *Hindus* consider as *incarnate rays*, or *portions*, of their several deities. Now JUPITER was the ISWARA of the *Hindus*, and the OSIRIS of the *Egyptians*; and HERCULES was an *Avatara* of the same divinity, who is figured, among the ruins of *Luxore*, in a boat, which eighteen men bear on their shoulders. The *Hindus* commonly represent this mystery of their phisiological religion by the emblem of the *Nymphæa*, or lotos, *floating like a boat* on the boundless ocean; where the whole plant signifies both the earth and the two principles of fecundation.

are not so distinctly marked, and the *Linga* is more conical. Behind the *Linga*, opposite the spout of the *Yoni*, is a projecting eyelet, or receptacle, perhaps, of a flower or wick; and near it is the appearance of another image having been on the rim, but it is broken off. *Fig*. 3. of PLATE 83. is a similar subject, neatly cut

The *germ* is both *Meru* and the *Linga*; the petals and filaments are the mountains which encircle *Meru*, and are also a type of the *Yoni*.

"Another of their emblems is called *Argha*, which means a *cup*, or *dish*, or any other *vessel* in which *fruit* and *flowers* are offered to the deities, and which *ought* always to be *shaped like a boat*; though we now see *arghas* of many different forms—oval, circular, or square: and hence it is, that ISWARA has the title of ARGHANATHA, or *Lord of the boat-shaped vessel.* A rim round the *Argha* represents the mysterious *Yoni*, and the navel of VISHNU is commonly denoted by a convexity in the center, while the contents of the vessel are symbols of the *Linga*. This *Argha*, as a type of the *Adhara Sacti*, or *power of conception*, excited and vivified by the *Linga*, or *phallus*, I cannot but suppose to be one and the same with the ship *Argo*; which was built, according to ORPHEUS, *Argon*. verse 66. by JUNO and PALLAS; and, according to APOLLONIUS, Book II. by PALLAS and ARGUS, at the instance of JUNO. The word *Yoni*, as it is usually pronounced, nearly resembles the name of the principal *Hetruscan* goddess; and the *Sanskrit* phrase, *Arghanatha* ISWARA, seems accurately rendered by PLUTARCH, (on ISIS and OSIRIS,) when he asserts, that OSIRIS was commander of the *Argo*. I cannot yet affirm that the words *p'hala*, or *fruit*, and *p'hulla*, *a flower*, had ever the sense of *phallus*; but fruits and flowers are the chief oblations in the *Argha*: and *trip'hala* is a name sometimes given, especially in the west of *India*, to the *trisula*, or *trident*, of MAHADEVA. I shall, in another place, show that the JUPITER *Triphylius*, of the *Panchæan* islands, was no other than SIVA holding a *triphala*, who is represented also with *three eyes*, to denote a triple energy; as VISHNU and PRIT'HIVI are severally typified by an equilateral triangle, (which likewise gives an idea of capacity,) and conjointly, when their powers are supposed to be combined by two such equal triangles intersecting each other."—*As. Res.* Vol. III. p. 365.

On the same respectable authority, whence the foregoing extract is derived, I shall insert, briefly, some of the legends connected with it, on the subject of the *Linga*, *Yoni*, *Argha*, &c. and then notice the representations of them offered in the plates of this work.

One day, as MAHADEVA was rambling over the earth, naked, he chanced to pass near the spot where several *Munis* were performing their devotions: MAHADEVA laughed at them, and insulted them in very provoking and indecent terms, enforcing his abuse by significant signs and gestures. The offended *Munis* cursed him; and the *Linga*, or *Phallus*, fell to the ground. MAHADEVA, in this state of mutilation, travelled over the world, bewailing his misfortune: his consort too gave herself up to grief, and followed him in a state of distraction, repeating mournful songs. This, *Mr.* WILFORD says, (*As. Res.* Vol. IV. p. 366.) is what the *Greek* mythologists call the wanderings of DEMATUR, and the lamentations of BACCHUS.

The world being thus deprived of its vivifying principle, generation and vegetation were at a stand; gods and men were alarmed; and having discovered the cause of it, searched for, and found, the sacred *Linga*, grown to an immense size, and endowed with life and motion.

Having worshipped the sacred pledge, they cut it into thirty-one pieces; which, polypus-like, each became a perfect *Linga*. The *Devatas* left one and twenty of them on earth, carried nine to heaven, and one to the inferior regions, for the benefit of the inhabitants of the three worlds. To satisfy DEVI, and

in hard black wood, from *Colonel* STUART's collection. It is of the size represented, having the kneeling bull on a level with the pedestal, with his nose near the orifice or spout of the *Yoni*; which has a beaded exterior, and a snake within it, its tail reaching nearly to the bull's nose. SIVA's five heads rise from the

restore all things to their former situation, MAHADEVA was born again, in the character of BALESWARA, or ISWARA, *the infant*; but suddenly became a man, under the title of LILESWARA, or ISWARA, *who gives delight*: and after various adventures, met his consort then in the character of SAMI RAMA,* (the SEMIRAMIS of the *Greeks*); who, by the sweetness of her voice in chanting her own metamorphosis and that of LILESWARA, attracted the notice of her former and future spouse in his present character—till now, entirely indifferent to the female sex. The goddess soon became LILESWARI, and was happily reunited to her lord.

The *Hindus* insist, that the *black stone* in the wall of the *Kaaba* (or sacred temple of *Mecca*,) is no other than the *Linga*, or *Phallus*, of MAHADEVA; and that it was placed there by MAHAMMED out of contempt: but the newly-converted pilgrims would not give up the worship of the *black stone*, and sinistrous portents forced the ministers of the new religion to connive at it.—*Ib*. p. 371.

In the dreadful war, above mentioned, between the *Lingancitas* and *Yonijas*, the former stood their ground pretty well at first, but were in the end defeated, and shamefully routed in the battle, through the potency of the sacred *Yoni*. MAHADEVA, enraged, was about to destroy them by the fire of his eye; but PARVATI interposed, and, to appease him, made use of the same artifice that BAUBO did to put CERES into good humour; and showed him the prototype of the *Lotos*: MAHADEVA smiled, and relented, on condition that the *Yonijas* should instantly leave the country. Whether this legend allude to a real war between the worshippers of the *Linga* and *Yoni*, or be a mere phisiological allegory, *Mr*. WILFORD could not determine.—*Ib*. Vol. VI. p. 334.

Mr. WILFORD, in the eighth volume of the *Asiatic Researches*, continues his Essay on the *Sacred Isles in the West*. I take thence the following description of *Meru*, the fabulous mountain so often referred to by eastern mythologists.

"*Meru* is the sacred and primeval *Linga*, and the earth beneath is the mysterious *Yoni*, expanded, and open like the *Padma*, or *Lotos*. The convexity in the center is the *Os tincæ*, or navel, of VISHNU: and they often represent the phisiological mysteries of their religion by the emblem of the *Lotos*, where the whole flower signifies both the earth and the two principles of its fecundation: the germ is both *Meru* and the *Linga*: the petal and filaments are the mountains which encircle *Meru*, and are also the type of the *Yoni*: the four leaves of the calyx are the four vast regions towards the cardinal points: and the leaves of the plant are the different islands in the ocean round *Jambu*: and the whole floats upon the waters like a boat.† The *Hindus* do not say, like the *Chaldeans*, that the earth has the shape of a boat, which is only a type of it. It is their opinion—I do not know on what authority, that at the time of the flood, the two

* In reference to what is stated by *Mr*. WILFORD, in the *As. Res*. Vol. VIII. p. 256. the goddess in this character ought rather, perhaps, be called SAMI DEVI. Some mention is made of her under the article AGNI, p. 301.

† At the end of this interesting essay are curious plates, representing *Meru* under the fanciful semblance of a *Lotos*, and other geographical extravagances of the *Hindu Puranicas*, or poetical fabulists.—See p. 270.

center of the *Yoni,* (or rather the *Argha,* the rim being in strictness the *Yoni,*) bearing on their summit a *Linga*; on which is an expanded lotos, over which a snake protrudes its head, its body convolving round the stem of the *Linga,* and around the foreheads of SIVA, form part of his *Jata,* or braided locks, in a

principles of generation assumed the shape of a boat with its mast, in order to preserve mankind. Enthusiasts among the *Hindus* see these two principles every where: in the clefts of rocks, commissures of branches, peaks, among mountains,* &c. The earth is typified by a *boat*; the *Argha* of the *Hindus,* and the *Cymbium* of the *Egyptians,* are also emblems of the earth, and of the mysterious *Yoni.* The *Argha,* or *Cymbium,* signifies a vessel, cup, or dish, in which fruits and flowers are offered to the deities, and ought to be in the shape of a boat; though we see many that are oval, circular, or square. ISWARA is called ARGHA-NAT'HA, (or the lord of the boat-shaped vessel): and OSIRIS, according to PLUTARCH, was commander of the *Argo*; and was represented by the *Egyptians* in a boat carried by men, who might, I think, be, with propriety, called *Argonauts.* The ship worshipped by the *Suevi,* according to TACITUS, was the *Argha,* or *Argo,* and the type of the mysterious *Yoni.* The *Argha,* with the *Linga* of stone, is found all over *India* as an object of worship: it is strewed with flowers, and water is poured on the *Linga.* The rim represents the *Yoni,* and the *fossa navicularis*; and, instead of the *Linga,* ISWARA might be represented standing in the middle, as they used to do in *Egypt.*"—*As. Res.* Vol. VIII. p. 274.

"During the general deluge, BRAHMA, or the creating power, was asleep at the bottom of the abyss: the generative powers of nature, both male and female, reduced to their simplest elements, the *Linga* and the *Yoni,* assumed the shape of the hull of a ship, since typified by the *Argha,* whilst the *Linga* became the mast. In this manner they were wafted over the deep, under the care and protection of VISHNU."

Mr. WILFORD adds, in a note, that "MAHADEVA is sometimes represented standing erect in the middle of the *Argha* in the room of the mast."—*Ib.* Vol. VI. p. 523.

"The most ancient oracle and place of worship at *Delphos* was that of the earth in a cave, which was called *Delphi,* an obsolete *Greek* word, synonimous with *Yoni* in *Sanskrit*: for it is the opinion of devout *Hindus,* that caves are the symbols of the sacred *Yoni.* This opinion prevailed also in the west; for per-

---

* To these instances, given by *Mr.* WILFORD, of mystical types arising, from contemplating any ordinary aberration of nature, in the mind of an enthusiastic *Hindu,* may be added a fancied mystery in any regular excavation.—If he dig a pond, the *Hindu,* if a *Saiva,* imagines it a type of the *Yoni,* or DEVI, and cannot fully enjoy the comforts it offers him until it be reunited to the other types of elemental nature. The water that this *Argha,* or *Yoni,* encloses is a symbol of VISHNU; who is, in physics, a personification of humidity in general: here it is his *navel.* After numerous ceremonies, expensive according to the means of the party, a mast is, on a lucky and sacred day, inserted into the center of the mysterious *Yoni,* or *tank*: the mast represents the *Linga,* or SIVA; and now the typical reunion of the original powers of nature is complete. The last ceremony of placing the *Linga,* or mast, is commonly called the marriage of the *Linga* and *Yoni*: strictly speaking, the brim of the tank is the *Yoni*; its area, the *Argha.* In front of most temples of eminence is seen a tank—some of them exceedingly beautiful; and in the center of the tank a mast, generally with wooden steps nailed up its sides to facilitate ascent to its cross-trees, for the purposes of hoisting a flag, or decorating the *Linga,* or mast, with garlands of flowers, or sprinkling it with water, or placing lights on it. In some temples DEVI is exclusively worshipped, by her votaries the *Sactis*; and the tanks attached to such temples have no mast, or *Linga.*

manner not very well represented in the plate. *Fig.* 5. of PLATE 83. is a group contained on a sort of throne, from a modern cast in brass, about three inches square, of rude design and execution. In the center is the *Linga*, &c. with the bull kneeling in its front, opposite to GANESA, who faces the spectator, having a cup, out of which he is eating, in one hand, and a ball, or cake, in another: two uplifted hands hold a hook and fan, as I can determine by referring to similar and more perfect subjects, but which in the plate, as well as in the cast, look more like two birds. On his right is a female, with a spouted vessel in one hand and a cup in the other, noted in my memoranda as PARVATI: on her right, BAL KRISHNA, in the infantine attitude represented in PLATE 60. On the other side of *Nandi*, or the bull, is *Naga*; his hooded head upreared; his length coiled under him: in his front is a cup: on his right, ANNA PURNA, in her usual attitude; as seen in PLATE 9. and as described in page 158. On her right are five heaped balls, called *pancha pinda*; typical, I have been instructed, of GANESA, DEVI, SURYA, and VISHNU, who, placed together, form a base for the central one, resting equally on them, a symbol of MAHADEVA.

This description of image, I learn, is chiefly used by *Brahman* females for their daily oblations of prayer, and offerings of flowers and fruits: about *Poona* they call it *Gawer*; and the adoration, *Gawer che puja*. The subjects differ in reference to the power propitiated and the object supplicated: that represented in PLATE 83. would answer for the usual prayers for children to the *Linga*; to GANESA, for prudence and propriety of conduct; to ANNA PURNA, for daily bread, &c. I have others, where, as in this, the figures are cast with the

forations and clefts in stones and rocks were called *Cunni Diaboli* by the first *Christians*, who always bestowed the appellation of devils * on the deities of the heathens. Perforated stones are not uncommon in *India*; and devout people pass through them, when the opening will admit of it, in order to be regenerated: if the hole be too small, they put the foot or hand through it, and, with a sufficient degree of faith, it answers nearly the same purpose.

One of the seven wonders of the peak in *Derbyshire* is called by a still coarser name, but very improperly; for this wonderful cave, or, at least, one very much like it, in the *Sacred Isles*, and particularly noticed in the *Puranas*, is declared to be the sacred *Yoni*. The cleft called *Guhya St'han*, in *Nepal*, answers fully and literally to the coarse appellation bestowed upon the other in *Derbyshire* by the † vulgar; and is most devoutly worshipped by numerous pilgrims from all parts of *India*."—*Ib*. Vol. VI. p. 502.

* A determined etymologist might, perhaps, attempt to deduce our popular name for the King of Hell, through some *European* languages, from the *Dev*, or *Deval*, of the *Indian* heathens: the latter word, meaning, indeed, a temple of a deity, is in many parts pronounced very nearly as we pronounce the name *Devil*.

† *Guhya*, or *Podex*.

throne, and the deities and objects contained within it nearly the same, but differently placed: in some, *Naga* seems the chief; and such are, I believe, more particularly invoked in cases of ill health. Images of *Naga* are very common: some, as in PLATE 84. where he overspreads the *Linga* or *Nandi*, or both; others, where his folds form a pedestal for either of them; and others, where the upper surface of the folds are flat for receiving an image, his head, overspreading, forming a canopy. Recurring to PLATE 83.—I have empty thrones, of different sizes and forms, in which deities may be placed, either singly or in groups, according to the nature of the intended offering or supplication: one of these thrones is nearly a foot square. *Fig.* 2. of PLATE 83. is from a very old rude cast of the same size, in which a tiger seems bound to a stake, with a *Linga* and *Nandi* beside it: a votive offering of gratitude, perhaps, in allusion to some personal adventure or escape. *Fig.* 4. has been before noticed as an *Argha* contained in a *lotos*, borne on the back of a tiger; used for sacrificial oblations to DEVI: this is from a tolerably well executed cast, of the same size, in brass. Three of these supported lotoses are given in the plates immediately under our descriptive notice; and I have many others, borne by Tortoises, GARUDA, a Bull, Lion, Tiger, &c. as requisite in different *Pujas*. Some have the *Argha*, without the *Kamal*, or lotos, fixed like a little table, with a lotos spread on it, on the back of the animal.

PLATE 84. contains varieties of the same subjects. *Fig.* 1. from a good brass cast of *Nandi* caparisoned, kneeling before a *Linga*: *Fig.* 2. nearly the same, but with *Naga* overspreading the *Linga*; the aperture, or *Yoni*, being beneath it, with the *panch pinda* opposite to *Nandi*: this is old and rude. *Fig.* 3. is more modern, and better cast: *Nandi* is here fully caparisoned, with bells, housings, horns tipped, &c. He rests in an easy attitude, with one leg uplifted; the others bent beneath him: the *Linga* under his nose, and surmounted by a large *Naga*, or rather its head; for it speedily terminates, being inserted in a socket, whence it easily lifts out, at the tail of *Nandi*: under the mouth of *Naga* is a little eyelet, in which a hook might be put for suspending any thing over *Nandi*—a flower, bell, &c. This subject is about seven inches high. The remaining *fig.* 4. has been before noticed: GARUDA kneeling beside a snake; his hands respectfully closed; he bears a cup, or calyx, out of which springs the expanded foliage of a lotos, containing an *Argha*, or *Patra*, to receive offerings in honour of VISHNU. GARUDA's tail, turned up, and terminating in a bird's head, forms, with his wings and back, a support to the cup: the cast is a pretty good one, in copper, of the size represented.

Figures 1. and 3. of PLATE 85. are *Lingas*, &c. in varied situations: in one instance, canopied by *Naga*, five-headed, with the balls and bull: in the other, single-headed, with the bull only: in both cases, however, although not well represented in the engraving, *Naga* is folded round under the *Linga*, forming its rest. *Fig*. 2. of this plate, is a five-wicked lamp, used in *Puja:* it is of brass, of the size represented, and has three short feet to be placed on at certain stages of the ceremony: the receptacles for oil, or *ghee*, are small, and of a mystic shape: a lamp thus shaped is called *pancharty*. I have others of different sorts, as noticed in p. 69. borne by women, elephants, and other animals; with one and with five places for wicks, generally of the same form. *Fig*. 5. is a *kamal*, or lotos, closed, in the style noticed in p. 337. borne by a *kurma*, or tortoise; used, when duly expanded, and bearing flowers, &c. in an *Argha*, in *Puja* to VISHNU in the *Kurmavatara:* it is well cast in copper. *Figures* 4. and 6. are spoons, used in such ceremonies for laving images with holy water: they are called *Sruva* and *Druva* in *Sanskrit*; by the *Mahratas*, and other *Hindus*, *Pulahi*, and *Atchwan*; and have different forms according to the rites, or object of adoration. *Atchwani* means, I believe, appertaining to lustration.

PLATE 86. has two more lustral spoons, of a more particular and ornamental sort: on one we see GANESA above the bowl, with an elegant female on each side; KRISHNA, in his character of MURLIDER, or the *Tuneful*, on the stem; and a head, crowned by a *Linga*, surmounted by a *Naga* five-headed, forming the handle. This implement is, I apprehend, used in *Puja* to congregated deities, adored by sects in common, or by that sect who endeavour to avoid the inconveniences of schismatic jealousies and ill-will by joining several deities in one general system of adoration; worshipping the deities conjointly, although, perhaps, their powers and attributes are particularly and separately propitiated. The other spoon, *fig*. 2. of PLATE 86. exhibits *Naga* overspreading GANESA, who has the *Linga* in his lap: this is, perhaps, used in *Puja* by *Ganapatyas* and *Saivas* generally.

The other two, *figures* 3. and 4. are the *boat-shaped Argha*, so particularly mentioned by *Mr*. WILFORD in preceding extracts. All the subjects in this plate are of the size represented, and are in the collection of *Colonel* STUART. The upper boat is spouted, so that liquids may be poured from it; but the lower is not so, and seems formed more to contain and retain: its shape is precisely that of some boats used in *Bombay*, and in other parts of *India:* the *Linga* of MAHADEVA, identified sometimes with the *Os tincæ* of VISHNU, and with the mountain *Meru*, and with many other mysterious allusions, is seen elevated in the centre of the *Argha*, or area, itself a symbol of the world, surrounded by the sacred *Yoni*, fancied in the rim of the vessel. These vessels are called *Argha*, or *Patra*, and *Argha-patra:* the first, meaning a boat, or vessel; the latter, a cup, or goblet; reminding us strongly of the *Patera* of the *Romans*. *Patra* is also a leaf, especially when formed into a cup or drinking vessel, as is very commonly done in *India:* the plantain leaf, of which it has been supposed the first aprons of our first parents were made, is easily formed into a convenient cup, and is retained in that shape by a skewer.

Lustral ceremonies are deemed very important by *Brahmans*, and are attended to, as prescribed in their books, with a degree of minute particularity that cannot but appear ridiculous to those not interested or informed in the points to which such lustrations are supposed to have reference. Images are frequently bathed with water, oil, &c. indeed there is no end to lustral ceremonies: to which the *Romans* also gave the greatest attention. *Lingas* are constantly washed: I will not offer an opinion, whether the goddess NANDINA, of the *Romans*, who presided over the lustral purification of infants on the *ninth* day of their age, have any probable connection with *Nandi*, that we have recently so often had occasion to notice as an attendant on the *Linga* and *Yoni*—objects peculiarly connected with lustral ceremonies; or with NANDINI, a cow spoken of in p. 139. NANDINA, I should imagine, was, from her office, a form of DIANA, who appears so often identified with DEVI, whose relationship to *Nandi* we have frequently shown: in some ceremonies dedicated to her, the *ninth* day is particularly marked.—See p. 156.

In a great many ceremonies, lustrations make a part: spoons and *arghas* are therefore in extensive use. The *Argha* in a circular form, when, however, I have mostly heard it called *Patra*, is an attribute of DEVI: it is sometimes called *pan patra*, and is seen in many of our plates, borne by her and others of her family, apparently both as a drinking and a ceremonial utensil.—PLATES 12. 24. 28. 37. 38. 39. 42. In PLATE 58. the infant KRISHNA is conveyed over the *Yamuna* in a flat domestic utensil, that mystic sectarists would not see merely as such. A similar vessel, filled with various animals, in PLATE 59. would, in like manner, be deemed by such visionaries as an epitome of the world; as is slightly noticed in page 197. NARAYANA in his watery cradle, as seen in PLATE 20. is a most mystical and profound subject: his boat-shaped *Argha*, its rim, its termination; the endless figure he assumes by the puerile conceit of putting his toe in his mouth, symbolical of eternity, furnish enthusiasts with fancies of a corresponding description—that is, endless, and puerile. The cradle is also styled *vat-patra*, meaning of the leaf of the sacred *pipala*; and *pan-patra*, or leafy vessel; as well as *Argha-patra*, and by each of the words forming the last. In marriage, and in funereal ceremonies, as well as in that copious sacrifice of *Srad'ha*, an *Argha* is an indispensable utensil.—See *As. Res.* Vol. VII. Art. viii. and ix. by *Mr.* COLEBROKE, who, in those, and in his other curious essays on the religious ceremonies of the *Hindus*, &c. has thrown a strong ray of light on a subject heretofore very obscure; and that still stands in need of his farther investigation.

The *Linga* is likewise seen in most of the plates referred to in the preceding paragraph, and in many others of our work. PLATE 22. shows a pious female in silent adoration of a *Linga*, as particularly noticed in p. 68. In PLATE 36. are two others, with *Lingas* and rosaries in their hands: such rosaries, when used to promote abstraction, are called *Jap-mala*. PLATES 25. 26. 29. 32. and others, exhibit *Lingas*, &c. connected with the adoration of the *Regenerator*, SIVA, or his *Sacti*, or *Energy*, PARVATI.

At the very extremity of a promontory on the island of *Bombay*, called *Malabar Point*, is a cleft rock, a fancied resemblance of the *Yoni*, to which numerous pilgrims and persons resort for the purpose of regeneration by the efficacy of a passage through this sacred type. This *Yoni*, or hole, is of considerable elevation, situated among rocks, of no easy access, and, in the stormy season, incessantly buffetted by the surf of the ocean. Near it are the ruins of a temple, that present appearances warrant us to conclude was formerly of rather an elegant description. It is said, with probability, to have been blown up by gunpowder, by the pious zeal of the idol-hating *Portuguese*, while *Bombay* was under their flag. Fragments of well-hewn stone are now seen scattered over and around its site, having a variety of images sculptured on their surface: many of those most useful in building have been carried away by the *Hindus* to help their erections in the neighbouring beautiful *Brahman* village, its fine tank, and temples.* With the view, neither pious nor sacrilegious, of dis-

* The village here noticed is a pretty specimen uf unsophisticated *Hinduism*; for, although situated on the populous island of *Bombay*, it enjoys a degree of tranquil repose that is rarely contemplated. It contains several temples, and is built round a fine tank, or piece of water, of considerable extent, with broad flights of steps down to the water at the north and south ends, having also steps at convenient situations at the sides. *Brahmans* are here found leading the life they love, although it would not, perhaps, be much relished by many *Europeans*: the ceremonies of religion comprise the business of their lives, and a literary and contemplative indolence form their negative pleasures: some of them, it is said, have lived here to an old age without once visiting the contiguous town of *Bombay*. Wealthy and devout persons pay occasional visits to these philosophers, and derive profit and consolation from their sage councils. At the distance of a mile to the northward from this village, and on the westernmost limit of the island, is situated,

covering to whom this temple was dedicated, I have particularly examined its remains; and, with the help of my servants, succeeded in removing the stones and rubbish from the surface of the ground, and discovering what was buried beneath. The temple appears to have been sacred to the *Hindu* Trinity in Unity; for I found a stone, a good deal mutilated, some feet under ground and ruins, well carved into the triform head so stupendously sculptured in the cave at *Ghari-puri*, or *Elephanta*, of which NEIBUHR gives a plate, and after him MAURICE. And it appears also in the *As. Res.* but, in my humble estimation, ill executed in every instance; and I have examined the colossal bust with the copies in my hand. Of the stone that I thus found, a good representation is given in PLATE 81. and it seems a fair model of its gigantic neighbour. The fragment is more than two feet high, nearly as broad, and about eighteen inches thick, and is of course very heavy. I brought this stone to *England*, and it is now deposited in the company's museum at the *India* house. The front face is BRAHMA; on his right, SIVA; to his left, VISHNU.

PLATE 82. is a representation of another stone that I, in like manner, found, similarly, in the same place. The subject seems the same with the other—the *Trimurti*, or *triform*; but a whole length, and the only one, I think, that I ever saw. It is about one foot thick, two feet high, and nearly as broad: the back is unhewn, as if it had been placed in a wall. This stone I also brought to *England*, and deposited it, with its ancient fellow, in the museum at the *India* house. BRAHMA here appears in a front whole-length figure, bearded, with his rosary and vase, as noticed in a former page: the sacred string hangs loosely from his left shoulder; and at the top of the united coronet appears a *Linga*, inserted in its receptacle the *Yoni*, or *Argha*. In this subject one body, given principally to BRAHMA, as the most *material* of the powers, serves the three heads: sometimes, as has been before noticed (p. 257), three heads and bodies stand on one leg.

Fig. 2. of PLATE 82. has no immediate connection with our present topic: it is taken from a sketch, by *Mr.* SALT, of a subject in the grand arched temple on *Salsette*; representing an individual of one of the many celestial bands introduced among the epic machinery of the *Hindus*.

almost amidst the rocks, a pretty temple of MAHA LAKSHMI, much resorted to, especially at the annual *Jatra*, or fair, by pilgrims and pious persons, who have the additional benefit of the optional regeneration offered them in the passage through the venerated type under our notice, on the neighbouring promontory. The tombs of the *Parsis*, of which a particular description is given in my NARRATIVE, contribute farther to the quiet and retirement of this most interesting part of the delightful island of *Bombay*.

Returning to the cleft, or *Yoni*, at *Malabar* point, I repeat, that it is a type much resorted to. When RAGOBA (as he is colloquially called, but more properly RAGONAUT RAO; classically spelled RHAGU-NAT'HA-RAYA), the father of the present *Peshwa*, BAAJY RAO, while exiled from *Poona*, was living in *Bombay*, he fixed his residence on *Malabar* hill, where he built a lofty habitable tower, since removed. He was in the habit occasionally of passing through the cleft in question; and being a *Brahman* of considerable piety, was doubtless much benefited by such regeneration. It is related of SIVAJI, the daring founder of the *Mahrata* state, that he has been known to venture secretly on the island of *Bombay*, at a time when discovery was ruin, to avail himself of the benefit of this efficacious transit: this relation is, I believe, in ORME'S *Fragments*, and other works, but I have them not at hand. SIVAJI was a *Mahrata*; proving that high and low sects have faith in this sin-expelling process. Women also, as well as men, go through this operation; and I have witnessed some ridiculous, and, indeed, some embarrassing and distressing, scenes in the unsuccessful efforts of individuals, loaded either with sin or flesh, or both.

It is necessary to descend some steps on rugged rocks, and then, by first protruding the hands, you ascend head first up the hole. After the feet be lifted from their last support, the ascent is very difficult, and sometimes impracticable: in which case the essayist remains with his head and hands exposed to the laughing or commiserating spectators above; and it is necessary that some one should go below to aid the disappointed aspirant in his or her descent. I have several times attempted this regeneration, but could never effect it; although I have often seen my superiors in bulk, and, I conclude, in skill, as well as faith and good works, perform it with apparent ease.

Another instance of piety, or by whatever other term it may be best distinguished, of the aforesaid RAGANATH RAO, I will give, on the authority of *Mr.* WILFORD, *As. Res.* Vol. VI. p. 538. I have heard the relation both at *Poona* and *Bombay*; and understood, that a cow of gold was actually made, but it may have been only an image of smaller dimensions; and that RAGOBA himself also was passed through the typical *Yoni*.

While in the exile before noticed, he sent two *Brahmans* on an embassy to *England:* they went by sea to *Suez*, and returned by *Persia*. On their return, they were treated as outcasts; for, although men of unexceptionable character, it was deemed impossible for them to travel through countries inhabited by *Mlech'has*, or impure tribes, and live according to the rules laid down in their sacred books.

After various consultations among learned *Brahmans*, convened from all parts, it was decreed by the holy assembly, that, in consideration of the good character of the travellers, and the motive of their journey, which was the good of their country, they might be regenerated, and have their sacerdotal ordination renewed. For the purpose of regeneration, it is directed to make an image of pure gold of the female power of nature, in the shape either of a woman or a cow: in this statue the person to be regenerated is enclosed, and is dragged out through the usual channel. As a statue of pure gold, and of proper dimensions, would have been too expensive, it was deemed sufficient to make an image of the sacred *Yoni*. RAGOBA accordingly had one made of pure gold; and his ambassadors having been regenerated by passing through it, with proper ceremonies, including immense presents to the *Brahmans*, were readmitted into the communion of the faithful.

Of SECTARIAL MARKS, or SYMBOLS—the GAYATRI—O'M—and other *Sacred Texts* and *Words*, reverenced by HINDUS.

THE *Hindus* are prone to fancying a type of something mysterious in almost every subject that can come under their contemplation: any thing hollowed out, conveying an idea of capacity, they deem typical of the *Yoni*, or *Argha*, itself a type of female nature, or the *Sacti*, or power, of SIVA: of this some notice has been taken in the preceding article. The sea, a pond, a well, a cave, the palm of the hand, or any thing similarly hollowed, convey to their enthusiastic minds an idea of the *Argha*; and their periphery, real or imaginary, an idea of the *Yoni*. In like manner, a mountain, a hill, a tree deprived of its boughs, a mast, a pole, an obelisk, a pyramid,* or any thing conical or erect, excites an idea of the *Linga*; and such subject they can fancy its symbol: a conical stone is particularly so esteemed, or fire, whose natural and necessary form is conical.—Hence a triangle, with its apex upwards, is the immediate type of MAHADEVA, who, in some relations, is Fire personified.—VISHNU is, in like manner, a personification of the principle of humidity; and water is symbolized by a cone, or triangle, with its apex downwards: these types correctly denoting the ascending and descending properties of their respective prototypes—elemental fire and water. The two conjoined, like our masonic symbol, (see *No.* 42. of PLATE 2.) express the junction or union of the two elements, or deities: this mark, or character, is said to represent also VISHNU and PRIT'HIVI, of whom an equilateral triangle is severally the type.

For this six-pointed diagram the *Brahmans* have several mysterious names; but it is generally called *Sherkun*, which, I believe, means little else than *six-*

* The larger the object the more venerable: the pyramids and obelisks of *Egypt* have been supposed of this origin.—See *As. Res.* Vol. II. p. 478. where a cone, in *Bengal*, is described of 363 feet diameter. The sea itself, or rather its containing concave, is, as noticed in p. 340, the *Argha* of the world. I have never heard it so called; but can fancy that a *Hindu* would see in the sea-shore the *Yoni* of PRIT'HIVI—in the concavity, an *Argha*.

pointed. If it have five points, it is also replete with mythological allusions: Siva and Brahma have, or had, five heads. The diagrams have also mathematical properties of a mysterious description; and they serve, like our fox and goose, or solitaire, boards, for a species of game, played with cowries, or with dice, guiding the movements of the men. It is a popular game, and the instruments of play are always at hand: the lines drawn in the dust with the finger, and a few stones picked up, will furnish the means of gaming: cowries being used as money, two or three of them are rarely wanting to a party disposed to play.

In a fine painting of the fort gate of *Agra*, by Daniell, an artist unrivalled in oriental scenery, exhibited at *Somerset House* last year (1808), this sexangular reunion is delineated, as sculptured in large dimensions on each side the gateway. Although the fort of *Agra* be mostly of *Mahomedan* architecture, it may probably have been constructed, like *Juanpore*, out of the ruins of *Hindu* masonry: I do not know that *Mahomedans* hold such symbols in any reverence: in charms, philters, amulets, &c. they, like *Hindus*, have great faith.

The triangle, *No.* 40. of plate 2. is called *Trikun*, which it literally means; and has been explained to me by a *Brahman* as the symbol of certain deities or powers, and as the type of triune coequality: and hence applied by some to the three great powers conjointly. A point, called *Purm*, represents the Deity; having neither length nor breadth—self-existing—containing nothing. A circle is Brahm, Eternity; having neither beginning nor end—unity—perfection. A circle enclosing a triangle, (44. of plate 2.) and a triangle enclosing a circle, (43. and 45. of ditto,) have also mysterious allusions, like similar hieroglyphics among *Freemasons* and others, to Trinity in Unity, and Unity in Trinity, not easily comprehended; and have been borrowed, perhaps, by the enthusiasts of one country from the enthusiasts of another: the less comprehended, the more such things are admired: with such people every thing mysterious is profound, and respected accordingly.

Mr. Paterson informs us, (*As. Res.* Vol. VIII. p. 77.) that the triangle is a symbol of Siva, uniting in himself the three great attributes; also of his consort, similarly gifted. If we inquire of a *Saiva*, or rather of a *Lingancita*, he will dignify the object of his adoration with every attribute of Divinity; as will a *Sacti*, or *Yonija*, varying the object from Siva to his consort, Devi. A *Vaishnava* will describe full-gifted Vishnu; with a *Gocalastya*, Krishna is the Almighty; with a *Ramanuj*, Rama, as we have frequently noticed in the course of this work, more especially under the head of Sects. Plate 2. shows, in

Nos. 40. to 46. the symbols that these sectaries would fancy to represent the object of their worship.

In the *Durga-puja, Mr.* PATERSON proceeds to inform us, the sacred jar, an essential article in the celebration of those mysteries, is marked with the combined triangles, (*No.* 42. of PLATE 2.) denoting the union of the two deities, SIVA and DURGA. The *Sactas,* worshippers of the *Sacti,* or female principle, mark the jar with 65. The *Vaishnavas,* in their *puja,* use also a mystical jar, which is marked 71. These marks, *Mr.* PATERSON says, are called *Tantra*; and are hieroglyphic characters, of which there are a vast number. He hence ingeniously deduces the identity of the *Hindu puja* with some *Egyptian* rites of a corresponding nature.—See his Essay on the Origin of the *Hindu* Religion, in the eighth volume of the *Asiatic Researches.*

Among the *Jainas* a sort of armorial-bearing seems to have been adopted, more commonly than is observable with other orientals: for it is not, I think, very general for *Indian* families—not even of noble or of royal rank, to adopt any distinguishing badge, as hath long been so universal in *Europe.* Such individuals as could not write, used a mark or stamp, which is now called *Byse:* TIPPOO SULTAN used one, although he could write; and had also a tiger for his emblem: and several of his copper coins, as exhibited by me in a former work, bore an elephant—others, an axe.

In a catalogue of fabulous *Jaina* kings, *Mr.* COLEBROKE (*As. Res.* Vol. IX. p. 305.) notices the signs or emblems of many: among them, a horse, an ape, a curlew, a lotos, the moon, the marine monster *Macara,* a rhinoceros, a buffalo, a boar, a thunderbolt, an antelope, a goat, a jar, a tortoise, a conch, a serpent, a lion. *Nos.* 72. 73. and 84. of PLATE 2. are marks adopted by three of them.

Mr. COLEBROKE, in a note on the last passage cited from *Mr.* PATERSON, says, that the jar is used at most festivals, as well as at that of DURGA; and is consecrated by prayers, invoking the presence of the deity, or deities, who are on that occasion worshipped; adding also invocations to GANGA, and other holy rivers. When the celebration of the festival is completed, the holy water contained in the jar is employed by the priests to sprinkle or bathe the person who commands and defrays the expenses of the celebration.

Various *Yantras,* or mystical figures and marks, are appropriated to each deity: such figures are usually delineated on the spot where a consecrated jar is to be placed. These *Yantras,* which are supposed by superstitious *Hindus* to possess occult powers, are taught in great detail by the *Tantras,* or *Agama Sastra;* but seem to be unknown to the *Vedas* and *Puranas.*

The words *Yantra* and *Tantra*, as well as to hieroglyphics, are applied also to a sort of invocatory incantation of a supplicatory tendency—*Tantra* especially; also a philter. *Yantra* means, farther, a sort of magic square, either of figures, or an *abracadabra*. By BRAHMA's carpet, PLATE 4. is one of these squares: another is seen in PLATE 20. and *No.* 89. of PLATE 2. is a *Tantra*, or *Mantra*, or *Yantra*, or something of that sort.

Mantra is an imprecatory incantation: it is generally composed of a passage from the *Veda*, in which the names of some tremendous deity occurs. The *Hindus*, and, indeed, the *Mahomedans* too, have great faith in the efficacy of propitiatory incantations, and great dread of those of a malevolent tendency.*

* It may be here remarked, although not particularly in place, that both *Hindus* and *Mahomedans*, of both sexes, and of all ages, ranks, and sects, are childishly fearful of ghosts and hobgoblins. Few individuals could be found who would dare to walk alone in the dark, especially in or near a place exciting sensations of melancholy or horror: a burying-place, or gibbet, for instance. When arguing on such idle apprehensions, I have been told seriously of the reasonableness of their existence; and there are few persons but can relate instances where danger has arisen, from departed or evil spirits, to natives: but they say that the holiness of JESUS CHRIST exempts his faithful worshippers from mischief arising from demons and witchcraft. *Mahomedans* also readily admit the divine mission of CHRIST, his miracles, and some other points of doctrinal *Christianity*; and, indeed, MAHOMED himself, in a manner almost unequivocal, bears testimony, in the *Koran*, to the pre-eminence of our SAVIOUR in power and place over his own prophetic rank.

A learned *Pandit*, discoursing on the history of JESUS CHRIST, observed to me, that the *English* were a new people, and hitherto, perhaps, had in our confined records a history of but one *Avatara*; whereas the *Hindus*, from their antiquity, and from the profundity of their sacred historical books, had an account of a great many, that took place in remote parts, as well as in *India*; and that very likely, if the *Puranas* were closely examined, the incarnation of Our SAVIOUR would be found recorded in them. Such disputants are ready to believe any thing; and disarm your resentment, if disposed to feel any at the capaciousness of their faith in their own monstrous legends, by the liberality of their concessions.

Both *Hindus* and *Mahomedans* have extensive belief in sorcery and witchcraft. I will, while in this digression, retail an anecdote of the late NIZAM ALLY KHAN, our ally of *Hydrabad*, commonly, but not correctly, called the *Nizam*. I take it from a letter, written in January, 1798, from *Poona*, to a political correspondent, and shall give it exactly as I find it.

"For some time past the *Hydrabad* newspapers have abounded with accounts of necromantic endeavours against the NIZAM's life, casting another ridiculous ray of light on the folly of that silly *durbar*.

"It seems suspected, that THYNIAT AN NISSA *Begam*, (SEKANDAR JAH's mother,) and the minister, (AZIM UL OMRA,) are jealous of the superior talents, spirit, and generosity, of FERIDUN JAH, his highness's second son, and are using these shameful practices to undermine his father's affections. Evidences, manifestly suborned, affirm, that certain incantations have been performed on a wooden figure, arrayed in a suit of clothes, procured for the unholy purpose by the mother of FERIDUN JAH, from the *Nizam's* wardrobe, and that this effigy of his highness was buried. The figure has been dug up, and produced, with some of the *Nizam's* hair found drawn into its side, corresponding with the local seat of his highness's paralytic

The following passage from the *Ramayana* will exemplify this; and, with those who have faith in such works, affords a sufficient reason to fear the effects of such curses.—

"Even he who cannot be slain by the ponderous arms of INDRA, nor by those of KALI, nor by the terrible *chakra* of VISHNU, shall be destroyed, if a *Brahman* curse him, as if he were consumed by fire." In page 372, *Brahmanical* potency, almost, it may, indeed, be said, omnipotency, is strongly enforced.

We will proceed to the more particular consideration of PLATE 2. and endeavour to explain its various symbols or hieroglyphics: and as the subject is likely to occupy more room than I can well allot for it, I, rather than abridge my remarks, prefer giving them in a smaller type; although in this, as in former instances, I may thereby detract from the uniformity of my page. But as I hope my readers will gain in matter a compensation for any diminution or irregularity in the appearance of my work, I confidently rely on their excusing it.

It is generally known that *Hindus* mark their foreheads, and have a superstitious regard for such distinctions. I have been told, that it is held necessary, where convenient, or no especial objection or difficulty exist, for these marks to be daily renewed, and, of course, by the hand of a *Brahman*. One of that sect cannot perform any of his daily sacrifices, ablutions, &c. without the completion or contemplation of this distinction; and it is irreverent in one of an inferior tribe to approach a holy man, or to ask his blessing, or to partake in the benefit of any religious rite, without, or in view to, this sectarial decoration. The race of *Hindus* are generally understood to be divided into the two grand sects of *Saiva*, otherwise called *Sivabakht*,

---

affection: his barber has been arrested, on suspicion of having furnished the hair. But the old man seems to have sense sufficient to disbelieve his son being capable of acting so basely; and says, plausibly enough, that if he hath been palsied by sorcery, a discovery thereof should, by all necromantic rules, break the spell, and restore his withered members to their functions: whereas he continues as decrepit and helpless as ever. A *Moghlani*,* in AZIM UL OMRA's family, who pretends to hold converse with spirits, has made all this stir: she affirms the *Nizam* to be under the influence of sorcery, and that his present disease is the effect of the incantations of no less than twenty-five magicians of *Hydrabad*, whom she offers to point out; and has named a nephew of MAMA BATCHU (an *asseel*, or bed-chamber woman of the *Nizam's*) as one of the number, and he has been apprehended. Other ladies of the *Mahl* (I omit their names here,) are sadly alarmed, lest this wizard, who is much with the *Nizam*, should pitch also on them." Ridiculous as it may appear, that such folly should have connection with politics, it is nevertheless true, that, in this case, they were closely combined; operating, or intended to operate, on the permanency of a ministry, the succession to the government, the influence of the *English* or *French* at the court of *Hydrabad*, and, consequently, on many points of great national importance.

* A female *Moghle*, or *Mogul*. It is common, in the *Dekkan*, to call foreign or northern *Mahomedans*, *Moguls*: it is assumed sometimes by *Dekkanys*, especially if a little fairer than others.

worshippers of SIVA; and *Vaishnava*, otherwise *Vishnubakht*, worshippers of VISHNU. These, as hath been so often noticed, are variously subdivided; but it is said, that the former are to be known by the horizontal position of their forehead-lines, and the latter, by their perpendicularity. This is, I believe, generally correct: but as we proceed to consider the subject more particularly, we shall, I think, find some exceptions to this rule, and some anomalies not, in the present state of our information, easily reconcileable to it.—PLATE 2. contains many of these marks; and they might, numerous as they are, have easily been extended. The three upper rows are, I believe, with two or three exceptions, to be found on *Vaishnavas*; and some of them also on personages appertaining in family and character more, one would think, to the other sect of *Saiva*.

One perpendicular mark, centrally between the eyes, is generally referrable to one of VISHNU's sectaries: it is not common. In PLATE 26. we see it, however, on SIVA, and on PARVATI: on her, as given (*No.* 1.) in the plate under our consideration, (PLATE 2.)—on him it is conjoined with a circlet, forming one of the three marks given in *No.* or square, 22. In the same plate (26.) we see VIRA BHADRA, an *Avatara*, or son, of SIVA, with the dot or circlet only; and in the same plate, (26.) *No.* 2. of PLATE 2. being two perpendicular parallel lines, is borne by NARASINGHA, an *Avatara* of VISHNU.

The next four numbers, or marks, 3. 4. 5. and 6. of PLATE 2. (to avoid troublesome repetitions, the reader will please to observe, that where it is not otherwise particularly expressed in this account of sectarial marks, PLATE 2. is to be understood as that referred to,) being two upright parallel lines, with a black or open circlet between or under them, are the commonest distinction of *Vaishnavas*, whether seen on pictures of VISHNU himself, or on RAMA and KRISHNA, or others of his *Avataras*: *Nos.* 9. to 14. inclusive, are also of this description. Many plates of this volume will exhibit some variety of these marks, and more would, had my frequent admonitions and corrections been more carefully attended to by the artists employed on that portion of our work. *Nos.* 2. 10. and 11. I imagine to be the same mark, varied by being double or single, joined or separate: they are seen on VISHNU, or his *Avataras*, in PLATES 6. 12. 13. 18. 76. 97. and others: in coloured pictures, mostly red. RAMA and KRISHNA have mostly *Nos.* 3. 4. 5. 6. or 9. red lines, with the circlet, or dot, black.—See PLATE 52. in which, both above and below, RAMA has *No.* 3. the lines being red, and the circlet black: the person behind him, LAKSHMAN I imagine, has the same. In one of the pictures whence that plate was taken, RAMA is blue; in the other, white, or copper-coloured; and LAKSHIMAN is of the same hues, but differing in each picture from his brother. RAVANA has *No.* 2. in red lines; which may, indeed, being side faces, be 2. or 10. or 11. as, in like manner, the others may be 3. or 9. In this plate VISWAMITRA, the *Guru* of the divine brothers, has the mark 51. or 52. in black lines; as he has also, and 53. or 58. in other pictures. One would not have expected the mark of a *Saiva* on such a character—but I do not think *Hindu* painters very particular in this point; for the same person, as I judge him to be, in the lower part of PLATE 90. has, as well as his pupils, their prototype, and *vahan*, the usual mark, 3.—but the circlet ought to be black; as it ought also, above, on HANUMAN and GARUDA. These two heroes have mostly this mark, but sometimes 2. without the circlet or dot, and sometimes 10. and 11. The like may be said both of RAMA and KRISHNA; and the colours too differ in different pictures. *No.* 10. or 11. is sometimes red, black, white, or yellow; as are 12. and 13. the central mark or line being also of different colours—red, white, or yellow, but mostly red. In one picture, not engraved, I observe 12. 13. or 14. on PARASU RAMA, and on the enemy that he is combating: the central mark, red; the exterior, white. In another, RAMA CHANDRA, LAKSHIMAN, and HANUMAN, have the same; and RAVANA, the white exterior only. Of KRISHNA, the same varieties are observable: and I will here notice two marks peculiar to this person; and I remark them each in one instance only.—These are 21. which is engraved in *fig.* 7. of PLATE 60.—and *fig.* 9. of the same plate, has the common mark 3. with a fine black line, shorter than the others, drawn through the circlet, otherwise it would be like 26.—I know not if it be any particular distinction: *fig.* 8. of PLATE 60. has 18. or 19. *No.* 3. and its fellows, are, on the whole, the commonest marks: as well as in the plates already referred to of *Vaishnavas*, we see it also in PLATE 23. on KANDEH RAO, an *Avatara* of SIVA: in 46. KARTIKYA, his reputed son, has it; and below, in the latter plate, which portion, I apprehend, represents some exalted marriage, as BRAHMA reads the ceremony, we see it again: but in these instances the circlet ought, as in the pictures, to be black. BRAHMA, we may here remark in passing, has 2. 10. or 11. in red. In the next plate (47.) BHAIRAVA another member of SIVA's family, has 3. in red, and a black dot, in one figure; in the other, 2. 10. or 11. in red: his male attendants all have the same. In PLATE 95. he has 18. or 19. PLATE 48. has 12. on the two first *Avataras* of VISHNU. The next plate (49.) exhibits some variety: VISHNU and BRAHMA have the same, 12. white, with red in the middle: SIVA has 82. crescent, white: RHEMBA (or LAKSHMI) has 31. red. PLATE 51. has varieties not in PLATE 2. but all relating to 9. or 12. INDRA, in PLATE 79. has both 2. and 3. or 9. in red, with the usual black spot in the latter: his attendants, 2. or 10. AGNI, in the next plate, has also 2. and 3. or 9.—PAVAN, 2. or 10. or 11. SURYA, in the original of PLATE 89. has 3. or 9. but the black circlet is omitted in the engraving: CHANDRA has 2. or 10. in red. The whole group in PLATE 96. (the *Vaishnava* story of which is yet to be related,) have 3. the lady excepted; who has, like many attendant females, on men of different sects, a red line parallel with her eyebrows, along her forehead. PLATE 97. has 2. the ladies, a circle, 22. I do not think any of my subjects have 15. or. 16. the forms of which I have borrowed from BARTOLOMEO; who says, (page 340.) that the former is painted on the breast and forehead with yellow, red, or white earth: the lateral strokes, white, or yellow; the middle, always red. It represents, he says, the *Medhra*, or womb, of BHAVANI, (see page 384.) from which every thing existing was produced; and is much used by the *Shivanites* and *Vishnuvites*: he calls the hieroglyphic *Triumanna*, the holy earth. *No.* 16. he calls *Shula*, which, like 74. (also borrowed from him,) *Trishula*, is the trident held by SIVA, as a symbol of his power over heaven, the earth, and hell. The *Shivanites*, he says, paint them with white earth on their forehead and breast; and some call it *Tirunama*, that is, the most sacred name of God. I have not copied 15. and 16. accurately: the round terminations are too large—but, indeed, if actually representing the *trisula*, should, I think, have been pointed, not round; 74. too, should be more equal at top, like turrets; and it is, I think, intended to represent the turretted crown of DEVI.—See pages 148. and 168.

No. 17. of PLATE 2. is taken from a coloured picture, not engraved, representing VISHNU, standing; one of his arms uplifted, in the other, a short gilt staff: he has large eyes; a robe of fine muslin, through which his blue skin is seen: his attendants are fair; one holds a looking-glass to him; the other, a *chawrie* of peacocks' feathers: both have mark 3. On this picture is written, in *Mahraty*, RANCHUR NAT'H, a name not familiar to me, under which VISHNU is worshipped in some northern parts—*Hardwar*, perhaps, or *Guzerat*. *No.* 18. and 19. I should class together, and with 3. and 4. but they are seldomer seen. KRISHNA, *fig.* 8. of PLATE 60. and in other pictures, has 18. or 19.—so has BHAIRAVA, PLATE 95. *No.* 20. is not usual: I observe it only in *fig.* 2. of PLATE 6. where VISHNU has it in the *Vaharavatara*; but it may only be a variety of 3. or 9. or 12. as seen in similar subjects in PLATES 48. 51. &c. *No.* 21. has been noticed on *fig.* 7. of PLATE 60. and 22. has been likewise noticed: the circle, with one line raised on it, is seen in PLATE 26.—the circle or dot, alone, is often seen both in men and women (see PLATES 11. 16. 26. 65. 36. 38. 39. and many others,) of both grand divisions, or sects. My *Pandit* fancied this circle or dot to have very profound relations: he called the dot *purna*, a *point*, typical of the Deity; having neither length nor breadth; self existing—containing nothing: the circle, he said, similarly, was BRAHM—without beginning or end—unity—perfection.

Three perpendicular lines, with or without dots or circles, 23. 24. 25. 26. I should judge to be of the same family with 12. 13. or 14.—and so I should, uninformed, have classed 15. and 16. on the general principle, that perpendicular lines appertain to sects of *Vaishnava*, and horizontal lines, to sects of *Saiva*. *Mr.* COLEBROKE, in the article so largely quoted from under the head of SECTS, (p. 121.) has noticed some sectarial marks.—*Nos.* 3. 4. 5. or 6. the lines white, the circlet red, he applies to the *Gokalastas* (adorers of KRISHNA and RADHA); and gives another mark to the *Ramanuj* (adorer of RAMA and SITA), who, he says, add an upright red line in the middle of the *double white* one: both make the circlet with red sanders, or with turmeric and lime.—This will apply to 12. 13. 14. or to 23. 24. or 25.—to the two last best, perhaps, as they have the circlet; and is not in strict accordance with what I have above related of the similarity, in many instances, of the marks borne by RAMA and KRISHNA, and their followers, whose circlets are generally black: we may, however, safely infer, that a particular mark is not at all times exclusively applied by, or confined to, the individuals of any sect. Three upright lines, 23. to 26. are by no means so common as two: *fig.* 9. of PLATE 60. is, as before observed, taken from a picture with the mark very like 26. *Nos.* 27. and 28. are taken from BARTOLOMEO. I do not recollect that I ever saw them as forehead marks, either in pictures or on men: I imagine both to represent the *Chakra* of VISHNU, before described. BARTOLOMBO says (p. 343.) that the oldest *Indian* kings used the wheel by way of sceptre, and were therefore termed *Chakra-verti*; a word that has occurred in earlier pages of this work.—(See p. 227.)

The mark 29. of PLATE 2. is seen on MAHA KALI, or DEVI, in PLATE 29.—in the original picture, which, indeed, is but an outline sketch, it is more lozenge-like, as in PLATE 2. one of her attendants has 49. (the circlet, however, between the lines).—This goddess has more distinguishing marks, as well as names, than any other: in PLATE 28. she has 35.—in PLATE 27. she has 38.—in PLATE 26. she has, rather unaccountably, the perpendicular 1.—in PLATE 24. wherein she, as *Ardha-nari*, is a moiety of SIVA, she has 83.—in the tinted originals, the crescents are white: the exterior of the central eyes, black, with a red tinge inside: one of the pupils, black; the other, with a white dot in its centre; both circlets below the crescents, yellow, of the hue nearly of the female moiety of the figures. If these trifling differences have, as I believe, different allusions—which, however, I shall not attempt to explain, although I fancy I have a clue to them, what an idea must they give us of the endless puerilities of *Hindu* rites, ceremonies, and rubrics; for every visible variety has its corresponding rite, and every rite its own appropriate rules and ordinances. But to return: in the same plate, (24.) *No.* 78. or 80. of PLATE 2. is borne by BHAIRAVA: the circlet in the eye, black; under the white crescent, yellow: the outline of the eye, which, as the hieroglyphic of DEVI, has a reference beyond the eye, is dark; the interior, red. PARVATI, in her variety of forms, has many other marks: in PLATE 5. she has 48.—in PLATES 17. and 18. she has *No.* 33. which, in the highly finished original of PLATE 17. seems to be *No.* 31. formed of an emerald, with pearls appended; whether meant for more than a mere ornament, I cannot say: I have many pictures of the goddess with it, as well as with 31. *No.* 32. is taken from PAOLINO, who says it is the *Pedma*, or lotos; a symbol of water, and a mark of the *Vishnuvites*: 31. and 33. being conical, may thus appertain to the *Sacti* of SIVA, or Fire.

Nos. 34. 35. 36. and 37. of PLATE 2. distinguish SIVA's and PARVATI's images and votaries.—See PLATES 5. 6. 9. 14. 15. 16. 28. 36. 40. &c.—not, however, exclusively; for in PLATES 9. 11. we see the same on images of the *Vaishnavas*: but the marks on images cannot be, in general, so well discriminated as in drawings. *No.* 38. we have noticed in PLATE 27. *No.* 39. is taken from PAOLINO, who says it is the *Linga*, borne on the neck, or arms, or forehead. *No.* 30 is also from the friar's Voyage, and he notes it as the same with 40. and calls it "*Agni*, or *Ti*; that is, Fire, worshipped as a symbol of SIVA, or the Sun." The triangle apex upwards, 40. has been before remarked as SIVA's emblem, he being Fire; and this element is appropriately denoted by such a triangle, or any thing conical, like 31. or 33. to mark its levity and property of ascension: *ti*, in *Malabaric*, is fire; *agn*, in *Sanskrit*; and *ág*, in several dialects derived from it. *No.* 41. is VISHNU's symbol—Water; well denoted by an inversion of the triangle, or as in 32. the form necessarily assumed by its descending gravity. In a former page (122,) it is noticed, that VOPADEVA, the poetical author of the *Sri Bhagavata*, endeavours to reconcile the theological doctrines of all sects of *Hindus*: his disciples are named *Bhagavatas*, who now are, however, merged in the division *Gokalast'ha*, their tenets tending mostly to glorify KRISHNA: from this source has, I apprehend, originated the notion of the union of the symbols of SIVA and VISHNU, Fire and Water, as seen in 42.—and hence too may have originated this symbol, so profound in the mysteries of Free-masonry, as noticed in an early page of this article; as have the next four numbers, 43. 44. 45. and 46.—We, therefore, dwell on them no farther here, but must notice them again, slightly, when we arrive at *No.* 89. where we see a circle within a triangle, itself circularly comprehended.

The two next rows of hieroglyphics, 47. to 64. the last number, perhaps, excepted, being horizontal lines, appertain to SIVA, PARVATI, their offspring, or adherents. *Mr.* COLEBROKE says, that the *Saivas* and *Sactas* draw on their foreheads three horizontal lines, with ashes obtained, if possible, from the hearth on which a consecrated fire has been maintained; adding a red circlet, which the *Saivas* mark with red sanders; the *Sactas*, when they avow themselves, (see p. 123,) with saffron, or with turmeric and borax. The *Sauras* also are distinguished, he says, by the horizontal triple line, made, as well as the circlet, of red sanders; while the *Ganapatyas*, or adorers of GANESA, use red minium for the circlet: but *Mr.* COLEBROKE does not notice what lines the latter delineate on their foreheads.—See page 124.

In PLATE 18. we have a variety of distinguishing forehead marks; not, however, exactly copied in the plate.—*No.* 47. of PLATE 2. is on GANESA; the two venerable men on his left, who are, perhaps, NAREDA and BHRIGU; on KARTICKYA, near them; and on BRAHMA, on the other side—these are all yellow; and the two lines are not in all cases well defined: VISHNU and GARUDA have 10. or 11. in yellow: SIVA has 83. but with only two faint lines from the crescent: PARVATI, as before observed, and all the choristers, have 33.—the two women with *chawries*, behind SIVA, have a white circlet, with a gold line raised on it, like 22. I have a picture (that mentioned in page 204, where KRISHNA mortifies his friend,) in which NAREDA has black lines joined at the ends, with a black circlet, like 64. but with three lines only: several pictures of GANESA are similarly marked—sometimes double, sometimes triple, lines. *No.* 48. or 49. is on a picture of SIVA, not engraved, wherein he is apparently running from VISHNU, who has *No.* 9.—both are two-handed; their skins, dark blue; their lines and circlets, white. In PLATE 5. also, we see the mark 48. on PARVATI: her consort has 34.—VISHNU, 8. the only instance I find of it: BRAHMA has 7. And here we may remark, that BRAHMA is found with both perpendicular and horizontal lines: this may be in allusion, perhaps, to matter, or the earth, partaking of both properties of SIVA and VISHNU—Fire and Water. In PLATE 5. he is marked perpendicularly as a *Vaishnava*; in PLATE 3. horizontally, as a *Saiva*: in the latter, he has *No.* 64. I have no other image or picture with four lines: *four* seems to be a number rather peculiar to BRAHMA; four faces; producer of the four *Vedas*, and the four tribes; four-armed; allusive also, it is said, to the four quarters of his own terrestrial creation. *No* 50. I imagine to be merely 48. or 49. with the lines connected at their extremities: I am not aware what difference, if any, there may be in the crooked or straight lines, or in differently coloured dots. I have a portrait of NANA FURNAVEESE with the double line, 50. joined at the ends; the circlet between, not under them, black. This portrait I obtained at *Poona*, and judge it to be taken from a native painting, after *Mr.* WALES's portrait; for in DANIELS's fine *durbar* print, as published by CRIBB, that great statesman is in the same attitude and dress, with the same mark as in my picture of him. The late *Peshwa*, MHADU RAO, in that print, has *No.* 9.—as he has also, in my portrait of him; yellow lines, and a black circlet. *Nos.* 9. and 49. or 50. seem the prevailing marks at that *Durbar*: BEHRU *Pandit*, minister for *British* affairs, has the latter.

We now come to three lines, open and closed at the ends, with and without dots; or the dots over, under, and central: the lines of equal and unequal lengths; the dots or circlets of different hues; and the central marks of different shapes and positions: what may be the distinction of all these varieties I shall not attempt to explain. Three straight lines, as 51. we find, in PLATE 52. as before noticed, on VISWAMITRA. *No.* 52. three straight black lines, connected, is, in PLATE 19. on NAREDA; while the other attendant, fanning SIVA, has *No.* 2. a double perpendicular red line, a mark of the *Vaishnava:* SIVA himself, on all his foreheads, has *No.* 67. but with *two* black lines, having yellow between them. Below, in PLATE 19. he has 69.—the central mark, or eye, is, however, like that of 67.—KARTIKYA, his son, has the *Vaishnava* mark, 2. or 10. or 11. in red: this is odd. *No.* 53. or 54. is borne by DEVI, in PLATE 30.—and in PLATE 22. she has both lines and circlet red. *Nos.* 55. to 56. are borne by DEVI, GANESA, and others of that family, in pictures not engraved. GANESA has the latter, the circlet black, in PLATES 32. and 45.—in the former, SIVA has 67. lines, &c. black: VISHNU, 18. or 19. lines red, circlet black: BRAHMA and INDRA, 2. in red. In other plates, MAHADEVA and his family are seen with the varieties of three lines, enclosing an eye, as exhibited in PLATE 2. *Nos.* 59. to 63. 67. to 70. In PLATE 25. VIRA BHADRA has *No.* 60.—I have fancied that the pupil of the eye, being full, or on the right or left sides, (67. 68. 69.) has reference to the phases of the moon; this deity (SIVA), his consort, and family, bearing such intimate relationship to the solar and sidereal hosts.

Passing rapidly *No.* 65. which has been noticed, *No.* 66. seen in PLATES 13. and 15. being nearly the same, I imagine, as *Nos.* 34. 35. 36. 37. and, perhaps, 38. as seen in PLATES 14. 27. 28. &c. also *Nos.* 71. to 74. already noticed, we arrive at the bottom row of crescents, variously accompanied. This lunar hieroglyphic seems exclusively the distinction of MAHADEVA and his family: I do not, in this instance, find any exception. *Nos.* 75. and 76. I have taken from PAOLINO *da San* BARTOLOMEO, who says, that the *Shivanites* paint them on the forehead in yellow, as emblems of SIVA and PARVATI—the Sun and Moon. In all my pictures the crescents are white: most of the varieties of PLATE 2. from *Nos.* 77. to 83. are seen, I believe, in PLATES 17. 18. 24. 49.—in these the pupil of the central eye varies its phases, as astrologers delineate the moon in her course; although such little distinctions have not, perhaps, been always attended to in the engraving of our plates.

No. 84. has been noticed as a sort of bearing, or arms, of a *Jaina Rajah*. *Nos.* 85. to 88. and many others of a similar sort, I have on pictures of KRISHNA, RAMA, or some form of VISHNU: 85. is on a coloured picture of the former, most gaily dressed, piping to a couple of admiring cows: on it is written, in *Mahraty*, MURLIDER. *No.* 86. is on a picture of VISHNU, or KRISHNA, four-handed, splendidly dressed and decorated: an attendant fans him, another offers him a goblet: it is titled, in *Mahraty*, GOKAL NAUT, under which name KRISHNA is worshipped in *Guzerat*. *No.* 87. is on RAMA, dark blue, two handed, holding a small bow and a three-pointed arrow; dressed and adorned very much like GOKAL in the former picture: SITA stands, with palms respectfully closed, on one side; LAKSHIMAN, with a *chawrie*, on the other; HANUMAN, in front: the central marks are very like *No.* 12. the side-strokes are green, the middle one, red. *No.* 88. is taken from the same picture as the lower part of PLATE 20. described in pages 81, and 103: all the lines are red; the crosses and dots between them, yellow; the upper row of pearls, white. The picture of HARI on the many-headed serpent, described in pages 26, 27, has mark 86. all yellow. In the large and elaborate picture of the same subject, mentioned in page 28, VISHNU on *Sesha*, and GARUDA, and RAMA, and KRISHNA, and others, have the usual mark, 3. or 9. lines red, circlet black: GANESA has 47. and VISWAMITRA, 63.—all the ladies, more than thirty in number, have, as is most common, one red line along their foreheads, about parallel to their eyebrows.

Of PLATE 2. the last subject, *No.* 89. remains to be noticed: this is a very curious article, but I am not able to explain the meaning of the characters on it: they have, I imagine, the same sort of ambiguous allusions as the astrological *scheme*, or *type*, at the end of MOORE's Almanac. It is taken from a stout piece of copper of the same size, rising, layer over layer, as the circles lessen upwards, reaching at last to the mystery within mystery—a circle enclosing a triangle (*No.* 44.) enclosing another circle, (45.) in which is *something*—

vastly profound, doubtless, as we see it accompanied by a *purma* (circlet, or dot, or point,) in others of the larger circles, but what I cannot say: the under side of the copper is concave, corresponding with the raised surface. This description of article, I fancy, is a sort of *hocus pocus* thing used in incantations, and other mysterious rites—a *mantra,* either for a tremendous or benevolent result, according to the tendency of the deities whose names it may bear, and the position or conjunction of their attributes. But we have dwelt so long on the various symbols represented in PLATE 2. that it is time the reader be relieved from the farther consideration of a subject, very copious, but not, I fear, very interesting. I therefore hasten to a conclusion of this article; but have to observe, that the important personage, BUDDHA, has hitherto been unnoticed among these sectarial distinctions. The *Jainas* and *Mahimans* do not, I believe, mark the foreheads of their images, nor, that I recollect, their own: but the *Brahmanical* BUDDHA is sometimes so marked. In one of my series of *Avataras,* where he is seated in the usual position in a temple, he has the mark 2. or 10. or 11. in white, tinged with yellow: he is represented as a very fair handsome youth, two-handed, decked with a gay coronet, earrings, garlands, &c. &c. and with an appearance of hair: two long-haired fair attendants fan him; and two cows are near his temple. In another, he is four-handed, without any mark: in a third, he is four-armed, with the mark 18.—the lines red, the dot black.

Major MACKENZIE (*As. Res.* Vol. IX. p. 254.) says, that " the *Jains* mark their foreheads with sandal powder; and some have a small circlet of red powder in the center of the sandal mark:" but the sort of mark is not hence discoverable.

As well as the forehead, it will have been observed that *Hindus* paint their arms and breasts also, and sometimes their throats: sandal powder, turmeric, *chuna,* or lime, ashes from a consecrated fire, cow-dung, and other holy combustibles, made adhesive by a size of rice-water, or sometimes rubbed on dry, are the ingredients and usages on this occasion. Several lines of white, ashen, or yellow hue, are commonly seen drawn across the arms and breasts; and I understand that *Yogis* and *Saniasis,* and other pious persons, frequently carry about them a little packet of these holy pigments, with which they mark those who show them respect, in repayment of their attentions.—See page 54.

The extreme importance that the *Hindus* attach to the supposed profundity of the *Gayatri,* renders it a text of more curiosity than, perhaps, indifferent readers will be able to discover in the words themselves, in either their familiar or recondite allusions.

I shall give several translations of it, by different *Sanskrit* scholars, premising that it is a text mentally recited, never articulated. I was, until lately, persuaded that none but *Brahmans,* and not all *Brahmans,* were taught this sacred text; but I am forced, somewhat reluctantly, to yield that opinion to the authority of better informants: at any rate, it is evident, that, whatever may be the existing practice on that point, it was the usage formerly to teach it as a matter of course, indiscriminately, to the three first classes—the *Brahman, Chetriya,* and *Vaisya,* unless the individual were rendered by vice unworthy of the "second birth" promised in the holiness of this mysterious regeneration.

There is no doubt but that pious *Brahmans* would be very deeply shocked at hearing the *Gayatri* defiled by unholy articulation, even if expressed in the most respectful manner; and would be distressed at knowing the characters and meaning to be in the possession of persons out of the pale of sanctity. I know a gentleman, on the western side of *India*, who has the characters; and their sound, if uttered, in our letters. He once, without, perhaps, being aware of the result, began to recite it audibly in the presence of a pious *Pandit*; but the astonished priest stopped his ears, and hastened, terrified, from his presence. I should be sorry, for my own part, if it were revealed so as to be uttered by individuals who might inconsiderately, and perhaps wantonly, wound the feelings of so many good and respectable men as would thereby become liable to—what they would conceive, such profanity: its promulgation, while distressing to many, would answer no desirable end either to science or literature. Nor would I have been the first to publish the character, that, if uttered, would yield the sound of O'M; or, being triliteral, better, perhaps, written AUM: but as it is already before the public, I have given it in my frontispiece, in a form of beauty heretofore unattempted, from the elegant pen of *Mr.* Wilkins, to whom, on so many occasions, my gratitude is so deeply due.

In the frontispiece, above the head of Ganesa, the reader will see the symbol, or character, that a *Brahman*, as I have experienced, would not contemplate with indifference. I once pointed it out, as it appears in the *Gita*, to my *Pandit*, in *Bombay:* he said nothing, but averted his face, half smiling, evidently pained by what he saw: unwilling to mortify him, I ever after avoided the subject.

I now proceed to give the promised extracts illustrative of the *Gayatri*.

Sir W. Jones says that the *Gayatri* is called the "Mother of the *Vedas*;" and in the conclusion of the preface to the *Institutes* of Menu, he intends a translation in the following passage, the words in *Italics* being those immediately of the text:—

"The many panegyrics on the *Gayatri*, the Mother, as it is called, of the *Vedas*, prove the author to have adored, not the visible material sun, but that *divine and incomparably greater light, which illumines all, delights all, from which all proceed, to which all must return, and which alone can irradiate* (not our visual organs merely, but our souls, and) *our intellects.* These may be considered as the words of the most venerable text in the *Indian* scripture."

Another translation occurs in the thirteenth volume of his work, in which the author seemed to intend making the translation as literal as possible:—

"*The* Gayatri, *or holiest verse of the* Vedas."

"Let us adore the supremacy of that divine Sun, the Godhead who illuminates all, who recreates all, from whom all proceed, to whom all must return;

whom we invoke to direct our understandings aright in our progress toward his holy seat."—Page 367.

The following paraphrase, or commentary, is by the learned *Pandit*, RHADACANT; and is evidently descriptive of BRAHME:—

"Perfect truth; perfect happiness; without equal; immortal; absolute unity; whom neither speech can describe, nor mind comprehend; all-pervading; all-transcending; delighted with his own boundless intelligence, not limitted by space or time; without feet, moving swiftly; without hands, grasping all worlds; without eyes, all-surveying; without ears, all-hearing; without an intelligent guide, understanding all; without cause, the first of all causes; all-ruling; all-powerful; the creator, preserver, transformer, of all things.—Such is the Great One: this the *Vedas* declare."*—*Ib.* p. 369.

* *Ins.* of MENU, Chap. II. v. 76.—" BRAHMA milked out, as it were, from the three *Vedas*, the letter A, the letter U, and the letter M; together with three mysterious words, *bhur*, *bhuvah*, *swer*; or *earth*, *sky*, *heaven*.

" 77. From the three *Vedas* also, the Lord of Creatures, incomprehensibly exalted, successively milked out the three treasures of that ineffable text, beginning with the word *Tad*, and entitled *Savitri*, or *Gayatri*.

" 78. A priest who shall know the *Veda*, and shall pronounce to himself, both morning and evening, that syllable, and that holy text, preceded by the three words, shall attain the sanctity which the *Veda* confers.

" 79. And a twice-born man, who shall a thousand times repeat those three (or *om*, the *vyahritis*, and the *gayatri*,) apart from the multitude, shall be released in a month even from a great offence, as a snake from his slough.

" 80. The priest, the soldier, and the merchant, who shall neglect this mysterious text, and fail to perform in due season his peculiar acts of piety, shall meet with contempt among the virtuous.

" 81. The three great immutable words, preceded by the triliteral syllable, and followed by the *gayatri*, which consists of three measures, must be considered as the mouth, or principal part of the *Veda*.

" 82. Whoever shall repeat, day by day, for three years, without negligence, that sacred text, shall hereafter approach the divine essence, move as freely as air, and assume an ethereal form.

" 87. By the sole repetition of the *Gayatri*, a priest may indubitably attain beatitude, let him perform or not perform any other religious act.

Chap. VI. v. 70.—" Even three suppressions of breath, made according to the divine rule, accompanied by the triverbal phrase *(bhurbhuvaswah)*, and the triliteral syllable *(o'm)*, may be considered as the highest devotion of a *Brahman*;

" 71. For as the dross and impurities of metallic ores are consumed by fire, thus are the sinful acts of the human organ consumed by the suppression of the breath, while the mystic words and the measures of the *Gayatri* are revolved in the mind." (The suppression of the breath is thus performed by the priest:—Closing the left nostril with the two longest fingers of the right hand, he draws his breath through the right nostril; then closing that nostril likewise with his thumb, holds his breath while he meditates the text: he then raises both fingers off the left nostril, and emits the suppressed breath, having, during its

In the *Asiatic Researches*, Mr. COLEBROKE, in his Dissertations on the Religious Ceremonies of the *Hindus*, and on the *Vedas*, has given several versions of the *Gayatri*, as used in different rites: they here follow.—

"On another occasion, the *Gayatri*, properly so called, bears the following import;—'On that effulgent power, which is BRAHME himself, and is called the light of the radiant Sun, do I meditate; governed by the mysterious light which resides within me, for the purpose of thought: that very light is the earth, the subtle ether, and all that exists within the created sphere; it is the threefold world, containing all which is fixed or moveable; it exists internally in my heart, externally in the orb of the sun, being one and the same with that effulgent power. I myself am an irradiated manifestation of the Supreme BRAHME.' —With such reflections," says the commentator, "should the text be inaudibly recited."—Vol. V. p. 359.

He, in another place, thus renders the important text:—"*Earth! Sky! Heaven!*—Let us meditate on (thee, and on) the most excellent light and power of that generous, sportive, and resplendent Sun; (praying that) it may guide our intellects."—Vol. VII. p. 259.

suppression, repeated to himself the *Gayatri*, with the mysterious names of the worlds, the triliteral monosyllable, and the sacred text of BRAHM. A suppression of breath is thus explained by an ancient legislator to imply the following meditation: "*Om!* earth! sky! heaven! middle region! place of births! mansion of the blessed! abode of truth!—We meditate on the adorable light of the resplendent Generator which governs our intellects: which is water, lustre, savour, immortal, faculty of thought, BRAHM, earth, sky, heaven."—See *As. Res.* Vol. V. Art. xxii. This, and other parts of this note, will explain a text cited in p. 372.)

Chap. XII. v. 93.—"Such is the advantageous privilege of those who have a double birth from their natural mothers, and from their spiritual mother, especially of a *Brahman*, &c."

Chap. II. v. 74.—"A *Brahman*, beginning and ending a lecture on the *Veda*, must always pronounce to himself the syllable *Om*: for unless the syllable *Om* precede, his learning will slip away from him; and unless it follow, nothing can be long retained." (A commentator on this verse says: "As the leaf of the *palasa* is supported by a single pedicle, so is this universe upheld by the syllable OM, a symbol of the Supreme BRAHM."—"All rites ordained in the *Veda*, oblations to fire, and solemn sacrifices, pass away; but that which passeth not away," says MENU, "is declared to be the syllable OM, then called *acshara*, since it is a symbol of God, the Lord of created beings."—See *As. Res.* Vol. V. Art. xxii.)

"169. The first birth is from a natural mother; the second, from the ligation of the zone; the third, from the due performance of the sacrifice: such are the births of him who is usually called twice-born, according to a text in the *Veda*.

"170. Among them, his divine birth is that which is distinguished by the ligation of the zone and sacrificial cord; and in that, the *Gayatri* is his mother, and the *Acharya* his father." (*Acharya*, or *Guru*, means spiritual preceptor.)

"The last hymn, or *Sucta*, of the third book of the first *Veda*, which book contains invocations by VISWAMITRA, consists of six prayers; one of which includes the celebrated *Gayatri*. This remarkable text is repeated more than once in other *Vedas*; but since VISWAMITRA is the *Rishi* to whom it was revealed, it appears that its proper and original place is in this hymn. I therefore subjoin a translation of the prayer which contains it, as also the preceding one, (both of which are addressed to the Sun,) for the sake of exhibiting the *Indian* priests' confession of faith, with its context; after having, in former essays, given more than one version of it apart from the rest of the text."—

"This new and excellent praise of thee, O splendid playful Sun! (PUSHAN,) is offered by us to thee. Be gratified by this my speech: approach this craving mind, as a fond man seeks a woman. May that Sun (PUSHAN), who contemplates, and looks into, all worlds, be our protector.

"LET US MEDITATE ON THE ADORABLE LIGHT OF THE DIVINE RULER (SAVITRI).—MAY IT GUIDE OUR INTELLECTS. Desirous of food, we solicit the gift of the splendid Sun (SAVITRI), who should be studiously worshipped. Venerable men, guided by the understanding, salute the divine Sun (SAVITRI) with oblations and praise."

"SAYANACHARYA, the commentator, whose gloss is here followed, considers this passage to admit of two interpretations: 'the light, or BRAHME, constituting the splendour of the Supreme Ruler, or the Creator of the Universe;' or 'the light, or orb, of the splendid Sun."—Vol. VIII. p. 400.

The passage in capitals appears to contain the whole of the *Gayatri*; and, with its context, is sufficient to prove that the *Hindus*, esoterically, are not polytheists. But it is difficult to conceive, why the text should be so sedulously kept secret; for its exposition, unconnected with the idea of mystery, and affectation of profundity, doth not appear likely to have the effect, so dreaded by priests, of "guiding the intellects" of the multitude to the discovery of truth.

In the article SURYA it is noticed, that the Sun is called SAVITRI in the *Gayatri*; and under the name of SURYA, SAVITRI is personified as a female married to SOMA, the Moon.—See SURYA, page 283. PUSHAN is also among the appellations of SURYA, in page 287.

The sacred monosyllable is generally spelled OM; but being triliteral, seems better expressed by AUM, or AOM, or AWM, it being formed of the three *Sanskrit* letters that are best so represented. This mystic emblem of the Deity was first introduced to the *European* world by the translation of the *Gita*; where

(p. 142.) we are told it is forbidden to be pronounced but in silence. "The first letter stands for the Creator, the second for the Preserver, and the third for the Destroyer."

Again: "*OM*, *Tat*, and *Sat*, are the three mystic characters" (which are given, but I have not the types,) "used to denote the Deity. The word *Sat* is used for qualities which are true, and for qualities which are holy: it is applied also to deeds which are praiseworthy. Attention in worship, zeal, and deeds of charity, are likewise called *Sat*."—*Gita*, p. 22.

Hence, perhaps, the *Satya yug*, the virtuous or golden age: *Sati*, a widow who burns with her husband's corpse: a name also of BHAVANI, implying constancy and virtue.

KRISHNA, describing his own excellencies, selects the first and best of many things to compare to himself. "I am," he says to ARJUN, "the monosyllable among words."—*Gita*, page 68. "Amongst harmonious measures, I am the *Gayatri*."—*Ib.* page 87.

Mr. PATERSON calls this mystic sign of BRAHM by the name of *Pranava*; and by making a sort of double cypher of the O M, and filling it up, and giving a body to the central and connecting part of the cypher, fancies he has discovered a mysterious triad represented at *Jagan-nath*: it is curious, but not easily explained without his plate.—See, therefore, *Asiatic Researches*, Vol. VIII. page 62.

This word, used like our *Amen* at the end of prayers, is used also, as we have seen, at their beginning. If uttered, it would express a sound not very different from *Amen*, as the word is sometimes drawled out, nasally, by a country parish clerk; or, perhaps, more like the half-groan, half-grunt, of the quakers, by which those good people express pious emotions. The sacred syllable is also called *Anghé kár*; meaning *yes, so be it*: implying consent, approbation, &c.

Of BALLAJI, WITTOBA, and NANESHWER, *Avataras* of VISHNU; and of KANDEH RAO, an *Avatara* of SIVA.

The *Brahmans* of *Poona* gave me the following particulars of the *Avatara* of VISHNU, which they call BALLAJI.

'In *Sanskrit* this *Avatara* is named VINKATYEISH; in the *Carnatic* dialect, TERPATI; in the *Telinga* country and language, VINKATRAMNA GOVINDA; in *Gujerat*, and to the westward, TA'KHUR, or T'HAKHUR, as well as BALLAJI: the latter name obtains in the neighbourhood of *Poona*, and generally through the *Mahrata* country.

This incarnation took place at *Terputty*, in the *Carnatic*, where, in honour of BALLAJI, is a splendid temple, very rich, and much respected. At present it is in possession of the *English*, who are said to derive from it and its dependencies an annual revenue of one lack and twenty-five thousand (125,000) rupees: about fifteen thousand pounds sterling.

It is related, that all acts of this temple, to which an extensive district is attached, are carried on in the name of VINKATREDDY-DESSYE, another appellation for this *Avatara*. *Brahmans*, and other *Hindus*, in the *Carnatic*, sometimes are sworn in the name of VINKATYESH. The temple is built of stone, covered with plates of gilt copper, and is held in high estimation; said, indeed, not to be of mortal manufacture.

Pilgrimages are made to *Terpati*, better, perhaps, spelled *Tripati*, from all parts of *India*, especially from *Gujerat*: the trading inhabitants of which province, of the tribes of *Bania* and *Battia*, and others, are in the habit of presenting five or ten per cent. of their annual profits to this temple, whose deity appears to be the tutelary patron of traffic: rich gifts and votive offerings are likewise received from other quarters.'

In this *Avatara*, or, as being of inferior importance, more strictly, perhaps, called *Avantara*, (see p. 14.) VISHNU, in his form of BALLAJI, was attended by his *Sacti*, LAKSHMI, and by another wife, SATYAVAMA; and they are generally seen with him. As well in his *Avatara* of KRISHNA, with whom SATYAVAMA appears to have been a favourite, (see p. p. 203. 215. 217.) we find her, with LAKSHMI, in immediate attendance on her divine spouse in his paradise of *Vaikont'ha*, as well as participating with her favoured associate in promoting the tranquillity of the *Preserver*, while reposing on *Sesha*, in *Chirasamudra*, or the sea of milk. —See PLATE 8. and page 28.

In PLATE 11. are BALLAJI and his wife, LAKSHMI, from brass images, as described in page 31; and in PLATE 12. is another representation of them, from a subject in gilt silver, noticed in page 32. In the first of these, he has the forehead mark, *No.* 34. of PLATE 2.—LAKSHMI, *No.* 1.—his may, however, be also *No.* 1. cut deeper: in PLATE 12. he has *No.* 10. He is in both these subjects, as he is also in many others in my possession, gifted with the same attributes as VISHNU; with whom, or with KRISHNA, he would most likely be identified, if his whole history were made out. His wives, LAKSHMI and SATYAVAMA, we see, in the plates just noticed, in the same attributes as LAKSHMI, when, as bearing the lotos, she is called KAMALA, as is mentioned in page 29.

Plate 76. gives another representation of this *Avatara* and his wives in another form: it is taken from a coloured picture, and the only one I have in which these persons are painted in that attitude with their arms *a-kimbo*; a position in which Wittoba and his wife are generally exhibited, as we shall notice presently. Ballaji, in the original of plate 76. is but two-handed; of a dark blue colour, with yellow waist-cloth, and a red scarf: on his forehead he has mark 10. or 11. of plate 2. in red; in the engraving it is too sharp at bottom: his wives have 31. in red.

Another representation of this *Avatara* is given in plate 97. taken from a good modern cast in brass, about nine inches high. This cast, like the silver one of plate 12. is in five pieces: the back lifts out of sockets in the pedestal, and admits the figures to slide backwards out of the grooves in which they are fitted: it is then seen that the seven-headed *naga*, joined to the figure, continues his scaly length down Ballaji's back, and making two convolutions under him, forms his seat: a second, shorter, snake, also part of the figure, protrudes its head, and makes a rest for Ballaji's right foot, and terminates with the other snake behind him. Unless this refer to the same legend as Krishna crushing *Kaliya*, I know not its allusion. Ballaji holds the usual attributes of Vishnu; his wives, the lotos, like Kamala, as before noticed and described, (page 29); but instead of her elegance of attitude and beautiful arrangement of the hair, Ballaji's wives are distinguished for the reverse: their form and attitude are clumsy; their dress, the scarf or mantle excepted, is inelegant; and their hair, badly arranged, with a rose at top, is braided, and hangs straight down their backs in a *queue*. He has *No.* 2. of plate 2. on his forehead; his spouses, the circlet of *No.* 22. The back part of this and similar subjects form a sort of glory to the figures, and has, I believe, that intention, and is, indeed, similarly called; for its name, *Prabhaval*, is, I imagine, derived from *Prabha*—light, splendour, glory. Two or three sockets or eyelets behind are for the reception of flowers, or, perhaps, lighted wicks, at the oblations offered to the power thus typified.

Ballaji is a frequent name among *Brahmans*, and other *Hindus*. Ballaji *Pandit*, or rather Ballaji Janardhana, was the name of that great and good man, so well known by his family and official appellation, Nana Fernaveese: Janardhana is likewise, as well as Ballaji, a name of Vishnu. Thus much as to Ballaji: let us now proceed to the consideration of the story of Wittoba.

This was one of the many subordinate incarnations of Vishnu. It took place at *Panderpur*, a very respectable town about eighty miles to the south east of *Poona*. The *Brahmans* speak of it as an event of not very ancient date; but say that it is recorded, perhaps prophetically, in the *Maha Bhagavata*. A splendid temple is dedicated to the worship of Vishnu, under the form of Wittoba, at *Panderpur*, usually spelled *Punderpoor*, in which he is represented, sculptured in stone, of the size of a man, standing with his feet parallel to each other; with his hands upon his hips, the fingers pointing forwards, (see plate 11.*)—

* The *Jainas* have a fanciful mode of representing the world by comparison to a woman with her arms a-kimbo; reminding us of Wittoba's and Ballaji's wives, as seen in plates 11. and 76.—her waist is the earth, the superior portion of her person is the abode of the gods, and the inferior part comprehends the infernal regions.—See *As. Res.* Vol. IX. p. 318.

he is covered with a sort of raised hat, crowned with a *Linga*: his hair is plaited, and turned up. In smaller temples beside his, are images of RUKMENY and SATYAVAMA. This account is as I received it from a *Brahman*, who well knew the temple and town; which I visited myself in 1792, and gave some account of it in a work published soon after.

Images of this *Avatara*, which seem very much akin to that of BALLAJI, are very common: I have many; and of his wife, or wives, with their arms in the attitude represented in PLATE 11. but only one, with the mark of a foot on WITTOBA's shoulder, and the hole in his foot, which will be farther noticed presently. The images in PLATE 11. are clumsily cast in copper, modern, considerably larger than there represented: his forehead is marked with *No.* 19. of PLATE 2.—his wife's, with 34.—the latter rather appertaining to PARVATI than LAKSHMI: there are, however, *Yonijas* among the *Vaishnavas*: the singularity of a *Linga* on WITTOBA's head, as seen in PLATE 11. has been before noticed.—See page 32.

The history of this incarnation, as related to me by a *Pandit*, I give, with some other particulars connected with it, in the note below.*

* A *Brahman*, named PUNDELLY, was travelling on a pilgrimage from the *Dekhan* to *Benares*, with his wife, father, and mother: his neglect of the two latter caused them many vexations on the journey; for he would sometimes ride with his wife, and leave them to walk, &c. Arriving at *Panderpur*, they took up their abode in a *Brahman's* house for the evening and night; during which, PUNDELLY noticed, with some self-abasement, many acts of filial piety and kindness on the part of his host toward his parents, who, with his wife, composed the hospitable family. Early in the morning, PUNDELLY observed three elegant females, attired in white, and richly decorated, performing the several duties of sweeping his host's house, and putting it in order; filling water, arranging the vessels for cooking, sanctifying the eating-place by plastering it with cow-dung, &c. &c. and, astonished at the sight, he proceeded to inquire who these industrious strangers were, he not having seen over night any such persons of the family: but his inquiries were received with repulsive indignation by the beauteous damsels, who forbad him, "a *chandala*, an ungrateful and undutiful son," &c. to approach or converse with them.

PUNDELLY, humbling himself, solicited to know their name, &c. and learned they were named GANGA, YAMUNA, and SARASWATI, and immediately recognized the triad of river goddesses. More and more astonished, he, after prostration, inquired how it could be that such divine personages, in propitiation of whose favour he, with his family, among thousands of others, undertook long and painful pilgrimages, should descend to the menial occupations he had witnessed. After reproaching him for his undutiful conduct, they replied to this effect: "You have witnessed the filial and dutiful affection of the heads of this family to their aged and helpless parents; for them they seem solely to live, and for them they find delight in toiling; they seek no pleasure abroad, nor do they deem it necessary to make pilgrimages, or even to go to the temples for the purposes of prayer. Know ye that these acts, necessary and holy as they may be, are nevertheless of no avail unless earlier duties have been attended to. Bad men, especially those who neglect their first duties to their parents, to whom all first duties are owing, may pass their whole lives in

Although, among my papers, I find an article purporting it to be an account of the marks on WITTOBA's *breast* and *foot*, the former only is discussed, as just given; the origin of the pierced foot is omitted. I recollect, that when inquiring of my *Pandit* the history of this *Avatara*, I wished for more particulars

pilgrimages and prayer without benefit to their souls. On the contrary, with those who are piously performing those primary duties, the outward ceremonies of religion are of secondary and inferior moment; and even deities, as you have witnessed, minister to their comforts ond convenience. He who serves his parents, serves his God through them."

Struck with remorse at this rebuke, PUNDELLY resolved amendment; and dropping his intended pilgrimage, remained at *Panderpur*, and for a series of years acted in a most exemplary manner toward his parents, exceeding even in attention and duty the pattern of his former hosts: insomuch, that VISHNU inspired him with a portion of his divinity, and he now assumed the name of WITTOBA. Two wives of VISHNU, in his former *Avatara* of KRISHNA, to which, indeed, this approximates almost to identity, were associated with him in this—RUKMENI and SATYAVAMA: some give WITTOBA three wives, adding RADHA to the other two. RUKMENY is represented in the same position as her husband, and has a temple beside his at *Panderpur*.

I have given this story at length, as related to me, to show that the history of the *Hindu* gods is sometimes made subservient to the inculcation of moral and social duties; and it is likely that most, if not all, of their mythological fables have allusions creditable to their religion and morality, although, perhaps, not in all cases discoverable.

In one of my images of WITTOBA, (see PLATE 11. *fig. 6.*) he has a print of a foot on his breast, and a hole in his foot: respecting the former, I find the following memorandum, which I took from the mouth of a *Brahman*.

In a divine assembly, BHRIGU was asked who, of the gods, was the most mighty: he said he would proceed to inquire, and first went to BRAHMA; on approaching whom, it was the necessary and decorous usage of BHRIGU to pay very respectful obeisance, which, on this occasion, he purposely omitted, and experienced in consequence a severe reprehension, including copious abuse, (for the *Hindu* gods, like HOMER's, are very abusive,) from BRAHMA; who, however, became pacified by seasonable apologies and respect on the part of BHRIGU. The moral of this, the *Brahman* thus explained: Our creation, or Creator, may be abused by our ill conduct; amendment, or contrition, averts the consequences.

He next proceeded to *Kailasa*, the paradise of MAHADEVA, and omitted, as in the case of his visit to BRAHMA, the usual tokens of adoration on entering the divine presenee. The vindictive deity was still more enraged than BRAHMA, but was in like manner pacified by BHRIGU's apologies, and showing him due respect. This, as far as I could understand it, means, that Destruction, although certain and deserved, may be rendered less terrible by contrition.

He then repaired to *Vaikont'ha*, the celestial residence of VISHNU, whom he found asleep, with LAKSHMI *shampooing* his feet. BHRIGU knew that the moderation, affability, condescension, &c. mild qualities of this gentle deity, were such, that a mere omission of respect would by no means move him to anger; and to make a trial of them, he boldly gave the god a severe kick on the breast. VISHNU awoke, and, seeing BHRIGU, arose; and, in place of anger, expressed apprehensions that he must have hurt his foot by striking it against his (VISHNU's) breast; and proceeded to lament it, and to rub and chafe BHRIGU's foot to remove any consequent pain. "This," said BHRIGU, "is the mightiest god: he overpowers by the most potent of all arms—affability and generosity." This I understand to mean, that Preservation, although continu-

than he had in his recollection, and especially as to the pierced foot; my note of which I deferred till he should consult his books on the subject. Other matters interfered, and the information was not obtained, which I regret; for I do not know of any mention of it in any author; and the following anecdote, coupled with it, renders the history of this *Avatara* the more desirable.—

A man, who was in the habit of bring me *Hindu* deities, pictures, &c. once brought me two images exactly alike: one of them is engraved in PLATE 98. and the subject of it will be at once seen by the most transient glance. Affecting indifference, I inquired of my *Pandit* what *Deva* it was: he examined it attentively, and, after turning it about for some time, returned it to me, professing

ally extended, we can never deserve or secure by our own merits or conduct; nor is the most intemperate daring always fatal.

VISHNU, in the character of WITTOBA, retains indelibly the impression of BHRIGU's foot; but why it is retained particularly by WITTOBA I find no mention of.

It will at once occur, that this story, lame as it may appear, inculcates the efficacy of mildness and forgiveness; bearing, with due respect be it spoken, some resemblance to the advice given by superior authority, of turning the unsmote cheek to an assailant. This mild quality, my *Brahman* endeavoured to make me understand, is a characteristic of VISHNU, called, in *Sanskrit, Satwa-goon*; implying infinite mercy or forbearance. BRAHMA is characterised by the term *Raja-goon,* which implies discriminative or circumscribed justice, or judicious temperament; while to the vindictive SIVA is applied the character of *Tama-goon,* meaning ever angry, with or without reason.

These terms of *Satwa, Raja,* and *Tama,* as well as applicable to the nature of the three supreme powers, are supposed to be descriptive of the conduct and temper of men: they are generic terms of temper, admitting and embracing manifold specific modifications. Metaphysicians may discover in these terms, descriptive of the dispositions of the three great gods, an appropriate allusion to their respective powers of Creation, Preservation, and Destruction. To all nature, creation is equally dispensed; BRAHMA, the creator, is equally just: to all, destruction, though delayed or averted, is certain, and is typified in SIVA's indiscriminate vengeance: while the infinite forbearance of VISHNU marks his equality of preservation.

In the *Gita,* the qualities of *Satwa, Raja,* and *Tama,* are discussed, and described as *truth, passion,* and *darkness*; or, as the words are sometimes used, *white, red, black.* Generally, *Sanskrit* words beginning with *Sat,* comprehend an idea of truth, purity, goodness; those beginning with *Tam,* of darkness, and its derivatives. In other places, the colours supposed to be appropriated to the three powers of the Deity, are noticed, and will be found to differ in their application. From what has just appeared, *White* is applied to VISHNU; *Red,* to BRAHMA; and *Black,* to SIVA: on other occasions, we find *White* the colour of SIVA, and *Blue,* of VISHNU; the latter, especially when seen as KRISHNA, is, and, indeed, in most of his *Avataras,* painted *Blue,* as SIVA is *White. Red,* as far as I recollect, is always BRAHMA's, although he is seldom painted of that colour: SIVA, as KALA, is black.

In MAURICE's Ancient History, Part III. p. 445. the outrage of BHRIGU is noticed; but the forgiving mildness is referred to KRISHNA: a farther evidence of the idea of identity between the principal and inferior *Avataras* of VISHNU. In p. 454. the story of the kick is again told of VISHNU: "who is KRISHNA; the same who exhibited to ARJUN his own exalted might."

his ignorance of what *Avatara* it could immediately relate to; but supposed, by the hole in the foot, that it might be WITTOBA, adding, that it was impossible to recollect the almost innumerable *Avataras* described in the *Puranas*.

The subject of PLATE 98. is evidently the crucifixion; and, by the style of workmanship, is clearly of *European* origin, as is proved also by its being in duplicate.* These crucifixes have been introduced into *India*, I suppose, by *Christian* missionaries, and are, perhaps, used in *Papish* churches and societies: the two in question were obtained in the interior of the peninsula, but I could not learn exactly where: they are well executed, and, in respect to anatomical accuracy and expression, superior to any I have seen of *Hindu* workmanship.— They are about the size of the picture; and although but small, I have chosen to give it in a plate by itself, lest the pious might be hurt at seeing such a subject mixed with the apparent grossness of *Hindu* idolatry. And, indeed, with this caution, I have some apprehension of giving offence; for showing my plates to a friend somewhat scrupulous on such points, he suggested the omission of PLATE 98. But I do not, as I then remarked, see much difference in such a plate among mine, and in the same subject among paintings of heathen deities seen without offence in the galleries of our collectors—even in the habitations of our most pious and gracious Sovereign.

* The reason why an exact duplicate of an image is a proof of its not being of *Hindu* workmanship will appear in the description of their mode of casting in metals. First, the artist makes in wax the exact model, in every particular, of his intended subject, be it what it may; whether an image of a deity, or the hinge of a box: over this he plasters a covering of fine clay, well moistened and mixed, leaving an aperture at some part: when dry, it is put on a fire, with the hole downwards, and the wax of course melts out. The plaster is now a mould, and receives at the aperture the molten metal, giving it externally, when cool, the exact form of its own concavity; or, in other words, of its original waxen model. The plaster, or crust, or mould, is now broken, and the image—say—is produced, sometimes sufficiently correct to require no after-polishing. The beautiful specimens of *Hindu* mythology, cast at *Benares* under the superintendance of *Mr.* WILKINS and some *Pandits*, have never since received the least polish or filing, but are now seen at the *India* house museum exactly as they made their first appearance from the moulds. From these classical subjects the following articles in this work have been taken, by *Mr.* WILKINS's obliging permission: PLATE 3.—*fig.* 2. 3. of PLATE 13.—PLATES 15. 48. 50. and 51.

That *Hindu* casts have but little muscular expression, is not, perhaps, to be considered altogether as defective, or attributed to want of skill in the artists: the human subject with them is rounder and plumper, less marked by angles and muscles, than the hardier and ruder persons of higher latitudes, who, of course, exhibit more "nerve and pith." The models from which *Hindu* founders have borrowed their forms partake of the roundness of APOLLO, not the muscle of HERCULES, as was before hinted at in p. 248.

Having in this article digressed a little from the, peradventure, dry, but by no means barren, subject of mythology, I will endeavour to relieve it by indulging myself, and I hope my reader, with extracting a few lines from the still eloquent, though for ever silenced, pen of the lamented JONES: if, as is probable, they be familiar to him, they cannot be unwelcome: if they be new, they will be the more acceptable. I must premise, that the subject is the philosophy of the *Asiatics*; and the following passage is illustrative of the ancient morality of the *East*.—

"Our divine religion, the truth of which (if any history be true,) is abundantly proved by historical evidence, has no need of such aids as many are willing to give it; by asserting, that the wisest men of this world were ignorant of the two great maxims—that *we must act in respect of others as we should wish them to act in respect of ourselves*—and that, instead of *returning evil for evil, we should confer benefits on those who injure us.* But the first rule is implied in a speech of LYSIAS, and expressed in distinct phrases by THALES and PITTACUS; and I have even seen it, word for word, in the original of CONFUCIUS, which I carefully compared with the *Latin* translation. It has been usual with zealous men to ridicule and abuse all those who dare, on this point, quote the *Chinese* philosopher; but instead of supporting their cause, they would shake it, if it could be shaken, by their uncandid asperity: for they ought to remember, that one great end of revelation, as it is most expressly declared, was not to instruct the wise and few, but the many and unenlightened. If the conversion, therefore, of the *Pandits* and *Maulavis*, in *India*, shall ever be attempted by protestant missionaries, they must beware of asserting, while they teach the gospel of truth, what those *Pandits* and *Maulavis* would know to be false. The former would cite the beautiful *Arya* couplet, which was written at least three centuries before our era, and which pronounce the duty of a good man, even in the moment of destruction, to consist, *not only in forgiving, but even in a desire of benefiting, his destroyer—as the* sandal *tree, in the instant of its overthrow, sheds perfume on the a e which fells it.* And the latter would triumph, in repeating the verse of SADI, who represents *a return of good for good as a slight reciprocity*; but says to the virtuous man, '*Confer benefits on him who has injured thee:*' using an *Arabic* sentence, and a maxim apparently of the ancient *rabs.* Nor would the *Mussulmans* fail to recite four distichs of HAFIZ, who has illustrated that maxim with fanciful but elegant allusions:—

'Learn from yon orient shell to love thy foe,
And store with pearls the hand that brings thee woe:
Free, like yon rock, from base vindictive pride,
Emblaze with gems the wrist that rends thy side:
Mark where yon tree rewards the stony shower
With fruit nectareous, or the balmy flower:
All Nature calls aloud—"Shall man do less
Than heal the smiter, and the railer bless?"

As. Res. Vol. IV.

We have still to notice another *Avatara* of VISHNU, under the form and name of NANESHWER; but as, in the numerical order of our plates, MAHADEVA'S *Avatara* of KANDEH RAO is first placed, we will first notice that character, and then proceed to the consideration of NANESHWER.

What I have to relate of KANDEH RAO is gathered chiefly from *Poona Brahmans*; who state, that SIVA became incarnate in this personage for the purpose of destroying an oppressive giant, named MANI-MAL, at a place in the *Carnatic*, called *Pehmer*. PARVATI, they say, under the name of MALSARA, accompanied her lord, who appeared as a man clothed in green, (but I have no picture of him so clothed): he is generally represented with PARVATI on horseback, attended frequently by a dog. Here follow some farther particulars:—

The giant MANI-MAL made a most desperate defence against KANDEH RAO's attack, but was at length slain; whereupon all the oppressed subjects of this giant paid adoration to KANDEH RAO, to the number, as the story goes, of seven *Kroor* of people, whence this *Avatara* is called *Yehl-khut: Yehl*, in a dialect of the *Carnatic*, being seven, and *Khut*, or *Koot*, being a *Mahrata* pronunciation of *Kroor*, (100,00,000,) a hundred *lakh*, or ten millions.

A handsome temple, dedicated to the worship of this *Avatara*, is at *Jejury*, a town of some extent, about thirty miles to the south-east of *Poona*. I have visited this temple: it is situated in a beautiful country, on a high hill, and has a very commanding and majestic appearance: the temple, walls round, and steps up to it, are well built, of fine stone. Some account was given of it in a former work; wherein is also a relation of the *Murliders*, or musical girls, attached to it, who were said to exceed two hundred in number, and, of course, the most beautiful that can be found—such as I saw were very handsome. A great many *Brahmans* reside in and about the temple, and more beggars than I ever saw in any one place.

I have had occasion to remark, and it has also doubtless been remarked by others, that the site of churches built by the *Jesuits* are always on the most healthy, beautiful, and picturesque points, evincing the judgment and taste of that wonderful order of men: the same may, I think, be observed of the situation of *Hindu* temples; generally, after allowing for the necessary proximity of water, the most beautiful the neighbourhood affords.

The obtrusive importunity of the beggars prevented my examining this fine temple at *Jejury* so fully as I wished; indeed, from their officiousness, I could scarcely examine it at all. The *Brahmans* informed me, on subsequent inquiries, that a stone is there, about two feet square, on which are two *Lingas*, one larger than the other, whence KANDEH RAO, and, I suppose, MALSARA, sprung: there are also two images of him, between two and three feet high, one of gold, one of silver; and one of gold, of MALSARA; all richly ornamented on great days, when they are mounted on horseback, or on elephants. If, however, there really be such massive images in metal, they could scarcely be carried by a horse: images of lighter materials are, I apprehend, substituted; or metallic heads are *embodied*, armed, and arrayed with clothes, and thus carried about or exhibited. I have several of these hollow heads, to which bodies, &c. could easily be appended: I have also several brass masks, some as large as a man's face, that may answer, and, peradventure, may have answered, on similar occasions.

Jejury temple is very rich: it is said to expend half a *lak'h* (50,000) rupees yearly in the expenses and establishment for KANDEH RAO: horses and elephants are kept for him; he and his spouse are bathed in *Ganges* water, rose-water—perfumed with *atr*, and decorated with gems. The revenues, like those of most other temples, are derived from houses and lands given by pious people, and from presents and offerings constantly making by all descriptions of votaries and visitors, according to their means, or their faith, hope, or charity. The *Murliders*, however numerous, are not, perhaps, any expense, but rather a source of revenue, to the temple. At the annual *Jatra*, or fair, which commences on the last day of the dark half of *Chaitra*, (in January,) a *lak'h*, or more, of persons visit *Jejury*: it is customary to sacrifice a sheep; and the *Brahmans* assured me, that twenty, or, on particular years, thirty, thousand are slain on this occasion, and to the honour and glory of KANDEH RAO.

There are few deities more domestically popular, throughout the *Mahrata* countries, than those of the *Avatara* under our consideration; more especially in the districts around *Jejury*, where KANDEH RAO has, I think, his principal temple, and where, indeed, it is said by some, that the incarnation was manifested. In all my images of this *Avatara*, of which I have many, (not fewer than ten,) KANDEH RAO is accompanied by his *Sacti*, under her name of MALSARA, on horseback, and frequently attended by a dog—a singularity that I cannot account for; although, doubtless, a legendary detail will be found of it in some of the poetical romances, the *Puranas*.

In the lower part of PLATE 23. this mounted pair are represented, from a coloured picture, in which they are of a fairish, or copper, complexion: he is four-handed; a sword, a trident, and his wife, occupy three hands; the fourth is empty: she holds the bridle. In the picture they have two attendants: the one before has a pouch, made of tiger's skin, with the tail forming a cover, or flap, of superfluous length, as is sometimes now carried by *Yogis* and holy persons. he behind has a parasol of that description, called, in *Persia* and in *India*, *aftabgir*. Both attendants have the forehead mark, *No*. 2. or 10. of PLATE 2. in red; and KANDEH RAO, before remarked as a seeming anomaly, has the *Vaishnava* mark, *No*. 3. or 9.—lines red, circlet black: his horse is white, and his dog blue.

PLATE 94. has four representations of this *Avatara*, from casts in brass. *Fig*. 1 is very old and rude: three of his four hands hold a short sword *(Kardgha)*, the cup *(patra)*, and double drum *(damru*, or *dindima)*, and the fourth is empty: his spouse is stradling behind him, and holds on by her husband's elbows: the horse is led by an armed female; a dog is on the other side; between the horse's feet is an animal's head, but not so much like a beeve's as in the plate; and a cup, or something circular, is at the leader's feet.

Fig. 2. is also very old and rude, and has evidently been buried. In this cast the lady sits foremost, and her good man is on the pad behind her: he has a sword and target; she, a cup, or dish, and apparently a lotos: in front of the horse are a *naga*, *linga*, and, what I take to be, two human feet; and beside the horse are the remains of, what I imagine to have been, the dog: a sun and crescent are in front of the pedestal.

Fig. 3. is more modern, and is better cast. KANDEH RAO is four-handed, holding *trisula*, sword, drum, and a full cup: his left foot rests on the pummel of the saddle, his knee and leg thereby forming a seat for his wife, who has a sword and cup in her hands.

Fig. 4. is likewise modern, and in good preservation: in one of his hands is a sword; by the other he holds a cloth or scarf, in which MALSARA stands, leaning against his arm and shoulder: she has a cup in one hand, and something like a rosary in the other: his shield is slung over his shoulder and his *zennaar* is conspicuous: his long-toed shoes are rather unusual: a curly-tailed dog is under the horse.

The description of article engraved in PLATE 95. is mentioned in page 166, being impressions on thin plates of copper, embossed by steel or iron dies, for the accommodation, being very rude and cheap, of such pious persons as are not in circumstances to obtain the advantage of a domestic image. KANDEH RAO is met with in this form as often as any of his divine brotherhood. We see him in *fig*. 1. of PLATE 95. with his wife, horse, dog, &c. pretty nearly as before described; and again in *fig*. 3. with more than their usual attendants. Of all the mythological subjects in my possession, this is, I think, the rudest and worst executed; it is much more so than the plate indicates, or, perhaps, than could be represented: the die was probably of wood, carved by a man too poor to purchase an object of worship: it is of the size of the engraving, and has a second sheet of copper forming a back, its edges overlapping, and thereby strengthening that embossed; and the space between the plates being filled with lak, or some bituminous substance, tends to preserve the impression from indentation or defacement:—See page 167.

PLATE 95. contains three other figures, inserted chiefly to fill it. *Fig*. 3. is an embossed head of BHAI-

RAVA, of whom sufficient notice has been taken in earlier pages; and the singularity of his having a *Vaishnava* mark on his forehead (*No.* 19. of PLATE 2.) has likewise been mentioned. *Fig.* 4. by the shield, staff, mustaches, and breeches, one would take for a hero; but my *Pandit* marked it as DEVI, under her name of FERINGAHI, and would not allow that he could be mistaken. The bow and shafts in the hands of *fig.* 5. of this plate (95.) denote PARASU RAMA: the two last, as well as the first, figures of this plate have the same forehead mark; not very well defined, but resembling *No.* 34. of PLATE 2.

In the early part of *Sir* CHARLES MALET's diplomatic residence at the court of *Poona*, that government, not, however, without some demur, yielded to his wish of being permitted to reside at a small distance from the city, rather in the house allotted for his accommodation within its walls, which, indeed, was, I believe, burned down; and he pitched on a spot as delightful, perhaps, as any in the *Mahratá* territory It is situated, and comprehends the portion of land, between the rivers *Moota* and *Moola*, which form a *junction* of their waters and name at the Residency, hence called *Sangam*; and in the rainy season spread to a great and beautiful mass of water, with ornamented islands interspersed. But I must not trust myself with the description of a spot that I ought to recollect with gratitude, having there formed and cemented some of my most valued and esteemed friendships, and passed, in other respects, a profitable and happy portion of my life. On this lovely spot *Sir* CHARLES MALET and his suite built convenient habitations; but it having been previously occupied by a *Deva*, rudely chiselled in stone, (which preoccupancy was, I fancy, a cause of the demur on the part of the *Durbar* at allowing an unsanctified association,) and his position interfering with a projected building, it was necessary to remove the god, or want the house; and it was rather apprehended that the stability of the deity could not be brought to yield to the convenience of mortals, those mortals not being *Brahmans*. But after a reasonable time taken for deliberating on so important a point, it was yielded, and permission was given to remove the *Deva*; and after, with due *etiquette*, settling the ceremonials of movement, a council of *Brahmans* directed and assisted in the operation, which was auspiciously performed on a lucky day at a lucky moment, music and various minstrelsy forwarding the harmony of the arrangement—*Sir* CHARLES, of course, not forgetting a seasonable donation to the *Brahmans* for expiatory oblations, in reference to the possible sin incident to the disturbance, and to holy men and temples, in view to a continuation of the benignant influences of the *Deva* over the favoured spot where he had fixed his shrine. After all, however, he was moved but a few feet—merely from the site of the intended house to the exterior of the surrounding wall, where he still reigns, in a niche, the tutelary *Daemon* of the *Sangam*, and the SYLVANUS of its groves and gardens.

Although, while at *Poona*, I daily passed close to this *Faun*, for he is situated in a garden between the upper buildings of the Residency and the breakfast-saloon, or hall of audience, at the junction of the waters, and have often seen women adorn it with flowers, and propitiate it by prostrations and prayers, I have yet no account or description of it; nor do I well recollect the name even of our sylvan deity: what I could have any day done, was, as is not unfrequently the case, altogether omitted. Referring for information on this point to my old and most valued friend *Mr.* UHTHOFF, he, I find, has also, and so has *Sir* CHARLES MALET, forgotten the name of our common acquaintance. *Mr.* UHTHOFF informs me, that he has, after its removal, frequently seen people sacrifice sheep and goats to the idol, and worship it; and he and *Sir* CHARLES think with me that it is of KANDEH RAO, who about *Poona* is also called KANDOBA; and it is not an uncommon name with *Brahmans* and other *Hindus*. In page 375, I find I have written the name of a *Brahman*, called, I imagine, after this *Avatara*, RAKPAT KANDHI RAO.

PLATE 96. refers to a story well known at *Poona*, near which city, at a village called *Alundy*, the event, the immediate subject of the plate, took place.

I will give the story as I find it among my memoranda: it was written down, as related to me by *Brahmans*, at *Poona* and *Bombay*.

NANESHWER is an *Avatara*, or rather, perhaps, (see p. 14.) an *Avantara*, of VISHNU, of recent date; by some stated to have happened twelve hundred, by others, six or seven hundred, years ago, at the village of *Alundy*, about six *kos* (nine miles) eastward from *Poona*. This village belonged, until lately, to SINDEA; and the *English* had a detachment of troops there in the late war with that chief.

NANESHWER was a *Brahman*, living at *Alundy*, and wrote a great book on religion, metaphysics, theogony, &c. in poetry: he is highly venerated for his learning and piety: his book is named after him, *Naneshweri*; is not scarce; indeed I believe it to be a metrical commentary on the *Gita*. It is said to be a work of such erudition, as not to be fully comprehensible without a knowledge of fifty-six dialects; that number of languages having flowed from the inspired penman through the composition of this work.

In the fulness of time NANESHWER was, as is not very unusual with *Saniyasis, Gussayns*, or *Yogis*, buried alive at *Alundy*, where his tomb is seen under a splendid temple; and he condescends to appear, for he is not dead, to very pious suppliants; and others he encourages by spiritual movements. In niches of the temple, or sepulchre, are statues of WITTOBA and RUKMENY, in stone, handsomely clothed and adorned with jewels; and the tomb is very rich. It is annually resorted to at a sort of fair, called *Jatra*, and is numerously attended from *Poona*, and from distant temples and towns. I have seen the *Peshwa* and his court go from *Poona* in great state; and I have been pressingly invited by *Brahmans* to visit the shrine, and particularly a *wall*, that will presently be spoken of; but either had no convenient opportunity, or neglected it till too late: wealthy visitors make handsome presents at the temple: its annual expenses in clothes for WITTOBA and his spouse, feeding *Brahmans*, and alms, are estimated at about eighteen thousand rupees.

NANESHWER's father, his name does not occur, having lost his wife while childless, was grievously afflicted, and vowed to become *Saniyasi*: after a lapse of some years, he found the report of her death untrue, and recovered her; but having entered on the austerities of his probation, such reunion caused great scandal among the *Brahmans*, who refused to consider him as one of their holy tribe.

They had now four children, by name NEWRATI-NAT, NANESHWER, and SUPANDEVA, sons; and MUKHTYE, or MUKHTEHBYE, a daughter; who were left orphans while young, and were considered by the *Brahmans* as *Chandalas*, or abominable outcasts, being the offspring of a *Saniyasi*. The poor children were sadly persecuted—could not marry, were not permitted to wear the holy string, and underwent sore mortification; but Providence relieved them from this state, by enabling them to perform several miracles, which satisfied the *Brahmans* that, although the offspring of a vile connection, they were yet sanctified and holy. One miracle was this:—

As a test, NANESHWER was desired by some *Brahmans* to endue a male buffalo, that happened to be approaching, with human faculties: he was at this time under reproach that he could not read the *Vedas*, and exclaimed that he would make the buffalo recite from the sacred volume; and he laid his hand on the beast, and commanded it to speak, which it immediately did, and accurately recited such portions of the *Vedas* as the sceptical *Brahmans* chused to point out.

The other miracle, of which PLATE 96. is a representation, was the following:—

Attracted by the fame of the miracle just detailed, a holy man, named CHANGA DEVA, or, as the name is pronounced in conversation, CHANGDEO, was coming toward *Alundy* to visit NANESHWER; who, with his brothers and sister, happened to be sitting on a wall: the sister intuitively knew of the approach of the holy man, and apprized NANESHWER of it, and of his business, and described his equipage. On his nearer approach, NANESHWER laid his hand on the wall, and commanded it to bear him and his relatives to their visitor; which, to the astonishment of all, it did, about a quarter of a coss, into the presence of CHANGA DEVA, who now appeared mounted on a *Bengal* tiger, and by a whip whirled a *cobra capel.* This wall is carefully preserved at *Alundy,* and held in great veneration: it is described to be about twenty feet long, and three feet thick, and seven high.

This CHANGA DEVA, otherwise called CHANGA-WAT-TESHWER, was an extraordinary person, having, by his ardent piety, himself performed some miracles, and was supposed to have been presumptuous and arrogant in consequence; and that of the walking wall is thought to have been wrought with the view of checking the progress of his pride: for although performed by a youth, it yet so far exceeding any thing in his power, that he humbled himself to the children; and acknowledging his inferiority, became thenceforth conspicuous for his humility and piety.

This *Avatar* of NANESHWER is very well known, and much respected, at *Poona,* and all its neighbourhood, and generally in the *Dekhan, Kokun, Gujerat,* &c.

On the equipage of CHANGA DEVA, it may be remarked as not unique, for other holy men have adopted the tiger as a vehicle.—A pious personage of this description was reported to have visited *Sri ranga patan,* (the city of SRI RANGA, or MAHADEVA, commonly *Seringapatam,*) about the year 1797, and, although a *Hindu,* to have been hospitably invited by the late TIPPOO SULTAN: he was attended by ten disciples, and declined the royal civilities, saying, a tree was sufficient shelter for him.

Of CHANGA DEVA I must also farther remark, that he was of that class which my *Pandit* called *Yug-saddan,* or *Yug-brasht,* or *Yug Vyasa,* who, by extraordinarily pious pains, obtains miraculous longevity: they prolong their existence, it is hyperbolically said, to some hundreds of years.

The performance of the *Yug saddan* is believed, without difficulty, by several *Brahmans,* with whom I have conversed upon it, to be the result of labour and study, superadded to ardent and persevering piety; but, perhaps, owing to want of a common language in which abstract terms could be conveyed, or to their not fully comprehending the theory of this feat, I could never satisfactorily understand how it is performed. As far as I could gather, it is the faculty of drawing, by degrees, all the breath (or, perhaps, the principle of life, or the soul,) into the upper part of the head, and thus continue for any number of years the aspirant may have previously determined on, or, as others say, in proportion to his piety, in a state of insensible absorption—exempt from the destructive operations of earth or water, but not of fire. The sect called *Byraggy* are apparently the most frequent and successful practisers of this extraordinary act. One of this description is now (November,* 1804,) described to me to be at *Poona,* of eminent attainment in this line of holiness: he is at present in this state of absorption, in a sitting posture, and is said to be many hundred years old.—I intend to make some farther inquiries after this personage.

Perhaps the following passage in the *Gita* may allude to this practice:—

"Some there are who sacrifice their breathing spirit, and force it downwards from its natural course; whilst others force the spirit, which is below, back with the breath." †—Page 54.

As may the following, in *Mr.* WILFORD's Dissertation on *Egypt* and the *Nile:*—

"On the banks of the *Cali* dwelt a *Brahman,* whose name was LECHAYANAS—a sage rigorously devout, skilled in the learning of the *Vedas,* and firmly attached to the worship of HERI; but having no male issue, he was long disconsolate, and made certain oblations to the god, which proved acceptable; so that

* This account is extracted from my memoranda, and I give it without alteration. I was unable, or neglected, to make the inquiries adverted to.

† *Hindu* mythology and metaphysics were but little, or not at all, investigated in the days of BUTLER, learned as he was, or that witty wag might be suspected of having borrowed some of his Hudibrastic lines from that source; those especially beginning his simile of—"wind i' th' *hypochondria* pent."

his wife, SANCRITI, became pregnant, after she had tasted part of the *Charu*, or cake of rice, which had been offered. In due time, she was delivered of a beautiful boy, whom the *Brahmans*, convened at the *jatacarma*, or ceremony on his birth, unanimously agreed to name HERIDATA, or given by the divinity. When the *Sanscara*, or institution of a *Brahman*, was completed by his investiture with the sacerdotal string, and the term of his studentship in the *Veda* was past, his parents urged him to enter into the second order, or that of a married man; but he ran into the woods, and passed immediately into the fourth order, disclaiming all worldly connections, and wholly devoting himself to VISHNU, he continually practised the *Samadhiyoga*, or *union with the Deity by contemplation*, fixing his mind so intensely on God, that his vital soul seemed concentrated in the *Brahma-randhra*, or pineal gland; while his animal faculties were suspended, but his body still uncorrupted, till the reflux of the spirits put them again in motion; a state in which the *Hindus* assert that some *Yogis* have remained for years. And the fanciful gradations of which are minutely described in the *Yoga-sastra*; and even delineated in the figures called *Shatchacra*, under the emblems of lotos-flowers with different numbers of petals, according to the supposed stations of the soul in her mystical ascent."—*As. Res.* Vol. III. p. 456.

The reader must not too nicely criticise the reduplications of persons observable in PLATE 96. where we see NANESHWER, both sitting on the wall and standing on the ground, assisting to raise up his prostrate adorer, CHANGADEVA; who, as well as kneeling at the feet of NANESHWER, is also, at the same moment, bestriding his ferocious vehicle. All the males of this group have, as noticed in the account of PLATE 2. the mark, *No.* 9. on their foreheads: the lines red, the circlet black.

Neither of the four *Avataras*, discussed in this division of my work, have, I believe, been before introduced to *European* readers; and although nothing very important be derivable from this transient notice, still, as forming links of that lengthened chain, which binds in its superstitious and idolatrous folds so great a number of *Hindus*, it may not be deemed redundant.

Into this division of my work I had intended to introduce a few lines on the question of converting the *Hindus* to *Christianity*; but so much has been recently said on this warmly-agitated topic, that men's minds can yet be scarcely brought coolly to its consideration. I was desirous to add to the arguments on this head my humble testimony against the ill-timed and ill-directed efforts that have been recently applied, in view to the promotion of so grand a scheme.—But I will leave the good cause in the able hands of *Major* SCOTT WARING; my liberal friend the "Vindicator of the *Hindus*," and, above all, to the vigilance and exquisite keenness of the *Edinburgh Reviewers*, whose talents, however reprehensibly applied on some questions, are on this directed to a benefit really national.

Those only who chuse wilfully to misunderstand, will affect to suppose, that I, that any *Christian*, that any good man of any religion, can desire that the *Hindus* should not be weaned from many enormities unhappily practised among them in the insulted name of, but, in fact, forming no legitimate part even of their, religion—the *Sati*, deliberate and meritorious suicide, infanticide, and others. So far as relate to our extensive territories, such practices are, or speedily will be, discontinued; and by the diffusion of our influence will happily, with Divine permission, be entirely so. We may hope and expect that many of their fooleries will follow their enormities, and that the great work of eventual conversion to the simplicity and holiness of *Christianity* may supersede the mummery and idolatry of *Hinduism*. But this must be the work of time, effected by the conviction resulting from example and instruction; not by *coercion*—a word said to have been used, and its effects enforced, by a dignitary of the *English* church. He, doubtless, means well; but if it were my misfortune to be in *India* at the time of acting on such a system, or to have a son or near connection there, I should take the earliest creditable opportunity of urging a withdrawal from the terrible effects that may reasonably be expected to ensue. Without such an interference, so devoutly to be deprecated, I should not see with indifference any material increase of the numbers of our zealous missionaries in *India*, especially if unwatched by our governments: it would induce me to dispose of my *India stock*, and to recal my property thence—not, perhaps, from the immediate fear of loss from expulsion or extermination, but of disquietudes and tumults, that would tend to lessen its value and its comfortable possession.

The work of the dignified divine that I have alluded to, I have not read; but if he actually uses the word *coercion* in its ordinary acceptation, and means thereby to force the *Hindus* at once to dismiss their *Brahmans*, and to renounce their religion, it would be difficult to find terms wherewith adequately to stigmatize so extravagant a proposition—our vocabulary of crazy epithets would be ransacked in vain; and, without meaning to give offence, I should really deem any one, who could seriously propose such a thing, more becomingly, as more safely, arrayed in a strait-waistcoat than in a surplice—better qualified for *Bedlam* than the pulpit.

Let us hope that the *Edinburgh Reviewers* will continue to expose, with their accustomed severity, the mummery of methodism; to "throttle the weazel" whenever they can catch it; and to view the grand question of converting the *Hindus* as progressive and remote; not likely to be brought about by schismatic enthusiasts, whose misapplied zeal must have the effect of hindering, and indefinitely protracting, the fruition of the great and good work that they, no doubt, are earnest to promote.

NOTICE

OF SOME

UNEXPLAINED PLATES, AND OF ANCIENT HINDU COINS AND MEDALS.

Several of our plates still remain undescribed, and others have been but slightly noticed; we will therefore now proceed to offer such farther particulars on that score as seems expedient.

The lower portion of plate 46. has been alluded to as representing probably a marriage of an exalted pair, as Brahma himself is reading the ceremony: it may be so; or it may represent Vishnu in his own person, or in one of his *Avataras*, with his wives, as seen in other plates, listening to a portion of the *Veda* relating to Fire, his foot being held over a mass that seems issuing from a pit: it may be in honour of Fire, or Agni, or intended to show the impotency even of that ardent element acting on a disciple of the *Veda* listening to its holy texts. The plate is taken from a tinted picture, in which the persons are all of the same copper colour.

Plate 75. has two subjects scarcely noticed. *Fig.* 1. is Vishnu, gorgeously attired and decorated, with his usual attributes, standing in the expanded foliage of a lotos, which forms an *Argha* for him; its stem, around which Sesha duplicated twines himself, his many heads canopying the deity, terminates with the picture. Vishnu is blue, Sesha white: lotoses scattered about indicate the scene to be in the water.

Fig. 2. of plate 75. is taken, like the preceding subject, from a pretty picture of *Colonel* Stuart's: it represents the mystical union of the three sacred rivers, the Ganga, Yamuna, and Saraswati, severally the consorts, or energies, of the three great Powers. This mythological junction is poetically called *Triveni*, or the *three plaited locks*; and is a female Triad, similar to what has before been noticed of the *Trimurti* of male powers. In the picture the fish is swimming, its head only being above the water: the fish, the clothing of the goddesses, and the glory encircling their heads, are of gold. The full-faced figure is white, and is therefore Parvati in her form of Ganga: she bears the forehead mark, *No.* 37. of plate 2. or rather its interior only, reversed: on Ganga's right, with a roll of paper, perhaps a *Veda*, in her hand, is Saraswati, indicated by her red face, the colour of her consort. Lakshmi, in her form of Yamuna, the genius of that river, is blue, the colour of her lord, or of water: she holds a golden vessel (of *amrita?*)

Junctions of any sort, especially of waters, are held sacred by *Hindus*; and above all, the union of the sacred rivers, Ganga and Yamuna, near *Illahabad*: the latter river had previously received the Saraswati below *Dehli*, so that, in fact, all three do unite at this famed *sangam*. But this is too tame for a *Hindu* poet, who therefore feigns a subterrene flow of the Saraswati, and a mystical union at the sacred point; where bathing is of course peculiarly efficacious, and where zealots are persuaded that suicide is of a most meritorious description. I once saw, at *Poona*, a well modelled group in clay, where Rad'ha's locks, *tripartite*, were plaited into this mystical *Triveni* by the amorous Krishna, who sat rapturously admiring the work of, and in, his hands.

Of PLATES 99. 100. and 101. slight mention has been made in page 179. The first contains eleven, picked out of several scores of similar, subjects; all of them bearing the appearance of great age, and many of having been buried. A staff, or two sticks, a cup, a bag, sword, target, are what they mostly hold: they are two or four-handed; some are five-headed; some are of single figures, some two men, others man and woman; the latter, in one instance, with a child: the figures are standing, sitting, or riding on horses, hogs, and non-descript animals: their sizes are various; some less than an inch in height; others four or five inches; some mere human figures, without attributes; others any thing but human, with surrounding glories, sun, moon, *linga*, a horse, a dog, balls, feet, cup, ropes, &c. &c. and hats, pretty much like the round hat of *Europeans*, are on or over the heads of many; some have the trident, others VISHNU's attributes. *No.* 1. of PLATE 99. is more defined and finished than the cast, where the figure is scarcely human: a cup and staff are in its hands, and below are apparently a *linga*, and either a rope or an animal's head and horns. *No.* 2. has the genuine rust of antiquity: the *zennaar* is conspicuous, and, with the sun, moon, and five balls, so often seen with more important objects of *Brahmanical* adoration, seem to refer this image to a sacred origin and rank; although some *Brahmans* that I consulted on the subject denied the fact, and said such images were not of an orthodox or regular description, but cast by ignorant individuals for particular and confined worship, not recognized by *Brahmans*, or assisted at by them. *No.* 3. is much more ancient and shapeless than the plate represents: it seems to be of a woman naked, or nearly so: of this description I have several, more modern, and of a larger size; very full breasted, with the hair rather curiously, and not inelegantly, twisted on the head: one, eight inches high, has silver eyes, with many ornaments, but no clothing; and is standing in an affected, but not indelicate, posture, with a fruit or flower-bud between the middle finger and thumb of the right hand. I was told this was of RUKMAS, or RUKMENY, spouse of KRISHNA; and it may be used in the singular and reprehensible ceremonies of the *Gokalast'has*, noticed in page 123. Another, in nearly the same attitude, has not even ornaments. *No.* 4. of PLATE 99. is of that description of image called *Yir* and *Vir* by the *Mahratas*, among whom they are chiefly in use, uncountenanced, it is said, by *Brahmanical* authority. *No.* 11. is of the same sort, extremely old and rude; as is *No.* 4. but has been modernized by the file: it is of brass, *No.* 11. of tin, or some composition of which that metal is the basis: its right arm is broken off.

Nos. 5. to 8. are apparently of the same manufacture and age, so basely executed as to be scarcely recognized as human beings: the plate represents them, in proportions and features, too fair; especially *No.* 8. which is the only one of this sort that I find with a child: the *zennaar* is on all the males, but put, unusually, over different shoulders: 5. has two *lingas*, and 6. five balls. *No.* 9. with the staff and cup, sun and moon, is also very old. Some *Brahmans* have called similar figures, of BHAIRAVA; others have turned up their noses, and examined them with apparent contempt, but evidently ignorant of their origin. Whether *No.* 10. be of man, woman, or beast, or what it may hold in its hand, it is difficult to determine: it seems to be very old, and rude in a degree not to be described by pen or pencil; as may be said also of the four strange things engraved in PLATE 100. from casts in brass of the size represented. Three of them hold the *trisula*, referring them to a sect of *Saiva*; and the horse may refer to KANDEH RAO. *Fig.* 1. has a cup in one hand, and the bridle in the other: a shield is on his thigh, and his *trisula* and *zennaar* are conspicuous: it has been buried. *fig.* 2. has a sword, shield, and *trisula*, but has, I think, only two arms: his hat is very like ours. What *fig.* 3. is, or has, it is not easy to say. The double drum and trident of SIVA may be traced in the hands of *fig.* 4.—the stirrups appear to be formed of a rope, passed over the saddle before and behind the rider. I have described these as male figures, but they may as well be called women, or, it may almost be said, any thing else.

In describing PLATE 101. I shall be forced to repeat the terms rude, barbarous, old, &c. equally applicable here as to the two preceding plates, although we have now to notice subjects of a different character;

but of what character, or age, I am equally unable to determine: the antiquity of some of them must be very great; and the information that I have been able to obtain respecting them is vague and unsatisfactory. Sometimes I have found a *Brahman* disposed to deny altogether the *Indian* origin of a subject, *No.* 1. of PLATE 101. for instance, but have staggered him on showing him one nearly similar, such as *fig.* 2. or 3. where five heads seem to connect them with their less monstrous brothers; or *No.* 4. or 7. where a *linga* and five balls offer still closer marks of relationship with acknowledged families.

It is rare to find a collection of curiosities, of any sort, made by *Brahmans*, or any *Hindu*: except in the instance of NANA FIRNAVEESE, I cannot call to mind a collection of any extent. He had a great many pictures, which cost him, I was told, a very large sum: they are carefully preserved in books and port-folios, wrapped in cloths. During the tumults of *Poona*, they were deposited, with other valuables, in the strong hill fort of *Logher*, half way on the *Bombay* road; and are now in the possession of DUNDU PANDIT, its late commandant, who resides under the *English* protection at *Tanna*, the capital of *Salsette*. I have examined some of these books, which contained very fine pictures, on mythology, and on various subjects; and from a general account of the collection, I concluded it to be very extensive and valuable—but still, perhaps, to be purchased at no very great price, although, doubtless, beyond my means. DOWLAT RAO SINDEA had also some pictures, which fell into the hands of the *English* in our contest with him, and were purchased at the prize sales by his victorious opponent, *Sir* ARTHUR WELLESLEY. This paucity of *Hindu virtuosi* I notice in view to the remark, that my *Pandit* and others were surprised, and, perhaps, reasonably enough, at my throwing away my money on such useless articles as old defaced images, coins, &c. and, when asked to explain their histories, would mingle, with some impatience and contempt, I thought, a little shame at their intelligence not keeping pace with the antiquity of the subject, or the extravagance of the artist. Most of my images were obtained at *Bombay* through the means of correspondents on the continent: a native or two, with the expectation of profit, sent people into the interior to purchase such things, to which the unhappy state of the *Mahrata* country, during the last years of my residence in *India*, gave too great facilities. I generally purchased all that were brought to me; as, if not wanted, or too dear, for my own collection, I bought them for a friend, who had greater means, and a greater disregard of money, than myself. I obtained many also through the agency of travelling friends, who, aware of my idle propensity, procured for me what they deemed curious: but, in happier and more peaceable times, I do not imagine that images are often obtainable. But to return to PLATE 101.

Nos. 1. 2. 3. and 6. I should judge to be of the same hero: their arms are nearly similar; *No.* 2. has, indeed, his sword broken, and *No.* 6. his left arm: and their dress and equipage correspond with each other, but not with any thing else that I know of; for whether the beasts they ride be meant for horses, dogs, hogs, rhinoceroses, or what animal, it is impossible to determine. *Nos.* 7. and 9. appear to be dismounted members of the same family: they are armed the same, with crooked swords. *No.* 7. which in the cast has greater appearance of breasts than in the plate, has the sword in the left hand: over the heads is a hat, bent down at the sides exactly like ours, but not well represented in the plate: five balls are at its foot, and other things that may be fancied a cup, a rope, sun, and crescent; most of which are found on *No.* 9. where a *linga* is also discoverable.

Nos. 5. and 8. do not, I imagine, belong to the same class of idols as the others of the three plates now more immediately under our notice, but, the latter especially, to the legend of DURGA slaying the monster, as represented in PLATES 34. and 35. and described sufficiently in page 152. *Nos.* 5. and 9. are older and less defined than the engraving represents: they are four-handed, holding a trident, sword, and cup, and bestride tigers: the latter is spearing the monster, on which her foot is placed, as formerly described.

PLATE 102. is taken from a curious and handsome cast, not modern, but in good preservation: for the possession of which, I am obliged to the oft-experienced kindness of my valued friend *Mrs.* DOUGLAS

RICHARDSON, of *Bombay*. It consists of a square pedestal: on each side of which is seated, back to back, 1. GANESA—2. VISHNU—3. MAHADEVA—4. PARVATI, as represented in the plate: the deities are full-dressed, and ornamented beyond what the engravings exhibit; and the cast is a very fine one. In our first view, GANESA fronts us—a pot-bellied squab figure, as he is often seen; holding an *ankus*, or hook, a rope, a ball, and, what I judge to be, a piece of his tooth, (see p. 172.) for in the cast one is considerably longer than the other: on his forehead he has the mark 35. or 38. of PLATE 2.

Turning to the right, we bring VISHNU to front us, *fig*. 2. likewise profusely decorated, and armed with his usual attributes: the *gadda*, or mace, on which his lower left hand rests, looks here like a sword; and the *pedma*, in the other inferior hand, is in the form of a blossom only. GANESA is now seen, with his short tooth, in profile to the right, and PARVATI on the left, (the spectator's left,) of VISHNU. Another turn of the subject brings her in front, *fig*. 4. but, without the positive assurances of my *Pandit*, I should not have guessed PARVATI to have been the person intended by this figure: it wants the fine bosom that this goddess, especially in this description of cast, (see PLATES 5. and 28.) usually exhibits: nor is it common to see her decorated with the *zennaar:* she is but two-handed, and I cannot determine what she holds: her right hand, in the cast, has, perhaps, the top of that implement seen in the inferior right hand of PLATE 28. and looks more like a *caduceus* than any thing else. Turning our cast again to the right, MAHADEVA, *fig*. 3. confronts us, in the same position and character, and with very nearly the same attributes, as in PLATE 5. which was probably taken from casts similar to the subject of PLATE 102. the attitudes of the lower portion of PLATE 5. and the style of ornament of 102. being so much alike: two hands hold the same things, the antelope and *parasha*, and the other two are empty: his earrings do not pair in either subject, and he bears the same description of forehead mark in both. On his right, in PLATE 102. we again see GANESA in profile, and his longer tooth: on the left of MAHADEVA we better see the article in the hand of PARVATI; but, in the cast, it is still more like the *caduceus* of MERCURY. Before we quit PLATE 102. I may remark, that my engraver, after my draughtsman, whose general accuracy and excellence are above my praise, has given rather more form and anatomical expression to the pendent legs, the lady's especially, than the cast in strictness warrants.

PLATE 103. is taken from another four-sided cast, of which I have also given four views: it is from the collection of *Lord* VALENTIA; is old, but in tolerable preservation, and comprehends such a variety of figures and subjects, row over row, that I scarcely know where to begin with my description. Four rude feet support a sort of platform, square, having at each corner a person—whether male or female, not positively determinable—kneeling or sitting in a posture of adoration: between them are several persons and things, that will be presently more particularly noticed: a kind of flag waves over and touches the heads of the persons at the lower corners, and the flag-staffs join the angles of a second, smaller, platform, rising on the first: this has at its four corners the *chank*, or shell; and between the shells, in the middle of each side, four figures, very similar to those at the corners of the lower platform. A third, still smaller, platform rises on the second: at its corners are a disk, crescent, a triangle enclosing a circle, and seven or eight balls apparently in a dish. From this upper platform rises a round cup-shaped—mount, shall I call it? widening to its summit; around which a *naga* convolves, overshadowing by its upreared head two feet placed in a lotos, spread on the back of a tortoise, whose fins extend to, and are supported by, the folds of the snake at the brow of the mount, nearly covered by the tortoise's breadth.

What this may all mean, it is difficult to say: had the tortoise been *under* the mount, we might have referred it to the *Kurma*, in that *Avatara*, supporting *Mandara*; the mighty serpent *Vasoky* serving as a rope, by which the mountain, so supported, was whirled about, when the gods and demons churned the ocean for the *amrita*, as is represented in PLATE 49.—this legend is most likely adverted to in the cast; and perhaps several others are conjoined with it.—We will notice PLATE 103. more particularly.

In the first view of it, we see the tortoise in front, &c. as already sufficiently noticed, until we come to the bottom, where, on the centre of this face, sits GANESA, and on his right is a standing figure with palms joined in adoration; between them, is something as much like a sword as any thing else: on GANESA's left is a shrub or tree, and beside it a quadruped. Turning the cast to the left, we have the tortoise in profile, *fig*. 2. and see, in the place of GANESA, the back of GARUDA, on one knee, with palms joined, in the same attitude as *fig*. 4. of PLATE 92.—on his right is a quadruped (a cow, or a sheep?) and a bird, and between them and GARUDA, what I judge from the cast to be, a fish; or it may be a shell, like those of the angles of the next platform: on GARUDA's left is a standing person, and between him and GARUDA is a human head; in the plate, as well as in the cast, it looks as much like a vase, but, on examining the cast, the features are discernible; it has, besides, just the outline of the *occiput* of its neighbours. Another turn to the left shows us the back part of *Naga*, or SESHA, or VASOKY, winding round the mount; and on the lower platform is HANUMAN, with his tail turned up to his head, in a similar position to GARUDA: he is supported by a quadruped on his right and left, like the others, of equivocal kinds: at their feet are a bow and arrow, and a sword, referring, I imagine, to legends of the RAMA's; the former being the emblem of the great RAMA, and a *Sword*, PARASU, being the name of another. On the fourth side, *fig*. 4. BRAHMA, four-faced, (the features not so plain in the cast as in the plate, for all the exterior points are worn, indicating its great age,) occupies, in the same attitude of adoration, the place of HANUMAN, &c. on the lower platform, having on each side of him a bird of different kinds, and, to his right, a vase (of *amrita*, or his usual implement of sacrifice?)—behind him, a sort of sceptre, (or may it be a roll of the *Veda?*) and a little boat-shaped *argha*.

Many of the persons and articles noticed in this account are referrable to the *Kurmavatara*, but not all; and I should judge this subject to epitomize several of the exploits of VISHNU, in his different *Avataras*, in the manner of PLATE 93. described in page 324.—and a close examination of the subject of PLATE 103. would lead to lengthened surmises of astronomical, as well as mythological, origin and tendency, that we have no room or time left for: two or three points, however, we will briefly notice.

The *Hindus* have reverence for feet, or the impressions of feet. On the top of the lofty *Ceylon* hill, that we, after the *Portuguese*, call ADAM's peak, is said to be the impression of a foot, or feet, called by the *Hindus*, *Sripada*, or *Sripad*, meaning the divine footstep; VISHNU having, they say, alighted on that spot—in his *Avatara* of RAMA, perhaps. There have been, I think, among *Christians*, some discussions implying *Ceylon* to have been the *Paradise*, or *Eden*, of our first parents, and the footstep in question to have been left by ADAM. *Hindus* make pilgrimages to the *Sripad*, both on *Ceylon* and in other places, where similar proofs of a *descent* have been discovered.

In the neighbourhood of temples it is not unusual to find a flat stone embossed, or engraved, with two feet: several are about the temples at the *Sangam*, near *Poona*; and I was told by a *Brahman* that they are in remembeance and honour of widows who have become *Sati* there, being their last earthly or human impression, carved on the stone which served to step by up to the pile of their husbands. At this affecting sacrifice I have observed a flat stone placed for this purpose, and that the family of the victim, and the attendant *Brahmans*, received her last blessings and adieus while she stood on it: having quitted this stone, she is no longer human; she commences a participation of the beatitude, to the fruition of which she is hastening. It chills me to reflect, that I have for several minutes been close to a beautiful young creature in this awful situation—even to the moment of the flames reaching her, when her soul could scarcely be thought more in this than in another world. What my feelings may have been, when witnessing this tremendous scene, I cannot say or recollect; but I know that I could not then, however much it would have relieved me, shed a tear, although, when reflecting on it, it cannot always be withheld.

But to return for a moment to PLATE 103.—We there find the mystical triangle, seen in *No*. 45. or 46. and 89. of PLATE 2. and in PLATE 59. as noticed in page 198.—the disk, crescent, balls, and most likely every part of this elaborate subject, have their meaning and allusions in mythological and astronomical legends, which we shall not here attempt to trace.

Among the valuable property of the late Tippoo Sultan that fell into the hands of the captors at *Srirangapatan*, was a cabinet of coins and medals, *Mahomedan* and *Hindu*; many of them very old and curious. They were sold at the public prize sales; and a part was purchased by my old and highly esteemed friend *Major* Price, one of the prize agents, who kindly enriched my little collection by such duplicates as his lot contained. Plate 104. shows some specimens: they are all of gold, of the size represented; and great care has been taken to give as exact copies as possible, both of the figures and the inscriptions: the latter, from the antiquity of the characters, are not easily read, and I shall not attempt to explain them. Some *Brahmans* have attempted it, but made out nothing interesting or profitable—"*I worship* Sri," or "*Praise to* Sri," and similar sentences, were the chief result of their discoveries.

The upper row, *figures* 1. 2. 3. 4. contains four *huns*, or what we call *Pagodas*, (see p. 346.) impressed with a bird two-headed, bearing an elephant in his beaks and claws: this bird I should suppose, but may be mistaken, to be Garuda. I have seen them called *Kanduba-rundup*: Kanduba, a provincial name of Vishnu, may also be a name of Garuda, or of some other fabulous bird, of which there are many in *Indian* romances; and *rundu*, in southern dialects, *Kanareese*, and *Malabar* among them, means *two*; *rundup*, *double*: hence, the bird being double-headed, or split, as in *fig*. 3. may originate the term. The coins are of pure gold, and in good preservation. *Figures* 5. and 6. having an elephant on one side, and a sort of interminable scroll or flourish on the other, are called, by *Kanareese Brahmans*, *Gajpati*—*Gaja* being an elephant; and they are said to be coins of the ancient *Rajas* of *Annagundy*, a name also referring to something *elephantine*. Years of cycles are not uncommonly named after animals, &c.—the lion on *No*. 7. and the boar on 13. may, like 5. and 6. refer to their corresponding years of that cycle.

No. 8. has Hanuman in an active and menacing attitude, as is usual with him.—See plates 91. 92. 93. The coin is very old and much rubbed, especially on the figure side, which is in bold relief. *No*. or *fig*. 10. is another description of coin, but it may be questioned if it ever passed in currency; for such things were, and are, as I have been told, used in sacred ceremonies: this kind of coin is deeply concave, and on the reverse correspondingly convex. The concavity of *No*. 10. exhibits the *durbar* of Rama and Sita, who, seated on a throne, are attended, as I conjecture from the accounts of pictures given me by *Brahmans* of that *durbar*, by these persons—on their right, by Rama's three brothers; on their left, by his *Guru*, Viswamitra, (I have a picture, by the way, on which Vasishtha's name is written as Rama's spiritual instructor,) *Raja* Janaka, Sita's mortal or adoptive father, Hanuman, and Garuda.—This, however, is mere fancy; for the inscription at their feet has not been explained, and the features and distinctions of the figures are nearly obliterated, although it is difficult to conceive by what means, protected as they are by their sunk situation. On the reverse are the remains of Hanuman's outline, and some letters, but the greater part effaced: this simian hero is, however, easily traced; and as other more perfect specimens of this kind of coinage are preserved, he would, if doubtful, be confirmed by their similarity. If I mistake not, all the hollowed coins contain a similar group, and the convexity, Hanuman: one is in the museum at the *India* house; and Hanuman is, if not on that specimen, on some other that I have seen, enclosed in the center of intersecting triangles, like *No*. 42. of plate 2. Not more than half a dozen of these hollowed coins were, I think, found in *Srirangapatan*, and I never heard of any others.

Nos. 9. and 11. of plate 104. are curious articles, called *coins of* Arjun: about twenty of these were found in a bag so marked, سکه ارجن and with the number of coins it contained, in arithmetical letters, of a sort of ابجد *abjd*—not like that in common use among *Persians*, *Arabians*, and other *Mahomedans*, but apparently invented or adopted by Tippoo; who had also a cycle of his own, which may lead astray those who, like me, attempt to reconcile the dates on his coins to common chronology, unaware, as I formerly was, of the existence of such a cycle.

In the bag with these ARJUN *huns* was a paper, which I had an opportunity of copying, containing the following account of the coins.—

ياحافظ

هون هاي مچه مُدراي يعني ضرب دوماهي يكطرف وطرف ديكر حروف بالبند بابت زمانه ارجن برادر پنج پاندو مطابق سنه ١٢١١ هجري محمّد عم هفت هزار سال ميشود

In *English*.—

"Oh PROTECTOR!"

"*Matcheh Mudraï huns*—that is to say, impressed with two fish on one side, and on the other side certain *balbandy* characters, relating to the age of ARJUN, brother of the five *Pandus*; corresponding (or compared) with the 1211th year of the *Hejra* of MAHAMMED, (on whom be the blessing of God!) giving seven thousand years."

What the "*balbandy* characters" may be, I cannot say—perhaps a quaint term, like our "pot-hooks and hangers:" if it were translated, it might mean *hair-tied*.

The blessing, within brackets, on the prophet, is usual with the faithful, at every recurrence of his name, in writing and conversation; in writing it is not, indeed, generally, put at length, but abbreviated to the initials of the two or three words that are supposed to be understood: above, the blessing is comprised in two letters عم which, I imagine, stand for, being the initial and final of, علہ اسلام "on whom be peace." As well as after the name of MAHAMMED, the pious ejaculate a blessing on the name also of his successors, or of any eminently pious person of their own sect. I have heard a *Mussulman* bless the name of CHRIST on having occasion to utter it; but this is, I believe, an uncommon liberality, and would not have occurred out of *Christian* company. Obnoxious individuals, both of their own religion, but of another sect, and of other religions, *Jews* especially, are piously cursed, separately or collectively, as their names or tribes are pronounced by the orator.—But this is irrelevant.

These *Matcheh Mudraï huns* are supposed to be very old; the metal is pure, and they are in good preservation: in this instance, as, perhaps, in some others, the coins are engraved the wrong way.

Nos. 12. and 14. have a standing figure of VISHNU, with his *chank* and *chakra*, and two empty hands, in the position so common to him and his *Avataras*, and others, and as seen in PLATES 5. 6. 9. &c. These coins, as well as the first and last four, and *Nos.* 15. and 17. are smaller than *huns* usually are: *No.* 16. is a modern *hun*, of the common size: *Nos.* 5. to 11. and *No.* 13. are, as represented in the plate, larger.

No. 13. I should judge to be, like 5. 6. and perhaps 7. a coin of the *Annagundy Raj*, or government: its reverse has the same sort of scroll as the two former; and, as said before, the different animals they bear may denote the year so designated in the cycle in use, which years are sometimes so distinguished in writings—the year of the *boar*, of the *lion*, of the *elephant*, &c.

Nos. 15. and 17. have VISHNU and LAKSHMI, she seated in his lap, as seen in PLATE 11. then usually called LAKSHMI-NARAYEN. *No.* 16. is a clumsy, modern, ill-executed, *Carnatic hun*; it is, I think, of that description called *Swammy*, as bearing the effigy of a deity, to distinguish it from the *star pagoda*: it is of base gold; and in this, and in the design and execution, strikingly contrasted with its chaste antique neighbours. The deities on *No.* 16. are, as indicated by the *trisula*, SIVA and PARVATI; in the same situation as LAKSHMI-NARAYEN, and as they are seen in PLATES 16. and 26.—on the coins, however, the ladies are, in point of size, more on an equality with their divine partners than in the casts and plates. What the *Arabic* ح can mean on a *Hindu* coin, *No.* 16. I cannot say.

The four remaining coins, *Nos.* 18. to 21. of PLATE 104. all relate, I think, to VISHNU, his two commonest attributes being, especially on 19. and 20. discernible. The originals of 18. and 19. are not at this moment within my reach, and are not, I judge, so perfect in their features as some of the others.

But little has hitherto been brought to light on the subject of ancient *Hindu* coinage, and this is no place for such discussion. BARTOLOMEO says, *Voyage*, p. 85. that "the oldest *Indian* coins have no inscription, but only the representation of a cow, an elephant, the *lingam*, or some deity. ANQUETIL *du* PERRON, however, asserts, that he saw some with writing on them, which, as he pretends, were coined before the period of VIKRAMADITYA; but I never had an opportunity of seeing any of this kind." Until the conquest of *Mysore*, such coins have not, I believe, been seen by *Europeans*: except such as were then developed, I never had either an opportunity of seeing any. There can be little doubt of most of the coins represented in PLATE 104. (I except, of course, *No.* 16. put in merely as comparative,) having been struck as early as the age of VIKRAMADITYA.

Our last PLATE (105.) still remains unnoticed. It is taken from a vase, fully as elegant as the plate indicates, of gilt copper, that had been long unclaimed and kicked about at the *India* house, but is now appropriately ornamenting its museum: its contents may be a quart; and it is certainly a very beautiful specimen of *Hindu* workmanship, and highly creditable to their skill. SESHA, or NAGA, or VASOKY, five-headed, with VISHNU holding a *chank* in his front, and GARUDA behind, forms a handsome handle: on the other side, in the place of a spout, is a lamp, artfully supported by a monster; and on its sides are two kneeling threatening figures, armed with sword and shield—coadjutors, perhaps, of DURGA, who, eighteen-handed, is in the act of spearing the monstrous personification of Vice, so often described in former pages: the wreath, or glory, round her, as well as a wreath round the body of the vase, are very elegant.

Although unable, from want of time and room, to give at length the article alluded to in a former page, on the *Vedas* and *Puranas*, and other points of *Hindu* literature; yet, in the hope that a short notice of their contents will be acceptable, I offer the following outline—chiefly, as acknowledged, from the writings of *Sir* WILLIAM JONES and *Mr.* COLEBROKE: beginning with a portion of the eighteenth article of Vol. I. of the *As. Res.*—" On the Literature of the *Hindus*, from the *Sanskrit*;" communicated by GOVERDHEN KAL.

OF THE

VEDAS, PURANAS, &c.

"There are eighteen *Vidyas*, or parts, of *true knowledge*, and some branches of knowledge, *falsely so called*.

"The first *four* are the immortal *Vedas*, evidently revealed by God; which are entitled, in one compound word, *Rigyajushsamat'harva*, or, in separate words, *Rich*, *Yajush*, *Saman*, and *At'harvan*. The *Rigveda* consists of five sections; the *Yajurveda*, of eighty-six; the *Samaveda*, of a thousand; and the *At'harvaveda*, of nine; with eleven hundred *sac'has*, or branches, in various divisions and subdivisions. The *Vedas*, in truth, are infinite; but were reduced, by Vyasa, to this number and order: the principal part of them is that which explains the duties of man in a methodical arrangement; and in the fourth is a system of divine ordinances.

"From these are deduced the four *Upa-vedas*;* namely, *Ayush*, *Gandharva*, *Dhanush*, and *St'hapatya*. The first of which, or *Ayurveda*, was delivered to mankind by Brahma, Indra, Dhanwantari, and *five* other deities; and comprises the theory of disorders and medicines, with the practical methods of curing diseases. The second, on music, was invented and explained by Bharata: it is chiefly useful in raising the mind by devotion to the felicity of the Divine Nature. The third *Upaveda* was composed by Viswamitra, on the fabrication and use of arms, and implements handled in war by the tribe of *Cshatriyas*. Viswacarman revealed the fourth, in various treatises on *sixty-four* mechanical arts, for the improvement of such as exercise them.

"Six *Angas*, or *bodies of learning*, are also derived from the same source."—(I omit their names and contents: their subjects chiefly are—1. of the pronunciation of vocal sounds; 2. detail of religious acts and ceremonies; 3. grammar; 4. prosody; 5. astronomy; 6. on the signification of difficult words and phrases in the *Vedas*.)

"Lastly, there are four *Upangas*,* called *Purana*, *Nyaya*, *Mimansa*, and *Dherma-sastra*. Eighteen *Puranas* (that of Brahma, and the rest,) were composed by Vyasa, for the instruction and entertainment of mankind in general." *Nyaya* is a collection of treatises, in two parts, on metaphysics, logic, philosophy, &c. *Mimansa* is somewhat similar, divided into two parts; the latter, called "*Uttara*, abounding in questions on the Divine Nature, and other sublime speculations, was composed by Vyasa, in four chapters and sixteen sections. It may be considered as the brain and spring of all the *Angas*; it exposes the heretical opinions of sophists; and, in a manner suited to the comprehension of adepts, it treats on the true nature of Ganesa, Bhascara, or the Sun, Nilakanta, Lakshmi, and other *forms* of One Divine Being."

"The body of *Law*, called *Smriti*, consists of eighteen books," &c. &c. "delivered for the instruction of the human species, by Menu, and other sacred personages."

* *Upa-veda*, *Upanga*, *Uppuran*, infer a work deduced, respectively, from its principal: *up*, like our *sub*, implies inferiority.—See Wilford, *As. Res.* Vol. III. p. 302.

"As to *Ethics*, the *Vedas* contain all that relates to the duties of kings; the *Pu anas*, what belong to the relation of husband and wife; and the duties of friendship and society, (which complete the triple division,) are taught succinctly in both. This double division of *Angas* and *Upangas* may be considered as denoting the double benefit arising from them in *theory* and *practice*."

"The *Bharata* and *Ramayana*, which are both epic poems, comprise the most valuable part of ancient history."

"*Sanc'hya* is two-fold—that with Iswara, and that without Iswara; called *Patanjala*, and *Kapila*: the latter, in six chapters, on the production of all things by the union of Pracriti, or *Nature*, and Purusha, or the *first male*," &c. &c. "These books are not really divine, but contain infinite contradictions."

"The *Mimansa*, therefore, is in *two* parts, the *Nyaya* in *two*, and the *Sanc'hya* in *two*; and these *six* schools comprehend all the doctrines of the theists."

"Lastly, appears a work written by Budha: and there are also *six* atheistical systems of philosophy, entitled *Yogachara*, *Saudhanta*, *Vaibhashica*, *Madhyamica*, *Digambara*, and *Charvac*; all full of indeterminate phrases, errors in sense, confusion between distinct qualities, incomprehensible notions, opinions not duly weighed, tenets destructive of natural equality—containing a jumble of atheism and ethics; distributed, like our orthodox books, into a number of sections, which omit what ought to be expressed, and express what ought to be omitted; abounding in false propositions, idle propositions, and impertinent propositions."

"Such," concludes the author, "is the analysis of universal knowledge, *practical* and *speculative*."—Page 344.

A very ingenious and learned commentary follows, by *Sir* William Jones, from which the following passages are selected.—

"The *Vedas* consist of three *Candas*, or *general heads*—namely, *Carma*, *Jnyana*, *Upasana*; or *Works*, *Faith*, and *Worship*. To the first of which, the author of the *Vidyadersa*, or *view of learning*, a rare *Sanskrit* book, wisely gives the preference; as Menu himself prefers *universal benevolence* to the *ceremonies* of religion."

"After all, the books on *divine knowledge*, called *Veda*, or what is *known*, and *Sruti*, or what has been *heard*, from revelation, are still supposed to be very numerous; and the *four* here mentioned are thought to have been selected as containing all the information necessary for man. It must not be omitted, that the commentaries on the *Hindu* scriptures, among which that of Vasishtha seems to be reputed the most excellent, are innumerable; but, while we have access to the fountains, we need not waste our time in tracing the rivulets."

"From the *Vedas* are immediately deduced the practical arts of chirurgery and medicine, music and dancing; archery, which comprises the whole art of war; and architecture, under which the system of mechanical arts is included."

"Next in order to these, are the six *Vedangas*: three of which belong to grammar; one relates to religious ceremonies; a fifth, to the whole compass of mathematics; and the sixth, to the explanation of obscure words or phrases in the *Vedas*."

"Subordinate to these *Angas* (though the reason of the arrangement is not obvious,) are the series of *sacred poems*, the body of law, and the *six* philosophical *sastras*."

"The first *Indian* poet was Valmiki, author of the *Ramayana*, a complete epic poem, on one continued, interesting, and heroic action; and the next in celebrity, if it be not superior to it in reputation for holiness, is the *Mahabarat* of Vyasa. To him are ascribed the sacred *Puranas*, which are called, for their excellence, the *Eighteen*, and which have the following titles:—1. Brahme, or the *Great One*; 2. *Pedma*, or the *Lotos*; 3. *Brahmanda*, or the *Mundane Egg*; 4. AGNI, or Fire—(these *four* relate to the creation); 5. VISHNU, or the *Pervader*; 6. GARUDA, or his *Eagle*; 7. the transformations of BRAHMA; 8. SIVA; 9. *Linga*; 10. NAREDA, son of BRAHMA; 11. SCANDA, son of SIVA; 12. *Marcandeya*, or the *immortal man*; 13. *Bhawishya*, or the *prediction of futurity*—(these *nine* belong to the *attributes* and *powers* of the Deity); 14. *Matsya*; 15. *Varaha*; 16. *Kurma*; 17. *Vamena*, or as many incarnations of the Great One in his character of *Preserver*—all containing ancient traditions, embellished by poetry, or disguised by fable.—The eighteenth is the *Bhagavata*, or life of KRISHNA, with which the same poet is by some imagined to have crowned the whole series; though others, with more reason, assign them different composers." *

"Of the philosophical schools it will be sufficient here to remark, that the first *Nyaya* seems analagous to the *Peripatetic*; the second, sometimes called *Vaisishica*, to the *Ionic*; the two *Mimansas*, of which the second is often distinguished by the name of *Vedanta*, to the *Platonic*; the first *Sanchya*, to the *Italic*, and the second, or *Patanjala*, to the *Stoic*, philosophy: so that GAUTAMA corresponds with ARISTOTLE, CANADA with THALES, JAIMINI with SOCRATES, VYASA with PLATO, CAPILA with PYTHAGORAS, and PATANJALI with ZENO; but an accurate comparison between the *Grecian* and *Indian* schools would require a considerable volume. The original works of those philosophers are very succinct; but, like all the other *Sastras*, they are explained, or obscured, by the *Upadersana*, or *commentaries*, without end."

"It results, from this analysis of *Hindu* literature, that the *Veda*, *Upaveda*, *Vedanga*, *Purana*, *Dherma*, and *Dersana*, are the *six* great *Sastras*, in which all knowledge, divine and human, is supposed to be comprehended. And here we must not forget, that the word *Sastra*, derived from a root signifying *to ordain*, means generally an ordinance, and particularly a *sacred ordinance*, delivered by inspiration: properly, therefore, the word is applied only to *sacred literature*, of which the text exhibits an accurate sketch."

"The *Sudras*, or *fourth* class of *Hindus*, are not permitted to study the *six* proper *Sastras* before mentioned; but an ample field remains for them in the study of profane literature, comprised in a multitude of popular books, which correspond with the several *Sastras*, and abound with beauties of every kind. All the tracts on medicine must, indeed, be studied by the *Vaidyas*, or those who are born physicians; and they have often more learning, with far less pride, than any of the *Brahmans*: they are usually poets, grammarians, rhetoricians, moralists; and may be esteemed, in general, the most virtuous and amiable of the *Hindus*."

"We need say no more of the hetorodox writings, than that those on the religion and philosophy of BUDHA seem to be connected with some of the most curious parts of *Asiatic* history; and contain, perhaps, all that could be found in the *Pali*, or sacred language, of the eastern *Indian* peninsula."

"Wherever we direct our attention to *Hindu* literature, the notion of infinity presents itself; and the longest life would not be sufficient for the perusal of near five hundred thousand stanzas in the *Puranas*, with a million more, perhaps, in the other works before mentioned. We may, however, select the best from each *Sastra*, and gather the fruits of science, without loading ourselves with the leaves and branches; while we have the pleasure to find, that the learned *Hindus*, encouraged by the mildness of our government and manners, are, at least, as eager to communicate their knowledge of all kinds as we can be to receive it. But if we wish to form a correct idea of *Indian* religion and literature, let us begin by forgetting all that has been written on the subject, by ancients or moderns, before the publication of the *Gita*."—Page 355.

In the commentary, whence the preceding extracts are taken, *Sir* W. JONES gives some of the reasons that induced him and *Mr.* WILKINS to believe, notwithstanding the fable of BRAHMA's *four* mouths, each of which uttered a *Veda*, that the fourth, or *Atharvaveda*, was written or collected after the other three

* And they are differently arranged and named by other authorities.

Vedas. He adduces arguments strongly confirming such inference; but however conclusively such arguments had enforced this belief on the minds of most who think at all on the subject, it has subsequently and recently been so cogently assailed by *Mr.* COLEBROKE, as will be noticed presently, that, without farther support, it must necessarily be much enfeebled, if not altogether driven from its position.

We now proceed to select some farther particulars on the subject of the *Vedas* and *Puranas,* chiefly from *Mr.* COLEBROKE's Essay, in the eighth volume of the *Asiatic Researches.*

"The *Hindus* believe that the original *Veda* was revealed by BRAHMA, and to have been preserved by tradition until it was arranged in its present form by a sage, who thence obtained the name of VYASA, or VEDAVYASA; that is, *compiler* of the *Vedas.* He distributed the *Indian* scripture into four parts, which are severally entitled *Rich, Yajush, Saman,* and *Atharvana,* and each of which bears the common denomination of *Veda.*"—Page 378.

"With the *Hindus* it is an article of their creed, that the *Vedas* were composed by no human author. It must be understood, therefore, that, in affirming the primeval existence of their scriptures, they deny these works to be the original composition of the editor (VYASA), but believe them to have been gradually revealed to inspired writers."—Page 392.

Mr. COLEBROKE notices the circumstance of *Mr.* WILKINS and *Sir* W. JONES having been led, by the consideration of some remarkable passages, to suspect the fourth *Veda* to be less ancient than the other three; and proceeds to enumerate several arguments, and to quote some texts on which that suspicion might be so reasonably grounded; and, afterwards, giving his own proofs in support of a contrary opinion: he thinking it "probable that some portion, at least, of the *Atharvana* is as ancient as the compilation of the three others; and its name, like their's, is anterior to VYASA's arrangement of them: but the same must be admitted of the *Itahasa* and *Puranas,* which constitute a fifth *Veda,* as the *At'harvana* does a fourth."—Page 379.

The sources of the *three Vedas* are thus given by a commentator, quoting from the scripture itself—

"The *Rigveda* originated from fire, the *Yajurveda* from air, and the *Samaveda* from the Sun.'

"MENU (chap. i. v. 23.) alludes to this fabulous origin of the *Vedas:* but a commentator explains it by remarking, that the *Rigveda* opens with a hymn to fire; and the *Yajurveda,* with one, in which air is mentioned. Another commentator has recourse to the renovations of the universe.—'In one *Calpa,* the *Vedas* proceeded from fire, air, and the sun; in another, from BRAHMA, at his allegorical immolation."—*Ib.*

"From this,* compared with other passages of less authority, and with the received notions of the *Hindus* themselves, it appears, that the *Rich, Yajush,* and *Saman,* are the three principal portions of the *Veda;* that the *At'harvana* is commonly admitted as a fourth; and that divers mythological poems, entitled *Itahasa* and *Purana,* are reckoned a supplement to the scripture, and, as such, constitute a fifth *Veda.*"—Page 381.

"The *Vedas* are a compilation of prayers, called *Mantras;* with a collection of precepts and maxims, entitled *Brahmana:* from which last portion, the *Upanishad* is extracted. The prayers are properly the *Vedas,* and apparently preceded the *Brahmana.*"—*Ib.*

"Each *Veda* consists of two parts, denominated the *Mantras* and the *Brahmanas,* or prayers and precepts. The complete collection of the hymns, prayers, and invocations, belonging to one *Veda,* is entitled its *Sanhita:* every other portion of *Indian* scripture is included under the general head of divinity—*(Brahmana)*—this comprises precepts which inculcate religious duties, maxims which explain those precepts, and arguments which relate to theology. But, in the present arrangement of the *Vedas,* the portion which

* I have not given the paragraph immediately preceding, and here adverted to.

contains passages called *Brahmanas,* includes many which are strictly prayers, or *Mantras.* The theology of the *Indian* scripture, comprehending the argumentative portion entitled *Vedanta,* is contained in tracts denominated *Upanishad;* some of which are portions of the *Brahmana,* properly so called: others are found only in a detached form; and one is a part of a *Sanhita* itself."—Page 388.

" Prayers, employed at solemn rites, called *Yajnyas,* have been placed in the three principal *Vedas:* those which are in prose, are named *Yajush;* such as are in metre, are denominated *Rich;* and some which are intended to be chanted, are called *Saman:* and those names, as distinguishing different portions of the *Vedas,* are anterior to their separation in VYASA's compilation. But the *At'harvana,* not being used at the religious ceremonies above mentioned, and containing prayers employed at lustrations, at rites conciliating the deities, and as imprecations on enemies, is essentially different from the other *Vedas.*" This is adduced by *Mr.* COLEBROKE as the true reason why the three first *Vedas* are often mentioned without any notice of the fourth; " which must be sought," he says, " not in their different origin and antiquity, but in the difference of their use and purport."—Page 381.

In a subsequent page, *Mr.* COLEBROKE resumes this topic.—He says, " I shall select, as a specimen, a passage, (from the White *Yajurveda,*) material, as it contains an enumeration of the *Vedas,* and of the various sorts of passages which they comprise; and tends to confirm some observations hazarded at the beginning of this essay.

" As smoke, and various substances, separately issue from fire lighted with moist wood, so, from this great being, were respired the *Rigveda,* the *Yajurveda,* the *Samaveda,* and the *At'harvan* and *Angiras;* the *Itahasa* and *Purana;* the sciences and *Upanishads;* the verses and aphorisms; the expositions and illustrations: all these were breathed forth by him."

" The commentators remark, that four sorts of prayers *(Mantra),* and eight kinds of precepts *(Brahmana),* are here stated. The fourth description of prayers comprehends such as were revealed to, or discovered by, AT'HARVAN and ANGIRAS, meaning the *At'harvana Veda.* The *Itahasa* designates such passages, in the second part of the *Vedas,* entitled *Brahmana,* as narrate a story. The *Purana* intends those which relate to the creation, and similar topics. ' Sciences' are meant of religious worship; ' verses' are memorial lines; ' aphorisms' are short sentences in a concise style; ' expositions' interpret such sentences; and ' illustrations' elucidate the meaning of the prayers."

" The *Itahasa* and *Puranas* here meant, are not the mythological poems * bearing the same title, but certain passages of the *Indian* scriptures, which are interspersed among others throughout that part of the *Vedas* called *Brahmana.*"—Page 445.

" The *At'harva Veda,* as is well known, contains many forms of imprecation for the destruction of enemies.—But it must not be inferred, that such is the chief subject of that *Veda;* since it also contains a great number of prayers for safety, and for the averting of calamities; and, like the other *Vedas,* numerous hymns to the gods, with prayers to be used at solemn rites and religious exercises, excepting such as are named *Yajnya.*"—Page 471.

* This distinction is important; inattention to it has led inquirers into error. " Every *Purana* treats of five subjects: 1. the creation of the universe; 2. its progress, and the renovation of worlds; 3. the genealogy of gods and heroes; 4. chronology, according to a fabulous system; and 5. heroic history, containing the achievements of demigods and heroes. Since each *Purana* contains a cosmogony, with mythological and heroic history, the works which bear that title may not unaptly be compared to the *Grecian Theogonies.*"—COLEBROKE. *As. Res.* Vol. VII. p. 202. This description is applicable to the eighteen mythological poems called *Puranas,* not to certain passages of each *Veda* bearing the same name of *Purana,* and interspersed throughout that portion of the *Vedas* entitled *Brahmana,* or *divine precepts.*

" The subjects and uses of the prayers contained in the *Vedas,* differ more than the deities which are invoked, or the titles by which they are addressed : every line is replete with allusions to mythology,* and to the *Indian* notions of the Divine Nature and of celestial spirits. For the innumerable ceremonies to be performed by a householder, and, still more, for those endless rites enjoined to hermits and ascetics, a choice of prayers is offered in every stage of the celebration. It may be here sufficient to observe, that INDRA, or the firmament, fire, the sun, the moon, water, air, the spirits, the atmosphere, and the earth, are the objects most frequently addressed; and the various and repeated sacrifices with fire, and the drinking of the milky juice of the moon-plant, or acid asclepias, furnish abundant occasions for numerous prayers adapted to the many stages of those religious rites."—Page 398.

Mr. COLEBROKE, after giving very strong reasons for believing the *Vedas* to be genuine compositions, in opposition to some assertions of their having been forged or grossly interpolated, proceeds thus—

" The greatest part of the books received by the learned among the *Hindus* will assuredly be found genuine: I do not doubt that the *Vedas,* of which an account has here been given, will appear to be of this description.

" In pronouncing them to be genuine, I mean to say, that they are the same compositions, which, under the same title of *Veda,* have been revered by *Hindus* for hundreds, if not thousands, of years. I think it probable that they were compiled by DWAPAYANA, the person who is said to have collected them, and who is thence named VYASA, or the *Compiler.*"—Page 483.

Other writers interpret the word *Vyasa* to mean the *divider;* and it is sometimes applied to an incarnation of VISHNU, under that name, assumed for the purpose of arranging, or dividing, the *Vedas.* In the third chapter of the *Bhagavata,* twenty-two incarnations of the Preserver are enumerated; and some of them are noticed in page 224.—The 17th: " As VYASA, he divided the *Veda* for the instruction of mankind." KRISHNA DWAPAYANA being the name of the supposed compiler, and an *Avatara* of VISHNU being, as we have just seen, resorted to for the work, some writers have attributed the arrangement of the *Vedas* to KRISHNA, the *Avatara,* for which I think there is no authority. It is common for *Hindus* to attribute *Vedas, Puranas, Mahabharat,* &c. all to VYASA.

The following is the concluding paragraph of *Mr.* COLEBROKE's Essay on the *Vedas,*—

" The preceding description may serve to convey some notion of the *Vedas.*—They are too voluminous for a complete translation of the whole; and what they contain would hardly reward the labour of the reader—much less that of the translator. The ancient dialect in which they are composed, and especially that of the three first *Vedas,* is extremely difficult and obscure; and though curious, as the parent of a more polished and refined dialect (the classical *Sanskrit*), its difficulties must long continue to prevent such an examination of the whole *Vedas* as would be requisite for extracting all that is remarkable and important in those voluminous works: but they well deserve to be occasionally consulted by the oriental scholar."—Page 497.

* " Not a mythology which avowedly exalts deified heroes, (as in the *Puranas,*) but one which personifies the elements and planets; and which peoples heaven, and the world below, with various orders of beings.

" observe, however, in many places, the ground-work of legends, which are familiar in mythological poems—such, for example, as the demon VRITRA, slain by INDRA, who is thence surnamed VRITRAHAN; but I do not remark any thing that corresponds with the favourite legends of those sects which worship either the *Linga* or *Sacti,* or else RAMA or KRISHNA. I except some detached portions, the genuineness of which appears doubtful, as will be shown towards the close of this essay."—Page 398. See, under *Hindus,* page 368.

The reverence in which the *Vedas* are held by the *Hindus* will appear from the following texts in the *Institutes* of MENU.—

Chap. I. v. 23.—"From fire, from air, and from the sun, he" (the Supreme Ruler) "milked out, as it were, the three primordial *Vedas*, named *Rich*, *Yajush*, and *Saman*, for the due performance of the sacrifice."

This origin of the *Vedas* has been adverted to in a former passage: the most popular origin is, that they, the *four Vedas*, issued from the *four* mouths of BRAHMA. BRAHMA, as we have seen, had once *five* heads, as SIVA, in some of his forms, still has; and, in a preceding passage, a fifth *Veda* is spoken of. Some authorities attribute them generally to AGNI, or *Fire*.—See p. p. 269. 298. In the *As. Res.* Vol. III. p. 47. this passage, by *Sir* W. JONES, occurs:—"The *Veda* is called also *Agama*; but this title refers more particularly to a mysterious book, or set of books, so named from having *come* from the mouth of SIVA, as the *Vedas* proceeded severally from the four mouths of BRAHMA. The same word means also the *Veda*."

Chap. IV. v. 124.—"The *Rigveda* is held sacred to the gods; the *Yajurveda* relates to mankind; the *Samaveda* concerns the manes of ancestors, and the sound of it, when chanted, raises therefore a notion of something impure."

Mr. COLEBROKE, however, in the *As. Res.* Vol. VIII. p. 458. informs us, that "a peculiar degree of holiness seems to be attached, according to *Indian* notions, to the *Samaveda*—if reliance may be placed on the inference suggested by the etymology of its name"—which "is expounded as denoting something which *destroys sin*." And this inference receives corroboration from the circumstance of KRISHNA, when enumerating, in the *Gita*, various orders of beings and things, to the chief of which he compares himself, declaring that, "among the *Vedas*, I am the *Saman*." It may be said, perhaps, that this *Veda* more especially relating to music, over which KRISHNA presides, he may advert only to its harmonious pre-eminence.

"125. Let the learned read the *Veda** on every lawful day, having first repeated, in order, the pure essence of the three *Vedas*; namely, the *Pranava*, the *Vyahritis*, and the *Gayatri*." (*Pranava* seems the same with O'M.—See page 414.)

Chap. XI. v. 262.—"A priest, who should retain in his memory the whole *Rigveda*, would be absolved from guilt, even if he had slain the inhabitants of the three worlds, and had eaten food from the foulest hands.

"263. By thrice repeating the *Mantras* and *Brahmanas* of the *Rig*, or those of the *Yajush*, or those of the *Saman*, with the *Upanishads*, he shall perfectly be cleansed from every possible sin.

"264. As a clod of earth, cast into a great lake, sinks in it, thus is every sinful act submerged in the triple *Veda*.

"266. The primary triliteral syllable, in which the three *Vedas* themselves are comprised, must be kept secret as another triple *Veda*: he knows the *Veda*, who knows the mystic sense of that word." (It is seen in my Frontispiece.—See page 410.)

Chap. XII. v. 109.—"Well instructed *Brahmans* are they who can adduce ocular proof from the scripture itself, having studied, as the law ordains, the *Vedas*, and their extended branches, or *Vedangas*, *Mimansa*, *Nyaya*, *Dhermasastra*, *Puranas*."

The age of the *Vedas* and *Puranas* is a point on which some discrepancies exist among the most respectable of *Sanskrit* scholars: in noticing them, I trust I do not volunteer an invidious task; for my object is to excite some farther investigation of a point in itself curious and interesting.

* The *Tamulians* and *Malabars* call these books *Vedam-am*, with them, being like the termination *um*, in *Latin*; a termination generally annexed to neuter substantives. In *Bengal*, the book is called *Bede*, or *Beda*, there being no *V* in the *Bengally* alphabet.—See *As. Res.* Vol. I. p. 146.

Sir W. JONES (*As. Res.* Vol. I. p. 238.) rejects the claim of the *Vedas* to the *very* high antiquity that some warm advocates were disposed to confer on them: he could never believe that they were actually written before the flood; but ventures to assert that they are far older than any other *Sanskrit* composition. And, in Vol. II. p. 305. he says, that he "firmly believes, from internal and external evidences, that three of the *Vedas* are more than three thousand years old: and, in Vol. III. p. 484. says they appear to stand next in antiquity to the five books of MOSES. In the preface to the *Institutes* of MENU, the learned translator deems the three first *Vedas* to have been composed about 300 years before the *Institutes*, and about 600 before the *Puranas* and *Itahasos*, which he was fully convinced were not the productions of VYASA. The *Institutes* are supposed to have received their present form about 880 years before CHRIST's birth. By one mode of reckoning, the highest age of the *Yajurveda* is carried to 1580 years before the birth of our SAVIOUR, (which would make it older than the five books of MOSES); and the *Institutes* must then be assigned to about 1280 years before the same epoch: but *Sir* W. JONES deems the former date of 880 years for the *Institutes* the more probable. This would give the *Yajurveda* an age, in 1809, of about 2990 years; or 2980, when the translator published MENU.

Mr. COLEBROKE (*As. Res.* Vol. VII. p. 284.) infers, from several *data* there given, the probability that the *Vedas* were not arranged in their present form earlier than the fourteenth century before the *Christian* era, but cautiously marks the inference as vague and conjectural: about 3200 years would hence be taken for the *maximum* of elapsed years since the present arrangement of the *Vedas*. And deducing, by *Sir* WILLIAM JONES's method, the comparative age of the *Puranas*, they will be 2500, or 2600 years old at most; and the *Institutes*, 2800.

Mr. WILFORD (*As. Res.* Vol. V. p. 244.) says, "The *Puranas* are certainly a modern compilation from valuable materials that I am afraid no longer exist: an astronomical observation of the heliacal rising of *Canopus*, mentioned in two of the *Puranas*, puts this beyond doubt."

Mr. BENTLY, (*As. Res.* Vol. VIII. p. 240.) after giving various reasons and calculations for the foundation of his opinion, says, "it must be evident that none of the modern romances, commonly called the *Puranas*, at least in the form they now stand, are older than 684 years, but that some of them are the compilations of still later times."

As far as the *Purana*, called the *Sri Bhagavata*, is concerned, *Mr.* COLEBROKE countenances *Mr.* BENTLY's opinion. He says, "I am myself inclined to adopt an opinion supported by many learned *Hindus*, who consider the celebrated *Sri Bhagavata* as the work of a grammarian, supposed to have lived about six hundred years ago."—*As. Res.* Vol. VIII. p. 487.

Mr. WILKINS, in the preface to the *Gita*, observes, that KRISHNA throughout the whole makes mention of three *Vedas* only, and those the three first in their present order: the fourth, proving itself a posterior work, mentions him. On this being remarked to some *Pandits*, who assisted in the translation, they expressed great astonishment at it, as it had escaped all the numerous commentators on the *Gita*. I will here notice, that I once communicated this circumstance to two learned and well-informed *Brahmans*, who were much struck with it; and were greatly surprised to find the *Gita* known out of their own pale. Desirous to know how far the copies of this work, used in *Bombay* and *Poona*, agreed with the translation, I have occasionally compared a small portion of it, line for line, with a *Brahman*; he listening to my rendering it from the printed book into *Hindvi*, and reciting to me, from memory, the lines immediately following. As far as I could judge, from so vague a process, there is no difference in the copies used in parts so distant as *Poona* and *Benares*; and the *Brahmans'* memory seemed no less faithful than the translation.

The term *Upanishad* has frequently occurred, and seems not to have, in general, any accurate idea annexed to it: it has been understood to mean *arcanum*, *mysterious*, *secret*, &c. senses connected with concealment or mystery. The proper meaning of the word *Upanishad*, according to *Mr.* COLEBROKE, on the authority of the best *Sanskrit* writers, is "divine science, or the knowledge of God; and it is equally applicable to theology itself, and to a book in which this science is taught." *Mr.* C. gives the derivation of the word; and says, that "the sense, properly deducible from that etymology, invariably points to the knowledge of the Divine perfections, and to the consequent attainment of beatitude through exemption from passions;" and that "neither the etymology, nor the acceptation of the word, has any direct connection with the idea of secrecy, concealment, or mystery."—*As. Res.* Vol. VIII. p. 472.

"The whole of the *Indian* theology is professedly founded on the *Upanishads.*" Some are extracts from the *Veda*; and the rest are also considered as appertaining to the *Indian* scripture: but whether they are detached essays, or have been extracted from a *Veda, Mr.* COLEBROKE is not certain.—*Ib.* p. 473.

Of these fifty-two theological treatises, entitled *Upanishads,* the titles are given by *Mr.* C. and a concise notice of their subjects or contents.

The word *Sastra,* by some writers erroneously spelled *Shaster,* we find to mean, generally, an *ordinance,* and particularly a *sacred ordinance,* delivered by inspiration; and properly applicable only to *sacred literature.*

The *Veda,* collectively, is the body of *Hindu Scripture.*

Of KAMA, the GOD of LOVE.

NOTWITHSTANDING the popularity of this deity in *India*, where, both in poetry and conversation, he is, as in most other refined countries, in person, or by allusion to his attributes and effects, so often introduced, I do not find one representation of KAMA among my images or pictures; nor do I recollect ever having seen an original of either in *India*. He is finely sculptured, with all his attributes, on the beautiful pantheistic *choultry* at *Madura*, built by the munificent TRIMAL NAIG; and a print is given of him—not, however, from that source, by SONNERAT, which is copied into KINDERSLEY'S Specimens of *Hindu* Literature. On the *choultry*, he is, I think, standing, and not mounted on his parrot, as in SONNERAT'S plate. Having no image or picture, I have given no engraving of KAMA DEVA; and it is owing to this circumstance, perhaps, that I, at so late a period of my work, introduce to my readers this deity, so important in the real history of man, as well as in poetical and mythological researches. As a matter of course, I commenced my series of plates with GANESA, the god of policy, sagacity, and prudence; and have thus unwittingly disjoined, by the whole length of my book, those subjects and KAMA, the god of affection and love, of whom I would gladly have given a plate, if I possessed, or could obtain, an original cast or sketch. This can have been no designed arrangement; nor has it so much meaning as the distich that it seems to reverse—

"*Love* seldom haunts the breast where *learning* lies,
For VENUS sets ere MERCURY can rise."

I will introduce KAMA by an extract from the argument prefixed to the hymn addressed to him by *Sir* WILLIAM JONES.

"The *Hindu* god, to whom the hymn is addressed, appears evidently the same with the *Grecian* EROS and the *Roman* CUPIDO: but the *Indian* description of his person and arms, his family, attendants, and attributes, has new and peculiar beauties.

"According to the mythology of *Hindustan*, he was the son of MAYA, or the general *attracting* power, and married to RETI, or *Affection*; and his bosom friend is BESSENT, or *Spring*. He is represented as a beautiful youth, sometimes conversing with his mother and consort in the midst of his gardens and temples; sometimes riding by moonlight on a parrot or lory, and attended by dancing girls or nymphs, the foremost of whom bears his colours, which are a *fish* on a *red* ground. His favourite place of resort is a tract of country round *Agra*, and principally the plains of *Mutra*; where KRISHNA also, and the nine *Gopia*, who are clearly the APOLLO and *Muses* of the *Greeks*, usually spend the night in music and dancing. His bow of sugar-cane, or flowers, with a string formed of bees, and his five arrows, each pointed with an *Indian* blossom of a heating quality, are equally new and beautiful. He has at least twenty-three names, most of which are introduced in the hymn: that of KAM, or KAMA, signifies desire, a sense which it also bears in ancient and modern *Persian*. And it is possible, that the words *Dipuc* and *Cupid*, which have the same signification, may have the same origin; since we know that the old *Hetruscans*, from whom great part of the *Roman* language and religion was derived, and whose system had a near affinity with that of the *Persians* and *Indians*, used to write their lines alternately forwards and backwards, as furrows are made by the plough.

The seventh stanza alludes to the bold attempt of this deity to wound the great god MAHADEVA, for which he was punished by a flame consuming his corporeal nature, and reducing him to a mental essence: and hence his chief dominion is over the *minds* of mortals, or such deities as he is permitted to subdue."—Works, Vol. XIII.

"The *Indian* MAYA, or, as the word is explained by some *Hindu* scholars, '*the first inclination of the Godhead to diversify himself*,'—such is their phrase, 'by creating worlds,' is feigned to be the mother of universal nature and of all the inferior gods; as a *Kashmirian* informed me, when I asked him why KAMA, or *Love*, was represented as her son. But the word *Maya*, or *delusion*, has a more subtle or recondite sense in the *Vedanti* philosophy; where it signifies the system of perceptions, whether of secondary or primary qualities, which the Deity was believed, by EPICHARMUS, PLATO, and many truly pious people, to raise by his omnipresent spirit in the minds of his creatures, but which had not, in their opinion, any existence independent of mind."—JONES. *As. Res* Vol. I. p. 221.

MAYA, or ADA MAYA, is a name of LAKSHMI: she is thus the general attracting power; the mother of all; the *Sacti*, or *energy*, of VISHNU, the personification of *Spirit*; (*Maya*, both in its subtle and more familiar allusions, has occurred in former pages — see 9. 16. 73.) she, as *attraction*, unites all matter, producing *love* in animated nature, and, in physics, the harmonization of atoms. KAMA,* or *Love*, is her offspring, and is united in marriage to RETI, or *Affection*, the inseparable attendant on the tender passion; and in friendship to VASANTA, (commonly pronounced BESSENT,) or *Spring*, denoting *Love's* season, both literally in regard to the time when most animals are impregnated and vegetables burst into existence, and metaphorically, touching the early portion of man's passage through life. We have before noticed (p. p. 52. 217.) the allegory of KAMA being an *Avatara* or son of KRISHNA, by RUKMENI; other names of VISHNU and LAKSHMI, and a farther instance (see p. 133.) of the correspondence of that goddess with our popular VENUS, the mother of CUPID. Riding, or dancing, by moonlight, allude to the love-inspiring serenity of the time; such nights, about *Agra*, and in the southern parts of *India*, affording, after the heat and tumult of the day, a delicious quiet feeling of happiness not easily communicated, nor conceivable by the mere experience of the unsettled cloudy skies of northern latitudes.

The banner of KAMA, a *fish* on a *red* ground, and his *vahan*, or vehicle, a parrot or *luri*, have doubtless their allusions; the former possibly to the stimulating nature of that species of food, stirring the blood to aid KAMDEO's ends; and, perhaps, the *ensanguined* colouring and extreme beauty of the *luri*, and, like the fish, (and the dove of western mythologists,) its supposed *aphrodisiac* tendency as food, may have had a share in guiding a selection of attributes for the ardent deity. The soft affection and fabled constancy of the dove may have weighed with the *Greeks*, although constancy may not, perhaps, be, in strictness, a striking characteristic of Love.

SONNERAT says, that the *Hindus* deified KAMA (whom he calls MUNMODEN; which is, I suppose, one of his names in the *Carnatic*,) merely from their *gusto* for voluptuousness: but the fable of his having been reduced from a corporeal nature to a mental essence, prettily inculcates the idea of the progress and refine-

* We may here, as usual with all *Hindu* deities, trace KAMA's genealogy upwards to the Sun, who is BRAHM. LAKSHMI, in a divine and mortal view, both as MAYA and as RUKMENY, is his mother: she is VISHNU, that is, his *Sacti*, or energy: VISHNU, or KRISHNA, KAMA's father, is the Sun, the source, literally and figuratively, of warmth and union—affection and love. Let me here notice, as the only place in which I can supply the omission, that when (p. 288.) describing the legless ARUNA, charioteer of SURYA, that is, the precursor of day, AURORA, it escaped me to remark, that ARUNA's imperfect form has been supposed, and not inexpressively, allusive to his partial appearance: his head and body may be seen, but his legs are yet in invisible night, or lost in the blaze of SURYA's brilliancy.

ment of passion, and marks that the mind shares largely in his influence. It must, indeed, necessarily be, that the fabulist who thinks at all deeply, cannot but notice his extensive dominion over both mental and corporeal feelings.

Poets perpetually recur to this mishap of KAMA; and allusions to it have occurred in some of our earlier pages. Here follows some farther notice of that celebrated event.—

MAHADEVA and PARVATI, playing with dice at the game of *Chaturanga*, disputed, and parted in wrath; and severally performing rigid acts of devotion to the Supreme Being, kindled thereby such vehement fires as threatened a general conflagration. The *Devas*, in great alarm, hastened to BRAHMA, who led them to MAHADEVA, and supplicated him to recal his consort; but the wrathful god answered, that she must return to him of her own free choice. They accordingly deputed GANGA, the river goddess, who prevailed on PARVATI to return to her husband, on the condition that his love for her should be restored. The celestial mediators then employed KAMADEVA, who wounded SIVA with one of his flowery arrows; but the angry deity reduced the god of love to ashes. PARVATI, soon after, presented herself before SIVA in the semblance of a *Cirati*, a daughter of a mountaineer; and seeing him enamoured of her, assumed her own shape, and effected a reunion: and in the place of reconciliation a grove sprang up, which was named, from the impression which her appearance there made on the uxorious deity, *Kamavana*, or the *wood of desire*. The relenting SIVA consoled the afflicted RETI,* the widow of KAMA, by assuring her that she should rejoin her husband, when he should be born again in the form of PRADYAMNA, son of KRISHNA, and should put SAMBARA to death. This favourable prediction was in due time accomplished; and PRADYAMNA was seized by the demon SAMBARA, who placed him in a chest, and threw it into the sea. The chest was swallowed by a large fish, which was caught and carried to the palace of the tyrant, where the unfortunate RETI had been compelled to menial service: it fell to her lot to open the fish, and finding the chest and its contents, she nursed the infant in private, and educated him until he had sufficient strength to destroy the malignant SAMBARA. He had before considered RETI as his mother; but their minds being now irradiated, the prophetic promise of MAHADEVA was remembered, and the god of love was reunited to the goddess of pleasure.—See *As. Res.* Vol. III. p. 402. whence the above legend is taken, and 52. 206. 208. 210. 217. of our preceding pages.

In the *Ramayana*, (book i. sect. 22.) the resentment of MAHADEVA is thus noticed: "KANDARPA, the wily one, wounding ST'HANU, the lord of the gods, while, with uplifted arm, he was engaged in sacred austerities, met the desert of his crime from the eye of the great RUDRA—all his members, being scorched with fire, fell from his body: he was thence called ANANGA (bodiless), and the place where it happened, *Kama* (Desire)."—Page 179.

We will here notice some of the names of KAMA, and then some farther particulars respecting his attributes and character.

KAMA-DEVA, or, corruptly, KAMDEO, is merely the god of love or desire. MAKARA-KETU alludes to the fish, *Makara*, in his banner: *ketu*, I believe, is a banner. KANDARPA means love: and KANDARPA-KETU is another of his names. PUSHPA-DHANVA, with the flowery bow. MARA. ANANGA, the incorpo-

* The lamentations of RETI, on this occasion, fill a whole book in KALIDASA's poem, called *Kumara-Sambhava*, or the birth of KUMARA.—(See p. p. 52. 175). This book Sir WILLIAM JONES's teacher, a learned *Vaidya*, was restrained from reading, considering the ceremonies of a marriage, that of KAMA and RETI, at which BRAHMA himself officiated as father of the bridegroom, as too holy to be known by any but *Brahmans*. I have several pictures (see PLATE 46.) where BRAHMA is assisting at weddings. RETI is sometimes represented, in pictures, on horseback, throwing a lance.

real. SMARA, the ideal, as the son of MAYA, or *illusion*. MADAN, or MADANA, and MADAMAT, are names derived, I imagine, from a root signifying both *sweetness* and *intoxication*: honey is called *mad*, or *mud*; so is intoxication. In like manner *shad*, شاد in *Persian*, and, perhaps, also in *Sanskrit*, means honey; likewise, adverbially, merriment, pleasure, intoxication, but not to a degree approaching drunkenness; it means too, marriage, but not of the first or most respectable kind: MAKADAMA is, perhaps, from the same source. His name of PRADYAMNA, son of KRISHNA and RUKMENY, has been noticed: ANIRUDHA was his son, whose adventures with USHA are the subject of a pretty tale, and a very interesting drama.

In the beautiful pastoral drama of JAYADEVA, called *Gita Govinda*, so often extracted from on former occasions, allusions frequently occur to KAMA and his attributes. RADHA is thus described bewailing the absence of her beloved KRISHNA:—

"Fresh arrows of desire are continually assailing her, and she forms a net of lotos leaves as armour for her heart, which thou, O KRISHNA! alone shouldst fortify. She makes her own bed of the arrows darted by the flower-shafted god; but when she hoped for thy embrace, she had formed for thee a couch of their soft blossoms. She draws thy image with musk in the character of the deity with five shafts, having subdued the *Makara*, and holding an arrow tipped with an *amra* flower."

The *Makara* is said to be the horned shark: it is a name also of the zodiacal sign *Capricorn*, which is sometimes seen to terminate in the tail of a fish; but I know not if any inference can be thence drawn; nor do I know the legend of KAMA's "subduing the *Makara*," as alluded to in the above quotation.

The inhabitants of *India*, whether *Hindu* or *Mussulman*, may be generally called a salacious race; and cunning and itinerant quacks avail themselves, as in other countries, of the follies and propensities of their wealthier brethren. One of this description, some years ago, pretended to possess a portion of a wonder-working fish, that he called *Mahi Sukkhun khur*; which, if spelled ماهي سخن خور may be rendered the *discourse-devouring fish*; but I should not judge that to be its real meaning; and, indeed, I have its name before me, spelled سقنقور but, having no books, I am not sufficient of a *Persian* to determine its derivation or allusions: I conclude, however, that they may be traced to KAMA's fish, both as to family and effect. Be that as it may, I have been told, that impotent and old men, who, in *India*, I think, more than elsewhere, are prone to "envying every sparrow that they see," seek with avidity this rare invigorating drug; and, at *Poona*, I heard, that NANA FIRNAVEESE, attracted by the fame of a *Mahomedan* traveller, who possessed a piece of it, was in treaty for its purchase at an enormous price, but prudently made a previous reference to some gentlemen at the *English* Residency for their opinion of its powers; and, on being discouraged, declined the offered bargain. I lately, however, learned, that this was a trick played on NANA by some *Mahomedan* gentleman. Having occasion, recently, to write to a *Poona* friend, settled in *England*, I mentioned, and made some inquiries after, this fish; and it happened, that a *Moghul* gentleman, who was one of the party at *Poona* that so many years back played this trick on NANA, was at the time on his travels in *Europe*, and, when my letter arrived, on a visit at my friend's house. The story had been long forgotten, and was thus, by a strange coincidence, called to the recollection of several former residents at *Poona*.

I may here notice another drug, to which the *Brahmans* ascribe great virtues, of a healing, rather than an invigorating, nature: this is the *Egyptian mummy*, which they call *mammuë*, strongly accenting the last syllable. It might be spelled *mohamahi*, and afford ground for an etymological speculation, that I shall not here enter upon; nor continue the notice of the *Brahmanical mammuë* farther than to remark its being somewhat curious that such a name should be applied by them to such a subject.

KAMA's *five* arrows are each tipped with the blossom of a flower, which is devoted to, and supposed to preside over, a sense: the flowers are of a heating, inflaming quality; and are named, and well described, in these lines of the hymn, which paint VASANTA preparing the bow and shafts for his mischievous friend—

"He bends the luscious cane, and twists the string
With bees, how sweet! but, ah! how keen their sting!
He with five flow'rets tips thy ruthless darts,
Which through five senses pierce enraptur'd hearts:
Strong *Chumpa*, rich in odo'rous gold;
Warm *Amer*, nurs'd in heavenly mould;
Dry *Nagkeser*, in silver smiling;
Hot *Kitticum*, our sense beguiling;
And last, to kindle fierce the scorching flame,
Loveshaft, which gods bright *Bela* name."

The *Chumpa*, or *Champa*, more classically called *Champaka*, is a *polyandrian polygynian* flower; the *Micheha* of *European* botanists: it is of two sorts, white and yellow; small, and in its foliage like an expanded rose-bud. Gardeners make, and expose in the shops, chaplets and long strings of the blossoms, which loose women, on the supposition that its fragrance excites favourable sensations in the votaries of KAMA, decorate their hair with, and wear round their necks: its potency is, however, so great, that nerves unaccustomed to it can scarcely bear its odour within doors. Another flower, commonly called *mugri*, or *mogry*, is of the same description, and may, perhaps, be one of those classically named in the hymn.

The fragrance of the *Chumpa* is so very strong that bees refuse to extract honey from it, a circumstance that could not escape the keen eye of the *Hindu* poets; and they accordingly feign the *Chumpa* to be sadly mortified at this neglect. They have, however, afforded it consolation, by dedicating it to KRISHNA, the black deity; as they, contrary to some *European* poetical naturalists, consider the union of yellow and black peculiarly beautiful. KRISHNA is mostly seen profusely decorated with garlands of flowers. The *Chumpa* is farther consoled by the preference it has obtained in bedecking the glossy locks of black-haired damsels, as just noticed; also in the following stanza, literally translated from the *Sanskrit*:—

"That thou art not honoured by the ill-disposed bee, why, O *Champaka!* dost thou so heavily lament? The locks of lotos-eyed-damsels, resembling-the-fresh-dark-clouds adorning-the-sky; let these embellish thee."—*As. Miscellany*, Vol. II.

I will here add another couplet, from the same work, a translation from the *Birj* dialect; premising, that *Hindu* ladies sometimes wear a little mirror, called *chury*, of polished metal, in a ring on the thumb, and that the *lotos* is the emblem of female beauty.

KRISHNA, who had concealed his passion from the parents of a damsel whom he secretly visited, unfortunately chanced to find her in the midst of her relations: how great his distress! He was averse to departing without expressing his passion—words were debarred—both were embarrassed—love prompted:

"He, with salute of deference due,
A *lotos* to his forehead prest;
She rais'd her mirror to his view,
And turn'd it inward to her breast."

The *Amer*, mentioned in the extract from the hymn, is also called *Amra*, and *Amla*, and is said by some to be the *mangoe* flower.

"Dry *Nagkeser*" is also called *Kesara*: it is a handsome flower, with yellow and white petals. The *Bela* is a beautiful species of jasmin.

Among a refined people, advantageously situated in a low latitude, we naturally expect to find love, in its vast variety of relations, no inconsiderable portion of their occupation and amusement. Books and tales on amatory topics are very abundant; and, in common life, allusions are constantly occurring to KAMA and his excitations. It will be recollected, that KAMA is the son of KRISHNA; who, being VISHNU, is called, in the second stanza of the ode that I am about to introduce, as he is in former pages, MADHAVA. The three first stanzas of the ode consist chiefly of compound words, forming names of KAMA: for instance—PUSHPADANVA, with a flowery bow; MAKARA KETU, fish-bannered, &c.

On the 13th and 14th of the first half of the month *Chaitra*, which must be about the full moon, a festive jollity, with music and bathing, is held in honour of KAMADEVA: on which occasion, the following is a popular canticle---

"1. Hail, god of the flowery bow; hail, warrior, with a fish on thy banner; hail, powerful divinity, who causeth the firmness of the sage to forsake him, and subduest the guardian deities of the eight regions!

"2. O KANDARPA! thou son of MADHAVA! O MARA! thou foe of SAMBARA! Glory be to thee, who lovest the goddess RETI; who springest from the heart!

"3. Glory be to MADANA; to KAMA; to him who is formed as the God of gods; to him, by whom BRAHMA, VISHNU, SIVA, INDRA, are filled with emotions of rapture!

"4. May all my mental cares be removed! all my corporeal sufferings terminate! May the object of my soul be attained, and my" (---and, gentle reader, thy---) "felicity continue for ever."---*As. Res.* Vol. III. p. 278.

FINIS.

INDEX.

C.

K.

L.

M.

N.

T.

U.

V.

W.

Y.

Z.

THE END.